THE RIVALS

THE RIVALS

The Intimate Story of a Political Marriage

James Naughtie

FOURTH ESTATE · *London*

First published in Great Britain in 2001 by
Fourth Estate
A Division of HarperCollins*Publishers*
77–85 Fulham Palace Road
London W6 8JB
www.4thestate.co.uk

1 3 5 7 9 10 8 6 4 2

A catalogue record for this book is available from the British Library

ISBN 1-84115-473-3

Typeset by Rowland Phototypesetting Ltd,
Bury St Edmunds, Suffolk
Printed in Great Britain by Clays Ltd, St Ives plc

For Ellie
with love

Acknowledgements

Many people have helped me to try to understand the relationship between Tony Blair and Gordon Brown. I am grateful to friends and acquaintances inside and outside politics for their observations. This is meant to be a story about character and not policy (anyone who wants an economic analysis or a step-by-step account of the Northern Ireland peace process will have to look elsewhere) and so I have drawn on conversations going back many years since I watched the young Blair and Brown begin their careers and first knew them. I did not ask them to cooperate with this book, however, and they asked some of their closest associates not to cooperate with me. This is an unauthorized story, I am glad to say. But I hope it is authentic, in catching the quality of their dealings with each other and explaining how they came to achieve and maintain such dominance.

Many of their friends and colleagues in government and in Whitehall have been kind in helping me. Inevitably, most of them could only do so privately: Cabinet ministers do not like talking frankly about each other in public, and civil servants are prohibited from speaking openly about their masters. As a result, I made a happy decision about footnotes. There are none. I thought the phrase 'private information' repeated too often would be too irritating. So everyone will have to cluster under a blanket 'thank you'. You know who you are, and I am grateful. I have tried to provide sources for published quotations in the text. This is not meant to be an annotated biography (in any case, the trio of Rentoul, Routledge and Macintyre have together done that job as well as anyone could expect at this stage) and I have tried to write about these two political lives in a different way, which I hope explains something of what makes them what they are. I am especially grateful to some old friends who have been generous with their thoughts and with whom, over the years, I've spent long nights puzzling over the subjects of this book. Peter Riddell, Andrew Marr, Martin Kettle and Peter Hennessy in particular will find their footprints on these pages. All my colleagues on *Today* have given me cheery support and Stephen Mitchell and Tony Hall, who now has to handle opera singers instead of journalists, have been stalwart and straight. I have other debts. My agent Felicity Bryan is a star, and my editor at Fourth Estate, Clive Priddle, is a brilliant companion on excursions into the political undergrowth, as he is on writing expeditions to Argyll. Thanks also to Richard Collins for his sub-editing. My friend and colleague Nick Sutton is a writer's dream researcher. Most of all I hope I can repay my wife Ellie for her support, and give back to Andrew, Catherine and Flora the time we have lost.

JN
July 2001

Contents

EURO
MIDDLE ENGLAND
OLD LABOUR
RIDDELL

Introduction: Two Into One

No pair of politicians in our modern history have wielded so much power together as Tony Blair and Gordon Brown. They met when the Labour Party was weak and writhing in agony and then single-mindedly, with the help of the accidents that often shape politics, they were able to create a single political personality for their party and themselves that dominated the affairs of the country at the end of the century. We have seen nothing like it before.

This creation was a phenomenon that seemed to spring from nowhere. Their party was exhausted, angry and divided when they arrived at Westminster and they had to learn their parliamentary politics deep in the shadow of Margaret Thatcher, in the force field of her ideological challenge. Yet when they were only in their mid-forties they were commanding a government with a bigger majority than any one party had known since the Great Reform Act was passed in the days of their great-great-grandfathers. They began their second term in 2001 with seemingly untrammelled power in government, a Prime Minister and Chancellor who had turned politics to their own purposes and whose style was imprinted on their era.

But this power has pain flowing through it. In building a partnership which in its closeness has no modern parallel, Blair and Brown have lived with an intimacy which has caused each of them intense anxiety and anger as well as bringing them the luscious fruits of power. They still live in a political embrace which neither has been able to escape. Each knows that without it he would not have been able to flourish alone. That union has given them everything, including the despair. Neither enjoys the description of their relationship as a marriage, but it is the one that their colleagues in government most often use because they can find no other way of explaining the deep mystery of how their moments of political intimacy are often disturbed by tensions and arguments that seem to well up from a history in the partnership that only the two of them can feel fully or understand. One of their ministers in the Lords – a woman – was trying to explain it to an outsider who wondered how this strange Downing Street relationship worked, and put it like this: 'When you're with them together, you find them finishing each other's sentences.'

Even the weary veterans of the Westminster village, gathering to gossip at the well, find it impossible to rake up a comparison. No Prime Minister and Chancellor in the modern era have operated like this. None of Thatcher's three Chancellors – not even her cherished Nigel Lawson – had a relationship like the one that binds Blair and Brown together. A distance always remained, and when Lawson resigned after their falling-out the Prime Minister tried to carry on as if this was just another of the sad squalls of politics that pass away. None of us who have seen Brown and Blair grow together from their early days and who observe them now in power believe that a parting could be anything less than an earthquake in politics, a shock that would disturb the deepest foundations of their government and their party. And for one of them at least it would be bound to be a tragedy.

Politics doesn't have to be like this. Chancellors of the Exchequer can pass across the landscape without leaving many footprints, and Prime Ministers can appear to command governments alone, taking seriously the title of First Lord of the Treasury engraved on the letter box of Number 10 Downing Street. Their names aren't always coupled together. Heath is Heath, without Barber. Early Wilson is usually not Wilson–Callaghan. Macmillan is Macmillan without the forgotten Heathcoat Amory or Selwyn Lloyd or Maudling. And are the closing years of the eighties thought of as Thatcher–Major? Blair and Brown are different and we can't think of them as characters with separate existences. Their party, dominating the Commons with 419 seats out of 659 in 1997 and 413 out of 659 in 2001, thinks of them as a duopoly, and when Labour MPs try to envisage a government that is not constructed on the Blair–Brown axis they find it hard. They seem to have managed to put a psychological spell on their party. Everyone talks about what life would be like if one or other of them were not there, but no one finds it easy to conceive. In Downing Street and the Treasury they speak of that distant day with an awful fascination. How and when will it come? The knowledge that one day the pattern is bound to be broken is infused with a frisson of fear, because this Prime Minister and Chancellor have expended great energy in persuading their party of their own indispensability. Blair giving way to Brown? An unexpected political cataclysm that destroys one and preserves the other? The decision of one to go off to lead a different life? These are the delicious fantasies of Whitehall, chewed over in the tapas bars of Westminster as enthusiastically as once the strategy and gossip of empire was traded across the tables of the gentlemen's clubs of St James's. Anyone with a foothold in politics in any party knows that it is the obsession of our time and they know why. Like two wrestlers locked in a complicated clinch in the middle of the ring, this Prime Minister and Chancellor twitch and strain but remain nervous of the big thrust to break free. They're absorbed in the complexity of their entanglement.

To watch them over the last twenty years has been to see a friendship develop, turn into a political alliance and, through a fiery clash of ambitions, end up as a mesmerizing and dominant public spectacle. No one who has followed their political careers as an observer now wants to miss the raised eyebrow or the whispered aside or the piece of telling body language because, between these two, nothing is neutral or without significance any more. Everything carries a weight of meaning which they may regret but can no longer wish away.

In the early days they exuded a relish for the games of politics which has been disciplined by their own arguments and by power. Blair was much the more innocent of the two, plunging into Westminster like a youngster pushed off a high diving board by an unseen hand. Meeting him the year before he became an MP when he was fruitlessly canvassing the dedicated Conservatives of Beaconsfield in Buckinghamshire in the by-election of 1982 was to encounter a picture of unsullied vivacity. He had nothing to lose. Indeed as you did the rounds of the villages and lanes, you felt a certain sympathy for this underdog candidate not only facing a Conservative majority of the sort that used to be weighed rather than counted after the polls closed, but having to deal with a rampant Prime Minister raucously rallying her troops to the sound of Falklands war drums. None of us spotted it at the time, but the whole experience sharpened Blair's political enthusiasm and helped him discover that he wanted more. Within a year he was engaged on a quick blitz in County Durham to win the Sedgefield nomination, throwing himself into it as if he had to do a barrister's all-night swot before court in the morning.

Brown's innocence had long gone by this time, and in Scotland he was carrying a political history with him while Blair was getting his first thrills. The student politician and radical intellectual was a fixture in Edinburgh. When you visited his book-strewn flat you were part of a kind of downbeat political salon. The oxygen of politics in Scotland was devolution and Brown was of a generation that felt it had lived half a lifetime in a few wild years. In the seventies, reasonably sane people used to stand in pubs in Edinburgh and talk about what was going to happen when devolution or independence came – next month? next year? – and there was a Parliament and the trappings of a state and even an Embassy Row where ambassadors would come to observe the New Scotland. This is the kind of inflated nonsense that was in the air, and it was known by (almost) everyone to be nonsense. Yet it gave Scottish politics an undeniable surge of energy to which no one objected, and an edge which everyone enjoyed. In this world, everyone knew Gordon Brown. To those of us who travelled home regularly from Westminster and pored over the political map, his tracks were already clear.

The story that began to unfold when the two met at Westminster in 1983 became an absorbing one almost at once. Such was the despair of their generation, in which power seemed nothing more substantial than a flickering mirage on a far distant horizon, they could fling themselves into reform in a way that wouldn't have been possible if they had arrived at a different moment and found themselves constrained by the disciplines of seniority and proper form. Instead, their party was lawless, rudderless, a blank piece of paper. It represented a delicious opportunity for young, inventive minds prepared to create a new identity for Labour.

The mid-1980s were dominated, of course, by Margaret Thatcher. The shrewder young Labour MPs understood that they should use this time to make their own politics. They knew they were probably out of power for the decade, and so Brown and Blair began to scheme their schemes. They were good company in those days round a Commons dining table or in one of the bars, gossiping, plotting tactics for the next day's Employment Bill or just lounging on the Commons terrace on a sultry summer night wondering if their party was ever going to be able to climb out of the pit. They were invigorated by involvement with Peter Mandelson, which changed their lives, and started the clambering of the greasy pole in the shadow Cabinet elections after Labour's 1987 defeat. Even then they seemed to have a plan with a controlled narrative, every chapter pointing to the next.

Their sense of obligation to each other comes from the years they spent together in the parliamentary desert. Their main difficulty, and the principal cause of the cold shaft that often divides them, is the leadership argument of 1994 that only came about because they were so close. The privacy that they insist on preserving for their own negotiations on policy and strategy is the consequence of the intensity that they cultivated when they were free to revel in youthful self-promotion in opposition. Everything is explained by their past.

Explained, but not necessarily made easy. Blair and Brown are a complicated pair. Civil servants puzzle over the contradictions they throw up – the modernizers who want less open discussion in Cabinet; the devolvers who want a stronger Downing Street secretariat; the Prime Minister and Chancellor who boast of decisiveness and let the euro argument float from their grasp; the friends whose supporting gangs fight in the street and fill the air with gossip. Labour MPs wonder if the tensions will destroy them; but ask them what comes next, after Blair and Brown have exploded or departed, and you'll wait a long time for an answer.

They engender mystery. For all the obvious power that flows from the huge majority and their public insistence that they'll stick together, the very consciousness of their pact is nerve-racking for the government. Their colleagues don't know what deals they have made, and find it hard to think themselves into a world that has its emotional boundaries policed by Peter Mandelson and Alastair Campbell. Even in government, most of the Cabinet feel outsiders. They find it difficult to get the measure of the pulse in Downing Street. You can feel it beating, but it comes and goes and always seems dangerously elusive.

Ministers, civil servants and journalists are fellow conspirators in their mystery, trying to unravel the enigmatic relationship. Even those of us who watched some of the fine feuds and love affairs of power under previous governments from the ringside find this one hypnotic. Government has not been so concentrated in modern times. Only the neighbours in Downing Street seem to count. If they are as one, nothing can intervene. If the word seeps out that there's a row, or that one of them is on the warpath, the Whitehall air starts to stir and preparations are made for a storm. Everyone is always ready with the defences against that battering, because they think about the relationship all the time.

People who deal with ministers – civil servants, journalists, back-benchers, businessmen – want to know how the land lies. They have to be able to take a reading on relations between Number 10 and Number 11 at any moment. A piece of gossip does the rounds, an inspired leak or a piece of poison over a lunch table spawns a new tale, some unexpected political event flares in the sky, and suddenly there is another question about the central relationship in the government. They have built their administration on that partnership, and the power it commands, and they are stuck with it.

If it were not for the scale of the electoral success of 1997, everyone around Westminster imagines that this way of running a government could not have survived. The most important strength of Blair and Brown together is that they have never been put to that test. The advantages given to them by the majorities of 1997 and 2001 are immense. These reduced the Conservatives to a number of seats well below the 209 that Michael Foot took back to the Commons in 1983, Labour's year of disaster. The strength of their relationship is not only a consequence of their own histories, but of the way that the collapse of a weary Conservative Party after eighteen draining years in power gave them a Parliament that they were tempted to treat as a poodle. Watch Blair at the despatch box on a Wednesday afternoon and you see a Prime Minister who would often rather be back in the office. He enjoys the stage, but the parliamentary audience is not his choice.

The centre of his world is not the cockpit of the Commons, nor even his seat at the centre of the Cabinet table. It is the small room at the back of Number 10 where he and Brown do their deals. From the start of their life in government they operated as they had done in opposition – privately. Blair's colleagues believed it was a secretive system devised to assuage Brown's hurt at the subordinate role he had to occupy after Blair became leader, but the habit also predated that crisis in their relationship, and was the result of the intensity with which they lived their political lives in the eighties. In government, that past was the genetic map that determined how they behaved.

Whether in strategic economic questions, or crisis in the countryside or Kosovo, or trouble from a Labour infatuation with the rich, or from the press, the central relationship was the lightning rod to which everything was automatically attracted. No serious problem in government could be solved without these two laying hands on it, and the thought that it might be otherwise seemed never to have been seriously considered. That fact gave the government its personality, and many of its problems.

The pact which they use to run affairs does give their government strength, but it is strangely vulnerable because it depends on emotions that run deep in each of them. When those emotions are under control, theirs is a partnership of political power unrivalled in the democratic world. Together they're greater than the sum of their parts, and they have succeeded in dominating the middle ground of British politics as a result. But ambition for power and togetherness are not natural bedfellows. For all their instinctive sympathy and old loyalty to each other, their relationship in power is at the mercy of events and the stray personalities of politics who cluster round the throne.

One of the great historians of modern politics and workings of Whitehall, Professor Peter Hennessy, observes that they have changed the rules of power fundamentally. 'A contemporary historian isn't what you need for this subject. You need a medievalist. This is a court. All the assumptions we've made about politics in this country since Lloyd George – that decisions are rational, collective, and conform to a recognizable machinery – have to be thrown aside. They operate quite differently.'

Blair's government generates a running commentary on itself with a gusto which outsiders would find astonishing, and unravelling it is like delving into a pile of eels in a basket. Everything slips and slithers from your grasp, and that elusive quality is one of the reasons for the fascination of ministers and officials with the Blair–Brown partnership. They glimpse it at work for a moment – an agreed new phraseology on Europe, a coordinated series of speeches on the New Deal, even a cheery joint appearance on a radio phone-in – and then it is gone, lost in a flurry of competing briefings from the camp-followers around Whitehall who pass on the whispers from the ante-rooms of power. 'Gordon chewed the carpet.' Or: 'Tony was livid with him.' Or 'Cherie is incandescent. In–can–descent.' The truth is never absolute: another interpretation comes along in a moment. No statement can be made about these two without a qualification or a contradiction coming fast on its heels. Tam Dalyell, the Labour MP who became the longest-serving member of the Commons and Father of the House after the 2001 election, says, with a typically eccentric touch, that the best guide to the government is not some Labour Party pamphlet or manifesto, nor an academic study of The Third Way, but the eighteenth-century memoirs of the Duc de Saint-Simon which he was urged to read at school as a guide to the world of politics.

Saint-Simon's *Memoirs* are the story of the court of Louis XIV at Versailles, observed from the inside. Courtiers cluster round the throne, and jostle for a place near the king at his *levées* and *couchées*, the monarch's flickering eye follows the comings and goings of those who wish him well and those who don't, the spies and tale-tellers feed the court with its lifeblood of gossip. It is the picture of a world of power driven by intrigue and vanity. Dalyell says simply of his party in power: 'It is a court.'

The Rivals is a story of character and power. They are indivisible. This is not a dual biography but a picture of parallel lives which have reshaped an era. Ours is an age in which personality and celebrity have became the dominant cultural forces and Blair and Brown have ridden that tide. Together they have built a political personality that is all-powerful. This is the story of how they did it, how it works, and how it often threatens to consume them.

PART ONE

"'ERE COMES A TOFF ... 'EAVE A BRICK AT 'IM."

1
The Thespian and the Flanker

Tony Blair and Gordon Brown were closer than they knew, before either of them had any thought of politics. In Edinburgh in the winter of 1967 they were only a couple of miles from each other, doing what they would enjoy most in their teenage years. Brown was submerging himself in the quiet excitements of Edinburgh University library, discovering history. Blair was wrapping himself into a toga to take to the stage at Fettes College as Mark Antony in *Julius Caesar*.

Tempting though it would be to imagine a hazy spring day in the mid-sixties with two familiar figures, young and scrawny and mud-streaked, cavorting on rugby fields on either side of the Firth of Forth, one in the deep pink of Fettes and the other in the navy and gold hoops of Kirkcaldy High School, it almost certainly never happened. That particular image of teenage doppelgängers, playing out the first stages of their destiny almost within sight of each other, would be rather too easy and very misleading.

They were not peas from the same pod. When they did arrive in Edinburgh it was from different ways of life and they were set on separate paths. Blair's school years under the Gormenghast-like turrets and pillars of Fettes were programmed by rigid rules that were still self-consciously drawn from the traditions of the English public school – all houses and dorms and sporting spirit.

Blair's father, Leo, had chosen Fettes because it was said to be the finest public school in Edinburgh, the city in which his son had been born in 1953. A pupil from the age of eight at The Chorister School, Durham Cathedral, near the family home, Fettes was a natural progression for Blair. The great central spire of the college seems to command a kind of island on the northern side of Edinburgh, a vast building surrounded by its own trees and grounds. In Blair's day it was its own world, a deeply conservative institution that would only start to indulge in tentative change during his time there. Fettes was for the sons of empire, a place for training administrators and men of affairs, a school in which the pursuit of excellence was often assumed to encompass public success. Leo Blair had lectured in law at Edinburgh University at an earlier stage in his career and was now practising as a barrister on the Newcastle-upon-Tyne circuit, so the Blairs were a comfortable middle-class family, well able to afford the fees at Fettes for their two sons, William and Tony. Going to Fettes was not an act of social climbing. To Blair's father, who held Conservative views, it was a sensible way of making the most of the rewards from his professional achievements.

It would have been odd if Gordon Brown had not become a student in Scotland. The grip of the four ancient universities, all founded before the end of the sixteenth century, was strong. St Andrews, Glasgow, Aberdeen and Edinburgh were *the* places of learning. Only after the new universities began to spring up in the mid-sixties was the old pattern broken. Until then, any student who ventured south of the border was an exotic bird indeed, and the Scottish tradition was for Oxford and Cambridge to be places for a second degree if they were to be contemplated at all. Only in a few schools were they seen as natural options for the high achiever. They were very distant places. And Brown came from a background which was rooted deep in Scottish soil. Growing up in Scotland in the 1950s was to be aware of the weight of tradition. All of us were influenced by the generation that passed on the Victorian values of school, church and self-reliance. Children like Brown, brought up in the manse or the schoolhouse, still the twin pillars of the village or town, were taught that self-improvement was an obligation and so was a commitment to the community around. Whatever the family's party politics, this was overwhelmingly a conservative society in which decency and proper form had to be respected. Radicalism and scepticism were important forces too, but they operated in a context that seemed unchanging, the echo of a settled society.

The label 'son of the manse' often feels like a burden to those who wear it. Images of black-clad ministers glowering from high pulpits, and church elders prodding worshippers out of their homes on Sunday mornings, have proved hard to dispel. The Church of Scotland in which Brown grew up was certainly an institution that clung to many old ways, but it was a world away from the caricature that places so many Scots in the same grim category as the 'Wee Free' Presbyterians in their tiny sect. Dr John Brown brought up his three sons, John, Gordon and Andrew, in quite a different atmosphere. The pressure on them came not so much from a strictness in the home, but from the natural difficulty that anyone has in growing up the son of a highly respected member of the community. They grew up with a father who was considered a saintly man.

Dr Brown was a striking figure, noted for the power of his personality and for his preaching. Theology and social concern were inseparable. His first two children were born in Glasgow, when he was a parish minister in Govan on the southern banks of the Clyde, and in 1954 the family moved to Kirkcaldy when Gordon was three. The town sits on the northern shore of the Firth of Forth within sight of Edinburgh across the water and in an area which Brown has never left. His constituency begins a few miles to the west. He lives on the Forth. His education was completed within twenty miles of his family home. The boys grew up in a manse which was teeming with local life, more of an advice centre and a place of refuge than a grand house. Sunday after Sunday Brown heard his father preach and has often spoken of the effect his words had. 'He taught me to treat everyone equally, and that is something I have not forgotten,' he said in 1995.

At about that time, when his father had just turned eighty, Brown and his two brothers collected a number of his sermons, many of them dating back to their childhood, and had them bound and presented to him. A senior Whitehall civil servant (a Scot) suggested to Brown, who was shadow Chancellor at the time, that the Conservative Lord Chancellor, Lord Mackay of Clashfern, might like to have a copy since he would be interested in those sermons. James Mackay was a member of the strict Free Presbyterian Church (with whom he eventually fell out for the 'sin' of attending a requiem mass). He was indeed struck by Dr Brown's sermons, and wrote to him about one in particular. The two men had never met, but the retired minister was touched to receive the letter. When his son next met the thoughtful civil servant, the shadow Chancellor put his arm round his shoulder in a rare physical gesture of intimacy to thank him for a thought which had given his father such pleasure, and was clearly very moved. Such feelings run strong in Brown, though to outsiders the surface offers few clues to what lies beneath. The ties to his family and his background are exceptionally strong.

That background meant that education was important. Scots of Brown's generation were still reared on the inherited assumption that nothing should interfere with schooling. It was a duty of self-improvement that couldn't be put aside. In his case, it involved starting nursery school at four and ending up at the local secondary school, Kirkcaldy High. In Edinburgh and Glasgow education was a more complicated business, with an expanding private sector and all the jostling and jealousy that it customarily involves, but in places like Kirkcaldy things were straightforward. He would progress down the usual path and, of course, go on to university.

By the time he was sitting his leaving exams in the senior school, he was a natural recruit for a scheme which had intrigued the headmaster, Robert Adam, and which was being taken up by quite a number of Scottish schools. There would be a fast track for pupils who might benefit from an earlier start at university. Brown was academically gifted, a fact obvious to all his teachers from the start, so he was a natural candidate. And off he went to Edinburgh to study history in the autumn of 1967. There appears to have been no concern at school that he might be too young. Any relish, however, was tinged with anxiety and some anger.

As a schoolboy, Brown had been limbering up for student politics by dabbling in embryonic journalism, putting together a crude newspaper with his older brother (which they sold to neighbours for pocket money). He was racing ahead, but the speed disturbed him.

One of his biographers, Paul Routledge, later winkled out a fascinating unpublished essay in which Brown revealed his feelings about the system that had sent him on his way so quickly. Many of his friends had been pushed too fast for their own good and were then confronted with what seemed to them to be failure. Brown wrote: 'Surely it is better for children to succeed at school, and leave with some qualification for work, rather than endure failure, ignominy, rejection and at the least, strain, for the ironic reason of averting failure at university?' The words reek of self-consciousness at his own success, perhaps even of some guilt that he was one of those singled out for glory. Certainly there is evidence of some sense of awkwardness at being set apart so soon from those with whom he'd played rugby and football and watched Raith Rovers, the local Kirkcaldy football team.

He became a student with that feeling of injustice done to friends evidently running strongly in his mind. On top of all that, his arrival in Edinburgh coincided with a crisis of a sort he had never confronted before. At school, he was keen on sport. In his last term he took his place as a flanker in the school XV playing against the old boys and in the course of the game he took a bang on the head. Months later he realized that it had caused a problem with his sight. In the very week that he started as an Edinburgh University student he went into the Royal Infirmary for an examination that led to a period of some terror. The retina of one eye was detached in such a way that the sight of it could not be saved, and there was a scare about the other eye. It might go the same way. He listened to recordings of books made specially for the blind. His first term was sacrificed to the consequences of that moment on the rugby field and there were regular interruptions to his university life, during which he had three more operations. He took a general arts degree in this period, going on to take an honours degree in history after the operations were over, and staying on at the university to study for a Ph.D in Scottish Labour history, a passion that would remain.

His first years in Edinburgh were gruelling. The ban on reading after his operations would have been a handicap and a frustration to anyone: to someone already bookish and intellectually muscular it was a nightmare. Everyone who knows him well recognizes that his single-mindedness and relentless determination must in part be attributed to that trial in his late teens. For them, it explains elements of his character which sometimes seem impenetrable to outsiders.

That first year in Edinburgh, therefore, wasn't for Brown quite the invigorating introduction to student life that the age was promising to be for others. *Les événements* in Paris in the early summer of 1968 were having their effect across Europe, even in Edinburgh, though there were no bonfires or water cannon in the streets. In the piles of paving stones and behind the barricades was the stirring of a radicalism that began to transform campuses (although that term didn't yet apply) for a generation that knew its own music but hadn't yet discovered its own politics. Optimism was in the air. Sometimes it was angry, sometimes it was complacent, but it was there. Around Edinburgh University, student politics was beginning to bubble. Brown's brother John, two years older, was making his name as president of the Students' Representative Council (SRC) – the established student body – and others were starting to find political footholds. One was a notably eloquent young man with red hair. His name was Robin Cook and, five years older than Brown, he was finishing his honours degree in English when the sixteen-year-old arrived from Kirkcaldy. People knew of Cook. He had political ambitions.

Across the city, on the other side of the Georgian New Town, life at Fettes College went on more sedately. While Brown found the world opening up for him at the university, Tony Blair was settling into an institution which would frustrate him and turn him into something of an early rebel, though his irritations had no formal political character. When he became a boarder in the summer of 1966, having just turned thirteen, the regime controlled by the headmaster, Dr Ian McIntosh, was one that would have been familiar to generations long gone. Junior boys could be caned by prefects, apparently with relish. The remnants of a 'fagging' system were still in place, with the young boys acting as valets for their elders, some prefects still enjoying the consequences of the discovery of an inadequately polished shoe or a burnt piece of toast. Blair was beaten more than once. The boys led a life that was cut off. They saw little of the city which surrounded the school. Richard Lambert, later editor of the *Financial Times*, who preceded Blair at Fettes, says: 'It's extraordinary to think that we lived in one of Europe's great cities for six or seven years and hardly saw it. We didn't know Edinburgh at all.' Blair seldom talks of Fettes, but Oxford friends recall unflattering descriptions of his life there.

Blair was lucky that unlike those who had preceded him – they included future acquaintances like Lord Woolf, who became Lord Chief Justice in 2000, and the head of the weapons decommissioning body for Northern Ireland, General John de Chastelain – his generation began to see changes. In particular, Blair came under the influence of Dr Eric Anderson, who was in charge of a new house – Arniston – which opened in his second year at Fettes. Arniston, nowadays populated entirely by girls, became a haven for relaxation, at least by Fettes standards. By the time Blair left for Oxford in 1972, girls had been admitted to the sixth form (to the sound of the gnashing of Old Fettesian teeth worldwide).

The reports of Blair from fellow pupils and staff over the years have been of a boy who always enjoyed attention. From the start, that was the Blair story. He is the first Fettesian to become Prime Minister – in the sixties the Conservative Cabinet heavyweights Selwyn Lloyd and Iain Macleod were the most celebrated old boy politicians – and on the eve of his election in 1997 a former member of staff was happy to ponder his suitability for high office, gesturing towards the school theatre and saying: 'That, of course, is where he was happiest.'

His first outing was as Mark Antony in a house play but he graduated to starring roles in the annual school play, which was taken very seriously, and by the time he was a senior boy he was very much the thespian Blair. Eric Anderson was largely responsible for this enthusiasm. He considered Blair a natural actor who had an ability to think himself into parts: when he was on the stage he believed in his character and meant what he said. His stage activities were combined with regular trips – some illicit, according to contemporaries – into the outside world of Edinburgh, which were the cause of some consternation, as was the length of his hair. He was frequently disciplined and it is clear that by the end of his time at Fettes he was very happy to be away. Although Fettes admitted its first girl in his last year (as a favour to a governor of the school), for someone such as Blair who preferred to listen to Led Zeppelin and had no interest in beating the thirteen-year-old boys being lined up as prospective fags, the place was fairly grim. It changed markedly in the decade or so afterwards, and now takes pride in the description 'progressive' which in Blair's day most of the masters would have taken as an insult.

Inescapably, those Edinburgh years are etched on Brown and Blair. The future Prime Minister never lived there again and it has always been obvious that, although Blair is proud of his Scottish connections (occasionally making time on awkward party conference trips to Glasgow to visit old relations), the school years don't glimmer fondly in his mind. In conversation, the happier times at Oxford always take precedence. Partly, this may be because Blair has never felt part of the kind of establishment whose sons he came to know at school.

As a Conservative, Blair's father, Leo, had harboured hopes of a parliamentary candidacy at one stage, and the pattern of his education was cast in an unsurprising mould, his older brother having gone to Fettes before him. Blair's evident unease as he grew up had less to do with some burning political radicalism – he has always acknowledged that he had no such feelings – than with an instinctive irritation at the rules and the expected form of behaviour.

By the time Blair headed south at the age of nineteen in the summer of 1972 in the hope of greater excitement at Oxford, life in Edinburgh for Gordon Brown had already become more adventurous. The university was on the boil, and the students were discovering the joys of rebelliousness. They were blessed in this enterprise by a principal and vice-chancellor, Michael Swann, who played into their hands. The more they demanded 'democratization' and greater representation on the university's governing bodies, the more he resisted. As a result, the leaders of the students got what they wanted: trouble. A typical incident was the sacking of the editor of the campus newspaper, *Student*, by the university because it had published an article about LSD. Swann announced that he had sent a copy of the paper to the Home Office. There was a minor riot. The editor was reinstated and they waited for the next explosion.

Brown arrived at Edinburgh young and shy, and within three years had turned into a student politician who was becoming adept at using the campus newspaper to make mischief. By the time he finished his history degree and embarked on research for his Ph.D he was stirring it up whenever he could. It was hardly revolutionary stuff, but this was the first phase of student radicalism in Britain, and the university authorities found that they were under siege. Students wanted power in the institutions and at every turn they were happy to bash the vice-chancellors and governing bodies. The student newspapers of the time paint pictures of universities as bastions of stuffiness and reaction, ripe for reform. Brown was in the thick of it.

Like all trainee-radical students of the time, he was helped by South Africa. The Springboks' rugby tour of Britain attracted huge demonstrations across the country in 1970, and universities across Britain vied with each other to get the most protesters on the streets and disrupt the games most effectively. In Edinburgh, there was another spicy ingredient. From somewhere in the university administration came the leak of a list of the investments it held, showing that it had valuable shareholdings in some of the companies which were the pillars of the apartheid regime. The list found its way to Brown and his friends. At the time, this was the kind of political 'crime' which could spark a demonstration, or the occupation of some university office. A special-edition of *Student* was printed and Swann found himself surveying a campus in revolt. It was an embarrassing revelation for him personally, because, like many middle-of-the-road public figures, he was prominently associated with the anti-apartheid movement. The leaked information was used by the students to make the university hierarchy seem hypocritical and secretive, a charge to which it had no convincing reply.

Those of us of the same generation elsewhere in Scotland heard of these antics with predictable interest and envy. Edinburgh was alive. The episode was a humiliation for an institution nominally devoted to academic freedom and the principles of the eighteenth-century Enlightenment which had been one of Edinburgh's glories. It was also embarrassing for a university justifiably proud of its Commonwealth links and its internationalism to be accused of double standards. A substantial number of students were determined to be unforgiving. The place was in ferment, and in Swann the likes of Brown realized they had found a soft target. Copies of *Student* from 1970 have an air of simmering expectation. The authorities were on the defensive.

Within a year students were able to force on the university a change which was resisted and deeply resented by traditionalists in the administration and the academic body: they elected a student rector. In Scottish universities, the post of rector is a remnant of a nineteenth-century concept of symbolic student representation in the government of the institution. The rector was obliged under university statute to be the voice of the student body. It was never a position of real political power, more an emblem of the student presence, but rectors are still elected every few years by the students to sit on the university's highest council, the court. Indeed, they have the traditional right to chair it. In practice, rectorial elections were carnivals at all the universities, with serious candidates outnumbered by eccentrics and oddball figures from stage and screen (although unlikely figures such as John Cleese and Clement Freud have both served as hard-working rectors in St Andrews and Dundee). In sixties' Scotland there were exceptions, like the Liberal leader, Jo Grimond, who was an active rector in Edinburgh and, later, in Aberdeen. From time to time a figure of real distinction was elected. But the idea of a student as rector was generally still too daring.

Brown's first rector was the journalist and sage Malcolm Muggeridge, who in 1968 was engaged in a moral repudiation of his earlier leftism and was an eloquent assailant of all that sixties liberalization represented. He chose Edinburgh for one of his most famous blasts, which he delivered from the pulpit of St Giles Cathedral. The High Kirk of St Giles on the Royal Mile is one of the city's most potent historical buildings, the place where John Knox and his followers hatched the sixteenth-century Reformation against the Catholic hierarchy. Muggeridge took to the pulpit to denounce student immorality and in particular the arrival of the contraceptive pill which, as a rigorous convert to Catholicism, he abhorred. Students in Edinburgh were slothful and self-indulgent. Instead of carrying the torch for progress into a glorious future they were leading spiritually impoverished lives demanding 'pot and pills, for the most tenth-rate form of escapism and self-indulgence known to man'. Muggeridge resigned as rector. It was an electric event in the university's life, dramatizing the widening gap between the lives of most students and the old order. For those who wanted change, Muggeridge's theatrical and tortured outburst was a gift. In *Student*, he was lampooned as a comic figure who had become a sour absurdity.

The temperature was high and the paper was lively. Brown gravitated naturally to it, and became editor in his second year. The tone of the paper was propagandist: student rents . . . university secrecy . . . censorship – they were the staple diet of the editorial. There were, however, distractions. Almost every issue had on its front page, as if by statute, a picture of some pouting female student, usually lying on a grassy bank or lounging on Georgian steps. This was the kind of appeal turned into a populist art form by the tabloids in the seventies, and excoriated by the Labour Party for it, but it seemed to cause Brown no agony at all in his student days. He encouraged it. Young women spread themselves across the page, usually displaying a generous thigh or two, and gave the paper a louche spirit that was obviously intended. One of the pictures inside during Brown's editorship carried the caption 'Marguerite de Roumanie', on the occasion of her election to the SRC. This was Princess Marguerite of Romania, a contemporary of Brown's with whom he was having a relationship. Many years later it led to barbed jokes from Cabinet colleagues about the relative merits of the chancellorship and the throne of Romania.

There are other poignant pictures. In October 1969 the president of the National Union of Students came north to Edinburgh to try to persuade the recalcitrant Scottish Union of Students to merge with it, a sensitive question among student politicians in Scotland (although no one else) at the time. He can be seen on the front page, haranguing the crowd in Edinburgh, all hair, black-rimmed glasses and waving arms. It is Jack Straw. He remembers two things about that visit: 'We won. And the next morning I had the worst hangover of my life.'

Most students cared nothing for the world of trainee politics, but it was fertile ground for those who did. Tremors ran through university administrations across the country and for Brown's generation the prospect of causing more tremors was a nice counterpoint to the ritual scorn which every self-respecting student politician of the left had to pour on the Labour government of the day for its various 'betrayals'. Harold Wilson might have abandoned radicalism; they hadn't.

In such an atmosphere as Edinburgh, it was inevitable that there should be talk of trying to elect a student rector. Within two or three years the idea had become serious enough to produce a candidate who might win. That candidate was Jonathan Wills, a geography student with a shaggy beard and an irrepressible urge for self-promotion, and in late 1971 he beat the satirical cartoonist and journalist Willie Rushton to become the students' representative on the university court. Brown was the chairman of the Labour Club, and Wills was their candidate. This was a symbolic change, in the sense that no one expected the university to be different on the day after the election, but a different kind of political era had indeed begun. Wills was on the court for a year before he resigned. He had been a successful irritant and little more. Brown was the candidate to replace him and in a contest in November 1972 with the future industrialist (later Sir) Fred Catherwood, effectively the Conservative candidate, he won by a huge margin in a campaign which wasn't entirely high-minded – his campaign posters had him promoted by girls called 'Brown's Sugars' (after 'Brown Sugar' by the Rolling Stones from the 1971 album *Sticky Fingers*). *Student* was ecstatic, in the manner of such publications, celebrating the election of one of its own. His margin of victory, it announced cheerily and ridiculously, was 'the equivalent of President Nixon's landslide'.

Brown was now established. As a badge of his election he enjoyed the fact that Michael Swann was sufficiently irritated by it to refuse to attend the formal announcement of the result. From the start they were at war, and the engagement didn't last long. At the end of the year, Swann announced that he would be leaving Edinburgh to become chairman of the BBC, where he thought he would find relative peace. He had no appetite for the struggles that were obviously about to begin. For three years or so, the university establishment had been flinching uncomfortably. Brown turned the rectorship into a campaigning pedestal. He chaired the court, and issued press releases as if they were statements from the court as a whole, which they were not. When one was torn up by the university before it could be issued he announced in *Student* that it was 'political censorship of the lowest and most dreadful sort'. The whole posture was of a democrat pitched against the forces of reaction. His hair was long now, his crowd of supporters were starting to have the feel of a claque, and he was honing a polemical style in his column in the paper. Some of his colleagues from those days – notably Colin Currie and Murray Elder, who had gone to school in Kirkcaldy with him – would remain in the tight inner circle nearly thirty years later.

None of this would be a surprise to colleagues who came to know him in his political career. Already, certain characteristics were obvious. He attracted supporters, who understood the rule that loyalty was expected. He was single-minded. He was fascinated by the power of the printed word in pursuit of a campaign. And he was delving into Scottish Labour history of the twenties for his academic research, work which was pulling him sharply leftwards. He was impatient with the party he had started supporting as a teenager, following his father's example. Like many ministers in the Kirk, Dr Brown was a Labour voter.

Young left-wingers in Scotland had a cause. 'Red Clydeside' was a phrase that had found its way back into politics. The sit-in at Upper Clyde shipbuilders in 1971 had a galvanizing effect on the left, pitting the Scottish unions against Edward Heath's Tory government elected a year earlier. Somehow the tone in Scottish politics changed, with events on the Clyde polarizing opinion. None of the principal objectives of the sit-in were achieved – the decline in shipbuilding and the loss of jobs went on when the tumult had died down – but for Brown and young Labour people of his generation it had a profound effect, allowing them to forget their frustrations with the Labour government of the late sixties. They enjoyed seeing the politics of the street and the shipyard return. Direct action was invigorating. It was no long-term answer, much more a burst of radicalism that passed away quickly, but it charged the atmosphere. For an ambitious young politician it was a good time. There was the smell of cordite in the shipyards, huge demonstrations in the streets and on the campus a university court to be challenged and harried. Brown celebrated Swann's imminent departure with a victory against the university in the High Court in a judgement on the powers of the rector in mid-1973 and demonstrated that at the age of twenty-two he had learned how to use political muscle.

Blair missed it all at Fettes. He was two years younger, marooned at school. The clandestine trips over the wall into Edinburgh, which the boys regarded as something like an escape from Colditz, and arguments with masters about the length of their hair were about as exciting as it got. One of Blair's fellow pupils in Arniston, William Primrose, remembers the atmosphere as quite intimidating: 'In those days the school was quite oppressive, with quite a bit of peer-group pressure to conform. Those who were not conventional in a public school way tended to be mocked.' Blair escaped that mockery, not least because his exploits on the stage gave him a certain profile in the school, and because his rebelliousness appeared to have a certain style to it. It was obvious that schools like Fettes would have to change – the old rules and attitudes would repel the next generation of prospective parents – but change was slow to arrive. Blair was frustrated. In his last term, indeed, he left the school to live at the home of Lord Mackenzie-Stuart, a distinguished Scottish judge (and an Old Fettesian), whose daughter Amanda was the first girl to be accepted by Fettes. It was a deliberate manoeuvre by Blair's housemaster, to keep a rebellious spirit in check. He was frustrated and unhappy and anxious to be away.

At Oxford, Blair was no student politician, and never tried to be one. He took no formal position in the set-piece left–right student struggles of the day. After he arrived at St John's College to read law in 1972 there was an occupation of the Examination Schools building, at the heart of the university which was a *cause célèbre* on the left, a repetition of a famous late sixties episode which Oxford had thought of as its answer to the Paris revolution. The demonstration was a passionate affair for those involved, and the object of curiosity for many others who visited the scene of the action like interested tourists, but for most students it was a distant political event which hardly touched them. Blair's college did have its political cliques, but the ritual elections for the committee of the student body, the Junior Common Room, were not always very serious. One of Blair's closest friends, David Furzdon, recalls finding himself unexpectedly listed on both the right-wing and the left-wing slate in one JCR election. The group around Blair was neither involved in the activity on the left, which was fierce in a teenage sort of way, nor in the High Tory japes of the playboys who clustered round outfits like the Archery Club.

Yet there were glimmerings of Blair's style. One postgraduate student who arrived soon after Blair, Robert Watt, noticed him early on. 'I clearly recall my first sight of him. Someone in the student common room after dinner said "That's Tony Blair over there." When I said "Who's he?" or "So what?", he replied in some awe "He's in a rock band." I've always remembered this – since long before Blair became famous.

'He had an aura about him even then; people noticed him; he stood out. There must have been fifty people in the room but he was the one who got the attention. That may well have been the point of being in the band. In other words, he was already deploying the sorts of assets – trendiness and charm – which have been in evidence ever since.'

The band was Ugly Rumours, a name taken from the cover of a Grateful Dead album which was in vogue at the time. Blair – who used to be listed in the Fettes school choir at Founder's Day concerts as a tenor – was lead singer. According to students in and around St John's at the time, it would be misleading to think of the band as a sensational outfit with much of a following. It was a more modest ensemble. Furzdon recalls being at parties where Ugly Rumours might have been playing in the corner, but no more than that. No one expected that they might one day try to remember where they were when they first heard them play. Did they play at the Beggar's Banquet in St John's in 1974, the alternative College Ball? Quite a few people who were there have no recollection. Yet it helped to give Blair a style. He had no interest in the parliamentary kindergarten of the Oxford Union, whose doorstep he appears hardly ever to have darkened, and never mixed with the radicals who were running the Broad Left group of student politicians at the time. It may be symptomatic of that Oxford atmosphere of the day that none of the campus figures on the left in Blair's time went on to make important careers in mainstream politics. It was a strange atmosphere. Melanie Phillips, the *Sunday Times* columnist was a left-wing student at St Anne's. 'The sixties generation had gone. We were an in-between generation. The only fashionable place to be political was in the IS [the International Socialists, later to become the Socialist Workers Party]. Anyone who was in the Labour [Party] was regarded by everyone else as an appalling lickspittle and creep just looking for a career.'

Like many - probably most - students, Blair let politics go its own way. He never flirted with the far left, and made no effort to connect with the mainstream parties. Robert Watt says that one of the college catchphrases was 'He's far too intense', used of people who showed enthusiasm for something, particularly politics. Blair was never accused of being too intense.

But he did work hard. David Furzdon says: 'You'd be at a party . . . and you'd turn round at about one o'clock and find that Tony had gone. He'd slipped away quietly a couple of hours before. You'd find that he was getting up at five o'clock to finish an essay or to read something that had to be read. He was popular and gregarious but he was always careful and determined with his work.' It was, however, an application which his friends thought would lead to the law and nothing else.

The other side of Blair that emerged at St John's was spiritual. He has often cited his discovery of the Scottish philosopher John

Macmurray as a turning point in his life, but perhaps more important is the character who turned him towards Macmurray in the first place, a priest with an exceptionally powerful personality called Peter Thomson. Thomson is an Australian with the gift of directness and hypnotic eyes, and he made an impression on Blair that lasts to this day. His forthright character is summed up in an incident that took place at Buckingham Palace in the 1990s.

Peter Thomson had known the Prince of Wales at school in Australia in the sixties and he found himself, more than twenty years later, at an informal lunch with Palace aides discussing, among other things, the standing of the royal family. Asked about the Prince, Thomson recalls with glee that he told his fellow-lunchers that he thought the future king was performing perfectly well and was 'a good bloke'. It was a pity, though, that in public 'he always looks as if he has a carrot stuck up his arse'. Thomson much enjoyed the long silence that followed.

The irreverent reverend imparted a Christian commitment to Blair, an Anglo-Catholic approach which was in keeping with the practices he'd learned as a boy at The Chorister School (but which at Fettes had seemed of little importance to him). Thomson had read Macmurray at theological college and considered him one of the most important British philosophers of the century. The part of Macmurray's philosophy which Blair absorbed was the simple dichotomy which was claimed between 'society' and 'community', a distinction which he has adapted for his political purposes. Community, in Macmurray's definition, is something based on friendship. He rejects the Marxist thinking that has influenced so many mainstream Labour figures that sees conflict as an integral part of any human system. For Blair the combination of a belief in communities built on partnerships and trust between individuals, and the obligation of the Christian to 'love thy neighbour as thyself' was potent. At that stage in his life it was a substitute for formal politics, and the attitudes he developed at Oxford have never left him. Macmurray's deeper thoughts about the need to remove all aggression from society – which made him in the end a Quaker – sprang in part from his rejection of organized politics, and Blair has never followed the argument through. But the celebration of 'community' which was held to be something wider and deeper than any particular kind of organized society was one that attracted him, and stayed with him. Macmurray's ideas have attracted a good deal of ridicule, because they appear to rest on a belief in everyone's capacity for good: communities worked when people were nice to each other. The significance of Blair's interest is that it reveals how much more he has always been attracted to theories of personal responsibility than to political ideology.

Contrast this with Gordon Brown's political journey in Edinburgh. While Blair was completing his second year at Oxford with the college president, Sir Richard Southern, noting in his end-of-year assessment that he seemed 'quite extraordinarily happy', Brown was quite extraordinarily angry. He was already a political figure of substance, and deep in the arguments which had been stirred up with the election of first seven and then eleven Scottish National Party MPs in the two elections of 1974. The politics of Scotland was alive again.

In the Labour Party, the established leaders were solidly resisting any concessions to the SNP by way of devolution. That constituted appeasement. Led by the schoolmasterly figure of the Scottish Secretary Willie Ross, the party establishment's attitude was one of utter antagonism to nationalism and to any kind of elected assembly. But there were some Labour MPs, and a growing number of younger activists in Scotland, who believed that the policy was not only doomed but wrong. They began to plan for a Scottish Parliament, to fulfil the pledge that Keir Hardie had given when he founded the Labour Party in 1899.

Gordon Brown's response to the exhilarating mood was to produce, in 1975, *The Red Paper on Scotland*, a collection of essays which was meant to be the socialist prospectus for a new Scotland. Brown's introduction, entitled 'The Socialist Challenge', gives a vivid picture of his political mind at that moment, and one which is startling to anyone who knows only Chancellor Brown. In it he wrote:

Political power will become a synthesis of – not a substitute for – community and industrial life. This requires from the Labour Movement in Scotland today a positive commitment to creating a socialist society, a coherent strategy with rhythm and modality to each reform to cancel the logic of capitalism and a programme of immediate aims which leads out of one social order into another. Such a social reorganization – a phased extension of public control under workers' self-management and the prioritizing of social needs set by the communities themselves – if sustained and enlarged, would in E. P. Thompson's words lead to 'a crisis not of despair and disintegration but a crisis in which the necessity for a peaceful revolutionary transition to an alternative socialist logic became daily more evident'.

The turgid style is characteristic of leftist pamphlets of the time and *The Red Paper* was a classic of the genre. It was fat, badly printed and bound, with tiny type, but it was stuffed with thinkers and their thoughts. All over Scotland (and in every political party) the serious argument about devolution was boiling. What kind of Scotland should it be? The thought that there might never be a Scottish Parliament was withering away. Margaret Thatcher, elected Conservative leader in 1975, was even having difficulty with the Scottish Tories, quite a number of whom were committed to change. Michael Ancram was appointed party chairman in Scotland (he'd sat in the Commons for Berwick and East Lothian between the February and October elections in 1974) and was having difficulty explaining to her what was going on in Scotland. At one meeting she saw him to the door with the memorable words: 'Michael, I am an English nationalist and never you forget it.' But it was in the Labour Party that the real agony came.

Part of the problem was that a majority of its MPs were anti-devolution. They loathed the SNP – the 'Tartan Tories' they called them disparagingly – and were in no mind to give ground to them. But when Harold Wilson resigned as Prime Minister in March 1976 he bequeathed to his successor, Jim Callaghan, a government without a majority. As well as the informal Lib-Lab pact concluded with the Liberal leader David Steel in 1977, Callaghan had to neutralize the eleven nationalists who might bring him down. So a devolution bill – covering both Scotland and Wales – was born. It was a disaster. The Welsh Labour MPs objected to it even more than the Scots and it fell. Its successors were two separate bills, each setting up an elected Assembly. The story of the three years of the Callaghan government looked at from Scotland was the story of devolution.

During the mid-1970s Brown progressed from student rebel, to *Red Paper* editor, to Labour troublemaker. Once he had finished his Ph.D he began to teach politics at Glasgow College of Technology (though still living in Edinburgh) and began to rise. Older MPs had marked him down as an awkward whippersnapper from the start and when he went on to become chairman of the party's devolution committee in Scotland in 1978 at the age of twenty-seven there was real rage among those of the old guard at Westminster who were fervently opposed to devolution. But the government had to lurch on. Without the SNP and the Liberals, both devoted to the idea of devolution, it could not survive. Though many of its Scottish MPs did not believe in it, the devolution minister in the Cabinet Office, John Smith, finally secured the bill, at the price of a referendum. Again, there was much moaning among old party lags. Away from Westminster, in Scotland, Brown was devolution's leading advocate. It did not make him popular with some of the MPs who trundled back home from London on the night sleeper on a Thursday night. You did not have to spend long in the all-night bar rattling north before you heard the phrase 'that bastard Brown'.

Although it cost him some friends and made him enemies, it was the making of Brown. Robin Cook, the student politician when Brown arrived at university, had been elected MP for Edinburgh Central in 1974 and was convinced that the devolution policy was wrong. But Brown organized students to work on Cook's campaign. Despite their differences on devolution, the personal hostility between them came later. Like Tam Dalyell, MP for West Lothian, who saw himself as the Cassandra of the devolution years, complete with the gift of seeing into the future and the curse of never being believed, Cook campaigned across Scotland against devolution.

When the government was forced to concede the referendum to get the bill through, it was with a built-in high hurdle inserted by the anti-devolutionists which meant that 40 per cent of all those *entitled* to vote had to vote 'Yes' for an Assembly to be established in Edinburgh. The campaign was a disaster for the government, revealing Labour's splits and the lack of enthusiasm for the scheme among some of those who were meant to be its strongest advocates. The vote was lost, on the 40 per cent rule, because the bare majority that voted 'Yes' wasn't big enough, and Callaghan was therefore obliged under the legislation to introduce a Commons order repealing the Scotland Act and stopping the Assembly. He played for time but the SNP deserted him. They tabled a vote of no confidence, the Conservatives seized their moment, and on 29 March 1979 the government lost a vote of confidence by one vote. Mrs Thatcher was elected Prime Minister five weeks later.

The agonies of the Callaghan government quickly matured Brown and a generation of young Scottish politicians. While in England Labour was starting to sink into the rows and splits of the Bennite years and the rise of Militant, Scotland was still gripped by a real constitutional argument over devolution. Brown fought Edinburgh South in the 1979 election but was beaten by Michael Ancram. He began to work in current affairs for Scottish Television in Glasgow, but no one doubted that he would soon find a safe seat.

In fact, he had some difficulty. It was late in the day, just before the 1983 election itself, that he managed to find enough support – much of it on the union left – to give him a chance at Dunfermline East. He won the selection conference easily, but even six months before it had seemed that he might find it hard to be selected anywhere. Anti-devolution figures resented him; the old guard in the party still considered him an upstart; he'd been ruffling feathers for years. When finally Brown was chosen by the voters of Dunfermline it was hardly a happy election night for new Labour MPs. They watched their party sink to its lowest share of the vote for more than sixty years – 27.6 per cent and 209 seats.

On that same night, 9 June 1983, Tony Blair watched the results in Sedgefield, County Durham. His arrival at Sedgefield was as late as Brown's although for different reasons. After he left Oxford his political education was slow and his interest patchy. He went to London to train as a barrister, coming under the magisterial influence of Alexander 'Derry' Irvine in chambers which also produced Cherie Booth, and married her in 1979 with Irvine present as a beaming matchmaker. Only then did politics start to grip him, and his marriage was part of the change. His wife was a budding candidate and had an appetite for party battles that was still undeveloped in Blair himself. Years later he would cheerily admit: 'It was late before I had any politics at all.' His enthusiasm for politics was certainly kindled by his wife. Before he came to London in the mid-seventies he had indulged in no political activity. With his barrister friend Charlie Falconer he began to attend Labour meetings and joined the party. With his wife trying unsuccessfully to win the Labour nomination in Crosby (for the by-election won by Shirley Williams for the SDP) and going on to fight Thanet North in 1983 their household was becoming, surprisingly for him, a political one. By 1982 he wanted to have a trial run for Westminster. He would be the Labour candidate in the hopeless (staunchly Conservative) seat of Beaconsfield in Buckinghamshire, a place of copper beeches, the chalky Chiltern Hills, and not far from the Prime Minister's country home, Chequers.

The by-election was widely covered, not because any of the candidates was particularly interesting or promising, but because it came at a time when the Labour Party was riven by fratricide, appearing determined to destroy itself in set-piece battles between right and left which weakened the leadership of Michael Foot to the point where it appeared beyond rescuing. To top it all, Blair fought the last week of the campaign to the sound of rejoicing from Downing Street as British troops landed in the Falklands to take the fight to General Galtieri, whose Argentine forces had seized them on 2 April. The Prime Minister was rampant and Labour was struggling to stem the tide of defections to the newly constituted Social Democratic Party: the landscape was bleak.

Blair's start was unspectacular, though he had some new advantages. Irvine, an ever-present father figure throughout this period, had introduced him to his old university friend from Glasgow, John Smith. Smith and Irvine were a pair of gossiping, hard-drinking cronies with a happy lawyerly cynicism about politics mingled with an old-fashioned Labour loyalty. Irvine delivered Blair to the Commons one night for his introduction to Smith. The two spent much of the night boozing happily and a friendship was struck which saw Blair through his first parliamentary decade. Without it he would have begun as a much slighter figure.

So just as Brown was closing in on Dunfermline East, calling in favours from the Transport and General Workers Union to try to scupper the local opposition, Blair was engaged in a similar operation. He had decided he wanted a seat that he could win. When he went to Sedgefield to try to win selection, the election of 1983 was all but under way. In a blitz which later became famous as an example of his blend of charm and ruthlessness he won it. With his agent John Burton, who thought he was the most likely of the hopefuls who were chasing the candidacy, he put together a gang of supporters (the 'Famous Five', including Burton, were Phil Wilson, Paul Trippett, Peter Brookes and Simon Hoban) who saw him through. Even in 1983 the seat was as safe for Labour as Beaconsfield had been for the Tories, and Blair was in.

Brown and Blair had arrived at Westminster by different routes which meandered through quite distinct and separate worlds. One was the product of a political machine which he had understood and manipulated and, in the end, mastered with ease. The other was a wide-eyed amateur at politics. His political ambition began to simmer late. One was ideological by nature; the other was intensely distrustful of ideology and had spent long nights arguing himself into an approach to politics which put attitudes and instinct above historical analysis. But perhaps the greatest significance in the long term was that when they took their seats in 1983 for the first time, it was as MPs who belonged to a party which looked as if it might disintegrate before their eyes.

2
The Room with No Windows

'This party has about eighteen months left.' The words were Blair's, heard by all of us, and it was a sentence that he uttered frequently in the months after the election that brought him to the Commons as the youngest member of the Labour opposition, to sit in a party that was the sullen remnant of a routed army. It was angry, divided and confused. Michael Foot's leadership had disintegrated in acrimony and humiliation and Blair found that the exhilaration of election was shot through with despair.

In the long summer nights of 1983 he and Brown discovered that they shared a deep pessimism about Labour's future. Blair, with none of Brown's background on the left, was the less inclined of the two to think of it in a historical context and exuded a simple sense of alarm. He was splenetic about the manifesto on which he had just fought. On Europe, defence and nationalization he had campaigned on party promises in which he – like many other candidates – didn't believe. To judge by his conversations at that time, the prospect of life at Westminster seemed intolerable unless his party changed. Labour in 1983 was the party that said: 'We will negotiate withdrawal from the EEC which has drained our natural resources and destroyed jobs', a view which the government he eventually led would associate with those in the political outback. He would sit in the darkness of the Commons terrace overlooking the Thames after some late night vote and talk with journalists and colleagues in apocalyptic terms about Labour. The constant refrain was: 'We haven't got long.' Knowing Blair then was knowing an MP whose obvious ambition was tempered by a fear that he might have landed in a party in terminal decline. Visits to the leader's office in those days were extraordinary. Michael Foot would be reading a new biography of Swift, or revisiting an edition of Byron's letters, in what seemed a conscious effort to forget what was going on around him. Across the Thames in County Hall, Ken Livingstone was running the Greater London Council and not only taunting the Conservative government with his policies. He was taunting Foot too, by pursuing a leftist agenda that the leader was trying to disown. Foot's agony was palpable. For young MPs like Blair it verged on pathos.

His first days at Westminster involved a slightly comic period of cohabitation in a room with the Militant-supporting Dave Nellist, an arrangement thought at the time to be a typical whips' office joke in making a relatively smooth public schoolboy share a desk with the party's most obvious outsider (genial though the gangly, bearded Nellist usually was). It didn't last, and by the time the summer recess came, six weeks after the election, Blair and Brown had already decided to become room-mates, crammed into a windowless, airless office just off the main committee corridor of the Commons. They had the advantage of a niche near the main thoroughfare of Parliament in the thick of things, where gossip fills the air. But it was little more than a cupboard with desks.

Brown commanded most of the space in the office with his piles of paper and dog-eared books. Colleagues would compare him to a street-dweller whose every possession was dragged around in a moving pile. Towers of paper leaned into every corner, toppling over now and then to reveal forgotten coffee cups and their furry dregs. When you were invited in you struggled to find a place to perch. Blair seemed the organized intruder in this chaos, complete with barrister's briefcase embossed with his initials. From the start they were a pair that seemed interesting more for their contrasts than for their similarities.

Brown was already an operator, blooded in those Scottish battles and with a mind always tuned to political strategy. Blair was an innocent by comparison. His experience in Sedgefield had left no scars; Brown was covered in them. Blair was a relative unknown when he came to Westminster. He was wide-eyed. The other new MPs recognized the relationship for what it was. Martin O'Neill, a constituency neighbour of Brown's, says that everyone watched Blair acquire his political education. 'Gordon was in charge . . . and Tony was happy with that. It's how he learnt everything.' Brown had networks, in the unions and in Scotland, which provided 20 per cent of the Labour MPs in the 1983 Parliament. He opened that maze of contacts and political folklore to Blair when they came together.

Brown's reaction to the catastrophic election defeat of 1983 – the worst for Labour since 1922 – was different from Blair's. Characteristically, Brown began to make allies and to plan. He never talked about the disintegration of Labour, only about political strategies for survival. He was still gripped by the story of Labour in the twenties and knew that, although his party's position was grim, there was nothing new under the sun.

The difference in their outlook is obvious in their maiden speeches, both made in July. Brown's was a detailed assault on government economic policy, with the hailstorm of statistics that would become his parliamentary trademark, and a claim that mass unemployment would produce mass poverty in his constituency and others like it. Blair had spoken three weeks earlier on 6 July, also about unemployment, but even at this stage in the political kindergarten he was drawing a distinction between his hopes and past Labour thinking. He took the trouble to say that he called himself a socialist 'not through a textbook that has caught my intellectual fancy, nor through unthinking tradition' but because he preferred cooperation to confrontation. From the start, socialism was a word with which he was very careful. He was sparing with it, and almost sounded as if he was grappling for some new way of describing what he was. Even in that first parliamentary outing there are glimpses of the impatience with his party's old ways, and a reluctance to use the old language.

Labour was a churning pot of impatience all summer. Thatcherism was at its high point and new Labour MPs were realizing that it would be a long time before they had a chance to sit on the other side of the Commons. They were right, of course: it would take fourteen years. In the shadow Cabinet, Gerald Kaufman, a veteran operator from the vanished world of Wilson and Callaghan, called the 1983 manifesto 'the longest suicide note in history' and that was the view of many in the parliamentary party, maybe a majority. When Tony Benn (who had lost his seat in Bristol) claimed that the election had been something of a victory for Labour because nearly eight and a half million people had voted for a socialist programme, he was engulfed in a tide of venom. John Smith, who had more personal affection for Benn than most of his front bench colleagues, having worked with him in the Department of Energy, would say simply, 'The man's mad.' He would shake his head in despair.

Foot's inevitable resignation announcement came quickly, and the leadership election that rolled through the summer turned into an orgy of breast-beating about the past. Change there had to be, though there was no agreement about which policies should go and which party rules should be rewritten. That would take years to settle. For the moment, Neil Kinnock and Roy Hattersley represented between them a commitment to some sort of modernization. They had many policy differences – Kinnock was still a fervent unilateralist and wanted to pull out of Europe and Hattersley thought the opposite – but they engineered an informal pact through their campaign managers, Robin Cook and John Smith, to sell themselves as a team. The so-called 'dream ticket' for leader and deputy leader duly scooped up more than two-thirds of the votes in the electoral college. Their dream wasn't that they might find a way of agreeing on policy in a few weeks, simply that they'd save the Labour Party from itself.

Neil Kinnock told the party conference where he was elected that the response to the election disaster must be 'never again', but he discovered quickly that among the unions especially there was little appetite for party reform. Moreover, his own loyalty to Foot, whose leadership campaign he had managed in 1980, meant that on his part there could be no sudden break with the past. Reinventing the party was going to be slow.

It is hard to exaggerate the depth of despair in the Labour Party of 1983. In the General Election campaign the Social Democrats and the Liberals, who together came within three-quarters of a million votes of Labour out of forty-two million cast, were issuing grandiose predictions that they would supplant Labour as the natural opposition – claims that seemed ludicrously inflated even to some of those making them, since they had only twenty-three seats in the Commons, but which helped nonetheless to make the natural story of politics the sickness of Labour and to prompt the whispered question, 'Is it terminal?' In addition, the Social Democrats, founded only two years earlier, were eating into Labour's middle-class support and a series of disastrous by-elections had sapped it of any self-confidence. Warrington, Hillhead (where Roy Jenkins was elected for the SDP), Bermondsey and Darlington were names to make Labour shiver. Margaret Thatcher, Falklands victor, was in command in the Commons with a majority of 144 and the Labour opposition was doomed to turn in on itself, in an orgy of policy rewriting and organizational reform, before it could imagine presenting itself to the country as a credible alternative government.

For younger MPs the only hope was that, in the phrase that Blair was to use as opposition leader way in the future, things could only get better. Kinnock was promising a new era, and that at least gave a pinprick of hope to those younger MPs who had concluded that it was pointless to wait for Thatcherism to explode and for lost Labour votes automatically to come flooding back. It wasn't going to happen like that. The sense of the era as a transitional one was sharpened by the event that hobbled Kinnock's leadership at the start. In retrospect it would be seen as part of the change that Blair, and Brown to a lesser extent, felt must come.

The miners' strike began in March 1984 and lasted for twelve weary months. Kinnock took a battering. Labour's heart was on the picket lines, but for a good many members of the parliamentary party the picture of Arthur Scargill leading the miners to what most of those around Kinnock believed was certain defeat was a nightmare vision brought to life. Kinnock described him with deliberate cruelty as a First World War general, whose troops were being slaughtered. Brown was one of many who was painfully caught. His was a mining constituency, and his maiden speech had been devoted in large part to the survival of the pits and the prosperity of the families around them. But like most Labour MPs he found Scargill's opposition to a strike ballot impossible to defend: in private he would talk of the strike as a disastrous mistake, and admitted afterwards that it had been doomed from the start. The strike prolonged Labour's agony: the unhappy entanglement with Scargill lasted a full year.

Backbenchers were walking through a valley of despair. Many of their constituency parties were sunk in poisonous combat between factions and they could scarcely believe that theirs was a party that had been in government only four years earlier. MPs were bitter about the reselection rules which had been introduced by the party conference as part of the Bennite response to the 1979 defeat, and many of them found themselves condemned to be parliamentarians whose relations with the activists in their own party in the country were hostile and sour. No one at Westminster, even oldies who had taken part in the struggles between left and right in the fifties, could remember an atmosphere quite like it. The prospect of government seemed to exist only beyond a very distant horizon.

Meanwhile, Margaret Thatcher's Conservatives were relishing their political struggle with the unions, the battle which she had long expected and for which she had prepared. Around her there were those who had doubts – no one could talk privately for more than five minutes to her deputy, Willie Whitelaw, without sensing the depth of his unease and the passion with which he roared his favourite word 'Trouble!' – but she was determined to resist any settlement that didn't give the government a clear victory in the miners' strike. She saw it as the latest test of her resolve.

When she spoke to her backbenchers in July 1984 just before the summer recess, the Prime Minister chose to put the strike in the context of the 1982 Falklands War: 'We had to fight an enemy without in the Falklands. We always have to be aware of the enemy within, which is more difficult to fight and more dangerous to liberty.' She said that the striking miners were 'a scar across the face of the country' and spoke of the threat of tyranny. This was redolent of a remarkable speech she had made at Cheltenham Racecourse just after the Falklands when she declared that Britain had 'found herself again in the South Atlantic' and said: 'We have ceased to be a nation in retreat. We have instead a new-found confidence – born in the economic battles at home and tested and found true 8,000 miles away.' Politics was being played out on the high wire, in an atmosphere of exhilaration and danger. The autumn of 1984, when the IRA bombed the Thatcher Cabinet in the Grand Hotel, Brighton, seemed to bring proof that this was an age in which the unimaginable might always happen. To stand on the seafront on that October morning and gaze at the ruined façade was to sense that this was a momentous political era. It was bizarre to talk to Cabinet ministers streaked with dust and watch the plaster fall from the walls. Everything seemed infected by the event. They were fevered times.

So the early parliamentary years of Brown and Blair – in those days the names were always in that order – were lived in a political hothouse. Their party was still shuddering with the consequences of defeat, and engaged in a messy civil war that forced dozens of MPs to expend most of their energy in battles in their own backyards. The Liberals and the SDP were digging themselves in as a serious political force, goading Labour on its policies on defence, Europe and the economy, and the government was engaged in economic reforms and changes to trade union law which many Labour MPs realized would change the rules of politics for ever. The clock was running too fast to be turned back. It was therefore a happier time for younger MPs than for the old warhorses who wandered round the Commons shellshocked by the pace of change. For the newcomers, the only way was up.

Blair was the first to get a front bench job, as a junior Employment spokesman. He was surprised but grabbed it. John Smith had passed word to Kinnock's office that young Blair, as Derry Irvine called him, was a likely talent. Blair was called to the leader's office where he was ushered in by Kinnock's chief of staff, the beaming Falstaffian figure of Charles Clarke, whom he scarcely knew. It was Clarke who seemed in charge; Blair didn't know why he was there. Seventeen years later, Clarke would join Blair's Cabinet and become party chairman. The employment role was Blair's chance to exploit his barrister's training in employment law and, more importantly for his future, it opened a door to the unions. From the beginning his relationship with them had its ups and downs, because he was privately less outraged by some of the Thatcher reforms than the union leaders with whom he dealt, but he had the chance at last to make himself known.

Gordon Brown played a canny hand with Kinnock, turning down his first offer of a job in the shadow Scottish team. He had enough sense to realize that he risked disappearing into the familiar but confined pastures of Scottish Office politics, which have been known to have a suffocating effect on a promising career. His decision was revealing. With his background in Scotland, he was a natural recruit as a Scottish Office spokesman, but he was already surveying a wider and more inviting landscape and ambition led him away from Scotland. His second chance was the one he wanted, joining John Smith's Trade and Industry team in 1985.

They continued to share their room, and started to enjoy opposition as front benchers. But around them their party was still in a terrible state. Those left-wingers who had abandoned the Bennite causes of the early eighties were beginning to assemble in what became known as the 'soft left' and quite a few were going through the miserable and embarrassing process of shedding their past. Everyone, it seemed, wanted to be in the Tribune Group. Instead of being the dissident voice of old, it now turned into the voice of the leadership. If you were a Kinnockite you were in Tribune, so Brown didn't find it difficult to take Blair along in 1985, although he would never share the affection of the likes of Brown and Cook for the history of the left that they still cherished. It was because of Brown that Blair joined Tribune. His mentor John Smith, part of the Hattersley camp that kept a deliberate distance from the left, would never have suggested it.

In those days Tribune was like some kind of rolling revivalist meeting, marked by personal confessions and recantations. Kinnock was disposing of many of the policies that Labour had put before the electorate in 1983 – European membership wouldn't be renegotiated and defence policy was beginning slowly to turn towards multilateralism – and it was obvious that he wanted to reverse some of the organizational changes championed by the Bennite left, though it would only be after Kinnock was long gone as leader that something approaching a one-member-one-vote system of party democracy would arrive, and even then in a form that gave the unions a powerful collective voice in the electoral college. Yet by 1985 things were on the move. Party conferences saw fewer combat jackets and more suits, and the modernization banner was the one to march behind if you wanted to progress in Kinnock's party.

For most Labour MPs, the event that lifted the sullen mood of defensiveness and promised better things to come was Kinnock's speech to the 1985 conference in Bournemouth, always a town in which Labour seemed slightly uncomfortable. Perhaps it was the right place, well away from the traditional party pleasure garden of Blackpool, to signal a turning point. Kinnock's assault on Militant and all its works – dramatized by his contemptuous attack on the Militant-controlled Labour council in Liverpool – was the lancing of a boil. No leader had attacked a section of his own party in such terms for a generation and more, and the sight of Kinnock vibrating with anger on the platform sent most of his MPs into a state of modest ecstasy. Brown and Blair were among those MPs who thought it was the boldest and most welcome display of leadership they had experienced. Some were appalled, of course. Eric Heffer stomped off from his national executive seat on the platform to denounce Kinnock as a traitor to his party. But the overwhelming reaction was one of light-headed relief. For MPs like Brown and Blair, it promised to be the beginning of the end of the nightmare. Many MPs believed that week in Bournemouth marked the end of Labour's lost years, although the momentary optimism was misleading too, lending a false feeling of recovery when long years in opposition still lay ahead. Both Brown and Blair regarded Kinnock's speech with relief. Neither had a Militant problem in his constituency, but they thought that until Labour was seen to reject the far left outright it would remain unelectable. They both supported the subsequent party purge of Militant members, denounced by the hard left as a witchhunt but enthusiastically promoted by the Kinnockites in Tribune.

In the midst of all this, Labour made a decision which had a profound effect on them. The first impact was wholly pleasurable, and helpful to their careers, but in time it would seem a moment that also created between them a bond from which they couldn't escape and which at times appeared able to suffocate them. In September 1985 Peter Mandelson was appointed director of communications for the party.

Mandelson was an exotic creature even then. The clinching interview with Kinnock and Hattersley was – they thought – dazzling, but afterwards Kinnock confessed privately that he wasn't entirely comfortable with Mandelson's style. He'd noticed that he was wearing lurid socks and showing them off. 'I know he's . . . that way', said Kinnock, a little agitated, to Hattersley, 'but why does he have to flaunt it?' There is a dispute about the colour of the socks. Hattersley thinks they were pink, Mandelson blue. The effect was the same. This was before gay lifestyles were widely accepted, least of all in politics, and although Mandelson wore his sexuality relatively discreetly at this stage he never saw much reason to disguise it among friends and acquaintances. He was going to bring a different style to the leader's office.

He displayed a blend of Labour loyalism and irreverence. The loyalism was a family inheritance. As the grandson of Herbert Morrison, Foreign Secretary and leader of the Commons in Attlee's post-war government, Mandelson had been aware of the party since he could walk. He played with Harold Wilson's children as a boy. So after Oxford and a typical phase of student leftism it was natural that he should end up as a Labour councillor in Lambeth in south London, and equally natural that he should resist the blandishments of the Social Democrats when they broke away in 1981. A number of his friends who were struggling with the hard left on Lambeth council did leave – notably Roger Liddle, who would return to play a Downing Street role in years to come – but although on many policy matters and in his attitude to the left he agreed with them, he stayed within the Labour fold. But for his family ties, friends believe he might have defected. He was close to several who did, and does not seem to have expended much energy dissuading them.

But he could not make the final break. Alongside that visceral sense of belonging, however, ran a streak of iconoclasm towards the Labour Party. He has always been impatient with it.

As director of communications, Mandelson began in a characteristic way. Even before he occupied his office, he recruited Philip Gould, a thirty-four-year-old advertising man of earnest disposition who had set up his own agency, whom Mandelson had met only a couple of weeks before. The first Gould memo, which was delivered within days and ran to sixty-four pages – they were still landing on Tony Blair's desk in Downing Street sixteen years later – and sketched out assumptions which would underpin Mandelson's work and the policy reforms of the late eighties. Labour, he said, was seen as a collection of minorities and not a party that represented the majority; it appeared to be more interested in its own activists than in the voters. Gould's remedy was simple. Campaigns should have one purpose – to influence electoral opinion. A strangely obvious conclusion, it was one that led to a period of more than five years of troubled change in the Labour Party.

Early on, Mandelson found Brown and Blair and they found him. In his three years at London Weekend Television, he had been aware of them, and when he had worked as a research assistant in the shadow Cabinet after 1979 (he had worked for Roy Hattersley's leadership campaign in 1983) he knew of Brown in Scotland, but this was the real start of their relationship. He needed talent to push towards television and radio editors to speak for the party, new faces unassociated with the traumas of the past. Within a year the three were operating as a team. Brown would sit in his Edinburgh flat at weekends talking to Mandelson for what seemed hours; and in Blair, Mandelson found a spirit as restless as his own. Tabloid articles began to pop up signed by one or the other. All of us who had these conversations in Mandelson's ceaseless round knew they were supposed to be the two golden boys. The daily line was: 'They are the future'.

At first he spent more time with Brown. Mandelson found in him a rich source of material for the press. Brown had privately cultivated a number of Whitehall contacts from where he would produce regular leaks to embarrass the government, something ministers find deeply irritating, as he would discover in later life. By the time the 1987 General Election came along, Mandelson was established as the conduit for what the Kinnockites called 'progressive thinking'. In turn, that meant that he also began to be hated by elements of the traditional left who had already decided that Mandelson represented the enemy. They were right.

A year after Blair's deadline for the party to review or perish had passed, reform had become more interesting than thoughts of disaster. The poky Commons room had become a little powerhouse. The air was thick with plans, and with ambition. Mandelson was a regular visitor and as the 1987 election approached the three were beginning to be a force in the party that couldn't be ignored by the senior members of the shadow Cabinet. John Prescott, in particular, was finding Mandelson, as he would put it frequently, 'a pain in the backside'. He would joke at shadow Cabinet meetings about what he thought was the absurdity of the new red rose emblem for the party (which Mandelson was championing, though the idea was an advertiser's and not his) and the concentration – obsession, Prescott called it – with advertising techniques and voter research as the bedrock of the campaign.

That campaign was a failure for Labour: the Conservatives returned with a majority of more than a hundred. But despite the fact that the result tossed Kinnock into a period of deep gloom from which it took him months to emerge, Brown, Blair and Mandelson saw it as the first vindication of their approach. If policy could be modernized still further – burying the non-nuclear defence policy which had proved a serious handicap – they believed that the party, for the first time since the 1983 election, might become electable. Neither Brown nor Blair had expected to win in 1987, and they weren't surprised at the scale of the defeat. Rather, they were reassured that a pattern was beginning to emerge for the future.

In particular, Mandelson cherished the memory of a Hugh Hudson film on Kinnock which had run as a much-hyped Labour party political broadcast. It had failed, in the sense that it didn't persuade vast numbers of voters to give their votes to Labour, but it set a tone that Mandelson was happy to commend to the party.

The joke around Westminster was that the film should have been subtitled 'Jonathan Livingston Kinnock', a reference to the syrupy and vacuous American book and film (*Jonathan Livingston Seagull*) about a bird which had a brief moment of fame in the mid-eighties. In the party machine it was considered a triumph.

Mandelson was particularly proud of the way it had revealed the real Kinnock responding to direct questions about his integrity, capacity and convictions. They had worked hard to get Kinnock in the right mood, throwing question after question at him to get him to rise to the bait and deliberately provoking a passion audible in his responses. The questions did not feature in the broadcast – only Kinnock's replies. The Fleet Street interrogator recruited to draw the best out of the leader was the *Daily Mirror*'s political editor, Alastair Campbell.

It was in this period, Brown and Blair's second Parliament, that a pattern of relationships was established which would condition much of Labour's internal arguments and style for the next decade. Promotions followed quickly: Brown was elected to the shadow Cabinet in 1987, and topped the poll the following year, when Blair joined him. Labour was visibly starting to change at the top. Some of the older warriors were eased aside, and anyone whose convictions ran counter to the new orthodoxy – as with Bryan Gould on Europe – was heading for demotion. With the first promotions and the perceptible stirring of ambition the shared office was abandoned in favour of separate domains – still tiny – on the shadow Cabinet corridor.

Brown and Blair were no longer a pair of juniors, backing up their bosses in the shadow Cabinet and deferring to the leadership. They were making their own way, and with Mandelson egging them on and advising them on how to sharpen their public faces they started to carve out separate careers. The three were still a gang – around Westminster you seldom saw one without one of the others nearby – but they were beginning to build up their own teams of advisers. Blair, for example, turned in 1988 to Anji Hunter, whom he had first met while he was at Fettes, who joined his office and ran his parliamentary life.

The shadow Cabinet as a whole was taking on a new character. Robin Cook was on the rise, and eyeing an important economic portfolio, with any luck at the expense of Brown. John Prescott was nursing grudges against Mandelson (who he believed had tried to marginalize him in the 1987 campaign, as indeed he had) and also against Roy Hattersley, whom he thought an ineffective deputy to Kinnock. He was persuaded to back down from an open challenge to Hattersley by Kinnock, an operation that he regarded as humiliating because it opened him to criticism for alleged disloyalty. From then on Prescott revelled in his natural disposition to distrust the architects of 'modernized Labour'.

Naturally, much revolved around John Smith, now shadow Chancellor. Brown, Smith's deputy, was pitched directly against the Conservative Treasury Chief Secretary, John Major. It provided him with the chance, eagerly seized, to make his reputation as a formidable force in the Commons, but it was also the time in which he sowed seeds of doubt among some colleagues about his approach; these he would reap (with regret) when his own leadership ambitions were put to the test.

One particular episode illustrates it well. Nigel Lawson's 1988 Budget revealed that he had money to spend. It was the pre-boom time, when the coming bust was never mentioned. Smith, leading the Labour Treasury team, was trying to devise a strategy for Budget Day. What would they recommend as spending priorities? Brown, whose commitments to social spending and measures to tackle poverty were the political badge he wore with pride, was nonetheless cautious. Even Smith, caution personified, was surprised. And others in the team were surprised to hear Brown, as shadow Chief Secretary, argue for prudence, his watchword of the future.

Brown had already concluded that Labour had to establish a reputation for fiscal probity if it was ever to be elected. A number of colleagues disagreed. One who was present at that meeting, and who came from the left like Brown, said: 'I realised then where Gordon was heading and I knew that I would not be supporting him in the end.'

The significance of such encounters is that they came at a time when Brown was already being talked up as a future leader, a message spread assiduously by Mandelson. Brown's profile was well known and his friends and rivals were lining up, as politics makes them do. Robin Cook, for example, had always resented Brown's capacity to gather round him a band of loyalists – not something that Cook had managed for himself – and believed that on policy he was heading in the wrong direction.

Visitors to Cook's office would sometimes be pointed towards a particular book on his bulging shelves. It was called *Scotland: The Real Divide*, published in Edinburgh in 1983, and the authors were Gordon Brown and Robin Cook. It was said at the time that Cook felt Brown had taken too much credit for the book, and that the resentment was one of the reasons for his irritation with him, but by the end of the 1980s Cook's complaint was different. He was a critic of the economic policy that was emerging under Smith and Brown, who were trying to rid Labour of the image of a spendthrift party on tax. 'That's what he used to believe,' Cook would say as he took the familiar volume in his hand. 'This is what we were going to do with the economy,' he would snort.

Brown had become a prominent figure, in part because his battles with Major on public spending made good parliamentary theatre. They really didn't like each other. Brown would always mutter of him, 'Not as nice as he looks.' Major, as Prime Minister, would tell his ministers that he never trusted Brown. Even now, fifteen years after they first met on the opposite sides of a Commons committee on the 1986 Budget, Major says he has barely spoken to Brown. While the Smith–Brown team was improving Labour's economic attack, Blair was spokesman on Energy and then, after 1989, on Employment. Although his public profile was still fuzzy, he was becoming better known in the party because of his willingness to unsettle the trade unions. They detected some unease about their attitudes. They were right.

1988 saw another change which shaped the careers of Blair and Brown and brought a reminder that politics is a trade driven as much by human frailties and eccentricities as by strategy, never mind logic. Just after the Labour conference in Brighton John Smith had a heart attack at home in Edinburgh. He was lucky to survive, and took three months off from politics. Brown immediately took over. Bryan Gould, who was Trade and Industry spokesman, had expected to deputize as shadow Chancellor since he was the next most senior Economic spokesman, but Brown was faster on his feet. Mandelson said at the time: 'Gould had no idea what was happening. He turned round and Gordon was making the running. He didn't even feel the stiletto.' In those days, Mandelson was delighted to see Brown prospering. He had an eye for a headline and a telling phrase in the Commons and he was exhilarated at the chance to take on the Chancellor, Nigel Lawson.

The shape of Labour in the nineties was starting to emerge. At the top the main characters had established the relationships that would determine the party's future. One of those which is most intriguing, because it is often misunderstood, was that between Brown and Smith.

The two had developed a close friendship during the eighties and Smith had championed Brown's rise to the top of the shadow Cabinet. It was shortly after Smith's heart attack that Brown overtook him, pushing Smith into second place in the poll. It is also true that Brown has written movingly about Smith's commitment to social justice, which he sees as the great purpose of politics. He cherished Smith's principles. They had become close friends and relied on each other's judgement. Yet there were complications.

Before Brown arrived at Westminster he and Smith were not at all close. Despite Brown's enthusiasm for devolution and his support for Smith when he was the minister in charge in the Callaghan government, they were from different political moulds. It is impossible to imagine Smith curling up in bed with a copy of *The Red Paper on Scotland.* He was quite out of sympathy with the left-wing critique of those later Wilson–Callaghan years and was an unashamed member of the pro-European Labour right – in favour of a mixed economy that didn't embrace more nationalized industries and against pretty well anything that became a rallying cry for the left in the late seventies. On these questions he was an ally of many of those who went on to form the SDP, though he felt betrayed by them and embarrassed by having it pointed out that on many of the insistent political issues of the time he was closer to the departed Jenkinsites than to Michael Foot.

Smith's loyalty to Labour had little to do with the approach crystallized in the 1983 manifesto. He described a number of its promises as 'bonkers' and never expected that Labour could come close to winning. Brown would, of course, abandon many of the commitments in that document as time went on, but he had come from a section of the party where Smith's views were regarded as reactionary and lodged in the past. Smith, in his pungent way, didn't bother to disguise his attitude to the left. About such prominent figures on the established left as Robin Cook, with whom he had fought over devolution, he had a lively scepticism. 'Wee Cookie's an odd one right enough,' he often said. So it would have been surprising had he been an early fan of Gordon Brown's. He wasn't.

All the factions and alliances were, however, shaped more by personality than creed. Brown and Cook were from the left, but they had fallen out for good. Smith was of the right – his ideological stablemates were Hattersley, Denis Healey, Jack Cunningham and Gerald Kaufman – but he respected Brown's intellect. Temperament and chemistry were more important than ideological positioning. His eventual bonding with Brown came about principally because of a shared attitude to politics, and it was in this that they demonstrated something which was quite distinct from the Blair approach which would develop in the nineties.

Smith is often misleadingly described as an Edinburgh lawyer. He was a lawyer and he did live in Edinburgh, but the description conceals more than it reveals. Though his demeanour and his style seemed to outsiders to define his character and his natural habitat, Smith was emphatically a West of Scotland man who kept with him a certain feeling for the radicalism that he had absorbed from his father in the schoolhouse in Ardrishaig in Argyll where he grew up and where the *New Statesman* would arrive by boat. He inherited the same kind of egalitarianism that was summed up in the title of a famous book about Scotland by George Davie called *The Democratic Intellect*. He believed in a society founded on equality of opportunity in education and a notion of individual worth that wasn't ordained by wealth or social position. Though Smith had never practised politics as a matter of class struggle, and was always uncomfortable with the language that went with that view, his instinct for the political trade was similar to the one Brown had absorbed in the manse.

This meant that on the scarred landscape that Kinnock inherited from Foot, Smith and Brown felt that they were engaged on similar business. Disputes about the 1983 manifesto were in the past: that document was somewhere in a dustbin that they hoped would never be opened again. Each was a party loyalist, willing to play it rough in Labour infighting if it was necessary, and were temperamentally committed to night-and-day opposition in the Commons, Smith the old student debater who loved cross-examination from the dispatch box and Brown the ferreter-out of government leaks who had a knack of embarrassing ministers with his revelations.

The ties were strong in the late eighties, but like so many political friendships they began to fray in the aftermath of the 1992 election defeat. Kinnock had started the campaign believing in victory, though he subsequently admitted that by the last weekend of the campaign he had sensed a decisive shift back to the Conservatives. Smith, oddly enough, hadn't felt it coming and was genuinely startled when his old friends Donald Dewar and Helen Liddell took him to one side at his own constituency count to tell him that he should accept that the plane waiting at Edinburgh airport to take the new Chancellor of the Exchequer to London in the small hours of the morning would not be required after all.

That election was a turning point because, once more, power began to shift. When Smith succeeded Kinnock in the summer – an assumption of leadership that seemed natural to most in the party – he began to pursue a policy that some of those who had become quite close to him believed was both cautious and defensive. Brown and Blair found themselves at odds with their old friend. He had acted as an opener of doors for Blair, as a benign boss to Brown, and he had schooled them in parliamentary tactics, first in the long all-night sessions on the 1983 employment bill when he led the attack for Labour with Brown and Blair in support. But those days were past.

In the few weeks before Smith succeeded Kinnock, Brown was tempted to stand for the leadership himself. But as well as supporters he had enemies. One union leader phoned a party official when he heard that Brown was wondering about a candidacy and said: 'If what I hear is true, it has to be stopped. When the mice start running around they have to be stamped on.' The recipient of the call believes it was prompted from Smith's office. Brown read the signs and decided to bide his time. Blair's reaction, however, was not altogether understanding. He told a close friend: 'Gordon's bottled out.' Instead, he himself considered running for the deputy's post under Smith. Brown couldn't, because two Scots in the top jobs would be unacceptable. But Blair was stopped too. He met Mandelson and agreed to listen to party soundings. However, another union leader, Bill Morris of the TGWU, emerged the next day to declare his support for Margaret Beckett, and within twenty-four hours Smith was giving interviews supporting her candidacy for the deputy's job. Blair was scuppered. Afterwards he was convinced that the intervention of Morris had been arranged by friends of Smith. These episodes confirmed that the subcutaneous rivalry of the previous couple of years could, under the pressures and fears of high office, be brought gasping to the surface. They showed that each, instinctively, wanted to get ahead of the other.

In mutual frustration Brown and Blair settled down to life under Smith, and found that they were thwarted. Blair was the angrier of the two. His affection for Smith went back to their first boozy meeting at the Commons in 1982 and he had learned the ways of Parliament at Smith's feet, but after the 1992 election he had become convinced that Labour was now the cautious party and that the tempo was all wrong. His own instincts were already leading him in a direction which ran counter to the party's received wisdom – on the role of the unions and on crime, most notably – and the target of much of his private criticism was Smith. Mandelson, now MP for Hartlepool, having left his party post just before the election, was another of the critics. Smith had never been a fan.

Mandelson now found himself in an outer circle of influence. There were other sceptics from the Kinnock circle of reformers. On the *Mirror*, Alastair Campbell's view was that progress was slowing down. Mandelson put it differently: 'It's not slowing down. It's gone into reverse.'

Blair was demonstrably unhappy. He would tell friends the same thing again and again: 'John is just so cautious. It's a disaster.' At times he appeared almost to be despairing, despite the Major government's own troubles after the ignominious and messy exit from the European Exchange Rate Mechanism (ERM) on Black Wednesday in September 1992. Smith was abroad on the day itself so his new shadow Chancellor, Brown, was in charge in London. Brown concluded immediately that this was the event that would in the end destroy John Major's government. Smith agreed, but his subsequent tactics dismayed Blair. He believed that the next election would now inevitably be lost by the Conservatives as long as Labour didn't foul up in opposition: his cautious instincts therefore led him to sit tight. Blair did not agree with him. Indeed, there are some (they claim to be tuned into the Blair antennae) who go so far as to say that he even wondered about getting out of politics at this stage. Blair now denies it, and there is no solid evidence to support the claim. There is no argument, however, about the distance that started to open up between Blair and Smith.

Blair found that he had an ally in the leader whom Smith had succeeded. He and Neil Kinnock had developed an affinity for each other in the late eighties, when Blair began to relish the kind of policy sallies that would later become one of the main characteristics of his leadership. He was on the move, and to his relief he found Kinnock – and, even more to his surprise, John Prescott – more supportive than he could have expected. There had been predictable and sometimes quite feisty union opposition, particularly to his formulations on secondary picketing which were designed to ditch a great deal of Labour lore on the subject, but he found that Kinnock's commitment to change was solid enough to see him through.

In the approach to the 1992 election, Kinnock had become a still more impatient leader. He wanted further change. So even when

Blair irritated parts of the trade union establishment and the parliamentary party by challenging some of the assumptions that had survived earlier Kinnock reforms, he found his leader more sympathetic than he might have expected. Blair remained scarred by the despair that had cocooned his party after the 1983 defeat and, like Kinnock, was determined to avoid its grip again. Both were given to dark moods and although Blair still cut a breezy figure he was ready with shadow Cabinet colleagues to talk about the chasm that might still await Labour round the next bend.

They shared that caution about the future, even when the bizarre upheavals of Margaret Thatcher's resignation in November 1990 appeared to give Labour some cause for glee. Offstage, however, Kinnock feared with some justification that the judgement of Michael Heseltine and the senior Tories who supported him was right: a Conservative Party with a new leader was going to be stronger in the coming election, whoever that leader might be. Blair thought the same. The run-up to the 1992 campaign had been bad enough, with Blair among those near the top of the party who sensed that a Conservative victory was imminent. That feeling of frustration was to become much worse.

With defeat and Kinnock's departure immediately afterwards, Blair and his friends wondered if they had given their lives to politics only to see them played out entirely in tedium on the opposition benches. And despite the problems the Conservatives were facing, in Europe and elsewhere, Labour was prey to a period of self-doubt.

There was little excitement in Smith's election in the summer of 1992. Denied the fireworks of a Brown or Blair challenge the contest was routine with hardly a moment of drama. Blair found that, in common with others on the front bench who thought of themselves as modernizers, his attitude to Smith had changed. Aware of Kinnock's raw feelings about his successor, who he believed had come close to conspiring against his own leadership when it was at its weakest, Blair's affection was now tempered with a sense that Smith's instinct for steadiness and safety was risking the whole enterprise into which Blair and others had been drawn in the eighties: the effort to reinvent the Labour Party. In those days it had been a rather ramshackle project. There was a good deal of back-of-an-envelope policy making and only a patchy intellectual coherence in what was afoot, but faced with the reality of a fourth Conservative term the pace for Blair and his friends was quickening.

In Smith's camp, there was a quite different view. On party organization, they thought he alone could deliver change, only he could cajole the unions into a one-member-one-vote reform for the party. Only because he was trusted by the custodians of the block vote could he get them to open it up. He was respected by those whom he would have to persuade. That was true as far as it went. Smith had never lost his affection for the unions. When asked in the early eighties why a traditional Labour right-winger like himself – passionately pro-Europe and contemptuous of Bennite thinking – had never contemplated joining with the Social Democrats he would say: 'I am comfortable with the unions. They aren't. That's the big difference.' But by 1993 Blair was wondering openly if that cultural commitment could still be regarded as a strength.

Even while Smith was deep in messy negotiations to change party voting systems, which had been the knot that Kinnock had been unable to unravel in his time, his very accomplishment was starting to seem to Blair and a few like him as too much of a series of compromises.

It certainly allowed Smith his sweetest moment in arguments with the party, at the 1993 conference. He squeezed through his compromise on one-member-one-vote in Brighton, though it nearly slipped away. Opening up constituency selections to members' votes was an assault on union power; and though there would still be an electoral college for leadership elections (one third of the votes each for the parliamentary party, the unions and the constituency parties) the parties would let all the members vote and the unions would ballot. At lunchtime on the day of the vote Smith thought he had lost it, because the MSF (Manufacturing, Science and Finance) union wasn't on side. He called for Prescott who, in a famous barnstorming speech, swung the vote. Smith told Prescott he was going to resign if he lost, and though the idea was to appeal for re-election on the issue of reform, in confidence that the vote would be won in the end, it would have holed his leadership somewhere near the waterline.

In the moments after the vote, won by a hairsbreadth after a traditional Labour conference day of vote switching, threatened skulduggery and a good deal of confusion, he had the high spirits of a man who has just been spared the gallows. To his team, the closeness of that vote was evidence of how his caution in negotiation had been justified: it could only be won by stealth. To Blair, it was evidence that the future held only the prospect of more deals and more fixing. He had been privately very critical of Smith's speech to the TUC a couple of weeks before in which the leader had gone far too far in reassuring traditionalists, Blair thought, on full employment and workers' rights. Smith knew he needed the votes at the coming party conference in Brighton in a fortnight: Blair found Labour's positioning with the unions increasingly dispiriting.

And Brown was frustrated too. Having become shadow Chancellor in Smith's team, his instincts were to maintain the pattern that had been set in the last part of Kinnock's leadership. He was much more reluctant than Blair to be open about his feelings but those around him were clear that he was more unsettled than at any time since he had been elected to the front bench. There was one important contributory reason for this which caused him to lose his foothold in the shadow Cabinet elections and gave Blair an opportunity to make ground.

Brown had inherited from Smith's own years as shadow Chancellor a strong commitment to British membership of the European ERM and, as a result, his attack on the government after Black Wednesday was undermined. Some of his shadow Cabinet colleagues who had doubts about Smith's European policy – notably Jack Straw, Robin Cook and David Blunkett – started to question the way Labour had prepared the whole argument. To Smith and Brown the priority was to exploit the government's manifest discomfort, by arguing that the party traditionally associated with sober economic management had lost its grip. But those who had never been keen on joining the ERM thought that there might be an easier case to make if Labour hadn't been pressing so hard for so long for membership. As so often in politics, Brown found that the tenor of the times told against him. Where a couple of years before he had been the most sure-footed member of the shadow Cabinet he was now finding life more difficult.

After 1992 he had the job of expunging from the public mind the memory of the 'tax and spend' label which the Conservatives had successfully hung round Labour's neck in the election campaign, helped by John Smith's 'shadow Budget'. By common consent in the shadow Cabinet afterwards, it had been a disaster. The sight of the Labour Treasury team posing on the steps of the Treasury – a most un-Smith-like piece of PR – had seemed hubristic, and so it proved. The spending plans duly unravelled. Now Brown was to tell the party that its attitude to economic management had to change if it was ever to win.

He was prominent, but his popularity in the party was weakening. In interviews he began to develop a relentless style, one that would become familiar in later years, which intensified the public feeling of a Labour Party that was strangely defensive, despite the government's trouble. In May 1993 Alan Watkins wrote in the *Observer* that Brown had been 'for some months now on a kind of automatic pilot which enables him to repeat meaningless phrases in monotone'.

By the autumn of that year he had slid to seventh, and bottom, in the vote for the constituency section of the national executive committee (NEC). Blair was sixth. It was the kind of result that was hardly likely to create a flicker of interest outside the fevered world in which they lived, but for Brown it was the first time that he had seen Blair edge ahead of him. He didn't like the feeling.

This was the background to a subtle but decisive change in their partnership. For as long as anyone in the Labour Party after 1992 could remember (the habit of recalling the days before the mid-eighties having been abandoned because it encouraged nightmares), the coming men had been Brown and Blair, in that order. In his beaming schoolmasterish way, Smith had blooded them and coached them through their parliamentary tests, and by the time the party was preparing for the 1992 election it was accepted well outside their circle – and emphatically believed by those around Brown – that they would never fight each other for the leadership.

At the time, that meant that Brown would be the candidate. From those first days in the windowless room he had been the senior figure, the wilier operator, the one who knew the most recondite byways of his party. He had worked the union circuit year after year and in the parliamentary party he was the star around which a group of MPs was starting to cluster, in the way that they do. By 1988, he had beaten Smith himself to come top of the shadow Cabinet poll and if, at any time up to 1992, the party had been asked whether it was Brown or Blair who would fight for the leadership under a modernizing banner the choice would have been clear. Blair knew it. Each considered one opportunity and decided against it – Brown to run against Smith for the leadership, aged forty-one, after Kinnock's resignation in 1992, and Blair to go for the deputy leadership. And it was at this stage that they discussed straightforwardly how they should proceed together. They agreed – and neither has ever denied what their friends acknowledge – that it would be foolish for them to fight each other. They pledged not to do so. At that stage, immediately after the third successive election defeat, Brown was clearly the more powerful figure. Therefore the deal was simple: Blair would defer to Brown.

This understanding has been the source of gossip and acrimony because it is held by some of those around Brown to constitute a promise broken. To any outsider, this will seem a rather literal interpretation of the kind of unwritten agreement that is made in politics all the time and is bound to be eroded by the ebb and flow of events. There was never a chance that such a commonsense discussion at a moment of transition for Labour after an election defeat could be expected to last indefinitely. But the way these conversations became elements in a subsequent struggle for supremacy, as if they were protocols to some great international peace treaty, reveals what was happening to their relationship. Inevitably it was changing as they began to feel that personally and individually they might be close to power.

The rivalry was conscious and was transmitted to the posses of camp followers who were beginning to gather around them. If Brown had his old network of allies and the advantage of his Scottish base, Blair had a much less secure place to stand. His time as Employment spokesman had made him more enemies than friends in some of the big unions, where he was already seen as someone ready to move too far too fast. In the party at large he was still a figure without the substance of Gordon Brown: his first conference speech, after all, had only been in 1990 and although his parliamentary performances had given him a certain Westminster profile it had none of the sharpness of Brown's. Now, though, the clearing of the undergrowth that always follows an election defeat offered space that they were both determined to fill.

Even then, those who watched these two trying to plan the way ahead – every journalist at Westminster, for example – were aware of how the natural laws of politics were almost bound to pit them against each other, as is the way of things. And among those who already appeared to have come to a cold-blooded assessment of what was most likely to happen were John Smith and Neil Kinnock.

Both had tilted towards Blair, Kinnock because his own experiences in the two general elections he fought as leader had moved him in that direction. One reason for this is obvious, though it is often overlooked. He had found that there was a great deal of English territory which was deeply inhospitable to a Labour leader from Scotland or Wales. All the pollsters told him that without recapturing what later became known as 'middle England' Labour could not win; he knew it to be true. After Smith was elected Kinnock suspected that his Scottishness would prove his greatest weakness, and in looking ahead to the next generation it was one of the reasons for favouring Blair. He came to believe – perhaps as early as 1990 – that Blair would beat Brown to it.

Smith's view was moving in the same direction, but his reasons were more complicated and, in the end, more telling in their effect on others in the party in the weeks ahead.

At this stage no one was preparing for a leadership election. Although Smith's health was a regular subject of mordant conversation, it was unthinkable to contemplate an election campaign under anyone else. He was enjoying the job, enjoying the government's difficulties, enjoying the first real prospect of power that he had known since the Callaghan government fell in 1979. Smith was usually beaming as he went about his business. He could claim (just) that Labour was now a one-member-one-vote party, and as 1994 began he seemed a confident figure.

It was against this background that Brown and Blair's prospects were changing: the names were starting to be mentioned in reverse order. Brown was having difficulties with some of his Treasury team and making demands on shadow Cabinet colleagues for disciplines on spending which they were reluctant to give. Blair was shadow Home Secretary and enjoying a freewheeling argument with Michael Howard, a good Labour bogeyman, which gave him the perfect pitch on which to talk about a new kind of Labour Party and to start to employ a moral rhetoric which came naturally to him. Some of his colleagues didn't like that, even at this early stage, but they acknowledged its usefulness.

Smith knew that one or the other would probably succeed him. In early 1994 he was talking to two colleagues in the leader's rooms about the future. One who was present remembers: 'Smith stood at the window and looked over the river. He said, "People say that when I stand down Gordon's my successor. They say he's the son I've never had. That's not it at all. Tony is probably the one."' Smith had been saying something similar in private conversations with journalists for some time. Many of us heard him say: 'Blair's the man.' Roy Hattersley has a slightly different version. When he went to see Smith in April 1994 to tell him that he was going to stand down from the Commons, they had a brief conversation about leadership. Smith said that Blair was ahead for the moment, but there was no vacancy. Brown, he thought, was likely to prevail in the end. Smith was probably being mischievously ambiguous but his long-term prediction has not yet been put to the test.

This was the atmosphere that prevailed at the top of the party at the beginning of 1994. The leader, on jolly form, convinced that the government's economic problems and ugly disputes on Europe would give Labour the opening that had been so elusive for so long, thought he would be the next Prime Minister. Around him, however, there was simmering unhappiness. The shadow Cabinet was burdened by the personal antagonisms that had grown up in the long years of opposition and in the weary slog of reform. It was not a relentlessly happy band of brothers.

But Smith felt in charge. There was no direct threat to his leadership. He was enjoying his outings at the dispatch box. He was relishing the splinters flying in all directions from the Tory backbenches. He thought that at last Labour was beginning to find itself in tune with a public mood for change. He appeared to be in fine fettle when, on 11 May 1994, he went to the Park Lane Hotel in London to speak about Europe at a Labour fund-raising dinner. Next morning came his second heart attack. It was over.

3
One Leader

A melancholy frenzy followed Smith's death. Those around him were tearful and deflated, and the press decided to let the emotion flow. Politics appeared to come to a halt for a few days. But away from the sound of the torrential eulogies, there was quiet business to be done, and quickly. That was why the Labour chief whip, Derek Foster, made his way a day or two later on a private errand along the corridor behind the Speaker's chair to the empty rooms of the leader of the opposition under Big Ben. He retrieved a document for his own safe-keeping and left. No one knew he had been there.

It was a private paper commissioned by Smith himself a few months earlier. He had asked the chief whip for an honest assessment of the performance of the shadow Cabinet. Who was up and who was down; who was causing the government the most difficulty. Foster did not want his judgements coming to light in the course of the leadership election which was about to begin because he knew how fraught the atmosphere would become.

He had written in straightforward terms and his conclusion mirrored Smith's own. Brown was thought to be 'wading through treacle' as shadow Chancellor against Kenneth Clarke, troubled by his arguments with front bench colleagues about spending pledges which they wanted to make and he wanted to stop.

Blair, on the other hand, had found the job that suited him. As shadow Home Secretary he was able to start to develop a moral tone to his politics which, as events would prove, suited him much more than it suited many in his party. The Conservatives could be made to feel uncomfortable about crime, an issue traditionally their own, by a shadow Home Secretary who managed to coin a phrase that gave him, at last, a public identity. 'Tough on crime, and tough on the causes of crime' would, like most such phrases, come back to torment him. But it did its work.

And where did it come from? As Smith had known when he teased Blair about it round the shadow Cabinet table, it was not his own. Indeed, it had come from Brown, who had heard it in the United States. He and Colin Currie – the medical thriller writer, Colin Douglas – had developed a fine line in rhetorical inversions since the days spent in the mid-eighties contriving Labour slogans with Mandelson, and the origin of this one was pure Brown. But Blair had now made it his own and, as Foster noted in his memo to Smith, it had turned him into a national figure as well as a more substantial front bencher.

By contrast, Brown's troubles with colleagues were sapping his energy. Mo Mowlam, in particular, had a spiky relationship with him. She was an over-the-top, rumbustious, tactile woman; he was a man whose personal disciplines meant that hard work and frivolity were supposed to exist in separate compartments. He said nothing without having thought about it first. Mowlam was quite different. They found that they were colleagues who really didn't want to work together. But she was distraught nonetheless to be shuffled out of an economics job. She had enjoyed speaking about City affairs and had become popular in the party and in the Commons. She might have expected an advance. 'The bastards have given me Women,' she complained when she emerged from Smith's office with a new portfolio. Brown could expect no future favours from that quarter. They have not been friends since.

It was a common enough view to be damaging to the shadow Chancellor. One of Brown's strong supporters at that time, later to join the Cabinet with him, says of that period: 'We all knew Gordon had the equipment to be the best leader. But could you imagine working under him? It was never on.' This came from someone whose ideological wellsprings might be thought to be the same as Brown's, and it was a judgement that was filtering through the front bench team. A shake of the head, the eyes turning upwards – 'Gordon's difficult,' they would say.

So Labour prepared for a leadership election with the rising generation in the shadow Cabinet elbowing each other around. After Smith's death, events moved fast. The trauma of those days transformed the relationship between Blair and Brown with the speed and force of a summer storm. Politics was transformed and the two men were left with a residue of hurt and misunderstanding which has never left them.

Twenty days passed between Smith's death and the public announcement that Brown would not challenge Blair for the leadership. It was a passionate time. Much of the personal drama was given decent cover first by a period of mourning and public reticence about potential candidates discussing the leadership and then by the demands of a European election campaign which had to be fought, however half-heartedly. But a political struggle was joined, and the relationship between Blair and Brown was now on fire. Rival camps were embroiled in battles that would be carried into government – the talk of betrayal and double-dealing had become especially bitter.

This was the whirlpool of events which turned Peter Mandelson in the course of a few days into the object of Brown's lasting disdain and at the same time the figure whom Blair believed indispensable to the team which he would install in Downing Street. In the end, instead of being the government's stabilizer, that triangular relationship threatened to unhinge it.

The previous ten years became a piece of history. The young brothers-in-arms had now outgrown all that. Politicians in every generation, in every party, find that the moment comes when friendships have to be put at risk or abandoned because the time is right to strike out alone, and Blair and Brown realized on the instant of Smith's death that, although those heady early days might sometimes help to rescue their relationship for the future, each was on his own now. In the previous months they had talked to colleagues about each other more openly than before. They were making their own ways in the shadow Cabinet, and Blair, for example, was discussing with Mandelson for the first time the possibility that he might overtake Brown and get to the leadership. He did not yet put it explicitly, but he wondered aloud with friends about whether Brown could recover the commanding position he once had.

Now, with Smith gone, Brown had to confront that political truth, which was exceptionally painful for him. Many of his friends and allies refused to recognize or simply did not believe the fact that in the later stages of Smith's leadership he had ceased to be the man most likely to succeed. The story of the six days between the leader's death and his funeral is the story of Brown's realization that he could not win.

The narrative has become muddied over the years, and some around Brown still insist that he did not reach his conclusion until the day before he met Blair to settle the leadership on the last day of May, the twentieth day after Smith's death. The occasion was the fabled Islington dinner – in fact an awkward and quite meagre meal – at which Brown formally told his old friend that he would not stand and would support him to make sure that the leadership would pass to him. In truth, Brown had known for more than a week that victory for him was probably not possible. He could fight, but the party would split and if he did win he would inherit a mess. If he lost to Blair, he would have to serve under a leader who would certainly believe him guilty of betrayal. The deal in 1992 that they would not challenge each other was hardly a legal document, signed in blood, but both of them felt it weighing on them.

Brown continued to listen to friends and family who produced elaborate explanations about how he might prevail in the party's electoral college, and he gave every impression to supporters in a wider circle that he was still game for the fight, but there were a few close to him who believe that even before Smith's funeral he had faced the truth.

This was the climax to the chapter that began with Smith's collapse in his Barbican flat at breakfast time on 12 May. Within a few minutes Murray Elder, the leader's chief of staff and Brown's friend from infancy, had told the shadow Chancellor. Brown immediately rang Blair on his mobile phone and found him in a car leaving

Aberdeen airport on his way to a European campaign meeting. He had already been alerted. Derry Irvine rang Blair a few minutes later to say that Smith had been pronounced dead at 9.15 a.m. On the intimate network which connected these characters at the centre of Labour's affairs, and the wider party that would choose a successor, there was an immediate mingling of grief and hard-headed calculation.

They were all in a state of shock. Elder had been close to Smith for fifteen years, when he left the Bank of England to work for the shadow Cabinet after the 1979 defeat. He had undergone the trauma of a heart transplant to save his own life in the late eighties and had a special feeling for Smith after his first heart attack in 1988. They climbed together, Elder the experienced mountaineer leading the rather more sedentary Smith to a series of highish Scottish peaks. Irvine was one of Smith's closest friends, a veteran of the uproarious Glasgow student days, and someone whose mind was turning to the possibility of a political career in government instead of a lawyer's swansong on the bench. And Blair and Brown, for all their irritation with aspects of the Smith regime, had lost their mentor. They didn't need to be told what that meant. In their shock, they had to start to plan.

It was not a choice between one and the other, mourning and scheming. Brown had been with Smith the night before at the Park Lane Hotel and it was a profound shock to be wakened seven or eight hours later to the news that he was dying. But no politician in his position is equipped to grieve in a vacuum. For someone who had even pondered a fight for the leadership after Neil Kinnock's resignation in 1992, and who had been at the top, or thereabouts, of the annual shadow Cabinet election since 1998, it was perfectly natural to think about what happened next while he was writing the tributes to Smith throughout the morning of 12 May. For Blair, it was the same.

All their expressions about Smith's leadership were subsumed in natural mourning. Now Brown was to be found writing obituaries. In the *Mirror* he wrote 'he put service to others first . . . his fearless sense of duty drove him on . . . like so many Scottish socialists before him his politics were shaped more by Kirk and community than by ideological theories'. There was an acknowledgement there of Brown's own long political journey, and it's hard to read what he wrote around this time without recognizing that he was instinctively writing elements of his own manifesto.

Although efforts were made to suggest that thoughts of the leadership election did not intrude, only a few hours passed before the first manoeuvres began. Politicians' instincts lead them to do this: the issue of leadership is never entirely submerged. It always disturbs the surface. Supporters of Blair and Brown found that they had been preparing subconsciously for this moment. The frustrations of the previous year ran deep.

Their irritation with the leadership had been obvious to all their colleagues, and so was the way in which they had become natural rivals. Others in the shadow Cabinet had nurtured leadership ambitions – Robin Cook was prey to them regularly, and John Prescott saw himself quite instinctively as a leader of a large group of MPs, many of them from the north of England, who considered themselves traditionalists rather than modernizers. But the centre of gravity seemed to be somewhere between Blair and Brown. To the hard-headed schemers of politics around party headquarters and the shadow Cabinet corridor that meant one thing. As the two had tentatively agreed two years before, they wouldn't split the forces of modernization. Only one would stand.

On the very day that Smith died, this was understood. The two most widely held assumptions around Westminster were that Blair and Brown could not afford to fight each other if one of them was to win, and that Blair had strengthened his position so much in recent months that he would not stand aside. At Brown's side at the time, Charlie Whelan's recollections are succinct: 'The idea that Tony and Gordon would ever fight it out to the end was always complete bollocks. As simple as that.' So what would Brown do?

He was in a black mood. But already the phones were ringing. A succession had to be organized. Around the principals, everyone could feel the first stirrings of a campaign. Once Blair was back from Aberdeen, and before the day was out, both camps had assembled. There was no sense of embarrassment in this. For politicians not to talk about succession at a wake would be very odd indeed, as Smith himself knew. He'd often enjoyed the old political adage 'where there's death there's hope', slapping his thigh with glee at the thought of some coming by-election. So across Westminster the first plans were laid. Mandelson called at Brown's flat briefly in the late morning and left more aware than ever of what he had long known: that the weight of Brown's personal history, his determination to lead and his single-mindedness about politics was still pushing him on.

Mandelson then did what came naturally: he began to talk to the press. The accounts of his private conversations with serious political correspondents late that morning agree that he was still trying out Brown's case. Told straightforwardly by one sage, Peter Riddell of *The Times*, that the augurs pointed to Blair, he said he wasn't yet sure and wanted to know why that was so. Like some others, Riddell read it as genuine uncertainty in Mandelson, a man who revels in his reputation as a Rasputin and enjoys slipping on a mantle of ruthlessness, but whose politics are emotional. A good deal of angst is often involved. The bond with Brown had been close. They spoke endlessly. The break didn't come in an instant.

But by early evening some of Brown's friends were gathering in a conclave and they were already disturbed by what they thought was happening among the Blairites. Smith had been dead only nine hours, but Douglas Henderson, MP for Newcastle North and an old friend of Brown's from Scotland, arrived from his own Millbank office with news. His room happened to be near Mandelson's, and he claimed to have heard conversations with Fleet Street from which he concluded that the Blair campaign had started to roll. 'We're half a lap behind,' he told them.

Over the next week, Mandelson gave quite contrary indications to some other members of the shadow Cabinet about his own preference, implying that he was not sure of what would happen. Bumping into Irvine, who expressed confidence that Blair would indeed become leader, Mandelson replied: 'I am not persuaded of that.'

The trouble was that Brown and the people around him no longer believed his old friend. If Mandelson was trying to preserve the tripartite relationship, the effort was doomed. Brown had gathered a team which had come to regard him with great suspicion. Although Mandelson had encouraged Brown to take on Whelan as his spokesman, the two were already operating in separate orbits as competitors. Whelan's interpretation of Mandelson's every move, relayed to Fleet Street in regular bulletins from his mobile phone, was that it was duplicitous. Mandelson had once been Brown's man, but no more.

On the afternoon of 12 May the Commons adjourned in mid-afternoon after formal tributes had been paid. Mandelson had arranged to meet an economist friend from New York who was in London and they repaired to the Pugin Room, a bar looking out from the Palace of Westminster over the Thames. While he was there, he received a paged message from Blair. Could they meet? The area around the Commons chamber was quiet. Everyone had gone home. So they sat down in one of the empty division lobbies that run alongside and talked alone for about ten minutes. Blair's message to Mandelson can be summed up in four words: 'Don't write me off.' Mandelson had since claimed that he was surprised at Blair's determination. If so, the surprise did not last long.

The *New Statesman* journalist Sarah Baxter, close to Blair, wrote in the London *Evening Standard* that afternoon predicting a Blair win. Alastair Campbell, who had been close to both men for years, appeared on BBC's *Newsnight* at the end of this first day and gave his view as a weather-beaten political editor: it would be Blair. The following morning, Mandelson's aide, Derek Draper, reported that his boss had decided on Blair. From the beginning, the Brown camp had decided that enemies had encircled them before they could organize themselves. A chorus was beginning, gathering strength in the papers the next morning. By the weekend Nick Brown, who was organizing MPs for the Brown team, could see the strength of the opposition. Three polls in the Sunday papers made Blair the public favourite to succeed, and Mandelson had popped up on Channel Four on Saturday night in anticipation – well-informed as to the polls' conclusions – to say that it was important for Labour to choose the leader 'who will play best at the box office'.

Smith's funeral was still five days away, but Brown is said by some of those closest to him to have absorbed the truth: it wouldn't be him. On Sunday the 15th he asked Philip Gould, the modernizers' pollster and focus group manipulator, to tell him who had the better chance of winning, and, by Gould's own account, got this reply: 'I said Tony, without hesitation. Gordon asked me why and I replied that Tony not only met the mood of the nation, he exemplified it. He would create for Labour and for Britain a sense of change, of a new beginning, which Gordon could not do.'

Gould was a weathervane for what Blair would call New Labour, his polling and voter research pointing in one direction: towards change. Gould's relentless pursuit of the Blairite 'project', a word of which he is very fond, has given him a reputation among non-Blairites for a mechanical pursuit of politics. His message to Brown that he could not change Britain was not welcome. Their friendship dissolved. Years later, when some of Gould's embarrassingly frank memos to Blair about the weaknesses of his government were leaked to *The Times* and the *Sun*, a Treasury colleague of Brown's said the Chancellor was greatly amused. They had restored relations by then but Brown retained some scepticism about the Gould number-crunching exercises with voters and focus groups.

It was now clear that Blair had the momentum in the race to be the candidate of change. Taken with the polls on that Sunday morning, and with the public declarations of Mandelson and Campbell for Blair (as they were interpreted by those around Brown), the sky was darkening. If Brown were to win, it could only be by pitting the party against what was claimed to be a public mood for Blair. In doing so Brown would have to challenge the very appetite for modernization that he had been trying to apply to economic policy in the previous two years. Even someone with less of a tendency to bouts of melancholy than Brown might have felt something of a victim at that moment. He was caught.

It was probably made worse for him by the insistence of many of those closest to him, friends and family, that he *must* fight and *could* win. Nick Brown and Andrew Smith were twisting arms in the parliamentary party; he had broad union support. One MP on the team reported that when he had suggested to John Edmonds, leader of the GMB (General and Municipal Boilermakers Union), that Blair might win, Edmonds had replied 'Over my dead body.' From his circle, Brown was under intense personal pressure to stand.

Smith's funeral was planned for Friday 20 May, and at the start of that week Brown was aware that Blair had secured a position in the public's and the party's mind from which he could not now be expected to retreat. It meant, Brown knew, that he would have to make the first move. Just at that delicate moment, when friends believe he was accepting that inevitability, the letter arrived from Mandelson that more than any other document in the whole saga settled the pattern of relations that would persist for years.

In it, Mandelson said that Brown was seen outside as 'the biggest intellectual force and strategic thinker that the party has' but that he already appeared to be running behind Blair, which made it difficult for Blair to withdraw. Brown already knew this. Mandelson went on to say that if Brown threw himself into an intensive campaign to recover his position it would weaken Blair, and added, 'Even then, I could not guarantee success.'

Mandelson wrote the letter on his laptop and before sending it round to Brown he showed it to Donald Dewar, a supporter of the shadow Chancellor. Dewar did not object to the wording of the letter, though he was distressed by the circumstances. Smith had been one of his oldest friends, and now he found himself involved in a leadership election that was bound to divide two of his close colleagues, Blair and Brown. Dewar's lugubrious commentary is remembered by many because it was often repeated: 'It's all most unfortunate. Most unfortunate.' Off the letter went.

By way of personal reassurance (at least in Mandelson's interpretation) it contained the phrase: 'Nobody is saying you are not capable/appropriate as leader.' The analysis continued: there were critics who would attack Brown's 'presentational difficulties' and he certainly had enemies, but the main objection was that the party would be damaged by a Blair–Brown contest. 'Because you would be appearing to come in as the second runner, you would be blamed for creating the split,' said Mandelson.

The wording is intriguing because in its use of the first person the letter reads as if it comes from Brown's personal adviser, a position from which those around the shadow Chancellor believed Mandelson had already removed himself. Mandelson has since insisted that he was still writing as the candid friend who had not yet abandoned Brown. He returned in the last poignant sentence to that voice: 'Will you let me know your wishes?'

This letter fizzed like an unruly firework in Brown's office. A member of his family could still describe it nearly seven years later as 'the most clever and devious letter I have ever seen'. It was viewed in the Brown camp as an effort to use his feelings of loyalty to Blair to force a guilty withdrawal from the contest, and moreover as an effort to portray Mandelson as a loyal colleague when they believed he had already become something quite different.

Mandelson has always expressed astonishment at that reading and (backed by Campbell) has insisted on the depth of his feeling for Brown and loyalty towards him. He told his biographer Donald Macintyre: '[If] Gordon had emerged there and then, and Tony had signalled his support, I would not have thought twice. My loyalty to Gordon was intense. He had always seemed to be the leader of the pack, the man whose brainpower, political judgement and personality were dominant.' But feelings were soured, and later in the week in the course of the funeral preparations, when reports carried back to Brown base camp that Mandelson was still talking around Westminster of his loyalty to Brown, they got worse. The common phrase was: 'Mandy's at it.' Henceforth he would always be 'at it'. Anything Mandelson did would be interpreted by those around Brown as part of a wider and inevitably hostile plan.

No other episode can catch quite as vividly the emotional fragility of the relationships that now linked these three. The very intensity of their dependence on each other over the years seemed to carry its own explosive charge. The draining days after Smith's death passed in an atmosphere that was inevitably heavy with personal recollection, so nerve ends were rubbed raw. With Blair and Brown thrown without warning into the contest that would decide their future, and the finely tuned emotions of Mandelson having to contend with accusations of treachery as well as the guilt that was evidently there, every contact was volatile.

Brown and Blair had spoken several times, the first in an arranged meeting at the home of Blair's brother, Bill, on the night of Smith's death. It was brief and they skated around the subject. Neither showed his hand. Each was being urged by groups of supporters to press on. Mo Mowlam was running Blair's campaign and her team calculated by that first Saturday, 14 May, that he already had a third of the parliamentary party in the bag; Brown's counters gave him much the same story. As with the soundings from the party outside, the message was unmistakable. In taking on Prescott, the nearest thing to a traditionalist candidate who was likely to emerge, one of them ought to give way or the cause of modernization would be put at risk. Most of the public comment suggested it should be Brown who should retreat. Tony Wright, from the vanguard of the modernizers, said on television that it now required from Brown an act of 'heroism and self-sacrifice'. By the start of the week of the funeral that was the dominant theme.

In private, however, Brown was being told something else, especially in Scotland, where his supporters were insisting that Blair seemed a weak candidate and was beatable. From the other side of the border the case that Mandelson had deployed for listening more carefully to public opinion and the box office – the 'middle England' argument – seemed much less important. Scottish Labour had escaped much of the trauma that had taken so much of England so far out of its reach. And Brown's supporters among MPs and in the wider party had, of course, none of the nervousness that was evident among English MPs about yet another Scot (after Smith) taking over. Despite the southern metropolitan current running strongly against Brown, some of those around him persisted long after he had realized that the fight was over.

Crucially, on the day before the funeral on 20 May, Brown knew that the political world was waiting for him and not Blair to decide. By this stage he had no realistic choice. He was still being urged to fight by his brothers, John and Andrew, and the inner circle that included Colin Currie, Murray Elder, Whelan and Nick Brown was still pressing him. In the shadow Cabinet Donald Dewar, now preparing one of the tributes for Smith's funeral, was already sensing that the cause was lost. Being a pessimist by nature, he read the runes clearly.

At Smith's funeral in Cluny Church, on a grey day in Morningside, Brown and Blair sat apart. There is a telling picture of them, separated by a couple of rows, both looking gaunt and pale and gazing straight ahead. Unlike most of their colleagues they knew the words of the hymns and seemed throughout to be a pair apart, which indeed they were. The service was a taxing one for everyone, deliberately plain and unadorned, with the 23rd Psalm sung in Gaelic unaccompanied. Dewar and Derry Irvine both spoke. The atmosphere was heavy. A few hours later, Brown and Blair met near the airport for a brief conversation. Each knew by now that Blair's momentum was increasing, with Fleet Street giving it a hefty push. Blair left for London and Brown went back home to his house in North Queensferry in Fife, overlooking the Firth of Forth. There he listened to his friends telling him, yet again, that he should fight on, but in the speech that they worked on through the night to be delivered the next day to the Welsh Labour conference in Swansea there is less evidence of that appetite for the struggle than there is of Brown's acceptance of the inevitable.

He chose to adapt one passage of Ecclesiastes – 'To everything there is a season, and a time to every purpose under Heaven . . .' This was a time to unite. 'Because we have travelled too far, too many miles together, for us now to lose sight of our destination. Together we have climbed too high for us not to achieve the summit. And it is near.' To some, these words were an indication that he would fight on. Blair feared as much. But they can be interpreted quite differently, as a laying down of the sword, an acceptance of the course of events and the need to do what was demanded of him. The words are intended to suggest that heroism, to use Tony Wright's word, is not always about a fight to the death. It is worth remembering that this was going on a mere nine days after Smith had collapsed, that no public campaign had yet occurred, and that Labour was about to try to maintain the fiction that only after the European elections at the beginning of June would minds be allowed to turn properly to the leadership issue. Brown's Swansea speech was misunderstood by some around Blair as a piece of grandstanding (it was delivered in the absence of Blair, who had originally been booked to speak and who didn't want Brown to go instead) but its tone, to those who knew Brown, was that of the man who was preparing the sacrifice that many MPs were now asking him to make.

Brown is an enthusiastic student of American politics, and he is fascinated by the rhetoric of campaigns. One of his close friends in Washington is Bob Shrum, who was one of Al Gore's principal advisers in his struggle with George W. Bush during the 2000 Presidential campaign. But in a previous life, Shrum was famous for something else. As a speech writer for Edward Kennedy in his effort to take the Democratic nomination away from President Jimmy Carter in 1980 he wrote most of the address that Kennedy gave to the party convention in New York. It was a celebrated speech in its day – remembered for one phrase in particular, 'the dream will never die'. As a concession it is remembered by everyone who heard it as a classic piece of political theatre. It was exactly that tone that Brown tried to capture in Swansea. His stage, of course, was a much more modest one, his audience relatively small, and the occasion was still overshadowed by the funeral of the day before, but reading the words now it is hard not to conclude that the speech was made by a man looking forward to a distant crusade in the future rather than to an imminent victory.

Whether or not Brown was preparing to give way, the speech struck the edgy Blair camp as an appeal to Old Labour, and made them nervous. After discussing it with Blair, Mandelson spoke to *The Times* which carried a story on Monday 23 May to the effect that Blair was not going to abandon the cause of modernization. Set against the Swansea speech, the implication was that Brown was doing just that. But although he was irritated, Blair was also anxious to preserve the relationship with Brown when – as he now expected

– he become leader. Friends who spent most time with him in this period say he agonized aloud about Brown's feelings. He would say: 'We have to take care of Gordon.' This was rather more generous than some of his remarks a year or two before, when the strains had first appeared, but it reflected the reality of his new superiority. The truth is that they both realized quickly after Smith's death that the outcome was likely to be a Blair leadership, and it was in that period of just over a week, encompassing their own awkward meetings, the to-ings and fro-ings of Mandelson between the camps and the funeral itself, that all was settled.

A final act remained to be staged, but before that there was a period of frenzied campaigning of the sort that had been avoided (just) before the funeral. Brown's team lobbied hard, still believing they could convince their man that he might win. Two pieces of evidence, one much stronger than the other, convinced them otherwise. A survey for *On the Record* on BBC television on 29 May gave Blair a solid lead in all three sections of the electoral college which would decide the leadership and two days before, in the *Scotsman*, a survey of a number of Scottish Labour MPs showed Brown with only fifteen solid votes (to Blair's six) but said that six others who were natural Brown supporters wanted him to stand aside for Blair. This was interpreted in Westminster as evidence that even in Scotland Brown was not impregnable.

In the march of history, the *Scotsman* survey changed nothing, but it became another cudgel with which to batter Mandelson. Years later, one of Brown's closest advisers in that period said: 'We knew what Mandy did with that poll. His misinterpreted it to everyone. He probably fixed it himself.' Mandelson says he didn't twist it, though he showed it to MPs as a piece of interesting research; and it is certainly not true that the respected *Scotsman* correspondents of the time had been put up to it. The truth is that by this stage it was all becoming deeply painful in the Brown camp, and any bad news had to have Mandelson at its origin. By Monday night, 30 May, Gordon Brown was ready to tell his team that it was over.

The *Scotsman* episode illustrates how the passions released by the leadership contest had now entwined around the main characters, and how difficult it would be to escape those feelings. By the time Blair and Brown broke bread at Granita, a restaurant in north London, on 31 May, they were looking ahead to life under a Blair leadership but also aware that the events of the previous three weeks had changed their relationship permanently.

The idea of the dinner came from Blair's office. The Swansea speech had alarmed them. Brown was a powerful orator, and was capable of causing immense difficulty for Blair with the party if he felt that he had been pushed aside. Blair had only come to realize in the previous year that he might overtake Brown and he was still hesitant. Mandelson, well aware of Brown's sensitivity and the crushing sense of disappointment that he must be feeling, told Blair straightforwardly that he would have to promise that in any Labour government he would be a Chancellor with more power than any of those who had served Major or Thatcher. No one used the phrase 'dual premiership', but they accepted that Brown would be offered something which might seem like it.

This calculation was based on fear. Blair would be a leader with no experience of politics at the top level, and alongside him he would have a master strategist. If he offended Brown at this juncture, he could expect endless trouble. Mandelson had spent days and weekends with Brown over the years planning speeches, campaigns and strategies and he knew how potent a force he was. They decided they needed to go even further. Remembering the pact of 1992, when Blair and Brown had agreed not to challenge each other, they now agreed that Blair should tell Brown that he wanted to see him succeed him as Prime Minister in due course if the chance came. Pitched so far into the future, the promise seemed a safe one.

This piece of planning has an other-worldly air. A General Election was some way off. Labour had no notion what power would be like, if it came at all. Blair had never set foot in 10 Downing Street and had never even sat on the government side of the Commons. Yet here they were, about to discuss what might happen at the end of a second term of a Labour government. Their readiness to look so far ahead is an indication, first, of the momentum which had built up in the party in the cause of modernization and, second, of the sheer brazen confidence which Blair and Brown had developed. When Mandelson spoke to Blair about what he might do as Prime Minister in the course of a second term, he was listened to seriously.

Mandelson has since admitted another factor to friends: 'I was scared of Gordon.' It rang true with those who had watched them over the years. Brown was in charge and dominant. Mandelson encouraged and advised, but he never led. Where with some other members of the shadow Cabinet he could be openly manipulative, with Brown he was always careful. As Blair and Mandelson prepared in Blair's home in Islington for the climactic meeting of the leadership contest, Mandelson was aware of the consequences if the two had a row. As a wounded antagonist, Brown could destroy Blair's leadership.

The shadow Chancellor never gave any sign that he would relish that outcome. He seemed to want a settlement. But on what terms? On Tuesday 31 May Blair set off alone for Granita, on home territory, not far from his house in Richmond Crescent, Islington.

Brown had begun the evening with drinks at Westminster with his inner circle. He had dined with them the previous night and told them that he knew he must give way. They were not surprised. Even his most enthusiastic head-counter (Nick Brown) couldn't find evidence for optimism. Ed Balls, Brown's adviser, a former *Financial Times* leader writer, went with him by taxi and they arrived a little late at the restaurant.

A few minutes earlier the waiting Blair had been approached by the journalist Allison Pearson who was dining there with her husband. She had never met Blair, but introduced herself. She says he seemed happy – even anxious – to talk. Bubbling. 'What should we do?' he asked her, meaning the Labour Party. She remembers an exchange about the power of enlightened self-interest for good in society and about the need to do away with old Labour attitudes, the theme that was going be Blair's message to his party. He was ready to talk politics. Then she heard him say: 'You know Gordon, of course?' Turning round, she realized that she had stumbled into something important. Brown was polite and they shared small-talk before she sped back to her table. Ed Balls stayed for a few minutes then left.

Blair and Brown sat in the back of the restaurant, facing each other with an exposed brick wall as a backdrop. As a place for a private conversation, Granita in those days had one of the worst rooms in London, its design fashionably spartan. It echoed. By chance, however, there was a diversion that night. The actress Susan Tully – who played Michelle in the BBC soap *EastEnders* – was sitting near the window at the front and was the evening's object of interest. The fact that Blair and Brown were carving up the next government at the back passed everyone by. They huddled privately, unnoticed.

There was practical business to transact. Brown wanted a decent deal for some of his supporters in the parliamentary party and for those close to him. Murray Elder, for example, stayed for a period in the leader's office. Then came the main subject, command over economic policy and quite significant chunks of social policy. There would be no difficulty about that, said Blair. A paper was subsequently negotiated, with Mandelson in the almost inevitable role of intermediary, and was published as a statement, an important indication of the place Brown would occupy in any future Labour government. But the most important words at that table did not concern such practical matters. They touched on a more distant future. What awaited Brown after a Blair premiership?

There has been a pretence on the part of some that Blair went to that encounter wholly unaware of what Brown would say. That is not true. The concession was coming, as Blair had known for two weeks that it almost certainly must. His problem was a different one. What could he say to preserve the loyalty that had developed between them but had been threatened in the course of the leadership contest? He had spoken around the time of Smith's funeral about his awareness of the agony Brown must be feeling, given his thundering ambition and his determination, and despite the moments of irritation in the previous few weeks, his friends believed he now wanted to soothe it.

One of Blair's most prominent characteristics now came into play.

As it is put by one colleague who was sacked by him, and has no particular political affection for him now: 'One of Tony's weaknesses is that whatever has just happened he always wants you to leave the room feeling happy.' He does not like awkwardnesses, or unspoken grudges. A discussion must end with both parties feeling as good as is possible. It is true of Blair that, unlike many other politicians, when he is behaving ruthlessly he likes it to be disguised. That is the view of a number of his closest supporters. So, on this occasion, faced with an old friend who'd been denied a long-held ambition and someone whose support he needed carefully to secure for the future, what did he do to allow him to leave feeling happier than he expected? Blair was guided by Mandelson's entreaties echoing in his head. Brown must be offered something more than a powerful Chancellorship. He needed to be given hope.

The combination, friends of both men believe, led them to discuss quite openly what might happen if Blair became Prime Minister and won a second term. As advised by Mandelson, Blair certainly made it clear that he hoped Brown would succeed him. Their assumption had always been that they would stick together and Blair saw no reason why that should change. But beyond that fraternal expression the accounts begin to diverge.

Blair was asked subsequently by one of his Downing Street intimates to answer a straightforward question. Did he say to Brown that he would stand down before the end of a second term in favour of Brown? Blair answered without a pause: 'Absolutely not.'

From the other side Brown has never claimed, even in semi-private circumstances, that such a promise was made but his colleagues were convinced at the time, and have been given no reason to change their minds since, that Blair expressed his hopes for an eventual Brown leadership in such strong terms that he gave the impression it would be a deliberate act on his part that would bring it about, not simply the passage of time.

Brown left the restaurant believing that Blair had committed himself to supporting his own succession to the premiership, if he was able to pass on the torch. No one in Brown's most intimate circle believes anything else. He has not spoken of it to anyone who would repeat it, and no one expects him to. But it is a hope – though it has been doused by *realpolitik* – that has been built into his Chancellorship.

Is it true? Blair wanted to soothe Brown and to keep his loyalty. His friends believe that he spoke directly about a succession. Who knew what might happen? There might come a moment when it would be possible to hand government on. But a promise? They doubt it. There is no such gift that a putative Prime Minister can offer.

As a historian, Brown knows that pledges of that sort are undeliverable. The attractions of office tend to grip you quickly and firmly. How often has power been handed over in a seamless transition amid conditions of stability and success. In British politics, there is no precedent. Circumstances change, the landscape alters, fate intervenes. But the next day, when they staged a comradely walk across New Palace Yard under Big Ben to announce that Brown would support Blair for leader, Brown believed that he had been given an assurance that Blair would try to time any departure from office to allow Brown to succeed.

None of this was written down. There is no firm evidence of what was said. Brown believed he had a near-promise of succession; Blair insists that nothing so clear could have been offered, and wasn't. The understanding was more like a misunderstanding. Like the princess and the pea it was there, even if no one could see it.

They had to pretend it wasn't there. Brown prepared his words in support of Blair's candidacy and Blair made sure that Robin Cook, in particular, was warned about what Brown was going to say and would leap on board. And then came the campaign proper, at last, in which Blair, Prescott and Margaret Beckett fought it out to what was a near-inevitable conclusion (Blair 57, Prescott 24, Beckett 19 per cent). Only then could Blair relax about Brown. When he appeared at the first public event of the campaign in Blackpool at the GMB conference with the other candidates for a question and answer session, broadcast live on *Panorama*, he was much more concerned about Prescott who seemed likely to be his deputy. But the words exchanged with Brown over dinner weren't a settlement that would last indefinitely.

Roy Jenkins, often described as Blair's history tutor, has compared the encounter between Blair and Brown in conversations with friends as reminding him of a talk he had with Harold Wilson as Prime Minister towards the end of his second administration, just before the 1970 General Election which he lost to Edward Heath. 'Roy,' said Wilson, 'you know I believe you to be my natural successor.' For all the imaginary plots which Wilson imagined Jenkins having organized against him, and for all their tension on Europe which was even then a difficult party problem, Jenkins believes that Wilson more than half-believed it when he said it. Might not the same have been true of Blair in Granita?

There is one piece of hard evidence which can be brought to bear on the conversation they had that night in relation to Brown succeeding Blair as party leader either during or at the end of a second term. Later, well into his leadership but before the election that brought him to power, Blair confided in a friend outside politics that he had learned the lesson of Margaret Thatcher, the Prime Minister who stayed too long. He'd seen from the opposition benches how her government split and sundered around her and how she couldn't see it; moreover, how her intimates huddled in a Downing Street bunker unaware of the coming catastrophe. Blair has often spoken of it. But on this occasion he said more. He would make sure to avoid it. He could not imagine wanting to serve a third term and he would find a way of making a timely exit.

Did Blair rehearse that thought with Brown as they dined together? It is the kind of political promise that is less a promise than a musing on what might be. Labour, after all, had not even won a first term, let alone a second. But it is the kind of talk to which politicians return again and again. It deals with the delicious uncertainties of their fate, one of the lures that draws them to their trade. Blair couldn't know whether he would ever be in a position to deliver on such a deal, before or after an election, or before or after a referendum. The fact that he has talked of it privately with others suggests it would be odd if he hadn't discussed it with Brown on that night. The political truth of that conversation is that Brown left the restaurant to return to his closest friends, defeated but not humiliated. He would remain publicly loyal to Blair but privately loyal to the ultimate ambition which had always driven his political progress. The lingering effect of the Granita conversation is obvious. Blair had made no binding promise of the succession, and Brown's character set him against wishful thinking. But even if there was no expectation, there could be hope.

From close to Blair comes this intriguing description of one of the great difficulties that continually faces him. 'We all know the truth about the second term. With every day that passes Gordon will make another cross on the calendar. Day after day after day.' And they don't need to ask why.

PART TWO

'Look Gordon, you'll have to accept the fact that the Glass slipper fitted my foot and not yours'

4
The Alchemy of Power

Behind the bow window to the right of the black door of Number 10 sits the Prime Minister's press secretary. Early one evening, not long after Labour had moved excitedly but uneasily into Whitehall, Alastair Campbell sat with his feet up on his desk and turned his head to look through the net curtains. A happy stream of people was passing up Downing Street towards Number 11. Gordon Brown was having a party. Campbell watched them go and said to a visitor from Fleet Street: 'I wonder what he's up to now.'

Ministers and their courtiers seemed to be afflicted by the kind of suspicion immortalized in the reaction of the French statesman Clemenceau to the death of a rival at the negotiating table: 'I wonder what he could have meant by that?' Nothing could be as it seemed. If the Chancellor was having a party – *another* party! – he'd be working the crowd and spreading his word. Something was up. Something was always up. The air was heavy with intrigue.

That intensity of feeling was something that arrived with the cars that took the new ministers to their departments on 5 May 1997. A rising civil servant at the time, later to become a permanent secretary, says it was all something of a surprise to official Whitehall, especially those parts of it which saw the Cabinet at work close up. 'Of course we knew quite a bit about them. We had all done the usual homework and we had watched them operating in opposition. But we thought they were going to be rather *nicer*. We found that some of them really weren't very nice to each other at all.' The civil servants were surprised by the maturity of these disputes, which had clearly bubbled away for years. The government which they were about to discover was defined by arguments and clashes of ambition in the years of opposition. It was these that Blair and Brown had to transform into the driving force of a government, like alchemists turning base metal into gold. But the last years in opposition were fraught with such volatility and uncertainty that there seemed no guarantee that the magic would work.

Insiders knew that power had come to Labour without the problems of opposition having been solved first. On the surface, the leadership contest of 1994 seemed to have been absorbed by everyone, and there was no direct challenge to Blair. Old grumblers did patrol the Commons corridors in search of a Labour Party they thought they had lost, and they would spit the word 'Blair!' at you in the way that the hard left had once said 'Kinnock!' or an earlier generation had learnt to say 'Wilson!' Long before the election, the leader knew that there were those who had already placed his name high in the pantheon of treachery, which was the certain fate of the modernizer. That was no surprise, and hardly a problem, since political victories at the polls have a way of encouraging subservience and good behaviour. The more serious dispute still pulsed just below the surface. In the eyes of Brown's circle, Blair's leadership was tainted with a touch of illegitimacy, as if he sat on a stolen throne.

'He wouldn't be there without Gordon and everybody knows it,' was the sentiment that drifted round the Commons. Blair certainly did know it. He knew that it was Brown's network that had first given him a route map in Labour politics and he acknowledged to friends that the hundreds of beneficial hours they had spent together had been his political education. The same did not apply to Brown. He was meticulously loyal in public, and even some who know him quite well have not heard him utter personal criticism of the leader, except with the occasional backhand stroke. But there is none of Blair's willingness to praise, as when he says 'Gordon is my Lloyd George'.

He kept his silence. Brown has never compared Blair to Attlee or Disraeli, because any such analogy would reflect their relative positions. He was not going to give Blair the satisfaction of a comparison that would emphasize his own position as the Prime Minister's junior partner.

The roots of the problem, that negotiated balance on which the Blair government would rest, are buried in the unresolved personal disputes which persisted long after the settlement of the leadership in 1994 and they also sprout from the nature of that deal, the sharing of power between Blair and Brown.

The divisions which were agreed in opposition gave Brown command over social, industrial and economic policy, and the advantage for Chancellor and Prime Minister was that power shared was not power halved. Indeed, they were able to appear as if by their division of the spoils each had become stronger, Blair as a quasi-presidential figure directing government strategy, making treaties and fighting wars and painting the big picture, with Brown as the all-powerful economic overlord. The disadvantage, however, was that the increased power generated by their arrangement seemed to be made more volatile by the division, depending on daily negotiations between the two. The deal made them stronger, but more vulnerable too.

The partnership had, of course, been nurtured by Mandelson and when the election was won it was he who stood at their shoulders. To Brown he was a reminder of the personal disaster of the leadership struggle, but to Blair he was the essential companion, the grand vizier whose presence at court was indispensable. Perhaps surprisingly, Blair was more convinced that his eagle eye was needed at his side than even Mandelson himself. On 1 May 1997 itself, the day Blair learned from his pollsters that he would win a majority which might be bigger even than Labour's in the fabled year of 1945, Mandelson was hoping for a ministerial post inside a Whitehall department – 'a proper job' – and told Blair so. He wanted to be a real minister running an administrative machine. Instead, Blair followed his instincts and made him Minister Without Portfolio in the Cabinet Office, through the corridor from Number 10 with fishing rights across Whitehall, a post which would play to Mandelson's strengths and encourage his weaknesses. He saw all but the most sensitive papers that landed on Blair's desk and stood at the confluence of all the streams of ministerial entreaty and administrative negotiation that flowed to the prime ministerial study. Blair told friends he needed him there. But from the Treasury across the street Mandelson's presence looked menacing and unwelcome. Mandelson was the necessary catalyst in the preparations for power. He was an essential part of the chemistry that sustained the partnership. His presence, however, had often been combustible.

The big breach between Brown and Mandelson had not come during the leadership battle itself, although Brown was furious and sore and many of his supporters had condemned Mandelson by the end of it. A second episode made the hurt worse. In the autumn of 1994, Blair decided (not for the last time) to try to apply his own balm to the wounds. At his suggestion the trio took the opportunity of a party meeting in southern England to repair in advance to the Chewton Glen Hotel in Hampshire for a long talk. They convened under the aegis of Colin Fisher, an advertising man who worked for the Shadow Communications Agency invented in the eighties by Mandelson as Labour's link with the world outside party headquarters. The idea was to dine and stay up talking, recapturing the bonhomie of late nights past and soothing the recent bruises of the leadership contest. The next morning all would be well. It wasn't.

At dinner in a private room Brown did what he always does: he demonstrated that he had been thinking and planning. He produced a blueprint for a party reorganization, worked out in detail. The substance of the plan is much less important than the reactions it provoked, and their consequences. Blair was embarrassed. He had prepared nothing similar and, according to those closest to him at the time, hadn't expected such a document to be produced. He noted that one of its main features was an important job at party headquarters for Michael Wills, a close Brown ally who would later become a minister.

It was Mandelson, not Blair, who seems to have intervened first, saying something like 'I don't think we can do this now . . .' He later told friends that Brown was livid and added: 'Gordon flashed me a look of such menace. It was terrible.' The evening limped on with Brown's plan put to one side. Blair went to bed, and Brown and Mandelson talked on their own. This conversation ushered in a period of nearly two years, leading almost to the election itself, through which their relations were so cool as to be in hibernation. Mandelson has referred to it since as one of the saddest passages of his life.

To an outsider this may seem excessively emotional. It reveals the passions that bound these three personalities together and their instability. What passed between Brown and Mandelson cannot be known for certain – the two were alone in Brown's room – but enough has been discussed with friends and recollected at regular intervals for it to be clear that Mandelson believed he was being challenged about his loyalty. One version has it that Brown challenged Mandelson about his reluctance to have Brown's reorganization plan discussed and said: 'If you and I agree, Tony will never resist. You've got to decide.' Brown's friends dispute the implied invitation to Mandelson to take sides against Blair, though they don't deny Brown's anger. Whatever the words, the outcome is not in doubt. Brown and Mandelson, warriors together in the eighties, parted and were never close again.

This was not a breach that could have occurred without intense emotion. The point at issue – Brown's reform plan – was hardly the Marshall Plan or the Treaty of Versailles. Yet it was a moment of high drama, infused with feelings which bubbled up from great depths. To Brown and Mandelson it was clear that the triple relationship was irrevocably over. In the years when there was none of the pressure of leadership, or the prospect of power, their feelings could be managed. Then it had been all for one and one for all. Now that Blair was clearly and solely the 'one', Brown found himself unable to be part of the brotherhood. Blair's primacy fatally disturbed the balance. All three had driven to Chewton Glen together the previous day. When Brown and Mandelson left, they went separately and in the knowledge that the breach between them might never be healed. Brown's sense of betrayal was much sharper than it had been four months earlier when the leadership was decided. Mandelson, he realized that night, would never be willing to side with him in a dispute with Blair. In that judgement, he was correct. 'He is the leader. We've got to help him,' Mandelson said during their argument in the hotel. Blair had Mandelson's loyalty, but there were miserable consequences. Meetings of the leader's team and senior members of the shadow Cabinet in Blair's room were often strange and prickly, leaving those who were not on the innermost loop puzzled and often embarrassed. Mandelson couldn't resist displaying his soreness at the rift with Brown. Brown showed no interest in restoring the old relationship. Blair, trying to find his own style as leader from a standing start, was wearied by the atmosphere.

'What can you do with Gordon?' Mandelson would say, about some Brown refusal to agree with a suggestion from the leader. And from Brown's cohorts the response came in a steady drift of stories about Mandelson's perfidy. Brown himself did not contribute to these. But shadow Cabinet colleagues began to recognize the closeness of the Brown group and the consequences of the loyalty which he demanded and received. MPs like Nick Brown, Nigel Griffiths, Andrew Smith and Douglas Henderson formed a phalanx of foot soldiers who were always on the move through the Commons corridors with news from Brown's office: some shadow minister's effort to push through a new spending commitment had been squashed; a new stratagem for the election was being drawn up with Gordon in charge; a Mandy criticism of Brown at some meeting had been slapped down by Blair.

Curiously, Charlie Whelan had arrived at Brown's side as the result of a request from Mandelson himself, when he was still helping the shadow Chancellor to build up his team towards the end of John Smith's leadership. Brown had got to know Whelan the previous year during the fight to get union support for the one-member-one-vote reform. He was working for the engineering union and demonstrating a streetwise grip of spin-doctoring (a term still unfamiliar at the time). His recruitment revealed much about Brown, his tactics and the nature of his gang. A cheery, rumpled character invariably wreathed in smoke and gossip, Whelan was an unlikely combination of public school communist (lapsed), City currency trader and Fleet Street intriguer. He loved the game, whatever it was, and played the part of the ragged-trousered boulevardier. News from Brown's office, or the latest whisper about Mandelson, was grist to a mill which ground away happily, with Whelan gleefully cranking the handle.

Whelan would have been an unimaginable component of the Blair circle that was being built. Where Brown's office thrummed with party gossip and kept some lines open to even the more exotic corners of the Labour left, Blair's was engaged (partly as a deliberate strategy and partly by instinct) in a different game. In the pursuit of power they were cultivating non-Labourites who might be brought on board, pursuing a determined Bowdlerization of political language to expunge the old words and setting out on a determined expedition towards the places in Fleet Street which no Labour leader had reached before. This was partly because Blair had no choice. If he couldn't find at least one feature writer on the *Daily Mail* who might be seduced into writing something pleasant about a Labour leader (and his spectacular conquest of Paul Johnson, though the infatuation wouldn't last, convinced him the effort was worthwhile), or make some progress towards an understanding with Rupert Murdoch, he might sacrifice some of those rightish votes which were beginning to detach themselves in great slabs from the Conservatives and pile up for Labour. But the tilt was more than a piece of strategy. Blair's restlessness, caught most dramatically in his assault on Clause IV in the first conference speech as leader, was obvious to everyone around him. He was patently fed up with the nuances of Labour lore that he saw as antiquated. Blair's enthusiasms lay outside his own party.

Brown, by contrast, has never felt that pull. Even when, as Chancellor, he was making a virtue of policing the spending plans inherited from the Conservative government he would happily socialize with parts of the union left, especially in Scotland. If there is a contradiction, it is one he has always tried to ride. Blair is different. When he made his last constituency speech on the eve of polling in 2001, at the Trimdon Labour Club in his Sedgefield constituency, he gestured to his agent, chairman and friend, John Burton, on the small stage beside him and said again what he had been telling his local party for eighteen years: that they had made government possible because they had been willing to change and to challenge the inherited ways. That, perhaps above all, was what he admired in them. It was a striking assertion of how he sees Labour's history in the eighties and nineties. Brown sees it differently, as just another turning in Labour's winding road. The fundamental direction, in Brown's view, remains the same.

In his constituency, Blair's union support came first from the right of the movement, through the GMB, and he has never spent much time cultivating the left. As Employment spokesman he was irritated by what he regarded as the reactionary instincts of the big unions on party reform and on legislation like the Shops Bill. They believed that he often paid lip service to the importance of the unions to the party; they were right. Brown's closeness to the union leaders, especially Bill Morris and Rodney Bickerstaffe, even as the party was changing its economic policy under his direction in ways that the public sector unions, in particular, did not enjoy, was as intimate as it had ever been. Those on the left who didn't like what they were learning about Blair, and had regarded John Smith as a helpful fixer rather than an ideological companion, now looked to Brown who had a particular nostalgic affection for some of the hard men of the left. In them he could feel some of the inherited passion of the Scottish socialists about whom he had written in his biography of James Maxton, the 'sea-green incorruptible leader of the Clydesiders'. He also admired their all-or-nothing attitude to politics. For Brown, the enemy's enemy is indeed your friend and once loyalty has been promised solidarity is everything.

With Whelan and Ed Balls, the Brown machine began to operate. There was one rule more important than all the others. Loyalty. Since his student days Brown was known as a leader of the pack. His natural authority wasn't expected to be challenged. In the three years between the leadership settlement and the General Election this was the most obvious feature of Brown's operation. Front bench colleagues became used to bruising interrogations and in the party at large it became obvious that Brown was fashioning a sphere of influence which would be controlled by him and which would be as powerful and self-contained in government as it was becoming in opposition.

In the preparations for power, Brown considered himself as important as Blair. Tax had been the undoing of Labour in 1992, and his job at its simplest was to make sure that the campaign would not unravel in the same way. The result was a period of what some members of the shadow Cabinet described at the time as brutality. The leader and the shadow Chancellor saw each other every day (speaking much more often than Blair and Prescott, his deputy) and they laid down policy. The idea that collective shadow Cabinet discussions could change Brown's mind was regarded by his colleagues as absurd, because they had reason to know better. They complained about it, mainly among themselves, but the urgency of the coming campaign suppressed revolts. For shadow ministers in their forties who had come into politics to serve in government the prospect of another defeat, stretching Labour's eighteen years of tormented opposition beyond two decades, was terrifying.

Those who got in Brown's way were eased aside. As health spokesman, Chris Smith irritated the Treasury team with speeches that seemed uncomfortably close to spending pledges. Asked privately at the time what he thought of one of Smith's hints about Labour's plans Brown's reply was emphatic (and accurate): 'Whoever is Health Secretary it will not be Chris Smith.' He was duly shuffled sideways by Blair soon afterwards. Brown's approach brought him some admirers, but lost him friends. One prominent front bencher at the time, a natural supporter of Brown's on the left, confessed after a couple of years in government: 'We were all right when we thought that Gordon was the one with the most brains and the best strategic mind. But we were also right about the way he behaved towards us. I hate saying it, but the thought of him as Prime Minister is unimaginable. Think of how he'd behave.'

Rough judgements of that sort were common in the couple of years leading up to the election. The party was being corralled and disciplined in ruthless fashion by Blair and Brown. The memory of the wavering and often feckless leadership of Foot; the knowledge of how it took Kinnock nearly ten years to create even the image of an alternative government; and their memory of the 1992 defeat – all this gave them their political justification for the way they ran the party. Brown was also a natural disciplinarian. He is a man always under control, and apart from the famous shambles he leaves in every office he inhabits, he believes in order. Decisions are made and then implemented; commitments are given and kept. His personality kept Labour in order.

If Labour was to find a creative space in which to reinvent itself ideologically it needed Brown's discipline and authority. But it also needed the iconoclastic impetus of Blair. Blair had developed a certain affection for the Labour tradition, but it always played second fiddle to his impatience for reform. Brown enjoyed addressing party meetings; Blair didn't. Brown was still wrestling with the intellectual problem of reconciling his embrace of many elements of the market economy with his affection for old ideals which he had always expressed in the language of socialism. Blair had very few items of such baggage on the voyage. His ideas had developed in the late seventies without any of Brown's painful rethinking and even recantation. One policy seemed to him to follow from the other – union reform, a resistance to high personal taxation, an admiration for the entrepreneurial spirit, a suspicion of collectivist solutions. When Stephen Byers, a junior spokesman on Employment, was fingered as the Blairite who had mused to journalists in a Blackpool fish restaurant at the 1996 party conference about the possibility of a break in the party's link with the unions, Blair was perfectly content. There was no reprimand. There was a good segment of the shadow Cabinet that thought their own definitions of 'socialist' were being cast aside, but Blair was carrying even the grumpy along with him. Blair was starting to invent a new Labour language; while Brown was playing the foundations for a new economic policy which would depend, he said, on rigour and prudence. Most of the malcontented and the frustrated did not have the energy to resist. If they were going to get to power, this was probably the only way.

From time to time frustration would break out in the open, usually followed by a claim by a shadow minister that remarks had been taken out of context. This was the case with a Robin Cook interview in the *Sunday Times* around conference time in 1996 in which he said this: 'There is a very real danger that we're ignoring the needs of a minority in society who find themselves in a very difficult position, usually through no fault of their own, so much so that when someone like me comes along and tries to redress the balance we're accused of having an odd political agenda.' Cook's reference to a balance that needed to be redressed was, of course, a straightforward criticism of Brown as well as Blair. In private, Cook and those with similar doubts were sniping at the shadow Chancellor often enough for Blair to become alarmed. He had the running feud between Brown and Mandelson, then at one of its peaks of antagonism, and he knew that there was a reluctant section of the shadow Cabinet which was making it obvious that it was being dragged along unenthusiastically by the shadow Chancellor. Frank Dobson, Chris Smith, Clare Short and John Prescott all wanted to make spending commitments that Brown denied them.

Strikingly, Prescott did little to use that uneasy mood to unsettle Blair further. There were a few minor explosions, but they changed nothing. Indeed, Prescott's acceptance of the drift of Blair's leadership was much more telling than any of his criticism. After all, the year before John Smith died he had told the party conference as Transport spokesman that if the railways were privatized they would be brought back into public ownership, and he had vented his prodigious rage after 1992 on 'the spin doctors . . . and people in smart suits who've never won an election in their lives', spreading his ire to encompass Bill Clinton's first winning campaign of that year – the one Blair admired so much – attacking 'Clintonism' as the kind of thinking that would destroy the Labour Party. That language melted away. He had sharp words with Blair in private about his attitude to rail privatization, which the leader was not minded to reverse, but their row was never taken to the airwaves by Prescott. He fumed with his friends, but carried on.

There was one early scare for Blair, when Prescott wasn't invited to a meeting with the party's new advertising agency in 1995. The deputy leader erupted, with good reason. It was a sizeable meeting, including several apparatchiks as well as Blair and Brown and Mandelson, of course, and it looked as if Prescott was deliberately being kept away. He was. It certainly wasn't his kind of gathering

– there were plenty of smart suits, and one of the main participants, Philip Gould, was well-established as the blackest of Prescott's *bêtes noires* – but his omission was a foolish mistake. Blair apologized personally, and subsequently took great care to avoid such gratuitous offence to Prescott who, if he had been tempted to resign at that time, could have caused awful trouble for his leader.

That meeting has another significance. It was held at the home of Chris Powell, chief executive of the advertising agency Boase, Masimi, Pollitt (BMP), which had been hired to make ads for the party. Chris is one of three brothers who have spun a thread that links the Thatcher and Blair governments. One, Charles (given a life peerage by Major), was Thatcher's private secretary for foreign affairs in Downing Street through all the turbulent years, seeing it through to the last days of stumbling resistance in 1990 when, with Bernard Ingham alongside him in the last ditch, he watched the members of the Cabinet peel away from her one by one. The second, Jonathan, was a Foreign Office man like Charles, enticed by Blair out of the British Embassy in Washington where he was a principal observer of the start of Clinton's Presidency. He took over the leader of the opposition's office and, in due time, took his place as chief of staff (a new role) in the Prime Minister's office.

Anyone sitting round Chris Powell's fireplace on that Saturday in 1995 would have seen how different this Labour administration would be from its predecessors. The Powell brothers exude exactly the kind of suave confidence that has Prescott's antennae twitching furiously. In the world of Them and Us, the Powells are Them – exactly the kind of confident, successful, public school-educated characters that part of the Labour Party still found sinister.

The only trade union figure in the room was Tom Sawyer, who had left the public service union, NUPE, to become Labour's general secretary and who was a veteran of the Kinnock reforms. He retained some scepticism about Blair, but he had jumped on board. There were two groups of participants in this meeting – Blair–Brown and the advisers. That was how the party was now being run. The roles taken by Mandelson, Gould and Alastair Campbell illustrated how the campaign would emanate from their thinking more than from any collective discussions the shadow Cabinet might have. Ten years before, in the mid-eighties, this collection of people would have been unimaginable.

A pattern was set. Although Blair's imperious leadership was developing from the memory of party nightmares past, and Brown's more from his conviction that only the rigorously steadfast survive in politics, they were agreed. There would be no nonsense. If they needed evidence to bolster their view they could watch the Conservative government benches, where Eurosceptics were gnawing away at John Major's premiership. He'd been at war with them since he signed the Maastricht Treaty barely a year after he succeeded Thatcher and Tory discipline was breaking down. Major's accidentally recorded remark after a television interview with Michael Brunson of ITN in 1993 in which he referred to some (unnamed) members of his Cabinet as 'bastards' allowed the public to savour for once the reality of life in government. From then on the public saw a Prime Minister wrestling with his party, even having to resort to the device of a surprise leadership election in 1995 to try to give himself new authority. For the opposition there seemed to be a lesson in all this.

Blair and Brown had spent almost all their shadow Cabinet careers in a Parliament gripped by one crisis or another. Nigel Lawson's resignation from the Treasury in 1989 and Geoffrey Howe's a year later broke the back of the Thatcher government, and the early part of Major's premiership from 1990 was defined not by his feisty defeat of Kinnock in the 1992 General Election but by Black Wednesday later that year and the fissure on Europe that opened up under his feet. Young reporters arriving to watch the comparatively arid Parliament of Blair's first term would hear tales from old hands of how the Commons had once been a place of melodrama and tears when votes mattered, rebellions shook the government, and the members' lobby outside the chamber in mid-evening was a bubbling pot of intrigue. Ministers couldn't afford to lose their fingertip feeling for the mood of the Commons or they'd be lost. From the late eighties until the Blair government was elected, Parliament was an unpredictable place with a will of its own. As in the seventies, when

Callaghan's Labour government was limping towards an election it knew it could not win, Major's government was finding it difficult to keep breathing.

By December 1995 it had lost, technically, its overall majority when the wilfully unpredictable right-winger John Gorst said he'd no longer cooperate with Tory whips because of a hospital crisis in his Hendon constituency. This came on top of a classic episode of slapstick politics, when the Chancellor, Kenneth Clarke, had to issue a statement through Conservative Central Office denying that he had threatened to resign over Europe. Denials of that sort from Chancellors are rare, with good reason. They speak of panic. Clarke's came in response to a BBC report by Jon Sopel revealing Clarke's frustration with Major, quoting a devastating phrase the Chancellor used to describe a Eurosceptical remark the Prime Minister had made to the *Daily Telegraph* – he called it 'a boomerang laden with high explosives'. Sopel's source was blown by fellow-lunchers in a Park Lane restaurant and Downing Street panicked.

This was life in the late Major years – crises and rumours of crises, trouble among ministers, trouble at party headquarters, Commons votes that always promised trouble and an atmosphere in which every phrase in every interview was assumed to carry a hidden meaning. By the turn of the year, a Gallup poll put Labour thirty-five points ahead of the Conservatives.

The scent of panic emanating from the government had a profound effect on the opposition. Blair became as obsessed by the sight of a crumbling administration as he was about his own party's past. Just as Kinnock had said 'never again' to Labour after the 1983 cataclysm, so Blair said to his shadow Cabinet: 'We can't ever let this happen to us.' It meant that Brown's natural taste for discipline and what some of his colleagues thought was an instinct for authoritarianism was allowed to flourish. He had one principal purpose: the construction of armour-plating around Labour's spending plans. Where Smith had made much of a commitment to 'full employment', that notoriously elusive concept, Brown spoke of fiscal caution and inflation-busting as the pillars of his policy. Colleagues who were looking forward to fighting an election in which they wanted to promise to outspend Major on public services did not enjoy the regime. Blair and Brown decided the priorities: even Prescott was kept at arm's length. He was often consulted only after announcements had been leaked to the papers and was unable to put his stamp on any significant piece of economic policy.

Blair had put Brown in charge of election strategy a few months after becoming leader. The manifesto would not be subject this time to the painful arguments on the national executive that had set previous election campaigns off to a miserable start. The NEC had been tamed so effectively that it was no longer a lion growling at the party leadership but a pussycat with manicured claws – and the bedrock of the campaign was to be the promise of economic competence. Labour knew – the whole country knew – that its reputation for economic recklessness was a folk memory that was embedded in politics. It had to be expunged. Brown's tactic was to announce at the beginning of the election year that a Labour government would preserve the Conservatives' lower and higher rates of income tax for the lifetime of a Parliament. When he revealed it, on the *Today* programme on 20 January 1997, his colleagues realized that it was the decision that would dictate their lives in government. Not that they had known it was coming. The strategy had been drawn up with Blair and Brown's advisers, with Prescott informed late on. The shadow Cabinet were not surprised by Brown's decision, though many of them grumbled about it in semi-private around the Commons, because they had been feeling the Brown lash for more than a year. And as for the secrecy? By now, it was all too familiar.

Brown knew the announcement was the most important, by far, that he would make before the election. He took very few colleagues into his confidence after it was agreed with Blair, until Sunday 19 January, the day before his speech was to be made. He had agreed to an interview on *Today* immediately after the 8 o'clock news on Monday morning. He then did two unusual things. He tried to speak to the rest of the shadow Cabinet, one by one. And Whelan started to put the message out that he'd be making a big announcement. *Today* presenters mingle in political circles and are used to pressure, unwelcome but unsurprising. But being rung at home on the night before an interview with a specific heavy-handed hint about what might prove a valuable line of questioning is unusual. 'You will ask about tax, won't you?' said Whelan. Was this an attempt to use the programme? Hardly. It suited their purposes; but it suited *Today*'s too. It was inconceivable that such an interview could have taken place without a question about tax. But it was handy to know how excited the Brown team was. They had something up their sleeves.

Meanwhile, Brown was ringing his colleagues. He had an amusing difficulty with Prescott, who was in Hong Kong. He was staying as the guest of the Governor at Government House and the plan was to send him a fax. But the Governor was Chris Patten, former Tory Party chairman. There was an election coming: what if Patten told his friend John Major? So a message was left for Prescott to ring Brown urgently.

Monday dawned. In those days *Today* was broadcast from the grubby but cosy Studio 4A in Broadcasting House and Brown arrived with not only Whelan in attendance but Balls too. This was unusual. They stood behind the glass with the editor and the studio managers as Brown, jacketless, made his announcement. Whelan was agitated when, after five minutes or so, the tax question hadn't been asked: had all his promptings been in vain? No. After dealing with public spending, we turned to the most important subject. But the statement by Brown, unambiguous as it was, was still a surprise. This is how the exchange went.

James Naughtie: Let's put this in context, because the other half of this equation is tax. Is all this really about personal taxation? Are you doing this so that you can say to people, 'I'm not going to put your taxes up'? Because you think that's a necessary condition for winning the election?

Gordon Brown: No, a taxation system has got to be based on principle. It's got to be based on the values of a society . . . It is because of the importance we attach to work and because people have been dealt such a harsh blow over these last few years that we will leave the basic rate of tax unchanged and we will leave the top rate of tax unchanged.

Naughtie: Ah, so this . . .

Brown: And what I want to do over time, when resources become available, is introduce what is absolutely vital for the low-paid in this country in particular, but to the benefit of everyone, a 10p starting rate of tax. But I will not make promises I cannot deliver and that will only be possible when we have the resources to do it.

Naughtie: Right, let's get this absolutely clear. This, at last, is the Brown statement on tax. In your first Budget, you will leave the basic rate and the top rate unchanged.

Brown: I will be making commitments for our manifesto which are commitments for a Parliament. And the basic rate and the top rate will remain unchanged.

Naughtie: Throughout the Parliament?

Brown: Yes.

There it was. Balls and Whelan were like a couple of football coaches who felt they'd scored a goal. They were gleeful. *Today* presenters, producers and reporters realized that a new front in the battle over tax had been opened. Fleet Street descended on Brown, which is what they had planned.

The most important phrase in Brown's revelation, delivered *in extenso* in a City speech that night, was 'the lifetime of a Parliament'. It was a commitment of the sort that no putative Chancellor had given before, and his party knew what it meant: Conservative spending plans would shape the first phase of Labour's first government for eighteen years. On the surface everything was about election preparation; underneath, the assumption was that they were heading for office and that discipline was all.

This meant that although power did thrust Labour's new ministers into the unknown, and they had to deal with the mystification and embarrassments of being Whitehall innocents, almost to a man and woman, they were expecting it. There was none of the slightly vague, rather naive, hopefulness that had kept the Kinnock team going in

1992, when one of them took a photograph of the leader of the opposition in his garden reading a briefing from the Cabinet Office and couldn't quite believe that the red box would have prime ministerial papers in it the following week. Five years later, Labour's leadership was serious. Peter Hennessy, Whitehall's most distinguished academic eavesdropper, chaired some training sessions for shadow ministers organized by the Fabian Society to explain what they should expect in their departments, and at one of them he was told by someone who he says remained close to Blair in government: 'You may see a change from a feudal system of barons to a more Napoleonic system.'

Striking though the phrase is, it only tells half the story. Napoleon wanted lucky generals, but none was lucky enough to share the imperial throne. From the outset, Brown had a place that none of his predecessors had occupied. At the start, it seemed to some startled officials as if the working day was one long conversation between the two, on the phone and in person, with interruptions for a few necessary meetings with others. John Major has spoken of his close relationship with Kenneth Clarke as Chancellor and records in his memoirs that they would always meet once a week. That does not tell the whole story, of course, because there would be other contacts day by day, but it describes the kind of relationship the Prime Minister thought it natural to have with his Chancellor. Blair's and Brown's was quite different, and it sent tremors through Whitehall from the moment they arrived in Downing Street.

Within a few days, officials were wondering what to do. Blair was working from a tiny room off the Cabinet Room itself on the ground floor at the back of Downing Street and there he would meet with Brown with the door closed. This broke a cardinal rule. Except in exceptional circumstances, or when there is a deliberate piece of late night political gossip to exchange over a glass, Prime Ministers and their senior ministers don't usually meet alone. Notes are always taken; as with Cabinet ministers generally, office phone calls are monitored by a private secretary listening on a line next door and notes kept unless there is a particular request that it shouldn't be done. Such a request is, of course, noted. Even the informalities of power are not allowed to pass unseen.

Instead, Brown's calls went straight through to the Prime Minister's study. He would drift in and out with no need to be cleared through by an official. Jonathan Powell guarded the approaches but Brown was not impeded. When he was not in the Treasury he took to working in a small room at the back of Number 11, just a short walk, via the connecting passage and straight down the Cabinet corridor behind the front door of Number 10, to Blair's office.

Civil servants eddying around that office realized that they had never seen a relationship of this kind before. Even the Cabinet Secretary, Robin Butler, who acted as a bridge from the Major to the Blair administration before he was succeeded on his retirement by Richard Wilson, and who had seen many strange things around Number 10 in his time, was taken aback. But when he was approached by some officials, early on, who were concerned that they were not able to monitor all the meetings between Prime Minister and Chancellor and were therefore in danger of losing the grip that it was their task to maintain, he used a remarkable phrase in giving them advice: 'Let them be,' he said. 'Blood is thicker than water.'

That Butler found himself referring to the relationship in family terms is revealing. He had seen close partnerships at the top of government before, but here was intimacy of a wholly different flavour. Thatcher and Lawson, for example, had been notably close from 1983 to 1987, when he was the intellectual engine of her second term and their mutual admiration was intense. But it soon soured after her third election victory, when Lawson believed she was jealous of the credit he received for it. Lawson tried and failed to stop the political disaster of the poll tax (to her fury) and found that she was ultimately more willing to see the resignation of her 'unassailable' Chancellor than to agree to remove from Number 10 her personal economic adviser and freemarket soothsayer, Alan Walters, with whom Lawson was battling over exchange rates and Europe and whose public interventions drove the Chancellor to despair. Even at its passionate height, Thatcher–Lawson hadn't seemed like a mingling of blood.

Blair–Brown always did. The relationship was not being forged in government. It was already established. In a government with almost no experience of the byways of Whitehall – Jack Cunningham, Gavin Strang, Margaret Beckett and John Morris were the veteran exceptions who had seen some minor action in the Callaghan years – there were no ministerial big cats prowling the corridors, familiar with the terrain. There were some, like David Blunkett, who had come from local government and had manhandled big budgets in their day, but many of them had spent their political lives running little more than a fax machine and a couple of secretaries. It was all a shock. In 1997 Blair was, of course, the first Prime Minister since Ramsay MacDonald, Labour's first Prime Minister in 1924, who had never set foot in a ministerial office occupied by a member of his own party until he became their master. A majority of his Cabinet had never even seen the Commons from the government side. In this atmosphere of enforced ignorance, Blair's team tried to establish control and it was not a surprise to the civil servants waiting for them (though it was still unsettling and often irritating) that they did it with a certain wild-eyed enthusiasm.

They had spent three years of preparation in opposition by exerting the sort of discipline that had not been seen within the Labour Party since the post-war government. Attlee had his own style, dismissing ministers from his office (and, on occasion from the government) with a single laconic sentence before turning back to the cricket scores rattling off the teleprinter he kept in his office for the purpose. Blair's regime was different, but it was meant to be similarly brisk. The result was an obsession with control. It was almost as if they were surprised it didn't come automatically with government and felt they had to try harder. Whatever nervousnesss lay underneath, they started to behave like enforcers.

The seeds of future trouble were sown. At the time, they thought it was the only way. A frantic pace was set. There is no clearer example of how the early exercise of power in government had its roots in opposition. Brown's announcement of independence for the Bank of England came after only three days, a shock to the system which disoriented officials in the Treasury who had read his speeches of the previous eighteen months without picking up the clues. He had argued the case for a different relationship between ministers and the Bank quite clearly earlier in the year, but in the preparations they made for how to deal with the new ministers the Treasury officials hadn't foreseen it. This was more important than the other matters of personal chemistry which made his relationship with his permanent secretary, Terry Burns, so tetchy and which led to his early departure. It also produced a rocky start to the Chancellor's relationship with the Governor of the Bank of England, Eddie George, who was surprised to have been brought late into the Chancellor's thinking. In the course of administering the shock, the Chancellor demonstrated one of his characteristics – the way that breezy good humour can spring out of taciturnity quite unexpectedly. At the same time that he was having such a difficult beginning with some Treasury officials, Brown made sure that weekend to ring a few ex-Chancellors to tell them what he was about to do, in a spirit that was somewhere between cheekiness and politeness. Norman Lamont, for example, had suffered a fairly humiliating defeat in Harrogate where he had fled from his redrawn Kingston constituency in the hope of staying in the Commons, and was rather touched to get a cheery call from Brown who told him: 'You'll be pleased to hear that I'm introducing your policy.' Brown was oozing confidence. Apart from the Prime Minister, only two or three ministers knew in advance and a handful of advisers in the Treasury and Number 10 were in on the preparations. Prescott and Cook were informed, but not consulted in a way that would allow them to object. The government as a whole did not know that interest rate policy was being handed over and that, as critics on the left would have it, the Bank of England was being privatized. It promised to introduce the oligarchic rule of the bankers that had been a bogey of the left for a generation. Brown, however, had convinced himself that it was the best way of conducting the anti-inflation strategy which he told himself was needed, so he did it without blinking.

When MPs unhappy with interest rates later complained to Brown that he had surrendered his power over the economy he told them that he could not have had stability without first putting the Bank in charge. He believes that it was the most important decision of the first term. He and Blair spoke about it just before the election. He said he was going to do it. Blair said: 'Fine.' That was the extent of the discussion. Brown's control of economic policy was absolute. Those around him knew that Blair wouldn't argue. The Prime Minister, at least for the first year or two, would not contest the central strategy of the Treasury. It was the Bank decision that caught the flavour of those first days, both Blair and Brown being anxious to appear virtuously decisive.

But the anxiety produced other kinds of decisiveness that were to cause trouble. Not many members of the public have read, or would want to read, Questions of Procedure for Ministers, though it is a document which is to each member of the government what Queen's Regulations are to a soldier. Blair's introduction to the 1997 edition (it is updated by every incoming Prime Minister) ends with the words: 'I commend the Code to all my ministerial colleagues.' This is misleading. The Ministerial Code, as it was to be called after 1997, consists of the instructions by which ministers live their lives – how they deal with each other across departments; what the chain of command is to the Cabinet Office; when the Prime Minister should be told of administrative changes and by whom; and how negotiations must be conducted with Downing Street. The point of publication, following John Major's decision to declassify the document in pursuit of 'openness', was to demonstrate the government's commitment to personal standards of behaviour. As it turned out, the rules were to cause Blair considerable trouble when the tide of sleaze began to lap around the government. But in the document there was one especially telling paragraph. It reads: 'In order to ensure the effective presentation of government policy, all major interviews and media appearances, both print and broadcast, should be agreed with the Number 10 Press Office before any commitments are entered into. The policy content of all major speeches, press releases and new policy initiatives should be cleared in good time with the Number 10 Private Office; the timing and form of announcements should be cleared with the Number 10 Press Office. Each department should keep a record of media contacts by both ministers and officials.'

This had several consequences. Leaving aside the brief spasm which passed through the proprietors of certain restaurants within a mile or two of Westminster, whose tables were playgrounds of ministerial gossip and mischief paid for by Fleet Street, some members of the government began to behave as if the last shreds of privacy and dignity had gone. Alastair Campbell, they realized, was now entitled by prime ministerial diktat to know everything about them – even their informal conversations with journalists – and they felt the formidable grip of the Number 10 Private Office tightening round them. The timing of Whitehall announcements has always been an obsession in Downing Street – any government needs to look as if its many arms and legs are roughly coordinated – but the new code went further. It established a new tone in government. Labour's pre-election effort to appear relaxed, unstuffy and loose-limbed and Blair's to present his team as a streetwise gang of individuals was now officially declared over. The era of control had begun.

The government's personality was defined as much by this preoccupation with a culture of command as by Blair and Brown's early efforts to appear decisive and quick, and it revealed a lurking fear under the confidence that had seemed to characterize the first days. Blair had spent much of his time since becoming leader in cultivating Fleet Street, and he had been well schooled by Campbell in the ways of the tabloids. The capture of the *Sun* as a Labour-supporting paper in the run-up to the election was the greatest prize, to be treasured over the years and guarded with near-obsessive care, but Blair, with particular help from Anji Hunter, had also calmed the troubled breast of the *Daily Mail.* He suspected it wouldn't last, but at least he was promised a period in which it would not try to destroy his government simply because it carried the label 'Labour'. All this manoeuvring changed Blair. Now he could barely think of a strategy without automatically considering how it would play in the papers. Talking with Paddy Ashdown about the future of Labour–Liberal Democrat cooperation he was often open about the importance of avoiding offence to the papers which had been so painstakingly neutralized or brought into Labour's camp. More than any predecessor as Prime Minister – including Major, who was the despair of his staff for his habit of chewing over newspaper headlines and plunging into late-night rages as a result – Blair worried about how his government was portrayed.

With Philip Gould, the perpetual pollster, ready with daily readings of the public mood and Campbell in a closer position at his shoulder than any Downing Street press secretary had been before, Blair was often being presented with dark tidings about the reaction to some speech or policy announcement. Prime Ministers tend to have few people around them who can talk frankly, without choosing their words carefully. Campbell is one of them. 'Bollocks' and 'crap' often pepper his conversations with Blair, even when they are not alone and someone from one of the outer circles of power is in the room. Ministers from past governments affect shock at this. One Thatcher veteran said he could not begin to have imagined what would have happened to him if he had walked into Her study and announced: 'This speech is complete crap.' Campbell can do it happily, and he does. He has none of the polished deference of the natural civil servant, which holds cheekiness to be the greatest sin, and he speaks to the Prime Minister in private as he would speak to one of his journalistic clients. Blair takes it, every day.

The significance of Campbell's influence is that it reveals Blair's acknowledgement that his government would do nothing without first taking trouble and time to find out how it would be presented to the public gaze. To members of the government this was portrayed as a strength, the mechanism by which the muddles and dithering of the Major years would be prevented. In truth, the conception of how power would be exercised was as much an expression of nervousness.

Blair's 1997 government had none of the confidence of experience. It was building defences against what Blair thought were its great enemies – indiscipline among ministers, a slackening of reforming zeal, and a turning of the Fleet Street worm. That reflected the obsessions of opposition and fear of what failure would mean for a party that had grown used to the wilderness. The call for discipline covered a basic lack of trust: Cabinet colleagues were not to be empowered because that would endow them with the potential to wreck the new government's scheme. And so the levers of power were held by just two people. It was safer that way, as long as the two individuals thought alike and trusted each other. What no one could know for sure in 1997 was how that relationship would change in government and whether the fault lines opened up by the leadership contest would widen. And so this was how the Blair government came into being, pulsing with what Robin Butler had identified as the ties of blood between Prime Minister and Chancellor, which gave it its air of wild intensity. The volatile spirit infected its whole life.

5
A Cabinet Made for Two

No Prime Minister since the nineteenth century has spent more time avoiding formal meetings with Cabinet colleagues than Tony Blair. When they happen, they are brief. The real deals are done elsewhere, usually in the Prime Minister's study with only three or four people sitting around: and, as often as not, with only two. 'We are not a very collegiate government,' said one Cabinet minister, just before he was sacked. 'I'm afraid we don't really see very much of each other. It's a strange outfit.' From the start, it was to be a government of individuals, moving in their various orbits round the pair at the centre like planets whose orbits wobble under the influence of competing suns.

The patiently crafted relationship with Brown, handled with the delicacy that you might expend on an unstable bomb, had to be watched and tended in government ever more carefully. So in power, privacy became Blair's stamp. Civil servants soon dispensed with the old Whitehall habit of clearing Cabinet ministers' diaries for all of Thursday morning, and putting putative lunch guests on standby for cancellation. Weekly Cabinet meetings ended in under an hour, as if the clock on the mantelpiece behind the Prime Minister's head would sound an alarm if they let the discussion drag and the Lord Chancellor might turn into a pumpkin. At least once, the Cabinet were out on the street in under thirty-five minutes. For officials who remembered the Thatcher Cabinets, or the rambling hours of Callaghan and Wilson days when ministers still indulged themselves with long interventions and arguments and semi-confessional outpourings, this was brevity that was almost indecent. Blair runs his

Cabinet as if it is a formal ritual, like some piece of parliamentary procedure that has to be observed, or a weekly church service from which everyone must be allowed to escape on time. The decisions are taken elsewhere.

Blair is quite open about how he would view a Cabinet that insisted on staging grand debates. With horror. He told Michael Cockerell on BBC television in 2000: 'The old days of Labour government where, I think, the meetings occasionally went on for two days and you had a show of hands at the end. Well – I mean – I shudder to think what would happen if we were running it like that.' He is unashamed, as usual, to use a Labour government as the example of how not to do things in Whitehall – his instinct to expunge his party's record in power is very strong – but he exaggerates. Harold Wilson certainly organized an occasional orgy of Cabinet meetings. Before deciding on his tour of European capitals in 1967 to discuss British entry to the Common Market, Wilson had seven full Cabinets between 18 April and 2 May, with two on the final day. Blair is wrong, however, about a show of hands being common. It wasn't. His horror is generalized and fuzzy, but it is real. He simply cannot imagine how a government can function with a Cabinet having to be consulted regularly. Think of what these warring ministers might do, he seems to suggest, and how long they would take to do it.

Blair sees ministers one by one on the secure territory of his own little office, with his own staff gathered around. He negotiates alone whenever he can. The Cabinet committee system, which Thatcher and Major still used as the engine of government, is much less important to Blair. It is even less important to Brown. This is despite his being given the prize by the Prime Minister of the chairmanship of the committee on economic affairs (EA in Cabinet Office jargon), which includes all the ministers with the big Whitehall budgets and is, alongside the overseas and defence policy committee, the most important sub-Cabinet group. Brown was the first Chancellor to chair this committee since Wilson retrieved it from his Chancellor in 1966 after the economic storms of his first two years in office. As part of his understanding with Blair in opposition, the committee chairmanship came with Brown's rations. But strangely he never seems to have relished it. Blair clearly doesn't regret not chairing it ('Tony doesn't like maths anyway,' says one sniffy spending minister) and Brown also does his main business elsewhere. A picture of Brown in the chair has been provided by a colleague sitting near him: 'He can't wait to get it over. Maybe that's why he's so rude to us. I don't know. But it's Gordon at his grumpiest. He's sometimes much more interested in what Balls says than he is in what we say. He scribbles away all the time on his pile of papers and sometimes doesn't seem to hear what we say. I'd say that they aren't anything like the meetings that outsiders maybe think we have.'

Like Blair, Brown operates on his own ground, in his own way. A nervous crocodile of ministers troops one by one to the Chancellor's Treasury sanctum for individual meetings round the huge meeting table where he often does his negotiating. From the moment he arrived in the Treasury, committed to the inherited Conservative spending plans and a stern regime for ministers who wanted to spend, this has been his mechanism for control.

In the early years of government, the surprising outcome of this tendency for Blair and Brown each to want to work alone, doing their deals in bilateral negotiations with individual ministers, was that it allowed them to preserve their own relationship as the real centre of government. Blair's ceding of economic authority to Brown and the Chancellor's contentment that the Cabinet was not to be allowed to become a powerful and potentially rampant force, meant that they could operate in their own spheres and settle the big decisions between themselves alone, with no interference.

Intimacies were reserved for their separate circles of advisers and, most of all, for each other. One Cabinet minister puts it like this. 'What's the thing I hear the Prime Minister say most often? "I've got to clear this with Gordon." Or: "I'll square this with Gordon and it'll be fine." Or: "I'll take care of Gordon." It's the same all day, every day. That's how we work.'

At the start, the Treasury hated it. They had a more private Chancellor than they had ever known. His door would close and nothing could happen until it opened again. His secrecy was famous.

When Terry Burns was still his permanent secretary, before the instabilities of their rocky relationship persuaded him to get out, he asked one of the secretaries in Brown's private office one day in July when the Chancellor was proposing to go on holiday. One of them looked at the closed door, behind which the Chancellor was thundering away on his desktop computer, battering out some memo to a Cabinet colleague: 'We don't know. He won't tell us.' The character of any department changes with the personality of the Secretary of State, and Brown brought to the Treasury exactly the air of closeness and near-obsessive single-mindedness that had caused difficulty with so many shadow Cabinet colleagues in opposition. Government didn't change him: his officials realized that the Brown they had watched from afar was going to be the Chancellor they had to work with. He didn't care that it offended some quite grand Whitehall figures, like the (anonymous) official who told Peter Hennessy: 'The Chancellor is an anorak. He has the social skills of a whelk.' The Brown bonhomie is reserved for out-of-office activities.

In the office, he got an early reputation for gruffness. Some Treasury officials resented his importing of his own team – Balls, Sue Nye and his adviser Ed Miliband were around him, and Whelan was exactly the kind of rough diamond which that department is never going to value. He did not have the Treasury style, which is one of the reasons for Brown's loyalty to him. The Chancellor liked to work alone, didn't like being patronized by some of the officials who tried to, and wanted to make it obvious from the start that he would make his own decisions, many of them in private. By comparison, the Kenneth Clarke regime under Major had been louche. This seemed the age of the hair shirt. Brown, in fact, is a convivial man when he chooses and he is a genial host. But the Treasury found that at work he behaved more like a headmaster than an eager prefect. Some didn't like it.

Blair had the same effect on the officials who had expected to run his life. He brought his intimate circle into Downing Street with him, and it was to them that he always wanted to turn first – to Jonathan Powell; to Anji Hunter, who acts as part-confessor and part-coach; and above all to Alastair Campbell. In the early stages, one of his important civil service private secretaries, Moira Wallace, used to find it difficult to get into Blair's study at important moments (particularly when the Chancellor was there) and expressed her frustration to colleagues. It was an awkward handicap because she was the official in Number 10 who was meant to monitor the comprehensive spending review, the most important negotiation in the government's first year. Those who knew Blair well told her that it was no reflection on her professionalism or discretion. That was the way he worked. The Downing Street joke afterwards, a good-natured one, was that her next job was a most appropriate one, based on her experience with them: she was to run the Cabinet Office's social exclusion unit.

The Cabinet is encouraged to get on with its life as best it can, individuals dealing one by one with the Prime Minister or the Chancellor – to get money, to clear a speech, to shape a new policy, to recover from some public blunder or to conceal one from the public gaze – and the consequence is that many of the inherited problems in their relationships were allowed to fester through the first term. If Cabinets are families, this is one with a fractious history and a love of combat that seems to come naturally.

Sitting round the family dining table, the Cabinet preserves some old feuds, whose roots are deep in the past, and it crackles with the jealousies of ambition and political disappointment. This is hardly unique to the Blair government, of course. Major's 'bastards' were a source of carpet-chewing angst to him, and ministers who witnessed Thatcher's persistent humiliations of Geoffrey Howe in front of colleagues, especially after she removed him from the Foreign Office, speak of them still as exercises in public cruelty, shaking their heads at the memory. Sometimes outsiders do get over-excited about the personal disputes in politics, and forget that in the fevered world of a Cabinet there are bound to be strong ties of loyalty and strong enmities too. It is true of all parties. Even as the Labour Cabinet was bedding down, and surprising Whitehall with the maturity of its family disputes, there was a spectacular example of this in the shadow Cabinet across the floor of the Commons. One serious national newspaper editor was astonished in the course of a conversation with a leading Conservative just after the leadership election of 1997 to be told of a piece of gossip which even he found startling. The story he was told was that the shadow minister to whom he was speaking had concluded that a fellow member of the shadow Cabinet was – literally – 'possessed by the Devil'. So serious was this belief that an exorcist was consulted, who was apparently taken aback by the suggestion but who nonetheless agreed to make a visit to the House of Commons to sit anonymously in the public gallery and gaze down – presumably thinking cleansing thoughts – on the object of the accusation during question time. The editor, a sober and respectable figure, reeled away from the conversation convinced that politics was even stranger than he had always known. It's a useful reminder that it is indeed a rough old trade, and it attracts all sorts.

Every Cabinet accommodates rivalry and some hatred. Throughout the Wilson years, Jim Callaghan and Barbara Castle had a relationship that throbbed with distaste and envy and after their struggle over trade union reform at the fag end of the second Labour government of the sixties it became mutual loathing. Callaghan's first significant act on becoming Prime Minister in 1976 was to sack her. No one in the political front line was surprised. Edward Heath, once asked about the role of women in politics, said of his successor, Thatcher: 'I had one woman in my Cabinet. One too many.' So it goes.

Blair's Cabinet, however, has a family character of its own. The central tableau throughout the first term was a picture that told much of the story. The table tapers slightly at the ends, like a coffin, to give more junior members out on the wings a proper sight of the main activity at the centre, and every eye is drawn to the axis of power which runs from the Prime Minister's chair in front of the fireplace to the Chancellor directly across from him, about four feet away. The floor-to-ceiling windows let in quite a bit of light and it is a room which inevitably carries a certain grandeur from its history. Ministers' chairs are the ones used by Gladstone's last Cabinet; everyone knows that this is the room in which politics has been distilled for the last two centuries and more. Brown habitually sits with a pile of papers in front of him and always with a pen in hand. He is flanked by Cook on his right and Derry Irvine on his left. They were the three big beasts in the first term, with Prescott on one side of Blair across the table and the Cabinet Secretary (Sir Robin Butler and, after 1998, Sir Richard Wilson) on the other. The most recent arrivals at the table sit, as tradition dictates, at the ends of the table, from where it is sometimes difficult to hear and where irreverent commentaries on proceedings on centre stage can be whispered quite safely.

In the group of three ministers facing Blair across the width of the table the body language was absorbing from the start. Brown's physical behaviour in Cabinet fascinates his colleagues. While the Prime Minister is talking, unless he is directing a question to the Chancellor or giving him the floor, Brown is usually writing. His apparent absorption in his own thoughts borders on the rude. He acknowledges his colleagues only rarely, in breaks from the stream of note making. He has a distinctive hand, with big, sprawling letters. Sometimes, if he is organizing his thoughts on paper, he will write very fast in capitals. It is an unmistakable style, and because he writes at speed it becomes an athletic business. His whole posture seems to be directed at making his pen work hard and the paper scrunches up as he goes. When Brown is writing in Cabinet you can't miss it, even if you are a minister well below the salt. He writes instead of looking around. With Cook the conversation would be limited; with Irvine, their unspoken rivalry for the Prime Minister's ear makes dialogue awkward. Some restless members of the Cabinet describe them as the two bullies, who always behave warily towards each other. Brown is such a dominating figure with such physical presence that in the course of routine and frankly tedious meetings he is watched by everyone. 'I have no idea what he writes,' says one colleague who sits well outside the central group, 'but there's a lot of it.'

Another, no longer in Cabinet, is less charitable. 'It's obvious that he doesn't want to look at anyone except Tony. That's how power is shared out in the government. Gordon acknowledges the Prime Minister – as an equal as much as the boss – but no one else.' Most members of the Cabinet agree that Blair is careful to defer to his Chancellor in formal meetings. Every minister knows that they have divided the world into two parts – Brown's control of social and industrial policy as well as the economy means he treats the ministers involved as Treasury satraps while Blair adds to the obvious prime ministerial concerns of foreign policy, defence and Northern Ireland the need to fulfil campaign promises on health, the subject that by the beginning of the second term had become the nearest thing to a Blair policy obsession. In Cabinet, as in the daily round of Whitehall meetings, they operate as a duopoly. They don't argue across the Cabinet table – that's left for their daily private encounters – and Blair defers to Brown in the policy areas in which he's been given command. At Cabinet meetings everyone else – Irvine, Prescott, Cook and Straw included – is an onlooker.

But around this central group the Cabinet's lesser power games are played out. Blair has gone to considerable trouble to involve Prescott, having learnt early in their relationship how easy it would be to leave him feeling slighted. A deputy prime minister who strayed off the reservation into parts of the Labour Party where Blair's name is spoken like a curse would be a dangerous beast indeed. Some of Prescott's friends, never reconciled to Blairite thinking and practices, accuse the Prime Minister of patronizing him and, frankly, of exploiting Prescott's vain streak. Richard Caborn and Rosie Winterton, both ministers, would not use those words, but would sympathize with that view. The defence from Prescott is that he was able to make use of the authority he was given – for example, in leading negotiations at the Kyoto climate change conference where he was probably at the zenith of his parabola in power before it dipped back into the mire of transport policy. The settled Whitehall view after four years was that his vast department of Environment, Transport and the Regions had proved an empire that stretched too far, whose distant reaches had slipped out of control. The lines of command were very tangled by the end. And just as he prepared for his arranged move to the Cabinet Office, settled privately with Blair months before, he had his election fist fight in Rhyl with Craig Evans, the most celebrated egg-throwing protester of all, who could not have expected the straight left to the jaw that he got from the light heavyweight deputy prime minister.

Blair, who was in his constituency on 16 May when titbits of news began to arrive in the early evening of a streetfight involving his deputy, displayed signs of panic. He'd had an awkward encounter himself on camera earlier in the day with Sharron Storer, the partner of a cancer patient in Birmingham, who accused him of neglecting the NHS. Blair had appeared stuck for words, and stumbled. He looked shaken by the verbal assault, to which it was hard to summon up a quick diplomatic reply, and for some of those back at his campaign headquarters it revived ugly memories of the wobbly Blair of the WI speech in June 2000 and the fuel protests of the autumn. This was the image of the Prime Minister that they least wanted to re-create, and they were preparing for the worst headlines of the campaign. Then came Prescott. For an hour or so it looked as if Blair might have to think of sacking him. He spoke twice to his embarrassed deputy on the phone, and soon the truth dawned on those around Blair: Prescott's escapade would get a good deal of comic treatment which would be rather easier to handle than persistently awkward questions about NHS waiting lists and, as a bonus, it was an episode that would clip the deputy prime minister's wings. After this he'd not be in a strong position to deliver grandiloquent speeches about the government's 'vision', nor to appear as a deputy with a hold on Blair. His punch cost him political weight.

In any case, that weight has seldom been used to try to destabilize Blair. The Prime Minister found one of the most surprising features of the Cabinet, as he has confessed to his associates, not the bad blood that still flows around the table between the likes of Brown and Cook but the fact that Prescott has not drifted into a position of opposition. He has had plenty of disagreements – he thinks Blair's interest in the Liberal Democrats is absurd, he still finds the language of entrepreneurship unsettling and shares late night regrets with his friends that Blair's Labour Party, as it seems to him, is irredeemably hostile to the trade unions. Yet he has never organized a Cabinet revolt of significance nor fomented organized discontent. There have been manoeuvres on regional policy and transport and efforts to promote the careers of his loyal friends, Caborn being the most obvious, running regional policy at the DETR then becoming trade minister at the DTI and finally Minister for Sport. But these have been matters of everyday politics, not major engagements. In his big arguments with Brown, on transport and especially the London Underground, he has often found himself more in sympathy with Number 10 than with the Chancellor. Compared with the activities of some senior ministers in the Major and Thatcher years Prescott's challenges have been expressions of dissent so polite that they have often passed unnoticed.

Prescott in government has been quite different from Blair's expectation of him in opposition. At the time of the leadership contest in 1994, Blair was worried. Although Prescott's formulation of 'traditional values in a modern setting' was an acknowledgement of the inevitability of change, Blair was conscious that he did not really understand him. 'I really am not sure if I can handle Prescott,' he said to colleagues during that campaign. 'I am never sure what he is going to do next.' But in government Blair has found Prescott easier to handle than any other minister. It brings him regular bulletins of thanks from Blair. Any visitor to Downing Street won't have to wait long for a prime ministerial tribute to his deputy. On the night the egg landed, Prescott benefited from that gratitude.

This is the (surprisingly) stable part of the family, enlivened by occasional talk of a Prescott late night explosion or a need for some tenderness, but in which there never seems to be the threat of fracture. There has never been a serious threat of resignation from him. Prescott has not played that game with any gusto. Even in his darker moods, roaring with frustration at the 'fancy boys' in Number 10 or another Gould memo based on voter focus groups ('all that glitters is not Gould' he once announced on the *Today* programme with a giggle), he prefers to boast of his loyalty, not his trouble-making.

But near the dormant volcano of the deputy prime minister at the Cabinet table rumbles the family feud that will not die. The old contest between Brown and Cook has swung back and forth between them for at least two decades. Most of the government believes that it was his knowledge of the depth of the feud and his fears about what it portended for the second term that caused Blair to take Cook from the Foreign Office on the day after his re-election and make him Leader of the Commons.

But strangely, it was not only a surprise to Cook, who spent a considerable part of the day inside Number 10 telephoning friends for advice about whether or not he should leave the government in anger. Brown didn't expect it either, and nor did the new Foreign Secretary, Jack Straw. As Home Secretary, he was preparing for an agreed move to the Department of Transport and the Regions, slimmed down as a result of the obvious difficulties which had caught up with Prescott. Straw had a meeting arranged with the permanent secretary of that department on election day itself. That move was anticipated by his own private office and Prescott's, which had organized the necessary briefings for an incoming minister and was utterly sure that it would be Straw. With David Blunkett given leave from Number 10 to drop broad public hints that he was to become Home Secretary, and Straw's move well-trailed with the usual string of prepared smoke signals from Blair's office, all seemed ready for a prepared piece of choreography at the top of the government. Blair had been talking for months about how he regarded Cook as a great success in Europe, and how his diplomacy in the Kosovo war had so impressed the Americans, and those around him took it as a signal that after all his early difficulties – in Kashmir with a silly hat and an ill-judged phrase, in Israel with a piece of bungled diplomacy, and with a public crisis in his private life in the government's first year – he had secured his place for the second term. So even Brown did not know what was about to happen when he flew from his own count in Fife back to London to join Blair at the outdoor celebration of victory at Millbank just after dawn on 8 June. Yet such was the history of the Brown–Cook relationship that it was assumed by their gossiping colleagues that it was Brown's pressure that made the change.

Even if the decision was Blair's own, without any direct suggestion from Brown, the belief that it was done to try to prevent a continuing public exchange of barbed speeches between Chancellor and Foreign

Secretary hardly reflects well on Downing Street. For most of the first term Cook and his circle had been complaining about Brown's coolness on the euro, often with only the thinnest diplomatic disguise. And soon after his demotion to Leader of the House (hailed by both Cook and Downing Street, in the threadbare language of such moments, as an exciting new challenge perfectly suited to his great talents) his former special adviser David Clark, who had long been battling on Cook's behalf with his counterparts in the Treasury, broke cover. On the very day that the new Parliament met for the first time, two weeks after the election, the Chancellor delivered his Mansion House speech and doused the euro enthusiasts with a cold shower. The watchword was delay. Clark gave an interpretation which chimed with Cook's own. He described the shuffling of the Foreign Secretary in words which members of the government could easily hear coming from the lips of the new Leader of the House: 'Mr Blair took the decision, we are told, to prevent the early months of his second term being dominated by headlines detailing Cook–Brown splits on the euro. There is, of course, a more orthodox way for the Prime Minister to prevent Cabinet splits: to reach a clear decision of his own and impose it on his colleagues. That he chose not to do so is a stark admission of personal weakness.'

The weakness claimed is not, of course, a failure to impose his view on 'colleagues' in the plural but on his Chancellor alone. Cabinet government in the Blair years has been seen by those at the centre of it as a simple struggle at the top of the government. The ministers who cluster round the throne can sometimes infect the atmosphere for good or ill, and they can succeed or fail in their own departmental endeavours with important consequences for the government, but only one among them matters alongside Blair. The result is that the Cabinet is seen by Labour MPs, and sometimes appears to see itself, as principally a reflection, even a victim, of that relationship.

In this case, Blair's moves had as much to do with freshening the top of his government as with a response to the difficulties between Brown and Cook. He confided afterwards to other members of the Cabinet that he wanted to keep Straw in the top three and not to be seen to be demoting him to Transport. The relationship between Blair and Straw had deepened considerably in the first term. That was part of the balance and the other changes were designed to keep Brown happy – the departure of Byers from the DTI to Transport and the arrival of Patricia Hewitt at the DTI, from the Treasury. None of Brown's supporters was eased out obviously and in economic and industrial policy, all the key positions were taken by ministers who looked first to the Treasury.

Cook hardly had time to feel aggrieved before he had an opportunity for glee. He was already meeting backbenchers with whom he had lost contact since he was sent to fly abroad for his country as Foreign Secretary in 1997, and had mischief in his eyes. He was careful not to be around when Downing Street and the chief whip's office made their blundering decisions about Select Committee lists which produced the biggest rebellion of the whole Blair era, and was able to say later that he advised against it, thus putting himself on the side of the backbench shop stewards who saw this as a test of parliamentary virility. Moreover, he could use the opportunity – and did – to promise procedural reforms which meant nothing to the public outside but were of immense importance to Labour MPs. For a deposed Foreign Secretary, it felt good to be seen as their champion in the Cabinet.

Blair, however, was cursed with the inevitability that, as with every reshuffle, the first of the second term would be seen again as a kind of tug-of-war between Brownites and Blairites.

The one that caused most anger in the Brown circle was the removal of Nick Brown as chief whip, a tearful episode for him which also condemned him to Whitehall's notorious house of nightmares, the Ministry of Agriculture, Fisheries and Food (MAFF). Brown had been his namesake's most assiduous supporter, a head-counter and arm-twister on the backbenches for more than a decade and one of his closest advisers at the time of the leadership struggle. The Chancellor believed that he could protect him; but Blair was advised that it was dangerous to have a chief whip whose first loyalty lay with Number 11. He agreed.

At each following reshuffle the counting went on: how many

Blairites in, how many Brownites out? In the nature of such games, much of it was absurd. It did the Chancellor more harm than good to fight for the positions of some of his friends. Why, his colleagues wondered, was it worth it for Brown to argue for a return to a junior government job in 2001 for Nigel Griffiths, the Edinburgh South MP who is one of his long-time supporters, who had been sacked as competition minister in the DTI the year before? The appointment was interpreted by some in Downing Street as pointing up Brown's refusal to let go, which they regard as his biggest failing. Brown doesn't see why he should apologize for what he sees as proper loyalty to friends. Each change of personnel had become a Downing Street–Treasury test, a weakness which Blair tells colleagues he has recognized but can't fully expunge. There was some panic among Brown's friends, for example, on the morning of the 2001 reshuffle when it was thought for an hour or two that Charles Clarke was being promoted not to the Cabinet Office and the party chairmanship, where he ended up, but to a job in the Treasury. He is regarded as an enemy of Brown's and his arrival in Great George Street (where his father, Sir Otto, was a famous senior mandarin) would have been explosive. It seems that Blair never intended any such thing: but the thought was enough to send a frisson through the Brown camp. When Blair has a reshuffle, that's life.

The zealots encourage this talk still, despite the fact that the gossip around rival team selections has become something of a joke over the years, and the subject of ridicule in the press. It seems to be in the government's blood. The language was invented by the rival camps themselves, after all, not by any Fleet Street conspiracy, although when it was up and running there wasn't a political journalist whose nose didn't twitch at another twist in the story of a struggle for supremacy between supporters who were happy to have the Cabinet seen as the field on which battle could be joined. Whose foot soldiers had the higher ground? Who had the heavy artillery? Almost any minister will take you through the line-up with glee, pointing to Brown's most enthusiastic supporters – the Treasury chief secretary Andrew Smith, the Social Security secretary Alistair Darling, with Margaret Beckett retaining enough distance from Blairism to be counted a friend. They'd note that the others are now outside the full Cabinet – Nick Brown, and a clutch of second-ranking ministers circling in an outer orbit.

Blunkett? Blair's new best friend. Straw? Blair's joint leadership campaign manager all those years ago and the man with most interest in stopping a Brown succession. Alan Milburn at Health? Strongly for Blair, with a bag full of Treasury secrets from his time as chief secretary. Stephen Byers? A Blairite who was given the black spot by Brown when he was at the DTI and has scores to settle.

But the difficulty in a Cabinet with such self-conscious dividing lines is that the whole business of government becomes a struggle of personalities and its energies are directed inwards. The balance of power is measured every day, as with the tap on a barometer in the front hall of Downing Street. And the demotion of Robin Cook has set the pressure gauge spinning. His antipathy to Brown is overlaid by a new fury at being forced to leave the Foreign Office. He was distraught. He owes Blair no favours now and there are many Labour MPs who believe that in the course of the second term he will be the natural conduit for the unhappiness that is bound to arise on the backbenches, the focal point of the inevitable sporadic troubles that will arise from that source. He will be well placed to sharpen their focus. Cook's story, the dilemma of a minister caught between the Scylla and Charybdis of Brown and Blair (it is the kind of grand reference that Cook might well make), is the story of how one of the great questions of the second term – whether or not to give Britain a European currency – couldn't be disentangled from the Cabinet struggles that, like so many Prime Ministers before him, Blair had seen take a grip of his government.

It became the most dramatic example of how personal conflicts came to seem more important in the public eye than the substantive issues themselves. They did so because Blair's Cabinets have had one striking and maybe perplexing characteristic from the beginning. They have not been Blairite.

This does not seem a contradiction to anyone who is inside the government. From the start, Blair saw himself in a position of some solitude. He enjoyed it. Thatcher-like, he revelled in the image of the party leader and then the Prime Minister who was willing to swim against the current. He took care to fix his lines of control into the party, and to have his allies organize a more supportive NEC, but he also craved a reputation for a kind of political loneliness. He enjoyed moments when he could seem *different*. When one of his close supporters, Harriet Harman, stirred up a traditional Labour kerfuffle in opposition with her choice of a selective school for her son, Blair refused to take the party's side (despite Alastair Campbell's fury both at Harman's decision and Blair's support for it, which he made no effort to conceal from the press). In his own decision to choose a selective school for his oldest child, Euan, Blair was happy to let it be seen as the kind of decision that defined the break he had made with Labour's past. Each time he could hear the roar of disapproval from many members of the party, and the grunts of discontent from some of his own ministers, but as with Clause IV he wanted such episodes to make a point. From time to time, he wanted to stand alone.

Almost no one around the Cabinet table, with the possible exception of Derry Irvine, would be with the Prime Minister on all these questions. He nurtured rising ministers like Byers and Milburn in the language and practice of Blairism, but in the first term they were still learners. Geoff Hoon at Defence was loyal, but it is a department that has a way of separating its ministers from the rest of the government: they become figures apart, spending their days trying to reassure a nervous military and fighting an endless war with the Treasury about funding. Brown did not have close collaborators in the Cabinet's most powerful posts, but neither did Blair have colleagues who were willing to express themselves in his language. He always seemed to be a few strides ahead. Blunkett, still with a rich dash of authoritarianism from his days on the left in Sheffield, would be a Blairite radical in Education but stayed well clear of wider arguments about Europe, for example. Jack Straw signed up at the Home Office to a regime of reform which many party critics savaged as illiberal, but he resisted Blair on much of his constitutional reform programme. And so on. Apart from Mandelson, whose Cabinet career was dominated by his two enforced resignations in three years, there was only one all-round Blairite at the table and he was the boss.

Towards the end of the first term a complaint was made regularly by the Prime Minister – his Cabinet had too many weak links. This Prime Minister, elected in 1997 with a bigger majority than any one-party government since the Battle of Waterloo, and re-elected four years later with one that was nearly as great, was tormented by the thought that he had so far failed to construct a Cabinet in his own image. Blair was racked at the turn of the century by the thought that he might not have done enough to bed his ideas down. It was partly for this reason that he continued to talk to Mandelson.

After his resignation as Northern Ireland Secretary, he was still in regular touch with Downing Street. He and Blair decided that he should not be seen to visit Number 10 – if he was spotted there would follow a new season of Mandelson stories and speculations which neither of them wanted – but they talked a great deal. Casual callers to Powell's office would hear talk of 'Peter's' latest call or piece of advice or commentary on events. And there was only one Peter. Blair, all his friends concluded, was lonely without him.

This was not simply because of their intimacy, going back over so many years and involving so many joint operations and clandestine manoeuvres, but because Blair did not even now have a Cabinet with whom he felt he wanted to confide completely. Every Prime Minister has a Cabinet composed partly of favourites and partly of rivals, but in Blair's case he came to believe that his Labour Party had not yet produced a crop of first rank ministers. 'Can you explain to me,' he asked a new friend towards the end of the first term. 'Where are the people? Why don't I have more of them? I need some better people at the top. I know it. Where are they?' As he approached the re-election campaign, a number of his closest friends saw this self-questioning becoming something close to an obsession.

His critics complained that he was much too cautious in fertilizing the lower ranks of government with new talent and was reaping the reward, and he has expressed some guilt-tinged sympathy with that view. He has spent a good deal of time cultivating backbenchers, who are brought in groups to sit with him at the Cabinet table by the chairman of the parliamentary party, and therefore he has been made aware of their grumbles, but he is privately convinced that he has not yet shaped a party that will produce future Cabinets which will be better than the one he started with.

The consensus among the mandarins who have watched the Blair government since it arrived is that the Cabinet has been weak for two reasons – partly because of the Blair–Brown division of power and the necessary private negotiations that make it work, and partly because man for man and woman for woman it was not a group that was able to give departments a real sense of purpose. It was this weakness that Blair tried to correct in June 2001 with the arrival of Charles Clarke, Patricia Hewitt, Estelle Morris, Tessa Jowell and the new chief whip in Hilary Armstrong. But it was still a reshuffle that demonstrated his limited scope for the kind of revolution part of him favoured.

The Scottish and Welsh Secretaries, Helen Liddell and Paul Murphy, stayed in place, for example. These have been awkward jobs since devolution, and each Secretary of State has had some difficult moments with the Parliament in Edinburgh or the Assembly in Cardiff, but Blair did not believe he could follow his instincts and abolish the posts. It would have been politically difficult, with menacing elections looming for Labour in both Scotland and Wales in the next couple of years, and the person who was most anxious to point this out to him was Brown. There is not a nuance in Scottish politics that he misses and he has kept up a stream of warnings to Blair about the dangers of the Nationalists: warnings which the Prime Minister was finding somewhat wearing even before the Parliament was opened in Edinburgh. He has a history of difficulty with the Scottish party and the Scottish press ('a bunch of wankers' in Campbell-speak) and displays in private the same kind of impatience that brought him trouble and embarrassment in Wales on the issue of 'London interference'.

So despite the government's rhetoric of change, it sometimes comes slowly. Blair believes he has no option but to run the Cabinet in the way that he has, because he would find a truly collegiate government a cumbersome animal, and because he has engineered with Brown a mechanism which delivers decisions quickly and irreversibly. They may have arguments and rows and each may stomp off from time to time. Each may complain to his intimates about the other. The early bloom of their relationship may have faded. But they still believe that the partnership works and that they need each other. Without Brown, Blair would find the conduct of economic, industrial and social policy a much more hazardous business because he believes that no alternative Chancellor could exert such formidable discipline, even if he were easier to placate at moments of anxiety. Brown also knows that Blair has conceded to him ground that all his predecessors in Number 10 have kept for themselves, and that, though he may feel a rising private frustration about his prospects for the succession, there is no value for him in creating an open Cabinet rift of the sort that occurred between the last five Prime Ministers and their Chancellors. Better to share power between two individuals who enjoyed working alone, than to invite a powerful Cabinet to line up behind one or the other on each important question. Nothing but danger could come from that.

In that sense the duopoly has remained stable, surviving despite the regular onsets in Downing Street of what feels like a political hurricane season, but the stability has come at a high cost. Blair has a Cabinet that at times has resented its impotence in policy-making, as well as some of the Prime Minister's own initiatives. When Derek Foster, the former opposition chief whip who was denied a Cabinet job by Blair, said this government 'wasn't fit to lick the boots' of the post-war Attlee government he irritated a good number of ministers but caused some others to mope privately about their powerlessness to influence the direction of policy.

But the signs at the start of the second term were not that there would be more attention paid to the Cabinet or to Parliament, but less. Blair's changes to the Downing Street machine, based on observations by a number of outside business figures who had looked at how decisions were taken and implemented, were building blocks to a Prime Minister's department based on the Cabinet Office.

It is not so named, but this central office of government which has always been the fear of the mandarinate is now in place. With

Powell, Campbell and Hunter in charge of three new sections the mating dance with the established civil service will have to continue until a final settlement is reached. No one doubts that the old Whitehall spectre of a Prime Minister's office more like the White House than the office of a parliamentary leader has now arrived. Whitehall now expects it to be the pattern for all governments in the future, and the centre to strengthen. Blair's command premiership has almost decreed that such a structure should be built. He will not dismantle it.

His relationship with Parliament is distant, compared to that of his recent predecessors. It is not surprising that a Prime Minister with a majority of 167 finds that he isn't fretting over the outcome of parliamentary votes, and he has been spared the horrors which John Major had to endure week after week when a Commons rebellion seemed to be scheduled on the weekly order paper. But Blair's attitude springs from something deeper than the comfort of a big majority. He has always been impatient with the Whitehall machine – a feeling sharpened with the approach of the 2001 election when 'delivery' of public services became the government's most pressing problem – and that restlessness about how government's work is done encompasses Parliament.

Blair prospered there in opposition, but he has never had the enjoyment for Parliament's habits or a lust for its charms in the way of John Smith and most of his predecessors in the Labour Party. When the Commons embroiled itself in a messy and sometimes ludicrous election of a new Speaker in the year before the General Election, he made it clear to his staff that his irritation went far beyond the fact that the process took seven hours. It seemed to him pointless that a Prime Minister should be wasting his time sitting in an office at Westminster waiting to complete a string of procedural votes. Why couldn't he get on with running the country?

He was unaware that the change of Prime Minister's Questions to a once-a-week outing would annoy some of his own backbenchers, though it did, and has tended to dismiss the possibility of genuine trouble among Labour MPs as fanciful. But at the start of the new Parliament, with a determined cross-party group of backbenchers, a sort of All-Star Awkward Squad, forming themselves into a campaign for changes to the select committee system, there were stirrings of trouble. They wanted a system that took power away from the whips and gave the Commons more freedom in calling the executive to account. With the wounded Cook, in place as Leader of the House, whose interest in reform converted him to support for proportional representation years ago, they believed they might be in a position to make serious mischief.

There were warning signs for Blair in the first term. As Speaker, Betty Boothroyd regularly scolded ministers who showed what she thought was contempt for parliamentary convention (the most common being the making of policy announcements to a morning press conference, or to the audience of the *Today* programme, before coming to make a statement at the despatch box). Her surprise retirement was interpreted by those closest to her as a clear signal to the government that she disapproved strongly of its way of working. Blair's attitude to Parliament is not unlike his view of Cabinet government. Formal respect, but little commitment. He lusts after streamlined executive government, and is irritated by anything that gets in the way.

By the start of the second term the Blair style was set in stone: a Cabinet of ministers whose most important negotiations were directly with the Prime Minister or the Chancellor and who would seldom be invited to have a general discussion round the table. Government rested on the axis that ran from Number 10 to the Treasury and Blair gave the impression that he had no interest in running affairs in any other way. Ministerial meetings were as small, as short and as infrequent as they could decently be. And Downing Street itself was expanding, placing new departments in the chief whip's former residence in Number 12, with the happy symbolism that it squeezed Number 11 in its embrace.

Above all the government remained a kingdom divided between two rulers and their courts, commanding their own domains and responsible between themselves for solving those territorial disputes that arose. Around Blair and Brown the architecture of government reflected their own relationship, built on privacy and intimacy and with carefully erected defences which they hoped could resist the wildest storm.

The relationship and therefore the business of government was frustrating – sometimes infuriating both of them – and it caused their officials and political bag-carriers to lead lives of anxious rivalry and intrigue. But it was one from which there was no escape. They believed it still worked for them. And while it did, its imprint was on everything the government did.

PART THREE

6
Definitely Maybe

Sometimes the Chancellor rushes into the Prime Minister's office at such a speed that a path has to be cleared for him. Officials stand aside; doors fly open. It happened like this one Wednesday afternoon a few weeks before the date had been chosen for the General Election. So agitated was the Chancellor that one official was knocked aside as Brown raced for Blair's office. The door closed behind him and soon there was the sound of angry voices. They were arguing about Europe again.

Such moments are familiar to the civil servants who are jammed around the desks in the office just outside Blair's office next to the Cabinet Room. This particular argument, however, was a special one. Europe had been a source of disagreement since their earliest months in government and four years on was threatening to disturb the careful election plans. Ministers were pulled one way and then another by the debate. On this Wednesday Brown felt the balance tilting away from him, so he demanded a face-to-face meeting with the Prime Minister alone. They were arguing, as so often, about a few words.

In the confines of the Prime Minister's small ground floor office looking on to the Downing Street garden, the significance of a phrase was being dissected. Blair had used it in the Commons an hour or two earlier. Brown was upset by it. Each knew that it was like the shift of a tiny weight on a pair of finely-balanced scales, a tilt more powerful than it seemed. Their discussion was intensely important to them both, yet it was just as important that the world outside should know nothing of their disagreement. The surface of the waters had to remain undisturbed, though underneath their feet were churning furiously.

The tumult had come about without warning. At Prime Minister's Questions that day, 7 February, William Hague had asked Blair to clarify his definition of five words – 'early in the next Parliament'. This is the weary phrase that every minister had been trained to utter as the formula for the timing of the Treasury decision on whether to recommend British membership of the single currency, the trigger for a referendum. Hague asked a simple question: did 'early in the next Parliament' mean within a couple of years?

Blair was able to appear almost puzzled by the nature of the question: wasn't the answer obvious? He replied: 'Early in the next Parliament means exactly what it says. Early in the next Parliament would, of course, be within two years.' In one sense, this revealed nothing at all. What could be more straightforward? Yet those words produced a fusillade of phone calls from the Treasury to Downing Street, the angry meeting between the Prime Minister and his Chancellor, and a memorable aside from Blair to a member of his staff, delivered with a revealing grin: 'Let's say it was a slip of the tongue.' That would not only be the explanation to the public, but to the Chancellor of the Exchequer too.

This is the kind of episode that would seem baffling to an outsider allowed a peek behind the curtain of politics in Blair's government. To those at the centre the pattern was familiar and the exchanges seemed to carry an electric charge. Throughout the first term, Europe was the great national question that could not be allowed to become the great national question. The dangers were simply too great, because Blair and Brown found themselves drifting apart on the question of the euro, and it became an emblem of their differences. The Prime Minister came to believe that his commitment to British membership had to be clear if a referendum was to be won; the Chancellor began to try at every turn to keep that commitment vague and to insist that the Treasury alone was the 'guardian' – he invented the word for the role – of the economic decision that would precede any referendum. So it was a struggle for supremacy. In Brown's view, the Treasury was not to be pushed around by Blair.

When he heard the Prime Minister's description of the timescale, unsurprising and almost banal as it was, he fumed.

Lurking behind these arguments and this sensitivity was an even more dangerous problem for them both. The European debate gripped the government, as it had gripped all its predecessors for more than a generation, and acted as a cipher, a kind of second language which revealed a government divided and uncertain on this question despite its majority. From the first months in power, when they decided that a decision to join the euro should be put off, Blair and Brown inevitably came to be seen as the leaders of two distinct groups of ministers – one in favour of getting Britain into the euro and joining the central core of the EU as quickly as possible, another which was innately cautious and even hostile. The problem for Blair was that Brown's group was bigger and seemed likely to remain so.

The argument churned through the government in the eighteen months up to the 2001 General Election. No other issue of strategy had the same resonance. Although in principle the Prime Minister and Chancellor were both publicly committed, it was complicated by huge difficulties in timing, and by the determination of Brown and the Treasury to be the arbiters of the five tests that would trigger the referendum. The European question was not a division of principle between Number 10 and Number 11, but it was an argument about tactics that swung to and fro with such rapidity that it had as much effect inside the government as if it had been a fundamental dispute about the policy itself. Fortunately for the government, the Conservatives' decision to play the 'keep the pound' theme in William Hague's campaign allowed Labour to play a dead bat. The Prime Minister and Chancellor could both say that they promised a referendum and the Conservatives didn't. That was the divide, not the difference between them in Downing Street about the economic tests. For an election campaign, that would do. But the argument went on.

Blair and Brown tried to take some of the sting out of the issue only a week after polling. Brown went to the City to deliver his speech at Mansion House and gave a signal to the City that a judgement on the tests might be some way off. The idea was to give everyone a cold shower: the Chancellor was telling the City to calm down. Immediately the assumption was that he was pushing Blair. Intriguingly, the truth is different.

Blair himself had been involved in the drafting of the Mansion House speech. He approved of the downbeat signal. Despite his anxiety not to appear wobbly on his commitment to deeper integration in Europe, he had learned in the previous year how dangerous for the government the timing of the argument could be. He, at least as much as Brown, wanted to turn down the heat.

Almost since the government was elected, the European argument has been monitored as a strategy for which the enthusiasm of one or other seems to wax and wane. The media's fascination is increased by the obvious way in which they have tried to keep their tactics on Europe to themselves.

A consequence of this is a remarkable one for the Cabinet, or at least remarkable for those outside who believed that their meetings might sometimes permit real debate. From the day it first convened on 8 May 1997, Labour's first Cabinet meeting for eighteen years, until the government was dissolved for the 2001 election there was not a single round-table discussion of policy on the single European currency. It was the unmentionable policy, the one that could only be handled by the Prime Minister and the Chancellor in their own way, between themselves and with selected groups of colleagues from time to time, as they saw fit. Just as set-piece arguments on the economy of the sort that marked important stages of the early Thatcher years were never encouraged, so the Euro discussion did not happen. Reflecting on this at the end of the first term, one minister said: 'I suppose you find it odd that we never had a proper debate about the euro round the Cabinet table. I'm afraid it isn't odd at all. This isn't a very collegiate government. We just don't debate things like that.' He shrugged.

Ministers had never been led to expect anything else. Prescott enlivened TV and radio interviews regularly by insisting that the euro decision would be a collective government decision when it came, but in practice that collective voice was a chorus which sprang to life when the Prime Minister and Chancellor had made their decision. There was no prospect that they would be overruled by their own Cabinet – the idea would strike Whitehall as absurd – and it was just as unlikely that the Cabinet would insist on arguing the subject through and forcing the pace if Blair and Brown decided that the moment had not come. So the balance was held between the enthusiasm in Downing Street for an early referendum if the conditions were right and a natural Treasury caution. Brown was no Eurosceptic, but he was determined to keep his own counsel. Above the door of that old Scottish changing house, Drummonds branch of the Royal Bank of Scotland at the top of Whitehall, there is a motto intended to be a cautionary word to any reckless customer. It says 'gang warily': proceed with caution. Brown was determined to gang warily towards the euro zone.

By the end of the first term, the reason John Prescott was saying publicly (and much more forcefully in private) that the decision whether or not to recommend British entry had to be taken by the Cabinet as a whole was not to emphasize that decisions of that sort were made collectively: it was to try to make sure that, for once, it did happen. On Europe, most ministers felt cut out and remote. They were distant observers. Outside Downing Street and the Foreign Office, ministers would hear of it on the Whitehall grapevine, in trembling messages that spoke of a tilt one way or the other between Number 10 and Number 11 or a new intervention by Robin Cook, as Foreign Secretary, another Mandelsonian ploy, or another snort from the Treasury in Mandelson's direction. As often as not it would be a message flashing up on the computer screens on ministerial desks around Whitehall, written by the Chancellor himself, reminding them that the position he had just repeated in the course of some remarks to the Cabinet remained the position of the entire government, and that his choice of wording was the only one that any minister could use.

No policy reveals more clearly the government's fault lines and the character of its principals. It ensnared them in personal feuds and struggles which were only controlled and kept largely from the public gaze by the lucky accident for Blair that he faced an opposition party that was continuing its own traditional internal struggle on Europe. But by the end of the first term, this was the issue that Blair knew he had to resolve. His Cabinet Secretary, Sir Richard Wilson, told his civil service colleagues that it was without question the policy that the government must settle early in the second term. Delay could bring untold political trouble. Yet in the week after their re-election, the Mansion House speech suggested that delay rather than decisiveness was the choice.

Every government since the fifties had found that Europe was a constitutional question that gnawed at their parties' vitals. The Conservatives were split on the Common Market from the moment it came into being, with the nationalist right at war with the emerging majority which thought of itself as internationalist and outward-looking. That division was given cover by the Thatcher victory in 1979. The Prime Minister was able to send semaphore signals with her handbag to those Tories who were instinctively hostile to European institutions, playing the part of the one-woman opposition to Brussels. But simultaneously, while the rhetoric was often antagonistic and sometimes even contemptuous of Europe, the Thatcher government followed broad Treasury and Foreign Office advice and dug in deeper. Thatcher's enthusiasm for the single market led her to agree in 1987 to the Single European Act, the piece of legislation which Eurosceptic Tories later came to regard as a pivotal moment in the history of integration.

The double game couldn't be played for ever: ultimately, Margaret Thatcher lost a Chancellor, Nigel Lawson, over exchange rate policy and a Foreign Secretary, Geoffrey Howe, over her hostility to Europe a year later. With Howe's departure in 1990, and his memorably savage resignation speech which thrilled half his party and horrified the rest, she turned within a month into a Prime Minister who could not command the support of her Cabinet and was gone. She paid for mistakes like the poll tax, but it was Europe that finished her. Labour's experience was less melodramatic but just as painful.

As Prime Minister, Harold Wilson weaved and dithered on Europe throughout his first two terms, but found when he returned to power in 1974 that this would no longer do. His own deputy,

Roy Jenkins, had led sixty-nine Labour MPs to the 'Aye' lobby to support Edward Heath's government on the principle of British membership and settle the matter in October 1971, and the only device Wilson could find to help him handle his party was the referendum, which he had dismissed with contempt when Tony Benn had first suggested it. The Cabinet were allowed to take different sides, thereby lifting the threadbare veil that was supposed to protect the government's divisions. But the party at large was not turned by the big Yes majority into a pro-European party. Michael Foot led Labour into the 1983 election waving a policy of renegotiation which was effectively a promise of European withdrawal, since the demands to be made of the other member states were known by everyone to be impossible to meet. Labour's gradual emergence as a pro-Europe party was greatly complicated by the presence of the Social Democrats. Jenkins, David Owen, Shirley Williams and Bill Rodgers had founded the SDP in March 1981 in large part as a challenge to Labour's anti-Europeanism and it was meant as a bolt hole for many on the Labour right who could not stomach it. The effect was to make it more difficult for some of Labour's most enthusiastic Europeans to argue their case inside the party: they were open to the charge of neo-Jenkinsite treachery.

So, as with the Tories, Labour's European scars were ugly. Blair is no political historian by instinct, but as he came to know Jenkins he absorbed the lesson of those battles.

Blair was only nine when the Macmillan government ran up against the 'Non' of General de Gaulle in 1963 with Edward Heath leading the British negotiations. As a student Blair hadn't attended the televised debate at the Oxford Union which was one of the few sparkling events in the 1975 referendum campaign. He had adopted the ritual hostility to the European Community as a putative Labour candidate in 1983 (it was hard to find a seat if you didn't in those days) and as part of the Kinnock generation shed it like a snakeskin sometime in the mid-eighties. But when he became Prime Minister he was still wary of economic and monetary union. The sight of the eviscerated remains of the Conservative Party after the 1997 election was testimony to the consuming power of the European argument,

John Major's government having devoured itself in the years since Black Wednesday on that very question. There were also plenty of ministers and Labour MPs who retained suspicions of the EU, and especially its plans for a single currency operating with interest rates set by one central bank. This central bank was the 'bosses' Europe' which had been demonized by much of the Labour Party in the seventies, the Europe that they believed wouldn't permit a British government to pursue its own economic and social policies.

So Blair had no stars in his eyes. Yet Roy Jenkins was on hand to try to instil some excitement. To many Labour MPs, Jenkins was a claret-stained ghost of battles long past but Blair enjoyed his company and valued his political wisdom. They dined together several times when Blair was opposition leader, Derry Irvine sometimes acting in his familiar role as host and sommelier. They talked about the Liberal Democrats and proportional representation, of course, but also about Europe. Jenkins, after all, had been trying to encourage a pro-Europe Labour government since the 1959 General Election, and for the first time he had one. He was also determined to impart to Blair the lessons of prime ministerial uncertainty on Europe: in his view it meant disaster. This was the Chancellor of the Exchequer who, in his own words, had warned Wilson in 1970 about his European attitudes: 'What is most damaging to your reputation and position in the country is that you are believed, perhaps wrongly, to be devious, tricky, opportunistic.' There was an echo of those words in his warning to Blair. In Jenkins's view, Europe was one of those great questions which had the power to destroy any Prime Minister who handled it in a slippery fashion. So he was determined that Blair's eyes should be directed across the Channel, and that he shouldn't blink.

But Europe wasn't an issue that Blair could address as an intellectual puzzle to be solved. It touched on the most sensitive relationships among those around him. Most of all, it fell squarely between the spheres of influence of the Treasury and the Foreign Office – between Brown and Cook.

There is an old political adage, coined by Lloyd George, and a special favourite in the Labour Party, which laid down that there could be no friendships at the top in politics. Sometimes debts of loyalty and trust can survive power, but in the sense that completely open relationships become almost impossible to sustain in the struggles and negotiations of government, the rule is true. And turned on its head, another truth jumps out. Old enmities seldom pass away in politics. The difficulties between Brown and Cook are a spectacular example. For years they have maintained a spiky relationship, which has often slipped into open hostility. Government has mechanisms for concealing such feelings – Cabinet ministers can stand on stately platforms and appear to be partners in power, pursuing joint objectives – but in the human exchanges that determine the character of an administration old grudges seldom disappear.

Putting a date on the start of what is considered by their colleagues to be a genuine feud between Brown and Cook is difficult. By the time Brown began his political career at university, Cook was up and away, already on the threshold of Parliament which he reached, as MP for Edinburgh Central in 1974, nearly ten years before Brown. For someone with Cook's ambitions and talents as a left-wing orator in those days it was galling, as it was for many others higher up in the Labour establishment, to find the young student radical making such waves. Despite his contribution to *The Red Paper on Scotland*, for the rest of the seventies Cook found himself on the opposite side in the devolution debate that gripped Scotland.

Cook, convinced that devolution was a mistake, pressed for a 'No' vote in the referendum on 1 March 1979. With Tam Dalyell, and fellow figures on the left like Brian Wilson, he pitched himself against his party. Since Brown was running the Scottish party's devolution campaign in Edinburgh, by arguing against it at Westminster, Cook became a natural foe. Later, it got worse. At the end of the eighties, when Brown began to get his teeth into Labour's spending commitments as shadow Chief Secretary, Cook was the spokesman on Health and Social Services. He wanted to promise to spend more. Brown wouldn't let him. Cook accused Brown of making speeches away from Westminster which played to the party's desire for higher spending, but of arguing behind closed doors with his shadow Cabinet colleagues for a much more restrictive policy. Cook accused him of double-speak, and from then on their coolness dropped a few more degrees.

It was obvious to Cook's shadow Cabinet colleagues throughout the Kinnock years that he had a gimlet eye trained on the shadow chancellorship. He never got it, Smith being the natural successor to Hattersley. Brown in turn became Smith's natural choice when he became leader: Smith would not have chosen Cook, because the two men weren't close at that stage. When they had been rival campaign managers for Kinnock and Hattersley in 1983 there was some bad blood. Smith had bonded with Brown, but not with Cook.

Despite his notable prosecution of ministers over arms to Iraq at the height of the Major government's difficulties, it was Brown who had the more senior job under Smith. And even when Cook managed in one year to come top of the constituency section vote in the NEC elections and to head the shadow Cabinet poll – he would ask his colleagues if they, like him, suspected it might be a record – he was not offered the job he wanted. Blair had made his promise to Brown, and it was Foreign Affairs for Cook.

Their personal history became an important part of the European debate. Brown devised his five economic tests in autumn 1997, the moment at which the government decided against using its majority to have a honeymoon referendum on the euro, and from then on found that the Foreign Office was forcing the pace, trying to ease Downing Street into a more enthusiastic posture. Cook had been no Euro-enthusiast at first – as a seventies left-winger he had campaigned for a 'No' vote in the 1975 referendum on whether or not to stay in the Common Market – but sitting in the Foreign Secretary's grand square room looking out to St James's Park, where so many of his predecessors had cast their moist eyes towards the empire beyond the seas, he began to relish the politics of the European Union.

This was greatly encouraged by his permanent secretary, his fellow-Scot Sir John Kerr, who was a former ambassador to the EU in Brussels. They did not have a good relationship – when Kerr retired in July 2001, Foreign Office gossip had it that he had enjoyed his four weeks with Jack Straw more than his previous four years with Cook – but on European matters they had a shared interest in massaging Downing Street, and giving the Prime Minister an occasional slap. Europe was their bread and butter, the diplomatic marketplace where momentous constitutional negotiations were moving ahead, new relationships were being built with Russia and Eastern Europe and where, in the considerable space left by the end of the Mitterrand–Kohl era, a new generation of leaders had taken over. Cook was enjoying himself at last.

In the Treasury, it was quite different. Brown had a number of officials around him who still bore the ugly scars of the Major government's painful ejection from the ERM in 1992 on Black Wednesday, which Brown believed was the event that had made the long-term disintegration of that government inevitable. His closest adviser, Ed Balls, had always been unimpressed by some of the claims made for a common currency. In his previous life at the *Financial Times* he had shown what the Foreign Office thought were signs of scepticism. So the two great departments entered a traditional stand-off, with Blair holding the ring.

In all his economic arguments with Brown – whether over the minimum wage, pensions or public investment – Blair was conscious that he had given his Chancellor guarantees which created a kind of dual premiership on these questions. It was the same with Europe but Blair, with a Prime Minister's sense of his international role, wanted to shine on his own.

He relished his European ventures. He was quite different from Brown in that respect. The Chancellor enjoyed taking his summer breaks in Cape Cod, Massachusetts, where he'd work his way through the latest American economic tomes and historical biographies between games of tennis, and drink the political gossip from the Harvard diaspora that headed for the Atlantic shore in the summer. For Blair it was Tuscany or Provence, sun and chilled wine on the terrace. He might break off to have lunch with Lionel Jospin or to greet the Italian Prime Minister for an afternoon, but they were brief interludes. His were the wanderings of a happy

European, perching on a balcony for the Palio in Siena, lounging on the terrace of a shady *palazzo*. He became the only British Prime Minister of the modern era to muster a French accent respectable enough to use to address the National Assembly, an accent honed in a Paris bar where he'd spent a student summer. (Margaret Thatcher had learnt her speech for the opening of the Channel link in Lille by rote from a phonetic script, though she did it with such panache that François Mitterrand was fooled for a moment into thinking she must be fluent.) From the start Blair wanted more of Europe.

There was an obvious political incentive. When he came to office, the European left was in a beaten and bedraggled state. He was fresh and he had a mandate that everyone envied. At first, this caused him to be carried away. He went to a meeting of socialist leaders in Sweden and spoke about the lessons to be learned from his election as if he were lecturing a class of delinquents yet to be persuaded of the error of their ways. They didn't like it. Jospin, in particular, was offended because he thought (quite correctly) that Blair was expressing disdain for his style of socialism. Considerable repair work had to be done on the relationship, which has never been a particularly trusting one. The French socialists continued to believe that Blair had been too dazzled by aspects of Thatcherism: for them, Blair's 'third way' was a treacherous path. But after his fumbling start, Blair began to tread the European stage with more confidence.

The twice-yearly summits are generally more enjoyable for heads of government than for finance ministers, who are not allowed to steal their superiors' thunder and sometimes don't even attend. Blair has always been in his element at these meetings, though they can turn into festivals of tedium. Brown, by contrast, has never enjoyed the wearying sessions of finance ministers and has a reputation in the corridors of the Commission in Brussels for brusqueness and for seldom taking any trouble to acknowledge one of the commissioners' most precious possessions, their own *amour propre*. Towards the end of the first term, one of his favourite themes was the tendency of the commissioners to interfere in his handling of the economy. Just before the election he said in a BBC interview: 'I am not prepared for the European Commission to give us lectures about what the level of spending should be in this country.' The commissioners were guilty of 'unwarranted interference in British affairs'. Even in a pre-election atmosphere sharpened by Eurosceptic rhetoric, this was revealing about Brown's attitude to the EU, expressed in language which Blair would never use, even after a pep talk from Rupert Murdoch.

Brown's determined pursuit of stability and prudence have not needed the help of the EU, he argues. The British government has done it alone. In all his repetitions of the formula agreed in 1997, the measures which the government will apply to the economy when it believes the time is right to join the euro, Brown uses phrases almost identical to Blair's, but he stresses the primacy of the Treasury in making the judgement. And even the Prime Minister has seemed to acknowledge that the process is being driven from there. Asked at the beginning of 2001 whether it was he or Mr Brown who would be deciding whether the test had been met he sounded hesitant: 'I very much hope it will be both of us together. That would be the normal way of doing it.' An extraordinarily tentative prime ministerial thought.

In that hint of doubt about how the decision will be made in the course of the second term lies the awareness of how their efforts to march in step have often seemed to falter. In the middle of the first term, Blair began to address the political nature of the euro decision; Brown always prefers to rest on the economic realities. He echoes the Prime Minister's commitment to a European future – telling the CBI in 1999 that the Labour Party of the eighties was wrong and irresponsibly anti-European – but for the second half of the first term he devoted considerable energy inside government to trying to rein in the European debate. When Mandelson and Byers strayed off the reservation fenced in by the Treasury and talked about the benefits of the single currency, they were told by Brown to stick to the line: nothing must disturb the policy of 'wait and see'. While Blair was being attacked by the most aggressively pro-euro figures in business and among Conservatives and Liberal Democrats for failing to give an early lead, Brown stuck remorselessly to his text: 'the decisive test as to whether and when we will enter will be based on the five economic tests', he said in New York in autumn 1999.

The timing would be a Treasury decision, and no one else's. The tests were sufficiently subjective to permit it to be made at a politically convenient moment. The judgements about the effect on jobs and on the City, the criteria for investment and flexibility, weren't matters of mathematical precision, and even the most difficult, the achievement of convergence of 'business cycles and structures', was loose enough to keep a roomful of economists arguing for a month. The tests didn't tie Brown down, they freed him up. And that was their point.

Brown's caution has never been fully-fledged scepticism. He gave a clear glimpse of his thinking in a private speech to a meeting of the Anglo-French Colloque, a political-economic discussion group, in Versailles in January 2001. Knowing that his words would find their way to the appropriate quarters quite quickly – they were in the hands of the French and German governments, not to mention Robin Cook in the Foreign Office, within a few hours – he delivered a notably enthusiastic pro-Europe speech, refusing to give any clear hints on euro membership but taking the opportunity to try to change his image as a grudging European. He also took the opportunity in Versailles to have a private meeting with the head of Nissan's European operations to discuss a big investment in north-east England. Nissan was worried about Britain staying outside the euro. After half an hour in private with Brown, the Nissan executive left happily and the investment was announced soon afterwards. The message was clear. Brown might be cautious, but he hoped one day, like Blair, to take Britain into the euro, as long as it was done on his terms and in his own good time.

From the moment he put the government's policy to the Commons in October 1997 he was determined to keep the decision to himself. The policy, according to one Downing Street adviser, became 'as much a matter of Gordon's psychology as economics'. No one could deviate from the formula; no one could rush the Treasury along.

One day the Chancellor would announce that the tests had been met, when it suited him. Until then, everyone could wait – including the Prime Minister. This caused immense frustration in the minority of the Cabinet that felt, with Blair, that it should be one of the purposes of their government to change the national mood on Europe and prepare for entry into the single currency. But Blair was unwilling during the early stages of his premiership to try to recapture ground he had already ceded to Brown. It was part of their compact.

Brown was allowed to set the rules and it meant that his long-standing dispute with Mandelson took a new turn, that his old rivalry with Cook became the talk of the government, and that the strains with Number 10 intensified in the last year of the first term. His reluctance to let the euro debate open up posed an awkward question which Blair would soon be forced to answer: how great was this government's real enthusiasm for Europe?

Its European difficulties are inseparable from its difficulties with its own personality. Blair's attitude has been markedly different from that of his Chancellor, and Brown's difficult relations with Mandelson and Cook have greatly complicated the stealthy progress on membership of the euro which has always been Blair's aim. In his pre-election assignations with the Liberal Democrats before 1997 he was perfectly clear that he was an enthusiast. Despite his efforts to reassure the Eurosceptic press that he was not what they would call a Brussels softie, he was evidently looking to the prospect of political operations on a wider stage; and when it opened up for him, he duly revelled in it. In Downing Street he made sure that the tone was aggressively euro friendly.

Blair's European policy adviser was Roger Liddle, Mandelson's old friend from the Vauxhall Labour Party, who left to join the Social Democrats in 1981 and spent more than ten years working closely with Roy Jenkins and Bill Rodgers in cementing the merger with the Liberals. After he rejoined Labour he was appointed by Blair to the policy unit and there were no ideological hurdles for him to surmount: it was a perfect fit. Like Derek Scott, a former SDP candidate who became an economic adviser in the policy unit (and whose relations with Brown had the quality of permafrost), he was evidence of Blair's contentment in shrugging off a sense of party loyalty. With Mandelson as minister in the Cabinet Office next door with a roving brief and a corridor taking him straight into Number 10 there was a pro-European whiff in the air.

Liddle is a bustling, rotund figure with a jovial obsession for politics. In the Labour Party, then in the SDP, then in the Liberal Democrats and once again back in the Labour Party he was a campaigner and fixer who did not seem to change. He is a man whose distinctive giggle can be heard in the next room and whose eyebrows shoot to the top of his head with excitement several times in the course of the briefest conversation. He had a brush with disaster in summer 1998 when he was alleged to have helped Derek Draper, a former Mandelson aide working as a lobbyist, with contacts in government. It was a classic minor political embarrassment for the government – and a significant illustration of Blair's style. Though Liddle, who was distrusted by some ministers simply on account of his SDP–Lib Dem past, could easily have been thrown overboard, Blair refused to do it. Liddle stayed in the policy unit working on European policy from the position of an ardent enthusiast for closer integration and the single currency.

Mandelson's appointment to the Department of Trade and Industry in July 1998 was intended as part of the preparation for the coming argument over the euro. The deal agreed in 1997, with Brown managing the famous five economic tests which were to settle the timing, committed the government to the principle. Every minister knew, however, that a rocky slope lay ahead of them. Brown's natural interest was in securing the economic stability at home on which his credibility rested. He knew that his decision before the 1997 election to stick to Conservative spending plans in the first phase of government, and to promise not to raise basic tax rates for the lifetime of a Parliament, would make him a deeply unpopular Chancellor in his own party unless he could prove within four years or so that it had delivered sustainable growth. He was uninterested in European adventures. He and Blair might repeat the same phrases about Labour's Europeanism and its friendliness in principle to the euro, but in his mind a referendum campaign was an unwanted distraction.

Pro-Europeans around Blair saw it as an issue that was putting more distance between him and Brown. They would gossip about Brown's dinners with sceptics like the American financier and journalist Irwin Steltzer (a courtier and fixer of Rupert Murdoch's) as evidence that he was playing the other side of the street. Not that Downing Street was ignoring the sceptic press. A great deal of energy was devoted to the reassurance of Murdoch and his editors – Alastair Campbell has a nervous system that is tuned carefully to the *Sun*, and a pen that is always ready to dash off a signed article by the Prime Minister saying that the national interest will never be sold off. Such articles, or friendly briefings to journalists on Eurosceptic newspapers, are carefully timed. Whenever the argument heats up a signed article will appear, almost always written by Campbell.

The 2001 General Election campaign provided a delicious example. Two weeks before polling day Blair captured the lead story in the *Financial Times* with an interview for the paper in which he sounded enthusiastic about the prospect of euro membership when the circumstances were right. A stream of soothing balm was directed at the City. On the same day the *Sun* carried an article under Blair's name which was carefully crafted to sit happily with the government's formula but to invite the interpretation that this was a Prime Minister who would never bounce his country into some foreign currency, an assurance which duly appeared on the front page in a form that made it sound like a sigh of relief from Wapping. In Downing Street, the judgement was that the crossover readership would be small.

Such moments were revealing because they displayed Blair's own uncertainty at the end of the first term. The most enthusiastic Europeans in his circle had no doubt about his cast of mind: 'He is intellectually committed to British involvement in Europe. That means inside the euro. He wants the influence that brings. He'll do it', one said, even as the traditional mixed smoke signals were pouring out of the Number 10 chimney in the run-up to the General Election. The trouble for the enthusiasts was that it seemed Blair's careful gavotte with Brown had been going on for so long that neither of them knew how to stop dancing.

Blair also knew that however much he might want to express more enthusiasm before the election there were two good excuses for caution. One was public opinion, still weighted heavily against the euro; the other was placating Brown. He didn't need a crystal ball to know what might happen if Brown felt manipulated. He had seen the results up close.

In the summer of 2000 there was a serious explosion on European policy. It was a bad time for Blair on other fronts and in May he was lucky to be able to ride out what could have been a destructive storm.

The trouble began, once again, with a phrase that seemed innocent enough. Just like Blair's later answer to Hague, the words themselves were innocent, but they were uttered by Mandelson, and that was enough to provoke a protest. On 17 May he observed: 'The fact is that as long as we are outside the euro, there is little we can do to protect industry against destabilizing swings in the value of sterling.' Nothing in that sentence would have disturbed Blair in the slightest. Indeed, Alastair Campbell's briefing to lobby journalists that afternoon was going to deal with it as an unsurprising statement of fact. That was the plan before Brown's arrival in Blair's office. The door was closed and those nearby heard what one later described as 'a hell of a noise'.

After the door was opened, Blair spoke to Campbell and the Downing Street line changed. Ministers were all to be bound by the 'prepare and decide' policy on the euro, which wouldn't be compromised by any pro- or anti- statements while the judgement on the five economic tests was awaited. All speeches on these matters would be cleared with the Chancellor before they were made. Mandelson's remark, of course, was considered by Brown to be a cheeky piece of propagandizing. The previous month Mandelson had told a GMB union conference in Belfast that Britain should 'take [our] place at its heart and shape it to our ends'. On the day of his second intervention, the Trade and Industry Secretary Stephen Byers told the Commons that the government mustn't slip back into its previously cautious posture of 'wait and see'. In the Treasury this amounted to something like insubordination. The relationship between Brown and Byers was already bad. The Chancellor had recognized in Mandelson as Secretary of State at the DTI someone who could prosecute the European case vigorously in industry and business: with Byers he wasn't so alarmed, but he was irritated for different reasons. Mandelson was a combatant on Europe worthy of a fight. Byers wasn't. Around Brown's office, Byers was a name to be bracketed with the weaker brethren in the Cabinet. With the bigger beasts – Mandelson and Cook – he was one of the three troublesome ministers who took every opportunity to speak positively about the euro. The Chancellor wasn't having it.

The euro affair coincided with the onset of a fever that weakened the government for nearly six months. Indeed, even as Mandelson was stirring passions with his remarks, Philip Gould was beginning a two-day session with one of his focus groups, which would be condensed in a memo which reeked of gloom, the most alarming report Blair had received from him since taking office. Gould's message to Blair in May 2000 was not only that Labour support was beginning to sag and sink – voters apparently thought he was 'soft on crime' and didn't like it – but that for the first time since he became Conservative leader William Hague was looking like a credible figure 'speaking for the mainstream majority'.

Far from allaying public disenchantment the government embarked instead on a wild summer of misjudgements and mistakes. Blair missed the early part of it so as to be able to spend time with his family after the birth of his son Leo on 20 May and he was fortunate in the interpretation of some of the pictures of a greying and seemingly weary Prime Minister which appeared on his trips to and from Chequers. The charitable assumption was that he was having interrupted nights and was helping out at home. This was only partly true. He was also going through his most difficult time as Prime Minister.

First there was Brown's speech on 26 May 2000 about elitism at Oxford – the Laura Spence business – which sent Downing Street into a spin and caused warnings to be given to Cook and Prescott not to be tempted into follow-up speeches that might be lumped together in the public mind as a resumption of some class war. Then, even more embarrassingly, there came Blair's own debacle at the Women's Institute conference on 7 June, which enlivened the country's television screens with the unexpected image of a Prime Minister being heckled and slow-handclapped by an audience which he might have expected to coo happily at tales of his new-born son. On the lonely-looking stage at Earl's Court he seemed an uncertain and shaken figure, unable to conceal his bewilderment. Here was a flustered Prime Minister who was starting to get it wrong.

Political luck sometimes turns like the run of a malign pack of cards, and on it went. Far from the summer recess bringing some calm to politics, everything seemed to heat up. Soon Blair was embroiled with the fuel protesters, who had managed to turn a popular grievance about the price of petrol into a kind of guerrilla campaign which blockaded roads and closed petrol stations, isolating refineries and turning a prime ministerial visit to John Prescott's Hull constituency for a celebration dinner into an embarrassing cross-country scuttle.

Blair had to get a grip. But the Treasury was horrified when he said in a press conference that the government would resolve the crisis in twenty-four hours – 'crazy' was the word that floated around Brown's office – and it was the Chancellor who argued successfully for a measured concession to the protesters, price cuts which were put in the context of an environmental strategy and which could be made to seem part of a long-term strategy. The policy worked, and it was seen in Whitehall as an illustration of Brown as a steadying influence. There had been distinct signs of panic in Number 10. It was an episode after which Blair had to reassert his authority. Europe was the obvious area in which he could demonstrate that after a shaky summer he was a Prime Minister back in charge. The ambassador to the EU, Sir Stephen Wall, was recalled to take charge of an EU unit inside the Cabinet Office which was to be the political powerhouse on matters European. Never mind that the Chancellor would keep the five tests in the Treasury; the Downing Street machine would set the political pace. From this point on, Blair began to acknowledge the political dimension of the debate in a way that he had resisted in the past. He agreed with Roy Jenkins's tart remark at the time: 'You cannot convert the British public in a fortnight after previously taking the view that the euro is a subject you must not discuss, rather like the Victorian attitude to piano legs.' The curtains around the piano legs would have to be swept aside.

Blair had felt it necessary to seize the initiative from his ministers because in the period of about six weeks that encompassed the latest Mandelson affair and the birth of his son, he was said by colleagues to be in despair about the state of relationships around him. Brown was fizzing about Mandelson's friskiness: Cook was newly resentful towards Brown – he'd had the humiliation of having to censor a European speech while he sat on the Commons front bench on Downing Street instructions to pacify the Treasury, the full text having already been made available to the Press Gallery upstairs. Foreign secretaries do not enjoy looking foolish. Everywhere Blair turned there was trouble. Philip Gould continued to warn that Hague was on the rise. And Campbell, the Cerberus at the gate, was having a hard time keeping the sceptical press at bay. Even he couldn't stop the *Sun* running a front page editorial on 24 June calling Blair 'the most dangerous man in Britain' because of his 'weakness' for the euro. The skies were darkening.

There appeared now to be two governments. Blair, his advisers and a trio of ministers were trying to keep the euro argument on the move, believing that the first groundwork had to be laid for the distant referendum. The Prime Minister was being told by pro-euro business leaders and union enthusiasts like Sir Ken Jackson of the AEEU that he had to show leadership, and he confessed to his staff that he was stung by the accusations of weakness that were flying around his head. But the Treasury was an immovable object. Brown knew that his caution reflected the views of a majority of the Cabinet. The Deputy Prime Minister John Prescott, the Home Secretary Jack Straw and the Education Secretary David Blunkett were all with him. So Blair not only appeared weak to the public – the satirists were beginning to get to grips with the grin and the glottal stops – but he knew that inside government his authority was also being undermined.

At the height of the trouble, on 15 July, Brown made his annual Mansion House speech. He laid out the policy – a successful single currency would be good for Britain, but the five economic tests were sacrosanct and couldn't be prejudged. There was a telling sentence about the origin of the policy. It was the Chancellor himself, of course, who had made the first statement to the Commons and he chose to underline that fact once more: '. . . the policy set out in October 1997, repeated by the Prime Minister in February 1999, has not changed and will not change'. Blair was carefully depicted in a supporting role.

There was to be no backsliding from dissident enthusiasts within the Treasury either. Three days before the speech, when the *Financial Times* published a story saying that Brown's officials believed that the tests might be met 'within two years', there was an unusual public denial from the Treasury. This was a subject on which no doubt could be allowed.

Everyone at 10 Downing Street knew that the problem was festering. As time went by Cook, Mandelson and Byers were bound to try to force the pace on Europe once more, such was their irritation with Brown. It was just as obvious that the Chancellor had set his course and would not be diverted. He was in charge of the timetable and he was convinced that politically it would be foolish for Labour to open up the European debate before the election. He wanted a prolonged silence.

Blair had to respond. He did so in two ways. First, he began to plan a European venture of his own. He'd try to transform the atmosphere with what George Bush Sr. had called 'the vision thing'. Work began on a speech to be made in Warsaw in October. Second, he'd adopt his characteristic approach to personal disputes. There would be a gathering of friends, after which everyone would feel much better.

He called a meeting in his office with Brown and Mandelson to thrash it all out. He meant this to be an opportunity to restore old bonds, and he dramatized the gesture by deciding that Brown and Mandelson would run the 2001 election campaign together. It might have been a statement of faith that the improbable could be made to happen and peace would break out. Those around him doubted it. One member of the Cabinet said: 'When I heard about it I thought for the first time that Tony had flipped his lid.' The scepticism was justified.

There were the traditional difficulties in arranging the get-together. The Chancellor was busy. Diaries were full. Mandelson suspected Brown of avoiding him; Brown suspected Mandelson of organizing the whole thing to reassert his influence. Blair finally got them to sit down together in his little room, between the Cabinet Room at the back of Number 10 and the officials' room on the other side. This is a plain but a sunny room, its windows giving out on to the garden, and it is notably uncluttered. There are Blair family photographs on the desk, and little else. Blair likes it that way. He and the Chancellor sat in the armchairs, Mandelson on the sofa. By the accounts of the participants that circulated immediately afterwards in their closest circles, the meeting was a grisly encounter and an utter failure. Blair was uncertain; Brown was irritable and aggressive; Mandelson was nervy and hesitant. He seemed to want to leave. If Blair needed a demonstration of how the old feelings still held them in thrall he had it.

Through the winter into 2001, the message was spread to the world outside that 'Gordon and Peter' were having a ball and cooking up a spectacular election campaign. It wasn't true. The preparations were certainly being made; both were turning their formidable tactical brains to the campaign; each was happy to answer questions in public about the other with a cheery assurance that they were friends, as ever. Underneath, however, there were familiar strains.

Brown wanted to suppress the euro debate entirely before the election. He and Blair had their scripts neatly dovetailed. Each insisted that there were no political objections in principle to membership and that when the moment came they would campaign with vigour for a 'Yes' in the promised referendum. But the moment had not yet come. In Seoul Blair said in October that if he were asked then to vote he would say 'No'; Brown said that he wouldn't rush in and put at risk 'economic stability or the discipline that has created sustained growth'. They marched in step. But the government was now carrying another burden: its reputation for news management, which spawned a phrase that clung to Downing Street – control freakery. Thanks in large part to the summer's weird cycle of events and the desperate efforts to fight back, the government was seen as an outfit that was as interested in appearance as the substance of policy. It was touched by the curse of spin.

One consequence was that the more carefully the statements on the euro were choreographed, the more they were interpreted as clever public relations. There was a problem of belief. Blair saw his Warsaw speech as something of an answer. He worked hard. Drafts were solicited from a gallery of euro thinkers. The historian Timothy Garton-Ash (a distinctly non-Labour figure) was asked for his thoughts; Charles Grant of the Centre for European Reform, a fervent Labour supporter of closer European ties, was an important influence. The phrase that lodged in the public mind after the speech, however, was inserted by Campbell. He suggested that Blair should say of the new Europe that it was 'a superpower, but not a superstate'.

Blair was bolder on Europe in this speech than he had ever been before, speaking of the importance of enlargement to the east – set in train by the Nice Treaty – and of reform in Brussels. And in one paragraph he summed up his own frustrations of the previous years: 'British policy towards the rest of Europe over half a century has been marked by gross misjudgements, mistaking what we wanted to be the case with what *was* the case; hesitation, alienation, incomprehension, with the occasional burst of enlightened brilliance'. He deliberately followed that sentence up with a restatement of the government's policy on the euro, saying that the five tests had to be met if Britain's economic strength wasn't to be put at risk.

But the signal from Warsaw wasn't a cautious one. Blair wanted to escape from the arguments in his Cabinet about Europe and, though he knew that public opinion and most of the press was vigorously hostile to euro membership, he appeared to have embarked on a new course.

The Warsaw speech was intended by Blair as evidence that he wanted to break free from the domestic argument about the euro and play on a wider stage. Like every Prime Minister since the fifties he felt the lure of the European challenge, just as even the instinctively suspicious Margaret Thatcher had been unable to resist the opportunity to plunge into the argument about national destiny and the European future. Yet Blair was still the cautious observer of the polls, the papers and the national mood. The message from Gould wasn't changing; the editorials were still bashing Brussels. He had to balance his enthusiasm with a public sense of wariness.

Just before the election, he spoke to Rupert Murdoch, which he does regularly. He valued the support of the *Sun*, which Campbell believed had been one of the foundations of the shift in opinion before 1997, and he was fearful that Europe could undermine Murdoch's decision to let that paper, and *The Times*, continue to support Labour. He asked Blair directly whether there would be an early referendum if Labour won. Blair assured him that there would not be.

This was not a difficult pledge to give, since the exchange rate would make a decision in the early part of the Parliament impossible and Blair had already committed himself to a sober assessment of the five tests on a Brown timetable. But nonetheless he felt it wise to be clear with Murdoch: he could guarantee that the editors of *The Times* and the *Sun* would not be embarrassed by his European policy if they urged their readers to vote Labour.

The plan was to dampen down the debate. Blair did not follow the advice of his party's more avid Europeans – the Mandelson-Liddle axis – and he decided not to make an early move to prepare public opinion for a referendum. Instead, he agreed with Brown to deliver the sober Mansion House speech and play for time. The Conservative leadership election helped, with Downing Street happy to make mischief at the possibility of the election of the pro-euro Kenneth Clarke, planting a story in the *Sun* to the effect that if he were elected Blair might consider having the referendum on the same day as the next General Election, forcing the Tory leader to argue for 'Yes' on one ballot paper in support of the government, but 'No' on the other against Labour. It would not need a Machiavelli to suspect that the intention was to encourage some Tory members to vote for Iain Duncan Smith instead, the preferred choice of Downing Street for opposition leader.

The government prepared for a long delay, happy to allow the impression to gain ground that there would be no referendum in this Parliament. The Treasury view was put nicely by Ed Balls in a contribution to a private Labour Party seminar in early July, which was tape-recorded and subsequently leaked (with a suspicious lack of embarrassment on the Treasury's part). He said: 'We have to be careful in the second term that we maintain our position as pro-European realists. We know there are big debates to be had on Europe, on taxation, on the euro, on economic reform, on political reform. The most important thing for us as a party is to keep focused on the need to stay united, stick to a long-term agenda and not to do anything in the short term which would divide us.' Stability and investment in public services might otherwise be threatened, he said.

That 'Euro realist' position contrasts with the enthusiasm which Blair has often embraced. But it was the authentic Treasury voice. For the moment, Downing Street seemed happy to let it set the tone for the government.

The desire shown by Blair in his Warsaw speech to break free had not yet reached its moment of fulfilment. Inside Downing Street Campbell was determined that public opinion was still far too hostile for the government to challenge it with a burst of euro enthusiasm. Jack Straw at the Foreign Office could be trusted not to go gooey-eyed at Brussels, given his distinctly sceptical political pedigree leading back to his days as Barbara Castle's bag-carrier in the early seventies. Both Blair and Brown hoped one day to operate in the euro zone, but Brown's characteristic caution at the consequences of a decision made at the wrong moment was the prevailing tone.

Officials in Downing Street who criticized the Treasury's nervousness at any speech or interview or casual remark that smacked of enthusiasm had to accept that, although Blair himself might express occasional frustration with Brown, the guardian of the five tests, it was the Chancellor who controlled the timetable.

The Cabinet waited and watched. Ministers gossiped, and some of them, like Byers and Cook, looked for progress. But the chances

The student Rector of Edinburgh University displays a physical echo of James Maxton, the spirit of Red Clydeside, fifty years on.

Labour Old and New. On the threshold of a parliamentary career, before his trial run in the 1982 by-election, Blair meets Michael Foot.

A leadership secured with a smile. The poignant moment of victory for Blair in 1994, and a squeeze of congratulations from the friend who stood aside, when friendship still seemed simple.

The other friend, Bill Clinton, in 10 Downing Street.

How Prime Ministers get it wrong. The women don't want to know that he and Brown don't disagree on the Euro.

The man behind the smile ... Alastair Campbell looks for trouble.

The Iron Chancellor as the Cabinet sees him, listening behind his defences.

One shirt-sleeved and one jacketed, but eyes dead ahead, the two campaigners move as one but stay apart, catching the cool flavour of the 2001 campaign at Millbank.

Fatherhood is wearing …

… but the thought of it is liberating.

of a round table discussion in which the government could set a collective strategy on the euro and the referendum were nil. Such things, they now knew, didn't happen. The debate was driven by Number 10 and Number 11 and the decision had been made to let it idle in neutral. Until that changed, no one would move. They were definite. Maybe.

7
Rival Obsessions

Paddy Ashdown is not a politician who sprays his audiences with cultural references. Nor does he have the irritating weakness of the political opera-goer who can't hear a ministerial speech without being tempted into a Wagnerian reference. Yet after the climax of his political affair with Blair had passed he did offer a telling description of the Prime Minister. 'I think he was a bit like Don Giovanni. He meant it at the time.'

The description is warm rather than bitter, and Ashdown had no reason to see himself as the victim of a serial seducer. There were more dangers for Blair in his pursuit of the Liberal Democrats than there were for Ashdown, who became the first third-party leader to sit in formal circumstances in the Cabinet Room since his long-forgotten Liberal predecessors had their last taste of coalition in the Second World War before subsiding into parliamentary obscurity for a generation. The recklessness was all on the Prime Minister's side. He was operating without the support of most of his Cabinet, and with no visible supporting tide of encouragement from the Labour Party at large.

For a Prime Minister whose leadership throughout his first term was overwhelmingly cautious, this was by far his boldest personal manoeuvre. He had intended it to be even bolder, musing about a formal coalition even when he had been told by his private pollsters in May 1997 that he was heading for a comfortable victory, one that might expand into a rout of the opposition. He drew back only at the last moment. But more than a year after the election, sitting on his huge majority and untroubled by any jitters in his Cabinet or his party, he was able to say to a close friend outside the Labour Party words which would have given most of his Cabinet the vapours: 'I still wish I had put Ashdown in the Cabinet.'

It was a remarkable revelation, and an insight into Blair's purpose in courting the Liberal Democrats even after he was convinced that he could govern comfortably on his own. This strategy was no lifeboat, painted yellow: it was a search for congenial travelling companions. And in these efforts he was more alone than in almost anything else he did in the first term.

In the early days of the government only Robin Cook among senior ministers was willing to behave benignly in the direction of the third party, and Mandelson, outside the Cabinet in the first year as Blair's ministerial fixer, was the oiler of wheels. For many Labour MPs Mandelson's enthusiasm was the proof that they should turn away. He had his supporters in the intake of young MPs in 1997 (there were a number who knew that their political careers had been largely invented by his successful remarketing of Labour) but more of them were hostile. They would smile at him as he flitted through the crowd at a Downing Street reception for new MPs, or in the Commons tea room, then turn and tell the latest story of some new piece of Mandelsonian gossip about his influence in the Prime Minister's office or about a new collision with Brown.

Blair appeared to care little about this. Mandelson was his most loyal operator, a one-man kitchen Cabinet with sensitive ears and flashing eyes: he heard all the secrets and missed nothing. His unpopularity among many MPs appeared to be of no consequence to the Prime Minister. Indeed, Blair seemed to value him as an opportunity to open up some distance between 'independent' Downing Street and the Labour Party. Like Thatcher before him he enjoyed from his earliest times in office the sensation of being a leader who could sometimes appear deliberately at odds with his party. Just as she had on arrival offended one-nation grandees and aristocrats, so Blair was prepared to use Mandelson to stir up the traditionalist Labour tribe. And if there was one issue guaranteed to make Labour MPs feel that they were being not merely stirred up but thrown bodily into a blender it was cooperation with the

Liberal Democrats. It was a deliciously volatile combination. In his support for cooperation with the Liberal Democrats in government Blair was challenging Labour to make a break with its recent past. He knew it was desperately unpopular among party activists, and that MPs were coming back from their constituencies reporting bewilderment among their members about why Ashdown was deemed to matter, but the Prime Minister wanted them all to know that he didn't care. One of his staff says: 'He enjoyed that feeling almost more than anything else.'

One of their intimates recalls Brown telling the Prime Minister straightforwardly, 'You're on your own. I'm having nothing to do with it.' That was an attitude shared by John Prescott (who fumed and giggled all at once when anyone mentioned the Liberal Democrats) by Jack Straw, by the then chief whip Nick Brown, and by a majority of other members of the Cabinet. Brown and Prescott told Blair from the first that they weren't interested and exuded a good deal of contempt for the exercise. They had never been part of Blair's cosy encounters with Liberal Democrats in opposition and found it even more extraordinary in government that a Prime Minister with a majority of 179 wanted to bring a third party into the outer chambers of government and continued to talk, vaguely but insistently, about coalition, proportional representation and a reshaping of the political system. But he did none the less.

And the truth about the constitutional arguments in the government just after it was elected is that Brown's suspicions about the dealings with the Liberal Democrats had a counterpart in Blair. From the start he was nervous about devolution, and expressed private doubts to many colleagues. But he found himself pulled along, for one inescapable reason: 'It's Gordon's passion. So we're doing it.' As things turned out, however, it was Brown's passion which turned into legislation and a Scottish parliament. Blair's came to nothing tangible – no moves towards coalition, a nervous drawing back from electoral reform and, after the 2001 election, a new distance from the Liberal Democrats.

Devolution did bring Blair some success, but great bursts of embarrassment and political trouble too. He claimed credit, naturally, for the referendums that established an Assembly in Cardiff and a Parliament in Edinburgh, coming back to the city of his birth on the afternoon of the 'Yes' vote to drive down the Royal Mile and hail the completion of the task which had first been handed to John Smith as a junior minister in the late seventies, who even then had thought it a poisoned cup. It sweetened over the years. Smith became a genuine reformer and by the time of his leadership the Scottish party had put aside the doubts and divisions of the seventies. So Blair could drink happily in celebration with the Scottish party. But in private he worried and fretted about devolution. It didn't stir him as it did Brown. The north-east of England MPs whom he'd known for fifteen years were still unreconciled to a local powerhouse Parliament to the north of them in Edinburgh, and Blair was being poked by Prescott to encourage regional government in England. Blair was, and is, deeply sceptical and the Whitehall advice has been that it promises to be an administrative nightmare. So although he was willing to be innovative in the composition of his government, thinking unthinkable things with the Liberal Democrats, he was conservative on devolution.

For the two principals, this was another awkwardness that had to be managed. Brown would have the Scottish Parliament that he's campaigned for through nearly three decades; Blair would have his way with the Liberal Democrats: or at least he would sit in the Cabinet Room with them, even if neither party could agree that coalition made sense. The two stories reveal how their partnership depended on an agreement that they could stay apart on these matters, following parallel paths that would never really involve any awkward political reconciliation. Pragmatic considerations would determine how long each journey lasted. Unsurprisingly, Brown's was better mapped and he had fewer policy issues to divert him.

The first meeting of the so-called Joint Consultative Committee with the Liberal Democrats took place in the Cabinet Room on 17 September and it was one of the more revealing tableaux of the early days of the Blair government. For the Prime Minister and the leader of the Liberal Democrats this was a picture that had shimmered in their minds for years. But there was no Chancellor or deputy prime minister present, no feeling of a Cabinet that had decided to make this happen.

This JCC brought four Liberal Democrats into the antechamber of government, letting them sign the Official Secrets Act and enjoy a first modest acquaintance with the machinery of government. Alongside the full Cabinet committees it was a minnow, but its very presence was important enough for the Chancellor to be careful to make a point of ignoring it. Various ministers were brought in by Blair as its remit was tentatively extended from constitutional reform, but Brown did not once sit at the table in the whole first term. It was his choice and Blair hardly tried to dissuade him.

Brown's absence had one happy consequence for Ashdown. He sat in the Chancellor's chair, directly across the table from the Prime Minister. The two sides were arranged as if for a negotiation, with Blair, Cook, Donald Dewar and Mandelson on one side and Ashdown, Alan Beith, Menzies Campbell and Lord Holme on the other. Brown's presence would have produced an amusing awkwardness. He'd have joined Blair on the government side and would have had to look at Ashdown sitting in his chair. It was never likely to happen. Another absentee whose significance was underestimated in 1997 was Charles Kennedy. He was never part of Ashdown's closest entourage.

Brown's distance revealed a powerful and insistent undercurrent that flowed just under the surface of the new government, attracting Blair and repelling Brown. It was a force that the Prime Minister encouraged, indeed had conjured up from the depths, and one that his Chancellor resisted. For both of them it became one of the ways in which they developed different political characters in power, showing how differently they regarded their party. No political question revealed more clearly in the early days how these two men who had made their pact on the economy and public services still saw Labour through different eyes. But it allowed each of them the minor luxury of a personal talisman to venerate in contrast to the other's. In a way, they both needed the Liberal Democrats.

For Blair they were the manifestation of his unease with his own party. He wanted to send a clear signal about the inclusiveness of his new party that distinguished it from the narrow tribalism of Labour in the 1970s and 1980s. From the moment he assumed the leadership he had begun to weave schemes with Paddy Ashdown which for both Labour and Liberal Democrat leader soon seemed to lead to one end – coalition. It was the logic in their minds and though Blair faltered at the last, and had moments of doubt throughout, he never lost the sense of a job uncompleted. For him it would remain 'the project'. Even after the 2001 election, when the Liberal Democrats' fifty-two seats and the Conservative disaster gave them every reason to distance themselves a little from Labour, Blair retained a belief that a centre-left alliance might some day make sense. In his mind, it was sleeping and not dead. He was prepared to breathe new life into it, to woo the Liberal Democrats again, if he needed to.

Brown never believed in it. He had been outside the Blair–Ashdown conversations in opposition and was brought in late in the day for one set-piece talk with Ashdown which he carried off without complaint but which was never followed up. For him it was a moment of politeness undertaken at Blair's request, and no more. To those unhappy at the general drift of policy under Blair and its consequences for economic policy, Brown could point contentedly to his own party loyalty when it came to contacts with the enemy. He was surprised that Blair attached so much importance to his session with Ashdown – there had been several requests for it before Brown agreed – and would joke about it to his staff.

But the striking difference in their attitude to the third party never became a *casus belli* between them. The truth about the politics of cooperation and putative coalition is that for each of them it was a useful way of backing away from the other, of staking out two separate territories among their MPs. Brown's apparent intransigence reassured the old Labour hardcore; Blair's intellectual engagement with another party's philosophy attracted the smart young things – Stephen Twigg, Tony Wright – and extended the natural boundary of his government.

For Brown, it made political sense to let Blair carry on and to keep his own distance. 'Gordon knows the movement hates them,' says one of his associates about the Liberal Democrats. In speeches and in conversation Brown deliberately calls them 'the Liberals' still, a quite conscious effort to irritate them. When Blair spoke of a 'new politics' that might be built on inter-party consultations, Brown muttered about what Labour might do on its own; while Blair was being pursued by amorous Liberal Democrats and calculating how best to respond to their advances, Brown was conspicuously elsewhere.

No episode in their preparations for power reveals more clearly how their different backgrounds in the party had produced quite distinct political strategies for government. For Blair it was a hope that he could persuade his party – or maybe bundle it – into cooperation with others, and eventually into some form of broad coalition. By the time he became leader he had almost reached that conclusion: within months it had become an objective of his leadership. An intriguing thought was becoming flesh. But for most of his ministers there was nothing in the least bit intriguing about it. For that reason it had to be kept secret, not only from the mass of the party – which would have convulsed itself had it known – but even from modernizing companions who were already disturbed by the suspicion that Blair was getting too cosy with Ashdown and who might have become dangerously agitated had they known anything like the truth.

When, three years after the event, one of Brown's closest colleagues was shown Ashdown's diary entries for the six months leading up to the 1997 election he was startled at the depth of the relationship. The Chancellor's men had thought they knew it all: they didn't.

For Blair, the idea had germinated early. At Smith's funeral itself he had revealed his thinking. After the service, and the departure of the funeral party for Iona, the company had repaired to the Signet Library in the Old Parliament House where in traditional fashion the funereal mood was leavened with drink and serious political gossip. A leading Scottish Liberal Democrat figure was speaking to Blair and decided to talk frankly: 'When you win, don't forget the

Liberals.' Blair's response was decisive: 'Don't worry. I can assure you that I won't.' This was before the leadership campaign proper, at a moment when any such talk in public by one of the candidates would have been damaging, perhaps even fatal. It was therefore a startling statement, almost sacrilegious to some, and it hinted at what was to come.

The previous summer Paddy Ashdown had been given a first glimpse of Blair's interest in what Liberal Democrats always call 'realignment', the moment when they imagine the trumpet sounding and the walls around the old parties tumbling down. The two men and their wives dined together for the first time, and when they met again at Ashdown's house in Kennington, south London, about six months later it was obvious that they shared an impatience with the way party politics worked. There was no talk of pacts or coalitions, but plenty about what Ashdown called in his notes a new pluralism.

Standing behind it was the figure who had done a great deal to manoeuvre Blair in this direction and who was still bent on a strategy for Labour that he had first conceived nearly forty years before, Lord Jenkins of Hillhead. Roy Jenkins was of course an ogre to most of the MPs and unions who had elected Blair. This was the Labour deputy leader who led the rebellion in 1971 that gave Ted Heath's government the Commons votes to take Britain into Europe; the Home Secretary who left the Labour government in 1976 for the fabled purlieus of Brussels as the first (and only) British President of the European Commission; the majestic soothsayer who had spoken of the coming disintegration of Labour in the depths of its trauma after the 1979 defeat; above all, the relentless old schemer who had put together the Gang of Four, founded the Social Democratic Party in 1981 and tormented Labour through the eighties. In short, the Traitor Jenkins.

Blair felt none of this. Having discovered his politics late, he was curiously immune to the folk tales of betrayal which were passed around among others. Instead, he discovered Jenkins the Political Sage. It was in the course of their conversations that Blair began to develop a theory of what had happened to Labour and how it could be changed. He become fascinated by the way that what he saw as the triumph of Victorian Liberalism had been dissipated in the century that followed. A nineteenth century that spoke of progress was followed by one that was marked above all by conservatism. So Blair concluded. It's a theme that he still brings up in conversations with colleagues, and evidently cherishes. Labour, the argument goes, failed to fulfil the promise of its founders and handed much of the century to the Tories. Rather than revelling in the stories of the 1945 Labour government, the staple diet of Labour MPs when the sky turns black, Blair developed an almost permanent sense of frustration with the past.

Brown looked back in a quite different spirit. He had become fascinated by 1920s politics as a student and it was to the Red Clydesiders that he turned for his Ph.D. They were rebellious socialists whom he admired and found inspiring and his biography of James Maxton, the most charismatic of them and the founder of the Independent Labour Party, showed that fire hadn't dimmed. Its opening sentence recalls a protest meeting in Glasgow in the early twenties which was said by those present to have demonstrated more enthusiasm than anything that had been seen since the campaign for the Reform Act nearly a hundred years before. Brown quotes a veteran of the march as saying that for many of them there it was the most inspiring hour of their lives.

Though it is a book that acknowledges the failure of the Clydesiders to change politics in the way that they wanted, and dwells on the reasons for it, it crackles with the kind of nostalgia for earlier Labour struggles which is quite absent in Blair's credo. They have different heroes.

So the ease with which Blair began to talk to Ashdown about realignment and another transformation in Labour sprang from an attitude to his party which was quite different from Brown's and the one cherished by most of his colleagues. Within four months of his election as leader he was insisting privately to Ashdown that his was no tactical manoeuvre but something more profound. 'You can trust me on this,' he said when Ashdown came to his home at the end of the summer in 1994.

For any Liberal Democrat leader this would be dizzying. However, Ashdown had enough sangfroid to be aware that it was likely that Blair would swing back and forth when questions of close cooperation and coalition arose, as they were bound to. And sure enough, he did. In the two and half years up to the election there were moments when Blair was preoccupied with the dangers of their association, not least from its possible discovery by the Conservative-leaning newspapers who were now the subject of Labour's most earnest wooing. Above all he continued to baulk at electoral reform for Westminster which for Ashdown was the key to everything but which Blair knew to be something even recruits to the newest of New Labour were not nearly ready to digest. To Ashdown, it was as if Blair wanted the world that proportional representation would bring without all the trouble of having to bring it about. And indeed in government Blair showed no more inclination to embrace PR, not only because he knew most of his party and a majority of his Cabinet were set against it, but because he seemed genuinely unpersuaded in his own mind. He had a radical view about the make-up of his government, but not about the voting system for Westminster. He was prepared to embark on the intellectual reform of Labour but not simultaneously to hand over the mechanisms of control that the first-past-the-post system bestows on clear electoral winners. To Liberal Democrats, this was not taking the plunge, but paddling with your socks on.

In May 1995, Blair was ready to talk to Ashdown in front of some of his colleagues at Derry Irvine's table, fuelled by his fine wine. Brown was not among them. Robin Cook, who had long been an enthusiast for PR, was chosen by Blair to work on a strategy with Robert Maclennan for the Liberal Democrats and there began a series of meetings which would tie both parties into some kind of arrangement in the event of a Labour victory or a hung parliament. There could be no going back now without causing severe embarrassment.

But even then Blair's difficulties were obvious. A mere month after the Irvine dinner Ashdown received a phone call of such nervousness from Blair that he concluded 'he's been got at', probably by Brown. The Cook–Maclennan meetings were to be kept secret until after the Labour conference in October 1996 and Blair was saying that he couldn't see the electorate, let alone the Labour Party, supporting PR. They were a pair of nervous suitors at this stage, neither of them sure of how far their parties would let them go. Ashdown knew that asking Liberal Democrats to stand aside in some seats to help Labour would be anathema to them; Blair knew that Labour blood boiled at the thought of deals with other parties, raising spectres of Ramsay MacDonald and alleged coalition traitors from Labour's past. When Blair gave an interview in *The Times* in September 1995, floating the idea of more inter-party cooperation, it gave Ashdown a fright. Elements in his own party did indeed want nothing to do with Labour and it gave him a few awkward moments at his conference. It was all very sticky.

But the truth, known only to a few, was that the groundwork for possible coalition was already being laid. Blair's talk was bold. Squashed together in John Major's plane coming back from Yitzhak Rabin's funeral in Israel in November 1995, Blair raised with Ashdown the possibility of seat-by-seat pacts in south-west England, and this time it was Ashdown who knew that his party would have a seizure. So it went, back and forth. Sometimes Ashdown prodded and pushed, sometimes Blair. Jenkins hovered overhead, feeding Blair with the historical imperatives that inspired him. Day by day Blair became more used to the idea that he might one day lead a government which had another party in it. It was in sustaining this relationship, maybe more than any other in opposition, that Blair had come to depend on Peter Mandelson. He was one of the few around the leader who had a relish for the cross-party conversations. Alastair Campbell, who had become Blair's spokesman in September 1994, had a robust suspicion of all Liberals. The vast majority of the shadow Cabinet, had they known of the sweet nothings being whispered between the leaders, would have paled at the thought. But Mandelson was different.

He was Blair's agent throughout, and Ashdown had presented him with a perfect partner in Lord Holme of Cheltenham, whose enjoyment of some of the darker arts of politics is a legend in his party. He had been an operator from the days of the Lib-Lab pact in the seventies, when David Steel did a deal with Callaghan's tottering government with the express intention of giving the Liberals a taste of the compromises of government so that they might lose virginity as painlessly as possible. It had no effect on government policy that anyone could discern clearly, but it served its purposes. Throughout the negotiations with the Labour defectors, the formation of the SDP and the eventual merger, Holme was the key figure, a suave and polished negotiator with a love of the good life and a tactician's political brain. His ploys against David Owen when he started to distance himself from the Liberals as SDP leader were famous, positively Mandelsonian in their exploitation of the press. He was Ashdown's closest collaborator and the natural link to Mandelson. They began to talk a great deal, and their instinctive love of the secret side of politics egged them on. With every contact and each proposal they sensed the leaders edging closer together, and were happy to nudge them on. Holme would say as the election approached: 'Mark my words. This will end with the spelling out of one word, and that word is coalition.' Even old colleagues, aware of Holme's closeness to some Labour figures, were wary. But he meant it, because Mandelson had told him.

Indeed, so confident had Mandelson become that he almost fell into an elephant trap of his own making. His old friend Roger Liddle was by 1994 a Liberal Democrat who was developing a convenient affection for Blair: it was the lack of leaders like Blair, he thought, that had persuaded him to join Roy Jenkins in the SDP in 1981. He and Mandelson decided to write an account of what a new Labour government would be like. In effect it would be a trailer for Blair's manifesto. As a result it was exceedingly carefully worded, to the extent that parts of it sank into banality, and chunks of it had to be approved by members of the shadow Cabinet, notably Brown, who vetted the economic chapters with a lack of enthusiasm which he did not conceal from Mandelson. At the Irvine dinner Cook was highly amused to find a copy of the book and a novel by Albert Camus side by side and asked Irvine what he could possibly find in common between them. Entitled *The Blair Revolution: Can New*

Labour Deliver?, it is a volume which has suffered much mockery over the years. Mandelson almost made it worse with an overenthusiastic chapter on inter-party relations.

What appeared to be a synopsis of the book's passages on cross-party cooperation and possible coalition found its way to the *Observer* and was published. There was a hurricane. Mandelson had to deny that he would contemplate any such thing: there was much talk of misquotation and misleading interpretation. And, sure enough, when the book did appear in 1996 it dealt with the difficult question of PR and 'realignment' in strictly neutral terms. The original version had been nearer the truth, of course. The enthusiasm which even then was being stoked up between Blair and Ashdown was still judged a little hot for the parties, or the electorate.

In this period, Blair can be seen in a position which would become familiar to him in office. Mandelson was by his side, ready with the encouraging word, the tactical ploy or the quick defensive play, but he was largely on his own. Cook would do the negotiating with Maclennan but he was never a genuine Blair intimate; Irvine would be supportive but could hardly be deployed in the party where he was still a somewhat shadowy figure; and most of the shadow Cabinet could not be trusted with the secret. If not alone, Blair was certainly not surrounded by supporters determined to see him through.

The thought of coalition politics was anathema to almost everyone who was preparing to serve in a Blair Cabinet. Cook was the only figure in the front rank who would speak enthusiastically about PR, and the idea of bringing the Liberal Democrats into a majority Labour government was not one that even he would be willing to argue for in public. Yet the messages from Downing Street convinced Holme and Ashdown that eventual coalition was in Blair's mind. He mused with intimates about Ashdown (probably as Home Secretary) and Menzies Campbell (as Defence Secretary) coming in. Blair enjoyed thinking these radical thoughts. His problem was the explosion in his own party that would follow and, much as he was willing to juggle the gelignite, with Blair there was a bedrock of caution. His leader's speech in 1995 in Blackpool dispensing with Clause IV, once the holy of holies in Labour's catechism, had been phrased carefully enough to prevent possible trouble in the audience in the Winter Gardens. He wanted most of them to realize the implications of what he had said well after he had finished and was safely off the platform. He wanted to shock and startle, but to protect himself too. With the coalition talk, it was much the same.

The curious twist in his relations with the Liberal Democrats was that he was still not convinced of the case for electoral reform for the Commons. He told Ashdown regularly that he wasn't persuaded of its benefits. Ashdown found it hard to understand how a Labour leader could think happily of coalition but not of the change to the system that would make it more likely, and from time to time inevitable. Usually the argument was put the other way round – the case for PR led to an acceptance of coalition as a consequence. Blair revealed in his conversations with Ashdown that he was less interested in a radical reshaping of the Commons than simply in jerking Labour out of old thinking, the urge that had driven him since his first rather bewildered days in the battered parliamentary party after its 1983 collapse. The evidence suggests that Blair had not thought the entire process of coalition politics through. He simply wanted to start. Ashdown, being leader of a party where talk of party realignment was the stuff of life, knew what it might mean. Two years into the Labour government, with the Joint Consultative Committee meeting regularly in the Cabinet Room, he was prepared to contemplate privately the winding up of his party in ten years' time. If Labour was changing in the way Liberal Democrats wanted, Ashdown would wonder aloud, then would there in time be any reason for the Liberal Democrats to exist? Like Blair he was taking a position that many in his party would regard as treasonable. With more than 3,000 local councillors by this time, his party was thinking of its own future.

Blair and Ashdown met like lovers in a clandestine affair, sometimes at Blair's home in Islington, sometimes at Ashdown's home near the Oval in south London where they would sit round the small kitchen table talking of revolutions that most Labour MPs had never contemplated. Their wives were sometimes present, and the relationship soon became much less of a negotiation and more of a political friendship of the sort that neither could have with some of their closest colleagues. The two wives embraced publicly when they went to the Strangers' Gallery in the House of Lords to hear Blair's first Queen's Speech being read in 1997. Blair simply didn't talk to Brown about cooperation between the parties in the way that he did with Ashdown, and Ashdown was aware that there was deep suspicion at the top of his own party about what he might brew up with Blair. When Brown went to see Ashdown in December 1996, after Blair's repeated entreaties, he expressed disbelief to his friends that in the course of their conversation about economic and social policy Ashdown had said he was concerned that there were some aspects of Labour thinking that might not go down well with Alan Beith, his deputy. Brown's staff say that there was hilarity in his office at the idea that Beith mattered at all.

But the affair went on. By the time the election came along on 1 May 1997, Blair and Ashdown knew each other's minds well. Blair was resisting a gold-plated promise on PR but he wanted Liberal Democrats in his government. Ashdown saw his opportunity to get a toehold in government for the first time in the modern history of British liberalism, but he had his own doubts. His party would be by far the weaker partner, unless there was an unexpectedly close result and a hung Parliament, and a number of his MPs feared that they would be swallowed up by the Labour Party in a messy merger which would bring them little but ridicule in their constituencies. So Ashdown asked Blair, when they spoke on polling day, to be careful. This was an extraordinary conversation. A Labour Prime Minister-in-waiting who knew that he was heading for a commanding majority, probably in three figures, was willing to bring a third party into his government and was being told by the leader of that party that he must watch his language, in case it upset some Liberal Democrat MPs. The word 'merger', Ashdown said, must never be used. They agreed that some participation in a Cabinet committee might be the best way to 'heal the schism', a phrase that Blair liked to use to describe his purpose.

To Blair, Ashdown seemed to be the one who was now showing the greater nervousness. Hence, a year later Blair was able to say ruefully to some intimates (though certainly not to Brown) that he wished he had gone further himself. Would Ashdown the Cabinet minister have been disowned by a significant section of his party for collaborating in the implementation of the Labour policies which had won the election? It seemed to Blair that it was just such an outcome that Ashdown feared. The picture of a Liberal Democrat leader being more nervous about coalition and merger than a Labour Prime Minister with a newly won majority of 179 still causes amusement, and a good deal of astonishment, in the Brown camp. They simply cannot understand Blair's attitude.

There were to be no Cabinet jobs, only the Joint Consultative Committee. Blair intended it to be seen as something more important than it was. It would meet in the Cabinet Room itself – many Cabinet committees labour away in much less grand surroundings – and the Cabinet Secretary himself would be on hand to give it the appropriate Whitehall imprimatur. Senior civil servants in attendance, however, saw it rather differently. 'They loved the Cabinet Room and all the officials fussing around,' one of them says. 'But frankly we thought it was all a bit of joke. I'm afraid we giggled quite a bit after some of the meetings. In terms of government business it was meaningless. Rather laughable, I'm afraid.'

If Blair's intention was to heal the schism that he believed had separated the anti-Conservative parties in an artificial way, this was a thin and temporary repair. It was not much strengthened by the government's reaction to the Jenkins Commission on electoral reform, which Liberal Democrats saw as the proper price of their involvement in government. When Roy Jenkins emerged in 1998 with his plan for a modified version of the alternative vote system it was set adrift and allowed to sail away towards the horizon. There was not a whimper of support from a single minister. Blair had other obsessions by then, and saw no need to pretend that he was more attracted by PR than he had been when he first started to see Ashdown. The Labour manifesto of 2001 touched on the subject only in the most cursory fashion, and as if to acknowledge the truth the Liberal Democrats' own manifesto reduced it to a lower priority than in any such document for more than thirty years. In his leader's speeches in the campaign, Charles Kennedy gave little more than a brief ritual genuflection to electoral reform.

When Ashdown was gone, Kennedy deliberately pushed part of his legacy to one side. He said on BBC television during the election campaign: 'We have a joint Cabinet committee which discusses constitutional reform issues. In the best part of my two years as leader, it's only met twice. Why? Because I'm not blinded by the lights of the Cabinet Room at Number 10 Downing Street and I'm not in favour of meetings for the sake of it.' Even allowing for the party loyalty which has to be on show during a campaign, this was a brusque dismissal of the strategy which had dominated the last years of Ashdown's leadership. Kennedy sees little for his party in the level of cooperation offered by Blair, and the tentative affair between the parties has turned into something close to estrangement. Charles Kennedy says:

> Since the 2001 election there seems to be a lessening in the appetite in and around Number 10 for further constitutional reform initiatives, something I regret, but perhaps in part a product of other internal Labour party and trades union tensions.
>
> But my hunch remains that the day will come when it becomes in Labour's longer-term interests to revisit certain of these issues – and when they do the Liberal Democrats should be ready and up for that moment.

Kennedy was from a different generation. He was the happy recipient of a surge in support for the Liberal Democrats and found that a campaign based on extra investment in public services was popular, seeming to outflank Labour. There was little point in talking about closer ties, even if he thought that Blair was still interested. He was seen by both Blair and Brown as a leader without the gravitas which they thought Ashdown had developed (to their surprise) and although his relations with Brown were perfectly cordial – they both swam in the Scottish pond – everything had shifted down a gear.

Ashdown is right to say that, like Don Giovanni, Blair 'meant it at the time', because he did have bursts of passion about his desire to change Labour's thinking about cooperation across party lines. But the ardour cooled quickly after each burst, helped by his knowledge that the Cabinet was not Blairite, in the sense that it did not subscribe to 'the project' as it had been hatched in the Prime Minister's mind. Ministers might be quite happy to contemplate some previously unthinkable things in economic and social policy but this was still a Cabinet representing a party that had spent long years out of power and wanted to enjoy victory. Labour MPs who had beaten Liberal Democrats in the General Election were telling the party whips of their fury at any suggestion of too close a relationship with the enemy. Fortunately for Blair, they did not know the whole truth. Nor did Nick Brown, the chief whip, who had little knowledge of the intimate nature of Blair's conversations with Ashdown. 'Healing the schism' with the Liberal Democrats would have produced an instant Labour schism of its own if he had.

In power, Blair understood that as well as his party not sharing his thinking, the Liberal Democrat members had not yet been won over by Ashdown. It was much easier to be cosy to Labour notionally in opposition than when it was a massively powerful party of government. So he kept his enthusiasm for the private encounters with Ashdown, which still took place, away from the prying eyes of his ministers. The JCC met regularly, and for most members of the government its proceedings mattered not at all. Different Cabinet ministers were taken along from time to time and the discussions were duly minuted, but in the life of the government it had little significance. One senior minister puts it like this: 'There are some Cabinet committees you want to sit on. It's important that you are there. You have input in some of the big decisions at least. With the Liberal thing there doesn't seem much point. It obviously means something to Tony but nobody else takes it very seriously at all.' That is a common view among ministers in the senior ranks; there are other views which are more hostile. It is one of the few subjects on which Prescott has often felt it safe to disagree with Blair in public. In many interviews he has said that everyone knows what he thinks about Liberals. He never has to add: 'Not much.'

Prescott would not serve in a coalition Cabinet and everyone knows it. But Blair has never abandoned his urge. From time to time it breaks the surface for a moment. He told Robert Harris in May 2000 in an interview: 'I've never given up on that goal, and I still believe it can be achieved.' Most of the time, however, this is a passion that dare not speak its name.

Blair's most radical thought about the kind of government he wanted to lead was, therefore, one that he couldn't easily share with his colleagues. He often had to conceal it. By contrast, the trouble with his most innovative change – devolution to Scotland and Wales – was not in concealing his enthusiasm but in keeping his misgivings private.

Blair did confess his doubts to a small group of Labour MPs who went to see him before the 1997 election. They were anti-devolutionists, still convinced that the policy was an appeasement of nationalism and would fail. They thought, as a large section of the Labour Party had thought in the seventies, that the SNP in Scotland would be energized, the Conservatives in England would be given a banner to raise and that the government would find itself paddling once more in the mire which had sucked down the Callaghan government in 1979. The MPs, among them the veteran anti-devolutionist Tam Dalyell, put their case to Blair. They were on a hopeless mission. They wouldn't be able to persuade him to abandon the party commitment to devolution, as they knew before they arrived. But Blair was surprisingly open with them. He revealed that he was troubled by the politics of devolution, and fearful that the constitutional complications would hobble his government. And he said something else: that his relationship with Brown was essential to the success of a future Labour government, and that it could not survive what Brown would consider betrayal on devolution.

Blair's interest in 'healing the schism' between the non-Conservative parties in British politics was a feeble thing compared to Brown's adamantine commitment to devolution. For a quarter of a century he had argued for a Parliament in Edinburgh, and his feelings about devolution had been a still point in the turning world of his economic views. The editor of *The Red Paper* in 1975 was writing about a Scotland with a Parliament, just as the Iron Chancellor, with his fiscal rules and his love of prudence, was determined that the Labour government would legislate for devolution in its first Queen's Speech. Blair's nagging worries about the consequences and his suspicion that it was a distraction from the government's main business were not going to be allowed to delay things.

But even Brown had to accept referendum procedures which infuriated some of the most dedicated devolutionists. Despite Labour's absolute commitment to a Parliament, on the model devised by the cross-party Scottish Constitutional Convention, Blair announced a year before the General Election that there would be a referendum with two questions, the second giving voters the chance to decide whether or not the Parliament should have tax-raising powers. For the true believers this was in itself a betrayal. What if the Parliament were approved but not allowed a measure of control on taxation? Its legitimacy would be sabotaged and all the old arguments about irresponsible talking shops would return. The Liberal Democrats, in particular, were furious. Blair wouldn't give ground to them. He told Ashdown that there were many English nationalists in his party who wanted devolution to die, and if it was to survive he had to have his hand strengthened by a two-question referendum. There was no other way. Blair needed the two-question referendum to give devolution legitimacy. If the Liberal Democrats didn't like it, too bad. He could hardly undermine a policy which had come to be seen as something of a memorial to John Smith but he had developed a nagging fear about what became known as 'the English backlash'. Without a referendum he believed he would find it hard to defend. His own Scottish party was deeply unhappy – any referendum had been ruled out repeatedly as unnecessary – and the Liberal Democrats spoke of betrayal, but Blair insisted.

It was held on 11 September 1997, before the late summer glow of the election honeymoon had faded, and the government duly won a clear 'Yes' answer to both questions. The legislation which had to follow was likely to provide more of a difficulty than the Scottish electorate which, after all, had voted overwhelmingly for devolutionist or nationalist parties in the five General Elections past. The legislation was based on a plan drawn up in the first fretful six weeks of the government's life and the Cabinet negotiations were further complicated by the oldest rule of politics, the one that says everyone knows everyone else's past.

The Scottish Secretary and First Minister designate Donald Dewar had to argue his case in a ministerial committee (DSWR – Devolution to Scotland, Wales and the Regions) chaired by Derry Irvine. They had been students in Glasgow together, but their friendship was broken. Long after their buoyant days as young debaters in a notable gang of livewires and wits that included John Smith and Menzies Campbell, Dewar's wife, Alison, left him for Irvine with their son and daughter. Not surprisingly, Irvine and Dewar were not regular companions thereafter. There was some nervousness in government about how they would work together. But Dewar got into the habit of coming off the sleeper from Glasgow to London every week and having private breakfasts with Irvine in his apartment at the Lords. They made it work, though it was not easy for either of them.

It wasn't surprising that other members of the Cabinet looked in on these devolution arguments with a certain awe and mystification. Everyone seemed tied up with everyone else in Scotland: different generations like Brown's and Dewar's seemed to be connected by shared experiences that were passed on down the years. Added to the wariness of ministers like Jack Straw about the devolution exercise itself – what would independent-minded northern constituencies like his in Blackburn do when the English complaints became too loud for comfort? – was a degree of irritation at the assertiveness of the Scottish mafia in Cabinet. But Irvine, in fact, was disturbed by the drift of Dewar's first paper to the committee: like Straw he did not want to see the centre of power in Whitehall weakened too much. Blair sympathized with that view. Brown did not.

Blair told Irvine that he did not want a plan that seemed in any way to impinge on Westminster's ultimate sovereignty. The subjects devolved to Scotland must be clearly delineated and Westminster's powers in other matters must be clear and unaffected. He also sought a promise to cut the number of Scots MPs at Westminster and said that when that could be agreed he wanted the Edinburgh Parliament reduced in size by the same proportion. This infuriated his Scottish ministers who disagreed profoundly with the view that the new Parliament should have to wax and wane with Westminster. But the issue of Scottish MPs was to be kicked off into the future, so that row was postponed.

During the Cabinet's arguments on devolution Irvine had the advantage not so much of prime ministerial patronage but of his own patronage of the Prime Minister. He found it difficult to avoid using the old description 'young Blair' when he was off duty, and in the early days of government every minister with well-tuned political antennae knew that he and Blair spoke to each other a great deal, a call coming on many mornings from Number 10 to the Irvine apartment in the Victoria Tower high above the House of Lords. They gossiped about everything. This gave Irvine the clout that comes with such intimacies. In the early days of the government, no one could afford to offend him. It was too risky.

Ministers found this galling. Privately, they complained about his style. One minister who had been treated at a Cabinet committee like a trembling witness who'd come to court with a threadbare story said after her first experience of the Irvine treatment: 'I don't think I have ever met a ruder man.' This was a high accolade. It made Irvine a few enemies, and he became the Flashman of the Cabinet, routinely described by his colleagues as a bully. Stories would circulate of humiliating interrogations of ministers who hadn't mastered a brief. As in a courtroom, he would pause to glance with a raised eyebrow at a colleague who was encouraged to share his scepticism about the case being made, and there would be the sort of derisory grunts that only come from the unpersuaded. 'You've got to remember that we can't stand him – but he probably doesn't know it,' one quite senior member of the Cabinet said in the early days. In fact, Irvine understood quite well that he wasn't especially popular. His position in the government had not come as the result of a conventional political career and his power flowed from one source alone: his old pupil. The advantage was that it gave him independence. He had no network of supporters that had to be nurtured and massaged. He dealt directly with the Prime Minister, and no one else was in a position to intervene.

Irvine mastered his devolution brief and got on with it. Having launched himself as a constitutional reformer, Blair wanted the legislation to pass quickly and with as little collateral damage to the party as possible. But no one believed that when Blair had gone anyone would find the word 'devolution' engraved on his heart. In conversation he would raise his eyes heavenwards and hope it would soon be over. He was encouraged in this by Straw, who spoke of the importance of maintaining 'executive democracy', by which he meant the power of the central bureaucracy in London, parliamentary sovereignty for Westminster in as many areas of policy as possible, and no change to the first-past-the-post system for election to the Commons. The ministers who agreed with Straw were reconciled to PR in Scotland – long since agreed by the Labour Party, largely as a defence against the chances of an outright Nationalist majority in Edinburgh in years to come – but the devolution argument was drenched in suspicion.

Blair's worries were compounded after the Scottish Parliament and the Welsh Assembly were elected. The campaign in Scotland was awkward, and in its later stages Brown was sent up to give it some weight. This caused some resentment on Dewar's part, but Blair was in a state of mild panic about what was happening beyond England's borders. 'He looked up there and saw nothing but trouble,' one of his officials says. Some of the trouble was of his own making. In Wales, the choice of Alun Michael as leader in the Assembly was unpopular and politically humiliating for Michael himself, who eventually had to give way to Rhodri Morgan, the party's popular choice, whom Blair had decided to oppose for his 'old Labour' sympathies (Morgan prefers the neat description 'classic Labour'). In Scotland, the new administration, a Labour partnership with the Liberal Democrats, stumbled into a series of embarrassing bungles, found itself in a street fight with the Scottish press and had a troubled infancy.

These constitutional innovations were radical steps by any measure, but they left Blair uneasy. His instincts for reform were just that: instincts rather than plans. Where Brown had beavered away on devolution for twenty years, and in common with every Scots politician of his generation knew every turning in the maze, Blair had inherited a commitment whose complications he had never had to bother to master in the way that he would have had to had he been a Scottish MP. When he began to ponder the likely unpopularity in England of a Parliament that appeared to give Scotland special powers, and therefore advantages, he got the jitters. Along with Irvine, oozing with the instinctive caution of the lawyer playing a canny hand, he watched the pace being set by Dewar, with Brown's support, with alarm.

The paradox of Blair's first term is that he led a government which produced more radical changes to the constitution than any since before World War I but couldn't shake off a nervousness about the whole exercise. Three years after he came to power, nearly two dozen bills had gone through the Commons reshaping the institutions of the United Kingdom, and yet he chose never to devote a major speech entirely to constitutional matters. It was almost as if he didn't like the very thing he had committed so much of his legislative time to. Brown was different.

Though he has in general been notably reluctant to involve himself in public debate about questions that aren't Treasury preoccupations he has pushed and harried on devolution. One of his colleagues, who watched the progress of devolution with Straw-like alarm, offers a picture.

'Gordon is obsessed by Scotland. Obsessed. He reads the Scottish papers. Talks about it all the time. Of course he's terrified that there will be separation. Devolution has always been his thing. He pushed the pace on. Tony went along with it. Not very enthusiastically, but he went along.'

But in politics such observations seldom come without an explanation that tries to identify the motive. 'Now Gordon talks all the time about regionalism and the need to solve "the English question". He knows, of course, that if England isn't reconciled to Scottish devolution and the regions are sorted out there will never be a Scottish leader of the party. The penny has dropped. It happened about two years ago. He talks about it all the time.'

That interpretation of Brown's motives may not be entirely unfair, but it ignores that pulse of devolution that those around Blair have sometimes been unable to feel. For Scots politicians of all parties the years of the constitutional debates of the seventies were invigorating, bloody, memorable ones. There was a comic demonstration of it at Dewar's funeral in October 2000 in Glasgow Cathedral.

Blair read a lesson from Isaiah about the obligation to help the humble and the needy and Brown delivered the principal tribute from the pulpit. It was a congregation which represented a Scotland whose byways Dewar knew intimately, representing every party and faction as if they were a small community gathered for a town meeting. Everyone seemed to know everyone else. Indeed the funeral arrangements were attended by arguments of the sort that Dewar the politician would have found hilarious – an emissary from London declaring that Glasgow City Council's finest china wasn't good enough for the reception after the service; officials of the Scottish Executive trying to reroute the cortege on its way to the crematorium to avoid the City Hall in George Square because of a dispute with the council leaders; a jockeying among clerics for position and the sight of one of the most distinguished among them being seated by chance behind a large stone pillar, to his evident discomfort. It was a melancholy day for Dewar's friends but not without the traditional piquancy of the political funeral.

Brown's address was delivered as if it was a political speech, almost a rallying cry. He turned from his recollections of an old friend (with whom he'd been having some painful arguments in the year or so up to his death) to his theme of social justice. In the day or two before, while Brown was thumping away at his keyboard in the Chancellor's office in the Treasury, writing a tribute that would match the occasion, there were discussions in Number 10 about how 'political' the address could afford to be. 'We decided that Gordon could push out the boat a little quite safely. It was quite right that he should talk about the importance of social justice and the rest of it,' an official said after the funeral. A friend of Brown's found it laughable. 'Can you imagine some prat from Number 10 telling Gordon what to say at Donald's funeral?' he said, sipping strong tea from one of Glasgow City Council's finest china cups, safely approved for the wake.

It was a tribal occasion. Blair, sitting in the front row with Brown, Irvine and the Prince of Wales, felt again the self-awareness of the Scotland that was being shaped by his own devolution of power. His colleagues believe that it's an awareness tinged with foreboding. A Parliament that begins to think for itself, an electorate that looks to Edinburgh and not London, Nationalists who are ready to exploit any dispute with London and win easy votes as a result – they are Downing Street nightmares. Devolution changed the shape of the British state within a year of the election of the Blair government. For the Prime Minister, however, it was a change that tingled with apprehension.

Blair's caution and his willingness to think the unthinkable always march hand in hand. For years before the election he was happy to contemplate coalition, whatever his party thought about it. About devolution, his inherited revolution, he was apprehensive. Alongside him, in Brown he had a Chancellor who saw radicalism in a quite different light. His was a party belief, a Labour loyalist's line. The Liberal Democrats wouldn't be welcome in the Cabinet Room if he were Prime Minister, all his friends knew, but on the constitution itself he'd draw on the beliefs of early twentieth-century Scottish socialists, who still cast a spell on him, and battle for a kind of Home Rule.

On the day of the referendum result, in September 1997, Blair flew to Edinburgh and then Cardiff to mark the moment. It was something of a triumph for him, and he grinned at the crowds. A friend of Brown's who was watching, said: 'What does it mean to him?' The unspoken answer was: 'Not much.' But Blair revelled in the success of the referendums like a professional. Eighteen years before it had been the Scottish referendum that marked the beginning of the end of the Callaghan government. This Labour government had succeeded where its predecessor had failed, and Blair could justifiably feel that he had completed the work that John Smith had begun.

His worries about devolution increased after Dewar's sudden

death; in Downing Street the leadership of Henry McLeish in Scotland was thought to be of a distinctly less commanding sort, and Blair's nervousness returned. A Prime Minister who worried as much as Blair about the efficiency of the Downing Street machine and wanted to streamline Whitehall was never likely to be a natural devolver, and Blair is not.

This was not as contradictory as it seemed. Brown, as is his habit, had built a strategy on one of his political principles, in this case devolution. That commitment was sacrosanct. If it meant a joint administration with the Liberal Democrats in Edinburgh, so be it. That was a consequence which would have to be managed. But for Westminster, Brown saw no principle involved. He did not believe in electoral reform for its own sake, nor in encouraging coalition. Scotland was important; the Liberal Democrats weren't.

Once again Blair and Brown came to a settlement from different starting points. Neither undermined the other's strategy, though neither felt it necessary to show great enthusiasm for it. They balanced their rival obsessions and let them flourish.

8
Money

Labour has often had trouble with money. It has always caused envy and guilt, and it brought squalls of uncertainty to the government. Blair may have exploited the sleazy episodes in the Major years to help swell his 1997 majority but when his own ministers began to slip and slide into the same muddy pools he found it even more difficult to deal with in public than his predecessors. He could boast of a Parliamentary Commissioner for Standards, a new Commons committee and new rules of disclosure for election donations but money made the government uncomfortable.

Clean government and financial propriety were not the only difficulties. Deep inside Labour there still lay a feeling of awkwardness about the rich, even about the half-rich. With Blair's regime came a new language as well as new policies. They intended to change the image of Labour as the party whose former Chancellor, Denis Healey, had promised to 'tax the rich until the pips squeak' in the seventies, turning it into a party that was at ease with wealth and its benefits. For Blair, the mantra of 'traditional Labour values in a modern setting' did not mean holding on to the value that equated wealth with greed and exploitation. Social justice and financial success were to be allowed to co-exist.

The sensitivity of the issue could be gauged by the awkwardness with which Blair spoke about it. At the start of the 2001 campaign he was asked by Jeremy Paxman on *Newsnight* whether he thought it was acceptable for the gap between rich and poor to widen under his premiership. His reply was evasive because Blair knew that he would offend his party with a more blunt one. Nonetheless he stubbornly refused to condemn the pursuit of wealth: 'It is acceptable for those people on lower incomes to have their incomes raised. It is unacceptable that they're not given the chances. To me the key thing is not whether the gap between those who – the person who earns the most in the country and the person who earns the least – is distant or not.' Blair's answer was revealing. His government was committed to a sustained attack on child poverty at home – a preoccupation of Brown's – and attempts at debt reduction across the developing world as part of a global effort to slow down and even reverse the spread of poverty around the world, another policy to which Brown has devoted a great deal of personal attention, and Blair has no difficulty with those objectives. Some of his warmest words for his Chancellor have been about them. But he has never believed that a concern about poverty should be matched by a nervousness about wealth.

On this question, perhaps more than on any other, his instincts have drawn him away from much of his party. Roy Hattersley, who for all his life in the Commons was associated with the loyalist Labour right, assumed the role of doom-laden pamphleteer from the Lords in his retirement from front-line politics, taking to the pages of newspapers right and left to denounce Blairism as a betrayal of Labour values because it was, above all, an elitist creed that had lost any interest in equality. Just after Blair's re-election, Hattersley said that he had even considered resigning from the party, which for a former deputy leader would have been an act with a guaranteed public effect. He had long since severed links with Downing Street, and is regarded there with some bitterness for obvious reasons, but his themes have unsettled Blair.

To the Blair of 1983, Labour seemed to have nothing to offer the professional middle classes. He went along with the party's election manifesto in public, despite his private doubts, but in the gloomy years that followed one of his preoccupations, much more than it was Kinnock's, was finding a political language that dispensed with the class envy which he still found uncomfortable. He was perfectly at one with the instincts of his constituency party, which, like most of the others in County Durham, leaned generally towards the right of the party, where he was not expected to indulge in bloodcurdling assaults on the rich and privileged. So early on, with friends like his agent John Burton, he experimented with a new language. A different attitude to wealth was part of it. Even during the height of Thatcherism, he wanted to associate Labour with a commitment to successful people as well as the downtrodden. His legal friends in London were comfortably off, even if most of them would not end up as Irvine-like millionaires at the Bar, and Blair was determined that Labour should not be a party that decried them. He had little idea where precisely such determination might lead, but in his early period in the Commons his private contempt was directed firmly at those on the left whom he believed to be imbued with a hatred of success.

This was hardly an incongruous posture for Blair. Before 1983 he had been a reasonably successful barrister who would probably have been making several hundred thousand pounds a year in the nineties had he stayed at the Bar and developed in the way that was predicted by Irvine, his head of chambers. Moreover, as a barrister he was self-employed. That status does not seem a particular hardship to those outside the law, given the rewards that are available for success, but it did mean that before entering Parliament Blair had become used to the fact that he was responsible for the size of his own income. If he was a success, he would probably become quite rich; if his cases dried up he would be scraping a living at the scruffy end of the profession. By the time he became an MP he was used to controlling his own financial destiny and was quite sensitive about money, a sensitivity no doubt sharpened by the fact that his income dropped by more than half when he was elected.

Blair came from a comfortable, though not spectacularly well-heeled middle-class background. His father, Leo, was a law lecturer in Adelaide, Edinburgh and Durham and practised as a barrister on the Newcastle circuit while Blair was at The Chorister School at Durham Cathedral. There was enough money to send Blair, and his older brother Bill, to Fettes. Theirs was not a household where money was a regular worry. When he began to show an interest in political ideas (as distinct from political activity) at Oxford, it was natural that he would match his creed to his own experiences. Blair never showed any sign of rejecting his family's status or outlook and was never one of those political figures who either buries the past or turns publicly against it. His father had been a youthful communist in Glasgow before the war, and Blair well knew the story of his disillusionment with the revolutionary left.

He has never shown an interest in class politics, unlike some members of his Cabinet who were formidable leftists in their day. Charles Clarke, his choice for Cabinet Office fixer and party chairman after the government's re-election, was left-wing president of the National Union of Students when Blair was in his last, politics-free year at Oxford. Alan Milburn and Stephen Byers both went on package tours to the far left in the seventies, all-in excursions to the self-contained world of Trotskyite certainty, when the clenched fist and the 'Internationale' were on show for the last time at party conferences. Blair was nowhere near such gatherings. His early years in the Labour Party, partly at the time when he shared a flat in London with his fellow-barrister Charlie Falconer, did not involve the kind of infighting that scarred the likes of Mandelson, and when he had his first electoral outing, in the Beaconsfield by-election in 1982, he described himself, safely, as a Labour centrist.

So when in power Blair spoke of his interest in allowing success to flourish, he was not adopting a new line. He was simply letting the old frustration show. He never accompanied his arguments for social justice, and equality of opportunity, with a balancing assault on the well-off and when Brown and he discussed the possibility of a 50 per cent upper tax rate in the run-up to the 1997 election Blair was strongly against an increase. He was certainly concerned not to lose the sympathy of some Conservative newspapers which were being won round to him, or at least tiptoeing towards disinterest, but he had no ideological appetite for higher taxes themselves.

Brown approaches the problem of wealth from the other end. While Blair has spent much of his political life finding a way of reconciling his belief in community obligations to his instinct for success and prosperity, Brown's had undergone a transition from the editor of *The Red Paper* who spoke about defeating the logic of capitalism and establishing street committees for an assault on the forces of privilege and power. By the time Brown fought Edinburgh South in 1979, he was a fixture of the conventional left and a pillar of the Scottish party. His attitude to taxation in those days was that the well-off should pay heavily for their success. The Brown of 1979 would not have supported the Brown of 1997 in holding the 40 per cent top rate: he would have been a rigorous pip-squeezer of the rich. At that time, the right was deeply suspicious of him, thinking him too young, too ambitious and far too sure of himself.

The confidence had a good deal to do with a certain kind of rage that he managed to preserve from his more radical days. His book on James Maxton was published in 1986, three years after he became an MP, and his visceral sympathy for the controlled anger that fuelled the Independent Labour Party of the 1920s and 1930s is still obvious. His account of Maxton's life acknowledges the failure of his political ambitions, but his conclusion on the last page is worth quoting. First he cites Maxton's defence of the individual, that 'people must never be allowed to become ants in an ant-hill,' then Brown adds:

> Cold, bureaucratic state socialism held no attractions for him. For Maxton the only test of socialist progress was in the improvement of the individual and thus the community. Greater educational opportunities would not only free exceptional people to realize their exceptional talents but allow common people to make the most of their common humanity, and ordinary people to realize their extraordinary potentials. The social equality he supported was not for the sake of equality but for the sake of liberty.

This is as good a summary of Brown's political outlook (or, at least, how he would like to have it interpreted) as there is. In his maiden speech in 1983 he spoke largely about poverty in his own constituency, in which he said that 15,000 people were dependent on means-tested benefits, and that in Scotland by his calculation more than a fifth of the population was living under the poverty line as defined by Whitehall. He went on: 'This is all because the government's philosophy is that the rich must get rich by way of tax cuts and that the poor must become poorer to ensure true prosperity.'

Brown's attitude was anchored in his background. His father was a minister who was more interested in social balm than fire and brimstone. He had often recalled that his family did not seem to want for anything, and though a Church of Scotland manse in the fifties was not usually a luxurious place, it was not uncomfortable either. The message he says he absorbed from his father's way of life and his sermons was that an individual's worth should be treasured and celebrated, and that social divisions should be ignored. This was the egalitarian strain that ran through church and school in Scotland (when they were at their best, though in some places they were often at their worst) and it explains much about Brown's own political wanderings thereafter. Kirkcaldy, where his family moved when he was three, was a typical Scottish town of its size, neither noticeably deprived nor obviously prosperous. There were substantial sandstone houses marching along the seafront, but little ostentatious wealth. The town's reputation elsewhere in Scotland came from a piece of doggerel from a poem of the day describing a train journey through Fife, which every schoolchild knew:

> And ye ken right well, by the queer-like smell,
> That the next stop is Kirkcaldy.

This was a reference to the town's linoleum factory, long gone now, which produced a distinctive pong, almost rivalling the heavy fumes from the Edinburgh breweries on the other side of the Firth of Forth but not as pleasant. More Scots of that generation would know Kirkcaldy for linoleum than for the fact that it produced Adam Smith, author of *Wealth of Nations*, who was the rediscovered hero of the Conservative Party at the time of Brown's arrival at Westminster, his formulation of the practical and moral force of markets having become the platform on which Margaret Thatcher wanted to build a new economy in the eighties. Brown had read Smith, of course, at Edinburgh and returned to him years later when he discovered the late night delights of the Treasury library where, after clearing his desk, he would repair and reread texts from eighteenth-century Scotland (especially David Hume) which – to the amazement of some less bookish parliamentary colleagues – he said he found relaxing and stimulating.

In his student days and afterwards Brown lived modestly. He was famous for muddle and never even flirted with an elegant phase. When he moved into his own flat in Marchmont Road in Edinburgh in the seventies it retained the flavour of a student nest almost until he left for the house he bought in his constituency in North Queensferry at the end of the eighties. He lived in a cocoon of books and papers in a flat that sometimes felt like a railway junction, because it was a stopping-off place for friends and acquaintances, a trading exchange for political gossip and intrigue and a place where people felt that if they stayed long enough they would eventually meet half of Edinburgh and many of its most interesting visitors. When Brown taught politics at Glasgow College of Technology in the late seventies, and worked in current affairs at Scottish Television in the early eighties, he still lived in Edinburgh and showed no sign at all of wanting to fit himself into a smooth professional mould. Even after he had been an MP for three years or so, when a visiting camera crew from the BBC arrived to film a long interview we found ourselves assisting in clearing a corner of his living room to create a suitable background – a temporary, tidy stage set – so that the subject wouldn't be surrounded by too much clutter. Brown's attitude to his own environment was not that of an aspirant social show-off. He needed enough money only to keep his political ambitions moving. It was never an end in itself.

The only show to interest Brown was on the political stage. He would devote a great deal of energy to political calculation – and, as some rivals in the Scottish Labour Party would have it, ruthlessness. He enjoyed hell-raising on a platform, but he was only Flash Gordon at these public moments. He dressed conservatively and never seemed to want to discard the ties which he had continued to wear even when he was a student railing against the Edinburgh University establishment, standing out from his fellow-troublemakers who were devotees of the stained T-shirt and the Che Guevara beard. By contrast, during his left-wing phase at Aberdeen University and later in Edinburgh politics, Brown's Cabinet colleague Alistair Darling was fashionably decked out in a combat jacket which in those days was a badge of earnestness. Thinking of Brown in a combat jacket is like thinking of Derry Irvine in a kaftan.

The outline of the radical young politician with a traditional side lies somewhere under the current figure of the conservatively dressed Chancellor doing his Whitehall rounds, like the first sketch for a painting lurking behind the final layers of colour. It is the authentic Gordon Brown. When Sarah Macaulay encouraged him to go shopping for new suits, he was persuaded only to choose four at the Savile Row tailors Norton and Townsend that were the 'cheap' cut, at £500 each, indistinguishable from the style of those that he had long favoured, usually dark blue or black with no fancy accoutrements. The four new ones were absolutely identical. They were to be his uniform for work. His wife-to-be was also allowed to choose him a tie for his first Budget, designed by Paul Smith. It was, like many of his other ones, red but with the merest hint of a distinguishing pattern. Brown the impatient intellectual radical of old has always been Brown the conformist about himself. Not much has changed.

Both Blair and Brown are of the generation that grew up while former rigidities of class were loosening, and an old order was turning to dust. It was no longer easy to know someone's social geography precisely. The children of the fifties were the generation that broke free from the austerity visited on their parents yet they were years distant from Thatcher's Children, born in the City big bang and raised to feel no embarrassment about money and material things, ready to chatter happily about the size of their mortgage as if it was another kitchen gadget. Life for that generation was increasingly about doing deals, shopping for financial services, buying PEPs and Tessas and ISAs and learning the language of money. Blair and Brown, in their own ways, reveal personally how difficult this transition has been for Labour. Brown is an uncomfortable propagandist for the world of liquid money and a life of risks, because his character seems set against it. Blair has tried to cast off all embarrassment about money with a swashbuckling defence of enterprise and success, and even a kind of hedonism among the winners who've made it, but he too has found it difficult to find a language which encompasses the public service commitments that are still Labour's boast and the freewheeling life he also admires.

The character who was the emblem of this difficulty in the first term was Geoffrey Robinson. He is a man who always seems to be smiling, even when he is not. He is a cheery glad-hander by nature, in politics and business, and for most of his time in politics he had a great deal to be cheery about. His successful career in the car industry which brought him the chief executive's chair at Jaguar allowed him to build on a fortune which he had been able to amass from his family firm. But it was a career of snakes as well as ladders, and the crash of an up-and-down outfit called TransTec because of its failure to deliver on a Ford contract (a failure of which Robinson has always insisted he was unaware) was expensive, not only in the loss of millions but in providing an episode that, despite his denial of direct investment, has dogged him, giving him the reputation of someone who always enjoyed sailing close to the wind. Robinson is a natural swashbuckler and a man of mystery. He made a fortune in the motor industry, bought a Tuscan *palazzo*, and moved into a Grosvenor House apartment on Park Lane with striped-trousered attendants on call. What other Labour MP can say that a shadowy Belgian millionairess left him a huge legacy which was tucked safely in an offshore trust for a rainy day? Madame de Bourgeois provided one of the exotic pages in the Robinson story which made him a most unlikely intimate of Brown's. Yet he was.

In the opposition years it was Robinson's money which, in part, funded Brown's extensive research operation, costing many tens of thousands of pounds. He oiled the wheels, and became part of the Brown circle, entertaining them and running a kind of permanent economic soirée for the team. Without him Brown's outfit would not have been the well-rehearsed gang it was when he got to the Treasury. Robinson, jovially and generously, gave it its private style.

He subverted Brown's straightforward tastes, and was the playboy of his team. In government it took less than two years for the rollercoaster to come off the rails, and for Robinson to be forced out, causing Blair's first personal crisis and exposing the government's intimate relationships to an unforgiving glare.

Everyone's character was revealed, sometimes cruelly but accurately, in the events that followed Peter Mandelson's request for a loan from Robinson to help him buy a house in the terminally trendy Notting Hill. He needed £373,000 and Robinson was happy to oblige.

When Blair appointed Mandelson to the Department of Trade and Industry in 1998 the arrangement could no longer remain the secret that it had been because Mandelson's ministerial activities could in theory have directly affected Robinson's business concerns. The Prime Minister should have been told. He wasn't. Mandelson's colleagues were astonished when the first leak of the story appeared. In fact it was a leak of a leak, because the information from an early copy of Paul Routledge's unauthorized biography of Mandelson found its way to the *Guardian.* Blair was angry that he hadn't known, and naturally suspicious that the information had come from the Treasury in the knowledge that it would probably force Mandelson from the government. He did not accuse Brown directly, but it deepened his distaste for the Chancellor's circle – led by Charlie Whelan and Ed Balls with sympathetic journalists like Routledge alongside – which he associated, simply, with intrigue and, now, the biggest political embarrassment of his premiership.

The first Mandelson affair threw the government into a state of panic. There was some quiet amusement at his predicament among ministers who feared him, but also mystification. One member of the Cabinet said: 'Peter is somebody who'll give you advice about a problem in a flash. He hardly has to think. In a few seconds he would have told any of us how to neutralize something like this – how to write to the Cabinet Secretary, the permanent secretary and so on – and how to take the sting out. You'd be safe; you'd be covered. But when it's himself, he can't see it.' Mandelson, the master tactician, walked to his doom. The DTI was investigating a company with which Robinson was connected. It was possible to argue that the Department's Chinese walls were sufficiently robust to allow Mandelson to say that it would be absurd to suggest that as Secretary of State he could intervene in a sensitive business investigation of the quasi-judicial sort that are always running inside the department. But the affair had such built-in drama and intrigue that it would not submit to such easy answers. For four days, over the pre-Christmas weekend, Mandelson tried to find a way out of the pit, but on the day before Christmas Eve he tumbled into it.

He tried to rearrange the financing of his house with the help of his family. He insisted that his arrangement with Robinson was a private deal between friends which therefore presented no conflict of interest for either of them. He said he had not breached the Ministerial Code. No law had been broken, no formal government convention had been breached. But, from the beginning, Mandelson's history made his position hopeless.

A good number of Labour MPs were luxuriating in his misfortune, just as he had been photographed luxuriating in a reclining chair in the elegant minimalism of his Notting Hill drawing room. Mandelson, who, in the opposition years could change a career with a raised eyebrow or a whispered word in the leader's office, was faced by well-populated backbenches whose MPs believed that their lowly status could be blamed on him. In this respect, his power was greatly exaggerated, but that hardly mattered. So enthusiastically and stylishly had he played the part of the Prince of Darkness that manoeuvres and plots of which he knew almost nothing were bundled up and laid at his door. Prescott and the others in the Cabinet who resented his power were happy to give the stories a fair wind. So when he began to slip and slide on the stories leaking out about the loan, a section of the party put on its happy face. You could have looked around the Cabinet table and missed the look of grief on the faces of Prescott, Cook, Straw, Blunkett, Mo Mowlam and, of course, Gordon Brown. Mandelson spoke to Blair (when the Prime Minister was in any case preoccupied with the renewed bombing of Iraq) at least twice over the weekend and they tried to find a way of rearranging his finances to wipe the Robinson slate clean. The effort lasted only two days before it collapsed in a heap.

Twenty-four hours later they were talking about possible resignation, the moment in such crises when resignation almost always becomes inevitable. The press was hostile, revelling in a story which had one of its favourite characters struggling against the kind of inexorable forces that had damned a series of Tory ministers and given Labour its pre-election air of moral superiority. The sight of the Prince sinking in the same muddy pond raised Fleet Street's spirits in those traditionally quiet news days before Christmas. The more he persisted in his explanations, in an increasingly desperate series of interviews, the more it was seen as a fruitless effort to stop a tide that was bound to overwhelm him. It duly did on Wednesday morning, Blair having told him straightforwardly the previous night that resignation was probably inevitable. He sweetened the conversation with the assurance that a clean break would allow the possibility of a quick return to the Cabinet, and an invitation to come to Chequers for the night after the resignation was evidence that he meant it. Mandelson knew he would serve a short sentence, and there would be time off for good behaviour. He was back in the government, in Belfast, in less than a year.

But Mandelson's conversations with Blair are only one side of the story. He spoke privately to Brown through the days up to resignation. Although the revelation about the loan was contained in Routledge's biography, and was therefore assumed by Mandelson to come from his contacts and cronies in the Brown circle, the two old friends spoke in what appears to have been a frank and emotional way. Despite the relationship's freeze before the election, they were now thrown together again for a moment. Brown told Mandelson he wanted to try to help. Mandelson's suspicions of those around Brown were temporarily eclipsed by the Chancellor's apparent distress at his predicament, and although he knew that the Chancellor had almost certainly known of the loan since the deal had been done in 1996, he did not appear to blame him directly for the way the story emerged. It seemed as if Mandelson wanted to believe in Brown's innocence. The closeness wasn't maintained for long, but for a day or two the pull of the old days almost brought the strange pair together once more. Those closest to Brown insist that despite the hostility which had built up over the leadership question, and the coldness that was often obvious between them, Brown was not one of those who enjoyed watching Mandelson's departure. They corresponded at this time, engaging in the kind of personal contact that had stopped after the falling-out in opposition. In the government's first crisis, the older loyalties did peep through the gloom, but only for a moment. Brown's sympathy was limited, and it was clear from his conversations at the time that he was much more concerned about damage to the government from the affair than the plight of Mandelson. A more cynical view is that Brown, having witnessed the removal he so longed for, could afford to be generous to Mandelson once his departure was inevitable.

As for Blair, he tried to save Mandelson until it became obvious that he could do no more. He was getting advice from Campbell, who knew over the weekend that Fleet Street thought Mandelson was finished, and that ministers seldom survive such judgements. In any case, he had long been aware of Mandelson's penchant for danger, always riding his bike with his hands away from the handlebars. This was true of his private life, of his conversations with journalists which produced colourful descriptions of ministerial colleagues in newspapers without much doubt about the source, and of the kind of impulse that let him accept the loan of a car for the election campaign from James Palumbo, proprietor of the London club, The Ministry of Sound. To some colleagues, anxious to avoid the impression of any financial indebtedness, that seemed rash.

Everyone in Downing Street also knew that Campbell often displayed some semi-public irritation at what he considered Mandelson's egocentricity. 'If he didn't think about himself all the time, we'd all be much better off – including him,' one friend heard him say. Campbell helped him to think through some possible survival strategies over the weekend but it seems certain that he never shared Mandelson's early confidence that the storm would subside in the Christmas glow. He knew that Fleet Street was showing an alarming interest in Robinson's business affairs, and the thrilling confluence of a secret loan, the Robinson millions and Blair's best friend was going to be irresistible. After the weekend he did not try to persuade Mandelson to stay and they both wept when the moment came for Mandelson to admit that his struggle for survival was over. Since then their relationship has never returned to the closeness that bound them together in the run-up to the 1997 election.

The loan affair revealed how tangled this web of feelings and obligations had become. These weren't ministers and advisers making executive decisions round a political board-room table; it was a family in agony. Brown still seems to have been both upset and relieved. Blair was determined that even if the proper course was for Mandelson to go, he was not going to lose his confidant – they wouldn't stop talking for a single day. And Campbell, reading the runes of the government's first public ministerial bust-up, was reinforced in his view that Mandelson, for all his tactical brilliance, always had a phial of poison somewhere on his person. Three years later, that judgement would help to condemn Mandelson once again, this time in circumstances which left him convinced that he had been the victim of an injustice perpetrated in panic. With Robinson, though, there was no such agreement. They both had to go and they knew it.

Compared with the effect of any of the policy arguments of the first couple of years, the Mandelson affair was draining on Blair. He skated along in the polls, which still seemed reluctant to display any serious weakening of the government's support, but he was damaged by it. The pubic had had its first glimpse of life behind the front door, and sensed the passions and the competing loyalties flowing between those who were in command. For the first time, Blair was pictured as a lonely Prime Minister. He still had the rest of the gang, with Brown the dominant Chancellor at his side, but somehow the world outside Downing Street sensed correctly that Mandelson's departure reinforced in Blair the feeling that continued to disturb him for the rest of the first term – that he was short of Cabinet friends. Any true Blairites were to be found in the learners' pool at the end of the table and not clustered around him in the centre.

Brown, whatever human pangs for Mandelson's plight he might have felt, was certainly strengthened by his departure.

In all the commentaries about the issues of judgement in the affair, Blair noted (though his newspaper reading is thin and selective and usually filtered by Campbell) that it was he who was being fingered as a Prime Minister who did not seem to be in control. Yet Brown had known about the loan for two years, and had also been the champion and protector of Robinson, whom he regarded as something of a magician in devising schemes for bringing public and private money together in capital projects. This rosy view was not shared across Whitehall, and there were places where Robinson's touch was not considered so sure. He was Brown's man. Yet while Brown appeared to shrug off the affair with a wave of his arm and a grunt, Blair saw himself portrayed as the man who had languished in innocence, who hadn't been told about the loan and had been powerless to prevent the self-destruction of Mandelson. Some around Blair fumed at Brown's success in stepping cleanly and completely out of the Robinson affair. The Prime Minister was often referred to in print as 'Teflon Tony', with a surface on which nothing unpleasant would stick. Suddenly it started to be said in Downing Street that an even more remarkable alloy had been developed in Number 11 next door. Brown's reputation never suffered seriously at the hands of Robinson.

There was a flurry in the press about a flat that he bought in an unprepossessing corner of Great Smith Street, Westminster, for £130,000 which had been sold by the receivers dealing with the collapsed empire of Robert Maxwell, but Fleet Street's best efforts failed to come up with anything remotely dodgy about the deal. Brown denied emphatically any knowledge of the flat's connection to a Maxwell company. Everyone concluded that it was indeed a coincidence. The flat in question was a small, plain affair in a grim modern block across the road from Church House, Westminster, and was a telling example of Brown's attitude to his personal finances. It was a good buy, a clever investment and a functional place to live. There was nothing showy about it. The spotlight passed over the Chancellor once more.

This pattern began to irritate some in the Prime Minister's circle. One or two of them who tended to stay out of the playground fights between Blairites and Brownites began to make a point of discussing with journalists the skill of the Chancellor, as they saw it, in being absent in times of trouble. They even argued that when Blair was deep in the Kosovo conflict, playing with the inevitable political risks that military action involves, Brown should have been more supportive publicly, and should have attended more meetings of the Cabinet sub-committee established to monitor the campaign, to which he often sent the Treasury Chief Secretary, then Alan Milburn, to fill in for him. The Treasury argument that diplomatic and military matters were not for the Chancellor, and that his role was only as banker and accountant for the Kosovo policy, was technically correct but by mid-term a view was settling on some of those close to Blair's office: 'Gordon's gone missing again.' It usually meant, they claimed, that there was trouble. Like Macavity the Mystery Cat, he often wasn't there.

As Prime Minister it was Blair who had to clear up after Robinson and Mandelson. Once Mandelson and Robinson were off the scene, however, one enduring problem remained. The Prime Minister, unlike the Chancellor, was stuck with the image of running a party which loved big money.

In opposition, Labour had begun serious fund-raising beyond its traditional base in the eighties under Kinnock. A few business people began to be attracted by reform, and the party worked them hard. Grand dinners were held in fine hotels and the well-heeled began to be drawn into Labour's circle. £500 here, £1,000 there, the occasional cheque for much more – by the time Blair became leader a rather healthy pattern was developing. With his own skills of persuasion he was able to open the pockets of some unlikely donors, businessmen who had never supported Labour before. He did so with the help, above all, of Michael Levy, who had made his fortune in the music industry and became almost a personal fund-raiser for the leader and his party in the mid-nineties. No one is sure how much of Labour's £25 million for the 1997 election campaign he raised, but the estimates go from £7 million to £10 million. By any measure, he has laid a huge clutch of golden eggs. Blair rewarded him with a peerage, and a role as an informal, back-channel Middle East envoy, an arrangement which (naturally) some in the Foreign Office did not like at all. Levy is a hospitable man, entertaining in high style in north London, but he also possesses the instinct for secrecy that makes good business. He seemed to be able to conjure vast sums from dinner guests whom he gathered round to meet and hear the Prime Minister, soliciting the cheques after the departure of Blair, in whose presence the sordid matter of fund-raising was not discussed.

Levy's style is not to everyone's taste. One business figure in Scotland, who was considering a donation to Labour, was outraged to be approached by Levy and asked the blunt question: 'How much are you worth?' He declined to answer. Later he complained to the Labour Party directly, claiming that Levy had followed up his first question with the suggestion that he might consider giving a million pounds, which is what Levy thought he could afford. Labour received nothing as a result.

This was the consequence of Labour's realization in the nineties that it was going to have to replicate the Conservatives' well-tuned methods of corporate and individual fund-raising to finance ever more expensive election campaigns. Though Blair argues that legislation passed in 2000 will put a hold on the ambitions of the super-rich to buy into political parties by placing limits on individual donations, stopping contributions from overseas and opening up detailed accounts to public scrutiny, his first term was financed by methods which had traditionally been attacked and scorned by Labour. It left him open to the charge that the 'purer than pure' government was behaving in exactly the same way as Tory governments of the past which it sought to portray as prey to special interests.

It was Levy who was instrumental in guiding to the Prime Minister's office one of the most unwelcome guests of the whole first term, unwelcome in the sense that he turned out to be the bearer of embarrassment and near-scandal. In the view of some members of the Cabinet – perhaps most – Bernie Ecclestone, the boss of Formula 1, should never have been allowed there. His route to the

Prime Minister was assisted by having as one of his advisers David Ward, who acted as a lobbyist for Formula 1 (he is mad about fast cars) and was formerly on the staff of John Smith. He has a high personal reputation with many Labour Party insiders and his presence at Ecclestone's side certainly smoothed his path. With Ward's help, and Levy's knowledge on the grapevine that Ecclestone was considering a large donation, he was invited into Downing Street.

Men like Ecclestone enjoy the frisson of the chief executive's handshake, and nothing less will do. The fact that his offer of a million pounds came at a time when the government was engaged in a sensitive and complicated argument about the future of tobacco advertising, a staple of Formula 1's success, was a disaster for Blair. To the outside world it was either conspiratorial or naive. Neither is an attractive prime ministerial trait.

So Levy's influence was valuable to Blair but dangerous, too. He operated from within the 'high value donation unit' – as might be guessed from its title, located in the party's Millbank headquarters, where politics was translated routinely into the style and practice of management. It was from this office that strange signals would sporadically emerge. Levy's deputy, Amanda Delew, wrote in one party memo not long after the 1997 election: 'Major donors expect to be invited to Number 10. If this cannot take place then income levels may be affected.' This memo, which reads like something addressed to a supermarket sales team, was discussing how far the door of the Prime Minister's office should be opened to the rich and generous. Blair's Downing Street has never operated on the scale of Bill Clinton's White House, where nights in the Lincoln Bedroom were arranged for important donors, but the natural desire to make the 'new' party a rich and successful one as well as the natural party of government brought some new habits.

Just as the first Mandelson resignation cast a shaft of light into the heart of the government and allowed outsiders to see the forces which drove it, so his second departure was the most telling and alarming political event Blair had to face in approaching the re-election campaign. Even more than the horrors of a foot and mouth crisis apparently mismanaged by the Ministry of Agriculture, which had long since become an object of contempt in his office – 'useless' was Blair's own description of the officials in charge at MAFF – the dangers posed by another Mandelson affair, in which an uncomfortable link between money and influence in government was again suggested, seemed to sound an ominous knell. The argument about what Mandelson said in a phone call to a junior Home Office minister, Mike O'Brien, about a passport application for the Hinduja brother became secondary. The Hindujas gave a donation of £1 million to fund the Faith Zone of the Dome – although the subsequent tax liability to the New Millennium Experience Company and tickets given to the family reduced the value of their donation to around £365,000. As well as 1,000 free tickets, their complimentary entrance passes were generous – allowing them, if they had wanted, to take a party of sixty people into the Dome free every day of the year. The controversy surrounding their name was persistent enough to ensure that any donation – even for a quasi-religious display in the Dome – was politically sensitive. The worry for Blair was the fear that there might be more awkward questions to come, and the knowledge that there were newspaper libraries with extensive collections of pictures of him as Prime Minister with the Hindujas unsettled him. Money, power, favours and friends became too potent a cocktail.

The report into the whole affair by Sir Anthony Hammond QC is not a document that explains Mandelson's resignation. It merely describes the confusion and uncertainty that surrounded a sensitive matter in which two brothers whose activities had long been the subject of warnings to the government from the security and intelligence agencies appeared to be able to get access to ministers which looked too easy. Unlike the Robinson affair of 1998, this one was not going to be allowed to run on. Although the first story of Mandelson's alleged role in supporting a passport application, which appeared in the *Observer*, did not signal the end of the Northern Ireland Secretary, within a few days Downing Street had decided that he must go. When Mandelson arrived in Blair's office it was to find the Prime Minister drafting a resignation statement for him. He emerged in a scene of memorable distress to say that he had decided to leave the government, and a few hours later he sat beside Blair shorn of his habitual jauntiness on the front bench in the Commons to listen to rampant Conservative mockery. Blair looked as if he had suffered a family bereavement: he and Mandelson had the look of a ruined couple. The closest of his friendships had been severed by the government's anxiety about its rich friends and its network of hangers-on, and the fear that the catch-all label of sleaze might yet stick to Labour in the way that Blair had managed to affix it to Major before the 1997 election.

The second Mandelson affair revealed how nervous Blair was about the danger that seemed to attach to his old friends – 'not again' was the Downing Street phrase of the moment – and something close to panic about the taint of bad money. There was nothing for it but a clean break. Mandelson would remain a friend, in more regular contact than almost any Labour MP knew, but his Cabinet career had to be terminated again. Blair's fear of another scandal was such that he had no doubt he must go.

Labour knew how sensitive these matters were. The party was awash with cash in the mid-nineties. The preparations for the 1997 election had identified a treasure trove of donations, and it seemed that everyone now wanted to be part of Blair's 'project'. They seemed likely to stay in power: why not jump on board? For those with the money to play a hunch, what was the sensible alternative?

Although the defence offered around Downing Street of the big donors was that none had landed the leader in as much trouble as William Hague found with Michael Ashcroft, Belize financier and Conservative Party treasurer, the gloss of New Labour was sometimes tacky to the touch. The early showbiz parties (discreetly toned down as the years went by) and the luring of such donors as the Tory philanthropist and businessman Christopher Ondaatje allowed the government to be portrayed as an outfit dazzled by the rich. The image was dangerous for Blair, because it meant, for example, that when the Millennium Dome became the butt of a national joke or the phrase 'Cool Britannia' became decidedly un-cool, he could be pictured as flighty rather than serious, a stylist and performer rather than a deliverer. This infuriated Downing Street, of course, when Blair was deep in the hands-on diplomacy and negotiations of Northern Ireland or Kosovo but it was an image that left its mark.

The government therefore developed a peculiar double personality. It was half-Prudence and half-Good-Time Girl. Brown's persona as Chancellor was uncompromisingly grim. From the start, he was the dark-suited bank manager gloomily wondering about the state of the overdraft. He wouldn't break his fiscal rules, invented by him and policed by him, and would never be anything but prudent. He would produce record levels of public investment, he said, but in his own good time. This attitude of unbending solemnity suited him, of course. There was a time, after a year or so at the Treasury, when it was suggested that he should try to smile more during television interviews. The party was concerned that he was appearing too dogged and downbeat. But give Brown a microphone and a camera and he is serious. It is his nature. His three-point plans, occasionally extending to ten-point plans, are famously grim litanies for interviewers to tangle with, and his style developed in government into a verbal reflection of his physical black-suited presence at the dispatch box or on the Treasury steps. He was immovable.

His policy was his personality. Having exerted a discipline on shadow Cabinet colleagues which would have been unimaginable a decade earlier (in the days when policy was made on the hoof in the Commons, and often didn't last until the end of the day) he was utterly convinced that success for the government depended on the tone being maintained in government. It did not make him popular. Though the City of London began to see a Chancellor who seemed to believe in the stability it held so dear, despite his refusal to put on a white tie for the Lord Mayor at his Mansion House dinner, the Labour Party felt uneasy. One minister recalls the early days: 'To be quite honest I dreaded going to my party meetings in the constituency. They were horrible. Here we were, the Labour government with the biggest majority in history and we were being told there were all sorts of things we couldn't do. Well, my people wanted them done. There's no doubt that when this government started, Gordon was not appreciated.' Yet everything had prepared him for this. No one could imagine a new Brown appearing at the dispatch box in a light grey suit, grinning from ear to ear and playing the economy like an accordion. Even when he produced his Budget surprises, at least one in each year's box, they were rabbits that seemed to be allowed out of the hat on sufferance. If they didn't behave, they were to go straight back in.

The first year was a difficult one for Brown. Although he was able to start to lay the foundations for the minimum wage, the welfare-to-work programme and to introduce some significant City reforms as well as give the Bank of England independence on interest rates, he found the euro tripping him up and in the spring he had the unhappy sight of a motion being debated at the Scottish Labour Party conference – and carried – which described reductions in benefits for lone-parent families as 'economically inept, morally repugnant and spiritually bereft'. The selection of words was guaranteed to send the Chancellor into a whirlwind rage, from which there was no chance of his backing down. He was the Iron Chancellor who would not bend, however hot the flames, and it was the image he cultivated just as naturally as he would conduct one of his broadcast interviews, refusing to give any ground. He had worked it out in his own mind, and that was that.

This was a political strength for Brown, despite the grumblings from his backbenches in the early days, with interest rates going up and a rigid spending regime in place. He was able to appear the solid figure alongside Blair whom it was impossible to imagine being dislodged. He spoke and answered questions on his own terms; he was resolutely a party man with no time for the rhetoric of the 'third way' or PR; he was assiduous in his conversations with backbenchers, trying to evangelize them in support of a fiscal attitude which those of them who had thought about it had never expected to see from a Labour government. He had one message: he would be the first Labour Chancellor who would finish a full term with a reputation which would rest principally on his management of the economy. That was the purpose of it all. In political terms, and crucially in terms of the media, Brown was massively successful. Four years of his dour uncompromising surface and barrage of statistics effectively machine-gunned any critics. When the electorate came to judge Labour's first term, the economy was hardly on the political agenda. He had made Labour safe, it seemed.

Brown's worst period coincided, of course, with Blair's. The troubled summer of 2000 reached its climax with the fuel disputes of the autumn. The danger for Blair was that he would look like a Prime Minister who was losing touch with the everyday concerns of the country; the danger for Brown, at least in his own mind, was that he might look like a Chancellor who could be pushed around. Where Blair instinctively tries to put himself in the position of those who are demanding a change of course – his technique is to try to demonstrate his sympathy with their complaint, and to mollify their feelings – Brown is more inclined to restate the policy and simply declare that if it is properly implemented it will work. This was illustrated neatly at a press conference in 2001 when the two sat side by side at Millbank, as they often did, to answer early morning questions. They were asked about the discontent felt by travellers on the railways. Brown laid out the policy – a thing of facts and figures – almost without taking breath. Coming in, Blair's message was, in effect: 'I feel your pain.' It was an encapsulation of their different instincts. In the fuel protests Blair was shaken by the image of chaos which was building up; Brown's concern was directed principally to making sure that no policy mistakes were made in conceding a quick victory to fuel protesters in a way that would prejudice his long-term economic game. Brown insisted that no immediate concession be made to the fuel protesters, reckoning correctly that the coherence of the protest would unravel as time passed. When, in his autumn statement, Brown finally acknowledged the issue, he was hailed. It was a command performance of economic authority.

Brown's handling of the fuel crisis was a microcosm of the two comprehensive spending reviews that dominated the first two years of the government. Brown had his disciplined strategy; he believed it would provide the revenues the government would want for public investment to build up into the first years of the century; he would give no ground. The first review was tough. Ministers who had expected to be able to argue politically for the exemptions and exceptions which are the stuff of spending negotiations with the Treasury found their paths blocked. Defence, in particular, found the Chancellor unsympathetic to their claims for increased spending. But they later found that Blair had been affected by the Kosovo crisis and the performance of senior military figures in it. He was on their side. So the then defence secretary, George Robertson, and Sir Charles Guthrie, the chief of staff, appealed directly to Number 10 over the Chancellor's head. They won. Brown was unconvinced by their arguments, and made it clear to Blair that he did not accept the settlement which the Prime Minister had approved. But of all the decisions in the two comprehensive spending reviews, this was the only significant one in which the Prime Minister most obviously took control. Otherwise, it was Brown's regime that ruled.

As the end of the first term approached, the same minister who confessed that he had found constituency party meetings difficult in the first years said: 'Nowadays, it's all forgotten. Gordon is God.' Apart from his stumble over pensions – the 75p increase was a piece of calculation that, unusually for Brown, misjudged the party mood rather badly – he was beginning to emerge as a consciously redistributive Chancellor. He spoke about poverty, and the minimum wage and the welfare-to-work scheme and more generous pensions – this was the message the party wanted to hear. While Blair began to try to lead his party on to yet another mine-strewn battlefield in the public services, opening up the debate about how best to inject private money without undermining the ethos of state provision, Brown was moving, rhetorically, in another direction. To listen to their speeches you might have imagined them in different governments, or at least in competing factions. They chose to emphasize different things – Blair talking about the need for radical solutions to pressing problems of public funding, Brown about the importance of creating a more equal society. They argued that the two were compatible, two sides of the same coin. If that was true, it was also true that their two faces were on different sides. In making the government's case they often seemed to take the same policy and interpret it in two entirely contrasting ways – Brown emphasizing his objective of pursuing a policy that was a development of what he was almost willing to say was socialist thinking, Blair arguing that if the urge to reform was allowed to slacken the old ways would return and decline would set in. In Labour Party terms they often sounded as if Brown was the traditionalist and Blair the iconoclast.

In the debate about the funding of private services, Brown appeared in his speeches to be the Chancellor who was trying to adapt the policies required in the new century to Labour's traditional instincts. While Blair was as impatient as ever, a weathervane searching for a new wind, Brown was playing the part of the reassurer. Compared with the Brown who alarmed his party after 1997 with his sternness, this was a Chancellor who wanted to reconnect to old networks.

Their public and private attitudes to money make up a prism through which it's possible to glimpse their characters. Brown retains an urge to redistribute wealth, though he has no interest in creating the kind of socialist society to which he was once committed, while Blair, although he argues the same case for 'fairness' and equality of opportunity as Brown, is relaxed about rich people remaining rich. It does not embarrass him.

Many of the Blair government's family problems were connected to money and its place in Labour's life. If it was to be 'New' Labour, surely the old nervousness about the rich must go. But if it was to be 'New' Labour it must also retain an ascetic probity, a sense of a government unbesmirched by the 'Loadsamoney' culture that had become such a part of the prosperous, devil-may-care nineties. In the personalities of its leading pair, it found an ideal solution: Blair the easy-going meritocrat, comfortable holidaying in Tuscan luxury; Brown the image of restraint down to the cut-price champagne at his own wedding.

Wearing their contrasting robes, they often find themselves together on a mission – or in arguing a case – and realize that although their political strength lies in staying together as a pair, they are pushing as hard as they can inside the relationship to nurture their own approaches and their own political personalities. Only by seeming to strain against each other can they claim for

Labour the broad, inclusive, political territory necessary to secure their place in power. In their approach to money, the big tent of politics is shown at its most inclusive. It was a technique, and an expression, that had a very specific origin that owed little to Dunfermline or Sedgefield, however, and rather more to Hope, Arkansas.

9
Brother-in-Arms

Bill Clinton was famous in the White House for losing his temper. He would rage. Especially when he was sinking into the mire of the Monica Lewinsky affair in the last two years of his presidency, he was capable of spectacular explosions which would erupt without warning and turn the President into a red-faced screamer. Blair was stoking up one of these Vesuvial displays during the preparations for the Kosovo war. Those who witnessed one telephone call made from the Oval Office to Blair in May 1999 knew that Clinton was displaying the telltale signs of an approaching storm and, since he and Blair spoke often enough to have dispensed with any need for diplomatic niceties, his staff expected the skies to break open.

The President was calling to remind the Prime Minister of the nature of their relationship. Friends they might be, but one was the leader of a modest European power and the other was President of the United States. Clinton saw no case for sending American ground troops to Kosovo to expel the Serb forces of Slobodan Milosevic until the bombing campaign which had begun in March had done its work – he'd told the American people in a televised speech on the first day of the bombing, 'I do not intend to put our troops in Kosovo to fight a war'. Blair disagreed. He was, according to a close adviser, 'possessed by that war' which he had spoken of as a moral crusade and had decided that, despite the reservations of other European countries and the United States, a ground force should be assembled. But Clinton was incensed. He spoke to Blair, in a conversation described by someone who heard it at the Washington end as 'testy', and the purpose was to remind him who was the senior partner in the operation. American troops would be committed by Clinton, not by Blair.

The conversation was remarkable not because it was tense and deliberately blunt on Clinton's side, but because it was the first time he and Blair had had an important strategic disagreement and, in the end, it occurred without the usual explosion. The President came close to letting loose one of his famous rages, which were kept private and seen only by West Wing staff or political intimates, a group in which Blair could be counted. But he was spared the blast. The call was evidence to those who heard of it in Whitehall and in Washington of how important the relationship had become to both of them. Blair was prepared to push Clinton to the limit; Clinton was prepared to control his temper, even with someone with whom he was accustomed to behave quite naturally and who he knew wouldn't mind hearing him in full ranting mode.

Afterwards, Blair did admit that they had had a frank conversation about his determination to prepare for a ground invasion. 'The bottom line for me was that we can't lose this,' he said in an interview on the American PBS network later that year. He insisted that Clinton had never ruled out using ground troops against Serb forces if they did not withdraw and allow the ethnically cleansed Albanian refugees to retrace the path of their trek through the hills and to return home. He knew, however, that Clinton was deeply reluctant to move, knowing that public opinion was unlikely to support a dangerous campaign and that few Americans had even the fuzziest idea of where or what Kosovo was. The Joint Chiefs of Staff were against a ground assault, and Clinton had no interest in trying to change their minds. Blair was as open about the fact that he believed a ground war might become necessary to back up the air campaign as Clinton was determined that it should never come to that.

The crisis was the moment when their relationship matured. It was also the most dangerous moment to date of Blair's premiership, as he acknowledged to his staff. There was no public appetite for a costly ground war, and in the Labour Party there was deep unease about NATO's airborne campaign against Serbia and Milosevic. After the seventy-eight days of bombing started in March, Blair spoke of the war as a moral duty. 'I was convinced that once we started it, we had to finish it. If we hadn't done so, it would have really given encouragement to dictators everywhere,' he said. He was on a course from which he was not prepared to deviate, and it was Clinton who felt that he had to try to calm the crusader spirit which was evident in Downing Street and the Foreign Office for what he suspected might be a step too far. But in the arguments between London and Washington Clinton had played something of the big brother to Blair.

For each of them the alliance was important. Clinton's staff believe that in the last two years of his presidency he spoke to Blair for longer than to all other world leaders put together. In Downing Street, Clinton is known to have had a huge personal influence on Blair. One of his aides involved in liaison with Washington even claiming that the political links between them ran as deep as any Blair had at home, apart from those with Brown. The connection with Clinton has been one of the most important strands of Blair's premiership, a personal channel that brought him political benefits, particularly in Northern Ireland, and also did a good deal to shape his style. They became so close that when he rang the White House in January 1998 to tell Clinton, 'I'm thinking of you', in the midst of the Lewinsky scandal that had seized Washington and was threatening his presidency, it was more than a polite gesture from a leader doing the right thing.

Apart from fighting a Balkans war, keeping a warlike presence to back up sanctions against Iraq and negotiating in Northern Ireland, they talked more and more as time went on about their own political obsession – the search for a language to describe the politics that they called, vaguely, 'the third way'. They developed an intimate friendship, though Blair had moments of incomprehension at Clinton's sexual escapades and confessed privately that he found some of Clinton's behaviour 'weird'.

Their first encounter was just after Clinton's election in 1992 in the campaign against George Bush Sr in which Clinton had styled himself a New Democrat. Labour had lost the General Election under Kinnock six months before Clinton's victory and Blair and

Brown decided together to go to the United States in January 1993 to try to identify the trick they had missed. The Democrats had successfully challenged a sitting right-of-centre President who was campaigning on a promise of 'no new taxes'. Clinton had somehow neutralized the tax question, appealing to traditional Democrat voters with an economic programme promising help for the lower-paid, while reassuring vast swathes of relatively prosperous suburban America where Republicans had been winning elections for a generation that his social thinking was no threat. It would be odd if there weren't lessons to be learnt from Clinton's experience. And anyway, Clinton was about to be President of the United States. So the New Labour embryos decided to go.

At home, their leader, John Smith, was not pleased. When reports began to come from Washington about Labour's 'coming men' riding into town, he rang Mandelson in a fury. What were Blair and Brown up to? Although Mandelson had just been elected for the first time in Hartlepool and was no longer a party official, Smith knew that he would be aware of exactly what was happening on the trip. He had always been suspicious of Mandelson, and immune to his charms, but this was an angrier Smith than Mandelson had ever experienced. The burden of the leader's complaint was that Blair and Brown were taking it upon themselves to import American ideas to the Labour Party. Why? He wanted to know the whole story, because he was suspicious that they were up to something. Of course, he was right. Smith bluntly rejected the need to study the Democratic example. The media baron and Labour supporter Clive Hollick had received a similar response six months earlier when, inspired by the Democrats, he wrote a memo called 'Campaign '96', in which he argued for 'a new Labour Party, new policies on tax and trade union links'. He presented these findings at a meeting with John Smith, Murray Elder and David Ward, Smith's policy adviser. Smith's reply reflected his confidence that Labour did not need to embrace the risk of radical change but could just wait for the Conservatives to implode: 'This is all very interesting, but I think you will find that it will be our turn next time.'

But Blair and Brown were plunging into bracing waters in Washington, refreshing themselves with the feeling of being among winners. From the moment they arrived there it seemed inevitable that the place would influence their outlook. The Clinton phenomenon, even then, seemed to Blair to be the kind of transformation in a political atmosphere that Labour should one day try to achieve. For Brown, his book-bags bulging with political biographies and economic texts, it was his dream city: everyone talked about politics, all the time. Obsessives were welcome. Brown would charge through the bookshops like a hoover, scooping up every political commentary he could find, while Blair was getting to know the diplomat at the British Embassy on Massachusetts Avenue who had been assigned to the Clinton campaign as the Foreign Office watcher, Jonathan Powell. Blair and the gangly, bubble-haired Powell, who had helped to plan the visit, have a natural physical symmetry. They gesticulate. Their enthusiasm is wide-eyed and they are instinctive people-watchers and gossips. So the two found themselves feeding each other's enthusiasm. Politics in that freezing January seemed fun. Washington was expectant. Back in London, Labour had nothing to look forward to, except five or so years of opposition. A weary, grey Kinnock was gone after nine embattled years as leader and although the two shadow Cabinet ministers knew that they would prosper under Smith's tutelage, and although they still counted themselves his close friends, they also expected a period in the party when their modernization plans were less prized in the leader's office than they had been. So they focused on Clinton: how had he fought a campaign in which he said there was one issue – the famous sign on his wall said 'it's the economy, stupid' – while dealing with the tax question that had bedevilled the two last Democratic presidential candidates and had haunted Kinnock? They wanted cheerful news for a change.

The trip was also a first, symbolic break with party thinking at home. In retrospect, Blair has identified it as a moment when a new vista opened up. Clinton was managing to harness some old Democrat principles of 'fairness' to a social agenda that reassured middle-income voters that they wouldn't find his administration a drag on their ambition – exactly the message that Blair and Brown would decipher and imprint on the Labour Party. But the intellectual departure would not be welcomed universally at home.

Two days after Clinton's inauguration, Prescott appeared on *Weekend World* on ITV and dismissed the Democrats as an outfit with nothing to teach Labour. Criticizing the advertising techniques and outside advisers who had clustered round Kinnock's office up to the election, he laid into the Democrats for engaging in cosmetic politics. 'It's not about strengthening a party – all the ideas from Clinton are an elite few running a party on the basis of the information they get from the polls. That is not the way the Labour Party has been run, and while we've tried it in the last couple of elections, it does seem that we've lost, doesn't it?' Prescott particularly enjoyed making the attack on a programme on which Mandelson had worked as a producer in the early eighties. He warmed to his theme: 'I do not think it's been proven that Clinton won the election because he broke his contacts with the trade unions . . . We've gone chasing the extra two per cent from the Liberals on this basis: if we get rid of the vested interest . . . we could have proportional representation. This has dominated our thinking. That is Clintonism.' Whatever it was, Blair and Brown were keen on it.

Some groundwork had been done over the previous five years. After the 1987 campaign one of the Democrats' veteran pollsters, Joe Napolitan, had written a report for Labour which expressed surprise that it was not employing the relatively new techniques of focus group research which, he argued, would identify much more clearly the voters' reasons for refusing to turn to Labour. In the years that followed, Philip Gould developed those techniques and by the early nineties, to the sound of contemptuous snorts from some on the left who saw them as another piece of Mandelsonian wizardry, it was established as Labour's way.

After the '92 election, American advice poured in. Stan Greenberg was the Democrat pollster who turned up in 1993 to try to impart the lessons of the Clinton campaign, on which Gould had worked. Between them they persuaded Blair and Brown that Clinton's experience could explain how to approach the economic issue. Labour had to resist promising what people did not believe they could deliver, but at the same time convince them they could promise them opportunity. What could be simpler? With the evidence of what the Conservatives had successfully pinned on Labour in the campaign ('Labour's tax bombshell'), it was this advice that helped to persuade them that the promises of Labour in opposition had to be underpinned by a commitment to fiscal discipline that voters would believe.

The other message from the Clinton campaign was, of course, that in fighting against an incumbent who was struggling with the economy there was no point in devoting every speech and every statement to criticism that sounded negative. There had to be 'hope', a natural word for Clinton to use for the corny reason that he came from Hope, Arkansas. So when Blair and Brown went to Washington they encountered a campaign team that had somehow translated the language of attack – against the Bush economic record – into something that seemed uplifting. It was what Labour had never been able to do at any time since Blair and Brown were in their early teens.

Both were fascinated by American politics. Brown's first visit had been to the Democratic Convention in San Francisco in 1984, where Walter Mondale was the presidential nominee preparing a challenge to Ronald Reagan that led to disaster. He said taxes would have to go up. His defeat gave a rampant Reagan a landslide second term. Brown watched the convention from the floor, absorbed in the politics of the Democrats' effort to find a way of thwarting Reagan, the Great Conservative. It was a catastrophe comparable to Labour's 1983 failure against Thatcher, but there was much to learn.

The first thing Brown heard when he arrived in San Francisco from London and stood at the back of the convention hall was a speech from Jesse Jackson talking about the young who felt dispossessed and in despair. Jackson said he wanted them to have 'hope in their brains, not dope in their veins'. Brown was aware that this was a preacher's style more suited to Harlem than downtown Dunfermline, but he repeated the phrase for days, apparently fascinated by how such a glib formulation could be turned to political uses. The other memorable speech at that convention was the speech of the Governor of New York, Mario Cuomo, about poverty and opportunity which brought him national celebrity and gave some lustre to an event which would otherwise be remembered only as a defeat in the making.

Brown's visit, which ended in his first immersion in Washington, made a profound impression on him. He saw a Democratic Party going through many of the same contortions that Labour was suffering, though without the implacable institutional party difficulties, and it was in the United States that he began to try to find ways of resolving the conflicts between his instincts as a socialist and the economic world that was beginning to take shape in the eighties. When the century ended he was still using the United States as a sounding board. Apart from his inevitable involvement with the George W. Bush administration, and the obsession shared with every finance minister for each utterance by Alan Greenspan, the chairman of the Federal Reserve, it was to America that Brown turned for new ideas – on welfare, particularly.

The 1984 visit wasn't simply a quick dip in America for Brown. It was obvious to all of us there that he was starting an affair with the place which has gone on ever since. Though he found himself in San Francisco dressed more for Edinburgh than California, it didn't stop him heading for the mountains of Yosemite National Park, in a suit. By the time he got back to London a few weeks later he was hooked on the USA.

Between them Blair and Brown were a pair who found the Americans at the right moment. Brown had fought four elections for Labour, the first as a losing candidate, and Blair three. They were impatient for a Labour government.

The Democrat evidence encouraged them in their view that Labour could not afford to wait for Major's government to make mistakes and expect to reap the automatic benefit. Smith was utterly committed to some aspects of party reform, but Brown and Blair felt that the years ahead might be overcautious. Smith's gifts at the despatch box were well known, but the lesson from the United States was that bashing Major would not be enough. The 1992 conference had been turned from the familiar Labour post-election wake into something different by Black Wednesday and the chaos of exit from the ERM. Politics was awash with stories of Major having come close to breakdown (much exaggerated), of the Chancellor, Norman Lamont, 'singing in the bath' despite the disaster, delighting in the break with fixed exchange rates. The Conservative government was sagging on the ropes. Labour enjoyed a false flush of optimism.

But neither Blair nor Brown believed that the next election could be won simply by claiming that Labour would be better than a bad bunch. Brown, appointed shadow Chancellor by Smith, had already decided that he should maintain a ruthless command of the party's spending plans. It was a decision which was reinforced by the 1993 visit to Washington.

They were hypnotized by Clinton's early days. And paradoxically, Blair absorbed one early lesson that had little to do with winning elections. After his first visit in 1993, during which Clinton's supporters had been talking of the whirlwind first months about to start in the White House, he watched in fascination as the new President stumbled into a series of political elephant traps and seemed about to throw away the advantages of goodwill he had won in the campaign. He became embroiled, most notably, in a row about gays in the military as a result of his desire to fulfil a campaign pledge to some of the interest groups which had supported his campaign. It turned into an ugly social battle which opened up old wounds and gave Clinton, the new Commander-in-Chief, unnecessary trouble with a military establishment that was already suspicious of him. Alongside that problem he found himself in a pickle over the MX missile programme. In the White House he had made the blunder of appointing a schoolboy friend, Mack McLarty, as chief of staff without establishing first whether he was up to the job. He wasn't. The place was running at half speed. From across the Atlantic, Blair was bemused. He had expected Slick Willie and he saw Blundering Bill. After he became leader he remembered this as clearly as he remembered Clinton's skill in the campaign. He told the shadow Cabinet before the 1997 election: 'Never forget that it's easy to throw it all away in six months.'

Clinton's slide to the Democrats' disaster in the mid-term elections of 1994 seemed to be an undoing of the campaign themes that he used to such effect in 1992. He'd been hammered by the populist Republican Newt Gingrich and his anti-government message, all tax cuts and lower federal spending. Clinton's response in the next two years was to absorb the evident rage of the electorate and, to the anger of some of his strongest supporters, to tailor his social and economic policies to assuage those feelings. Liberals were despondent, but fortunately for him the Gingrich revolution on Capitol Hill spiralled out of control. Clinton was able to force the Republicans into a Budget crisis which at one point briefly shut down the whole Federal Government (because there was no authority to pay day-to-day bills), after which he was able to present himself as the defender of government programmes like medicare and social security against the radicals of the right. It saw him through the 1996 re-election campaign.

Blair's first proper meeting with Clinton was in the spring of that election year in Washington. The agent of the rendezvous was Sidney Blumenthal, a writer on *The New Yorker* who had become convinced in the eighties that the Governor of Arkansas, though young and Washington-innocent, was a good bet for 1992. Blumenthal played his hunch in the magazine, got to know the Clintons and such was the chemistry that he found himself translated eventually to the White House as special assistant to the President after Clinton's 1996 victory. There he sat in the boiler room of the Clinton political operation, a natural adviser and campaigner, gripped by the melodramatic dips and dives of American politics. He comes from Chicago, where at the age of twelve he spent his first campaign as a precinct runner for the famed Democratic Party machine, and saw his first presidential candidate at a torchlit Kennedy rally in 1960. Leaving newspapers for magazines in the early nineties, Blumenthal was becoming more interested in Bill Clinton than journalism. Having met Blair on his 1993 visit he was a natural host in 1996 when the Labour leader came to Washington and he gave a dinner for Blair at his home to introduce him to Hillary Clinton. The next day, Blair spent an hour at the White House with her husband.

When Blumenthal joined Clinton's staff, part of his job was to develop the network with Labour which had been growing for years, in the expectation that Blair would be in Downing Street within a year. The relationship was carefully planned, and was certainly helped by Clinton's desire to make a contrast with the White House–Downing Street relationship in the Major years.

It had been undermined by Clinton's stubborn belief that during his 1992 campaign Major's government had helped his Republican opponents to scour Home Office records to find any information that might be held on Clinton from his time as a Rhodes Scholar in Oxford in the sixties. The story, broken by Blumenthal himself during the 1992 campaign, was that the Republicans hoped to turn up something embarrassing, perhaps a drugs revelation, that would damage Clinton. No matter that Major denied it, the Home Secretary denied it and the American ambassador in London at the time – Ray Seitz – denied it. Clinton believed that there had been a dirty deal, and he never forgot it. As a result his relationship with Major was civil, and at times verged on warmth, but was never close. When Blair came along in 1997, Clinton knew not only that they shared some political ideas about how to harness a market economy for public purposes but that whoever Blair was, he was not Major. The consequence for Blair was an even jauntier welcome than he might otherwise have received.

While Blair, as opposition leader, was matching Clinton and getting regular memos from Philip Gould on Clinton's re-election campaign, Brown was developing his own distinctive network across the Atlantic. He was especially fascinated by Robert Reich, Clinton's first Secretary of Labor, who left the administration in the first term fed up with Clinton's paling social objectives and apparent fiscal conservatism. His willingness to go as far as he did in compromising with the Republican majority on Capitol Hill over the federal budget distressed Reich, who became disillusioned with the drift. In the Labor Department, he was well known for his frustration and, for the e-mails which arrived regularly from his wife, a left-wing economist, which often circulated round the office. One of the regular refrains was: 'Your President is an asshole.' Reich went.

In office, while Blair developed his own relationship with Clinton (Chancellors not being involved in wars, peace negotiations and missiles) Brown renewed his own links. His key contact became Larry Summers, now president of Harvard, and Clinton's last Treasury Secretary. Summers is a large, jowly, jovial man who was known in the White House as a somewhat shambling figure, whose shirt tail often dangled behind him. He liked Brown when they became involved in the inevitable business of G8 summits and the IMF at which the administration and the Blair government were always doing deals. Summers had taught Ed Balls when he was a Kennedy Scholar at Harvard in the eighties and he had first met Brown in the course of the 1993 visit when he was deputy Treasury Secretary to Lloyd Bentsen.

Brown became fascinated by the American economists who were in Summers's circle. He began to take holidays on Cape Cod. Anyone who thought Brown was heading for Massachusetts for a spot of whale-watching or gentle surfing on the Atlantic swell was mistaken. He would head off to a small town called Wellfleet, on the curve of the tail of Cape Cod, south of Provincetown. This was the summer home to a group of American economists who cluster there, like painters at St Ives but with calculators instead of oils in their beach bags.

Labour MPs would not be surprised to find Brown there, as happy as a sandboy. Among those who go there for the summer are the economists Barry Bluestone and Bob Kuttner, who is sometimes described as the nearest American equivalent to Old Labour. Summers comes down from Harvard and is in some ways the centrepiece of this beachside salon. It is a congenial atmosphere for Brown: books, talk, social theories, with the odd tennis match to stretch a muscle or two. He couldn't imagine a happier way of spending a summer holiday.

In his effort to build a bridge between his intellectual background and the marketplace in which the Treasury has to operate he finds American ideas on welfare stimulating. How do you balance an assault on welfare dependency with proper care for social provision? How can a tax system be geared to encourage enterprise but lift the low-paid, especially against the background of an American tradition tilted against direct provision by the state? His Treasury officials say that Brown comes back from the United States, every time, as if he's found a new supply of adrenalin.

Blair has not been to Wellfleet. It would not be his scene. A beach barbecue with economists, with their Laffer curves and growth theories and graphs, comes near to his idea of hell. Instead, he had Clinton.

The President rang Blair on the night of his election in his car travelling from Stansted airport to the Royal Festival Hall for the victory party. Jonathan Powell had kept in close touch with Clinton's staff after he left the Diplomatic Service to become Blair's chief of staff in 1994 and from the first day in Downing Street the channel to the White House was open, with the telephone on Blair's desk marked with the single word 'Washington' in frequent use from the start. Between those who would work in Number 10 and those in power in Washington there was already a patchwork of contacts. Philip Gould had worked with the Democrats' pollsters for years. Now the President's and Prime Minister's staffs were intermingling.

The significance for Blair was not simply in having a President with whom he could have a good personal relationship and whom he could persuade, for example, to throw his energies into the Northern Ireland negotiations, but in feeling that he had a kindred political spirit. Clinton saw himself as the inheritor of a progressive tradition that embraced Franklin D. Roosevelt and Harry Truman and, before them at the start of the twentieth century, Teddy Roosevelt and Woodrow Wilson. The essence of it, in his view, was a determination to shape change rather than be shaped by it.

In a speech at Princeton University in October 2000 Clinton quoted FDR, saying that orthodox government had to be replaced with 'bold, persistent experimentation'. In the same speech he argued that progressive politics wasn't defined by a particular set of policy programmes but by the underlying belief that new economic and social conditions always demanded 'a new approach to government'. Clinton's approach to government changed several times in his eight years in the White House, veering from liberal to quite conservative on the old scale, but his argument was an appealing one to a British Prime Minister who was anxious to break away from what he thought was a stultifying tradition in his party. To Blair, anxious to develop in office some kind of intellectual momentum that could build on the party modernization that had begun a decade before, Clinton seemed heaven-sent.

But there was much less enthusiasm elsewhere on the Labour front bench. Prescott had clambered on board, but he was still suspicious of modernization. He equated closeness to Clinton with a desire, as he had put it in his *Weekend World* interview four years before, to break the party's links with the trade unions. This was a struggle, he thought, 'for the heart and soul of the Labour Party'.

He was right to believe that Blair wanted to move on from the removal of Clause IV from the party constitution to a reconstruction of the party. He felt no commitment to the place of the unions in its councils, which he thought anachronistic. He wanted to pitch a 'big tent' into which, as Clinton had done with the Democrats, he could persuade people who felt no visceral connection to the party. The enlightened self-interest of voters was to be the engine of reform. If the Labour Party spoke to them about their aspirations, they would support it without worrying about whether they were 'socialists' or not. These were the ideas that demanded Blair part company with the left of his party for good. A *Tribune* editorial said that his purpose was to make Labour 'even more bland in pursuit of elusive affluent working-class and centrist middle-class votes'. He might not want to accept the adjective bland, but Blair would not deny his search for those lost votes. If the Clinton experience helped, so be it.

The criticism of the 'third way' approach from the left was that it appeared to be insubstantial, maybe even vacuous. Blair, it was argued, had understood some important lessons about campaigning and public appeal from Clinton, but was there a genuine new approach to economic management and social change in the two countries, as was claimed?

The language Blair used to describe government that steered a course between abandoned ideas of state socialism and a society of unfettered free markets seemed nebulous. It was neither old left nor new right: but was it something which was best described in the negative, a prescription that got its character from what it *wasn't*? Even Clinton, speaking a few weeks before leaving office, described the concept in terms that seemed almost infinitely malleable and incapable of giving offence to anyone: 'a way back to enduring values; a way beyond a government profoundly indifferent to people's problems; a way forward to meet the challenges of today and tomorrow'. This was the kind of formulation that Brown found infuriatingly vague, all aspiration and no bite. He has never liked the 'third way' as a description of his own policy, preferring to leave the label to Blair.

Debate with Clinton about the future of left-of-centre politics went on through their negotiations over Northern Ireland and the Balkans and the worries over the state of Russia, the three subjects that occupied most of their time together. In Ireland, Blair was able to play to Clinton's obsessive interest in hands-on negotiations; Clinton happily plunged into the thicket of Belfast politics and spent three years engaged intimately with leading figures in all the parties, turning his St Patrick's Day parties in the White House into outings for almost anyone in Dublin or Belfast who had a connection with the peace talks. He took great care to include the Ulster Unionists, with David Trimble a regular visitor, and he smoothed paths for them on Capitol Hill which had previously been blocked. Having granted visas to Gerry Adams of Sinn Fein during Major's time (against the firm advice of his ambassador in London) he was in a position to exert some influence on the Republicans, which he did several times on Blair's behalf. By the time he left office it had not been enough to produce the progress of decommissioning which Blair needed, but in their valedictory messages to each other Blair acknowledged – accurately – that without Clinton's energetic absorption in the process the Good Friday Agreement of 1998 might well have been still-born.

The practical Clinton was a valuable friend. Blair, however, got more from him than assistance in tight spots. He was a Prime Minister who had never seen the inside of a ministerial office before he took office and indeed had only visited Downing Street once before May 1997 – when Major invited him to a reception for Clinton. So ready access to the White House was an extraordinary bonus. They behaved together as if they had been operating in the international arena for years, even when Blair was still learning how European summits worked (or didn't). Anyone observing Blair's first visit to the White House in February 1998 was granted a vivid picture of the enthusiasm of Clinton's embrace.

Clinton held the biggest dinner that the White House had seen since Richard Nixon left office. It was deliberately staged to surround Blair with glamour and glitz. The tables in the East Room were set with 'Eisenhower gold baseplates, Reagan china and Kennedy Morgantown crystal'. The vermeil and silver historical candelabra centrepieces were surrounded by hypericum berries with gold tapered candles.

The Blairs stayed until midnight, with the 240 guests. Clinton's Hollywood gang was out in force with a surprised Blair finding himself hugged by Barbra Streisand in the White House lobby. Stevie Wonder and Elton John did a cabaret in an auditorium erected above the White House swimming pool. The high command of the Senate and the House of Representatives was in attendance and Clinton's Cabinet hobnobbed with some slightly overawed Blair ministers who had come out with him for a seminar at the White House on the Third Way. One of them, Alan Milburn, announced that he discovered that in the official guest house across Lafayette Square from the White House (with the appropriate name of Blair House) he was sleeping in Eisenhower's bed. No one knew whether or not to believe him. After it was over, and Blair was heading to Camp David for the weekend, he remarked to an acquaintance: 'Not bad, eh?' and laughed. Clinton had put on a show.

Blair also witnessed the President's handling of pressure at the height of the Lewinsky scandal, which had reached a new peak just as he arrived for his official visit. Clinton's popularity was plunging, his critics were advancing on him in force, and he was facing the American press for the first time for weeks (since the obligatory East Room press conference for a visiting head of government couldn't be cancelled). As he waited with Clinton in an anteroom before entering the arena, Blair told his colleagues later, he was astonished by the President's seeming calm. Knowing that his presidency was in peril, and knowing that his dissemblings about Lewinsky were almost certain to emerge some day, he nonetheless managed to behave as if this were a normal press conference on another Friday morning. To Blair's surprise he betrayed no sign of nervousness, let alone panic. A few minutes later, at the twin podia in the East Room, Blair looked much the more nervous of the two, even when the CNN White House correspondent Wolf Blitzer put one of the celebrated questions of the whole affair to Clinton: 'Mr President, what is your message to the Lewinsky family today?'

Puzzled as he was by Clinton's handling of the scandal, just as he was bewildered at the stupidity of the affair with Lewinsky, Blair saw in Washington the opportunity to establish a powerful personal alliance that was invaluable to him. He was the least experienced leader in the bigger countries of the European Union, yet his relationship with Clinton was by far the strongest. His willingness to press Clinton on the ground troops issue was evidence of how he understood the advantages of his position.

At the height of the Balkan crisis, by chance, NATO leaders met in Washington to celebrate the 50th anniversary of the Alliance. Cook went with Blair and so did George Robertson, who would end up as Blair's candidate for the NATO secretary-generalship, with Clinton's strong support. In this conflict, to the despair of elements of the Labour left who were appalled by the decision to launch air strikes against Serbia, just as they were trying to persuade Blair (with no success at all) to change his support for sanctions in Iraq, Blair found himself lifted by the challenges of action in the field. He was well into his second year in power, and those around him noted a new phase in his style. He was less nervous about attacks from his critics in the party than ever before and was revelling in his foreign role which, in Kosovo, would be bound to stir up more criticism. Despite the horrors of the Bosnian war in the mid-nineties, there were many Labour MPs who would not support the bombing of Serbia. Sixteen of them signed a Commons motion condemning NATO's policy.

The first half of 1999 was an extraordinary period for Blair. In

January he went on an official visit to be received by Nelson Mandela in Pretoria, in May he received the Charlemagne Prize in Aachen and said he wanted to end 'uncertainty and Europhobia' in Britain, and in the intervening period he found himself in what was called 'a war of liberation' in Kosovo. After the Albanian refugees began to return to Kosovo under the protection of NATO troops in July, the reconstruction of a civil society would prove difficult, violent and long but Blair became so committed to the campaign against Milosevic that he emerged in those months as the most hawkish of the European leaders. He was pushing Europe, and he was pushing the Americans. One White House official told a senior British correspondent in Washington just before the NATO conference in April: 'The leader of this NATO coalition isn't Bill Clinton, it's Tony Blair.'

He became convinced, despite the nervousness of the Foreign Office, that ground troops would be needed in Kosovo if refugees were to come home in sufficient numbers to justify the action. The air campaign would not be enough. The displaced had fled through the mountains, to Albania and Macedonia, and the issue was whether the Serb forces in Kosovo could be stopped by an air campaign, with troops coming in afterwards, or whether there would be a ground war. The difficulties were huge, with terrain which was inhospitable to any quick action on the ground, and Clinton was clearly disturbed by the enthusiasm which Blair displayed for a ground war when he came to Washington in April for the NATO summit. The State Department and the Pentagon were alarmed, and Clinton was told that public opinion – the barometer that always hovered somewhere in sight – was not ready.

The American strategy in Kosovo had been implemented by General Wesley Clark, who was sacked six weeks after the campaign ended successfully. He reflected in his memoirs that this was the war that Washington did not want. The White House was intensely nervous, the State Department and the Pentagon were at loggerheads, and the President simply wanted to avoid being drawn in too deeply. In that context, Blair's urgings to Clinton about the prospects for a ground campaign were unwelcome.

The crisis passed with Milosevic's decision to draw back, under the pressure of the air campaign and diplomatic muscle from the Russians, and the crossing of the Macedonian border into Kosovo by the international force in the early summer was an almost bloodless exercise. In the effort to restore civil society in Kosovo there was much violence to come – the KFOR force of troops found none of their subsequent manoeuvres as easy as the entry into Kosovo itself – but for Blair the episode demonstrated the importance of clarity and determination. To his critics it was exactly as they expected when he invited Margaret Thatcher to Downing Street soon after his election and praised her because 'she knew the direction she was going in'. He had, in their view, succumbed to the temptations of semi-presidential power. On this occasion, however, the real President had been more cautious. Blair has never subsequently expressed regret for having tried to persuade Clinton to commit ground troops. Indeed, since he thinks that Clinton was persuadable (although there is no objective evidence for the belief) he wonders if he should have pressed harder.

The Kosovo episode as a piece of prime ministerial politics rather than military strategy is an intriguing part of the Blair story. To Cabinet colleagues around him it was the time when he found his confidence. Not all of them approved of his enthusiasm. 'I couldn't believe how fond he became of the generals,' one of them said at the time. 'It happens to all of them I suppose, but with Tony it was very quick. He loves the way they work.' By the time NATO troops assembled on the Macedonian border with Kosovo at the beginning of June, Blair was immersed in the politics of war. 'He was energized by it every morning. It was one of the periods – like the Northern Ireland negotiations – where he became completely absorbed and thought of very little else.' Critics found the leadership style a little messianic, and the left began to assemble its caricature of the Prime Minister as a trigger-happy sidekick of the United States who was content sometimes to criticize the White House for hesitation or lack of purpose. The picture is caught in the Kosovo cartoons of Steve Bell, Blair's most savage assailant, in the *Guardian* where the Prime Minister appears as a bulging-eyed Dr Strangelove driven by demons to launch another air raid or press another button.

When a fifty-mile-long military convoy moved into place in the darkness of a June night in the Macedonian hills ready to enter Kosovo, the British troops squeezed into the trucks did not feel they were part of an American-led NATO force. They spoke of it as Blair's campaign. At first light on Saturday 12 June the order was given to move at 4 a.m., on a balmy morning in the hills. The first sound was of a huge swarm of helicopters coming out of the gloom, Chinooks with trucks and armoured cars suspended under them filling the sky. The sight was extraordinary. At the front of the convoy, at the Blace crossing where the first entry into Kosovo would be made, a soldier who knew his cinema and knew his Prime Minister recalled the scene from *Apocalypse Now* where the helicopters fly in to the sound of the *Ride of the Valkyries*. 'The question this morning,' he said as he prepared to drive over the border with his men, is: 'Who does it better? Francis Ford Coppola or Alastair Campbell?'

Blair saw the campaign as a moral duty. He wasn't dragged into it. He leapt at it. Although the Kosovo campaign did not recast the political landscape at home, for him it was the first moment of danger in Downing Street. Even with a majority of 179 a war that went wrong would be fatal. If the war had become a catastrophe for NATO it would not have been a responsibility which Blair could have passed to anyone else. The decisions were his, and he was the leader in the Alliance who had become the most hawkish. And it had become especially obvious that Brown was not prepared to connect himself to the military crisis in the Balkans. Around Blair it was asked if the Chancellor's silence was the action of a minister concerned to preserve diplomatic propriety or a minister saying, once again, you're on your own. Without Kosovo, Blair's subsequent premiership might have had a different tone. It helped to persuade him that Downing Street should be the centre of a 'command and control' administration, not simply the enabler of collegiate government. In the first half of 1999 the hesitant, cautious Blair of the first two years, talking radically but proceeding gingerly in many policy areas, changed in the course of the military campaign. The Prime Minister with no experience was now a Washington intimate who had tangled with a President in war. In Germany and France he was seen as a restless (and perhaps reckless) leader with a greater relish for action than they had expected.

The surge of energy that clearly affected Blair during the Kosovo campaign was not entirely beneficial to him. He was different from the Blair who had taken Clinton's call of congratulations on 2 May 1997. With someone else in the White House, without the Balkan crisis, without the fascination for American campaign techniques which he was importing for the Labour Party, the Blair years would have taken a much more tentative course. Clinton was the Big Friend who made a difference. Only Thatcher's relationship with Reagan in the post-war era compared with the Blair–Clinton alliance.

John Prescott's worries about Clintonization were becoming flesh. Blair was talking to the White House night and day and Clinton was acting as a supplementary Northern Ireland Secretary in trying to keep the Good Friday Agreement alive. And in the Treasury Brown was nurturing his own American influences. They were as strong as Blair's, but they were inevitably absorbed elsewhere than in the Oval Office and its environs, where only Prime Ministers are allowed to do their deals. Each of them was revealing an absorption in Clinton's America, Blair as a student of the exercise of presidential power and Brown as the Chancellor who had a cultural fascination with the temple of capitalism and its high priests, especially Alan Greenspan. Their government was doomed to fret about Europe, like all its predecessors, but in adopting models for government they had become Atlanticists. The American experience revealed them as they are – Brown at the beach, but with economists talking markets and politics, and Blair in Washington, itching to play his role on the biggest stage, a map of the world.

PART FOUR

Rough guide to the Brownies

10
Friends

One night in 1998, just before the World Cup began in France, Gordon Brown was entertaining the Scotland football manager, Craig Brown, and some of his players to wish them good luck. He had filled the first-floor reception room in Number 11 with friends and acquaintances. Half of Scotland seemed to be there, and the joint was jumping. Brown made a cheery speech (with the traditional misplaced optimism) and so did Donald Dewar, then Scottish Secretary. The Prime Minister was standing by the door, having just slipped in without fuss. Someone said to him: 'Great gathering.' He laughed and said: 'It certainly is. The alternative government?'

Brown pulled Blair into the throng and they worked the crowd together, the Prime Minister's throwaway line forgotten in the hubbub. It had certainly been a joke, but one that evidently leapt naturally to Blair's lips, without much effort. Brown was in his element, his court at play. And Blair, whose own court is just as important to him, had understood the scene the moment he walked in. They were swept up together a moment later, mingling as best friends, with Brown (who had been a resolute travelling fan at the fiascos and passing moments of excitement at Scotland World Cup matches since the seventies) indulging in what seemed like some good-natured patronizing of his neighbour and guest. They were with friends. But whose friends?

There is no parallel in the modern era in Britain for the rival gangs of supporters who follow Blair and Brown. Although most successful politicians can count on an assemblage of loyalists and camp-followers who are willing to fight their cause year after year

– it is almost impossible to survive for long at the top without one – the role of friends in the relationship between these two is remarkable. Each depends on a group of close supporters, connected to a wider army, and they have survived as distinct armies in government. Indeed, one of the characteristics of the relationship is that power has not brought the two courts together but has tended to exaggerate their individual characters. They exert such a powerful influence on their two leaders, and the atmosphere inside is so intense, that they have become as much the architects of the relationship as Blair and Brown themselves.

At moments of crisis each man turns inwards to his supporters. In Number 10 and its environs Blair has four or five intimates, led by Alastair Campbell and Anji Hunter, who circle him from morning to night. In the Treasury, Brown depends in the same way on Ed Balls, his personal secretary Sue Nye and Ed Miliband. Beyond these inner rings are the orbits of friends and political supporters with relatively little overlap between their respective constellations. After the 2001 election, for example, Campbell, Hunter and Blair's political secretary Sally Morgan (elevated to a peerage and a ministerial job for the second term) all knew that Robin Cook was to be moved from the Foreign Office before Brown did.

The two personalities have created this universe, because they crave intimacy and privacy. When they are not together they enter their own worlds, which seem to have separate existences inside the government. Blair's aides work for a man, not a team of ministers; in Brown's office every speech is crafted to build up the Chancellor, not the government. The duopoly, bringing together two self-contained men with their own ambitions and pride, means that parallel teams were bound to spring up. The result was rivalry.

When the fuel protesters managed to summon up chaos from nowhere in September 2000, Blair and Brown had to decide quickly how to respond. From the Treasury came one interpretation: 'Blair's panicking. Gordon's going to have to sort it out.' From Number 10, a different line. 'Gordon's got to get this one right. Tony understands how serious this is.' Afterwards, the argument from the Blair camp was that he had managed the crisis, getting Brown to make the modest concessions that would get the tankers moving again. From Brown's side, it was said that the prime ministerial hand had to be held and his nerve steadied (the more convincing story). At every turn, the supporting chorus picks up its champion's theme and sends out the signal. In a government with two centres of power, there was no alternative. They were doomed to compete.

With two men who have a great capacity to inspire personal loyalty, any competition is bound to be passionate. But in the groups of friends one in particular has given the rivalry an ongoing emotional instability. Mandelson's dispute with Brown was one of the obstacles around which Blair had to construct his government, as awkward as if it had been a physical barrier built across Downing Street.

The first election campaign imposed its own discipline, and the early days in government were marked by a studied civility between Brown and Mandelson as if distant memories of the old days were being revived. But it was only a brief interlude. The pattern had been set in the opposition years and it was still the underlying template of government. Many ministers who've had enough proximity to the three of them to get a glimpse of the passions have chosen the word 'marriage' to describe the setting, because they're struck by the instinctive pull that Blair and Brown have for each other and the sense of obligation that lies between them, and also because they see Mandelson as the complicating agent in the *ménage*, a figure who fascinates each of them almost, but not quite, as much as they fascinate each other.

Blair has been tempted into using the word 'marriage' himself once or twice, but only in private. He dislikes it as a description, hardly surprisingly. He cannot, however, stop some of those around him looking at the bonds that tie him to Brown and Mandelson as links which they suspect that he feels (or fears) are as indissoluble in politics as is the anchor in his private life that binds him exceptionally strongly to his family.

The friends of Blair and Brown circulate around the separate points of this triangle, and over the years they have absorbed the passions that it contains. In turn, they have given back to the two men loyalties which are coloured by the tempestuous quality of the relationship and one consequence has been a heightened atmosphere and lots of trouble. Mandelson has never been the leader of a gang and has made his relationships one by one – close friends they may become, but they are not friends who run as a pack. It's possible, by contrast, to see Blair and Brown as the street fighters in *West Side Story*, leading the Jets and the Sharks through the alleyways on some new adventure, all flying fists and exuberant yells. There's always a scrap to be had, and always a new buzz to enjoy with the gang.

After one Budget a story spread around Whitehall that Blair had taken Brown to Chequers to work over his Budget speech because the Prime Minister thought it needed a new tone. From the Treasury came quite a different tale, of Downing Street ideas overruled by the Chancellor, who alone had the strategic vision. That kind of running commentary on their personal dealings became the daily conversation of Whitehall. Where the truth lay, or whether the story was accidental or malign, became increasingly difficult to know. Blair and Brown dealt with each other so much, on the phone and in person, and kept so much of their conversations to themselves, that they preserved the mystique of whatever passed between them. Even if there hadn't been a row, no one could prove that there hadn't been. In politics, a remorselessly speculative trade, that meant gossip and trouble.

Their friends were their sustenance and sometimes their weakness. The most striking characteristic of these groups, and the telling evidence of their importance, is that they have hardly changed in years.

When Blair reshaped Downing Street after his re-election, taking another step towards the creation of a Prime Minister's department in all but name, it was no break with the practices of the first term. The three pillars of his reconstruction were Jonathan Powell, Alastair Campbell and Anji Hunter. Blair was building on the existing foundations. It would be the old gang who would make his office more powerful and it was clearly intended that it should direct policy from the centre in an even more rigorous fashion than in the first four years. He told one questioner on a train journey during the election campaign that he was still frustrated after four years with the sluggishness of Whitehall, using the slightly chilling phrase: 'The Prime Minister's writ must run.' The foot and mouth crisis, in particular, convinced Blair in spring 2001 that the government machine was antiquated and he solicited outside advice from business and academia about how best to rebore its cylinders. Business people like Don Cruickshank, chairman of the London Stock Exchange, were asked for prescriptions. Blair appointed Wendy Thomson, from the independent Audit Commission, to run the reform programme for the civil service. But inside Downing Street he turned to old friends.

He has known Anji Hunter since they were teenagers in Scotland. Apart from a short break in the early nineties, she has worked for him since 1988. She is two years younger than Blair, attended boarding school in St Andrews and met through a mutual friend when he was seventeen. He has lightheartedly suggested that he attempted a seduction and was sent packing: 'My first defeat.' The fact that he feels secure enough to make the joke illustrates the kind of relationship they have. It is settled.

At first Hunter was a secretary, but with Blair on the shadow Cabinet she had assumed a different role, the kind of half-fixer, half-adviser that politicians need as their conduit to the outside world. It involves a level of trust which must be absolute, because there is no one outside the family who will know as much about the frailties and foibles of the boss. In his public life, she has been by Blair's side for most of the last twenty years and has seen every turn in his transformation from gawping new boy to greying Prime Minister. Her husky voice and the plume of cigarette smoke that often trails behind her are part of the Blair picture. Whether at the Women's Institute annual conference or in the White House, her mobile phone is close by, vibrating with the messages which flow to and fro in the Blair circle. She hears and sees almost everything.

As a result she has been the object of jealousy and some hostility. To Labour MPs anxious to get access to the inner reaches of Downing Street she is the keeper of the key who must be persuaded; to those who have criticized the side of Blair which is usually caricatured as 'presidentialism' she is the unelected courtier who is as likely to bite your head off as to let you through. Senior ministers may not have to negotiate to pass her portals but almost everyone else does. And for Blair she operates not only as a filter, keeping out unwelcome visitors and problems, but as an emissary in the parliamentary party, Fleet Street and beyond where she carries messages to the world outside and returns with the answers, with news and with the latest gossip fresh for the Prime Minister's office.

She is part of a wider intelligence network. All governments need them, so that in Downing Street they can feel the trembling from the most distant corners of the web. Intelligence is the bloodstream of politics, bringing news of danger. For example, after the 2001 election it was believed that one junior minister was having an affair which, if it had been revealed, would have been particularly damaging to the government. The minister was not reappointed.

Hunter is an important cog in that machine and Blair also uses her for personal tasks – soothing a bruised colleague, dealing with an MP whose marriage is in trouble or who's been bereaved, fixing a necessary social encounter with a newspaper figure who needs some timely massage, and all the other tasks that a political machine demands, day and night. Outside Blair's family there is no one closer. It's his constant refrain and the easiest way of pushing aside any problem: 'Speak to Anji.' With the family itself her relationship has a different quality and there is some strain with Cherie Booth, who is much closer to Baroness (Sally) Morgan. Hunter and Morgan had an up-and-down relationship in Number 10 before Morgan left for the Cabinet Office and the Lords at the start of the second term. The two women were competitors for the Prime Minister's ear. But it was Hunter whose throaty whisper was usually the one he heard first. Her intimacy is strictly at work, not at home. But for Blair-watchers it was not surprising that she prospered after the second election victory. Although her role as advance scout at the South London school where he launched the campaign was made public, and she was criticized for recommending a performance that became the first embarrassment of the campaign and the subject of jokes for weeks, the ties are as strong as ever.

In the newly created post of Head of Government Relations based in 12 Downing Street, from which the chief whip was asked to decamp, Hunter's power has been formalized and she will remain one of Blair's essential political limbs. He tells friends that he needs her. One of her tasks over the years has been to cultivate parts of the press that are more difficult for other members of the Blair circle to reach. While Alastair Campbell has tried to play most of the tabloids like an old violin, with only the occasional screech and broken string, it has been Hunter who has been one of the links in the all-important relationship – in Blair's mind – with the *Daily Mail*. It was she, for example, who played the part of Cupid in Blair's strange waltz with Paul Johnson, the irascible but gushing columnist once memorably described by Richard Ingrams as looking like 'an explosion in a pubic hair factory'. She spoke to him a great deal, and arranged the meetings which allowed the infatuation to develop. Johnson fell for Blair in the mid-nineties, writing in the *Mail* of their dinners and discussions as if he were announcing the discovery of a personal treasure trove of political talent and telling readers that they might be witnessing the coming to power of a great man. It went spectacularly sour, as such fevered dalliances in Fleet Street mostly do, but it served Blair's purpose well. The Labour leader who was happy to cultivate a 'middle England' appeal, and have it described as such, had found, albeit temporarily, a trumpet to make the appropriate noise. Subsequent blasts from Johnson announcing the turning of Blair from promising statesman to near-corrupt control freak weren't a surprise, and the Downing Street view was that his purpose had been served in opposition. Goodbye.

Hunter's speciality has been the use of antennae which stretch well outside the Labour Party. Before power made it easier to find newspaper acolytes, the widening of Blair's circle in Conservative newspapers had a great deal to do with her skills. She didn't look or sound like a political hack and she appeared to epitomize a change of style in the Labour leadership. It was valuable for Blair to have an intelligence operative who could also wield a steely charm.

The charm of Alastair Campbell escapes some people. With Hunter, he has been the backbone of Blair's operation since soon after he became leader. Campbell does, in fact, have a soft side to his personality, but it is usually concealed behind impenetrable layers of rigid muscle and some of those with whom he deals, in press and broadcasting as in politics, have hardly seen a hint of it.

One of the moments when his defences came down briefly was early in the first term on a Blair visit to New York where Campbell shared with reporters some of the family difficulties that came with his job. He'd argued with one of his children before leaving and as he departed his son said to him: 'You want a good soundbite? Here's one – you're a crap dad.' Blair told his first biographer Jon Sopel that just as he was sure his name would be mud in his house for spending so much time writing, the same was true in the Blair home because of his many enforced absences. The Downing Street gang have the feel of an extended family about them. It is not a controlled office environment of the sort that Blair's business heroes cherish.

Campbell and Hunter have often played a 'tough-cop-soft-cop' routine, with Campbell almost always in the role of the baton-waving thug. Eyes blazing, mouth curling and finger jabbing he can reduce a young reporter, or a feeble backbencher, to jelly. Hunter's techniques are more subtle, entreaties for help that sometimes work where directness has failed. Since Campbell's arrival at Blair's side in 1995 her job has not been to deal directly with journalists day-to-day, though she knows a vast number, but to persuade the hostile or the fearful that Blair's office is not just an organized bullying shop. It is an equally ruthless tactic.

No press secretary in the history of Downing Street has been as famous as Campbell or as influential. He was bequeathed part of this fame unintentionally by his predecessor but three, Bernard Ingham. Ingham was the voice of the Iron Lady and created for the public mind the image which Margaret Thatcher wore like a perfectly-tailored dress. He understood her appeal and her instincts because he sympathized with them, and gave them a language, all decisiveness and instinctive action. In turn, she conducted her premiership in character, the character which he had accurately sensed and described to Fleet Street and the broadcasters. He did so behind the flimsy veil of the unattributable lobby briefings which he fought successfully to preserve for a little longer. It was his skill and flair in the Thatcher era that was the foundation for the Campbell years.

Ingham's relationship to his Prime Minister, however, was quite different from Campbell's. He played by civil service rules – he couldn't imagine attending a Conservative Party conference, for example – and was never part of the kind of circle that Campbell helped to create around Blair. Ingham was the professional servant in the outer office, not the courtier at the bedroom door. His devotion to Thatcher was probably as great as Campbell's to Blair but even at the end, when he gave his last despairing advice to her as she headed for catastrophe in the leadership election of 1990, there was a little distance. No outsider has ever heard him call Thatcher 'Margaret'. By contrast, except in formal gatherings in the Westminster village, Campbell would hardly bother to refer to his boss as 'Prime Minister'.

As a lobby correspondent for part of the eighties Campbell understood Ingham's brilliance in sculpting the outline of Thatcher for those he was briefing. Before long they knew what she would think about almost anything, how she would respond to any political situation, what language she would use. Thatcher was herself, but 'Maggie' was Ingham's creation. Campbell learnt his lesson, and when he began to advise Kinnock informally and to sense the rhythms of an opposition leader's office while he was at the *Mirror* as political editor he adapted Ingham's techniques. It was, he thought, what Labour needed.

Campbell was Ingham with a souped-up engine and twin exhausts, a pulsating propaganda machine that was meant to spin routine announcements into something interesting every day, with powers sanctioned by the Prime Minister giving it a terrifying energy. Campbell was everywhere. He was playing the Fleet Street field, picking off cowed backbenchers to help in some piece of mischief against the Conservatives, reminding ministers that their loyalty lay to one man (and his press secretary) and, most of all, sitting at Blair's side when he made most of his decisions. With Mandelson, before he was promoted from the Cabinet Office to the DTI, he was the omnipresent adviser.

His old acquaintance Ingham was horrified at what had happened to his former job: 'The things this lot do . . . I couldn't begin to have contemplated some of it. They're bullies. They break every rule. I'd have been thrown out on my ear in a minute if I'd tried any of it. They're an appalling bunch.' The eyebrows jump with Healeyesque ferocity and he snorts. The unattributable briefings of his day had gone and Campbell was speaking for direct quotation. This gave the Number 10 briefings a bogus flavour of excitement, which can be dispelled in a moment by a visit to the official Number 10 website, and it heightened the aura of Campbell himself. He was, said the opposition and many a Labour MP, more important than some Cabinet ministers.

Everyone knew it to be true. No significant announcement could be planned by any department without Campbell approving, in meticulous detail, the timing of the statement, the wording of the press release, the arrangements for interviews with the minister on radio and television and the decision as to whether it might be worthwhile flying a kite a day or two in advance in a friendly newspaper.

The criticism became familiar as Campbell bedded down. He demanded more Number 10 control of the individual press offices in Whitehall departments, almost always manned by senior civil servants who were meant to be able to work as easily for ministers of either party and who were professional information officers. Some of them moved jobs or took early retirement, and nearly all of them grumbled. Andy Wood at the Northern Ireland Office, whose Whitehall service stretched back through the Thatcher years to Callaghan's Number 10 press office, was dismissed by Mo Mowlam, the Secretary of State, because of problems of 'chemistry' and he made public his disgust at what he thought was happening to the Government Information Service, always conceived as a source of straight information and background free of party-political embellishment.

The Campbell style took shape, with the crafted slogan and the message carved in stone as its main elements. There was always a line, and it had to be followed. In Blair's mind there was still the spooky memory of life in the early eighties, when Labour had no style, no consistency and, as a result, no message. That was why he resisted the efforts of some of his colleagues who tried to persuade him, as delicately as they could, to rein Campbell in. 'Ali is the best. He is loyal. He stays,' was Blair's response. No other Prime Minister in the media age had created and sustained a professional friendship like it. There were odd rows about a headline that had gone wrong, a briefing too far or a piece of gossip. Blair was furious when stories appeared after a family holiday in the Seychelles implying that he had rescued a drowning man. He hadn't. He had encountered a Scandinavian tourist. But they subsided as surely as the sun rose the next morning. What Campbell wanted, he got.

The more the metropolitan cynics giggled and the broadsheets sniffed (especially the *Guardian*, which Campbell regarded as a puffed-up enemy and not a friend) the more he bent to his task. Through the first term he controlled his office like the operations room of a ship at war. The tiniest blip on the radar screen was monitored, and the guns would swing round. Campbell is a regular caller to the BBC in the early morning. If there's a headline on Radio 4 at six o'clock which he doesn't like, he'll complain. Why was a headline about Geoffrey Robinson's business affairs or the troubles of the Leicester East MP Keith Vaz more important than some 'good news' announcement coming later in the day about lower crime figures or good results in primary schools? Among his favourite words are 'garbage' and 'crap'. The theory is not that a rude phone call will change a headline (it won't, unless there is an obvious factual inaccuracy) but that a regular sense of being watched will induce a sense of defensiveness. BBC producers and correspondents try to make sure it doesn't.

During the 2001 campaign the style was exported to Millbank Tower. Radio and television editors would receive organized barrages of calls after news programmes giving lists of complaints about the choice of interviewees or the adjectives used by a presenter. The opposition parties played the same game, of course, but without the same practised ease.

Campbell runs his regime as if it were a firm of nightclub bouncers.

An editor needs bawling out. A correspondent may have to be singled out for a humiliating aside at a lobby briefing (as one left the room early one day, Campbell called after him, 'Need a drink, do we?'). A backbencher may be reminded that the Prime Minister might find room in his diary for a visit to the constituency if a loyal silence is preserved. He once outraged the *Mirror*, the government's most loyal cheerleader, by passing one of its scoops to the *Sun*. He commands Blair's guest lists, even arranging for Richard Desmond, the porn millionaire who bought the *Express*, to visit Blair at Downing Street and Chequers, a favour which outraged dozens of sacked *Express* journalists and especially the former editor Rosie Boycott, a friend of Blair's whom Desmond had discarded.

Campbell's chamber was the political heart of the government, the place where all the lines crossed. In Cabinet, ministers found it difficult to plug into each other's lives. There were old friendships that could provide networks across departments, and of course ministers tried to help each other out in struggles with the Treasury or in swinging the balance in the Prime Minister's mind on the minimum wage, or the tube, or pensions, or the housing budget. But one Cabinet minister put it like this: 'We don't socialize very much. The Commons is quiet these days, because late night votes hardly matter. We just don't hang around much. It's quite strange. There's not much mingling at all.' More than in any government since the sixties ministerial lives were being lived inside departments. But they all had to have a lifeline to the centre and from the start Campbell, and Mandelson in his first year as Minister Without Portfolio in the Cabinet Office, saw a vast amount of prime ministerial paperwork.

They didn't see such documents as the weekly 'Red Book' from the Joint Intelligence Committee, with its update from the security and intelligence agencies, or more sensitive material from the Foreign Office or Defence, but almost everything else passed across their desks. Describing Campbell as a press secretary missed the point. By the time they all arrived in Downing Street he was part of Blair's personality, a component in every strategy and a presence in every room where the Prime Minister had to operate. During the Kosovo war he sat in on meetings with the Defence Chiefs of Staff. He was not the still small voice in his head, but the big loud heckler at his shoulder.

The Campbell phenomenon is a clue to the nature of Blair's gang. He was a fabled Fleet Street figure in his day, a boozer and bagpipe player whose history was exotic. From Cambridge he went on a whim to train half-heartedly as a casino croupier but ended up as a kilted busker round Europe, and then wrote amateur porn for the magazine *Forum* before throwing himself on the tabloids. He played rough with the hard men of the newspaper trade who knock on a victim's door all day and all night before they give up, and loved the wild life of the Street in the last days of its heady self-indulgence, before the accountants and the computers took over. About that time, the bottle clobbered him and he broke down. He hasn't touched alcohol since, but in an odd way he is still the same over-the-top character. And that is what Blair enjoys.

For this Prime Minister has a weakness for the charismatics. It would be hard to find someone less like Campbell than Blair's student spiritual guru Peter Thomson, and yet there is something they share – a certain gift of the glittering eye. Blair seems always to have been attracted by that kind of intensity and directness. Sometimes their relationship seems to have a theatrical quality to it. It allows Campbell an openness in the Prime Minister's office which has astonished some visitors. Campbell has no inhibitions. Though Blair only draws on ripe language in moments of real anxiety – even Milosevic is a mere 'shit' – and never does so in front of outsiders, Campbell lets his vocabulary run free. He also has a characteristic grunt, often accompanied by a twist in the upper lip, which is a challenge to the person who has just spoken. Tell me why I should not be contemptuous of this, it says. Blair gets it regularly.

Blair's critics interpret it as weakness. He himself argues that there is never any doubt who is boss, and can cite instances where Campbell has had to apologize to him for a foul-up in the press. But Campbell is so powerful that he is assumed to be the source, rightly or wrongly, of almost every word that comes out of Number 10. The most famous phrase in this category, which infuriated and wounded Brown in the middle of the first term, was the claim in the *Observer* on 18 January 1998, that someone close to Blair in Number 10 had described Brown as having 'psychological flaws'. Campbell was everyone's favourite culprit, because in such circumstances he always is. He has always denied, on and off the record, using the phrase. He insists it did not come from him and in evidence to the Commons Public Administration Committee denied briefing 'against any member of the Cabinet'. Around Brown these denials still ring with an uncertain note. The Chancellor himself doesn't talk of it: some of his staff do, and they still believe that the trail leads back to Campbell's office.

The report on 18 January 1998 was one of many critical of the Chancellor around that time, and the reason was obvious. Paul Routledge, the *Mirror* commentator and dedicated sceptic of all things Blairite, had published his biography of Brown, a detailed and sometimes racy account of his life which was prepared, as the book announced on its cover, with the Chancellor's 'full cooperation'. Perhaps it was the 'full' that set Downing Street off. Although Brown was not quoted in the book as criticizing Blair directly, it fairly reflected his grudges and grumbles and gave them voice. In Downing Street, it was as if a hand grenade had landed in the front hall. Through the next few weeks newspaper front pages were pockmarked with the fallout, a shower of anti-Brown stories. The 'psychological flaws' accusation was the most biting, but there were others. Outsiders glimpsed for the first time how trust might reside inside the two circles of advisers but not often between them.

Campbell and Hunter form the circle of intimates who are Blair's armour. Brown wears a similar protective suit. His most important adviser is Ed Balls, who was only twenty-seven when around the same time as Charlie Whelan he joined Brown in 1994. After Whelan departed, to gasps of relief in Blair's office and in Campbell's, in January 1999 Balls was left as the Chancellor's principal political lieutenant. He is a disarmingly cheery soul, given much more to laughing than to dark conspiracies, but he has created a fearsome reputation for himself. When he arrived at Brown's side from the

Financial Times, he was thought of as a hired economic brain. He was; but he came to be much more. With Whelan he was a partner in an operation that had as much interest in preserving and enhancing Brown's political power in the government and the party as worrying about the next spending round or the preparations for entering the euro. They weren't Treasury men, they were 'Gordon's men'. 10 Downing Street was therefore an outfit which had to be treated like any other part of government. The centre of their world was Brown's office and it was from there that they sent their messages to the world, not from mission control in Blair's office or, worse, from Campbell's.

They knew from the start that Blair found Brown's affection for Whelan a puzzle and had tried to persuade Brown not to bring him into government. Campbell defended him when the first euro row blew up in the autumn after the election, though he told Blair directly that he thought Whelan had behaved dangerously and foolishly in his telephone briefings and in his loose talk. Fortunately, they thought in Number 10, the Chancellor had been embarrassed too. But it took Blair's office eighteen months to lever Whelan out and fill the Treasury press secretary's job with a career civil servant once more, just as in the old days. Brown kept his loyalty to his old bodyguard – he continued to see him regularly and to solicit his advice – and Whelan and Balls are still a pair seen together around the watering holes of SW1 on the Chancellor's business. As Campbell and Hunter ride shotgun for the Prime Minister, so do Whelan and Balls for their man.

Blair's relations with Balls are civil, because, after the difficult first days in which officials complained to the Cabinet Secretary about their exclusion from Blair–Brown meetings, an arrangement was reached by which many of their discussions would be attended by one official from each side. Jeremy Heywood, a Treasury civil servant seconded to Number 10 as Blair's principal private secretary, was one such official until he moved on in July 2001, and the other was Balls. Officialdom was relieved that a regular pattern had been re-established, and some precious aides-memoires recorded for the files, despite the habit of Blair and Brown of huddling together alone almost every day, and of talking on unmonitored telephones at all hours.

So Balls straddles the official and the personally political in Brown's office. He helps to write speeches, though Brown will still sit for hours at his desk working on his own words, and he deals with many financial journalists. 'It's not Brown, it's Balls,' Michael Heseltine crowed in an unusually 'risqué' analysis at a Tory Party conference of one speech from the Chancellor. This irritates Downing Street a great deal, because, especially in the arguments over the euro, the Prime Minister's office believes it can spot a Balls briefing when they see it fashioned into an elegant column in one of the broadsheets. It is a suspicious relationship, because the stakes are high. Even if Brown were a minister who had been promoted to Chancellor they would still keep a sharp watch on his people (whom they saw, where they lunched, where their networks stretched – all the human intelligence of politics) but with his installation as the twin pillar of the government Balls became a quite different creature, whose every move had special interest and significance.

The contacts are strained. If a particularly disturbing story has appeared touching on either the Prime Minister or the Chancellor there will be an atmosphere for a while. Whether because of Brown's fury about the 'psychological flaws', Blair's anger at Treasury briefings about the euro, irritation at rival interpretations being circulated about disputes over the tube or Post Office privatization or BBC funding, a story will take wing and fly. Campbell will be asked by Blair to explain to Brown what happened; or Balls will have to account for his movements. They are all used to it now, and one of the frustrations which Blair has confessed to his circle is that it has almost become the way of the world. There is no genuine prospect of a stop to it.

One channel does exist which has been used to defuse some of the personal tension. Brown's secretary Sue Nye is Hunter's old friend. In opposition days they were matey in the shadow Cabinet corridor and could be found together in a wine bar from time to time consoling each other by sharing, in strict privacy, their latest worries about one of their bosses. From the start they managed to have a solid relationship even when Blair and Brown were paddling in choppy water. Nye is married to Gavyn Davies, a Brown adviser of long standing, Goldman Sachs economist and, from 2000, vice-chairman of the board of governors of the BBC. She is a Labour Party veteran, having toiled at party headquarters and in the parliamentary party before Brown had arrived at Westminster. She knows the party intimately, and although she shares the contempt of the Blairites for some past periods – her years in Kinnock's office when he was leader pitched her into battle with the hard left – she has the characteristic that Brown has tried to preserve in his office: a residual warmth for Labour history. Nye's importance for Number 10, however, is not simply in her party loyalty (which is almost as impregnable as her loyalty to Brown) but her resilient friendship with Anji Hunter. They sometimes talk more freely one to the other than their employers, and they are in the fortunate position of knowing (with Campbell and Balls, and sometimes Powell and Mandelson – the only others in that innermost loop) the detail of what has passed between Blair and Brown and, perhaps just as importantly, the state of mind of each of them when a particular encounter is over. Between them they form a safety valve.

These are the individuals who are the closest to Blair and Brown in their offices and they set the tone for the wider groups of friends who operate in Parliament and beyond. They illustrate, too, one of the most striking features of the Blair–Brown relationship, the presence of strong women.

Each of them is married to one. Cherie Booth is a woman of strong opinions – still to the left of her husband. However, despite her decision to pursue her career at the Bar with as little interference from government duties as possible (indeed, sometimes challenging government decisions in her field of employment law without worrying about comment in the press) she has been careful to avoid the Hillary Clinton model. Her references in public to any issue of political significance can be counted on a few fingers: she has resisted almost all temptation. But anyone who has the faintest brush with the Blair family is aware of her importance to the Prime Minister, and her refusal to hide her opinions under some affected simpering exterior. This has caused some friction with the Chancellor. Those who see most of them together are convinced that theirs is now a very cool relationship indeed. Each is possessed of an eloquent body language. Even when the words are friendly, Booth and Brown don't demonstrate any physical warmth.

But they have had to learn to be close neighbours. On coming to power, the Blairs moved into the flat above the shop in Number 11, because it provided room for a family. Number 10's flat did not. Number 11 is hardly spacious, let alone palatial, but it accommodates the Blairs and their four children, three of them in their teens. Brown moved alone into the flat at the top of Number 10. Towards the end of the first term, of course, the personal focus and the long lenses shifted dramatically from Cherie Booth and the Blairs' baby, Leo, born in June 2000, to Brown. His marriage to Sarah Macaulay in August was a surprise, not because she had emerged out of the blue (she hadn't) but because Brown, in character, managed to keep the wedding a secret. He rang Whelan the night before and the late editions of the newspapers managed to break the news, but Brown succeeded in having the ceremony he wanted, not in his local church in Inverkeithing, but in his own front room with the local Church of Scotland minister performing the traditional ceremony before a group of only their closest friends. His brother John was best man. The bridesmaid and pageboy were the children of Sue Nye and Gavyn Davies and there was no place for the metropolitan glitterati: everyone there was either a member of one of their families, a close professional colleague or a lifelong friend. Whelan, for example, was not there. Nor were the Blairs, who were due to begin their summer holiday and had learned of the wedding plans only twenty-four hours before they took place.

For Brown this was an extraordinary day. It was not only the culmination of a relationship stretching back over a few years and the start of a new era in his personal life, but it marked the end of a period in which his bachelor status had caused him trouble and misery. Long before he turned fifty in February 2001, his marriage plans – or, more accurately, the lack of them – were a source of good copy for the diary columnists. When he did allow a photograph to be published of a dinner date with Sarah Macaulay before the 1997 Budget it was widely described as some kind of put-up job, contrasted with his famous reluctance to be open about his private life. Brown was irritated and offended by this, but typically reluctant to do much about it. His unhappiness was compounded by his knowledge that for some years past his single status had given rise to rumours that he was gay. As with many such Westminster whispers, which attach themselves to the most unlikely characters from time to time, no one could produce a sliver of evidence for the assertion. This was not surprising, because Brown's friends insist that the story has no basis in fact. It did not stop it being peddled, often with the friend-of-a-friend attribution which many politicians know to their cost can quickly appear to become something more substantial in the retelling.

The closest Brown came to a public discussion of the matter came in a recording for *Desert Island Discs* on Radio 4 in the year before the 1997 General Election. At the time, at least one Conservative front bencher was stating 'as a fact' in various Westminster bars that Brown was gay. Some newspapers were said to have startling material which would find its way out. It was a cloud that hovered around him, and he knew of it. So when Sue Lawley interviewed him about his eight records, his book and his luxury, she decided to raise the question. He said that in some ways he was surprised that marriage hadn't happened and Lawley carried on. Surely it wasn't surprising that people were curious: 'It is something that middle-aged men and women have to put up with. People want to know whether you're gay or whether there's some flaw in your personality that you haven't made a relationship.'

Brown waffled in what was evidently some embarrassment and irritation, saying again that he had thought marriage might happen and it hadn't, but he left Broadcasting House furious. There was not much he could do, except to depend on Whelan to offer laddish hints about his love life and his interest in women – hardly a happy media strategy on which to have to embark. His best hope was that the questions would simply subside, but he was well aware that his natural tendency to keep his private life private would allow the old rumours to linger. Even in planning the wedding, however, he wasn't persuaded to ignore his natural instincts. The ceremony was private, the party was deliberately modest, and he left for his American honeymoon in his brother's car. The one concession to the media was a scrambled photocall in the back garden that included an exchanged kiss between Mr and Mrs Brown of some awkwardness. There are few more authentic pictures of the real Brown than those from his wedding, portraits of a man uncomfortable at the mingling of the public and private, ill-at-ease with the expected opening up of a life for public observation and comment. The bride was elegantly attired in an ivory two-piece silk dress. The bridegroom did not, however, use the excuse of his wedding to deviate from sartorial orthodoxy: a sober suit with the regulation red tie was his choice. He could have been delivering a Budget statement.

Brown has usually conducted himself like this. Although the student affair with Princess Marguerite of Romania had an inescapable air of improbability and panache about it, subsequent relationships have been conducted privately. For much of the eighties his close friend Marion Caldwell, then an Edinburgh solicitor, stayed well out of the public eye, and in the nineties a relationship with the broadcaster Sheena McDonald was kept very discreet. Brown has always been reluctant to open himself up as an object of public curiosity, and still shies away from personal interviews which might demand that too many innermost thoughts spill out. He has always been determined to keep the curtains drawn round his private life.

There was a touching illustration of his concern for privacy on the morning after his wedding. Whelan was touring the TV and radio studios as the obvious commentator on proceedings, indulging in some happy observations of the I-told-you-so sort. After saying on GMTV that, of course, the wedding wasn't really a surprise because the couple had been more or less living together for years, he received a phone call at the TV studios from someone close to Brown. It had not been prompted by Brown himself, but the message was that perhaps Whelan shouldn't have said what he had, because Brown's mother might have been watching. Even the shock-proof

Whelan was surprised that a Chancellor of the Exchequer in his fiftieth year might have to worry on such grounds.

The point of the story is not that Brown comes from a grim or straitlaced family. He does not. It is that he has a natural feeling for the boundaries between the private and the public which, in his mind, are inviolable. To many others in public life, and Blair is among them, this caution seems excessive and sometimes off-putting but it has always been a part of his character. Public displays of emotion, unless in pursuit of the political cause, are not enjoyable.

Brown the university radical grew out of Brown the conventional schoolboy, and one has not entirely replaced the other. His politics were always personal and energetic, but the sixteen-year-old who arrived in Edinburgh in 1967 and was thrown immediately into the trauma of his eye operations, with the fear of blindness in the background, was a character who had to leap from spotty adolescence to self-reliance very quickly. Colleagues from that era recall someone who was never a carefree youth. Adulthood, like political seriousness, came on quickly.

His lifetime at that time was his family, his father especially. He and his brothers, the older John and the younger Andrew, have stayed close and supportive. It is inconceivable that he would take a major turning in his life without talking it through with them first. Brown is not someone who seems ever to have felt his family slipping into a more distant orbit with the years. It is as close as it was when he was growing up in Kirkcaldy, listening to his father preach on Sunday mornings. His view has always been that these solid foundations must never be allowed to erode in his mind.

The closeness extends to the circle outside his Treasury office. It is striking that three of his most intimate friends are veterans of his student days. The thriller writer Colin Currie was a contributor to *Student* when Brown was editor. Wilf Stevenson, who became director of the British Film Institute, was also part of the gang. Murray Elder – now Lord Elder of Kirkcaldy, sitting on the Labour benches in the Lords – goes back even further. He and Brown went to nursery school together, played rugby and went to Edinburgh as students, coming together in politics again in the eighties when Elder emerged from a period at the Bank of England to work for Denis Healey and then John Smith, whose chief of staff he became in 1992. These are Brown's closest friends; they have all known him for well over thirty years. It is still to them that he returns. With his wife and his brothers, they are the private circle to which he confides his deepest feelings. They seldom travel any wider.

Rigorous privacy has never been of such concern to Blair. From the beginning, the circles that influenced him have been looser. Some of this can be traced back to his youth. Unlike Brown's youthful and traumatic immersion in university life, Blair was nineteen when he left Fettes and had a carefree air which may have concealed some of his ambition and his working habits at Oxford, but was nonetheless in character. He enjoyed being the centre of attention, whether at the microphone for Ugly Rumours in the seventies gear that pinpoints the year almost exactly, or at a St John's College party eyeing up an elegant woman who used to walk around the college leading a kitten on a lead. His gang then was eclectic and so it has remained.

He is still in contact with some of his student friends, none of whom went into serious politics. Socially his contacts are as likely to be from the law, or from the Islington circles in which the Blairs used to live before Downing Street, as from the Labour Party. He is close to his agent and chairman in Sedgefield, John Burton, with whom he won the selection in 1983 and who supported him during the early days of modernization against some awkward opposition, but in London his private circles have never been politically obsessive. Campbell and Hunter are office figures who, despite their professional closeness to Blair, are not fixtures at home. Brown guards his private life with determination, but it is paradoxical that his private and public lives are intertwined more completely than Blair's. With Brown it is hard to say where politics stops and the other life begins. They are tributaries of the same stream.

Blair, though he is less concerned at the inevitable intrusions that come with high office than Brown has always been, has separated his lives more clearly. Some episodes have alarmed his family, usually involving schools. Public comments made by the headmaster of the

London Oratory School, the Catholic school in Fulham where Euan was sent from Islington, are known by friends to have infuriated both of his parents. But Blair himself was able to make a joke at the time of the election of the incident in which Euan's friends left him drunk in Leicester Square and he was delivered home by the police. Although it was embarrassing and something of a family torment, it could eventually be spoken of lightly. In private, Blair has little of the obsessive concern with control that has come to be associated with his government. He finds it possible to relax.

Blair and Brown's political friends tell much the same story. Blair's political soulmates are a colourful, even eccentric bunch. The lead trio sets the tone – Mandelson, Irvine and Lord Falconer of Thoroton, never known in Downing Street as anything other but Charlie. They appear to provide Blair with much of what he needs.

Mandelson tells friends that, despite his two resignations, 'our relationship has never missed a beat'. Those who are in a position to know believe it to be true. Blair has despaired of Mandelson from time to time but it never seems to last for more than a few hours. He always comes back. During his first period out of Cabinet Mandelson was staying with friends one weekend while Blair was at a summit abroad. In the course of the Saturday the phone rang several times for Mandelson. It was the Prime Minister seeking advice. The disasters for Mandelson which led to his two resignations were seen in Downing Street as lapses of judgement on the part of someone who had always flirted with danger in public and in private, the moth that flew too close to the flame. But they did not destroy Blair's relationship with Mandelson. Although Campbell, even before the election, became greatly irritated by what he regarded as Mandelson's egocentricity – he told friends that he found his self-preening to be a pain – Blair has never wavered. On the day of the second resignation the stricken faces of the Prime Minister and the Northern Ireland Secretary suggested that they had been driven asunder, and the next day Andrew Grice, political editor of the *Independent* and an old friend and contact of Mandelson's, wrote words which were taken at Westminster to reflect Mandelson's own feelings – 'it's a parting of the ways'. It wasn't. To the irritation of

Labour MPs who rather enjoyed seeing Mandelson cut down from on high, Blair retains him as a trusted confidant. They talked before and after the 2001 election on the phone daily.

It is the same with Irvine. Blair's debt goes back to his pupil-barrister days in 1976 and to the introduction he provided to John Smith and the top of the Labour Party. Irvine's 'young Blair' shivered through the public relations disaster of Irvine's choice of Pugin-design wallpaper for his official apartments in the House of Lords, and an absurd row about the modernization of the Lord Chancellor's formal garb which turned into a Trollopian debate among officials in the Lords about his wig. When Irvine made an ill-judged speech to the Society of Labour Lawyers soliciting funds from people whom he could promote to the bench if he so wished, some of Blair's colleagues hoped it might be the end. When Irvine's apology to the Lords turned out not to be an apology at all, but a simple assertion of his own integrity and honesty, the Downing Street view was that it was another perplexing blunder. Everyone knew that, in the Lords most of all, a grovelling apology from a minister in trouble worked wonders and cleared the air. Yet there was never a hint in the post-election reshuffle that there would be a new Lord Chancellor. Blair's gratitude and affection run too deep. The phone calls may not be as frequent as they once were but he still talks to Irvine more often than to any other member of the Cabinet save Brown.

Falconer, too, had to walk through fire. As the inheritor of the Millennium Dome from Mandelson he found himself in charge of one of the great political disasters of the Blair years. Despite the figures showing that it was Britain's most popular visitor attraction in 2000 and the opinion polls claiming that most visitors would come back a second time, Falconer struggled to give any substance to a project which by the turn of the century seemed metaphorically as well as literally empty. By the start of the second term it was a forlorn sight on the Thames at Greenwich, with its insides ripped out. The lights at the top of the metal arms supporting the roof still winked over London; but the Dome was dead. Nothing was heard of Blair's boast that it would be the first paragraph of Labour's election manifesto, because it symbolized so much about the new

Britain that his government was bringing into being. Indeed, such was the nervousness about the Dome being used by the Conservatives as a symbol of emptiness and a costly triumph of flummery over substance that Labour was startled, as well as relieved, to find that the Tories decided to make little of it in the 2001 campaign.

Charlie Falconer is not a politician who looks as if he has had to soak up many punches. Indeed in some ways he is not a politician at all. A friend of Blair's from Scotland (Falconer also knew Amanda Mackenzie-Stuart), he carries the easy bonhomie of the confident and slightly louche lawyer, a few locks of hair splayed over his collar and a cheery smile usually completing the picture. He is well-fed and witty, a natural Blair companion who manages never to appear too serious, even when his brain is trying to work out the latest line of defence for the Dome, which kept it busy for many months. One senior civil servant, who is privately rather fond of him, says: 'Charlie is marvellous in a way. And he is obviously important to the Prime Minister. But the truth is that he is not really very political, in the sense of knowing things that most politicians expect to know. He's quite different. Derry is much the same – hopeless at some of the obvious political things. You could say they know nothing. But they're terribly important.' Falconer, however, did become a fixture at the Millbank election headquarters in the re-election campaign and displayed the energy for which his frame is often a disguise. On the night of the Prescott punch he turned instantly into the defence lawyer, scrutinizing television pictures again and again to come to a conclusion about the incident. One who was there said: 'He was transformed. It was as if he was at the police station having a first look at the evidence. He was making a legal judgement about what exactly had happened. When he slapped his hand and said "that's it – we're OK, I think", I thought the place was going to erupt in applause. His advice to Blair on the night was an important element in the Prime Minister's tactics with Prescott.'

Some of Blair's closest colleagues, excepting Mandelson who is steeped in Labour lore, were not cast in the political mould. And these are often the ones he would socialize with by choice, perhaps over a fine bottle of wine from Irvine's cellar. He would enjoy it more than an evening of heavy politics with some of his more earnest Cabinet colleagues.

Earnestness is more of a quality in the Brown camp. Although Balls and his friends exhibit a fair streak of hedonism – they are capable of spectacular drinking sprees – the Brownites have a high seriousness that is encouraged from the top. Geoffrey Robinson, Paymaster General before his fall over the Mandelson home loan, is an intriguing exception. Robinson is a high roller, whose business affairs have been subject frequently to critical scrutiny and investigation, and who seems at first glance to be a most unlikely Brown intimate. He lives during the week in a rented Park Lane apartment and has large houses in England and in Tuscany. He is gregarious and generous with his favours, feeding guests to their limits and acting as a rumbustious host. Brown and his entourage enjoyed Robinson's company and political gossip, Brown even taking to using the Grosvenor House health club for a period where he could be found on some mornings pedalling away on the cycling machine in a fair old sweat. Although party-loving Robinson was loyally on-side throughout, especially in pressing the case across government for public-private partnerships which had become a treasured Brown mechanism for pulling more money into the public sector while policing the golden rules of fiscal prudence. Robinson, whose business inventiveness has got him into trouble as well as bringing him a personal fortune, was a supporter who stayed signed up to the team.

From each of the groups of friends comes some of the character that makes Blair and Brown what they are. Blair's is a more relaxed circle, and not only because as Prime Minister he is not consumed by the usual political ambitions about how to take the last step to the summit. It is a reflection of his character in office as well as his personality. He has resisted complete absorption in politics, even in Number 10. Brown, on the other hand, has an attraction to the intricacies of the political world which never flags. He wakes up to political thoughts, and takes them to bed at night. Since his student days he has wrestled with the effort of pulling together a set of socialist instincts with the practical demands put on a late twentieth-century government in a global economy. That is where his energy goes.

The result is that with rare exceptions like the exotic Robinson, by Brown's standards a flamboyant dandy, his political friends tend to have seriousness in common. Alistair Darling, Secretary of State for Work and Pensions, is a little cheerier than he sometimes appears. Andrew Smith, chief secretary to the Treasury, is not. In the junior ranks of the government those who take their lead from the Treasury tend to adopt the style of Douglas Alexander, promoted spectacularly by Brown to an important role in the re-election campaign at Millbank although he was only elected in Paisley South in a by-election in November 1997 and appointed Minister for E-Commerce and Competitiveness after the 2001 election. As a clever economist who used to work for Brown (and whose sister, Wendy, is a minister in the Scottish Executive in Edinburgh), Alexander epitomizes something of the spirit of those whom the parliamentary party identifies as Brownites. They are serious-minded but they are not political innocents. They know how to play the game and understand the thrill of the cut and thrust of the deft political manoeuvre. Although Blair's Cabinet at the start of the second term showed a tilt away from established Brownite figures – Charles Clarke's appointment to the Cabinet Office being the most obvious evidence of the shift – there is still a gang of supporters sprayed around the backbenchers and throughout the government who regard Brown as the leader of a movement to which they belong. They don't plot directly against Blair, and will always protest their collective loyalty to the government, but they doff their caps first in the direction of the Chancellor's office.

Blair's inner circle is fiercely loyal and protective and will struggle for him in the last ditch; so will Brown's. The difference between their wider circles is that where Blair has wide support among those who have prospered under his leadership and who stand to gain most from his patronage, there is an anxiety among some ministers most loyal to him that Blair's political commitment may not be as strong as they would wish. A Blairite Cabinet minister bluntly articulated an anxiety shared among New Labour sympathizers: 'My fear is simple. It is that many of Tony's friends are there because the weather is still fine and that they could disappear very quickly in a storm. If he were to go suddenly, or if we were hitting really serious, serious trouble, I'm not sure what they would do. The difference with Gordon is that he has believers. Some of us don't want Gordon to be Prime Minister – but maybe his people want it more.'

That is where the story of the friends turns into a story about the future, and about the way Blair and Brown are appealing to their party. With their closest advisers and confidants helping them on they are engaged in a double game. Day by day they are continuing to make their established partnership work. Rows come and go but the decisions are made. There is no serious threat that Brown will resign, nor that Blair will walk away. They make it work because they must. It is how the government functions. But alongside the daily meetings and phone calls, entreaties and passages of angry silence, there was, at the start of the second term, a new game starting to take shape.

Blair, the Prime Minister who turned Labour into the most dominant electoral force Britain had seen for more than a century, was beginning to look to a second term as the period in which, like all long-serving Prime Ministers, he would try to find and secure his place in history. Where would he find it? And Brown, aware of a stirring deep in his party that spoke of coming discontent and trouble over the drift of policy, was wondering how to preserve the public loyalty which he has shown to Blair while building an alternative future for Labour under his direction, which his speeches, writings and political strategy all suggest that he sees glimmering somewhere ahead.

11
I Believe

The Arab League ambassadors who came as observers to Labour's conference in 2000 had a surprise when they met the Prime Minister on the penultimate day. At the party's reception for them he quoted from the Koran. Those guests who enquired as to whether a helpful handbag of quotes had been provided by the Foreign Office found that the source was not an assiduous diplomat's briefing but Blair himself. He was able to do it for a remarkably straightforward reason. He had the Koran by his bed, and was reading it.

Blair may be the only Prime Minister elected in the twentieth century to have opened the book with intent, apart from Anthony Eden, who studied Persian and Arabic at Oxford and may have had recourse to some of its exhortations when, in his wife's unforgettable phrase, the Suez Canal was flowing through his drawing room in 1956. Blair had no such background, and it was not Saddam Hussein or the debate about sanctions on Iraq that took him to the Koran. He was intrigued by its moral code. It is safe to say that there is not another member of his Cabinet who keeps a holy book by the bedside. Blair is alone among them in having a burning fascination for the spiritual, and no one can explain him without understanding that sometimes that feeling is more important to him than politics.

And despite saying in the year before he became Prime Minister that he was not fond of politicians who wore God on their sleeves, in the American way, Blair can easily be tempted. Indeed he revealed that his interest in the Koran was kindled by Chelsea Clinton, the President's daughter, who carries a copy everywhere, and he has picked up the habit. 'I carry a copy of the book with me whenever

I can, to give me inspiration and courage,' he told *Muslim News* in March 2000, saying that he found the Koran clear and reflective, revealing 'the concept of love and fellowship as the guiding spirits of humanity'. And all from a President's daughter.

Notwithstanding Margaret Thatcher's recitation of a prayer of St Francis of Assisi taken from her handbag on the steps of Number 10 in 1979, this is the kind of remark that no other modern British Prime Minister would have made. Not since Gladstone has a party leader spoken of religion like Blair. It's a practice that makes most of his Cabinet colleagues uncomfortable. A number of them are practising Christians, but most are not. None would be willing to slip so easily into spiritual mode.

Some of them find it scary. When he said in an interview in September 2000, after the miserable summer of fumbles and mistakes, 'I am a man with a mission', it rang true to ministers who have come to know him as someone driven by something inside. They have come to realize that it is not a conventional political philosophy that keeps him going. Many politicians live for the hours when they can tease out policy arguments, test them against political history, ruminate on the character of governments and ministers past. They think of themselves as pieces in a fascinating though sometimes infuriating political jigsaw that can never be complete. In their different ways, Brown, Cook, Blunkett and Straw are all like that. Blair is not. He has as much political energy, but it seems to come from a different source. He doesn't draw on the usual wellsprings of politics.

He doesn't feed on Labour's tradition, for the simple reason that even after he became leader he was unable to shake off the feeling that the story of Labour and the twentieth century is a story of failure. He contrasts the success of Gladstonian and Asquithian Liberals over a period of about fifty years from the last quarter of the nineteenth century onwards with the patchy story of Labour in the twentieth. He is as ready as the next Labour politician to eulogize the Attlee post-war government for the invention of the NHS or the strengthening of the welfare state – although at moments of high frustration with Labour he will point out that Beveridge and Keynes were Liberals – but underneath Blair has a more melancholy view of his party's history. His address at the Labour Party's 100th birthday at the Old Vic in February 2000 betrayed some of that unease. Any of his predecessors as leader would have been happier at the event. His rather gloomy view of Labour history was one of the reasons for his conference speech about the 'forces of conservatism' in 1999, which was not driven simply by a desire to appear more combative and perhaps partisan. Paradoxically, he found himself in trouble for making a speech which appeared to dismiss all Conservatives as hopeless reactionaries, when the convictions revealed in the speech derived more from a sense of failure on his own side.

Much of his politics flows from that negative feeling about his party. His own political convictions sprang from his interest in ethics at Oxford, rather than from an enjoyment of political activity, and he was aware when he was first attracted to Labour that it was a party which was burdened by a heavy sense of defeatism. In the seventies it was riven by ideological disputes and weary of government. Soon after he joined it, he concluded that it was facing schism and might splinter into fragments. His parliamentary career in the eighties consisted of dispensing with many of the attitudes and policies he had adopted as a young candidate. It was a bonfire of the promises. Unilateralism, opposition to the Common Market, support for nationalization, opposition to the sale of council houses – into the flames they went. Consequently, for Blair, there wasn't much in the ashes of old policies or in the litany of failed Labour governments from which he could draw inspiration. No Labour character figures in Blair's mind in the way that Maxton engrossed and spurred Brown. So he looked to other sources for his political energy and vision.

Such was his sense of distance from Labour's past that he developed a habit of sometimes referring to his party as 'they' instead of 'we' and to the embarrassment of his staff he has not managed to lose it in Downing Street. In arguing in the nineties for New Labour and then 'the third way', Blair was not simply trying to invent a new political language – as Thatcher had – but was consciously trying to put to rest the first hundred years of Labour's history. He might give the traditional conference speech boasts about the party's achievements, but twenty-two years of power in a hundred years didn't strike Blair as anything but failure.

Additionally, he had grown up with no sense of belonging to the Labour Party. His father had been an active Conservative and his own party membership came long after he had assembled a package of beliefs that weren't absorbed from formal politics. His religious interests at Oxford, which have remained with him almost unchanged ever since, led him to his interest in ideas of community from which he found his way to politics. Blair's political beliefs are unusual for a British leader in not coming from a framework of ideology. Even John Major was more steeped in his party's ideology than Blair.

The feeling of disaffection with his party's history, a history which has never gripped him in the way it mesmerized Brown as a teenage student, explains a good deal of Blair's impatience with colleagues and party traditionalists. When Roy Hattersley began his running commentary on the failures of the government after 1997, usually targeted directly at Blair, Downing Street affected to be amused. When the former deputy leader wrote savagely about Blair on the morning of a conference speech in Blackpool, however, there was genuine anger; and by the start of the second term the tone in Blair's office was contemptuous. 'How much did he get for that one?' they'd ask of the latest piece of savagery in the *Daily Mail*. 'When did he last say anything sensible in the Lords?' Publicly, the Prime Minister was said to be untroubled by anything Hattersley said; privately he seethed. Part of the reason is that he sees his own leadership as the natural and logical consequence of the Kinnock–Hattersley reforms and, according to his friends, he regards his old colleague as 'gutless' in refusing to accept it.

There's another reason. Blair knows that he has indeed been engaged on exactly the kind of rewriting of the Labour idea that Hattersley finds offensive. When he wrote just after re-election that Blair's devotion to meritocracy was a *coup d'état* against Labour's 'legitimate philosophy' because it betrayed the disadvantaged by its concentration on rewarding success, his ringing crescendo peaked with: 'I do not know what distresses me more, the apostasy or the naivety.' Blair would not plead guilty to naivety – his approach has been studied. Apostasy he might regard as a compliment. He would accept that he has indeed abandoned what he'd call 'old thinking' about equality of outcome, replacing it with a commitment to equality of opportunity. Hattersley's words wound only because Downing Street knows that the transformation – which he describes as a betrayal – is undeniable. It can't be disguised. It was Blair's specific intention.

Blair's beliefs involve a conscious rejection of the past, almost for its own sake. Throughout the Thatcher years he watched from the sparsely covered opposition benches as she wrote a new political language, with Nigel Lawson its supervising grammarian and Bernard Ingham and Norman Tebbit the trumpets who gave it voice. Blair used to listen in wonderment. Before he and Brown began to stir together just before the 1987 election, with Mandelson shaping the relationship, Blair would talk wide-eyed of Thatcher's success in reworking the geometry of politics. 'She's changed it all,' he would say. 'She speaks in a different way. She's made her own style.' It had a profound effect on him. Here was a Prime Minister who came to power determined to make amends for the failures of Edward Heath's last Conservative government, as she saw them, and to assuage her own guilt for her part in it. In doing so she turned her party to her way of thinking (or enough of it, at least, to allow her eleven years in office). This was achieved, Blair thought, more by stubborn attack than by negotiation. She simply demanded new thinking, persisted and got it. That was the lesson he absorbed. He admired her for that, and made no apologies to colleagues who were startled and privately appalled when he invited her to Downing Street after the 1997 election to talk about the early days of government. No other member of his Cabinet would have contemplated such an action. Blair, however, enjoyed the sense of being made in a different mould and was amused by the fuss. She hasn't been back – but he doesn't regret it. Just after he became leader in 1994 Thatcher said in a BBC interview: 'I see a lot of socialism behind their front bench, but not in Mr Blair. I think he genuinely has moved.' It didn't bother him.

Blair in pursuit of political ends is a Prime Minister who shows little concern about the means. If his party thinks it is being insulted, he doesn't care. If he's accused of being too close to the Liberal Democrats, he cuddles up closer. If he is said to be too ingratiating towards George W. Bush, he takes the chance once more to defend the Americans' thinking about national missile defence. When he decided to bring Charles Clarke into the Cabinet as fixer and all-purpose government voice in the Cabinet Office ('Minister for the *Today* programme' and 'enforcer' are two of the titles that traditionally go with the job) he made him party chairman without dreaming of consulting Labour's national executive, which for generations has elected chairmen by the happy rules of Buggins's Turn, to preside over the monthly meetings and have a week of celebrity by the seaside chairing the party conference. Like Thatcher, Blair is often his own opposition, relishing the collisions with his party. They animate him and are one source of his political energy.

Belief for Blair is an attitude to life rather than a set of conventional political positions. He revels in his *difference.* In politics he is an outsider who has found his way in, and who seems determined not to be constrained within the usual boundaries. Brown, by contrast, has spent his life on the inside and is the politician who only steps out on his own terms. He does not see politics as a pond into which he's chosen to dive but as the natural habitat which nurtures him and lets him breathe. This is one of the differences between them that has enabled them to survive as a pair. They are not doubles who replicate each other's instincts and attitudes, but creatures from fundamentally different environments.

As much as Blair never wants to lose the feel of the outsider, Brown cherishes the opposite. From the moment he started to write in *Student* and fall for the charms of campus politics in Edinburgh, he has been on the inside looking out. The attitudes he strikes in government lead directly back to his early politics. Like Blair he went through the process of ditching early obsessions, in his case the heady assault on 'the logic of capitalism' in the *Red Paper* period, and although he was never as strident either on unilateralism or in the anti-Europe cause as many of his generation on the left, all that had been cleared away by the mid-eighties. Yet with Brown there were threads that always led back to early days. His rhetoric as Chancellor, even as the iron disciplinarian of the spending reviews, is still replete with references to equality and social justice. Although the word 'redistribution' was held to be too much of a reminder of Labour tax-and-spend attitudes long gone, and was therefore buried, Brown has always been happy to argue for his politics as natural products of an egalitarian instinct, which he interprets as a commitment to equality of opportunity.

As a schoolboy he'd written about poverty. His father insisted that his children understand what it meant to have to struggle in life; Brown always says that one of the debts he owes him is the importance of a feeling for equality. It explains a great deal about Chancellor Brown, but of course it also poses some questions. He was the minister who fought the backbenches on benefit changes – forced by the Treasury on the Social Security department – and who tangled with the sprightliest old warhorse of them all, Barbara Castle, on pensions and refused to budge in the face of her entreaties and campaigns to accept the restoration of the earnings link.

He was defeated on pensions at the 2000 party conference, and in his re-election campaign Blair said he regarded the 75p rise as the biggest mistake of the first term. It was a mistake he was quite content to lay at the Treasury's door, saying pointedly in his leader's speech at the conference: 'I tell you now – as Gordon made crystal clear yesterday – we get the message.' Brown appeared to believe that, with his big increases in the minimum income guarantee, he was making his commitment obvious, but within a month he had to backtrack and announce increases in the basic state pension of £5 for a single person and £8 for a couple so that 'all pensioners – the very poor, those on modest incomes and the relatively comfortable – share in the rising prosperity of the nation'. He was scrambling to recover lost ground.

Brown has presented a dual personality to his party and the public. One half of him is the austere accountant and stealth-taxer, the Silas Marner of Great George Street. In the first comprehensive spending review in 1997 he bullied the Cabinet into accepting

Conservative spending plans and even those who had got used to his methods in opposition were surprised at the ferocity with which he guarded his defences. There would be no backsliding. He told his colleagues that it was the election promise on which the government would stand or fall. Blair managed a joke about it in his 1999 conference speech, telling the party: 'You've never had it so prudent.' This was the Brown who gazed beetle-browed at the electorate after each of his early budgets promising that the pain would allow some later pleasure. But it couldn't happen without the pain. The message was unwelcome among some colleagues who began to talk about a Labour government seeming not to be a Labour government at all. Weren't they supposed to spend more than Major? Brown said no. He had his fiscal rules and they would not be broken, above all the Golden Rule laying down that, over the course of an economic cycle, borrowing would all be used for investment and not for current spending, the day-to-day running costs of government. In real terms spending rose by only 1.3 per cent a year over the Parliament, a lower average figure than the Major government managed, and in his first two years it actually fell by an average of 1 per cent a year in real terms. Fiscal rules, prudence and the bogey of boom and bust became the building blocks of every Brown speech and the patois of Whitehall. In the way that politicians always tune instinctively into a new dialect, just as schoolchildren will pick up the slang of the moment, Brown's disciplined repetitions ensured that the whole government began to speak in the language of the Treasury.

But Brown insists that he is not a mechanical Chancellor, concerned simply with the economic efficiency and progress which it is his job to produce. His obsession with stability is indeed an obsession: it is a belief that drives him. When he is asked to write or speak about his political beliefs he invariably chooses a theme of social justice. His own justification for everything he does in the Treasury is assessed in these terms. If the prudence of which he speaks cannot be shown by the end of his Chancellorship to have improved social justice he will, in his own terms, have failed. He convinced himself in opposition that rigour was necessary if the economic conditions he required were going to be produced. He therefore found no difficulty in arguing to sceptical colleagues that Conservative spending plans had to be respected for two years, and that the agreement to stick to existing tax rates for the whole Parliament be kept. The Bank of England decision, disliked by the left because it was deemed to put interest rate policy in the hands of the City, was similarly not awkward for him because his political thinking was dominated by the end rather than the means.

By the end of the first term, although the word 'redistribution' was still outside the approved lexicon and Brown talked about 'balance' instead, he was almost willing to put himself in the context of a socialist tradition. On the morning after the Budget in which he had decided to offer no direct tax cuts but a substantial new investment in health and education he was asked on the *Today* programme if he thought of himself sometimes as a socialist Chancellor. He replied: 'I think of myself as being fair – yes.' Explaining what he meant, he said: 'If it means equality of opportunity so that more people in our country have the chance of realizing their opportunities, then that's what I want to do.' He did not suggest that it was an outdated label, only that he wanted to interpret in his own way what it might mean.

Brown's language is interesting, because although it replicates Blair's themes about the economy so that there is no danger of gaps appearing between them, the Chancellor has always tried to retain for himself the mantle of the minister who thinks about the poor. It was the subject of his maiden speech, his 1983 book about Scotland with Robin Cook, and his efforts to promote the cause of debt reduction in the developing world. Nothing is more important to Brown than reminding his party that he hasn't lost that concern, an accusation heard often during the first couple of years of austerity from the left-wing Campaign Group and individual critics like Ken Livingstone.

One way Brown responded was to try to turn the question of debt in the developing world into a personal crusade. In opposition, he and Clare Short were not especially close, and when she spoke on transport they had the familiar battles about spending commitments. Brown thought she was a loose cannon whose opinions arrived loudly and long before her thoughts were in order. In government, as International Development Secretary, she and Brown shared one of the more surprising alliances in the Cabinet. Had Blair wanted to move her in 2001, Brown would have fought to keep her in post. He didn't have to, but the message to Number 10 was clear. Their bond was a strategy on debt devised between them which Brown claims offers the hope that child poverty can be greatly reduced and, in some countries, virtually eliminated. He has spent a great deal of time on the subject, with fellow finance ministers and leaders in the development movement, and his colleagues, Blair in particular, are happy to acknowledge it as a genuinely original effort. Brown insisted by mid-2001 that twenty-three countries had had their huge debts cancelled because of their efforts, although aid agencies are still arguing that on average only a third of debt repayments have been removed and many of the forty-one countries identified as being in need of help in 1999 were still crippled.

For Brown, however, it was a significant area of his chancellorship. It is a part of his job that confers no political benefits directly, either to Brown personally or to Labour. Elections are not won and lost over arguments about Third World debt. But Brown has made time for his debt reduction strategy to matter deeply to him. It is particularly his own. When he delivered the Gilbert Murray Memorial Lecture at Oxford at the beginning of 2000 to mark the founding of Oxfam in the early forties, a passionate Brown in full flow could be heard: 'John F. Kennedy once warned us that if a free society cannot help the many who are poor, it cannot save the few who are rich. But I believe that we start our considerations from something more fundamental – our dependence on each other.' This led to a perhaps unlikely friendship with the Archbishop of Canterbury, George Carey. Carey, who has entertained Brown and his wife privately at Lambeth Palace, found himself a welcome guest in the Treasury, his first experience of such intimacy with a Chancellor. 'I think he is a quite remarkable and deep man,' says Carey of Brown. The relationship is not one which Brown has publicized but it is strong.

Brown's main public boast is the New Deal programme but he

is just as proud of his work on debt relief. For Brown, sometimes assailed as the man who told the first Blair government it could not spend enough on the things it wanted, it is an important touchstone. Without it, he would feel greatly diminished.

He would also be seen as a dour and ruthless Chancellor, because he and Blair conducted the first comprehensive spending review, laying down plans for three years, with the vigour of an inquisition. It was a two-man job, with Brown the driving force. There were moments when Blair might feel it necessary to moderate Treasury enthusiasm for a particular figure, after being lobbied by some minister concerned that his department's great causes were going to be jeopardized, but it was an operation of notable joint ruthlessness. The two Cabinet committees – on economic affairs and public spending (both chaired by Brown anyway) – were effectively bypassed. No collective discussions were allowed to disturb the course of the spending discussions which were conducted with individual ministers who found they had no right of appeal. They were given the figures for the next three years of spending, and that was that. There was no star chamber of the sort that Willie Whitelaw had to convene in the early Thatcher years to hear appeals and adjudicate on tricky disputes with the Treasury. The Blair–Brown regime was less forgiving at the start than the Iron Lady's. What is more, the system of public service agreements introduced by Brown, which were the instruments by which the spending plans were controlled, meant that departments could only get the next tranche of their entitlement when they had demonstrated that the policy objectives set for them had been achieved. They had to defend their 'outcomes', the word that along with 'delivery' was to become almost an encapsulation of the purpose of power under Blair and Brown.

Nothing like this had been done before. In the post-war era, no Chancellor had been given so much raw power. The Whitehall wiring all seemed to run back to Brown's desk. With the Cabinet structure giving way to something close to a dual premiership – or at least a partnership in which the Prime Minister did not lay much store by his second title, First Lord of the Treasury – Brown was able to put an imprint on the government that was a statement of his own conviction, that without discipline there could be no progress.

Brown is a politician whose beliefs are obvious, never far from the surface of his performance in government. Though he tries to play down the redistributive effects of his policy, aware that it may open up some difficulties for the 'third way' talk of Blair, he has been a Chancellor who has manipulated the tax system with zeal in ways which he believes will shift money to the right places. He is criticized in the opposition parties for having done it in ways which have produced more damage than benefits – the 'stealth taxes' on pensions and business would have been a juicy target for a stronger Conservative Party in the 2001 election – but as ever with Brown his purposes are obvious. It is the same with his notion of 'fairness'. Where Blair is ever-anxious not to appear to decry success, Brown is much readier with rhetorical assaults on 'fat cats'. They are, of course, pursuing the same policy, in particular a top rate of tax which they have never seriously considered raising since 1997, but describe the objects of their policy in different ways. Brown still has a penchant for regular attacks on privilege. It sometimes unnerves Blair, who is vulnerable to the charge that his education was a gilded path. But Brown enjoys it. It led him, however, into one of his most embarrassing blunders.

It became the Laura Spence affair. Laura, an A-level student in north Tyneside, had a headmaster who decided to make public his disappointment that, despite having ten of her eleven GCSE results at the top A-starred level (the other being a mere A) she had failed to get a place at Magdalen College, Oxford, and was bound instead for Harvard. There was no argument about Laura's brilliance. Her school expected her to get A grades in all her A-level subjects. It was pointed out that she was also a Grade 8 violinist (the most advanced level) and was about to reach the same grade on her viola. The local press took up her cause, noting that Oxford took fewer than 2 per cent of its students from north-east England (the Cambridge figure was only 3 per cent), compared with 43 per cent from London and the south-east.

That week Brown was due to address a TUC lunch to mark

thirty years of the Equal Pay Act. In his office, his adviser Ed Miliband (whose brother David, now MP for South Shields, was head of the policy unit across the street in Number 10) briefed him about the case. Alastair Campbell had already discussed it in Number 10 after the Newcastle *Journal* headline had been spotted by Blair's 'media monitoring unit' and they realised Brown was due to be speaking about equality. Maybe there was a point to be made here? Miliband gave the Chancellor the bare bones of the story. Brown was sympathetic and angry. He told the lunch that he and the Education Secretary, David Blunkett, thought Laura's story was an 'absolute scandal'. He then spoke in a language which, for the obvious reason of his public school background and Oxbridge education, the Prime Minister would not have used: 'This is an interview system that is more reminiscent of the old-boy network and the old-school tie than genuine justice in our society. It is about time we had an end to that old Britain when what matters to some people is the privileges you were born with rather than the potential you actually have. I say it is time that these old universities open their doors to women and people from all backgrounds.'

Brown let it all pour out. His feelings about privilege were on display, and all the more obvious because as Chancellor he has tended to speak so cautiously, making his points with a machine-like monotony. In this speech, the brakes were off.

But unusually for Brown, who seldom utters a sentence without having considered carefully all the possible consequences, his facts were garbled. Laura had applied to read medicine at Magdalen, where there were twenty-three applicants for five places, and a dozen of the other candidates had GCSE scores as good as hers. (Brown had referred mistakenly to her A-level results: at this stage she hadn't sat the exams.) Of the five who were accepted for the course, two were from state schools and three from ethnic minorities. Laura didn't go to Harvard to read medicine: she decided to read biochemistry. Oxford colleges insisted that it would have been very unlikely that she could not have found a medical place elsewhere in Oxford. She was not sent packing with no alternative but to leave the country. And the Harvard 'scholarship' was not equivalent to a scholarship award in Britain, only the usual means-tested assistance offered by that university (a place, as Brown's critics pointed out, which could easily give Oxbridge some lessons in 'elitism'). But Laura had already become a symbol of 'old Britain', stuffy attitudes and the persistence of class-based education. She seemed less bothered about it than some of her supporters, telling the *Harvard Crimson* campus newspaper that she was 'kind of upset at the time' after an intense interview but adding: 'I wasn't thinking that I had been discriminated against.'

Brown found himself in trouble. In Number 10, Blair was furious although the two men did not have a face-to-face row about it. He was made vulnerable by Brown's sally, because everyone writing or commenting on the case would, naturally, contrast the Fettes–Oxford path that he followed with Brown's from Kirkcaldy High School to Edinburgh as if they were evidence of a great social divide. *The Economist* was typical: '. . . the whole government, in pressing home this attack, while being led by Mr Blair, a privately-educated, Oxford graduate who sends his son to an "elitist", selective school, is guilty of hypocrisy and opportunism'.

Advisers in Number 10 spoke of the Chancellor with real bitterness. Later in the summer, after Blair had slipped into his own stream of troubles they were blaming him for raising the Old Labour spectre. Brown's friends know that he was embarrassed by the revelations of his factual inaccuracy – nothing can make him lose his temper faster than the knowledge that he's been lured into an avoidable mistake – but, just as importantly, they say he has never expressed any regret for the question he raised. He appeared not at all disturbed that senior Oxford dons, a number of them Labour supporters, turned on him and accused him of ignorance, like the scientist Richard Dawkins, who said cheekily that if he did represent New Labour he should do something new and depart from political precedent by apologizing. The fact that joining in the chorus was the Chancellor of the University, Roy Jenkins, did not, of course, increase the chances of a Brown apology, although Jenkins managed a barb aimed with characteristic accuracy: 'If he had wanted to launch a great attack I would have thought his alma mater, Edinburgh, was a better target, since it has more Etonians than Oxford at the present time.'

Brown, although irritated at the revelation of the muddled facts, has never revised his general attitude to the Oxbridge system. He was happy for it to be known where he was positioned. He didn't like the system, and he wanted to say it.

The episode is telling. In the wider Labour party, Brown found that there was sympathy for his approach. What if he had mangled the odd fact? He was talking, at last, about 'them and us'. And for Brown it was important that his party credentials were burnished. His 75p a week pension award had been announced in the Budget only a few weeks earlier, giving him by far his worst bout of personal publicity since coming to office. The Social Security department could be blamed by some of those in the Chancellor's circle, but that strategy was scuppered by the knowledge, enthusiastically peddled by the Treasury for three years, that nothing in that department could happen without passing through the Chancellor's all-powerful hands. There could not be a better moment for him to take an attitude of the sort that characterized the Laura Spence affair: here was a Chancellor who, though he might make mistakes on pensions, was willing to declare a passion for fairness.

Laura Spence was the unwitting agent of his effort to recover ground lost in the pensions argument: a political point was made. Brown thought he was seen to be on the side of those who wanted more access to excellence – among them women and pupils from state schools. It probably suited Brown that one of his assailants in the row that followed his speech was Blair's old housemaster from Fettes, Eric Anderson. He wrote in the magazine of Lincoln College, Oxford, of which he was the recently retired Rector, that Brown's remarks were deeply offensive: 'I have not seen Oxford so angry about anything.' But the fact that Anderson had left Oxford to become Provost of Eton was seen by those around Brown as useful. Forget the efforts of most Oxford dons to recruit more widely from state schools . . . this had become a political battle of attitudes. Brown was happy to send out his signal. The party would know where he stood.

For some of those on the Labour backbenches who were grumbling about Brown's 'fiscal terrorism' it was a welcome, even overdue, signal. Wasn't it the historic role of Labour ministers to challenge the establishment? In the parts of the party where Brown had his strongest traditional support, the parts that were deeply unsympathetic to Blair's approach to government, the incident was a blast of heat from the old days, fetid though it may have seemed in the senior common rooms of Oxford and the rarified corridors of Whitehall.

In the wide sweep of the first term, the Laura Spence affair did not have serious consequences for the government and was quickly overtaken by events that were much more alarming for Downing Street. Yet it demonstrated a fundamental aspect of Brown's political persona. He is not a minister who will ever be willing to change his fundamental attitudes. Despite the political journey he made from the seventies to the nineties he was displaying the political beliefs which he has kept with him. They are attitudes about wealth, power and social balance. Blair's beliefs are more philosophical than political, a series of instincts which are unconnected in his mind to party-political strategies or obligations.

Where Blair has been anxious to demonstrate that there are no sacred cows grazing on his patch, and has enjoyed the role of the iconoclast who sees a virtue in dismantling the history of his party, Brown has played the opposite role. Even as he espouses some of the language of the supply-side economists of the Thatcher–Reagan years, he is making an effort to remind his party that he retains some of the instincts of the traditional Labour man. Prime Minister and Chancellor often use the same words to describe their beliefs – a hatred of poverty, encouragement for the innovative, a commitment to educational opportunity, a modernized country – but in the accompaniment that runs underneath they reveal their different preoccupations. Blair is anxious to break free, and Brown wants to hold on.

One of Brown's strongest ministerial supporters puts it like this, without embarrassment: 'If you read Gordon's speeches you can see the shape of the party that he would run if he became leader. It's obvious that it's different from Tony's even though they've agreed on the direction the government has taken up to now. Gordon thinks of himself as a Labour man. Tony doesn't. It's the real difference between them.'

Clive Soley, former chairman of the parliamentary party, has had many conversations with Blair about his beliefs and attitudes, and speaks from the position of an agnostic who is interested in Labour's history and beliefs. He expresses the relative positions of Prime Minister and Chancellor thus: 'Tony is a Christian Radical and Gordon is a Christian Socialist. That's the distinction.' By that he means that Brown keeps with him a system of beliefs with which to apply prescriptions in the hope of achieving his ends, and Blair does not. He operates much more by instinct. Soley's acknowledgement of a shared link between their attitude to power and their policies, and their private beliefs is significant.

Blair, of course, is open about his religious life. He is a member of the Church of England but usually worships with his family at a Catholic church; his wife and children are baptized Catholics. Since his time with Peter Thomson at Oxford he has been, more or less, a practising High Anglican though without some of the ritualistic obsessions that sometimes come with that particular strand of Christianity. He is not afraid to draw on it, to the bafflement of some of his colleagues. Prescott, for example, who is resolute in his agnosticism, will not criticize Blair directly for his religious stand but finds it slightly mystifying. From inside the Catholic Church many have speculated that he will one day convert. He did take communion regularly from at least one Catholic priest but after a discussion with the late Cardinal Basil Hume, a close friend, that technically improper practice stopped. Blair could not resist a slightly waspish remark. After agreeing that he would refrain from receiving communion if the Catholic Church was troubled by it he added, 'I wonder what Jesus would have made of it.' Intriguingly, he used a formulation that has become something of a catchphrase among evangelical Christians. No apology there.

Blair's beliefs have caused him some difficulty, and not only from those in his party who find public expressions of religious faith unsettling and inappropriate in government. With the late Cardinal Winning in Glasgow, Blair had a very rocky relationship. In the West of Scotland, Labour is closely associated with the Catholic Church and the Cardinal was a figure of some importance, a Labour-supporting man on social questions but a churchman who was deeply conservative on theological matters, notably abortion. He objected to Blair's position on abortion – that he and his family wouldn't practise it but that he respected the right of others to take a different view. It was evidence, the Cardinal thought, of hypocrisy. Blair was offended. They managed to avoid running into each other on several prime ministerial visits to Scotland, and relations remained badly strained. Despite such problems arising from his willingness to discuss religion – no other post-war Prime Minister showed such an inclination, nor attended church so regularly – Blair has been happy not to retreat.

By chance, he found himself having to address a Faith in the Future conference, made up of a largely black evangelical audience, the very day after his son Euan's escapades in Leicester Square. Blair made a suitably chagrined reference to the incident and then departed from his text to quote a Longfellow poem: '. . . for thine own purpose, thou has sent the strife and the discouragement . . .' He said it was a poem he had turned to the previous night. He went on: 'Faith is important for another reason, too. Faith is and should be in the end the best expression of community, the best expression that there's something bigger than us as individuals.'

Speaking to Hunter Davies in the *Mail on Sunday* during the election campaign, he was frank about his feelings, and even the fact that he had to deal with the incident alone:

> I was very worried at the time. But now, looking back, it was pretty hilarious . . . It had been such an awful day for me. I can't remember all the exact details of the day, but it was bad. I think it finished with me being pretty rubbishy at Prime Minister's Question Time. Then next day I had an important speech to make. So I had lots to think about. Plus Cherie was away with her mother and the baby on a short holiday. That left me in charge of the family. At first, I was so busy I didn't have much

time to worry about Euan's absence. I wasn't in best shape anyway, with all the other things going on. It was quite late when I started getting worried. I rang some people to find out where he was. Then the police got in touch. It wasn't till 1.30 in the morning that he was located. When he did get home, he wasn't, er, all that well. I was desperate for a good night's sleep because I had a busy day coming up, but I didn't get much sleep that night at all. It was terrible at the time, with all those other things happening, but now in retrospect I can laugh about it. Next morning I was making a speech to some black church leaders. The news about Euan had come by then. They said they were going to say a prayer for me. That was sweet. I was touched by that.

It is impossible to imagine Brown speaking publicly in this way, not because he might not agree with some of the sentiments, but because he is not a politician who can mix the personal and political with Blair's insouciance. He keeps what religious feelings he has to himself. Though he does not go regularly to his local Church of Scotland in Fife, his wedding was conducted with the traditional ceremony and he has never appeared to lose his ties with that faith.

His public attitude to belief, however, is conditioned by a tradition that is quite alien to Blair. In Brown's childhood, religion was a private matter. Outpourings of enthusiasm were not encouraged, nor appreciated. Displays of fervour were generally regarded in Scotland as deeply improper. Religion was about private codes of behaviour. The Catholic way, with which Blair is familiar and very comfortable, has a style that is much less constrained. Reared in a cathedral choir school where Anglo-Catholic practice was the life-style, Blair gravitated naturally into the enthusiastic Christianity of the sort practised by Peter Thomson. It was not the over-the-top evangelism of the university 'God Squad' but it had an unselfconscious character which would not have seemed at home in fifties Kirkcaldy. Blair, though not a tub-thumping zealot, has built into his politics an overt spiritual tone which he finds comfortable, even necessary as a motivational reminder of why he's there. Brown keeps his religious beliefs private – even some quite close friends are not sure what they are. He much prefers the echoes of an old socialist language to the ethereal 'peaceful, very beautiful religious faith' which Blair finds in the Koran, though occasionally he is prepared to admit the truth of the adage that Labour owes a greater debt to Methodism than to Marx. A particular Scottish instance is described by Brown in his biography of Maxton, as the newly elected Red Clydesiders departed for London in 1922 from St Enoch's Square, Glasgow, on the night train to the sounds of vast crowds singing Psalm 124 ('Now Israel may say and truly, if that the Lord had not our cause maintained . . .'). Brown adds: 'Not sentiments widely heard in Bolshevik Russia, and the declaration issued earlier in the day owed more to the Bible than to Bolshevism, more to the traditions of the Scottish Covenanters than those of Soviet Communism.' The crowd also joined the William Morris Choir in singing 'Jerusalem', not an anthem often associated with Glasgow.

Cabinet colleagues who wonder why the rows – whether about the benefits policy or Mandelson or Campbell or Laura Spence – have never severed the link between Brown and Blair speculate privately about whether they have enough of a 'belief in belief' in common to retain a fundamental relationship. In the Cabinet there are very few who have been quite so marked by early religious and cultural influences (Blunkett, a serious Christian Socialist, being one notable exception) and some are repelled by Blair's overt attraction to religion. 'Tony's in his Jesus mood again,' one minister has said more than once, without much affection. Brown has none of that tone, but his politics are shaped as much by his background, in which a moral code was important, as Blair's.

Brown's private attitudes may be a deliberately protected mystery, but a description of the Chancellor without reference to the benign Calvinistic influences of his youth would be pointless. Blair, the Koran and the Bible packed carefully by Downing Street staff for every trip, can't be understood without his spiritual baggage. And their relationship, beset by gales and storms, gets some of its surprising resilience from that background. If Blair's public professions of religious faith seem soupy and off-putting to some of his colleagues, and Brown springs from a religious tradition which is often accused of implanting a repressed and guilt-ridden conscience, it nonetheless gives them something in common. At Donald Dewar's funeral, when Blair read from Isaiah and, a few minutes later, Brown delivered his own address, part sermon, part political rallying cry, each seemed at home and both knew it.

Blair lacks the armour of ideology; he has cast aside the shield of clannish party obligation. And what has allowed him to do this is a fundamental inner confidence – the confidence of a natural philosopher who has found a still point around which the intellectual and moral challenges of everyday politics can swirl and be dispatched. Blair's spiritual sense is, like his politics, inclusive rather than dogmatic. God lives, it seems, in a big tent as well.

The crucial distinguishing feature is not a doctrinal one, however, but in the distinct quality of the belief that each man has. Brown, a historian by training, a traditionalist by nostalgic instinct and a technician in practice, has a robust exoskeleton of conviction that roots him in his party. His certainties straddle the inner world and the political world outside. To him, they seem one.

12
Blair and Brown

The Cabinet table is like a psychological chessboard. The games are multidimensional and the lines of attack and defence cross each other in a pattern that is always changing. With each move, a new prospect opens up. But whatever the game plan, one axis never shifts.

The pulse that beats between Blair and Brown is their government's supply of nervous energy. Yet that same strength, which has allowed a Prime Minister and Chancellor to pool their powers and dominate a political era, has given their government a vulnerability, an inner contradiction that it is doomed to resolve in the end. Ministers argue about who is weak and who is strong, and who is the more manipulative of the two. They wonder how Blair and Brown can hold the balance between their personal commitment to each other and their rivalry. So they watch every move with eyes trained to spot the slightest shift of power and the moment when the endgame begins.

When Blair and Brown are together, they behave like brothers or young friends, leaning into each other, Blair touching and Brown grinning, making natural eye contact, understanding each other's reactions as only a close couple can. The notion of an estranged pair of battling ministers, each trying to outdo the other, is inconceivable. Their disputes and sulks don't undermine the closeness; they are the dark reflection of it.

Being part of the government involves studying this psychology. No one in the Cabinet can treat the duopoly of Prime Minister and Chancellor simply as the mechanism by which power is exercised in government. They are all drawn into the undercurrents of the relationship. Blair and Brown seem to their colleagues to need each other, aware that each provides something distinctive. Blair continues to speak of his admiration for Brown's intellect and force; Brown accepts Blair's skill in having colonized a vast tract of the political middle ground for the Labour Party. Each knows that without the other he would be much more feeble. So there is dependence, and that has bred a closeness which gives their government a distinct flavour. It's too strong for some tastes, imparting emotional tension to much of the business of government, but it is inescapable. More than most political partnerships, this one is psychologically compelling to those around.

At Chequers, alone except for perhaps one or two advisers and perhaps one minister involved in a specific subject to be thrashed out, they'll try to sort out some difficulty with a White Paper, or a Budget speech. Those who have been present at these almost private moments report that they are still capable of presenting the old picture of a pair of collaborators who speak an exclusive private language accompanied by an exchange of physical gestures – a grunt, a raised eyebrow, a dismissive wave – that comprise a personal code that they both understand without having to think. They're aware that it was their bonded, concentrated power at the centre of government that allowed an administration of more or less completely inexperienced ministers to manage the first term in a way that produced the second big majority. At those moments, the axis seems the most solid in politics.

But they complicate that simple contented image by the frustration they both display. Blair has wondered aloud to more than one colleague, on a number of occasions, whether he might have to sack Brown. Brown has grumbled about Blair and some of his social policy objectives, and allowed his friends to continue to put about the belief that there is a promise of the inheritance, given by Blair, that must be fulfilled. This parallel contest is as absorbing as the unified front that allows them to divide and rule, the means by which they control their government.

At least one colleague has grown weary of the difficult side of the relationship, especially as it seems as if it is the one that now dominates. He has known them for more than fifteen years and watched every move. 'It was a warm, bonded relationship. It really was. Now it is merely a professional relationship, not underpinned by warmth or much emotion any more. It's sustained simply by the need to exist.'

That bleak account of a union drained of the old passion portrays them as a close couple whose knowledge of each other is as intimate as ever, but whose relations have become routine. Through the re-election campaign it was obvious that some of the fire has cooled. Blair would throw his jacket off at a press conference and plunge into one of his head-shaking, confessional mini-speeches, apparently asking questions of himself. Brown would remain dark-suited beside him, eyes down and unflinching, scribbling away in his large scrawl on sheets of paper piled on top of newspaper cuttings and a copy of the Red Book. The physical relaxation just would not come, and the flow of jokes seemed strained.

By 2001, Brown, his colleagues thought, might have been sunnier. Mandelson was gone. The double act which Blair had planned for the campaign was destroyed before it could begin by Mandelson's unexpected departure from the Cabinet for the second time in January. Yet Brown did not relax. With his friend and loyalist, Douglas Alexander, they ran an efficient campaign with hardly a serious blip, but it was thought by the Blair camp to have a rather grim flavour. One member of the Cabinet put it like this at the end: 'We had a campaign run by two Presbyterians, two sons of the manse. The result was that it was serious and bloody boring. At the party afterwards you'd almost have thought that we'd lost.' This seems a harsh judgement on any campaign that produced an overall Commons majority of 167, but it reveals how the personal styles of Blair and Brown are becoming more distinct in the eyes of their colleagues. One resolute and dark, the Iron Chancellor, the other more relaxed than he was for most of the first term and apparently less concerned about the difficulties that lie ahead than his partner.

People close to Brown dismiss this as a caricature which is put about by Blairites. They point to Brown's last Budget of the first term, laying exactly the foundations he had promised the country would see when he entered the Treasury in 1997. They cite instances when the Prime Minister deferred to the Chancellor at important strategic moments in the government's life. Each side claims the stronger champion. To Brown's cohorts, he is the man who dominates the government and leads Blair. The Prime Minister's side instead claims to be led by a subtle operator who can play Brown's game and win the big battles cunningly, without hang-ups.

Most of the Cabinet are still trying to decide what these men are really like underneath, what drives them, and what keeps them together despite the increasing tensions and the always obvious differences in temperament.

Blair, the natural showman, has enjoyed the physical side of politics – the stage presence, the speech that moves an audience, the close encounter with an elector or another leader. Watching him with one of the audiences in the round assembled for meetings he did throughout the first term and the election campaigns was to see someone comfortable on the swivelling stool in an arena, jacket off, hands pointing, brain whirring. In the same way, he has a relish of the intimacies of contact with other leaders like Clinton.

Blair seems to be able to shake off the tremors of the office when he is at home. He'll want to talk about how he wishes most of all that he could have been a great tennis player, or about his last game against one of his bodyguards at the courts he uses near Chequers, or about how much time he's trying to spend in the gym discreetly built inside Downing Street. Political conversation is not theoretical or academic, but about people. How can so-and-so behave like that? Why can't people in the Labour Party realize what an extraordinary man David Trimble is and why he must be supported? Don't people realize that Paddy Ashdown and I moved everything forward by years? He talks about a political game of chess that takes different turnings and swings in unexpected directions. To Blair, politics is an unfolding pattern of the unexpected, a jigsaw without a picture on the box.

He also retains a feeling for his own inexperience. He'll recall his first G8 summit when Clinton, joking at the new boy's expense to

Boris Yeltsin, recommended that the Russian President, with his experience of the Chechen war, might go to Belfast to help as an intermediary in Northern Ireland – and how, to his horror, Blair watched Yeltsin listen to the translation and reply seriously that he thought it was an idea which he would take up – offering Cossacks on the Falls Road. The early days with Yeltsin were a diplomatic testing ground, in finding a way, for example, of resisting an invitation to have a summit meeting on a Russian submarine under the polar ice cap.

Even when Blair talks of public services, the obsession at the start of the second term, he enjoys the sweep of the subject and the personal anecdote rather than the painstaking argument. As a politician, he flies by his instincts and acts quite often on impulse. One visit to Cumbria during the foot and mouth crisis convinced him that the 2001 General Election should be postponed from 3 May, the date to which his team had been working for more than a year, the date to which a detailed timetable had been attached. A majority of his Cabinet colleagues thought he was wrong; the election team, led by Brown, was strongly against postponement. He wouldn't hear argument. The decision was made.

The private and public Blair are the same. His personal credo – a bit of Anglo-Catholicism, a bit of the philosophy of John Macmurray, a bit of the Koran – is applied to everything. It means that he tends to try to think the best of everyone, even in the most unlikely circumstances. He startled the Foreign Office, for example, by saying that he thought Binyamin Netanyahu, when he was Israeli Prime Minister, was deep down a peacemaker committed to a deal with the Palestinians on the kind of basis that the Americans had been negotiating for years. Robin Cook had to persuade him that perhaps he was allowing his hope to overrule his judgement. Blair, in the end, is an enthusiast.

Brown's enthusiasm is intellectual. It sustains an ambition that is unyielding but everything comes from mental effort. It is how he operates. Deep inside him is a set of attitudes and principles – about poverty, about equality of opportunity, about a society like the one his father imagined – and they sometimes seem to control everything. He thinks about politics all the time. Mandelson would say of him, when they were close, that he lived and breathed politics twenty-four hours every day. He'd never relax. Even with a glass of whisky watching *Match of the Day* there would be a strategy to think through, or a phrase to be minted for a speech or a mental note to be made of a book someone mentioned that had to be read. Brown relaxes with tennis or in watching football or rugby (indeed, almost any sport can get his attention, but not quite as easily as a *Financial Times* leader) but most of his life is a self-controlled piece of concentration.

Though he laughs and jokes with friends, his public appearances often have a sombre air. In interviews he is notoriously difficult to warm up. Face to face in a studio he is more mellow, but the sound of the Chancellor announcing a three-point plan down a phone line from Brussels, or from a distant radio car, is sometimes a trial. The lists and statistics are fired out like a Gatling gun. Anyone who can't see the issue of the moment in the terms that he has already sorted out in his own mind does not deserve much consideration, he seems to imply.

Blair is capable of annoyance too, and disguises his occasional tetchiness badly, but on most occasions adopts a take-or-leave-it attitude, in the knowledge that interviews are ephemeral and momentary. The sun will rise tomorrow; there will be another speech or another interview; yesterday will pass away.

Since their instinctive reactions are so at odds, they have had to develop a set of unspoken rules by which they can carry out their private discussions and preserve the precious bond that has served them so well. One of the most senior members of the Cabinet says: 'I have never seen Tony take Gordon on full-frontally. I don't think it has happened. He simply won't do it. We know that they have their disputes. But Tony avoids public battles with him.' At least one of Sir Richard Wilson's senior officials who watches many Cabinet meetings and has attended on past Prime Ministers, sees this as a shortcoming. 'It means that whether or not it really is weakness, the Prime Minister's Cabinet colleagues see it as that,' he says. 'Brown is stubborn. Extraordinarily so.' Each displays strength and weakness. Blair can allow an impression of deference to Campbell or Brown to spread without flinching, although it disturbs some of his colleagues. Brown has to cope with a manner, involving a great deal of impatience, that suggests fragility – but rests on a rock of conviction which gives him his foundation. The trick of Blair and Brown's relationship is that each understands the mental architecture of the other.

It is difficult for Blair to pick up every challenge: if he did the government would proceed by means of a series of rows. When he does pick a moment he insists, usually quietly, that his mind is made up. A favourite Brown response is: 'If that's your instinct, that's it.' The reference to instinct, which each of them makes quite often, reveals the extent to which they understand that their closeness has produced a way of working that depends more on 'feel' than on structured argument.

This means that when they fall out it is often over something apparently quite trivial. The funeral of the Princess of Wales was a case in point. In the hasty arrangements made by Buckingham Palace, with Alastair Campbell drafted in from Downing Street as a tactical adviser to assist in the panic of those days, the senior members of the government who were invited to Westminster Abbey were Blair, Prescott, his ceremonial deputy, and Robin Cook, who had been given a personal invitation by the Spencer family because he had spent a great deal of time with the Princess discussing landmines and their removal, a cause to which she had become devoted.

Brown was not on the list. He was furiously offended, possibly because Cook appeared to be pulling rank. Downing Street had to douse his anger for the two days leading up to the funeral. One of those close to it says it was a row fought with a passion which Blair found puzzling. The outcome, though its origin was never publicly admitted, was an announcement from Downing Street just after the funeral in September 1997 that Brown would chair the Diana, Princess of Wales Memorial Committee charged with the responsibility of finding a suitable way of commemorating her life. It was a chairmanship which few in the Cabinet would have wanted. It was daft to burden the Chancellor with it. But it was a necessary palliative, a peace offering from Blair, and it was accepted.

The episode illustrates the confined nature of many of their arguments, which are often petty irritations that spring up and throw one of them off balance for a while, before order is restored. They have found that they cannot run government any other way. They have come to rely on direct but private negotiating channels, the habit that is partly a reflection of Blair's personality and partly the best way of preserving the working partnership with the Chancellor.

Their government has become something of a metaphor for their personalities. Blair, for all his tendency to theatricality and his relaxed style, is surprisingly remote from most of his party; he is not a gregarious Parliamentarian. MPs tend to be brought in groups to see him: he doesn't mingle naturally with them. His family is a private cocoon which is jealously guarded and which is kept, as far as possible, away from his 'working' friends. The reason the Blairs spend a great deal of time at Chequers – much more than the Majors – is that it allows them to shut out the crowd.

Brown, of course, seems to worship at the altar of privacy too. The tendency to try to conceal his emotions was endemic in the society in which he grew up. Metropolitan types are often puzzled by his reticence about his private life before his marriage, but for children of fifties' Scotland sex outside marriage would be something conducted with the vision of an aged aunt standing at the end of the bed watching disapprovingly. You were taught to draw a veil over quite a lot. It means that he finds public displays of emotion uncomfortable, unless they are channelled through politics. It was striking that on the morning after the announcement, in July 2001, of the coming birth of his child he was seen smiling for the cameras with a relaxation that looked new. 'He looks as if he feels free at last,' a close acquaintance said.

Their own characteristics dictate the personality of the throng around the throne. It comes from four people: the Prime Minister, the Chancellor, Campbell and Mandelson. One of them is no longer there, technically, but his influence pervades Number 10 still. At the height of the government's difficulties with foot and mouth, a Labour MP rang the Prime Minister's office. He spoke to Jonathan Powell, who asked, as agile aides do, what the MP had thought of the coverage of the government on radio and television that lunchtime. How did we come across? The MP gave his answer, and got the reply: 'That's exactly what Peter thought.' This conversation took place at about 2 p.m. It was clear to the MP that Mandelson was plugged in to Blair's office as closely as ever, offering advice on the hour, every hour. He had resigned two months before but, once again, as everyone in Number 10 knew, he was a presence at the Prime Minister's side, the ghost in the machine and the political essence without which Blair seems sometimes to lack confidence in himself. Although Mandelson had been removed from Brown's side as joint coordinator of the election campaign – to the relief of staff at party headquarters who had dreaded the explosions that the arrangement would produce – he was helping to write speeches for the campaign, offering strategic advice and acting as a day-to-day sounding board for the Prime Minister who told his staff that he still depended on Mandelson's advice.

The survival of Mandelson as one of Blair's principal courtiers reveals the unchanging quality of the court. On its outer reaches, ministers come and go and rise and fall in influence. Inside, the old loyalties and rivalries dictate everything. Mandelson, despite the anger which he felt at his second resignation, cannot let go. One minister describes it in a cruel sentence: 'When you're on heroin, it's hard to get off.' The drug is influence and power, and Mandelson's attraction to the source of power hasn't waned, despite the deep resentments which disturbed him after he was removed from government for the second time. Nor has Blair's addiction to his old friend's advice.

Mandelson's principal grudge is against Jack Straw who, as Home Secretary, told Downing Street that he believed that his call to one of his junior ministers, Mike O'Brien, in support of a passport application by the Hinduja brothers was the exercise of improper pressure. Sir Richard Wilson, the Cabinet Secretary, went to some trouble to ensure that the Hammond report on the affair commissioned by the Prime Minister did not suggest that he was the principal agent of the 'resignation', but he still has a place in the Mandelsonian pantheon of villainy. These feelings, however, are separate from the intimacies of the old gang, which zing with a special passion.

As Blair and Mandelson faced the inevitability of his second resignation when they talked in the Prime Minister's study on 24 January, it was Campbell who oiled the trapdoor. Asked by journalists late that morning whether Mandelson would still be Northern Ireland Secretary by the end of the day, Campbell said he didn't know. From a Downing Street press secretary, that was a death sentence. When he said it, no decision had been taken but he knew that Blair would have to face the truth: despite his hopes of survival, harboured until that morning, Mandelson could not survive. The newspapers were rampant, the government was shivering at the thought of a pre-election financial scandal – in the Foreign Office, the Home Office and the DTI it was known that the Hindujas had been fingered by the security and intelligence services as dangerous friends who should be avoided – and for at least two days Campbell had known that resignation must come. The scene in the Prime Minister's study was simply the ritual act of preparation for parting. Campbell came in as Blair and Mandelson spoke and all but said 'get on with it'. Within a few minutes Mandelson stepped into Downing Street to say that he had decided that it would be better if he left the government.

An hour and a half later their faces in the Commons were a ravaged tapestry of despair – Blair distraught at the inevitability of losing the friend whose attraction to the dangers of politics was too great, and Mandelson whitened by the shock of a departure which he had thought only the day before that he could avoid. It looked like a family tragedy.

That Mandelson remained afterwards a trusted courtier, a friend always ready with a strategy or a piece of tactical advice, is evidence of their mutual obsession. The intensity of the relationships binding the quartet transcends the usual networks of loyalty and obligation and rivalry that always run through politics and gives Blair's Downing Street a heightened emotional air. The first four years put the relationships under the sorts of strains more usually associated with a creaky marriage but they could not be severed.

Campbell and Blair are a unique pairing of press secretary and Prime Minister. The nearest equivalent, of someone who could talk to the boss with vicious bluntness, is Joe Haines, who served Harold Wilson for much of his time in Downing Street. Towards the end, in 1975–6, Haines was able to tell Wilson that he was drinking too much, once pointing out to him in his room at the Commons that the very large brandy which he had started to need before Prime Minister's Questions had been rather too large, and his answers had been slurred. But even Haines, a laconic and sometimes acerbic man, would not have told the Prime Minister that a speech or a suggestion was 'fucking crap'. Campbell is not someone who puts on a different character when he enters the Prime Minister's study: if anything, his natural aggressiveness intensifies. Even in front of visitors he will make his boredom or his contempt or his anger quite obvious. Ministers are sometimes mystified by it. They fear Campbell because of his power, but one Blair loyalist in the Cabinet says this: 'I do not know how Tony can take it. Alastair treats him like a child sometimes.'

Blair is untroubled by the reaction to Campbell. Though he is capable of being irritated by the brutal satire of Rory Bremner (which resulted in him being banned from the campaign bus) he has never indicated any embarrassment about his closeness to Campbell or his willingness to be the recipient of blunt advice and criticism. He soaks it up, and it is a symptom of his own confidence. A less secure Prime Minister couldn't live with Campbell for a week. Blair's irritations are minor, usually about briefings which have gone wrong. But there has never been a serious breach with Campbell. He is ever-present, and even when his public role has led to bad publicity for Blair his relationship, in the phrase that Mandelson used to describe his own bond with Blair, has never missed a beat.

But Campbell's dealings with Brown are different. They have many similarities. Both are tall, dominating, forceful characters who use physical intimidation in argument as a natural part of their weaponry: they glower and they loom. Campbell, whose bagpipe-playing is as important to him as his support for Burnley FC, is an emotional Scot and believes he understands the churning depths inside Brown. This does not make them soulmates. It makes them suspicious of each other.

Campbell denies utterly the 'psychological flaws' remark attributed to him. Brown does not believe him and was not only angry but deeply hurt when he read it. He complained to Blair that Number 10 was getting out of control: an accusation which the Prime Minister found almost risible, because it was exactly the charge which he and his closest advisers had been laying against Brown's office. The political outcome in the Downing Street family was that relations between Brown and Campbell now had an extra layer of suspicion attached.

There is one particular problem, which disturbs Brown no less than it disturbs a number of members of the Cabinet. Campbell keeps a diary. He has taken notes since he joined Blair's staff in 1994 and there is very little of substance in the story of New Labour and the Blair government that he does not know. He has been present for every crisis and he has seen, more often than almost anyone else, the agonized arguments between Prime Minister and Chancellor. Mandelson has told friends that everyone knows Campbell will publish his diary some day, when the Downing Street days are over, and says this: 'Gordon is frightened of Alastair.' He's not the only one.

Fear is an important ingredient in the life of the quartet. Mandelson, famed as the great schemer, has a fear of the Prime Minister. He speaks of Blair and not himself as the manipulator: 'he uses me all the time'. At the height of his powers, when he was a formal courtier in the Cabinet Office next door to Number 10 in the first year of the government, the Cabinet (of which he was not yet a member) thought of him as the most powerful figure in the government apart from Blair and Brown. Mandelson saw it differently, and believed himself to be someone used by a Machiavellian Prime Minister, whose relationship with him was quite different from the one popularly portrayed. Blair, who remains deeply fond of Mandelson, was seen by his friend not as a weakling in need of sustenance from a fawning court (the caricature built up by some of Brown's friends) but as a more cunning tactician in personal dealings than Mandelson himself. One of the reasons for Mandelson's despair at both his resignations, apart from the stings of public obloquy and the simple loss of power, was that he believed his relationship with Blair was misrepresented. Far from being the dominant, manipulative half of the relationship, Mandelson thought himself to be the victim. He still does.

These are the kinds of feelings which flow around the quartet. The Hinduja affair released feelings of betrayal and anger on Blair's part, followed by ruthless decisiveness, then incredulity on Brown's, fear and bitterness on Mandelson's. Everyone was unbalanced and the feelings that lie just under the surface poured out again. Blair and Brown have been unable to escape that fate because the network trembles with deep feelings of friendship, disappointment and betrayal – an amalgam of emotions which can no longer be broken down into its constituent parts. Everything is fused. One of the reasons is that in quite different ways Blair and Brown have created a kind of personal politics which neither is able to unravel. Each relies in part on the other to preserve the relationships which brought them to power and have sustained the dominance of their government. They are trapped because of their success.

The duopoly brings together two different kinds of politics. Blair and Brown have different attitudes to loyalty, one practical and one much more emotional. Mandelson says of Blair that he sees political loyalty as a deal, in which favours are traded. This is certainly true in the Cabinet. Prescott is not especially close to Blair. They talk a good deal, but each knows that Prescott has never been a figure in the government with the clout of Brown, nor of Campbell. Blair, however, has traded loyalties with his deputy. When he became leader in 1994 he was worried about Prescott. He did not know him well, and Prescott's Labour background was one which Blair knew that he only vaguely understood. Yet Prescott has been loyal to Blair, keeping his explosions private. For all his contempt for some aspects of the government he has not destabilized the Prime Minister. In return Blair has protected him and talked up his role.

Brown's friends cannot imagine him dealing with a deputy in that way. The relationship would have to be more intense for it to survive. If Brown were in the position of appointing a deputy, he would select from the group of acolytes who have over the years demonstrated unquestioning loyalty to him. Despite his experience – half a lifetime's – in the arts of the political manoeuvre, Brown is a figure whose instincts and personality still dictate his behaviour. From his days as a student he has always operated in a close group. He still takes advice from his brothers and from a circle of friends who go back to Edinburgh days, and, in the case of Murray Elder, to nursery school. They are a trusted political family. In the Commons, his friends know that he will repay loyalty by defending them – but only if that loyalty is absolute. Ministers like Andrew Smith, Nick Brown, and Alastair Darling are utterly loyal. Others who served in the Treasury and became critics – notably Alan Milburn and Stephen Byers – are aware that there is no going back. 'With Gordon,' says a former Treasury minister, 'you know that deals are signed in blood. He won't let you down, but only if you promise the same. He's that kind of man. No mucking around. Are you for me or against me?'

Like Brown, Blair has some close friends to whom he is absolutely bound but, significantly, the two friends to whom Blair shows complete loyalty are not from Parliament – Campbell and Anji Hunter. They are trusted in part because they cannot be corrupted by political ambition. No one outside Blair's own family understands him better than Hunter. Irvine, scarcely a politician, is still close, but Blair's other friends are outside politics. He has no gang with whom he will unwind by replaying the latest government crisis or plan. Brown does.

Because each knows that the other brings to the relationship something that it needs, they have had no choice but to stay locked together. Brown, with his night-and-day political obsession, brings a sense of drive and conviction that Blair knows is on a different level from his own. Brown also understands, although the recognition shivers with an angst dating back to the leadership capitulation, that Blair has a political skill in enticing voters into Bill Clinton's 'big tent' that surpasses his own.

Brown is well aware that Blair's achievement in the first term was to occupy so much of the political middle ground that the Conservatives found it impossible to find territory in which they could wage a successful fightback. They were squeezed out, and the arguments in the leadership election that followed demonstrated that a substantial section of the party recognized that the Blair 'project' had done what it set out to do. However much they might argue against aspects of economic policy, or the domineering tone of the government, or its confusion on Europe, they could not argue away Blair's occupation of the centre of the political battlefield. Blair has harnessed Brown's intensity which has given the government its discipline, and in return Brown has acknowledged that it is Blair who sets the political tone. They have succeeded, at least if the re-election campaign and the result are to be taken as the measure.

But the dependence on each other makes their government vulnerable, especially when the two personalities fail to back each other up. Chaos ensures when the mechanism which allows one's failings to be compensated by the other doesn't work. Appropriately enough, one of the best analogies for the failures of Blair and Brown is drawn from below the surface – the debilitating row over the financing of the London Underground.

Blair has always been fascinated by Ken Livingstone and nervous of him. When he arrived at Westminster in 1983, Livingstone was leader of the Greater London Council and the embodiment of the leftism that Blair thought was threatening to destroy Labour. Although the Bennite tide had started to recede nationally, Livingstone, to the delight of Fleet Street, was refusing to retreat. The GLC taunted the Thatcher government and the Labour opposition too. Why wouldn't Michael Foot support him, asked Livingstone. Foot had realized that although the GLC had support for some of its radical policies on transport, for example, it had been successfully caricatured as the repository of all that was known in those days as 'the loony left' and had to be distanced from the party. Foot's aides were scarcely on speaking terms with Livingstone in the period just before the 1983 election. They hated him. Foot himself, who is a kindly man by nature, was bitter about Livingstone, whom he regarded as a factionalist and a destroyer. When the Conservatives abolished the GLC, Neil Kinnock, by then the Labour leader, believed it was an act that would have been impossible to put through Parliament had it not been for Livingstone.

So Blair feared Livingstone's destructive power, hence one of his most serious political mistakes. The whole Labour Party knew that Livingstone was more interested in being the first elected Mayor of London than in remaining MP for Brent East. But Blair could not contemplate the notion of a Livingstone victory. Despite polling advice which showed Livingstone as by far the most popular candidate, he insisted that the party find another one. The result was farcical. Frank Dobson was reluctantly persuaded out of the Department of Health to challenge Livingstone and was duly installed as a candidate.

Labour used an electoral college to select their candidate even though the London minister, Nick Raynsford, had told the Commons in May 1999 that 'the Labour Party will elect its candidate on the basis of one member, one vote. That is clear.' It wasn't. Each section – Labour members, union and affiliated societies, and MPs, MEPs and Greater London Authority candidates – had one-third of the electoral college, which was a desperate mechanism to produce the right result. Even Dobson thought it 'stupid'. He won by 51.5 to 48.5 per cent. But Livingstone had won 60 per cent of the votes of party members and 70 per cent of the union votes. Dobson's candidacy, after a period of political brutality in the London party directed from Downing Street, was a joke. It humiliated Dobson and embarrassed Number 10. Predictably, Livingstone launched his independent candidacy and won, with the Tory Steve Norris kicking Dobson into third place.

It was a re-run in technicolour of the championing of Alun Michael as first secretary in Wales despite the obvious unpopularity of a strategy run from London and in the end he had to accept the victory of Rhodri Morgan, whom he had opposed on the grounds that he had too many 'old Labour' leanings. The ploy failed, to Blair's surprise, despite the warnings given to him by Welsh MPs. London was worse.

When Livingstone challenged the government on the financing of the tube the problem was compounded. As well as Blair's instinctive opposition to Livingstone, and his fear of him, he stirred up Brown's deep antipathy.

Brown had good reason to dislike Livingstone, since as early as 1998 he had suggested publicly that the Chancellor should be sacked for running a policy that he interpreted as a surrender to the financial markets. He opposed the independence of the Bank of England and turned this into a personal campaign against Brown. The two were not on speaking terms. Brown regarded Livingstone as a party factionalist of the sort that he thought should be extirpated; Livingstone regarded Brown as a bully who wouldn't change his mind when it was made up. There was some truth on both sides. So when Blair stumbled into the mayoral mess, Brown had no interest in championing Livingstone's cause. And when Livingstone decided to oppose the Treasury's preferred public-private partnership (PPP) for the tube there was a predictable explosion.

Livingstone had undergone a metamorphosis in the Mayor's office. He was talking enthusiastically to the City and to business about how he wanted to build a partnership with them for the good of London; he seemed determined to be flexible in his thinking. GLC looniness had gone. Here was a Mayor talking about competition on the buses, cuddling up to business, operating across party lines. In re-inventing his political personality, his most dramatic stroke was in bringing in as transport commissioner Bob Kiley, an American who had revived the New York and Boston subways. Kiley thought the government's plan for a public-private partnership wouldn't work and was a safety risk, because it separated the running of the trains – by a publicly owned London Underground – from the maintenance of the track, signals and stations to three privately owned consortia. Brown had decided early in the life of the government that this was the best way to put the potential costs (and the almost inevitable overrun) on the backs of the private contractors and not on the taxpayer. Livingstone sailed into battle.

Blair met Kiley several times to try to find a way out of the impasse. Prescott was pulled in by Blair to try to change Brown's outright opposition: he failed. Kiley, Prescott announced, was going to be allowed to redraft the PPP proposals to try to devise an alternative that would satisfy both sides. The Treasury simply refused to let it happen. The Chancellor would not budge. By the time Kiley was sacked as chairman of London Transport (although he remained Livingstone's Transport Commissioner) after months of discussions with government in an effort to get a deal, Brown had still never met him.

The dispute then headed to the courts, with Livingstone hoping to turn the episode into a ground-breaking challenge to central government by one of the devolved institutions of which it boasted. He failed.

The mystery in all this was Blair, who knew that Livingstone's plan was popular with the public. All the polls carried the same message. Among London Labour MPs (who dominated the capital's politics) it was more popular than the Treasury alternative. Kiley, despite being criticized in Treasury briefings as a man whose reputation was greatly inflated and who didn't understand the British public sector, was popular too. Why not move?

The mystery deepened. Of all the disputes with Brown in the second half of the first term this was the one which appeared to give Blair the opportunity for a clean victory. Cabinet colleagues realized that he could make a popular decision and at the same time demonstrate his supremacy in government. For once he could be First Lord of the Treasury. Livingstone sent that message to him directly. But Blair would not overrule Brown. No episode in government reveals more clearly the dependence they have on each other. The political benefits were not sufficient for Blair to force the Chancellor to change his mind.

Brown's argument was simple. He held the view that money had been squandered on London Transport in the past and would disappear down a black hole once again if the Treasury surrendered control to Livingstone. He argued that his duty was to keep public money on this scale under his own control. He told Blair that this was a principle on which he would not budge. The politics of the issue would not change his mind. It was a classic Brown piece of defiance.

Kiley, a former CIA officer, who then used his skills to deal with the endlessly wily politicians of New York and Boston, was astonished. Livingstone had told him in typical style when he arrived that he would find dealing with Whitehall strange after his American experience. 'You'll find it's a bit like East Germany,' he told him, 'except that we have elections every four or five years.' After one of his efforts in Whitehall to get the government to abandon the public-private partnership, Kiley returned and told Livingstone: 'You're wrong. It's not East Germany. It's bloody North Korea.' In a splendid mixture of metaphors he linked North Korea with Kansas, because his nickname for Brown is the Wizard of Oz. Kiley came to believe that when you got to the end of the Yellow Brick Road you found that there was nothing there, only an illusion. Brown thinks exactly the same of Livingstone.

In the story of the Underground are distilled the forces that drive Blair's government. The Prime Minister's own nervousness at his party's past, epitomized by Livingstone; Brown's refusal to give way to an old enemy and his determination not to change a policy once settled in the Treasury; above all, Blair's refusal to overrule his Chancellor on an important matter of public policy even when it carries the prospect of popularity for the government and the likelihood that it will allow him to be portrayed as the Prime Minister who can't be pushed around by the Treasury. Although advised inside 10 Downing Street to challenge Brown directly and appeal for a change of heart, which he did, with the help of Prescott, Brown was resolute. Blair backed down, irritated but resigned.

This was a dispute about character and willpower. Brown was determined not to concede a financial argument. And Blair did not want to overrule him in public. The circumstances in which he has refused to let the Treasury prevail have been on issues that have not been argued out in the open. They have not involved a public repudiation of Brown, although sometimes Blair has refused to give way with a Brown-like resolve. The two had an abrupt series of exchanges about the funding of the BBC, which is a good example. In Downing Street it became the source of a great deal of anger, though little of it seeped into the public domain.

Brown was convinced that the government should impose a tougher financial regime on the BBC, involving an extra levy which the corporation would have to charge for its digital services. This had been recommended in a government report commissioned from Gavyn Davies, soon to be appointed vice chairman of the BBC and the economist closest to Brown. Blair disagreed; Brown believed he had been 'got at' by the BBC. As usual, the dispute got nowhere near the Cabinet. A series of meetings took place in Blair's office to try to resolve it. Brown was adamant. 'I am having nothing to do with this,' he said at a meeting in which Blair indicated his unhappiness at the Treasury view. Blair told him directly: 'I'm sorry, I've made up my mind.' The decision was made. Brown was angry, but impotent.

Such episodes find Blair in a determined mood, ignoring what ministers claim are Brown's 'insults' – their interpretation of his broody silence when Blair argues a case with which he disagrees. But in public, as with the tube, he is deeply reluctant to be seen to be at odds with the Chancellor. On Europe, the most obvious public argument swirling back and forth between Downing Street and the Treasury, they worked together on the speech Brown would give at Mansion House just after the 2001 election to try to make sure that they could buy time with a form of words that would not open a new burst of speculation. It worked. There were some headlines the next day, but the argument over the euro then went into a quieter phase. Blair had neutered it.

At every turn, when irritation or rivalry threatens the stability of the relationship there is an effort to stabilize it. In the nature of things, that effort usually comes from the Prime Minister. He has spent his leadership in the knowledge that Brown's ambition has not gone and has to be managed. Brown, on the other hand, is aware that he is acknowledged by Blair as the government's biggest thinker and strategist, the Chancellor who, in Blair's own words, 'has sixteen times the firepower of Ken Clarke' (Brown's old opponent in the Major government). This arrangement seems to some of Blair's friends to be one that the Prime Minister should resent more than he does; to Brown's friends it is simply a recognition of his place at the centre of the government, the Chancellor who engineered economic stability in the first two years (at the cost of popularity in the Labour Party) to allow the prospect of greatly increased investment in public services in the second term.

Blair has often been exasperated by what he considers Brown's stubbornness. More seriously, he believes Brown's supporters on the backbenches, around him in the Treasury and in Fleet Street to be damaging to the government because they portray government decisions and its standing in public esteem in terms of the Chancellor's decisions or outlook or prospects of succession. He is rigorous in support of Brown in conversation with outsiders, but does hint at the difficulties they encounter day by day. He will express a degree of mystification about the tactics used by his old friend: he understands the ambition that still burns, and the political determination that drives him, but he cannot share his all-or-nothing approach to politics.

On Brown's side there is a frustration born of the passing of time. Brown had been swallowing the consequences of the Granita dinner for seven years by the time of the re-election, with no obvious end in sight. No wonder he appeared to be chewing over a somewhat indigestible future. The Chancellor turned fifty in February 2001 – no great age in politics, but a milestone nevertheless. His colleagues believed that he was finding it more difficult rather than easier to deal with Blair in government. 'Gordon will never be reconciled to Tony as leader. It's as simple as that. It's part of the furniture.' That is the judgement of one minister who has attended many meetings with them, and who believes that one of the principal reasons for Brown's dislike of collective meetings is simply that he finds it difficult to recognize Blair's supremacy in front of colleagues. Brown himself denies this: he believes that such interpretations come from people close to Blair who have an interest in putting him down. He is right in that judgement. His view of some Downing Street courtiers is a mirror image of Blair's contemptuous description of some of the Chancellor's own crew. He argues that the Prime Minister does not take such a conspiratorial view of his behaviour in government, and does not believe Brown to be as reluctant as some suggest to accept the Prime Minister's authority.

But Blair's frustration does run deep. He has told close colleagues that he believes Brown's strengths are undermined by great weaknesses – even claiming that he has 'saved' Budget speeches by working them through with Brown at Chequers on the weekend before they are delivered. In turn, Brown has often expressed to friends his doubts about Blair's grip on strategy and has indicated a degree of disbelief at Blair's distance from his party. Such gripes have gnawed at their relationship over the years.

The admiration which they profess for each other is undermined by these feelings. Blair's regular choice of Lloyd George as his historical figure with whom to compare Brown has a touch of irony, and not only because Lloyd George was the most famous Liberal of them all. It was he who coined the phrase 'there's no friendship at the top', a motto of politics which hangs inevitably over a government like Blair's. Blair and Brown can still accurately be described as friends, in the sense that there are ties of loyalty which neither wants entirely to sever, but the intensity of their dependence on each other has gone as the intensity of the rivalries at the top of government has increased.

Each is more of his own man now than he was when the government was formed. Their personal lives, away from the office, reflect it.

The birth of the Blairs' fourth child in May 2000 was, obviously, an important event for them all. Those who know the Prime Minister well are aware of how profoundly it affected his outlook. He is the father of three teenagers and a child, and theirs is a close family. Unlike some politicians, he knows his children well, and is absorbed in discussion about their future. He is married to a powerful woman – the person who, more than anyone else, drew him into politics – and his family life looms large. They spend a great deal of time at Chequers together and Blair's ability to turn his gaze from government to his family is striking to all who watch him there. He is not obsessed by the premiership.

The importance of family ties is central to Blair, as he made clear by naming his fourth child Leo, after his father. Blair's childhood and youth were affected by two traumatic events involving his parents. His father's stroke in 1964 when Blair was eleven was an event which changed everything. It was three years before Leo Blair could speak properly again. It introduced a sense of deep uncertainty in the family. Secondly, Blair's mother, Hazel, to whom he was reportedly very close, died of throat cancer at the young age of fifty-two, just after he graduated from Oxford. She was of Donegal Protestant stock and his utter absorption in Northern Ireland is thought by some of those who know him best to reflect in part a commitment to her memory. In addition his sister, Sarah, developed a form of arthritis at a young age. The Blair family was marked by a series of tragedies.

Such a history is bound to have shaped his own attitude to his children, just as the background of Cherie Booth, whose parents parted from each other, has left its own scars. Their closeness to their children, and their determined religious commitments, are a striking part of Blair's character: it is part of the reason for the self-contained image which he wears.

The equivalent in Brown's life of the birth of Leo Blair in 2000 has been, of course, his marriage. His relationship with Sarah Macaulay went back to the mid-nineties after the break-up of his friendship with Sheena McDonald. The wedding was not for him the routine formalization of a long-standing relationship, but a commitment, with all the seriousness that he brings to everything. However, the public awkwardness which was displayed in the performance for the wedding photographs only seemed to evaporate properly when they announced in July 2001 that Sarah was pregnant.

Brown holds to tradition. He is close to his mother, who lives in rural Aberdeenshire, the part of Scotland where her own roots lie and where she and Brown's father moved when he retired from the ministry. His death was a blow to Brown, who had immense pride in him, and the concept of family is one that he and his brothers cherish. One inheritance which Brown was fortunate to escape was a family name on his father's side. Had Dr John Brown's middle name been passed on to his middle son, it might have caused some amusement among the Chancellor's Cabinet colleagues. His father was christened John Ebeneezer Brown, and any hard-pressed spending minister would have been happy to point out that it is a name chiefly associated these days with one figure, Dickens's Mr Scrooge. Gordon Brown's wedding has evidently not changed his determination to keep public and private lives apart. Sarah Brown (as she wants to be known) deliberately played no part in the election campaign, holding to a silence even more resolute than that famously practised by Ffion Hague, wife of the Conservative leader. She has been close to Brown's inner circle for some years, and, as before, they evidently intend to keep themselves to themselves.

The carefree young front benchers of the late eighties have aged. With the passage of time their political relationship has changed with their personal lives. They have grown apart. In government there are the same rows and moments of intimacy, and the same sense of dependence. But the familiar story is now played out against a different background. Blair is in his second term and has a new baby. Brown is fifty, married and looking forward to being a father. Almost like youngsters who drift away from each other as their lives take them on different paths, Blair and Brown find themselves thinking ahead in different ways while locked together at the heart of government. The absorbing question for their ministerial colleagues and their friends is the most obvious one of all, and the one that carries the heaviest weight of expectation and suspense: for how long?

13
A History of the Future

The war room in Millbank Tower which was the command centre for Labour's re-election campaign was a huge space for dozens of people, taking up the whole first floor, with only two private bolt holes to allow an escape from the throng. One was for Blair and one for Brown. The party planners placed them in the most natural configuration, as if by instinct. Blair's was along a short corridor leading from one corner and Brown's was in the corner diagonally opposite. They could not have been further apart.

No feng shui expert is needed for the message of that geography to be understood. Though Prime Minister and Chancellor often huddled together in the course of the campaign, and made a careful point of appearing as a practised double act at a string of press conferences, their private spaces were far apart. The two sets of advisers operated in different spheres and, despite the running conversation between their principals, they seemed happiest when there was no contact and each group was absorbed separately in the business of one man. The diagonal line from corner to corner was not only the axis along which power flowed, but the measure of a distance between the two camps that had been growing for four years.

After the election result was known, when Blair arrived back in London from his constituency to thank his staff, Brown had already flown down from Edinburgh and was on the stage set up outside Millbank looking over the Thames. They greeted each other with smiles, but betrayed not even a momentary hint of ecstasy. David Hill, a veteran party spokesman and arm-twister of the sturdiest denizens of Fleet Street, had been brought back from his lobbying firm for the campaign, and was spreading extravagant words: 'All of you in the media have to understand something about this result – it's probably the most astonishing victory in British electoral history.' Looking at Blair and Brown, it was hard to believe it.

Euphoria had been banned at the moment of victory. Any repeat of the 1997 frolics at the Royal Festival Hall risked looking arrogant, they had decided, so there was meant to be no public rave. Behind the controlled façade, however, the feeling that was struggling to find a way out was not one of wild celebration. It was a deep frustration. Blair was impatient with his Cabinet and with Whitehall, and Brown was impatient with Blair.

In Number 10, all the anxiety about 'delivery' in the public services and about the need to confront the public cynicism revealed in the General Election turnout (the first to dip under 60 per cent since the arrival of universal suffrage) was focused once again on the central partnership. Only if it worked did the government seem to function, and yet it was also seen by those around Blair as a great impediment. On Europe and on relations with the Labour Party, troublesome territory for Blair, Brown was seen as a problem, the right-hand man who was pursuing his own course and taking the opportunity at every turn to indicate that he was different from the Prime Minister. The reason why the melancholy air seeped through Number 10 after re-election was the recognition that the problems in the relationship were doomed to remain. There was no known surgical procedure in politics that could remove them cleanly, because the Prime Minister was bound to his Chancellor by a promise which could not be broken without destroying the government and starting again.

When Blair was elected in 1997 he told Mandelson that he was depressed by the persistence of the personal difficulties of opposition in government. After his re-election he had a matching frustration, in the knowledge that the problem of 'handling Gordon', which he had first identified ten years before, was still there. And he knew that on Brown's part there was a sense of impatience which pulsated just as strongly, and which Brown believed to be entirely justified.

When he started to reshape the government and Downing Street, he knew that their unsettled business was a destabilizing force which was likely to get more powerful as the second term went on.

Brown was entitled to believe that, as the election strategist, he had delivered everything. In 1997 he'd set out to change the public attitude to Labour as managers of the economy and all the polls told him that he had succeeded. The devaluation bogeymen of the past were exploded. But for Brown, this was a bittersweet sense of victory. The strength it gave the second Blair administration would surely postpone any hope he harboured of an early accession to the premiership. Which Prime Minister in the political history of Britain that he knew so well had handed over power at a moment of such dominance? Even Wilson, who unexpectedly organized the slickest departure of the modern era, had waited carefully until he had beaten Asquith's record of prime ministerial longevity and only went after a dozen years of dominance in the political arena.

Sometimes a civil servant around Downing Street would wonder idly whether Blair was enjoying the job, and then there would be a Kosovo or a Northern Ireland crisis or a foot and mouth operation and the Prime Minister would cease to be the man with the one-minute attention span and become again the obsessive commander. For Brown, the signs were of a premiership that was not ready to wane.

One of the signals was paradoxical. Blair's first order post-re-election was unexpected. He told Campbell: 'We've got to pull back. Pull back.' These were words that zipped round Whitehall like an order. Everyone on the inside knew what he meant. The government had spun itself into a tangled ball. A play called *Feelgood* was filling the Garrick Theatre every night, a few hundred yards from Number 10, and spraying Blair and his friends with merciless satire, depicting a political world in which nothing is real, only contrived for attention and deceit, and in which no motive is pure. A Prime Minister searches for a new empty phrase, the spin doctors scheme and contemplate murder, a government seems about to go up in flames. Twenty years ago, Denis Thatcher was happy to be seen being a good sport at John Wells's affectionate romp, *Anyone for Denis?* But Alistair Beaton's *Feelgood* was on a different plane. In his *Daily*

Telegraph review, Charles Spencer wrote that the 'manipulators and self-important creeps' who ran the country would be too scared to go to see it, but everyone else would know that New Labour could not be taken seriously again. Ministers and Whitehall advisers who crept into the stalls after the lights went down were reminded that, despite the biggest Commons majority of their lifetime, a troubling undercurrent of resentment and disaffection was running strong outside the gates of the citadel.

For Blair, who continued to convince himself that he had high motives and had kept his personal integrity, the palpable discontent was painful. His relationship with Campbell was portrayed generally in the media as that of the weak master dominated by the chain-swinging bully. Brown appeared in every cartoon as a smouldering presence about to burst into flame and consume Blair. When Blair wasn't the weakling he was the dandy, a flibbertigibbet. Like most Prime Ministers (with Major a notable exception) he had given up reading newspapers closely after a year or two in office, concentrating on the *FT*, and leaving the rest to Campbell to summarize, but he was aware that, although he was the most powerful holder of his office the country had seen since the Thatcher of the immediate post-Falklands era, he was being painted as a creature of feeble impulse, devoted to gesture politics.

For someone who believed his absorption in Northern Ireland over four years had been proof of statesmanship, and who revelled in his iconoclastic approach to his own party, the caricature was hurtful, more so than he let it appear. Hence 'pull back'. It meant something simple. With Campbell retreating from the front line, and Hunter and Powell running the three new departments in Number 10, the tone would change. Downing Street briefings would be taken over by Godric Smith, Campbell's deputy and a career civil servant, untainted by the tar brush of party spin. Campbell's move, conceived by Blair himself, was meant to make a practical difference and to send a message from Number 10 that the frenzy of control over Whitehall announcements and the effort to manipulate Fleet Street with their fingertips was over.

Blair's difficulty was that he had a competing instinct. When he commissioned outsiders to look at the machinery of government before the election, he knew the answer he wanted. The Number 10 machine needed to be strengthened and the streamlining of Whitehall had to go on. The command premiership had not yet reached its peak.

The Cabinet changes were meant to do the rest of the job, the arrival of Charles Clarke and Patricia Hewitt in particular freshening the team to give it extra bite. Blair was aware of a circle being completed, since they were the two stalwarts of Neil Kinnock's office when it was set up just after Blair himself had been elected. In his first year at Westminster they were much more influential than he was. Now they were all Cabinet colleagues, but with him at the top. He found the symmetry satisfying rather than piquant – Clarke, in particular, is seen by Blair as a potential successor, a judgement which may surprise some in the Cabinet but which is a sober one on Blair's part.

The importance of the changes was dramatized by the biggest revolt in the Commons of his whole period in office, the Select Committee revolt over the dumping of Gwyneth Dunwoody from the Transport Committee and Donald Anderson from Foreign Affairs. They were symbols of discontent. The vote was a scream of pain, forced from the backbenches by what many of them saw as an arrogant executive. For Blair, there was an even deeper problem. Some of his backbench supporters conceded in a dark corner, in the week of the rebellion, that the leader was badly out of touch. 'He is not loved by people he should be loved by,' one of his loyalists said. She pinned her hopes on Clarke as a new link between the party, Number 10 and the Cabinet Office but admitted that it was a serious problem for Blair. Unchecked, it was a danger to him.

Tony Benn, retired but still a Commons presence thanks to the Speaker's decision to give him access to the precincts in recognition of his fifty years as an MP, catches the flavour of the malcontents in a typically elegant way: 'The third way was invented to provide some sort of an ideological cover for the strategy of abandoning the trade unions and the historic commitment to a socialist society. It never had any base in public support and with the low turnout in 2001 the Labour vote is lower than it was in 1992.

'New Labour is probably the smallest political party in the history of British politics, but because they are all in the Cabinet it seems very strong. For the first time in my life the public seems to be to the left of a Labour government.'

This is the challenge to Blair. If he is to demonstrate that the 'third way' is more than a collection of things that it isn't – state socialism on one side and free-for-all capitalism on the other – he has to persuade more in his party of the claim. He could begin by getting the Chancellor to use the phrase, if he will. Brown is reluctant for a good reason. He doubts if it is a philosophy with bottom or with staying power.

Blair is well aware of the unease which he has been happy to stir up around him. The TUC general secretary, John Monks, put it to him like this: 'the trade unions and the party are like Ernie Wise and you're Eric Morecambe. When you're in trouble and you need a cheer from the upper gallery – that's where the *Daily Mail* and Middle England are sitting – you give us a good hard slap on both cheeks. We're your prop.' Blair gave him a wry grin. He could hardly deny the telling accuracy of the observation. Monks gives him a message that he hopes is tinged with alarm. 'We are all very, very apprehensive in the unions. We will try to find a way through and we will try not to put you up against the wall but it is going to be difficult.'

The union alarm centres on Blair's urge to reform the public services by inventing imaginative mechanisms for bringing in private money without destroying the public ethos. He believes, with the faith of a traveller on the 'third way', that it can be done. Public service unions don't believe it for a moment. For Blair this is another political hairpin bend that must be taken with the necessary screeching of tyres. For Monks, it is an example of the culture of New Labour which he has described directly to Blair as an urge to kick somebody on your own side when you're in trouble.

That practical unease among unions worried about jobs and the future of the public sector has an ideological counterpart among some of those who were the earliest cheerleaders for New Labour. Matthew Taylor, of the Institute for Public Policy Research, the thinktank which has given Blairism much ballast over the years, comes up with a simple prescription: 'To Blair and Brown the message has to be – a plague on both your houses. It's time for the rest of the Cabinet to get off its knees.'

These two critiques illuminate the problem in Downing Street. Blair's urge is to drive on with a relentless programme of reform. For Brown, anxious to maintain fingertip control of public finance, the extension of the command premiership has an obvious attraction. Yet for him the siren voices sound an insistent and alluring note of hope. Is this the moment when the ideology of the 'project' begins to splinter?

The challenge to Blair is profound. Brown could claim credit after re-election for an economy which would produce the money for him to present himself as the successor to Labour Chancellors of the past with the difference that he has the resources to fulfil his objectives. Prescott puts it like this to other ministers: 'It's the long game. Gordon has been saving the money. He's played the long game from the start.' Prescott's expectation, like that of others round the Cabinet table, is that Brown expects to emerge clearly in the course of the second term as a Chancellor with the money and the vision to appear the certain successor to Blair.

'Succession' is the word that hangs over the second term like a raincloud ready to burst. Blair and Brown have worked together and maintained their civility in public, and remnants of the old intimacy survive in private, but their relationship is one that is bound to change. It has withstood the burden of the emotional intensity of the first term to remain the centrifugal force in the government. After re-election, it was still the command mechanism. But if it changed, so would everything.

Brown is restless and ambitious. The evidence is in his demeanour. He is still uncomfortable in rooms where the Prime Minister is in command, still determined to exploit his personal link with Blair for decision-making and to bypass the usual Cabinet channels. One of his senior colleagues, who sits close to him in Cabinet, says this: 'For goodness sake, why doesn't he enjoy it? He's the most redistributive Chancellor since 1945. The most progressive Chancellor since Dalton. He's probably the most powerful Chancellor there's ever been. Why doesn't he enjoy it? It's extraordinary.' The reason advanced by this minister is that there is insecurity under that solid armour that Brown displays in public, an uncertainty about whether the brilliant student – a political shooting star – will ever streak across the sky in his full glory.

Brown believes that he will be Prime Minister. He wants it. He has wanted it since he arrived in Parliament. He believes he should have had it already, which makes him want it more. And he believes that Blair has gone as far as any Prime Minister can go in promising it to him. Brown's tragedy is that he also knows such promises are undeliverable. A Prime Minister who fixes a moment for departure is a rare bird indeed. Departures are difficult and dangerous. Brown knows, though he doesn't confess it to any but his nearest and dearest, that the prize may never be handed over. For him, that would be a tragedy, and that possibility condemns Blair's government to a strange life.

Around the Cabinet table there are ministers who believe that Brown can and will succeed. Irvine, who sits alongside him across from Blair, is one. But the majority could not now be expected to troop into a curtained voting booth and put a cross against the name of Brown. Too much emotion and energy have been expended in government for that natural succession to be seen by them as desirable. Most of Brown's colleagues in the Cabinet believe that it is more likely that the partnership will end in tears.

Brown will continue to be the Iron Chancellor. He will try to deliver the social benefits that he wants to produce, even if to his colleagues he will continue to illustrate the truth of P. G. Wodehouse's immortal observation, that it is not difficult to tell the difference between a Scotsman bearing a grievance and a ray of sunshine. But as time goes by he is almost certain to have to confront the fact of Blair's determination.

Blair has made up his mind to fight the next General Election as Prime Minister. Any hope Brown may have of Blair's voluntary retirement rests on one unlikely premise, a euro referendum in the course of the second term which Blair loses. It is an outcome that the Prime Minister is determined to avoid.

No one close to him doubts that he has two objectives. One is to win a referendum and take Britain into the single currency. The other is to win a third term in office. Blair sees in the European decision the opportunity of that place in history which second-term prime ministers naturally crave. Northern Ireland, once the repository of that hope, no longer shines with promise. Making the trains run on time, and delivering investment to public services in ways that bring visible dividends, are second-term obsessions in Whitehall, but they don't have the lustre of the national statement that a referendum result would give. Blair wants to ride the tide that will carry him across the English Channel. His ambition is fraught with fears, of course, because after the re-election campaign it was clear that public scepticism was as strong as it had been in the first term. The judgement from Campbell and Gould was still that a sea-change in opinion would have to occur to make it safe for the government to embark formally on a referendum campaign.

That very danger has helped to crystallize Blair's thinking about his future. If a referendum is postponed because of uncertainty about the outcome, he is determined to fight for a third term with the promise of a referendum to come. Euro-wobbles make him more likely to stay, not less. The paradoxical effect of his nervousness about public opinion is that it has simplified his options for the future. He has to hold both possibilities in his mind – a campaign late in the second term, with an election soon afterwards to capitalize on a Yes vote, or an election fought on the certainty of a referendum campaign to come. Neither can be ruled out. So he carries on. He has often talked about an eventual life outside politics – and still believes there will be one – but the mists surrounding the referendum have pushed that thought far ahead. His Shangri-La is a distant dream.

Even if political disaster were to strike for Blair, Brown's prospects would not be transformed. If the Prime Minister misjudged the public mood and held a referendum in the second term which he lost, it is difficult to imagine how the Chancellor (the guardian of the five tests) could be the beneficiary. Similarly, if an economic whirlwind engulfed the government how could the Chancellor be positioned to pick up the crown? A second-term succession for

Brown seems to depend on an Act of God, a runaway Number 24 bus in Whitehall or a sudden change of heart on Blair's part which would astonish those who know him best.

The politics and the personalities are pulling against each other. Blair's political judgement carries him down a path which will make it more difficult for Brown to succeed; the warm words of hope which Blair gave Brown in 1994 which were meant to preserve their relationship, and did, seem part of another age. When Brown left Granita on that Monday night in May, wanting to believe that he had struck a deal, and decided to rejoin his friends Balls, Whelan and Nick Brown to eat steak and chips it was maybe an implicit acknowledgement not only that New Labour food and the Islington ambience were not for him, but that there was an illusory aspect to the whole experience.

Blair still says that he hopes Brown will succeed him, but the transition is not spoken of in Number 10 as an event that is in sight. The second term is meant, with luck, to have its climax in the referendum, and not in Blair's retirement. A Prime Minister who won that campaign would not be one who could resist the prospect of a third election victory which it would be certain to make more likely. Brown, who would share the credit for a successful referendum and could hardly choose the moment to mount a *coup d'état*, would have to decide whether he wanted to be Chancellor for the third time or whether to step away from government. No one can imagine him as Foreign Secretary – its lack of executive power would frustrate him – and any other job would be subordinate to a new Chancellor. So unless he was prepared to wait he would go.

Brown is a political animal from head to toe. But intriguing thoughts are floated by friends and Treasury colleagues. The International Monetary Fund? A possibility. The World Bank with its role in dealing with development and debt round the world? An attractive thought. The European Central Bank? Don't rule it out. The last time the top IMF job came round, Brown was not seriously interested, but still took the trouble to talk it over with some fellow finance ministers around Europe, spreading the message that he was not someone who necessarily saw himself spending his life in

Whitehall. At some moment in the future, if Blair is settling into a third term, and Blunkett and a clutch of younger ministers are starting to burnish their leadership ambitions, Brown might decide to make the break. He has friends in America and Europe who would encourage him, and have already.

These are distant thoughts for them both. But they will be distilled in the next two or three years as the politics of the referendum are clarified. Blair will test his hope against public opinion; he will try to impart the idea of inevitability about the euro. He will also work on Rupert Murdoch. When he first attended a conference of Murdoch's News Corporation in Australia in 1995, the proprietor introduced him by saying that if they were going to have an affair, as had been suggested, they would do it as porcupines make love. Very slowly. Blair has been careful with him ever since, and will weigh the passions of the *Sun* and *The Times* in his decision (to the despair of many in his party). That will be as important to Blair and Brown as the assessment of the five tests, and then they will decide whether the risks have been minimized to the extent that will let them launch the referendum campaign.

Not until then will the patterns in the sand start to settle and give Brown an opportunity to study the lie of the land. He has support in the unions and the party – new MPs elected in 2001 got invitations to Number 11 in the first week, just as the 1997 intake had – and though his Cabinet allies are in the minority his political power is immense. Blair himself says he is Labour's most formidable force, and he only turned fifty in 2001. While he waits, there are battalions he can mobilize.

But Brown is the challenger who can do little to advance his chances of inheriting the crown. He cannot precipitate Blair's departure without a charge of disloyalty that would make his succession improbable. The partnership which took them into government and which has made their government work can't be broken without consequences which would almost certainly be politically fatal for both of them. On the euro, the more there is talk of division between them the more they must try to cling to each other, because they both need success in the referendum and defeat would be a disaster. Even as they start to look ahead to the next phase of politics and consider their individual prospects they have to stick together more closely.

Blair is well aware of the pain that this conundrum may cause them both. Roy Jenkins told him once about his own relationship with his old student friend, Anthony Crosland. They were young blades together, ambitious MPs, and they were two of the principal intellectual forces in the Labour Party of the Gaitskell era. Jenkins leapt ahead. On the ministerial merry-go-round he was Home Secretary while Crosland was at Education, Chancellor when Crosland was at Environment. Then in 1976 he progressed from Home Secretary to be the first British president of the European Commission, just as Crosland reached the Foreign Office for the last eight months of his life. Jenkins explained to Blair the difficulty this caused in their relationship, which was to both of them the most important they had apart from that with their wives. Crosland was the older by a couple of years (the very gap between Brown and Blair) and, according to Jenkins, had the better brain. Yet he didn't quite make it. Now and again when Jenkins and Blair meet, the Prime Minister gives a smile and says: 'Tell me the Crosland story again.'

Blair and Brown know that their partnership cannot last for ever. It has delivered them, and their party, an extraordinary period of untrammelled power and a capacity to influence their era in a way that few governments have an opportunity to do in their short time in the sun. Yet it has also given the two of them a sharpened sense of the melancholy undercurrent of politics, the understanding that every agreement brings in its wake the chance of failure, disappointment and personal tragedy. Their partnership is also their struggle.

Each knows now that the long years of apprenticeship and then achievement have taken them to a zenith from which they may well now be fated to begin their descent. They will start that journey together, but they know they will end it as they began – as friends whose rivalry is inescapable. They are bound together, until the life they have chosen to lead drives them apart.

'He loves me not!'

Chronology of Events

Blair		Brown		Events	
		20 Feb 51	Born in Giffnock		
6 May 53	Born in Edinburgh				
				10 Jan 57	Macmillan PM
1961–6	The Chorister School, Durham	1961–7	Kirkcaldy High School	15 Oct 64	Labour elected. Wilson PM
1966–71	Fettes College, Edinburgh			31 Mar 66	Wilson re-elected
		1967–73	Edinburgh University	18 June 70	Labour defeated. Edward Heath PM
				28 Oct 71	Jenkins rebellion
1972–5	St John's College, Oxford	1972–5	Rector, Edinburgh University	1 Jan 73	Britain joins EEC
28 June 75	Mother dies			28 Feb 74	Labour elected. Wilson PM
				10 Oct 74	Wilson re-elected
		1975	Publishes *Red Paper on Scotland*	5 June 75	Referendum on continued EEC membership
1976	Trainee barrister in Irvine's chambers			5 Apr 76	Wilson resigns. Callaghan PM
		1978	Chairman, Labour Devolution Committee	1978	Scotland Act passed
				1 Mar 79	Devolution referendum
		3 May 79	Contests Edinburgh South	3 May 79	Labour defeated. Thatcher PM
29 Mar 80	Marries Cherie Booth				
				3 Nov 80	Foot elected Labour leader
				Mar 81	SDP formed

Blair		Brown		Events	
				Sep 81	Healey defeats Benn for Labour deputy leadership
				25 Mar 82	Jenkins wins Glasgow Hillhead for SDP
				2 Apr 82	Argentina invades Falklands
27 May 82	Contests Beaconsfield by-election				
		1983–4	Chairman of Scottish Labour Party		
20 May 83	Selected for Sedgefield	16 May 83	Selected for Dunfermline East		
9 June 83	Elected MP for Sedgefield	9 June 83	Elected MP for Dunfermline East	9 June 83	Thatcher re-elected
		Oct 83	Publishes *Scotland: The Real Divide* with Cook	2 Oct 83	Kinnock elected Labour leader
				8 Mar 84	Miners' strike begins
7 Nov 84	Junior Treasury spokesman				
				5 Mar 85	Miners return to work
				24 Sep 85	Mandelson appointed director of communications
		Nov 85	Trade and Industry spokesman		
		1986	Publishes biography of James Maxton		
				11 June 87	Thatcher re-elected
8 July 87	City and Consumer Affairs spokesman	8 July 87	Shadow Chief Secretary to the Treasury		
				Oct 88	Smith suffers heart attack
Nov 88	Shadow Energy Secretary				
				26 Oct 89	Lawson resigns

Nov 89	Shadow Employment Secretary	Nov 89	Shadow Trade and Industry Secretary		
				11 Feb 90	Mandela released
				8 Oct 90	UK joins ERM
				1 Nov 90	Howe resigns
				28 Nov 90	Thatcher resigns. Major PM
				9 Apr 92	Major re-elected
				13 Apr 92	Neil Kinnock resigns
				18 July 92	Smith elected Labour leader
23 July 92	Shadow Home Secretary	23 July 92	Shadow Chancellor		
				16 Sep 92	Black Wednesday – Britain leaves ERM
Jan 93	Visits Washington, D.C.	Jan 93	Visits Washington, D.C.		
				12 May 94	Smith dies
31 May 94	Dinner at Granita	31 May 94	Dinner at Granita		
		1 July 94	Announces he won't stand for leader. Backs Blair		
21 July 94	Elected Labour leader				
				31 Aug 94	IRA announce ceasefire
4 Oct 94	Announces review of Clause IV				
				29 Apr 95	Special Labour conference approves new Clause IV
				22 June 95	Major resigns
				4 July 95	Major re-elected
				9 Feb 96	IRA break ceasefire – Docklands bomb
				29 Oct 96	Cook–Maclennan talks announced

Blair		Brown		Events	
				5 Mar 97	Cook–Maclennan talks reported
				1 May 97	Labour elected. Blair PM
Government 1997–2001					
2 May 97	Prime Minister	2 May 97	Chancellor		
		6 May 97	Independence of Bank of England		
8 May 97	First Cabinet meeting: 'Call me Tony'				
				9 May 97	Format of PMQs changed to one thirty-minute session a week
				14 May 97	Queen's Speech
				29 May 97	Clinton addresses Cabinet
				19 June 97	Hague becomes Conservative leader
				30 June 97	Hong Kong returns to China
		2July 97	First Budget: windfall tax on private utilities, new tax on pensions		
				20 July 97	IRA ceasefire restored
				22 July 97	LibDems join Cabinet Consultative Committee
				6 Sep 97	Funeral of Diana, Princess of Wales
		7 Sep 97	Appointed Chairman of Diana, Princess of Wales Memorial Committee		
				11 Sep 97	Referendum on Scottish Parliament
				17 Sep 97	First meeting of Lib-Lab Cabinet Committee

				18 Sep 97	Referendum on Welsh Assembly
				29 Sep 97	Livingstone beats Mandelson in NEC election
30 Sep 97	First Labour Party conference speech as Prime Minister				
13 Oct 97	Meets Gerry Adams at Stormont				
16 Oct 97	Meets Bernie Ecclestone at Downing Street				
		18 Oct 97	*The Times* headlines interview: 'Brown rules out single currency for lifetime of this Parliament'		
		27 Oct 97	Tells Commons that UK will not join the launch of euro in 1999		
				11 Nov 97	Ecclestone admits £1 million donation to Labour
16 Nov 97	Apologizes for handling of decision to exempt Formula 1 from proposed ban on tobacco advertising. Denies any wrong-doing				
				29 Nov 97	Geoffrey Robinson admits £12 million offshore trust
				1 Dec 97	Jenkins Commission established
				10 Dec 97	Forty-seven Labour MPs rebel against lone-parent benefit cut
11 Dec 97	Adams becomes first Republican leader since Michael Collins to meet Prime Minister at Downing Street				

Blair		Brown		Events	
5 Jan 98	Launches British Euro presidency at Waterloo				
				18 Jan 98	Source close to Blair despairs of Brown's 'psychological flaws'
				20 Jan 98	Robinson rebuked by Parliamentary Standards Commissioner for not declaring offshore trust
4–7 Feb 98	First official visit to United States as Prime Minister				
		17 Mar 98	Budget: introduction of Working Families' Tax Credit		
24 Mar 98	Address to French National Assembly				
				10 Apr 98	Good Friday Agreement signed
				22 May 98	Voters in Northern Ireland and Irish Republic back Good Friday Agreement
11 June 98	With Paddy Ashdown, releases joint declaration for constitutional reform				
		18 June 98	Announcement of national minimum wage £3.60/hour		
		14 July 98	Comprehensive Spending Review: triple-counting of public spending plans		
27 July 98	First Cabinet reshuffle – Peter Mandelson in; Harriet Harman and Frank Field out; Nick Brown demoted				

				15 Aug 98	Real IRA bomb in Omagh kills twenty-nine
21 Sep 98	Third Way seminar in New York with Clinton				
				29 Oct 98	Jenkins Commission recommends 'alternative vote plus'
				18 Nov 98	Standards and Privileges Committee publish report recommending Robinson makes an apology to the Commons
				16 Dec 98	US and UK military forces launch cruise missile and air attacks on targets in Iraq
				22 Dec 98	*Guardian* reveals that Mandelson kept £373,000 loan from Robinson secret
				23 Dec 98	Mandelson resigns as DTI Secretary. Robinson resigns as Paymaster General
				1 Jan 99	Launch of the euro in eleven EU countries
		4 Jan 99	Charlie Whelan announces he is to give up his job 'as soon as an appropriate opportunity becomes available'		
				20 Jan 99	Ashdown announces intention to retire as LibDem leader

Blair		Brown		Events	
23 Feb 99	Launches National Changeover Plan to prepare UK for the changeover to the euro				
		9 Mar 99	Budget: introduction of new 10p income tax rate and 1p reduction in basic rate to 22p		
				24 Mar 99	NATO airstrikes launched against targets in Yugoslavia
3 May 99	Visits refugee camps on Kosovo–Macedonia border				
				6 May 99	Elections for Scottish Parliament and Welsh Assembly
				20 May 99	Biggest backbench rebellion in first term – sixty-five Labour MPs vote against government's proposals for reform of incapacity benefit
				10 June 99	Yugoslav generals sign peace deal with NATO ending Kosovo war
				9 Aug 99	Kennedy elected LibDem leader
11 Oct 99	Cabinet reshuffle – Mandelson back as Northern Ireland Secretary				
				14 Oct 99	Launch of Britain in Europe

				26 Oct 99	Deal between government and opposition peers ends the right of most hereditary peers to sit in the Lords
4 Nov 99	Blairs are the guests of honour of the Hindujas at the Indian Festival of Light event in London				
18 Nov 99	Cherie Blair's pregnancy announced				
				1 Jan 00	Millennium Dome opening fiasco
16 Jan 00	Pledges NHS spending will be brought up to the European average				
				20 Jan 00	Wakeham Commission recommends a partially elected second chamber
				10 Feb 00	Welsh First Secretary Alun Michael resigns before a vote of no confidence
				15 Feb 00	Welsh Assembly appoints Rhodri Morgan as new First Secretary
				20 Feb 00	Frank Dobson defeats Livingstone to become Labour's candidate for London Mayor
				6 Mar 00	Livingstone announces intention to stand as an independent
11 Mar 00	Travels to Russia. Becomes first EC leader to meet Acting President Vladimir Putin				
		21 Mar 00	Budget: extra funding for the NHS		

Blair		Brown		Events	
				19 Apr 00	Mandelson makes positive speech on the euro
				4 May 00	Livingstone elected Mayor of London
				16 May 00	Mandelson speech about the damage to Britain if it stays outside the euro
20 May 00	Cherie Blair gives birth to baby boy, Leo				
		26 May 00	Criticizes Oxford University for elitism over Laura Spence		
7 June 00	Heckled at Women's Institute conference, Wembley Arena				
30 June 00	Proposes £100 fines for drunken or antisocial behaviour				
6 July 00	Euan Blair arrested in Leicester Square for being drunk and incapable				
17 July 00	*Sun* and *The Times* publish leaked memo written by Blair saying the government is perceived to be 'out of touch' with gut British instincts				
		18 July 00	Comprehensive Spending Review: extra £43 billion for public services from 2001–4		
		3 Aug 00	Marries Sarah Macaulay at his home in North Queensferry		

				8 Sep 00	Blockades of petrol refineries begin
				14 Sep 00	Fuel protests called off
26 Sep 00	Admits mistakes over pensions and the Dome at Labour Party conference				
				27 Sep 00	Leadership defeated at conference after delegates back motion calling for restoration of link between earnings and pensions
				11 Oct 00	Donald Dewar dies
				17 Oct 00	Labour and LibDems in Welsh Assembly agree to form coalition
				26 Oct 00	Henry McLeish appointed new Scottish First Minister
		8 Nov 00	Pre-Budget report: rise in pensions and cut in motoring costs		
				2 Jan 01	Lord Hamlyn revealed as mystery £2 million donor to Labour
				4 Jan 01	Labour announce further £4 million in donations from Lord Sainsbury and Christopher Ondaatje
				24 Jan 01	Mandelson resigns from Cabinet for the second time
				20 Feb 01	Britain's first case of foot and mouth for twenty years found in Essex
23 Feb 01	Becomes first European leader to meet President Bush				

Blair		Brown		Events	
				5 Mar 01	Increase in minimum wage to £4.10/hour
		7 Mar 01	Budget: more money for health and education. Increased children's tax credit		
				9 Mar 01	Hammon Report published. Clears Mandelson of acting dishonestly
2 Apr 01	Announces delay in local elections until 7 June				
				26 Apr 01	Phoenix the calf saved from slaughter
8 May 01	Announces General Election in a speech at St Saviour's & St Olave's Church of England School in Southwark				
16 May 01	Heckled by Sharron Storer, disgruntled partner of an NHS cancer patient			16 May 01	Labour launch manifesto *Ambitions for Britain* in Birmingham. John Prescott punches protester in Rhyl after being hit by an egg
17 May 01	Tells morning press conference 'John is John'				
				22 May 01	Margaret McDonagh alleges broadcasters colluding with protesters

Government 2001–

7 June 01 Blair re-elected

8 June 01 Cabinet reshuffle – Cook from Foreign Office to Leader of House of Commons; Straw becomes Foreign Secretary; Blunkett becomes Home Secretary

20 June 01 Mansion House speech – euro referendum unlikely to be called before 2003 and might not be held at all during the lifetime of this Parliament

16 July 01 Government defeated in the Commons. One hundred and twenty Labour MPs rebel over membership of Select Committees

18 July 01 Announcement that Sarah Macaulay is pregnant and expects to give birth in February 2002

Bibliography and Illustration Credits

Ashdown, Paddy, *The Ashdown Diaries, Vol. 1, 1988–1997*, Allen Lane, 2000

Brown, Colin, *Fighting Talk: The Biography of John Prescott*, Simon & Schuster, 1997

Brown, Gordon (ed.), *The Red Paper on Scotland*, Edinburgh Student Pubs, 1975

—, *James Maxton*, Mainstream, 1986

Gould, Philip, *The Unfinished Revolution: How the Modernisers Saved the Labour Party*, Little, Brown, 1998

Hennesy, Peter, *Cabinet*, Blackwell, 1986

—, *The Prime Minister: The Office and Its Holders Since 1945*, Penguin Books, 2000

Jenkins, Roy, *The Chancellors*, Macmillan, 1998

Kampfner, John, *Robin Cook: The Biography*, Phoenix (revised edn), 1999

Kavanagh, Dennis, and Seldon, Anthony, *The Powers Behind the Prime Minister: The Hidden Influence of Number Ten*, HarperCollins, 2000

Langdon, Julia, *Mo Mowlam*, Little, Brown, 2000

Lawson, Nigel, *The View from No. 11*, Bantam, 1992

Macintyre, Donald, *Mandelson and the Making of New Labour*, HarperCollins, 1999

Major, John, *John Major: The Autobiography*, HarperCollins, 1999

Mandelson, Peter, and Liddle, Roger, *The Blair Revolution: Can New Labour Deliver?*, Faber & Faber, 1996

McSmith, Andy, *John Smith: Playing the Long Game*, Verso, 1993

Oborne, Peter, *Alastair Campbell: New Labour and the Rise of the Media Class*, Aurum Press, 1999

O'Farrell, John, *Things Can Only Get Better*, Doubleday, 1998

Pimlott, Ben, *Harold Wilson*, HarperCollins, 1992

Rawnsley, Andrew, *Servants of the People: The Inside Story of New Labour*, Hamish Hamilton, 2000

Rentoul, John, *Tony Blair: Prime Minister*, Little, Brown, 2000

Riddell, Peter, *Honest Opportunism*, Gollancz, 1995

—, *Parliament Under Pressure*, Gollancz, 1998

Routledge, Paul, *Gordon Brown: The Biography*, Simon & Schuster, 1998

—, *Mandy*, Simon & Schuster, 1999

Seldon, Anthony (ed.), *The Blair Effect: The Blair Government 1997–2001*, Little, Brown, 2001

Sopel, Jon, *Tony Blair: The Moderniser*, Michael Joseph, 1995

Stephens, Philip, *Politics and the Pound*, Macmillan, 1996

Woodward, Bob, *Maestro: Greenspan's Fed and the American Boom*, Simon & Schuster, 2000

Young, Hugo, *One of Us*, Macmillan, 1989

—, *This Blessed Plot: Britain and Europe from Churchill to Blair*, Macmillan, 1998

plate section

1 Portrait of James Maxton by John Lavery © Scottish National Portrait Gallery
Brown as student © The Scotsman Publ. Ltd. Edinburgh

2 Tony Blair with Michael Foot © PA Photos

3 Brown congratulates Blair © Graham Turner/The Guardian

4 Blair and Clinton in silhouette © PA Photos

5 Tony Blair giving a speech to the WI © PA Photos

6 Campbell and Blair © PA Photos
Gordon Brown © Martin Argles/The Guardian

7 Tony Blair and Gordon Brown at Millbank © PA Photos

8 Tony Blair with his son, Leo © PA Photos
Gordon Brown and Sarah Macaulay © PA Photos

cartoons

Page xii © Chris Riddell (first published in the *Observer*)
Page 1 © Richard Wilson (first published in *The Times*)
Page 77 © Charles Griffin (first published in the *Express*)
Page 127 © Peter Brookes (first published in *The Times*)
Page 231 © Dave Brown (first published in the *Sunday Times*)
Page 318 © Nicholas Garland (first published in the *Daily Telegraph*)

Index

'GB' indicates Gordon Brown and 'TB' Tony Blair.

KT-415-792

THE END OF FASHION

william morrow and company, inc. | new york

THE END OF *Fashion*

the mass marketing of the clothing business

TERI AGINS

It is the policy of William Morrow and Company, Inc., and its imprints and affiliates, recognizing the importance of preserving what has been written, to print the books we publish on acid-free paper, and we exert our best efforts to that end.

Library of Congress Cataloging-in-Publication Data

Agins, Teri.
The end of fashion : the mass marketing of the clothing business / Teri Agins.
p. cm.
Includes bibliographical references and index.
ISBN 0-688-15160-4
1. Clothing trade. 2. Clothing and dress—Marketing. I. Title.
HD9940.A2A35 1999
687'.068'8—dc21 99-27075
CIP

Printed in the United States of America

FIRST EDITION

1 2 3 4 5 6 7 8 9 10

BOOK DESIGN BY GRETCHEN ACHILLES

www.williammorrow.com

to my parents,

Gene and Phyllis Agins

contents

acknowledgments

JUST LIKE THE fashion designer who bows alone on the runway, the book author is rewarded with a byline in boldface, when backstage there are many individuals whose deeds are indispensable to such endeavors.

I cannot adequately expess my gratitude to the scores of designers, retailers, publicists, consultants, and analysts whom I have enlisted during the past ten years that I have covered the fashion beat at *The Wall Street Journal,* especially those who weighed in during the nearly three years I spent researching and writing this book. Their trust and willingness to "open the kimono" have been a godsend in my quest to get the story right. I hope that I have succeeded in depicting their situations in a truthful and even-handed way.

I wish to acknowledge my agent, Joel Fishman, of Bedford Book Works, who first approached me to write this book and was a terrific sounding board and hand holder along the way. Joel introduced me to Paul Bresnick, executive editor at William Morrow, and his associate editor, Ben Schafer, who demonstrated their unflagging support and keen interest in my project. Two skillful freelance editors, Charles Flowers and Ed Shanahan, helped me to whip the manuscript into shape.

The Wall Street Journal, my professional home for the past fifteen years, is a repository of America's best reporters and editors who continue to challenge and inspire me. Managing editor Paul Steiger generously granted me a twenty-month book leave and put me back on the fashion beat when I returned.

I am fortunate to have many close relationships at the *Journal,* including Johnnie Roberts (now at *Newsweek*), Alexandra Peers, and Wade Lambert, who came through in the crunch with critical suggestions, while veteran book writers George Anders, Jeffrey Trachtenberg, and Roger Lownstein shared their experiences. Reporter Wendy Bounds kept the *Journal*'s fashion coverage lively during my absence. Bruce Levy, the *Journal*'s most valuable researcher, unearthed valuable nuggets, and computer whiz Phil Chan rescued my lost files on several occasions. Among my *Journal* colleagues who deserve my thanks are copy editor Betty Hallock, and editors Cynthia Crossen, Ellen Graham, David Sanford, Carolyn Phillips, Ron Alsop, Mike Miller, Laura Landro, and Dan Hertzberg.

Jane Berentson, a lifelong fashionista and big-picture editor, volunteered to help me map out the book and kept me on track. Veteran fashion writer Cathy Horyn is the world's most unselfish reporter, whose extraordinary talents are matched only by her friendship of a decade.

I've sharpened my fashion instincts by tapping the experts: Caroline Rennolds Milbank, Vicki Ross, and at the Costume Institute at the Metropolitan Museum Richard Martin, Deirdre Donohue, and Stephane Houy-Towner. I miss my mentor, the late Alan Millstein—the Quotron—who knew the ways of Seventh Avenue better than anybody else. Joan Kron, who first carved out the fashion beat at the *Journal* in 1983, came through and hooked me up with Andrea Miller, a skilled transcriber, and editor Ed Shanahan. In Paris, Pamela Golbin, of the Musée de la Mode et du Textile, was also an invaluable resource.

Several leading fashion journalists shared their astute insights: Bernadine Morris, Constance White, Robin Givhan, Mary Lou Luther, Ruth La Ferla, Christy Ferer, Elizabeth Snead, Anna Wintour, the late Elizabeth Tilberis, and *WWD*'s Patrick McCarthy, who permitted me to use the archives at Fairchild Publications.

Every nonfiction work benefits from having a broad range of key sources, and I am indebted to them all, including those who asked not to be named. My profile subjects kindly granted me extensive interviews and their staffers obligingly responded to my many inquiries: Ralph Lauren, Tommy Hilfiger, Emanuel Ungaro, Giorgio Armani, Zoran, Dan Skoda at Marshall Field's, Isaac Mizrahi, John Idol, and Robert Gray.

I gleaned pertinent insights from many others, listed here in no particular order. In New York: Bud Konheim, Joel Horowitz, Philip Miller, Victor Lipko, June Horne, Audrey Smaltz, Gary Galleberg, Hamilton South, Mallory Andrews, Jim Fingeroth, Dennis Walker, Jerry Chazen, Rick Rector, Bill Blass, Henry Hacker, Josie Esquivel, Faye Landes, Michael Toth, Christy Ferer, Carl Steidmann, Domenico De Sole, Maryanne Wheaton, Arnold Simon, Stephen Ruzow, Arnold Aronson, Allen Questrom, Terry Lundgren, Catherine Fisher, Michael Sondag, Craig Reynolds, Silas Chou, Lawrence Stroll, Kim Johnson Gross, Jeff Stone, Martha Nelson, Lynn Wyatt, Grace Mirabella, Michael Clinton, and Hal Rubenstein.

In Paris: Carlo Valerio, Ferrucio Ferragamo, Laura Ungaro, Rene Ungaro, Nino Cerruti, Ralph Toledano, Karl Lagerfeld, Didier Grumbach, Robert Bensoussan-Torres, Bernard Arnault, Tom Kamm, Amy Barrett, Pier Filipo Pieri, Jacques Babando, André Leon Talley, Denise Dubois, and Jacques Mouclier.

In Milan: Pino Brusone, Kevin Doyle, Maria Sturani, Rosita and Tai Missoni, Aldo Pinto, and Luigi Maramoti.

In Chicago: Sharon Stangenes, Genevieve Buck, Dorothy Fuller, Sugar Rautbord, Teresa Wiltz, Judy Byrd, Homer Sharp, Phyllis Collins, Connie Jackson, Gloria Bacon, Gary Witkin, and Dayton Hudson Corp.'s Michael Francis and Gerry Storch in Minneapolis.

In Los Angeles: Lisa Bannon, Wanda McDaniel, Michael Sharkey, and Bob Mackie.

Friends, indeed, are those who shared my pain and raised my spirits on the phone and through E-mails, and my tribe is the best: Wendy Urquhart (who came up with the idea for the book cover), Gay Young, Diane White, John Dwyer, Veronica Webb, Benjamin Borwick, Christine Bates, Peter Greenough, Chuck Stevens, Kevin Merida, as well as my sister Genie Agins, her husband, Chris Nunes, and Aunt Dorothy Wilson. Back home in Kansas City where I grew up, Bette Dooley, my stylish next-door neighbor, taught me to love high fashion.

Finally, I count as my biggest blessing, my parents, Gene and Phyllis Agins, whose love, guidance, and sacrifices have allowed me to pursue my dreams.

TERI AGINS

THE END OF FASHION

introduction

WHAT HAPPENED TO FASHION?

Supermodel Naomi Campbell has a killer body, a sassy strut, and a $10,000-a-day attitude. Famous for being fashionably late for work, she has left more than a few designers in the lurch right before a big show, wondering when—or if—she would appear. But the supermodel wasn't quite so cavalier when it came to Isaac Mizrahi, her buddy and the darling of America's designers. Nobody lit up a runway the way Isaac did during the 1990s. His witty, high-energy fashion shows were always the highlight of the New York collections.

On the evening of April 10, 1997, Mizrahi's fashion spectacle took place near Madison Square Garden, at the Manhattan Center on West 34th Street. At a quarter to six, with more than an hour to spare, the diva of the catwalks made her entrance, in sunglasses, $500 Manolo Blahnik stilettos, and a stunning spotted coat. On cue, bounding down the stage steps, emerged the man in black, Isaac Mizrahi, brandishing a Camel Light like a conductor's baton.

"There she is! *Na-o-mi!*" he exclaimed, swooping in to buss her on both cheeks. "Fab-u-lous." Mizrahi ooohed and ahhed, checking out her genuine leopard wrap. Evidently, the antifur era was over and out. Campbell was sporting the most politically incorrect of furs; leopards had been an endangered species since before she was born.

Naomi did a little pirouette, then swung open her vintage coat. The bronze satin lining was embroidered with the name of its famous original owner: Ann-Margret. "I got it in Los Angeles from this dealer," she explained in her girlish-British lilt. Suddenly, André Leon Talley, *Vogue*'s main man-about-Paris, stormed in to boom: "Girl, that coat is *major*!" The trio huddled for a dishy chat, then Mizrahi scooted her off backstage to get made up with the rest of the "girls," models like Kristen McMenamy and Shalom Harlow. As Campbell slipped away, her Hermès tote let out a "brrring," from her cellular phone. A cigarette ash fell to the floor as Mizrahi spun around, his arms flying as he jabbered some directions to his backstage crew. "I just *love* this," he muttered to no one in particular.

This drive-by vignette from fashion's fast lane harked back to *Unzipped,* the lively 1995 documentary that followed Mizrahi through the exhilarating fits and starts during the months when he prepared his 1994 fall collection. *Unzipped*, which won the audience award at the Sundance Film Festival, captured all the hyperbole, razzle-dazzle, and parody of high fashion, juiced up by the ebullient Mizrahi, a showman so delicious you couldn't make him up.

Straight out of Brooklyn's well-to-do Jewish enclave, Mizrahi got fixed on fashion early in life. His elegant mother decked herself out in Norman Norell and Yves Saint Laurent, while his father, a children's-wear manufacturer, bought Isaac his first sewing machine when he was still in grade school.

By the time Mizrahi was fifteen, he was stitching up a storm, designing a collection called "IS New York" which he sold to friends and a few neighborhood boutiques. He was also an imp and a cutup who in the 1970s starred onstage at the High School of Performing Arts and as an extra in the movie *Fame*. After studying fashion at New York's Parsons

School of Design, he moved on to Seventh Avenue, where he became an assistant to designers Perry Ellis, Jeffrey Banks, and Calvin Klein.

Ambitious and fast-tracking, Mizrahi was ready to do his own thing by the time he reached twenty-five. He invested the $50,000 trust fund his late father had left him to launch his eponymous fashion house in a brick-walled loft in downtown SoHo. His March 1988 debut runway show was one of those rare and unforgettable moments that left fashion editors agog. They knew they had just witnessed the start of something big.

That spring, Bloomingdale's rushed to put Mizrahi's debut collection in its windows on Fifty-ninth Street and Lexington Avenue, where Mizrahi showed up in person to greet shoppers. The most enthusiastic fashionistas swallowed the hype and splurged on their first Mizrahis. Kal Ruttenstein, Bloomie's fashion director, remembered: "We sold Isaac to the customer who was aware of what he was doing."

What Mizrahi was doing was cool and high-concept. He had a sophisticated take on American sportswear, inspired by fashion's modern masters, Claire McCardell and Geoffrey Beene, with a nod to Mary Tyler Moore, Mizrahi's favorite TV muse. But he also pulled a few tricks from up his own sleeve.

Throughout the 1990s, Mizrahi stood out as America's most prolific idea man, turning out one innovation after another, in a splash of Technicolor delight: paper-bag-waist pants, a tartan kilt strapless dress, fur-trimmed parkas, and boxy jackets. He spiked his fashion-show programs with puns to describe fabrics and colors: "Burlapse," "Fantasy Eyelet," "Lorne Green," and "James Brown." The fashion editors lapped it up, with page after page of pictures and kudos. But among retail buyers, there was decidedly less of a consensus. Barneys New York and Ultimo in Chicago were among the handful of stores whose fashion-forward clientele craved the labels with the most buzz. Accordingly, such retailers could move a few racks of Mizrahi's $800 jackets and $350 pants most every season. But Mizrahi barely caused a blip at chains like Neiman Marcus and Saks Fifth Avenue, where his spirited fashions got buried in the broad mix of up-and-coming designer brands.

Gilding the Mizrahi mystique was his colorful, megawatt persona. With a bandanna headband taming his frizzy black hair, he was an adorable cartoon. Isaac was fashion's funniest Quotron, who chirped frothy declarations with the push of a button, just like Diana Vreeland, the legendary *Vogue* editor of the 1970s whose snappy sound bites ("Pink is the navy blue of India") have entered fashion's lexicon. "Le Miz"—as *WWD* dubbed fashion's wonder boy—once exclaimed about a chubby fake fur jacket: "It looks *divine* in beast." He held forth to *WWD* about his 1992 spring collection: "It will be all about irresistible clothes. The *only* kind that will sell."

But what merchandise actually sold was of little concern to the members of the Council of Fashion Designers of America and other fashion industry groups, who showered Isaac with a number of "best designer" awards during his first years. All Mizrahi needed now was solid capital backing to take his business to the next stage. "All my life, I dreamed of a design house like that of Calvin Klein, Armani or Yves Saint Laurent," Mizrahi once wrote in a pitch letter to potential financiers. His dream seemed like a foregone conclusion by 1992 when the venerable house of Chanel in Paris stepped in to help, signing on to become Mizrahi's financial partner. Chanel certainly had the expertise, having successfully staged its own renaissance in the 1980s, with management's deft handling of Chanel's perfumes and accessories, bolstered by the ingenious Karl Lagerfeld, who had become Chanel's couturier in 1982. Chanel was poised to parlay Mizrahi's marquee image into profits with the 1994 introduction of "Isaac," a bread-and-butter department store collection of $150 dresses and $300 jackets.

Meanwhile, Le Miz continued to reign as Mr. Fabulous on the high-fashion runways, as he mined his bottomless pit of creativity. And after his wacky performance in *Unzipped*, a star was born. Among his TV and movie credits, playing a fashion designer, naturally, was his bit part in the Michael J. Fox comedy *For Love or Money*. He was also a jovial guest on the TV game show *Celebrity Jeopardy!*, where he was the winner.

But while Isaac, the stylish personality, was in high demand, his clothes weren't. By 1996, Mizrahi's runway collections weren't wowing the fashionistas anymore, as Gucci and Prada were now the favorite flavors of the moment. Meanwhile, the Isaac collection on which Mizrahi banked his future just didn't click with shoppers, who were far too savvy to fork over $150 for a cotton shift designer dress when chains like Bebe and The Limited were turning out similar styles for as little as $49.99. As reality bit harder, Mizrahi had no choice but to close his Isaac division at the end of 1997, leaving his struggling fashion house hanging by a thread.

That's fashion. And that's the curious way success plays out in the fashion world. A designer can be deemed hot by buzz alone—as Mizrahi was from the start—even though the sales of his collections were barely tepid. But people outside the fashion loop would never be the wiser, because fashion coverage in newspapers and magazines was all about style, not substance.

The fact that Mizrahi's sportswear was thoroughly modern should have worked to his advantage, but his business habits were pretty old-fashioned. He saw himself as a latter-day couturier who designed for supermodels and the coolest fashionistas—but not ordinary women. Mizrahi couldn't connect with the critical masses because he didn't relate to them. For example, when retail buyers once begged him to repeat one of his few best-sellers—paper-bag-waist pants—Mizrahi couldn't bring himself to do a rerun. "I just got *bored* with them," he later recollected.

Flashing back to the final scene in *Unzipped*, Mizrahi showed what really mattered to him. There was Mizrahi, in post-fashion-show anxiety at a Manhattan newsstand, hovering over a copy of *WWD*, which applauded his latest collection, proclaiming "the man has a hit on his hands." The camera zoomed in on a giddy Mizrahi, who was bouncing down the street. But what was missing from this happy ending was the only review that counted in the real world: sales in stores.

Mizrahi, aloft in a cloud of chiffon, had yet to get serious about the bottom line. He was an artiste who refused to become another Seventh Avenue garmento. "Look, it is all I can do to make fabulous collections and fabulous clothes," he explained in July 1997. "That is *all* I can do. You know I can't imagine after all these years, *I can't imagine* how it will translate at retail."

On October 1, 1998, the curtain finally came down on Mizrahi's fashion show. Ten years of terrific reviews added up to little; the House of Mizrahi chalked up no more than an estimated $15 million at its peak in 1996—and zero in the profit column. The money men at Chanel, realizing that Mizrahi's moment had passed, slammed the door on America's most beloved Little Fashion House That Could. Mizrahi unzipped played like an obituary across the bottom of the front page of *The New York Times*. Out of fashion and headed toward a career in Hollywood, Mizrahi was sanguine—leaving the door open for his possible comeback. "I will always have a great love of fashion. I'll always be a fashion designer," he told *WWD*.

There's no better example than Mizrahi to show what has been happening lately in the real world of fashion. It's not only the end of the millennium, but the end of fashion as we once knew it.

Mizrahi is a direct descendant of the trickle-down school of fashion, the aspirational system in which high-fashion designers, their affluent clients buoyed by scads of publicity in *WWD* and *Vogue*, dictated the way everyone dressed. The old order was starting to unravel when Mizrahi first went into business in the 1987. But failing to read the shifts in the marketplace, Mizrahi became the quintessential fashion victim; he arrived on the scene just when fashion was changing. By the early 1990s, a confluence of phenomena arising from retailing, marketing, and feminism began transforming the ways of fashion forever.

For all of its glamour and frivolity, fashion happens to be a relevant and powerful force in our lives. At every level of society, people care greatly about the way they look, which affects both their self-esteem and the way other people interact with them. And it has been true since the beginning of time that people from all walks of life make the effort to dress in style.

Yet fashion, by definition, is ephemeral and elusive, a target that keeps moving. A clothing style becomes fashionable when enough people accept it at any given time. And conversely, fashions go out of style when people quit wearing them. Traditionally, the fashion system has revolved around the imperative of planned obsolescence—the most familiar examples being the rise and fall in skirt lengths, and for men the widening and narrowing of trousers and neckties. Every few years, when the silhouettes change, women and men have been compelled to go shopping and to rebuild their wardrobes to stay in style.

In America's consumer society, which burgeoned after World War II, apparel makers, designers, retailers, and their symbiotic agents, the fashion press, were the omnipotent forces pushing fashion's revolving door. They have been responsible for creating new fashion trends and inducing people to shop until they dropped, to scoop up the novelties the industry promoted. This order was a mighty mandate that prevailed throughout the 1980s, a system which established a consensus that kept millions of consumers moving in lockstep. Perhaps that's what William Shakespeare foresaw when he wrote: "Fashion wears out more apparel than the man."

But in recent years, a number of circumstances caused a revolutionary shift that upset the old order and wrested control away from the forces in the fashion industry. In 1987, designers missed the boat when they failed to sell women on short skirts. They misfired again, a few seasons later, with the somber "monastic" look and other fads, resulting in millions of dollars of losses to the industry. By the mid-1990s the forces of fashion had lost their ability to dictate trends. Increasingly, the roles have reversed. The power now belongs to us, the consumers, who decide what we want to wear, when we buy it, and how much we pay for it. And nowadays, consumers are a lot savvier and more skeptical when it comes to fashion.

Four megatrends sent fashion rolling in a new direction.

- *Women let go of fashion.* By the 1980s, millions of baby-boomer career women were moving up in the workplace and the impact of their professional mobility was monumental. As bank vice presidents, members of corporate boards, and partners at law firms, professional women became secure enough to ignore the foolish runway frippery that bore no connection to their lives. Women began to behave more like men in adopting their own uniform: skirts and blazers and pantsuits that gave them an authoritative, polished, power look.

Fashion's frothy propaganda no longer rallied the troops. The press beat the drums for a decade, but the name Isaac Mizrahi still drew a blank with millions of American women who hadn't bothered to notice.

A defining moment in high fashion occurred in 1992 with the closing of Martha, the venerable dress salon on Park Avenue. Starting in the 1930s, Martha Phillips, a feisty entrepreneur with impeccable taste, began her reign as one of America's leading standard-bearers for snob appeal and Paris originals. And for nearly six decades, elegant women beat a path to the pink-walled emporium on shopping trips that took hours as Phillips and her attentive staffers put their clients together in head-to-

toe perfection. Such was the drill during an era when rich women derived much of their self-worth from wearing the best couture labels.

Martha's demise was the latest casualty in a rash of salon deaths, coming just months after the closing of such salons as Loretta Blum in Dallas, Amen Wardy in Beverly Hills, and Sara Fredericks in Boston. Martha Phillips and her exquisite counterparts couldn't hack it anymore because the pace-setting socialites who once spent a fortune on their wardrobes no longer devoted so much time and money to getting dressed up. Park Avenue style maven and decorator Chessy Rayner, who used to be a front-row regular at the Paris fashion shows, was among those who had made the conversion from clothes horse to fashion renegade. In 1992, she recalled: "Today my style is totally pared-down and non-glitz."

As such salons folded, many of their suppliers, namely the couture houses in Paris, faced a precarious future. For most of the twentieth century, Paris designers had set the standard, introducing the full-skirted "New Look" after World War II, the "sack" silhouette of the fifties, the "space age" sleek of the sixties, and the "pouf" party dress in the eighties. Such were the trends that Seventh Avenue manufacturers slavishly copied and adapted for the mass market. But by the 1990s, most Paris designers couldn't set the world's fashion agenda anymore. Styles were no longer trickling down from the couture to the masses. Instead, trends were bubbling up from the streets, from urban teenagers and the forces in pop music and counterculture with a new vital ingenuity that was infectious. The powers in Paris were taken aback when their captivated clients awoke from the spell of couture and defected in droves. And thus, the fortress of French fashion came tumbling down.

- *People stopped dressing up*. By the end of the 1980s, most Americans were wedded to jeans, loose knit tops, and Nike shoes, which became the acceptable standard of everyday dress even in offices. Leading the charge for informality were men, in their rejection of the business suit, which since the start of the industrial age had been the symbol of masculine authority and the uniform of the corporate workplace.

Starting in the 1980s, the bespectacled computer nerds at the helms of America's buoyant high-tech industries broke the pattern of stuffed-shirt formality in business. Microsoft Corp. founder Bill Gates emerged as the world's wealthiest man—and the personification of the Internet-set look, dressed for success in chinos and sports shirts.

In America's more traditional corporations, the men's fashion revolt first erupted in Pittsburgh, of all places. In the fall of 1991, Pittsburgh-based Alcoa, the giant aluminum concern, became the first major corporation to sanction casual office attire. The move came about after Alcoa had allowed employees who contributed to the United Way to dress casually during a two-week fund drive. The perk proved so popular that Alcoa decided to give its employees the option of never having to dress up again. Even Alcoa's top honchos stopped suiting up. One typical weekday morning in March 1992, Ronald Hoffman, an Alcoa executive vice president, was working in his suite on the thirty-seventh floor wearing a yellow V-neck sweater, an open-neck shirt, and slacks. "There used to be a time when a white shirt went with your intelligence," Hoffman told *The Wall Street Journal*. "But now there's no reason to do this anymore."

Before long, the rest of corporate America had shifted into khakis and knit shirts at least one day of the week, which became known as "casual Friday." Computer giant IBM went so far as to go casual every day, starting in 1995. Levi Strauss & Co., the world's biggest apparel maker, caught the wave in the early 1990s with its loose-fitting Dockers casual pants, which quickly became a popular wardrobe staple for men. It took less than five years for Dockers to explode into a $1 billion-a-year business.

Without enough suit buyers to go around, many of America's fine haberdasheries and boutiques suffered the fate of Martha. Charivari, a flashy New York chain known for its dressy and expensive European designer imports for men and women during the 1980s, planned to ride out the dress-down trend. In 1991, Charivari plastered on billboards: "Ripped Jeans, Pocket Tees, Back to Basics. Wake us when it's over. Charivari." Instead, seven years later, it was Charivari that was over—and out of business.

Indeed, it seemed as though not only dress-up clothes, but good taste, had fallen by the wayside as millions of Americans sank into sloppiness, wedded to their fanny packs, T-shirts, jeans, and clunky athletic shoes. "Have We Become a Nation of Slobs?" blared the cover headline of *Newsweek,* February 20, 1995. The accompanying article provided a mountain of evidence that people were no longer dressing to impress, including a Boston funeral director who said that some families were now asking for their loved ones to be buried without a coat and tie.

- *People's values changed with regard to fashion.* Most people used to put "fashion" on a pedestal. There was a sharp delineation between ordinary clothes from Casual Corner and Sears and true "fashion" from Paris couturiers and boutiques like Charivari and Martha. But such a divide existed before so many options for fashion became widely available at every price level. Stores like Ann Taylor, The Limited, Gap, Banana Republic, and J. Crew turned out good-looking clothes that deflated the notion that fashion belonged exclusively to the elite. In effect, designer labels started to seem like a rip-off. Increasingly, it became a badge of honor to be a bargain hunter, even among the well-to-do. Discounter Target Stores struck the right chord with this tagline in its ads: "It's fashionable to pay less."

Many people like Deirdre Shaffer, a thirty-one-year-old part-time psychotherapist from a New Jersey suburb, learned this lesson quite by accident. In 1994, Shaffer and her husband attended a cocktail party at their local country club to which she wore a black dress from Ann Taylor and $12.99 black suede sandals that she had just purchased from Kmart. Earlier that day, Shaffer didn't have enough time to comb the upscale malls where she usually bought her clothes. So, while she was shopping in Kmart for paper towels and toothpaste, she wandered over to the shoe racks, where she found the sandals. That evening, Shaffer was feeling quite satisfied with her budget find. "I got more compliments on the shoes than my dress," she recalled, noting that her friends were "impressed when I told them they came from Kmart."

Indeed, seeing was believing for Shaffer and millions of folks who wised up. It was akin to a Wizard-of-Oz discovery: Behind the labels of many famous name brands was some pretty ordinary merchandise. Increasingly, the savviest shoppers started paying closer attention to details like fabric, workmanship, and value—and thus became less impressed with designer labels. *Consumer Reports*, which is best known for its evaluations of kitchen appliances and cars, helped millions of shoppers see the light when the magazine began testing different brands of clothes for durability, fiber content, and wear. The truism "You get what you pay for" was proven false. In a 1994 test of chenille sweaters, *Consumer Reports* concluded that a $340 rayon chenille sweater from the upscale Barneys New York "was only a bit higher in quality" than a $25 acrylic chenille sweater from Kmart. In another trial in 1997, the magazine gave its highest ranking for men's polo knit shirts to Honors, a store brand that sold for only $7 at Target, but whose quality scored well above those versions by Polo Ralph Lauren at $49, Tommy Hilfiger at $44, Nautica at $42, and Gap at $24.

Marketing analysts describe consumers' new embrace of the most functional and affordable clothes as the "commoditization" of fashion. Beginning in the 1980s, more apparel makers shifted most of their manufacturing from the U.S. to low-cost factories in the Far East, where they were able to provide more quality at an attractive price: good-looking polo shirts and other apparel that were perfectly acceptable to most people—with no sustainable difference between one brand or another. As more people had no reason or burning desire to dress up anymore, they had no qualms about buying their clothes wherever they could get the best deal—just as Deirdre Shaffer did at Kmart.

The commoditization of clothes coincided with the most popular clothing trends of the 1990s: the "classics," "simple chic," and "minimalism." This comes as no surprise. Such mainstream styles are far easier for designers to execute on a commercial scale, in that they are cheaper and safer to produce, with less margin for error in the far-flung factories in China, Hong Kong, Korea, and Mexico, where much of today's apparel is made.

Furthermore, there's a whole generation of people under forty who don't know how to discern quality in clothes. Generation X-ers born in the 1970s didn't grow up wearing dresses and pantyhose in high school, nor did they own much in the way of "Sunday clothes." These young people are largely ignorant of the hallmarks of fine tailoring and fit. Jeans, T-shirts, stretch fabrics, and clothes sized in small, medium, large, and extra-large are what this blow-dry, wash-and-wear generation have worn virtually all of their lives. While their mothers and grandmothers donned slips and girdles—and pulled out the ironing board before they got dressed—these young people had already formed the habit of wearing comfortable, carefree clothes.

• *Top designers stopped gambling on fashion.* Isaac Mizrahi mistakenly believed that there were enough fashion mavens still willing to put their trust in his taste level. But the best-selling designers nowadays know better. Liz Claiborne, Polo Ralph Lauren, and Tommy Hilfiger are among the fashion houses that grew into billion-dollar empires of apparel, handbags, cosmetics, and home furnishings. Such fashion houses just also happen to be publicly traded companies, which must maintain steady, predictable growth for their shareholders. The upshot: The big guns can't afford to gamble on fashion whims. Fashion as we have known it requires a certain degree of risk-taking and creativity that is impossible to explain to Wall Street. Even though the leading designers tart up their runways with outlandish, crowd-pleasing costumes, they are grounded in reality. The bulk of the actual merchandise that hits the sales floor is always palatable enough for millions of consumers around the world, thus generating the bottom line that Wall Street expects.

WITH SO MUCH consumer rejection of fanciful fashions, will the world turn into a sea of khakis and T-shirts? Will Paris couture and the likes of Mizrahi and Charivari ever rise again? And moreover, will fashion ever matter as it used to?

"The fact is that women are interested in clothes, but the average consumer isn't interested in the 'fashion world,' " observes Martha Nelson, the editor of *In Style* magazine. Women want attractive clothes that function in the real world, "not something that is impossible to walk and drive in. You know, clothes that fit into your life."

So, that's why we've come to the end of fashion. Today, a designer's creativity expresses itself more than ever in the marketing rather than in the actual clothes. Such marketing is complicated, full of nuance and innovation—requiring far more planning than what it takes to create a fabulous ballgown, as well as millions of dollars in advertising. In a sense, fashion has returned to its roots: selling image. Image is the form and marketing is the function.

Nowadays, a fashion house has to establish an image that resonates with enough people—an image so arresting that consumers will be compelled to buy whatever that designer has to offer. The top designers use their images to turn themselves into mighty brands that stand for an attitude and a lifestyle that cuts across many cultures. Today's "branding" of fashion has taken on a critical role in an era when there's not much in the way of new styling going on—just about every store in the mall is peddling the same styles of clothes. That's why designer logos have become so popular; logos are the easiest way for each designer to impart a distinguishing characteristic on what amounts to some pretty ordinary apparel.

Having burnished his image through millions of dollars of advertising, Calvin Klein towers as a potent brand name and leverages his CK logo across a breadth of categories—$6.50 cotton briefs, $1,000 blazers, and $40 bath towels—even though there are plenty of cheaper options widely available.

Image, of course, works in conjunction with the intrinsics—the style, quality, and price of each actual item—and image comes from everywhere: the ambiance of the location where the clothes are sold, the advertising, the celebrities who wear the clothes, and so forth. Image is how the Gap sells a $12.50 pocket T-shirt, how Ralph Lauren pushes a $40 gallon of wall paint, and how Giorgio Armani moves $1,500 blazers.

These designers assault the American public with their ubiquitous advertising, most typically seen in the fashion press. But the roles have reversed there as well. Fashion publications like *WWD*, *Vogue*, *Harper's Bazaar*, *GQ*, and the rest have lost their power in their editorial pages to make or break fashion trends—the same power designers have lost to the consumer. Nowadays, the mightiest fashion brands, by virtue of their heavy-duty advertising, take their message directly to the public—unfiltered by the subjectivity of the editors: Ralph Lauren's ten-page advertising inserts in the front of *Vogue* and *Vanity Fair* are more arresting than any fashion spread featuring his clothes in the editorial pages of the magazine.

It was always confounding, this business of selling fashion. And now the industry has become fragmented into so many niches in which scores of companies churn out more and more merchandise at every price range, season after season. The fashion-industry powers at the head of the class prevail because they swear by retailing's golden rule: The consumer is king.

The following chapters capture some of the industry's best-known players in recent years, as they've succeeded—and sputtered—in their quest to make fashion for profit, as well as for glory. Fashion, which began in the hallowed ateliers of Parisian couture, now emanates from designers and retailers from around the world, reaching the masses at every level. In today's high-strung, competitive marketplace, those who will survive the end of fashion will reinvent themselves enough times and with enough flexibility and resources to anticipate, not manipulate, the twenty-first-century customer. There's just no other way.

chapter 1

PARIS: THE BEGINNING AND THE END OF FASHION

We will know twenty years from now what fashion is in Paris. Right now, there is general confusion.

KARL LAGERFELD, April 24, 1998

The stock market crash of October 19, 1987, left the world in stunned suspension, as millions of people pondered how their lives would inevitably change after nearly a decade of fast fortunes, high living, and conspicuous consumption. Just days after the big bombshell, New York's financial district erupted again—but this time for a glorious celebration inside the World Financial Center, the gleaming new office towers that were the home of American Express, Merrill Lynch, and Dow Jones and Co., the publisher of *The Wall Street Journal*. On the evening of October 28, New York's social glitterati headed downtown to pay homage to Christian Lacroix, French fashion's *it* man of the moment.

Except for the unlucky timing, the venue was perfect. Overlooking the Hudson River in lower Manhattan, with a distant view of the Statue of Liberty, the World Financial Center's glass-covered public courtyard provided a glamorous backdrop for a fashion-show stage and dozens of candlelit tables arranged around the sixteen live palm trees that rose forty-five feet from its marble floors. Partygoers would long remember the Lacroix gala, which concluded with a fireworks show as exuberant, excessive, and eerily off-key. It was an event where over-the-top fashion mirrored Wall Street, on the verge of collapse.

To the fashion establishment, the arrival of Lacroix had been like the second coming. With his dark, slicked-back hair and cherubic face, he was an extraordinary talent with a heavy-handed flair for the baroque. He had come to save haute couture, the pinnacle of French fashion, whose legendary practitioners included Yves Saint Laurent, Hubert de Givenchy, and Emanuel Ungaro. Lacroix had burst on the scene initially as the couturier of the house of Patou in the early 1980s, when haute couture was suddenly back in style for the first time in years. Luxurious suits and party frocks that cost as much as suburban homes became the badge of wealthy Arab ladies, nouveau riche trophy wives, and international socialites, who delighted in supporting high fashion's noblest tradition. "The fact is that fashion needs Lacroix—needs somebody new to bring along the next generation of couture customers," Holly Brubach raved in *The New Yorker*.

Serving as chairwoman of the Lacroix benefit, Blaine Trump, the beautiful, blond sister-in-law of real estate mogul Donald Trump, decked herself in a purple brocade Lacroix confection, in keeping with the fairytale frippery Lacroix sent down the runway that night: enormous *fichu* portrait collars, bustles, farthingales, pouf overskirts and underskirts—in a riot of vibrant colors, festooned with embroidery and jeweled trimmings. Balancing strange headdresses atop their tightly coiffed updos, the models moved gingerly down the catwalk. Also laboring under the weight of Lacroix luxe—and suffering gladly through the night—

were a number of guests, such as millionairess Gloria von Thurn und Taxis, who was done up in a black bustle number. Sitting next to Donald Trump, she whispered: "You know, you can't go to the bathroom in these dresses."

Lacroix took his runway bow to a shower of bravos and red carnations. No one was prouder than Lacroix's French benefactor, Bernard Arnault, a thirty-seven-year-old mogul on the rise. With the help of investment bank Lazard Frères in 1984, Arnault had acquired the bankrupt Agache Willot, whose most valuable asset was the Christian Dior fashion house. A couple of years later, he bankrolled the House of Lacroix, with an initial $8 million commitment. Over the next years, Arnault would become the luxury world's most active predator, creating, through a series of hostile takeovers and buyouts, LVMH Moët Hennessy Louis Vuitton, the world's largest luxury-goods empire. By 1998, the $8-billion-a-year LVMH had amassed a formidable lineup, including Hennessy Cognac, Moët and Dom Pérignon champagne, airport Duty Free Shops, as well as other fashion houses: Louis Vuitton, Céline, Givenchy, Loewe, and Kenzo. But Lacroix was Arnault's favored son, the only enterprise he had started from scratch. From the start, Arnault held high hopes, especially after Lacroix garnered so much breathless publicity for his signature pouf gown. He was destined to become the next Yves Saint Laurent.

But despite his triumphant debut, Lacroix would turn out to be the soufflé that refused to rise. No one had expected that there would be a run on $40,000 Lacroix ballgowns. But even Lacroix's earliest enthusiasts got cold feet—and cooled on the couturier. Georgette Mosbacher, the red-headed wife of U.S. Commerce Secretary Robert Mosbacher, admitted that she felt forced to buy a Lacroix dress, but never wore it, and ended up donating it to a museum. Likewise, the retail collections Lacroix created were fanciful eye-candy—but flops on the sales floor. The definitive proof that there was no more helium left in the pouf came when Lacroix brought out his first signature perfume, C'est La Vie, in 1994. Despite its Calvin Klein–size $40 million marketing sendoff, C'est La Vie retailed so poorly that Lacroix pulled the fragrance from the market.

During its first five years of business, the house of Lacroix waded in red ink—more than $37 million in losses. Profits were still elusive in 1997 when Lacroix, at forty-six, celebrated ten years in business, having run through almost as many managing directors.

Unapologetic, the earnest couturier vowed never to surrender to commercial pressures. He wrote in his fashion show program in July 1997: "I believe I have not given in to systems whatever they might be. . . . A Lacroix style has been born and even if it doesn't appeal to everyone, so much the better. The barefooted, jewelry-less woman, skimpily dressed in worn-out togs, creates a ghost-like vision that only satisfies the most pessimistic, of which I am not one. . . ."

Bernard Arnault wasn't so much pessimistic as he was frustrated by the couturier who couldn't be king of French fashion. By the end of the 1990s, Arnault would be forced to face the naked truth: that Lacroix was the end of fashion.

Bernadine Morris, the former *New York Times* chief fashion reporter, admitted years after the fact that she, too, had gotten carried away by what was a Lacroix moment. "When I wrote [my reviews], I believed it at the time. When you see an extraordinary collection, it does set you up. What we didn't know was what the fallout was going to be from the stock market crash. And now, looking at Lacroix ten years later, the demise of couture was irrevocable at that stage, the kind of elaborate clothes which looked so exciting in a show just weren't conducive to modern life."

THE TANKING OF Lacroix summed up all that had been going wrong with Paris fashion in the last decade. As the ranchers like to say in Texas: Big hat, no cattle. Throughout the 1980s, the Paris fashion establishment had many glossy components—haute couturiers, famous ready-to-wear designers, and loads of perfumes, handbags, and trinkets flashing their logos.

But underneath French fashion's broad brim was a sinking industry, outmoded and out of touch, suffering from hubris and denial. The upbeat reports that couture had bounced back during the 1980s were greatly exaggerated because the couture houses were still losing millions on such collections. With few exceptions, French designer clothes in general were too contrived, too uptight, or just too weird looking. "It's the same ten old men doing a boring rehash of what they've already done, like the hobble skirts that are too tight and too expensive," remarked Vicki Ross, an independent buyer for retailers in Asia.

The state of French fashion was shaky in the 1990s, but Paris still stood on ceremony as the fashion capital of the world. To be sure, the City of Light prevailed as the world's most visible stage, where the international press and hordes of fashion groupies converged every season to cover the designer shows. But French fashion just wasn't selling the way it used to—having been upstaged by fashion labels from Italy and the United States. Nevertheless, the French, smug in their superiority, maintained that Paris would always be the guardian of high fashion, if not high commerce. But the reality was that by the mid-1990s, the French designers, who invented couture and set the standards for high style for more than one hundred years, were now hopelessly passé.

LIKE VINTAGE CHAMPAGNE, haute couture appointed the French as connoisseurs of the good life. It came as no surprise that the homeland of Versailles and Madame de Pompadour would serve as the birthplace of couture and high fashion. "Nowhere else in the world was elegance taken so seriously or supported by such a reservoir of talent, skilled craftsmen and cooperative clients," wrote Marilyn Bender in her 1966 study of pop fashion culture, *The Beautiful People*.

The couture industry began in the nineteenth century as a vehicle to stimulate growth in the French economy. In 1858, monarch Napoleon III summoned Charles Frederick Worth, an innovative English dressmaker practicing in Paris, to whip up a magnificent wardrobe for his wife, Empress Eugénie, who would become the world's first fashion model. Worth, who invented the bustle dress, came to design all of Eugénie's official court clothes and his label—the first in fashion history—bore the royal crest. Thus, Worth became known as the first Parisian couturier and the preferred dressmaker of the crowned heads of Austria, Italy, and Russia, which fueled the demand across Europe for fashion, jewelry, and other finery made in France.

French fashion stood for snob appeal and the height of elegance for ladies whose lives revolved around their wardrobes, the ones whom Parisian gentlemen playfully ordered: *"Sois belle et tais-toi,"* or "Shut up and be beautiful." By the 1920s, fashion would become France's second largest export, employing thousands of workers and establishing the benchmarks for quality and style around the world.

"The fashion system here is a reproduction of the aristocratic tradition in which the couture represents the establishment," observed Pascal Morand, an economist who heads the Institut Français de la Mode, a fashion industry graduate school in Paris. "Couture sells a luxury image that makes people feel that they are belonging to an elite. In the French vision, the creativity comes strictly from the product. But with the Italians and Americans, creativity concerns all parts of the business."

DURING MOST OF the twentieth century, couture was a vital cog in the French economy, funneling big business to countless fabric mills and craftsmen trading in feathers, buttons, embroideries, and so forth. The French government lent a hand, providing subsidies and organizing the industry under the Chambre Syndicale de la Couture Parisienne, the powerful trade group that promoted high fashion.

As long as French couture was selling briskly, there was little incentive to industrialize the French clothing trade for the mass market. This was the stark contrast between France and the United States, where commercial apparel began to take on steam at the turn of the twentieth century alongside the nation's burgeoning department stores such as R. H. Macy in New York, Marshall Field's in Chicago, and John Wanamaker in Philadelphia. France had no such retailing boom, and thus the trade of handmade clothes and tailoring continued to thrive unfettered.

Even if department stores had cropped up across France back then, it was unlikely that the couturiers would have been inspired to sell to them. "They were all snobs," asserts Gerry Dryansky, a Paris-based journalist who reported on the couture houses for *Women's Wear Daily* in the 1960s. "Coco vowed she'd never do ready-to-wear because she didn't want to dress everybody. [The couturiers'] ambitions weren't so high. They were rich and lived well, but they never intended to build colossal businesses. Their snobbism was greater than their greed."

DESPITE THEIR AVERSION to outfitting ordinary women, the couturiers nevertheless did just that—in a roundabout way—as they opened their elite salons to American retailers and manufacturers, who went to Paris twice a year to get a few good ideas. These commercial clients gained admission into the French showrooms where fashion shows were held by paying a fee called a "caution," or by ordering one or two couture dresses, often priced a notch higher than what private customers paid.

Everyone who attended the shows back then knew the rules. Fashion-show guests were allowed to take discreet notes, with stubby gold pencils that were handed out with the printed programs. The members of the press agreed not to circulate photos or sketches from the shows until after the official "release" date one month later.

To further safeguard exclusivity, the couturiers staggered deliveries: The private clients received their orders first, about a month ahead of stores like Ohrbach's and Marshall Field's. In those days, all of Seventh Avenue breathlessly awaited for the couture samples to hit American shores. *Women's Wear Daily* reported on August 24, 1965: "The first batch of Paris couture models for New York is slated to arrive at John F. Kennedy Airport Wednesday at about 8 P.M. on Air France flight 051."

This crude form of protectionism, no better than a gentleman's agreement, was always prone to leaks. During one fashion show in the 1950s, Christian Dior darted out from backstage to confiscate one woman's notebook full of sketches. But most copyists didn't get caught. "Right after the shows at Chanel or Christian Dior, I'd run to the nearest sidewalk café and start sketching the collection from memory," said Shannon Rodgers, a designer who worked for a number of New York dress houses back then. His drawings came to life as affordable ensembles sold in the "French Room" at L. S. Ayres in Indianapolis.

Dior, who was one of the first couturiers to offer a mass-produced retail collection, fought a losing battle with the knockoff artists. As early as 1957, Dior wasn't moving fast enough; copies of Dior's hobble skirts were hanging on Macy's racks well before his couture customers got their originals. Retailers awaiting shipments from Dior's retail collection shifted into spin control, pleading for women to be patient, advertising that it was "better to wait for perfection."

The couturiers didn't need to convince French women about the virtues of fine craftsmanship, for their countrywomen had an affinity for custom-made clothes. Until the late 1950s, in fact, most middle-class Frenchwomen were still having their clothes made by local dressmakers, many of whom used bootlegged couture patterns. Most every French home or apartment contained a *lingerie*, a tiny room off the *boudoir* designed for the care of clothes, where seamstresses worked when they made house calls.

Thus, groomed in the habits of countless fittings and creative clothes-making, middle-class Frenchwomen dreamed of trading up, and eventually wearing the top-of-the-line couture. And before the cost of skilled labor rose sharply in the 1970s, which forced the couturiers to keep raising their prices, many Frenchwomen could afford to splurge occasionally on a simple couture outfit.

GREASING THE PATH for Parisian designers—and fashion in general—were the members of the fashion press, who were the best unpaid publicists a designer could ever want. Before the late 1970s, when designer brands became household names with million-dollar advertising budgets, fashion houses relied on powerful editors—Carmel Snow of *Harper's Bazaar*, Diana Vreeland of *Vogue*, and Eugenia Sheppard of *The New York Herald Tribune*—enthusiastic fashion buffs who relished their omnipotent role as kingmakers and arbiters of taste to the masses. The women of the fashion press were a clubby lot, who got used to being wined and dined and discreetly wardrobed—either at discount or for free—by fashion houses who were keen to curry their favor.

Raising her hand high, Carmel Snow did her part to ensure that the French couture houses, which had been shuttered during World War II, would rise again. She said: "I was no more willing to concede the permanent fall of Paris than was General de Gaulle. . . . Since fashion is the second largest industry in France, I felt my personal contribution to the Allied cause could be to help the revival of that industry." It was Snow, in fact, who coined the term "New Look" in her breathless description of Dior's pivotal 1947 collection of long, ankle-grazing skirts that rendered every woman's prewar wardrobe of short dresses obsolete.

Fashion journalism would always be known for its relentless boosterism, as fashion writers typically slanted their reviews to flatter their designer buddies with shameless flackery ("his best collection in years") and rarely a discouraging word.

"The women who covered fashion generally didn't do a good job," said James Brady, publisher of *WWD* in the 1960s and of *Harper's Bazaar* in the 1970s. According to Brady, "The major papers would send reporters to Paris twice a year to get competent fashion show reviews—and they got to lunch with the designers. But I'm not aware they ever did a serious business story. *Vogue* never did serious stories inside the fashion business. The average reader didn't know a helluva lot what was going on. Back then, women were fascinated by fashion trends and not by anything else."

Flexing its editorial muscle with stylish irreverence was the omnipotent *Women's Wear Daily,* the garment industry paper that turned into a lively social chronicle in the 1960s under the reign of John B. Fairchild, the Princeton-educated heir to Fairchild publications, the trade-newspaper empire founded by his grandfather in 1890. John Fairchild was twenty-seven in 1955 when he became *WWD*'s bureau chief in Paris, where he began transforming his sleepy, rag-trade rag into a gossipy must-read that raked over the personalities of high fashion: the couturiers and their socialite clients.

Becoming the editor and publisher of *WWD* in the 1960s, Mr. Fairchild, as he was always so respectfully addressed, drummed up delicious little dramas, pitting one designer against another—while blithely shunning those like Geoffrey Beene and Pauline Trigère, who didn't strike his fancy. The intrepid Fairchild weighed in annually with his famous IN and OUT list and his roast of the year's "fashion victims," those ladies who dared to wear the worst of fashion.

In his 1989 biography, *Chic Savages*, Fairchild writes: "The real issue is that in the fashion business, it's almost against the law to tell the truth, and anyone who steps behind the silk curtain to show how raw the business is can expect a rough time. Designers go to grotesque lengths to exaggerate their concepts to the press. And the press is just as guilty when it swallows the bait and spews forth huge headlines. The self-importance of our profession is appalling."

DESPITE THE GLAMOROUS world portrayed and promoted by the press, by the 1960s, the first hairline cracks in the couture world began to appear. Rising labor costs were steadily erasing profits, and in 1961, the French government stopped providing subsidies to couturiers who did not agree to use at least 90 percent French textiles in their collections.

But economics aside, Paris fashion was being upstaged by London, where the miniskirt was born. The impact of the mini was tremendous. Beyond its saucy, knee-baring silhouette, the mini represented a change in women's values as it rendered the matronly, hat-and-glove standard out of style. "What was amusing about the fifties was that women didn't care about looking young," recalled Karl Lagerfeld. "An eighteen-year-old wanted to look like a woman with jewelry and a mink coat because this was the fashion. The fashion of sexiness and youth didn't come until the sixties with the miniskirt and Brigitte Bardot."

Fashion's youthquake of the 1960s revolved around the joy of shopping, the onset of what was known as the "boutique mystique," as Marilyn

Bender noted in 1966: "From then on, most of the high and mighty fashion leaders wanted it known that their clothes came from the small shops with the low prices. . . . Shopping in boutiques was like altering the birthdate on a passport. It certified that a woman was a swinger."

The boutique phenomenon quickly spread to France in the 1960s, where such couturiers as Emanuel Ungaro and Yves Saint Laurent introduced ready-to-wear collections for their own shops. But this diversification turned into the quintessential catch-22: As more wealthy women got hooked on the more affordable frocks at boutiques, they began to lose interest in collecting expensive couture clothes.

AS THE FRENCH couturiers created boutique collections, they discovered that the easiest way to offset their mounting losses on couture was to sign up licensees, which provided a reliable money machine and a lifeline for their businesses. The father of fashion licensing was Christian Dior, who in 1948 signed up with Prestige, a New York hosiery company, which produced his Christian Dior nylon stockings. Dior rejected an initial offer of a flat $10,000 licensing fee and held out for a revenue stream—a sliding royalty based on a percentage of sales—which became the industry standard for such contracts in the future.

In fashion licensing, a designer collects a royalty payment—between about 3 percent and 8 percent of wholesale volume—from an outside manufacturer who produces and markets the merchandise. Licensing enabled designers to put their trademarks on handbags, jewelry, shoes, and bedsheets—as well as clothes—quickly and relatively painlessly. Millions of American women who would never see the inside of an exclusive Paris atelier nevertheless shared the allure of filling their closets with affordable designer merchandise that was blessed with a couture pedigree.

Long after Dior's death in 1957, the house of Dior continued to milk its vaunted trademark, with more than two hundred licensees by the late 1980s, when the royalties ran deep. "From 1983 to 1989 we had licenses that were getting 20 to 25 percent increases every year and we didn't understand why," said Marie Fornier, who worked at Dior at the time. "The system was so great; Asia was just opening and there wasn't a lot of competition outside the traditional designer brands. So it was, why not more? We even licensed Dior slippers with Aris Isotoner."

But "more" resulted in schlock instead of chic. Marc Bohan, Dior's couturier for nearly thirty years, became more and more disgusted as the Dior label ceased to reflect all that was elegant and chic. Once in the late 1980s when Bohan and Arnault were canvasing the floors of Bloomingdale's in New York, Bohan was aghast upon seeing "all that horrible luggage with the Dior name on it!"

While Arnault could take pride in Dior's popular fragrances such as Diorissimo and its chic Baby Dior infant's wear, the Dior trademark nevertheless suffered from "inconsistency," admitted Colombe Nicholas, who ran Dior's U.S. division in the 1980s and signed up many of its licensees at the behest of Paris headquarters. Quality control became exceedingly difficult to maintain because the licensees were more interested in making money than genuflecting to the House of Dior.

For example, the licensees refused to make merchandise that complemented the fashions designed by Marc Bohan. According to Nicholas, Bohan's "ready-to-wear [collections for Dior] never sold well in the U.S. because the clothes were all wrong—too expensive, too formal, too French-looking, and not lifestyle-driven. Marc would set styles; he would say, for example, that green was the color of the season and half of the licensees would say 'you can't give away a green coat in America.' So, they tended to ignore him, rightly or wrongly."

But the licensees were driven to safeguard their profits by any means necessary. They were already on the hook to pay Dior guaranteed minimum royalty payments, regardless of sales or profit levels. So it was in their best interest to jack up sales—to cut corners on quality, to make a handbag in a vinyl-trimmed canvas, for example, so that the handbags could retail for a lower price, making them easier to unload to department stores. Most high-fashion designers barred their licensees from shipping their merchandise to discounters like Loehmann's. But if nobody was watching—and the French fashion houses were lax when it came to monitoring—the licensees would surreptitiously ship merchandise to any stores they pleased.

In fashion licensing, Nicholas said, "It is very difficult to balance image and to make money. The challenge is standing up to the licensees, telling them that whatever limitations in price, there should be a certain quality level. But when you are sitting across from a licensee with whom you do $100 million of business, it is a difficult position to be in. They tell you, 'You don't know what you are talking about.' "

The licensing boom saturated the world with designer merchandise that hardly lived up to its prestigious labels—polyester scarves and handbags stamped with brassy logos. Hurting the French mystique even further was the flood of illegal counterfeit T-shirts and handbags hawked on the streets of big cities like New York. By the late 1980s, American shoppers in particular had had their fill and were no longer fascinated by most French designer labels.

WITHOUT A DOUBT, Pierre Cardin took fashion licensing to dizzying new lows. By the late 1980s, Cardin had signed up a staggering eight hundred licensees worldwide, in apparel, cosmetics, chocolate, home furnishings, and appliances. Cardin raked in the millions, selling his name so many times over that his cursive signature itself was a valued commodity. There was always a manufacturer somewhere in the world ready to slap "Pierre Cardin" on hair dryers, alarm clocks, bidets, and frying pans. "My name is more important than myself," Cardin once said.

Pierre Cardin became the couturier the French loved to hate—an artist who got swallowed by marketing madness. Cardin's gold-plated credentials dated back to 1947, when he was a top Dior assistant and renowned as the author of Dior's best-selling "Bar" suit—a fitted white jacket over a full black skirt. Cardin was also a trailblazer in menswear, the Giorgio Armani of his time. In 1961, when smartly dressed gentlemen favored the boxy suits from Savile Row, Cardin broke the mold with his dandy Edwardian-cut suits, with high armholes and nipped waistlines, that were soon worn by everybody from the Beatles to Rex Harrison.

Cardin, the son of Italian working-class immigrants, was always disdainful of couture's aristocratic pretensions. He could hardly wait to begin selling to the masses after he opened his own couture house in 1949, at the age of twenty-seven. Eight years later, he cornered the Japanese market, staging his first fashion show in Tokyo. And on the heels of President Nixon, Cardin conquered China in the early 1970s, where the screaming Chinese mobs awaiting Cardin's arrival mistook him for the president of France. "Cardin is a very excellent promoter and he was a salesman before anything else," said Henri Berghauer, who managed Cardin's business back in the 1950s. "Pierre realized early that he wanted to be more of a label than a designer. He wanted to be Renault."

Cardin's road to riches was paved with licensing contracts from a reported ninety-four countries—deals that the intrepid couturier made so fast and furiously that he had trouble keeping up with all the products he licensed. His haphazard ways landed him in court, when he was forced to pay $600,000 to settle a dispute over Pierre Cardin cigarette lighters, which he had mistakenly licensed to two different parties.

In 1981, Cardin paid $20 million to buy Maxim's, the legendary Paris restaurant, on which he lost millions as he turned it into a licensing machine. Nevertheless, Cardin was still filthy rich, one of the wealthiest individuals in France, with an estimated net worth of more than $300 million in 1987. Cardin-label products reached an estimated wholesale volume of about $1 billion in 1991, according to his biographer Richard Morais, who concluded: "His fortune was built on the back of rapidly changing media, which in the period of his lifetime had shrunk the world into one easily accessible market."

The eccentric tycoon was still on the move well into the 1990s, running his far-flung empire from Paris. In January 1997, he was taping a TV interview at Espace Cardin, the theater and exhibition space he owned across the street from the American embassy in Paris. Pale, thin, and angular in a drab gray business suit, Cardin feigned utter indifference to the plight of the French fashion houses in the 1990s. "I don't understand what they're doing. It makes no sense." He shrugged. "Anyway, I already did all of that."

As the septuagenarian spoke, his head tilted cockily to the side, he wasn't exaggerating. Indeed, the designers in Paris were now scrambling to pursue the same path he had pioneered twenty years earlier. "Pierre was considered too rough for this market at the time, but nevertheless, in the end, everybody wants to sell," said Berghauer. "You look at what has happened to these big fashion labels. They aren't selling caviar; they are selling T-shirts, jeans and underwear."

WHILE CARDIN, FRENCH fashion's most colorful enigma, was in a class by himself, it was left to the reigning king of couture, Yves Saint Laurent, to wave the flag for French fashion. After Dior's sudden death in 1957, it was the twenty-one-year-old Saint Laurent, Dior's able apprentice, who carried on designing the Dior collections without missing a beat. The fragile and introverted Saint Laurent founded his own fashion house in 1962, together with his shrewd and tough-as-nails business partner, Pierre Bergé.

For more than twenty years, Saint Laurent was revered as French fashion's most progressive designer for modern women, in the spirit of Chanel. Saint Laurent prospered as a couturier and a retailer through his chain of Rive Gauche boutiques, where he marketed such liberated looks as "safari" pantsuits, "*le smoking*" tuxedos, and pea coats.

But the house of Saint Laurent, too, couldn't resist the siren call of licensing, stacking on more than two hundred licensees, including YSL cigarettes. Bergé pontificated on the excesses of fashion licensing as practiced by the likes of Cardin, telling *The Wall Street Journal* in 1984: "A name is like a cigarette, the more you smoke it, the less that is left." Naturally, he avoided discussing the slew of mediocre Saint Laurent–labeled umbrellas, scarves, and handbags—not to mention cigarettes—that were dragging the trademark down.

Saint Laurent managed to hold on to his prestige longer than Cardin and Dior because of his stunning success in marketing perfumes. Years before Calvin Klein took over the perfume counter, Saint Laurent had already scored a blockbuster with his 1978 fragrance Opium. A spicy Oriental scent that was as exotic as its controversial name, Opium made its New York debut with a splash: Saint Laurent hosted a lavish bash on the *Peking*, a Chinese junk moored in the East River. Opium continued to be a bestseller for more than a decade, joining the ranks of dozens of other popular French designer perfumes.

French perfumes, whose essences were composed of the exotic flowers from France's southern Grasse region, used to be prized by women around the world. Thousands of American G.I.s returned from World War II with bottles of Chanel No. 5 for their mothers and sweethearts.

For years, perfumes had been a nifty, image-enhancing sideline for couturiers, producing such legendary classics as Arpège from the house of Lanvin, Joy by Jean Patou, and L'Air du Temps—in its famed René Lalique–designed bottle—by Nina Ricci. But in most cases, the perfume sideline threw couturiers off the track from their fashion main line and eventually became a distraction, albeit a profitable one.

"The perfume business is the worst thing that ever happened to French fashion," observed Patrick McCarthy, the editorial director of *WWD*. "Once perfume came on the scene, the French didn't have to worry about selling clothes. Any major fashion house, if you had a reasonably successful perfume, you could do what you wanted. The designer could tell the stores, 'I'm not changing the way I'm cutting the dresses; I am doing whatever I want.' The money would still be coming in from that little perfume license.

"That's why somebody like Giorgio Armani could come in and change the way men and women all over the world dress and take over all the space in stores," said McCarthy. Meanwhile, "the French were still selling some perfume—but nobody was buying their clothes."

Nevertheless, Saint Laurent and Bergé would go on to make enormous sums in their fashion house, which was valued at $500 million when it went public on the Paris Bourse in 1989. In the next years, Saint Laurent himself would visibly deteriorate, the legacy of more than three decades of nervous breakdowns and bouts with depression. In the early 1990s, he teetered and trembled down the runway, underscoring speculation that his future was precarious.

In 1993, cosmetics giant Elf Sanofi bought the house of Saint Laurent for $650 million, leaving Bergé and Saint Laurent in charge of the couture operations and with employment contracts for several more years. But Elf Sanofi made it clear that its long-term future was in its still-buoyant YSL fragrances and cosmetics. Elf Sanofi's chief executive, Jean François Debreq, told *Vanity Fair:* "If he dies, I think I make even more money because then I stop the [couture] collections." He said at the time that the couture was losing $5.4 million a year.

LICENSING WAS INDEED an opiate that had greatly enriched the French houses while handicapping them for the long run. By handing over their trademarks to licensees, the French designers escaped the rigors and nuances of mass production, international retailing, and marketing. So when the licensing bubble finally burst, the couture houses were hard pressed to find a new way to whip up a heady froth to revive their brands.

While the French were on their licensing binge in the 1980s, the Italian fashion industry was steadily making inroads, having gained its footing in Milan, in close proximity to the country's leading textile mills in the Lake Como region and factories that promote homegrown talents such as Giorgio Armani, Gianfranco Ferré, Krizia, and Genny. The Italian manufacturers, who had a history of competition and cooperation with the apparel, footwear, and textile sectors, "developed a marketing plan to increase Italian exports with the objective to make a large footprint in Italian fashion in the U.S.," asserted Armando Branchini, a Milanese management consultant.

"In one sense, the Italians have won the battle of fashion," wrote *WWD*'s John Fairchild in 1989, noting that French designers Emanuel Ungaro, Christian Dior, Christian Lacroix, Sonia Rykiel, Claude Montana, and Jean Paul Gaultier all manufactured much of their apparel in Italy. "The Italian monopoly is even more complete because in addition to clothes, the Italians are responsible for designing and producing some of the most beautiful fabrics in the world."

The French didn't worry much about the rise of the Italians during the 1980s because couture had gotten a shot in the arm with a new generation of fans from the Middle East and America. The couture revival coincided with the OPEC oil cartel in the 1970s, when wealthy Arab ladies began taking their petrodollars to Paris for shopping sprees. Middle Eastern women loved opulent couture gowns and they bought liberally, especially for weddings, for which they also bought couture dresses for their young daughters. In 1984, Arab women represented only about 15 percent of the clients, but they bought more than half of the reported $24 million of garments sold by the twenty-three official Paris couturiers that year. The Middle East gravy train continued until couture sales dropped dramatically with the outbreak of the Persian Gulf War in January 1991. Ironically, most of the couture ensembles destined for the Arab world hit a dead end, never to be photographed and never to be worn in public. As was the custom in Muslim countries, women wore their couture finery behind closed doors, only in the company of other women.

By the early 1980s, the Arab ladies were joined by the Americans, the Reagan-era charity-ball set—women like Ivana Trump, Ann Getty, and Lynn Wyatt—who headed to Paris via Concorde for the couture shows. Such clotheshorses were known to blow $100,000 or more on a couture wardrobe on a single Paris trip.

DURING THE EIGHTIES the rising couture tide lifted all French fashion, as Parisian designers like Claude Montana, Jean Paul Gaultier, Sonia Rykiel, and Thierry Mugler flourished alongside the couturiers.

The designer boom was running at full gallop and sparking a new type of rivalry: the war on the catwalks. It was Pierre Cardin who had paved the way back in the 1960s when he first began filling his runways with outlandish costumes, as he cleverly sensed that a sensational runway picture was worth far more than a thousand words.

The international fashion circuit included women's and men's designers who staged fashion shows twice a year in Paris, Milan, New York, and London. By the early 1990s, there were a staggering 1,500 major showings on the calendar. Television cameras joined the parade, capturing runway footage for such fashion news programs as CNN's *Style with Elsa Klensch*. High fashion turned into high entertainment. And always, the loudest noise was coming from Paris, where avant-garde Japanese creators like Issey Miyake, Yohji Yamamoto, Kenzo, and Rei Kawakubo joined the local lineup.

The shows took on a life of their own as everyone tried to outdo each other with seminude costumes, strange hair and makeup, and gimmicky staging—starring those $10,000-a-day playmakers known as supermodels. Jean Paul Gaultier, Paris fashion's kilt-wearing enfant terrible, was idolized by avant-garde fashion groupies, only to be one-upped from time to time by Thierry Mugler, whose 1994 fall fashion show, televised live, was a sci-fi spectacle of Jetsons-like creations, featuring celebrity model Patty Hearst and soul singer James Brown in a musical finale. The reported cost: $3 million.

Mugler could afford to splurge on such lavish shows, which were partially underwritten by Clarins, his publicity-hungry perfume licensee, who was glad to oblige as long as the shows created a big buzz. And the fashion magazines just couldn't seem to get enough of the wild and crazy images from the Paris catwalks.

Distracted by all that fashion-show hoopla, French designers missed out on the shift that began in the late 1980s when sales of high fashion stagnated and American retailers began searching for new ways to sell designer clothes. Retailers came up with a new marketing vehicle known as "bridge"—collections that carried a designer label but were priced at least 30 percent less than the top designer lines. Bridge jackets, for example, retailed at $350 to $650, compared to designer jackets at $700 and up. The bridge brands enabled American department stores to generate big volume in designer brands, without selling the most expensive goods. In 1996, bridge brands such as Donna Karan's DKNY, Anne Klein II, and Ellen Tracy accounted for about $4.7 billion, or 12 percent, of all women's wear sold at retail and represented the top price range at most department stores. By comparison, top-tier designer lines accounted for about $1 billion in retail sales and were available only at select locations at Saks Fifth Avenue, Nordstrom, Neiman Marcus, and Barneys New York, as well as the designers' own boutiques.

Given that French suppliers were accustomed to selling to independent boutiques rather than big American chains, most houses didn't grasp the bridge concept. Instead of shifting more of their production to the Far East, where most bridge brands were made, the majority of French designers continued to use high-cost factories in France or Italy. Thus, French designer brands weighed in at the loftiest prices, which virtually locked the French out of U.S. department stores and, consequently, the world's primary clothing market.

There was another fundamental problem: the look of the clothes. Retailers agreed that too many French designers had made some bad fashion calls. Even when Mugler, Montana, and Gaultier eventually marketed so-called "*diffusion*" or bridge-style brands, the styles were usually too avant-garde for most women—and were cut too tight for American bodies.

"Mugler and Montana were sexy and hot in the 1980s, but now women want something that is more contemporary and less aggressive," said Armand Hadida, the owner of Eclaireur, a seventeen-year-old chain of four high-fashion Paris boutiques. As for Jean Paul Gaultier's whimsical designs, Hadida considered them ridiculous. "Gaultier is doing only theatrical collections for the *défilé* [fashion shows], which are good for a moment, but try to sell this. Nobody wants to buy it. . . . It is a joke."

More affluent American women were gravitating toward bridge brands—and increasingly ignoring the noise coming from the high-fashion shows, which played on warp speed. The Paris shows continued to be media happenings, chock-full of buyers, press, and miscellaneous stylish groupies. This was the clubby world of the fashionistas, the women who dress alike in all-black, in a sea of studied nonchalance. The fashionistas reinforced each other's importance by being there, in the thick of the action, during a glorious, expense-account whirl, to cover the shows twice a year under the pretext of fashion news.

The American newspapers covering the shows—*The New York Times*, *The Washington Post*, the *Los Angeles Times*, and *The Dallas Morning News*—were caught in a tougher bind. They were passing judgment on clothes that would never be seen again—and that their readers thought were ridiculous. So the fashion writers strained to characterize fashion as a high art form—and they looked hard for any common themes on the runway that they could pinpoint as the coming trends that would soon trickle down to department stores. But once readers saw the pictures and read the copy, they knew high fashion was more and more a series of publicity stunts.

In 1995 *USA Today* stopped covering the shows in Europe and New York altogether, at the suggestion of Elizabeth Snead, *USA Today*'s fashion editor at the time, who volunteered to quit going. "I just couldn't justify going anymore. It didn't make sense to call the shows fashion 'news' when they weren't anymore." Snead transferred from New York to Los Angeles, where she started covering fashion on movie stars and celebrities, who had become the new fashion role models of the 1990s.

Retail buyers continued to ply the international circuit, but they were grounded by what their stores could actually sell—and not what fashion editors considered cutting-edge. "We're really not influenced by what we read," remarked Joan Kaner, fashion director of Neiman Marcus. The

Dallas-based retailer bought as much as 70 percent of its collections in the showrooms *before* watching a single fashion show, with most of their choices being the styles that the designers thought were too bland to be shown on the runway.

BY 1995, FRANCE was facing a bleak economic climate that affected fashion and other local industries. Consumer spending was down, unemployment stood at 12 percent, and the overvalued franc was hurting France's ability to increase exports of consumer products, from automobiles to clothes. Moreover, the French image was taking a bruising in the U.S. as many treasured symbols of French refinement came under siege. Sophisticated New Yorkers no longer treated themselves to classic French cuisine; Italian food—lighter, healthier, and more creative—was now the preferred choice of many. Champagne was still divine, but more connoisseurs also respected fine wines from California, Italy, and Spain. And on Mother's Day, men were more likely to buy their wives Beautiful by Estée Lauder than Joy by Jean Patou. The French mystique simply wasn't holding up.

In a telling sign that struck closer to home, French President Jacques Chirac appeared on the cover of *Paris Match* in an oxford-cloth, button-down-collar dress shirt with a Ralph Lauren polo-pony logo on his first day on the job in May 1995. (Lauren's officials back in New York sent Chirac a thank-you note and a box of shirts.)

The French mystique could no longer coast on inertia alone. French fashion needed to be repositioned, updated, and most of all marketed to a new generation of sophisticated consumers. "When you look back to the 1950s and 1960s, Paris designers had an ability to create a fashion look that everyone wanted to have," observed Carl Steidtmann, a New York retail industry economist. "The French felt they didn't need to market to consumers because their brands were very strong. But now that the focus has shifted away from designing, and if you have enough money and are good at marketing, you can create a strong brand."

Throughout Paris in department stores such as Galeries Lafayette, a number of the world's most powerful fashion marketers like Gap, Calvin Klein, and Ralph Lauren began winning over Parisian shoppers. In 1995, Calvin Klein had brazenly splashed his sexy underwear ads on billboards all over town and planted his retail flagship on the swank Avenue Montaigne—the best shopping street in Paris—directly across from Christian Dior. Klein's success didn't come from creating *true* fashion, maintained Didier Grumbach, the managing director of Thierry Mugler, who declared in 1997: "It is better to be known for a beautiful embroidered dress than for underwear."

By the mid-1990s, fashion's klieg light shone brightly on Milan with the onslaught of Italy's big three: Giorgio Armani, Prada, and Gucci. Ever chauvinistic, the powers in France ignored the Italians—at least for the record. The prevailing French group-think went like this: stay the course in promoting traditional French savoir faire, which will outlast them all. The Chambre Syndicale trade group took Paris runway shows on the road to such places as Belarus, Beijing, Shanghai, and Budapest, where the locals remained enthralled with classic French labels and now had the freedom to buy them.

Just as Arnault's LVMH went about acquiring the house of Givenchy in the 1990s, other fashion industry investors in France were also keen to revive couture's most fabled names from the 1940s and 1950s—namely Balmain and Balenciaga—instead of starting from scratch with an unknown designer. "Fashion in France is considered a national patrimony," said Morand, the economist. "You don't even pose the question whether one of the traditional houses is obsolete or not. That is why you have some financial people who will be ready to buy brands that don't mean anything anymore, because they are linked with history and status, whether or not they have a concept which is still valid."

But valid or not, reviving a long-forgotten couture brand was no different than launching a new name; both scenarios required millions in marketing and advertising to position the brands in the public consciousness. But heavy-duty advertising simply wasn't the French way, least of all in the fashion sector, where designers had long put their faith in the free plugs they got in the fashion press. Counting on getting a steady blast of publicity from one of Seventh Avenue's most beloved designers, the House of Balmain hired Oscar de la Renta to be its couturier in 1995. While Balmain did draw more business from de la Renta's American socialite clients as a result, the Balmain trademark and its Ivoire perfume remained in obscurity.

FOR ALL THEIR bluster about their eminence the beleaguered French houses were becoming more prickly and paranoid about their future. Perhaps that's why certain designers suddenly became obsessive about stopping knockoffs, which were the oldest gambit in fashion. Knockoffs had always provided the grist for countless fashion dramas as designers staked their reputations and won awards from their peers—by being original, by being first with the next Big Idea, whether they made money on it or not. The irony of it all was that designers around the world had stopped staring at Paris to get their best ideas. The most successful houses were pragmatists, grabbing trends from the present, from the past, and from the trendy kids on the street, making it impossible for any designer to claim ownership of a particular style. In any event, the end of fashion in the 1990s made pedantic arguments over creativity and originality irrelevant.

Nevertheless, the powers at the Chambre Syndicale decided to get tough on knockoffs, zeroing in on the hundreds of freelance photographers and video cameramen whom French designers had accused of leaking fashion-show photos to their foreign competitors. In 1995, the Chambre Syndicale dreamed up a regulation in which photographers attending the Paris shows were told that they could publish photos only for "journalistic information," and not on the Internet. Then the Chambre Syndicale instituted a throwback from the 1930s: an official photo "release date," three months after the shows were held. An impossible dream in today's media age? "*Mais non*," vowed Jacques Mouclier, director of the Chambre Syndicale. Mouclier claimed that "a French prosecutor" was all set to press charges against *First View*, a website that published fashion-show photos during the collections. "We are seeking to make an example," he asserted in 1997. But *First View* said that other than receiving a few threatening letters from Mouclier, nothing happened.

In 1994, a knockoff war erupted over a sleeveless tuxedo gown between Yves Saint Laurent and Ralph Lauren. Saint Laurent charged in a French court that Lauren's $1,000 tuxedo gown was a spitting image of his $15,000 couture version. (Ironically, though it wasn't widely known, Saint Laurent himself was a convicted plagiarist, who had been fined in 1985 after a French court found him guilty of copying a toreador jacket credited to couturier Jacques Esterel.) Sleeveless tuxedo gowns had been on the market for years, but that didn't stop a French judge from concluding that Lauren was guilty as charged and slapping him with a $411,000 fine. To further shame the American, the judge ordered Lauren to advertise the court decision in ten publications.

The judge, Madelaine Cotelle, wasn't a lawyer but a fashion expert of sorts, by virtue of her ownership of two boutiques in suburban Paris. During the proceedings, live models paraded through the courtroom dressed in both versions of the tuxedo gown. Judge Cotelle's remarks during the trial left little surprise as to Lauren's ultimate fate. "I know something about fashion," Judge Cotelle said. "Clearly there are differences in the two dresses. Saint Laurent's dress is made of a different fabric and has pockets, unlike Lauren's. And his buttons aren't gold, while Mr. Saint Laurent's are. The Saint Laurent dress also has wider lapels and I must say is more beautiful, but of course, that will not influence my decision."

Eagerly awaiting an expected victory in court, Saint Laurent's Bergé gloated. He told *WWD* that Lauren was "ripping off" the Saint Laurent tuxedo dress "line for line, cut for cut." Judge Cotelle ruled that his premature outburst defamed Lauren and fined Bergé $93,000. Indignant, Bergé later crowed that Saint Laurent's victory was a "great shot in the arm for our fellow designers. It's a clear warning that so-called designers, especially from America, cannot get away with lifting original ideas of true creators of fashion." (The case was eventually settled with both parties paying lower fines, and Ralph Lauren wasn't forced to run ads to publicize the decision.)

IT HAD BECOME increasingly harder to make a case that French fashion had kept up with modern women, including those from France, who were searching for practical fashion solutions, not just prestige, from a label. In 1994, Faces International, a Paris-based market research firm, surveyed three hundred European women about their attitudes toward fashion. The French respondents sounded just like American women, as they unanimously agreed that their "dream world of fashion" was "designer labels at affordable prices," and not couture. Answering the question "Who or what do you emulate when you try to be fashionable?" only 2 percent said "the models in magazines," while 70 percent said: "No one. I just want to maximize me."

ANY DISCUSSION ABOUT the stamina of French fashion always came back to Chanel, the house that underwent a spectacular makeover during the 1980s with the help of designer Karl Lagerfeld, who began creating Chanel's collections in 1982. By the end of the decade, Chanel was more than just viable—it was red hot, more popular than it had been under Coco Chanel, who died in 1971. By the mid-1990s, the Chanel empire, which included forty-one boutiques, had racked up an estimated $1 billion a year in clothes, cosmetics, and accessories—without enlisting a single licensee.

While Lagerfeld would get a lot of the credit, the fact was that Chanel owed its renaissance to a confluence of circumstances. Before Lagerfeld, Chanel was a prestigious, if faded brand that hadn't been compromised by the far-flung licensees that bastardized Dior's image. Chanel also benefited from its stash of enduring marketing symbols created by Coco Chanel: the tweed suit, the camellia, the interlocking CC logo, the quilted chain handbag, and the famous, black-tipped slingback pump.

Above all there was Chanel No. 5, the most popular designer fragrance of all time. Alain Wertheimer, who took over the Chanel empire in 1974, began aggressively marketing the famous fragrance in clever TV commercials, such as the one featuring a morphed image of Marilyn Monroe holding a gigantic bottle of Chanel No. 5.

Meanwhile, Lagerfeld got busy tarting up Chanel's dowdy tweed suits to make them status symbols for executive women. With his white powdered ponytail, sunglasses, and black Yohji Yamamoto suits, the German-born designer was the most experienced hired gun in high fashion. Since the 1970s, Lagerfeld had designed collections for Chloé in Paris and for Fendi in Rome, as well as his own namesake collections.

Chanel also got plenty of tailwind from Lagerfeld's close friendship with one of the most influential people in fashion, *Vogue* editor Anna Wintour, who frequently wore Chanel suits and practically lived in oversize Chanel sunglasses. "Karl is a terrific designer; he has everything going for him," said Bernadine Morris, the veteran fashion journalist. "He knows how to sell, how to seduce the press—he does it in five languages."

Lagerfeld admitted that he came to Chanel at the right time, in the early 1980s when he was able to concentrate on revamping Chanel's image with substance rather than pure hype. "All this media stuff didn't exist when I started at Chanel," he observed. "I made over the image with things that would sell. I didn't have to be outrageous."

While Lagerfeld resided most of the time in Paris, inside a splendid eighteenth-century estate on the Left Bank, he considered himself a foreigner and an outsider to the French fashion establishment, which he loathed because the French kept clinging to the past, while the rest of fashion had moved on.

Consumers around the world, Lagerfeld maintained, are "no longer impressed with the prestige of Paris. The Italians are very clever marketers and the Americans are making modern and interesting clothes, capturing the right mood of today. . . . You don't think of French perfume; you think of Calvin Klein, which the Europeans are also buying."

OBSERVING CHANEL WITH a mixture of envy and admiration was Bernard Arnault, the hard-charging chairman of the LVMH fashion empire. Arnault had spent about thirteen years building LVMH, exercising his penchant for strong-arm tactics. Everyone who had observed the unflappable Arnault wrangle one company from the grip of another wondered if he could also marshal his executives to master the subtleties of the high-strung world of high fashion. Arnault was considered a maverick whose steamroller style was anathema to France. "Behind his angelic appearance there lurked an authoritarian proprietor," wrote Arnault biographers Nadege Forestier and Nazanine Ravai in *The Taste of Luxury* in 1992. "He liked to increase tension in his various companies. His managerial credo became American-style management. He was not worried about charisma. What mattered to him was efficiency."

Born in 1949 to a wealthy family in northern France, Arnault majored in math at École Polytechnique, the prestigious French university that bred corporate titans and government ministers. Arnault spent three years in the United States to develop his family's real estate business in Florida before returning to France in 1983, when he began to build LVMH, starting with Christian Dior in 1984.

People close to Arnault believed that his original strategy was to recast Dior as a mirror image of Chanel. Colombe Nicholas, who oversaw Dior's U.S. operations in the 1980s, recalled: "There was always some envy when he looked at Chanel, which stayed pure without licensees and secondary lines, and Arnault is saying to himself, 'Dior is just as good a name and I'm going to make it pure again.' "

Tall, gangling, and pale, with heavy, dark eyebrows, Arnault was low-profile, aloof, and mysterious. He sat on the front row at fashion shows, stone-faced and silent, his bodyguards planted nearby. An accomplished pianist whose second wife, Hélène, was a concert pianist, Arnault never professed to be a fashion expert. He did profess that his obsession to collect so many of the world's top luxury brands dovetailed with his love of money. Arnault once said: "My relationship to luxury goods is really very rational. It is the only area in which it is possible to make luxury profit margins."

While he struggled with his pet project, Lacroix, Arnault put his faith in Dior, which had a thriving perfume and cosmetics business that would generate revenue and visibility for the brand as he went about canceling most of Dior's licensees in an effort to reposition Dior to be as upscale as Chanel.

Starting around 1994, designer handbags suddenly became the rage in fashion and Dior was lucky enough to ride the wave with its Lady Dior handbag, a quilted box in buttery lambskin, distinguished by the gold-plated letters D-I-O-R dangling from its double handles. At $1,200, the Lady Dior bag was a pricier version of Chanel's $960 quilted bag. But what a difference Princess Diana made! French First Lady Bernadette Chirac gave the Princess of Wales a Dior bag in 1995 and she began carrying it everywhere, within full view of the paparazzi. Before long, retailers had a hard time keeping Lady Dior handbags in stock and more than 100,000 Lady Diors flew off the shelves in 1997.

Employing his adopted American sensibilities, Arnault took advantage of the power of publicity. He recruited a few of the darlings of the fashion press to design for LVMH's brands. From London came John Galliano, who went to Dior, and Alexander McQueen for Givenchy. Arnault chose three Americans for LVMH's other leather-goods divisions: Marc Jacobs for Louis Vuitton, Michael Kors for Céline, and Narciso Rodriguez for Loewe. None of the new charges had couture experience, nor had they run financially successful fashion businesses on their own. Whatever their talents were as designers, they all held the promise of generating lots of press. Indeed, in the case of Rodriguez, he had made his name on a single dress. As an assistant at Cerruti 1881, Rodriguez created the much-photographed slip wedding gown worn by Carolyn Bessette when she married John F. Kennedy Jr. in 1996. Labeling McQueen and Galliano as "two of the greatest creators of our time," Arnault told *Paris Match* that he chose them "for the simple reason talent has no nationality."

The fashion world watched in awe while Arnault went about his grand restructuring. *WWD*'s McCarthy observed in December 1997: "It is a massive investment and it's fascinating to watch. For every ten times you try, there is one time you succeed. Who knows if Galliano will make Dior sing again? This is the biggest gamble anyone has taken in fashion in a long time."

Galliano—a Salvador Dalí caricature with a skinny mustache and alternating wavy and dreadlocked hairstyles—had a fitful start, first spending a year at Givenchy only to be shifted to Dior by Arnault. Known for his dramatic bias-cut evening gowns, Galliano staged many theatrical fashion shows, including a 1998 couture show with a Pocohontas theme, complete with a moving train. Rumors flew that the artisans in Dior's workrooms despised Galliano, and retailers conceded privately that his clothes weren't selling.

As for McQueen, the chubby son of a taxi driver, his claim to fame as a London designer were his low-riding, cleavage-revealing "bumster pants." The impudent McQueen liked to shock the French establishment, such as the time he told *Le Monde* that handmade couture embroidery looks "like vomit." His retort to his many critics was a dismissive "Fuck you." After the press criticized his first quirky-looking collections, McQueen lashed out: "People aren't going to get wonderful things overnight. I don't expect everyone to do what I do right away. . . . I do what I do and people can take it or leave it." Arnault was obviously taking it; he signed McQueen to a three-year contract in October 1997.

While the fashion press stopped short of writing off the designing Brits, other observers were pointedly dismissive. Lagerfeld sized up McQueen as "crude and vulgar," while David Wolfe, a New York retail consultant, pounced: "For Bernard Arnault to hire McQueen to do Givenchy is such an exercise in bad thinking; it goes against every idea of common sense and marketing imaginable. If any publicity is good publicity, then this works. But I will be surprised if it does."

If Arnault had learned anything from Lacroix, he knew that fashion shows would take Galliano and McQueen only so far. Colombe Nicholas wondered: "What is the press value of couture? If you have a strong accessory business your brand will work. Galliano is getting a lot of press but is the twenty-year-old buying that product? I don't think so. I don't understand where it will lead to."

Arnault had little to worry about with Louis Vuitton, the $1-billion-a-year leather-goods company that no young turk designer could destroy. Yet he believed that a Vuitton fashion collection would put some sizzle back into Vuitton, the same way that Tom Ford had done for Gucci in the 1990s. That's why Arnault chose Marc Jacobs, the New York designer who put the downtown grunge look on the runways when he worked for Perry Ellis in 1989.

Jacobs, a cute, chain-smoking favorite of fashion editors, began locking horns with Vuitton's strait-laced executives right from the start. It was an uneasy fit: Jacobs was a high-concept designer working for Vuitton, which catered to conservative, bourgeois tastes. In his first months at Vuitton in 1997, Jacobs had experimented with a boiled, matted cashmere that he adored because it was "guaranteed to pill with age; beautiful but a little fucked up." Jacobs delivered a few samples of his cashmere scarves, which Arnault passed out to his friends. They didn't get it. But Arnault told Zoe Heller of *The New Yorker* that Jacobs would nevertheless bring a "trendy, fashionable edge to Vuitton," which would broaden its traditional base. "It is an easy idea," Arnault said.

AROUND THE CORNER in 1998 was a new, jarring reality that nobody in Paris was ready for: the collapse of Asia. The most buoyant market for luxury French designer brands was suddenly hit with a monetary economic crisis that effectively froze consumer spending on fashion brands across the board. The Japanese superconsumers, who once collected Chanel handbags as if they were trinkets, put the brakes on their spending. Scores of designer shops in Singapore, Hong Kong, and Thailand closed. Economists predicted that the Asian crisis would last for a while, at least through 2000, before any recovery would begin. And everyone knew that once the crisis subsided, the Asians would return to the marketplace with a sobering new mindset—just as the Americans had done when they shifted from ostentation to practicality in the aftermath of the 1987 stock market crash. In the midst of the crisis, Japanese shoppers were getting into the habit of buying simple, affordable sportswear from Gap, which opened ten stores across Japan in 1998.

The so-called Asian flu stung the luxury-goods sector badly in 1998, when LVMH's earnings plunged 29 percent, dragged down by $37 million in operating losses from its Duty Free Shops division, which was hit hard by the weaker yen and reduced Japanese overseas travel.

In the meantime, Bernard Arnault, the protector of French high fashion and luxury-goods raider who some dubbed "the wolf in cashmere," took a stunning detour in 1999. Instead of simply hiring a few more British and American designers to pursue LVMH's French agenda, Arnault began aggressively shopping for American and Italian fashion brands to call his own.

During a March 1999 interview at Dior's Fifth Avenue showroom, he explained his new, multinational strategy. "It isn't a question of country, but a question of power of the brand and its capacity to be developed on a worldwide scale. Fashion is very different in today's world. It is very important to link up with each other."

In 1999, LVMH spent $1.5 billion to secure a 34 percent stake in Gucci Group, the Florence-based leather-goods and fashion house that was among the hottest, most profitable fashion brands in business. Arnault coyly explained that his interest in Gucci was a friendly attempt to forge a partnership. But his sneaky way of buying up all those Gucci shares without launching a formal bid for all of Gucci was viewed as a "creeping takeover"—an approach that incensed Gucci's CEO, Domenico De Sole, who began waging a down and dirty fight to escape LVMH.

As if Gucci didn't keep him busy enough in 1999, Arnault extended his overtures in March to another Italian designer, Giorgio Armani, to effect some type of "partnership" with LVMH, presumably to link up with Armani's connections with some of the best Italian factories. Praising Giorgio Armani to the hilt, Arnault called him a "fantastic designer and a businessman whom I admire very much. He is an incredible talent and extremely successful worldwide. I don't see any other brand that can compare with Armani with so many different lines with a separation between them. Armani is a unique example."

Arnault was also teeming with pride with regard to his best hire so far, Michael Kors, who had accomplished in a little more than a year something that Galliano, McQueen, not to mention Lacroix, had failed to accomplish. Under Kors, Céline was starting to attract significant retail business from American stores. Arnault was so pleased with Kors, in fact, that in March 1999, LVMH bought a 50 percent interest in the modest fashion business Kors continued to operate in New York.

Unlike the artistically obsessed Lacroix, "Michael Kors is very interested in commercial success," Arnault observed. "He goes to the Céline shop to talk to the customers. The reason to be a designer is to sell. Fashion is not pure art. It is creativity with the goal of having as many customers as possible wearing the product."

LVMH rounded up more American companies in March 1999, buying a 70 percent interest in a trendy New York spa called Bliss, and curiously, a 25 percent stake in Gant, a solid but undistinguished maker of men's sports shirts sold in department stores.

The new-look LVMH, stacked with more Americans and perhaps a couple of Italians around the corner, heralded the end of French fashion as the world knew it.

c h a p t e r 2

FASHIONING A MAKEOVER FOR EMANUEL UNGARO

The great question which I have not been able to answer despite my thirty years of research into the feminine soul is "What does a woman want?"

SIGMUND FREUD (posted beneath a picture of Freud in the studio of Emanuel Ungaro)

On the balmy morning of July 8, 1996, about an hour before his couture show at the Paris Intercontinental Hotel, Emanuel Ungaro was at peace, and oblivious to the backstage commotion of models and makeup and hair people rushing around like Keystone Kops.

For thirty-one years, Ungaro had performed this drill to perfection. Dressed in a black turtleneck tucked into black pants, he slipped past the racks of the exquisite creations he had worked on for nearly four months. Short and sturdy, Ungaro wore facial stubble, his thick, graying hair in a brushed-back shag setting off his heavy-lidded blue eyes. He was a sexy, good-looking sixty-two. A charming gallant, given to hand-kissing and to passionate analogies, he made fashion his mistress. "My colleagues always tease me when I plunge my nose into fabric," he once said. "I caress it, smell it, listen to it. A piece of clothing should speak in so many ways."

Keeping his distance backstage, Ungaro found a quiet spot where he sat down and closed his eyes to meditate, as he always did before the storm on the runway. He had more on his mind than usual. Just days earlier, he had announced that he had sold his fashion house to Salvatore Ferragamo SpA, the Florence-based footwear and fashion empire owned by the Ferragamo family.

The takeover of the House of Ungaro was far from hostile. It was actually more like a marriage of two businesses that, by all appearances, dovetailed quite neatly. Ferragamo's marketing and international retailing expertise enhanced Ungaro's extraordinary skill at making fine garments.

The House of Ferragamo respected Ungaro's heritage and promised to preserve his couture and possibly to strengthen it, even though couture would inevitably generate losses. Ferragamo saw high fashion as an invaluable legacy that would enhance the cachet of the Ungaro trademark (as well as that of the Ferragamos)—and would keep Emanuel Ungaro toiling away happily for years to come.

So Ungaro was ready to take a big—and belated—step into the brave new world of high-fashion marketing. Ferragamo was prepared to roll out a new generation of Ungaro boutiques, to overhaul Ungaro's licensees, and to position the couture house in a more modern way. Ungaro looked forward to a prosperous new future. "I want this house to grow, to reach its fullest potential," he said.

Yet while he talked a big marketing game, Ungaro remained an old-school couturier who had a lot to learn. Handbags were now the hottest designer trinket on the market. But to Ungaro, a handbag wasn't a stand-alone that got stamped out by the thousands; he created a handbag to *accessorize* a particular outfit. Selling the fashion house he built from the ground up was "very difficult, both from an objective and sentimental perspective," he told *WWD* in July 1996. "It was a decision that took a long time. I *did not* and *do not* want to change the house."

But changes were inevitable. As Ungaro pondered the many possibilities in those moments before his fashion show, he was also thinking about his new partners, the Ferragamo family, who would be in the audience ready to view their first Ungaro collection.

EMANUEL UNGARO WAS a proud member of that rarefied circle of haute couturiers who started in the sixties: Andre Courrèges, Yves Saint Laurent, and Paco Rabanne, among others. Ungaro had burst onto the scene in 1965 with kicky minidresses—and not ballgowns. He was the renegade whom *WWD* had nicknamed "the terrorist" and the "new cat for couture."

During the mid-1980s, Ungaro reigned as one of couture's finest artisans, whose trademark burned the hottest when such international socialites as Lynn Wyatt in Houston snapped up his body-hugging, draped silk dresses which came in a kaleidoscope of layered prints and patterns. "Emanuel had such a definite style, a focus. Those jackets were unforgettable. You *knew* what you were looking at," remembered Grace Mirabella, the editor of *Vogue* from 1971 to 1989 and Ungaro's most enthusiastic sponsor in the fashion press.

Ungaro had indeed made it, but he never reached the critical mass that would have made him a household name. By 1995, Ungaro had only nineteen shops, with just three in America, and his once-popular Diva perfume had fizzled and was practically forgotten. Nearly all of the House of Ungaro's $280 million revenue in 1995 had come from royalties from twenty-five licensees, many of which were in Japan. Ungaro's first love would always be couture, of which he sold only about three hundred outfits a year, at a loss of $3 million.

With his 1996 marriage to Ferragamo SpA, Ungaro, a proud perfectionist, became one of the last couturiers to sell out, joining Dior and Givenchy—both owned by LVMH, Bernard Arnault's luxury goods conglomerate, and Yves Saint Laurent, which became a division of Elf Sanofi, the big pharmaceutical concern. "These are huge financial powers with lots of means," Ungaro said. "I cannot really compete by myself in this situation."

After watching the venerable business of his contemporary, Hubert de Givenchy, lose its identity after being swallowed up by LVMH, Ungaro was determined not to allow his trademark to lose the classy, romantic French image that had always been the signature of the house.

EMANUEL UNGARO'S JULY 1996 couture show took place in one of the most magnificent venues in Paris, the Salon Imperial at the Hotel Intercontinental. A baroque ballroom with a frescoed ceiling, the Salon was designed in 1878 by Charles Garnier, the architect of the Paris Opera house—a heritage underscored that day by Ungaro's choice of music, which included the recorded arias of Maria Callas, one of his favorite artists.

The Salon resembled a regal theater, its mottled mirrored walls reflecting the endless runway bisecting the room. A glossy crowd of fashion's high court of socialites, private clients, fashion editors, and other international guests streamed in, creating a multilingual din of French, English, Italian, and Japanese. They took their assigned places in tight rows of gilt chairs lining either side of the runway, with each seat bearing a name card written in calligraphy, and secured with a fuchsia ribbon—Ungaro's signature color. As the room grew stifling from the bright overhead stage lights and the clash of perfumes, shiny-faced women fanned themselves furiously with their fashion show programs.

Milling around the doorway, the fashion paparazzi snapped the usual couture suspects, the tucked and titled social X rays now in their sixties, such as Park Avenue socialite Nan Kempner and the swan-necked Viscountess Jacqueline de Ribes, who ran her own couture house for a while in the 1980s.

French actress Anouk Aimée was greeted by a bolt of flashing strobes when she entered. Aimée had had a long love affair with Ungaro in the 1980s, and she provided the inspiration for his Diva perfume, which she helped him promote at its introduction. Although they were no longer a couple, they remained such friends that she always made it to his shows. Wearing huge sunglasses atop her chiseled cheekbones, the sixty-two-year-old actress was just as fetching as she had been more than thirty years earlier, starring in *A Man and a Woman*.

Three members of the Ferragamo family had flown in from Florence for the show, but they were nowhere to be seen. Pier Filipo Pieri, Ungaro's plucky public relations man, had stashed them in the hotel's coffee shop—a little scheme he hatched to heighten the drama when the Ferragamos entered the packed Salon just moments before the lights went down.

Right on cue, the photographers swooned at the sight of the Ferragamos. First came Wanda Ferragamo, the sixty-eight-year-old matriarch, a short woman with wavy reddish hair, in a crisp summer dress. Her modest demeanor belied her stature as the executrix who had spent the last thirty-five years steering her family's firm to international prominence following the death of her husband, Salvatore.

She was followed by her son Massimo, who ran Ferragamo in the U.S., his wife, Chiara, and her eldest son and heir apparent, Ferrucio, age fifty, who managed to look distinguished on crutches, his right leg in a cast after a soccer injury.

It had been Ferrucio's idea to buy Ungaro. Investment advisors had brought the parties together, and then Ferrucio and Ungaro negotiated in secret for about nine months. During that time, Ungaro and Ferrucio communicated using the code name "Rosa"—roses were the flower Ungaro often used in his advertising.

It was easy to see why they clicked, for Ungaro and the Ferragamos had a lot in common. Ungaro's parents were Italian; he was married to an Italian and his CEO, Carlo Valerio, was Italian. Ferrucio and Ungaro spoke to each other in Italian, and they were like-minded in their serious and conservative approach to business—both were committed to quality and the snob appeal of high fashion. Salvatore Ferragamo SpA bought a controlling interest in Emanuel Ungaro S.A., which had an estimated value of about $40 million, leaving Ungaro with a minority stake and an employment contract that left him in place as couturier through 2002.

As the searing soprano of Maria Callas permeated the Salon Imperial, the fashion show was under way. The Ferragamos watched attentively, marveling at the fifty-four couture confections under the trademark that now belonged to them. Out came the models in Ungaro's gold-embroidered decorative jackets, worn with flowing silk pants. The evening gowns were opulent, festooned with handmade lace and intricate beading. The grand finale was a magnificent pearl-encrusted wedding gown.

The applause swelled and a few people rose to their feet as Ungaro, beaming and blushing a bit, came down the runway to take his bow. All eyes in the room watched as he paused midway to extend his hand to the Ferragamos, who looked happy, yet reserved. They joined Ungaro backstage for champagne after the show to greet well-wishers Aimée and other clients.

A couple of hours later, the Ferragamos met with Ungaro for their first joint board meeting in the conference room back at Ungaro's atelier at 2 Avenue Montaigne. There wouldn't be a whole lot to discuss. The Ferragamos weren't ready to make any moves yet; they had just hired Bain management consultants in Boston to do an extensive study of the couture house. So Ungaro had to sit tight for a while. All he could do now was go along for the ride. And keep meditating.

EMANUEL UNGARO WAS born in 1933, in Aix-en-Provence, in the south of France, where his Italian parents, Cosimo and Concetta, had emigrated during the 1920s to escape Mussolini's Fascist regime. In Aix, Cosimo Ungaro, a tailor, opened a storefront haberdashery, where the eldest of their six children, Eugenio, began his grooming to take over his father's shop when he was fifteen. His second son, Emanuel, first sat down before a Singer machine when he was five and quickly took to the craft of making men's suits. The Aix shop was a serious yet jovial workplace where *La Bohème* filled the air, as rendered by Cosimo Ungaro, who "had a perfect voice for Rossini, a lyric tenor light, seductive and airy that he coached us in at work in our tailor's shop," Ungaro later recalled.

Emanuel inherited his father's passion for opera, but by the time he was a teenager, he already had set his ambitions far from Aix, in Paris, where he dreamed of designing couture for the world's most elegant women. Emanuel was twenty-three in 1957 when he arrived in Paris, settling in the Montparnasse district, the community known for its artists, intellectuals, and musicians. The next year Ungaro got his big break. He was hired as an assistant to the legendary couturier Cristobal Balenciaga, at the recommendation of one of his assistants, Andre Courrèges. For the next six years, Ungaro toiled under the wings of the great master, who was the archetype of the suffering artist. Ungaro once wrote: "What I can try to describe is the emotional effect of my encounters with him, the genuine and powerful feeling of having been brought into contact with knowledge, rigor, strength and greatness."

Even in the lofty leagues of Paris high fashion, Balenciaga towered above them all. Coco Chanel once asserted, "Balenciaga alone is a couturier in the truest sense of the word. Only *he* is capable of cutting material, assembling a creation, and sewing it by hand. The others are simply fashion designers." Balenciaga had first made his name in his native Spain, where at age forty he opened his first couture shop in Barcelona in 1935. Two years later he had established another atelier in Paris on the exclusive Avenue Georges V, which for more than thirty years attracted the world's most elegant and discerning clients, women like Gloria Guinness and Babe Paley.

Balenciaga ran a modest but thriving business between his Paris and Spanish workrooms, where he toiled relentlessly in silence, for he tolerated no talking at the office. Balenciaga marched to his own exigent drummer as he invented styles like his famous chemise, or sack dress, that flattered the rounded, matronly figures of the ladies who sought him out. Where Balenciaga led, buyers followed, like Beverly Rice, who ran the French room at L. S. Ayres department store in Indianapolis during the 1960s. Back then, Ayres hosted a chic luncheon, "Paris Calling," where local ladies listened as Rice, via transatlantic hookup, breathlessly related the latest news from the runways. "When Balenciaga changed the width of a seam, *that* was news," she recalled.

The Balenciaga mystique was further heightened by his inaccessibility and indifference to the rest of high fashion. The reclusive master took no bows on the runway, nor did he give interviews. He refused to introduce retail collections and rejected all licensees, except for perfumes. Resigned that the future of fashion was in retailing—and not couture—Balenciaga abruptly shuttered his couture workrooms in 1968 and died four years later.

Indoctrinated in the ways of Balenciaga, Ungaro rose to become his chief assistant. Courrèges left Balenciaga to open his own house in 1961 and Ungaro left a couple of years later, but then spent a few months helping out Courrèges, to whom he was indebted for having recommended him to Balenciaga.

Finally, in 1965, Ungaro was ready to go on his own. He scraped together a few thousand dollars and opened his business with his partner and girlfriend, Sonia Knapp, a fabric artist. Knapp hocked her blue Porsche to raise enough money for three months' rent for a tiny Right Bank studio on Avenue Macmahon. Ungaro's atelier-on-a-shoestring included three seamstresses and Knapp, who helped design fabrics and served as the house model. Meanwhile, Ungaro wore many hats as couturier, bookkeeper, delivery man, and janitor, sweeping up all the pins and fabric scraps after hours.

By then, Courrèges had made a splash as the hottest couturier in Paris, by virtue of his 1964 futuristic "space" collection of white minidresses worn with short white boots. After Courrèges's instant fame, the fashion world anxiously awaited the debut of another promising Balenciaga protégé. Days before Ungaro's July 1965 show, *WWD* reported: "One name on everyone's mind is Emanuel Ungaro. Paris needs a new force. The press needs a new attraction and Emanuel Ungaro is here." He didn't disappoint.

Ungaro's collection of twenty shift minidresses and coats in double-faced wool in pastel colors would have made Balenciaga proud. It was now Ungaro's turn to be the toast of Paris, as influential clients such as

Marie Hélène de Rothschild and Jacqueline Kennedy rushed in for fittings at his studio. And *Vogue* began its love affair with Ungaro, prominently featuring his creations in its fashion spreads.

Alongside his popular couture, Ungaro signed his first licensee, Gruppo GFT, to make a boutique collection called Parallèle in 1967. Based in Turin, Italy, GFT began in 1865 as a manufacturer of uniforms for the Italian army. Military uniforms were among the first apparel mass produced after the sewing machine was invented in the 1850s, ushering in the era of commercial clothes making. A century later, Ungaro would take his couture expertise inside GFT's factories to spearhead the company's diversification into women's wear. "GFT said, 'Here is a factory and 200 people. Do it,' " Ungaro recalled. "I spent three days a week in Turin teaching them how to make the clothes. I was a pioneer; I paved the way for the others," which included Giorgio Armani and Valentino, who later also became GFT licensees.

By the seventies, GFT was also turning out Ungaro menswear, under the direction of Ungaro's younger brother, René. But the couturier wouldn't wear his own label, preferring instead the fine hand-tailoring of his other brother, Eugenio, who made all of Emanuel's suits at their father's shop in Aix.

DESPITE HIS PIONEERING moves into industrial clothes making, Ungaro adhered to the doctrine of Balenciaga. "He makes what he wants—the best," explained Catherine de Limur, the director of Ungaro's couture salon from almost the beginning. "He designs like a writer writes a book. He's not commercial; he's a couturier." Consequently, Ungaro didn't factor in the feedback he got from his clients. "Research just shows what women liked in the past," he explained. "I project myself into the future. I don't even remember my last collection."

INSIDE UNGARO'S SECOND-FLOOR design by studio on Avenue Montaigne, daylight streamed in from a wall of windows where creativity took place in the Balenciaga tradition. Even the short lab coat Ungaro worked in had a ceremonious cut, featuring an unusual kimono armhole. Hanging from a cord around Ungaro's neck was a flat, beige pouch containing a stash of straight pins and a tiny pair of scissors.

Balenciaga taught Ungaro to design by working first with the fabric and then sketching afterward—which was just the opposite of the way almost every other designer created. Ungaro began by cutting toile, or muslin, after he had his "dream," or concept, figured out. Using a live model, Ungaro used hundreds of pins to baste every seam, pleat, and tuck. His smooth, blocky hands were nimble and quick, as he took the utmost care when he got to the armholes. "I sew the sleeves myself; I have a *passion* for the sleeves," Ungaro murmured.

As the weeks went by, a long rack of toiles—so full of pins that each piece stood stiffly at attention—sat in the studio's hallway, ready to come to life in whatever fabric Ungaro chose. Pamela Golbin, the curator at the Musée de la Mode et du Textile, the fashion museum at the Louvre, said of Ungaro: "Everything evolves from the fabric, so your relationship with the fabric will change the outcome. If you choose chiffon or wool—two fabrics that have nothing to do with each other—the result of each will be different. Balenciaga and Ungaro let the fabric dictate what will happen, as opposed to using a technician to figure out how to produce a garment from a sketch."

Not surprisingly, Ungaro cut and pinned in twelve-hour stretches, in solitary confinement, while chamber music by Beethoven and Wagner played in the background. The act of designing was exhilarating at times, but always, he sighed, "full of suffering."

Over the years, his private clients also suffered—before and after they received the invoices for their couture garments. The pinnacle of fashion perfection required patience—a client had to troop over to Ungaro's atelier at least three times for fittings. On the floor below Ungaro's studio were his two primary workrooms where the *petit mains*, the "little hands," in white lab coats actually fabricated the garments. There were sixteen sewers specializing in the *flou*—dresses and gowns—and fourteen other seamstresses in the *tailleur*—jackets and suits. They used irons and sewing machines—but only to stitch the primary seams on each garment. Everything else—the buttonholes, the zippers, the pleats, and the tucks—were sewn and finished entirely by hand.

Et voilà! Perfection was indeed divine: an exquisite garment that looked as beautiful turned on the inside as it did on the outside. Couture garments were often embellished with hand embroidery or beading, work that was farmed out to a dwindling breed of artisans around Paris. A simple daytime dress took a few weeks to make; an embroidered gown took months. The high cost of such exacting handwork was what drove up the price of couture, which in the 1990s ranged from about $15,000 to $150,000 for the fanciest beaded and embroidered gowns.

Couture had been the calling card of his atelier, and Ungaro doubted that his couture workrooms could survive without him. He was confounded by the limitations of his assistants, who could sketch well enough but couldn't sew. "I try to teach to young people [that] to be able to do what I am doing means that you have to work twelve hours a day every day of the week. They don't do it anymore. They don't have patience for a fitting. There is a young man here who has fantastic taste but he can't control the construction of the drape. Maybe, if he has a good *premier* [first assistant], he could tell him how to do it. It is very complicated."

And even more complicated than producing couture was making couture viable again after the go-go eighties, when Ungaro seemed poised to take off internationally.

"The Heat Is On. Fashion Goes Feminine and Ungaro Leads the Way," blared a coverline on an April 1988 *Newsweek* in which Somalian model Iman was pictured in Ungaro's polka-dotted pouf cha-cha dress. "After twenty-three years of perfecting a combustible formula of silk fabrics and a seductive fit, his draped dresses are the hit of the year," wrote *Newsweek*'s Jennet Conant.

The eighties had been good to Ungaro. One of his most devoted clients, Lynn Wyatt, said: "Emanuel puts a woman on a pedestal and that's why I feel so feminine and romantic in any Ungaro gown." Wyatt, the perky, petite wife of Houston oil mogul Oscar Wyatt, made a stunning entrance at Count Volpi's ball in Venice in 1988, dressed in Ungaro's yellow-and-black tartan ballgown.

Such famous fashion plates adored Ungaro, but the workaholic, reclusive couturier didn't hobnob with them. Before he was married, Ungaro continued to live as a haute-bohemian in a rented studio apartment, and he drove around Paris in a beat-up Austin Mini Morris. He had season tickets to the opera and to the symphony, and his big indulgence was a country house in his hometown of Aix-en-Provence, which he decorated with Italian baroque furniture and flea market antiques he liked to collect.

Not surprisingly, Ungaro was on "the miserly side," remarked *WWD*, noting that in 1986 he drew a yearly salary of about $500,000 but ran around the office turning off lights. "I have complete freedom in this house," he said. "I'm not working under the pressure of finance. I use my freedom in the haute couture."

While couture always conferred prestige on the Ungaro trademark and some one thousand pages annually of editorial spreads in fashion magazines, Ungaro was still largely unknown—undoubtedly because he never spent more than $1 million to advertise his fashion lines at a time when other houses were spending tens of millions on advertising by way of their perfume licensees. Ungaro would have to wait until the 1990s for his name to become a bona fide hit in America—and his commercial coup didn't come from couture or Parallèle. Instead, Ungaro scored with his lowest-tier label, Emanuel, a women's bridge collection of $475 silk blazers and $250 pants—a collection that he didn't design.

Introduced in 1991, Emanuel vaulted Ungaro ahead of all the other French fashion brands, to become *the* top-selling French apparel brand in American department stores, selling more than $150 million at wholesale in the late 1990s.

Emanuel was a tale of "The Licensee Knows Best." Watching its sales of $2,000 Parallèle ensembles decline steadily, licensee GFT dreamed up a new cash cow for American department stores called "Emanuel by Emanuel Ungaro." Emanuel went from being a literal interpretation of Ungaro's bright prints and romantic styling in its first seasons to becoming a polished, tailored collection of suits, jackets, and vests in neutral shades. "We have a living French couturier, which is our heritage, but we had to make something that would sell in the States," said Maura De Visscher, the founding president of the Emanuel division. "Ungaro trusted us and gave us the license to make the right decisions."

Ungaro was immensely proud of Emanuel, even though he hadn't done any of the heavy lifting. Still, this was a man who got off on psychic rewards, not fat royalty checks. It must have galled him that most American women didn't know who the Emanuel behind Emanuel was. Actress Kyra Sedgwick, hired in 1997 by GFT to appear in Emanuel's advertising, was initially among the clueless. "I knew the name but I wasn't that familiar with the designer," she said. Before she became the poster girl for Emanuel, the wide-eyed blond actress said her wardrobe consisted "mostly of vintage clothes from secondhand shops."

WITH THE STABILITY and prestige that Emanuel delivered, Ungaro celebrated his twenty years in business by designing a family life for himself. In 1990, the fifty-six-year-old couturier married the well-connected Laura Fafani, a thirty-year-old divorcée from Rome whose father was the director general of Italy's three state-owned TV stations. The couple said they hit it off at their first meeting, during a business lunch, when Laura was a publicist for GFT. *Vanity Fair* pictured the happy newlyweds on their wedding day, and writer Ben Brantley noted that "hearts were shattered in Paris" when the news of Ungaro's marriage broke. "Here, after all, was the end of the long bachelorhood of fashion's most flaming heterosexual, a man who claimed to make clothes and love with monomaniacal devotion to the unfathomable in women. 'I design dresses for women I would like to take in my arms,' he said. . . . Laura represented 'one of the few times in my life that I seduced the woman [rather] than her seducing me.' " The Ungaros had a daughter whom they named Cosima, after Emanuel's father.

Slender, pretty, and highly animated, Laura Ungaro became director of communications for her husband's house, where she became the modern muse Ungaro now needed. Laura imparted her own sense of style to Ungaro's socialite look. When she tossed on Ungaro's exquisite embroidered jackets over a T-shirt and a pair of tight pants, she made them look sassy and very youthful. She had her own discreet way of dropping fashion hints to her mate. "I like to play a little game with him," she said, recalling the mornings when she got dressed in something that wasn't designed by Ungaro. "I may ask him to zip me up." Ungaro, of course, wouldn't utter a word, but Laura would discover later that he had been asking his assistants about her clothes.

Laura worked alongside Carlo Valerio, the seasoned, forty-six-year-old Milanese executive whom Ungaro hired as his first managing director in 1993. Bringing in Valerio was Ungaro's first step toward modernizing his business. The professorial Valerio, who favored blue oxford-cloth shirts and sweater vests, had a degree in nuclear engineering and was previously an executive at Ratti, the giant Italian fabrics producer. He set about developing a restructuring plan for Ungaro, which culminated with the sale to the Ferragamos.

Ungaro was among Ferragamo's first outside acquisitions in a diversification plan designed to provide future positions for nineteen members of the youngest Ferragamo generation who were coming of age and were expected to join the family empire. As with Ungaro, the story of shoemaker Salvatore Ferragamo was one of ambition and big dreams. Born in 1898, Salvatore was the eleventh of fourteen children who grew up in poverty in the Neapolitan village of Bonito. He was just nine years old when he crafted his first footwear: white shoes in canvas and cardboard, made specially for his little sister's first communion. At sixteen, Salvatore was already a skilled shoemaker on his way to Boston, the capital of America's footwear industry, to learn about mass production.

But Salvatore Ferragamo was frustrated when he saw the tradeoffs required to execute factory-made footwear. The mass-produced American shoes were "heavy, clumsy and brutal, with a toe like a potato and a heel of lead," a far cry from what he was capable of turning out by hand.

So he headed to the West Coast, where he opened a handmade-shoe shop in Santa Barbara, California, in the shadows of the motion picture industry. Salvatore became famous for his innovative and comfortable footwear used in movies. His private clients included screen legends

Douglas Fairbanks, Mary Pickford, Greta Garbo, and John Barrymore, who relied on the Italian cobbler to resolve his problem of flat feet. Salvatore perfected his signature fit by taking anatomy courses at the University of Southern California, where he learned everything he could about the foot.

When Salvatore Ferragamo returned to Italy in 1927, he had retail orders from Saks Fifth Avenue and Marshall Field's—and a burning desire to grow. He began to expand with the help of dozens of shoe contractors around his Florence headquarters. He later married Wanda Miletti, the daughter of his hometown mayor. During his fifty-seven-year career, Salvatore Ferragamo created some twenty thousand styles of handmade shoes, including his patented cork wedge heel, an innovation he concocted during the leather shortages of World War II. Later, in the 1950s, he invented the first pair of stiletto heels for Marilyn Monroe, in alligator skin.

In 1960, Salvatore died after a long illness at age sixty-two and left his homemaker widow in control of his business. With the help of her children, Wanda continued her husband's dreams of building Ferragamo into a full-line fashion house that dressed men and women from "toe to head" by adding scarves, men's silk ties, sweaters, and other sports wear. While these collections rounded out the Ferragamo empire, they were fairly staid, never matching Ferragamo's innovations in footwear.

That's why many fashion insiders jumped to the same conclusion when they learned of a Ferragamo-Ungaro partnership: How could Ferragamo, which had no track record in high fashion, orchestrate a makeover at Ungaro when Ferragamo's own collections were so conservative? In apparel, Ferragamo's bestsellers included men's silk ties and a wool cardigan sweater with gold-logo buttons, a perennial in its line for more than a decade.

Set against Prada and Gucci, which marketed trendy fashions alongside their core leather goods, Ferragamo never became a force in apparel. It wasn't as if Ferragamo hadn't tried. Steven Slowick, an American designer and former Calvin Klein assistant, was barely in his twenties when the Ferragamos hired him in 1989 to create its women's collections. Slowick, who reported to Giovanna Ferragamo, Ferrucio's older sister, had tweaked Ferragamo's conservative look in his fashion shows, but neither the merchandise in the boutiques nor the advertising seemed to reflect his new mood. His first fall collection in 1990 had a sixties/Andy Warhol mood, with mirrored-fabric minidresses and lots of leather. He recalled: "For *them,* it was too forward, but for the press, it wasn't crazy. After that fashion show, Giovanna told me how the family members felt: 'This is too extreme for us. We have to, kind of, tone it *down.*' "

Slowick, who left Ferragamo in 1996 to open his own fashion house in Paris, has fond but mixed feelings about his years at Ferragamo, where change occurred at a snail's pace. "They are great people, very serious and all that, but they are not fashion people," he reflected in July 1997 from his modest studio on the Left Bank of Paris. "Their view of fashion is very conservative. Very, very conservative. And my personal view is that you have to be a little out there. You can make a product that's really classic that you can sell to a twenty-year-old and an eighty-year-old. That's hard to do, but Hermès does it. But you have to make an image. I told [Ferragamo], 'You have to do something about that image because it's the pits. People think you're an old-lady house.' I think of my grandmother when I think of Ferragamo.

"I worked the best I could within the structure of the family and the company. It was more like, 'Well, we don't want to lose our old customers; we don't want to confuse them, but we want to get more modern.' Which I can understand. But at some point you have to go a bit one way or a bit more the other way. I would say to myself, 'Be patient—you know this is the way this family works.' But other times my American business side would come out and say, 'Oh, why can't you just change things quicker?' "

Likewise, at Ungaro the Ferragamos were locked into their cautious Goldilocks strategy: Not too fast, not too slow, just right. But in fashion, where momentum counted for much, they needed to strike while the irons were hot. Instead of making a great leap forward, the Ferragamos liked to enlist outside consultants to study their situation. The Bain review, which came out a year later, didn't contain any monumental revelations. The only bit of new marketing came in the October 1997 fashion show, when a model in a floral dress bounced down the runway caressing a huge bottle of Fleur de Diva, a new Ungaro perfume launched in a joint venture between Ferragamo and Bulgari, the Italian jeweler. But for a fragrance sendoff, Fleur de Diva's was altogether pitiful; the perfume wasn't even advertised in America, Ungaro's prime market.

While Ungaro's name was still on the door and Valerio was the managing director, the de facto CEO was Ferrucio Ferragamo, the formal and often terse micromanager who acted as if he knew more about high fashion than he probably did. During the summer of 1997, Ferrucio took several early morning flights from Florence, arriving at Ungaro's atelier at about 9:30, ready for a full day of board meetings with Ungaro and Valerio. Ungaro always detested these drawn-out meetings, which took him away from his work in the studio, yet he sat through them, mindful that he had to be involved in planning the future of his house. Aware of his short attention span, Ferrucio avoided the minutiae of profit margins and market share when he was in the room. "We know he gets a little bored, so we try to make the meetings as interesting as possible," Ferrucio said.

But during the meetings, the person who was squirming was Carlo Valerio, whom Ferrucio had effectively pushed out of the loop. After Ferragamo bought Ungaro, Ferrucio had dispatched one of his accountants to work in Paris, bypassing Valerio altogether.

Meanwhile, in New York, Peter Arnell, the fashion advertising wunderkind who had produced the first ads for Emanuel, had read about Ferragamo's big plans for Ungaro and thought it might be time to check in. But when he called Valerio in Paris in the summer of 1997, Valerio admitted that he didn't know what was up: "The decision process has suddenly become very slow."

Valerio had been eager to start rolling out Ungaro boutiques, while gradually phasing out certain licensees. But Ferrucio's plan was to sever most of the licensees immediately, especially the ones in Japan. The Ferragamos, who owned all but three of their fifty signature boutiques, didn't believe in licensing in most cases; all Ferragamo merchandise was made in Italy through a network of selected contractors, and tightly controlled through a central distribution center in Florence. Valerio worried that if Ungaro canceled so many licensees, the company would lose not only a royalty stream, but visibility at retail. Valerio preferred to phase out the licensees slowly, while simultaneously promoting Ungaro on other fronts.

But it was clear that Ferrucio would prevail and that Valerio would soon be out of a job, substituted by a managing director of Ferragamo's choosing. Valerio resigned quietly, having accomplished his goal of finding a financial partner for Ungaro. While Ungaro didn't balk at Valerio's leaving, privately his associates said he was upset, yet resigned that he was no longer running his company.

Ferragamo wasted no time cleaning house. The first licensee to go was a line of Ungaro bathroom tiles made in Italy, which had yielded "zero for the bottom line or our image," Ferrucio explained. As expected, the House of Ferragamo immediately took over production of Ungaro's shoes and leather goods, canceling Ungaro's licensee in Europe.

The next group to tackle were the twenty-five Japanese licensees representing about $100 million, or 44 percent, of Ungaro's 1995 revenue. Ferragamo had sound reasons for wanting to discontinue most of the Japanese licensees. The Asian business had come at a heavy cost to Ungaro's image. Over the years, Ungaro had allowed Takashimaya, the Tokyo retail giant and its main Japanese licensee, to adapt the look of Ungaro's clothes to appeal to a broad range of Japanese shoppers. But Takashimaya, wearing two hats as licensee and retailer, always had a conflict of interest. There was little incentive for Takashimaya to sell Ungaro merchandise to Japanese retailers that competed with its own stores. Consequently, in Japan, most people saw Ungaro as a Takashimaya house brand—a fact that was underscored because the fashions by Ungaro carried a "made in Japan" label. As a consequence, when Japanese tourists visited Paris or London, for example, they weren't inclined to shop for Ungaro fashions they thought they could find at home.

Ferrucio's strategy centered around moving all of Ungaro's production either to France or to Italy, with the exception of Solo Donna by Ungaro, a women's brand sold only in Japan through Takashimaya.

Initially, Ferrucio had considered Japan the biggest problem area, but in 1997, Emanuel, Ungaro's U.S. juggernaut, took an unexpected body blow. American department stores were overstocked with bridge designer merchandise from Dana Buchman, DKNY, Ellen Tracy, and Emanuel that wasn't selling as briskly as it had in the past. But Emanuel's executives hadn't anticipated the retail slowdown when they charged ahead, aggressively shipping merchandise into department stores during the worst of seasons. As loads of Emanuel clothes languished on the markdown racks, Emanuel failed to meet department stores' profit benchmarks, obliging the company to pay steep rebates, known as "markdown money." The division had planned for sales of about $150 million, but less than half of that sold. The upshot: Ungaro would receive lower royalties for 1997—and again in 1998, when sales had slumped by a third, to an estimated $100 million.

Right before the Emanuel crisis came to light in early 1998, Ferrucio hired a replacement for Valerio. After a drawn-out search, he made an underwhelming choice: the reserved and soft-spoken Thierry Andretta, a forty-one-year-old former managing director at Belfe Group, an Italian outerwear maker whose biggest licensor was Giorgio Armani. Andretta was hardly the hard-nosed presence whom everyone expected Ferrucio to choose. Andretta said he was taken aback initially when the headhunter from Egon Zendher International described the Ungaro position as a "difficult opportunity."

Looking more like an advertising creative director than a high-fashion mogul, the balding, sun-tanned Andretta favored Armani sport jackets paired with casual pants from Banana Republic. Andretta had five interviews with Ungaro in Paris, where they talked about the history of the house and his mentor, Balenciaga. "I like the history of Ungaro," Andretta said. "We had a lot of discussions about marketing. I see there is a lot of potential here, especially in menswear."

Andretta knew what Ungaro was up against: his own favorite designer. "Armani is the best industrial designer in the world," Andretta said. "There is a line, a signature look that he is always evolving. Ungaro has a history of creativity. It is hard to make a comparison because these are two different worlds of the fashion business. It is more simple for Armani; he changes a few details, whereas Mr. Ungaro, he makes a lot of new things each season."

In April 1998, Andretta moved into Valerio's old office at the atelier and got busy carrying out Ferrucio's orders, signing up new licensees—all Italian companies—for eyewear and jeanswear. It had now been nearly two years since the Ferragamo takeover, and nothing major had happened to jump-start the Ungaro trademark. Other than a few paparazzi shots of *Vogue*'s Anna Wintour and actresses Elizabeth Hurley and Sharon Stone wearing Ungaro out on the town, there was no buzz. Instead of opening new stores in 1998, Ungaro was closing shops in Bangkok, Singapore, and Jakarta, where the Asian economic crisis had hit hardest. By contrast, Calvin Klein, Dior, Gucci, and Prada were rolling out new boutiques and running advertising everywhere you looked.

Meanwhile, the boss's wife had done her best to shake things up. Laura Ungaro hit the gas pedal, hiring five different parties to work on Ungaro's marketing campaigns, prompting Andretta to reel her in. Ever outspoken and anxious, Laura fretted, pointing to Ferrucio, who was holding things up. She spoke up one afternoon in the hallway of Ungaro's Paris atelier: "Ferrucio is more rational and cold, he is slower than me . . . maybe it is good, I give him the push to go forward, but he has to think about it. . . ."

Ferrucio, she insisted, was still on a learning curve. "There is the difference between the way you go with leather goods and haute couture and prêt-à-porter. You can't go slow and take your time in fashion. Since he has entered our world, only in a short time, Prada and Gucci are moving. He is starting to learn. It took a long time and now we begin to move forward."

Laura had a dream: "Money, money, money. I have a plan, we just need money to go fast and it will explode!" she exclaimed, rubbing her fingers together. "I feel that this is the right moment for Emanuel Ungaro. It is now. The company needs to invest in the priorities, the boutiques, the advertising campaign, because Ungaro—as far as the fashion crowd is concerned—is understood. He is following the needs of the market."

While Laura prattled on, her husband was upstairs, sequestered in his studio as usual, fixated on pinning another toile. Recovering from a cold, Ungaro looked weary and became testy when the question was put to him again: What was taking the Ferragamos so long?

"The Ferragamos are very clever, reflective people. They don't do things like that," he said, snapping his fingers for effect. "They have to be sure everything is good. They take their time, to think and to check. I am still the chairman and the family is part of the company. We make all our decisions together. We are completely compatible and complementary. I have a serenity about the future for the house. I'm not paralyzed with haute couture, I'm not mummified. Many houses aren't selling clothing. We are still selling clothing, two million pieces a year. I want this to be a young house. . . . The house is full of projects and energy and young people working all around me."

Ungaro was now concentrating on improving handbags and shoes, the weakest part of his business. "That is difficult—to find an identity with accessories is very difficult. We must find an emblem that is elegant and identifiable. We are working on a handbag now. I don't know when it will be ready; that is a dream. The moment you have it, that is fantastic."

BUT UNGARO NEEDED more than a dream and Laura needed more than just money. In addition to all those millions that Ferragamo had yet to spend on the House of Ungaro, the company desperately needed a deft, well-executed game plan—and some luck. Ferragamo's go-slow approach was designed to avoid making costly mistakes. But going too slow had also resulted in missed opportunities. Then there were those inevitable, unforeseen banana peels: the Emanuel setback and the Asian crisis.

What seemed inexplicable, however, was that the fashion house wasn't keeping its name in lights. Ungaro's solitary, one-page advertisement in the September 1998 *Vogue*—the most high-profile issue of the year—said it all. Ungaro was anonymous and becoming even more so.

Intense and reflective as he was, Ungaro must have second-guessed himself often. Had he erred in selling out to the Ferragamos? Clearly, the partnership was a good fit when it came to footwear and leather goods, but now it was clear that the Ferragamos were out of their league when it came to orchestrating a turnaround.

Ferrucio Ferragamo kept on taking his time while Ungaro was barely coasting on his famed couture heritage to keep his brand afloat. But the Italian owner made no apologies for sticking to his plodding approach. "We can't force the situation," Ferrucio declared during an April 1999 interview. He lamented that Ungaro had lost visibility and sales, after cutting off eighteen licensees. But he vowed that the next steps to remodel Ungaro's remaining boutiques, to expand further into menswear, and to introduce a unisex Ungaro fragrance in 2000 would bear fruit in due time. In three to five years, Ferrucio predicted, the Ungaro label would be back on track.

Following his penchant of enlisting outside professionals before making any costly move, Ferrucio called upon New York investment bankers at Goldman, Sachs & Co. to assist in negotiating a better deal with Ungaro's longtime licensee, GFT.

In the meantime, fashion insiders around the world were convinced that the House of Ungaro was stuck in a rut and steadily slipping off the radar. Ferrucio appeared to be unfazed: "Are we doing this for pride or are we doing the right thing to revive the brand? We don't want to waste money.

"It could be that [Emanuel] might be more anxious to have more visibility, but I told him that I will invest more money at the right time."

So for the short term, the House of Ungaro would lumber along without doing much to establish a more arresting and prominent image for the couturier who more than thirty years ago had basked in the reflection of the great Balenciaga. Until Ferrucio Ferragamo figured things out, Ungaro would likely remain a stagnant, fading brand, like so many others in France.

As for Thierry Andretta, the job that was originally pitched to him as a "difficult opportunity" wasn't worth the wait. He resigned from Ungaro in order to follow the big money and fast company at LVMH. Andretta jumped ship to run a business that by the looks of things was well on its way to becoming a player in the new millennium. In March 1999, Andretta became managing director at Céline, whose designer Michael Kors was now the darling of LVMH chairman Bernard Arnault.

chapter 3

BOUND FOR OLD GLORY: RALPH LAUREN AND TOMMY HILFIGER

I don't respect Tommy Hilfiger as a designer. Everything he did he got from me. He has nothing new to say.

RALPH LAUREN, April 1997

In July 1998, Ralph Lauren took ownership of the American flag for a cool $13 million.

Not since eighteenth-century seamstress Betsy Ross stitched up the original stars and stripes had any individual American been even remotely tied to the flag. It was a sweet moment for Ralph Lauren, American fashion's first billionaire, to give back to the land that had given him so many opportunities. The designer's Polo Ralph Lauren Corp. had donated the millions to restore the gigantic 185-year-old star-spangled banner—the very flag that inspired national anthem writer Francis Scott Key—which was hanging, tattered and threadbare, on a wall of the Smithsonian's National Museum. With the stroke of a pen, Lauren, the marketer of stars-and-stripes sweaters and "Betsy" coffee mugs, had catapulted himself into the league of America's great benefactors.

And what must have made it all the more sweet was that Lauren had one-upped Tommy Hilfiger at the same time. Lauren couldn't get over the fact that Hilfiger, his archrival and the hippest designer of the 1990s, had snatched *his* symbol, the American flag, and was waving it all over his advertising, which further validated Tommy's own red-white-and-blue logo. The Gap had ripped off Ralph as well, with its own flag sweaters, but it was Hilfiger who had stolen much of Lauren's thunder in the 1990s. So Ralph had a burning desire to get the flag back from Tommy. A once-in-a-lifetime opportunity came along in 1998. During his January State of the Union message, President Bill Clinton made a public appeal to recruit donors to save America's historical treasures. Lauren heard about the speech and made his move.

On July 13, at a ceremony to officially present his gift, Lauren looked every bit the statesman in his Purple Label pinstripes, standing onstage at the National Museum next to President Clinton and Hillary Rodham Clinton, pledging allegiance to the flag, *his* flag. The designer beamed broadly when President Clinton declared in his speech: "You know, most of us have, maybe not most of us, but a lot of us, including Hillary and me, have these great Polo sweaters with the American flag on it."

To dispel any notion that Old Glory was for sale to the highest bidder, the Polo organization had promised not to parlay its deed into a public relations bonanza. "We've been assured that this is a philanthropic gift and not a marketing gift," said A. Michael Heyman, a Smithsonian spokesman.

But the media quickly connected the dots. *The Washington Times* ran an editorial cartoon of an American flag with a Polo logo in the corner. *New York Times* columnist Frank Rich observed: "A shopper at a Ralph Lauren Polo outlet store should only get such a bargain as Ralph Lauren got in Washington. . . . an avalanche of publicity that would cost more in the open market, even if you could get it wholesale."

Ironically, at the same time, Congress was considering a law to safeguard the sanctity of the American flag that would bar its use in paintings and other flag motif merchandise flooding the market in recent years. If enforced, such a law would put Lauren in the precarious position of being both a savior and a desecrater of the flag. Lauren "[risked] being thrown in jail for body scrub with a flag logo," Rich ventured, then added: "Is this American justice? Tommy Hilfiger, who's given not a dime to flag preservation and whose own red, white, and blue flag logo knocks off Old Glory without reproducing it, will escape scot free."

Indeed, Hilfiger had been making out like a bandit by copying the style of Lauren, who himself was fashion's most flagrant usurper. For more than thirty years, Lauren had splendidly co-opted the props of the establishment—the polo shirt, the English country look, and even the Ivy League's L.L. Bean—imparting them with his own pedigree and a Waspy snob appeal that millions of people loved.

Without Ralph Lauren, there would be no Tommy Hilfiger Corp., which was for all intents and purposes a clone of Polo Ralph Lauren. Opening his business some seventeen years after Lauren, Hilfiger imitated Lauren's business model to perfection, having hired a number of Polo executives and alumni to help pull off his coup. Hilfiger had been a quick study and even an innovator. He was the first designer who dared to identify with the inner-city street style that was pure melting-pot America—a move that paid off quite handsomely. For both Lauren and Hilfiger, it was Old Glory that had been the most effective marketing tool and a blatant symbol of their redefinition of fashion the American way.

BY THE LATE 1990s, fashion had come to this: a tug-of-war over marketing. In Paris, Bernard Arnault's LVMH empire had its hands full, attempting to revive classic French brands while chasing Gucci, Armani, and other fashionable American trademarks that looked promising. Meanwhile, the last of the great couturiers, Emanuel Ungaro, was stuck on a slow boat, trying to market his way into the millennium. But on the other side of the Atlantic, Ralph Lauren and Tommy Hilfiger were living proof that the end of fashion was already here.

Both men had captured the hearts and minds—and the money—of millions of consumers by being *out* of fashion. Designers without portfolios, neither had apprenticed in Paris, nor studied fashion in school or anywhere else. They didn't sketch; they didn't sew; they hardly *designed,* so to speak. Their clothes weren't so original. Still, they remained ahead of the fashion curve by largely ignoring it. Each stayed grounded in the classics: the khakis, blazers, shirts, and sweaters which they recycled every season in new colors and fabrics, adding a little new detail here and there, all cleverly packaged with arresting, resonating images. They were the haute couturiers of marketing.

All you had to say was Ralph or Tommy. Like Madonna. They were the masters of the fashion universe, galloping lengths ahead of the rest of the fashion pack. Founded in 1967, Polo Ralph Lauren had sales of $1.7 billion in the fiscal year ending April 1999—translating into more than $5 billion at retail—turning out apparel for men, women, and children, sheets, towels, furniture, cosmetics, china, crystal, and even designer paint in hues of denim, suede, and thirty-two shades of white. Likewise, Tommy Hilfiger tallied $1.7 billion in sales in the fiscal year ending March 1999—or nearly $4 billion at retail. He was destined to overtake Polo sooner, rather than later, since Hilfiger had only just begun to diversify from menswear and cosmetics into women's apparel, home furnishings, and the rest. The surefooted Hilfiger had already beat Lauren to the New York Stock Exchange by five years, and his stock consistently rode high above the other apparel stocks. Hilfiger's stock had traded as high as $70 a share during all of 1998—or more than twice the price of Polo's shares. Although Lauren didn't make it to Wall Street first, he got there in time to run with the bulls. Polo's 1997 stock offering allowed Ralph to hang on to 90 percent voting control of Polo, while yielding him a $440 million jackpot, turning him into a billionaire.

Welcome to the era of designer as powerful brand name, with the clothes as the expression of the designer's personality. Lauren and Hilfiger both enjoyed pole positioning, front and center in America's malls, where they drew shoppers into more than 1,500 department stores such as Macy's, Bloomingdale's, and Dillard's, where they each had in-store boutiques, as well as to their own chains of specialty stores and discount outlet stores.

As menswear designers from the start, both figured out early on just what it took to sell clothes. Neither Hilfiger nor Lauren veered off into fashion land, the avant-garde styles that women's-wear designers created to tantalize the fashion press. It was pointless to try to sell men on high-fashion novelties. Menswear designers had no choice but to flex their creativity in the way they packaged the familiar—pants, shirts, and jackets—to make them more desirable than the anonymous store brands offered on the main floor. And by the late 1990s, when women's-wear fashions gravitated to more classic styling, fashion in general turned entirely on marketing. "It's not the jeans or the shirt but the image," said Terry Lundgren, vice chairman of Federated Department Stores, owner of Macy's, Bloomingdale's, and Rich's. "Customers want to be like Ralph and Tommy; those brands relate to the image of what [consumers] are. Marketing is more important today than it has ever been."

In fashion, as in baseball, there's nothing quite like fast company. Ralph Lauren and Tommy Hilfiger were like Mark McGwire of the St. Louis Cardinals and Sammy Sosa of the Chicago Cubs. As they traded homers during the 1998 season, the dueling sluggers lifted each other to peak performances, leading both of them to break Roger Maris's thirty-seven-year-old record—thus elevating the overall tenor of Major League Baseball. Driven to win, Lauren and Hilfiger stole each other's best moves as they took the lead in ushering American fashion into a modern era.

The triumph of Tommy and Ralph was made possible when fashion washed up on America's shores in waves of blue denim, that all-American staple that Calvin Klein and Gloria Vanderbilt recast as designer jeans, starting in the late 1970s. At the same time, Seventh Avenue's Liz Claiborne stepped up to offer career women a spread of affordable mix-and-match sportswear options, imparting a new respect for the American look that would gather even more steam over the next decade, culminating in the 1990s with the advent of the Gap.

Ralph Lauren, who had always preached "the appropriateness of American sportswear," believed that fashion would someday catch up with him. "The American sensibility has become a very important international sensibility," he explained. "We created sportswear. Ours is a more modern culture because of the way people live. We travel, we're athletic, we move. Americans are the leaders because we know how to do sportswear better here than anywhere else."

So just how did these two middle-aged white men capture the imagination and the wallets of people of all ages from every walk of life around the world? The secret was their ability to fulfill a deep-seated desire among all consumers: to belong. Traditionally, fashion had derived much of its power and allure from being original, unique, and exclusive—from the fact that no two women will own the same piece of couture. But that fashion is over. The new fashion is about inclusion, belonging to a world or lifestyle that feels good, looks good, and above all else, is accessible. Like the American dream, the new fashion has to appear available to all—regardless of the economic reality most people live. Perhaps more than any other designers, Ralph and Tommy intimately understood this desire to be an insider, rather than an outsider. And a look at their careers, how they mirror and how they differ, reveals why their fashions reign supreme. Not surprisingly, their business practices are methodical and painstaking, not to mention very similar.

RALPH LIFSHITZ WAS born in 1939, the youngest of four children and the son of Russian Jewish immigrants. His father, Frank, painted murals and houses for a living, raising his family in a two-bedroom apartment in the Bronx. Young Ralph set his aspirations high, having gotten his first close look at America's upper classes during the summers when he worked as a waiter and camp counselor at Camp Roosevelt in the Catskills during the 1950s.

A devoted movie buff, Ralph soaked up the dapper, insouciant style of matinee idols like Fred Astaire and Cary Grant and aimed to dress just like them. Ralph stood out at Dewitt Clinton High School as the prince of preppy, dressed in tweeds, corduroys, and sweaters tied around his shoulders, "as Brooksy as you can get," he later recalled. This was around the time that Frank Lifshitz was said to have changed the family surname—which the kids were always teased about—to the smooth, patrician-sounding Lauren. The name change marked the beginning of Ralph's social climb from Bronx striver to Fifth Avenue baron. Next to his senior picture in the 1957 *Clintonian* yearbook, Ralph Lauren listed his ambition in life: "millionaire."

After high school, Lauren began taking classes at night at City College of New York, but soon dropped out to begin his first stint in the rag trade: selling suits at Brooks Brothers. During the early 1960s, he would ply the pavements in the scrappy world of wholesaling, peddling ladies' gloves and men's ties, and became known as the nattiest road man in the garment district. On his modest salary, he still managed to tool around

Manhattan in a Morgan, a jaunty English convertible, and to buy his wardrobe at the posh Paul Stuart on Madison Avenue. "Nobody was interested in style as much as Ralph," remarked Clifford Grodd, Paul Stuart's chairman, to Jeffrey Trachtenberg, Lauren's biographer, who concluded: "Ralph didn't fantasize about becoming a fashion designer, he became a designer to fulfill his fantasies."

And so finally, in 1967, Lauren's fantasy came to life as he became a designer—of neckties—opening a modest showroom in the Empire State Building. He named his brand "Polo," which he figured evoked just the right amount of snob appeal. Bloomingdale's sold "Polo by Ralph Lauren" ties for $15—which was twice the price of other fine ties—and promoted them as status symbols, with ad copy like: "The age of elegance inspires the unique design of our 'Regency' tie by Polo." Lauren's tony ties flew off the counters and soon he was well on his way to making shirts and suits to go with his ties, buoyed by a $50,000 investment from Norman Hilton, the suit manufacturer that became Lauren's first financial partner.

Lauren will go down in fashion history for introducing the concept of "lifestyle merchandising" in department stores, where each fashion brand was segregated in its own appetizing ambiance. In 1970, Lauren convinced Bloomingdale's to put all his ties, suits, dress shirts, and raincoats together in his own special little boutique. Lauren designed this outpost to feel like a gentlemen's club, with mahogany paneling and brass fixtures. Once enveloped in the Polo lifestyle, shoppers who intended only to pick out a shirt would instead browse around and buy an entire outfit.

Through the years, Lauren festooned his in-store shops with walking sticks, antique alligator luggage, and other slick props, which went a long way to weave a spell around Ralph's rich man's look and stirred all kinds of longings in people, the dream that the upwardly mobile shared for prestige, wealth, and exotic adventure. Whether it was a $200 Fair Isle sweater or a $7,000 mahogany highboy with tartan-lined drawers, Polo's dream merchandise seemed to belong to aristocrats, Ivy Leaguers, and adventurers, who rode horses on ranches, took safaris in Kenya, and yachted in Newport.

"I elevated the taste level of America," Lauren often observed, reflecting on the nuances and the fine details he used to rework fashion's old standards. Polo's tweed hacking jacket, for example, came in richer-looking wool with real horn buttons and grazed a man's body with soft, natural shoulders. His knit shirts with a discreet polo-player logo embroidered on the chest had a faded patina that made them more comfortable, as if you'd worn them for ages. Lauren's ersatz old-money look was more expensive than usual, but still within reach of those who lusted for a piece of the good life. And millions of Americans did.

More than anything, Lauren burnished his fantasy world in the evocative imagery of his advertising, shot by Bruce Weber, the fashion photographer who also created some of Calvin Klein's most memorable ads. In blocks of as many as twenty pages in *Vanity Fair* and *The New York Times Magazine* and *W*, the advertising spreads were seductive movie sets that showcased Polo's extensive lines of apparel, accessories, and home furnishings in the most appetizing way: in stately mansions with roaring fireplaces, replete with distinguished gentlemen and lithe brunettes, all outfitted in character. Much of his elegant staging rang true. "I would be hard pressed to find any photo from my boarding school or summer days that placed side by side with a Polo ad would show its artifice," wrote Lang Philips in an article headlined "Confessions of a Young Wasp" in *New York*.

But not everybody could abide Polo's packaged affectation. "The only difference between a parvenu in a sharkskin suit and a parvenu in a Lauren blazer is that the latter has pretensions," wrote Jonathan Yardley in *The Washington Post* in 1986.

The underside of such resentment against Lauren was a mix of old-fashioned snobbery and jealousy. The hard-line Wasps wore their pedigree in boxy Brooks Brothers suits, cashmere sweaters, faded rugby shirts, and Top-Siders, which represented quality and tradition, but never fashion. So when Ralph came along, he was an easy target for Waspy curmudgeons. Here was this Jew from the Bronx who had co-opted their town-and-country style and had turned it into fashion. He did such a good job that the British royal family—the ultimate Wasps—loved to wear Polo too.

Certain members of fashion's old guard in Paris were naturally contemptuous of Lauren's stunning success. In an effort to bring him down, Yves Saint Laurent sued Lauren, alleging that he copied one of his couture gowns, and a French court found Lauren guilty as charged.

While Lauren would develop a thick skin against his detractors, he would never be defensive about his important contribution to fashion: "I don't put myself in with Saint Laurent or Ungaro," he later reflected. "But I am doing something they aren't doing that is original, and I am proud of that." (LVMH's Bernard Arnault would later pay Lauren the ultimate compliment in declaring that Polo was the American fashion house that he admired the most.)

IN THE MID-1980s, Tommy Hilfiger was just getting his feet wet on Seventh Avenue when Ralph Lauren had already set the agenda as the most successful designer in America. He had pulled off this feat with the assistance of his longtime business partner, Peter Strom, a former executive at Norman Hilton. By 1986, the year Lauren was ready to pull out the stops to make a historic footprint in the world of retailing, Polo's licensees generated about $400 million in annual sales.

In the tradition of America's nineteenth-century department store founders like Marshall Field in Chicago and John Wanamaker of Philadelphia, Ralph Lauren opened his own retail palace on the corner of Madison Avenue and Seventy-second Street in the former Rhinelander mansion. In 1894, the wealthy Gertrude Rhinelander Waldo had ordered up the five-story limestone French-style château, which took five years and more than $500,000 to build, complete with bowling alley and billiard room.

Ralph Lauren took on a long-term lease on the fabled Rhinelander, where he spent an estimated $33 million to create retail's most sumptuous *mise en scène*—an investment that paid off, not for the profits the store generated, but for the fabulous way it depicted Lauren's posh imagery so completely. Even the most jaded shoppers couldn't help but be bowled over by all the mahogany, the magnificent floral arrangements, the vintage paintings of noble gentry on horseback. With Cole Porter tunes filling the air, it was easy to get carried away, as many dazzled American shoppers and foreign tourists did, trooping home with armloads of navy Polo shopping bags.

Most shoppers would never get to see where all this merchandise was created—which since 1991 was inside another palatial setting farther south on Madison at Sixty-first Street, at Polo's headquarters inside a steel high-rise. A swift elevator ride to the fourth floor delivered visitors to Polo's reception area, known as the Reading Room. As regal as any library inside an English country estate, the high-ceilinged, mahogany-paneled Reading Room was replete with an exposed balcony, a majestic staircase, and lush appointments all around: cushy sofas, a well-worn leather wing chair, and a hassock covered in zebra skin. Down the hallway of this "Upstairs Downstairs" facade was a stark contrast: white-walled cubicles with computers and file cabinets, where the serious work got done.

Amid the stuffy grandeur of the Reading Room was an unexpected, whimsical note: a pile of M&M's in a huge oriental bowl. All day, employees and visitors scooped up handfuls of candy. "Everyone loves M&M's," explained Lauren. "For twenty years I've always had bowls of M&M's around. This is a happy place."

M&M's might have sweetened the ambiance, but Ralph's definition of a happy place needed further elaboration. Happy, as in fat and happy and prosperous—well, he was certainly right about that. But happy, as in kicky and happy-go-lucky—that interpretation wouldn't fly. The house of Lauren was buttoned up and dead serious—full of tightly wound people with a Moonie-like devotion to the man whose name was on the door. Polo Ralph Lauren didn't get to be the mightiest oak in American fashion by taking it easy.

In an industry where high-strung personalities, creative tension, and second-guessing are par for the course, Polo was renowned as being the most complicated, the most obsessive of all. "Ralph is demanding and the politics are difficult," explained one former design assistant. "Everybody is scared to question Ralph."

Another former staffer shared his view about what went on behind the walls of the Reading Room: "Ralph was always telling us that we're the standard, that everybody is always imitating everything we do, that everybody wants to be like us. There was always this arrogance about who we were and that bred an elitism among everybody who worked there. People at Polo just thought they were just better than anybody else."

So it was easy to understand how an $8-an-hour sales associate working behind the polished counters at Polo, outfitted in a $1,500 suede safari jacket and $300 jodhpurs, could slip into the role of a country squire, thanks to Polo's generous employee discount. "The salespeople were totally sucked in. We were romanced by it all," recalled a former salesman, who waxed wistfully about the late 1980s, the years when Polo employees were treated to gourmet catered lunches of dilled chicken salad and couscous, free of charge. "The chitchat in the afternoon wasn't about the *Dallas* episode last night. All we talked about were clothes, like Ralph's latest $600 crocodile moccasins which had just arrived and that everyone wanted to buy."

The Reading Room, just like Polo's in-store displays, makes for that all-important first impression, which is the essence of Ralph Lauren, the quintessential, keep-up-appearances man. The man, the merchandise, the company are one seamless facade maintained by his troops with dogged devotion.

The people at Polo often spoke in Hollywood metaphors. "Think of this as a movie," a Polo executive once told the salespeople at the Madison Avenue store. "Ralph is the director and you are the actors, and we are here to make a movie."

And indeed, Lauren once fancied himself as a leading man. "I always see a movie running in my head," he once told the *Los Angeles Times*. "I'm the star of the movie and it's a vision of what a particular world represents to me."

So it stood to reason that he would star in his own fashion ads. For years, his handsome, perpetually tanned face set off by wiry gray hair jumped from the pages of magazines. Once, in the 1980s, he portrayed a leathery Steve McQueen, in a T-shirt, beat-up jeans, and cowboy hat, slugging a bottle of beer. After his hair grew whiter in the 1990s, he turned into a suave Cary Grant, as the role model for his top-drawer Purple Label suits, made in England.

Cary Grant was a Ralph obsession. One New York evening when Lauren presented an award to Audrey Hepburn, he stood onstage wearing oversized Cary Grant spectacles. The dapper actor himself never had it so good. "Now I think my life is so much better than what I wanted," Lauren told the *Los Angeles Times*. "A few years before he died, Cary Grant came to my house for lunch with his wife. [Grant] said that my life is a real example of what people think *his* was. The interesting thing is, I'm more Cary Grant than Cary Grant."

But more people likened Lauren to the self-made mogul and master of reinvention, Jay Gatsby, from F. Scott Fitzgerald's novel *The Great Gatsby*. (Coincidentally, perhaps, Lauren designed the costumes for the 1972 movie of the same name, starring Robert Redford, another actor whom Lauren had idolized.)

Over the years, Lauren invited the world to ogle his lush life in a number of glossy magazine profiles. Those upbeat stories always depicted him as larger-than-life, no doubt because he wielded a big stick, as one of the most formidable advertisers in fashion. With his immense ad budget, Lauren didn't have to bother with wooing the press with free lunches and clothes. Only a few editors were treated to his special gift: "designer" steaks from the steers raised on his Colorado ranch that arrived in a wooden box with an RRL brand on it.

It is little wonder that so many people insist on calling him Ralph Lo-REN—the affected pronunciation just sounded more exclusive and otherworldly. In the pages of *W* and *Town & Country*, Ralph lived large in residences that resembled the dreamscapes in his ads. His homes included beach-front spreads on Long Island and in Jamaica, a Fifth Avenue duplex apartment, a baronial estate in Bedford, New York, and—the place where those steaks come from—a fourteen-thousand-acre cattle ranch near Telluride, Colorado, named Double RL (for Ralph and Ricky Lauren). The ranch even had a teepee, a rustic hideaway furnished with log furniture, a bearskin throw, cowboy hats, and Navajo blankets—"stuff inside there an Indian never dreamed of," one of the ranch hands told *W*.

"It's a Wonderful Life" was the cover line for the December 1996 issue of *Town & Country*, where Ralph, clad in a black turtleneck, military-style navy blazer, and weathered jeans, strolled hand in hand with his fetching blond wife, Ricky, who wore Polo's flag sweater over her jeans. Inside *Town & Country*, the Laurens canvased their leafy Bedford estate alongside their three Polo-perfect offspring, all in their twenties: David and Dylan, both graduates of Duke University, and Andrew, an alum of Skidmore College. The kids hadn't gravitated to fashion, but the eldest, Andrew, had pursued his father's fantasy, as he struggled to be an actor.

Meanwhile, inside Lauren's Hollywood workplace, he starred in the role of *working* designer. His PR people bent over backwards to convince inquiring reporters that yes, it was Ralph who designed every sock, every sheet pattern, every napkin ring that bore his label. Once, when a reporter sought to speak to Ralph, a PR woman crisply begged off: "Ralph is busy *designing*."

Reporters obligingly listened to this storybook spiel—and rolled their eyes. Everybody knew that though Ralph Lauren stood alone on the runway to take his bow, he was running a design machine, like so many others, where dozens of assistants and licensees performed much of the creating. All that mattered was the outcome. And the Polo machine—ever-rigorous in its standards and practices—churned out a slew of fine merchandise at many price levels, better than anyone else in fashion.

The French couture houses, which paid a steep price for having ignored their licensees in the 1980s, could have learned a lot from Ralph Lauren. He was never careless with the merchandise that bore his label. Every shirt, every bathrobe, every armchair had to uphold the Polo image. "We work with them as though they are part of our company," Lauren said of his twenty-odd licensees. "We design everything including the ads. We retain as much control as we can without owning the company."

And under Lauren's vaunted control, "Every year the bar goes up," said one person who formerly worked for Westpoint Stevens, maker of the sheets and towels for Lauren's home collection. "[Lauren's people] say they want everything to be perfect. But all they really want to do is to please Ralph. But sometimes they don't even know what he wants. So we're always paranoid. Small mistakes get magnified. The people at Polo are the best in the business, but they can be difficult to work with."

Ralph Lauren had arrived at a pinnacle of consistency in a creative process that people who have worked with him have described as painstaking and plodding. Lauren was always more verbal than visual, and he liked to recite his concepts to his design team. Lauren would often begin by describing a little vignette of his idealized customer, such as a sophisticated woman with a casual, elegant style, who loved to travel to Europe. Lauren's design staff returned weeks later with prototypes of actual sample garments, which were placed in meeting rooms, along with sketches and storyboards, with antique books, fabric swatches, pictures, and other props. The staffers prepared their samples, taking inspiration from the closets of vintage clothing and furnishings Polo had collected over the years.

Lauren himself would get most involved when it was time to review the sample garments, when he rejected, tinkered, and asked many, many questions. Such meetings dragged on for days, turning into a game of office politics as everyone jockeyed to impress the boss. "Ralph is the king of meetings," said one of his former high-ranking assistants. "He's always running late and when he walks in, there are twenty people in the room, his staff and some people from the licensee. Then somebody would start sucking up and would say, 'Ralph, what you are wearing today is brilliant, those boots are terrific.' Everyone else would join in. So, before the meeting starts, Ralph then spends another twenty minutes talking about his woven belt or whatever he's wearing."

This assistant said: "Ralph is a great editor, but he can't draw it. You have to design a dozen samples. You have to present the right alternatives and you must give him enough of them so that he can pick from the group. But still, he can't make a decision. He chews over the location of every ad, of every possibility, of every concept. Then he comes back the next day and changes his mind."

Was it indecisiveness or an obsession for perfection? his staff often wondered. They watched him waffle when he decorated his homes or when he dickered over whether he needed a haircut. Once, when Lauren decided to repaint his prized antique Mercedes, one of the eight vintage cars in his collection, he polled everybody in the office. The former staffer explained: "He had six gray cards and he called me in his office and asked me what color did I like. I swear that they all looked the same. No difference between them. He held them up to the light. Then he walked over to the window. Then he had to show them to everybody, even the receptionist, to get her idea."

People with money and power have always gone to extraordinary lengths to get what they want. So how did his assistants get inside the head of the man whose ideas are so innate and full of nuance, who only knows what he wants when he sees it? Lauren surrounded himself with like-minded people who shared his taste level and his Waspy sensibilities—such as Kelly Rector, a stunning brunette and accomplished horsewoman who grew up in Connecticut, who later worked for Calvin Klein, whom she married in 1986.

So when Lauren told his charges to make a tartan that was "more Scottish" or to redo a raincoat that wasn't "army surplus enough," they had a pretty good idea of what he wanted. And perhaps one of their hardest tasks was helping him choose a scent for his fragrances, after he lost his sense of smell following a brain tumor operation in 1987. "Do I need a focus group? No," he once explained. "My talent and the company's talent is the ability to have instincts and sophistication. To travel, to feel, to get a sense of the public and a sense of visual things. We are constantly feeding off of each other."

The most loyal of Lauren's staffers, who learned to put up with his precarious ways, stayed on for years and became indispensable acolytes, known in house as the "Ralphettes." The queen of this sorority came with a Polo-esque name: Buffy Birritella, who served as Polo's senior vice president of women's wear. Birritella joined the company in 1971, leaving her job as fashion editor for *DNR* (*Daily News Record*), the menswear version of *WWD*.

Birritella even looked like Ricky Lauren, with her straight blonde mane, slender figure, angular face, and outdoorsy flair for fashion. She instinctively knew what was "very Ralph" and what was "not Ralph enough." For Polo's Madison Avenue emporium, it was Birritella who picked out the styles that would go on one hundred brass doorknobs, which took a year to make. She also climbed the scaffolding to supervise the workmen cleaning the mansion's limestone facade. "Ralph wanted the patina left in certain spots, so I pointed them out," she told *Avenue* magazine.

For Ralph Lauren to engender so much loyalty and dedication in so many people reflects the charisma of this complex, low-key man. "When you see him in meetings, he has an enormous presence. You never thought of him as short," said one employee about Lauren, who looks to be about five four. In 1992, *The Washington Post*'s Cathy Horyn wrote about the effect he had on his employees: "There probably isn't a man or a woman on his staff who hasn't felt the soft stroke of his voice, fallen for the tenderness of his gaze and suddenly found themselves wanting to turn cartwheels for him just because he happened to stop them in the hallway or at a design meeting and say, 'Tell me what you like. Tell me what you're going to wear tomorrow, Saturday night.' "

Ralph Lauren entered the 1990s in terrific shape. The fashion house that he and Strom had built was now generating sales at retail in the billions, rock solid and in for the long haul. As Strom prepared to retire in 1995, his succession would be as orderly as the changing of the guard, for waiting in the wings was Michael Newman, the financial chief and fifteen-year Polo veteran who would become vice chairman and chief operating officer—responsible for much of the heavy lifting for Ralph, who served as Polo's chairman and CEO.

AS OTHER DESIGNERS jealously looked at his long string of incredible hits, they had to admit: Ralph was *the man*. Lauren had stayed true to his classic design aesthetic, which virtually insulated him from fashion's changing whims. But being on top was never as comfortable as it appeared. Lauren worried about becoming too complacent, losing focus, and going right out of style. As worthy competitors such as Hilfiger, Gap, and J. Crew took on Polo in the mid-1990s, Lauren was forced to raise the bar. Every season, he once reflected, designers are "gobbled up and spit out every two seconds. To be a classic in this day and age is a real challenge."

Lauren couldn't help but be haunted by what had happened to his contemporary, Calvin Klein, Seventh Avenue's other Bronx sensation, who had launched his fashion house around the same time Lauren did in 1967. Throughout the seventies and most of the eighties, Calvin and Ralph played out Seventh Avenue's most spirited rivalry. Klein had built a mighty empire, fortified by his fragrances, jeans, and underwear that were cherished by consumers the world over, thanks to his sexy, cutting-edge advertising. But for reasons other than fashion, the house of Klein, in 1991, was on the verge of coming undone.

Having successfully bounced back from drug rehabilitation in the late 1980s, Klein was fighting demons in his own business. In 1990, Calvin Klein Inc. reported revenue of $200 million, with $4.3 million in net losses—the third time in the previous five years the company had been unprofitable. The house of Klein was being dragged down by its core jeanswear division, which accounted for 80 percent of Klein's revenue—and $14 million in operating losses in 1990. The problem was fundamental: Klein's famous jeans were stone cold at retail because he had lost his magic touch with the youth market. The jeans division was also the culprit of a bigger distraction: the huge junk-bond debt the company had accrued in the 1980s when it bought Puritan Fashions, its former jeans licensee. In 1991, Calvin Klein Inc. still owed a staggering $55 million in junk-bond debt—and had only three years to pay it all off.

As Klein appeared to be headed toward bankruptcy, his day of reckoning never came. The next year, Klein got an unusual reprieve: a helping hand from his buddy, David Geffen, the billionaire Hollywood mogul and founder of Geffen Records. Geffen paid off all $62 million of Klein's debt securities—effectively providing the company with a generous loan. Then Geffen jumped in to assist Klein and his longtime business partner, Barry Schwartz, to restructure their company away from manufacturing into a house of licensees. From then on, nothing came between Calvin and his Calvins. The designer threw himself into making over his jeanswear division to recapture America's youth.

Klein's reversal of misfortune was swift. By 1994, the company's turnaround was right on track, and Klein was able to dig out of his hole and repay Geffen. Klein bolstered his management by hiring a new president, Gabriella Forte, a plum executive he lured away from Giorgio Armani. Then he began his push into home furnishings and retail boutiques around the world. Klein's experience was a close call—and a textbook lesson—that fashion, even in the major leagues, was always a slippery slope.

SO LAUREN WASN'T about to rest on his laurels through the company's midlife years. Throughout the 1990s, he would be consumed with making over the house of Polo, skillfully repositioning the business to make it more populist by adding lots of lower-priced lines to be in step with the Gap generation—*and* more attractive to Wall Street. Like a plastic surgeon performing a face-lift, Lauren left no visible scars of demarcation, in a balancing act to turn on young, urban shoppers without turning off his maturing, elite fans. After years of spotting Tommy Hilfiger in the rearview mirror, Ralph now faced his rival in the passing lane. From then on, the designers would bob and weave around each other—sometimes colliding head-on.

WHILE RALPH LAUREN prevailed as the merchant prince of Madison Avenue, Tommy Hilfiger was busily monitoring Polo's every move. Not surprisingly, Hilfiger—the second in a family of nine children, whose father, Richard, was a jeweler and watchmaker in upstate Elmira, New York—got his start on the sales floor. He was a toothy, mop-topped high school senior in 1969 when he and two friends scraped together $450 and opened "People's Place," the only boutique in Elmira specializing in bell-bottomed jeans. People's Place flourished for a few years before going bankrupt in 1977. Three years later, Hilfiger moved to Manhattan, where he landed a freelance assignment designing Jordache jeans. Then he was discovered by Mohan Murjani, head of Murjani International, maker of the hot-selling Gloria Vanderbilt jeans and Coca-Cola sportswear, which launched him as a menswear designer in 1985.

Born in India, Mohan Murjani was a flashy, ambitious scion of a Hong Kong apparel contractor, who had come to New York with an agenda: to leapfrog into the forefront of America's burgeoning designer fashion boom. He saw the squeaky-clean Hilfiger as the ideal marketing vehicle to introduce what was essentially Polo at popular prices, what Tommy liked to call "preppy classics with a twist." Murjani's Polo-lite debuted with a $40 "public" pant in khaki ("made to fit the public"), a $25 "Harvard" button-down shirt, and a $30 "Newport" polo knit shirt. Tommy's answer to Ralph's embroidered polo pony insignia was a Bavarian crest which he found in the public library.

Hilfiger had only been on the market for a short time when Murjani went for the gusto when he made Hilfiger the centerpiece of a controversial campaign created by the famous adman George Lois. In the summer of 1985, a huge billboard high above Times Square telegraphed: "The Four Great American designers for men are R—L—, P—E—, C—K—and T—H—." Another print ad brazenly declared: "Every decade someone with talent and a sense of the times takes a good look at the great classics and makes them better. That's what Tommy Hilfiger did when he redesigned the button-down shirt, the polo shirt, the sweater, the classic chino and everything else modern men and women wear. Style marches on."

Fashion insiders were taken aback. They considered Hilfiger's bravado as crass—and a lie. Hilfiger hadn't paid his dues on Seventh Avenue and was clearly a fake. "He may have well-styled, well-made products, but I don't like the connotation that he is a creative designer," sniffed Jack Hyde, a longtime men's fashion writer and professor at the Fashion Institute of Technology in New York.

But there was no denying that Hilfiger's cart-before-the-horse approach was catchy and original. It was also working. Shoppers began asking for that new designer they often called "Hil-finger"—because the sportswear looked great and didn't cost too much. Paul Cavaco, a fashion industry stylist, noted in 1990, "To the consumer, Tommy is a classic. . . . The ad campaign—as much as I don't like it—is brilliant."

Hilfiger would never live down his public relations pole vault into fashion's major leagues. As Lauren's most visible facsimile, he was branded with the scarlet letter as fashion's great pretender. In those early years, the forces on Seventh Avenue often likened him to the Monkees, the prefabricated rock group who starred in the hit TV series of the 1960s and were modeled explicitly after the Beatles. The more popular Hilfiger became, the more fashion cognoscenti snubbed him. No doubt it unnerved many struggling designers that Hilfiger was living proof that deft packaging and deep pockets could turn any ambitious nobody into a fashion sensation. Years later, when Hilfiger said that he was ready to introduce an expensive women's collection, Amy Spindler, *The New York Times* fashion critic, pounced: "By setting his sights on fashion, as opposed to clothing which has earned him his good name and fortune, he runs the risk of revealing in larger-than-life runway proportions the undeniable banality that informs his esthetic . . . the wizard could just be a small man with a megaphone."

In reality, Hilfiger was hardly a swaggering braggart. He was reserved and somewhat square. He looked downright foolish when he starred in his own ads in the late 1980s. There he was, grinning, leaning against a vintage convertible above the caption: "Tommy and His T-bird," or astride a motorbike, "Tommy and His Harley." He looked stiff instead of hip. To his credit, he had the good sense to quit.

Tommy finally changed his tune starting in the early 1990s, with the help of adman Michael Toth, who helped him fashion a more believable persona. From then on, Hilfiger left the modeling to groups of grinning, well-scrubbed young models, who captured the feel-good side of the American dream, of Fourth of July picnics and downtown parades—a niche that hadn't been filled in designer imagery. Lauren had cornered the Wasp aesthetic while Klein had cornered the market for sex. So that left a wide-open field for Hilfiger. "Tommy came down the middle and said, 'Here's Norman Rockwell, you can aspire to being fun and having fun in your life.' And more people identified with that," Toth said.

Tommy clearly was having lots of fun when he pressed the flesh with his customers. He made in-store appearances his trademark, clocking in at least a dozen appearances every year at department stores such as Belk's, Dillard's, and Macy's. Most designers rose above such grassroots stumping after they hit the big time. "I haven't done a store appearance in maybe twenty years," Ralph Lauren remarked in 1997. "I lead a quiet life. People buy Ralph Lauren because they love the product. They don't care that I'm in the press every day. I'm happy that I'm not."

But when Tommy hit the retail hustings, he became a natural politician, with the earnest appeal of *American Bandstand*'s Dick Clark. Tommy turned on like a TV—flashing his perfect set of teeth, set off by dimples. He was one of those gee-whiz guys who just hadn't gotten over the fact that he had really made it—and his very presence could create a scene. Once, a crowd of about a thousand turned out at Macy's in New York, when Hilfiger stood at the end of the runway and ripped off his windbreaker and sunglasses, tossing them to the squealing spectators, just like a rock star. The young, delighted fans—a rare blend of white, black, and Latinos—roared. Later, Tommy planted himself at a table and stayed for more than an hour to sign autographs and pose for pictures.

Such retail road shows served another purpose as well—the chance for Tommy to check out first-hand what the coolest kids in Atlanta and Dallas were wearing. He chatted up shoppers to learn how he could make his collections more appealing and then he took that information back to his staffers in New York.

Hilfiger's reputation as an affable, approachable designer even resonated with celebrities, who were just as star-struck upon meeting Hilfiger. *GQ*'s creative director, Jim Moore, was present during a photo shoot with former New York Knicks coach Don Nelson in the locker room at Madison Square Garden. When Knicks players John Starks, Patrick Ewing, and others heard that Hilfiger was on his way over to be photographed, "They couldn't believe it," Moore remembered. "They were all running around grabbing basketballs for him to autograph. It was a funny dynamic. It was like, *who is the celebrity*?"

AS "HONORARY CHAIRMAN" and principal designer for his namesake house, Tommy Hilfiger was the face man, an effective image-maker, with seemingly boundless energy to spare. Hilfiger attended key meetings where he put forth his opinions, but he rarely talked to the press about designing or even managing his company. In showroom presentations to retailers, he could be commanding—unfolding sweaters, pointing out fabric details, and even reciting wholesale prices. But mainly, he put his trust in company management and dozens of staff designers who kept all the plates spinning at his headquarters, an eleven-story brick building at 25 West Thirty-ninth Street in the heart of New York's garment district.

The house of Hilfiger was built with a number of executives who were once associated with Polo Ralph Lauren, notably its three principals: Silas Chou, chairman; Joel Horowitz, chief executive officer; and Lawrence Stroll, vice chairman. Through the years, these three had poached many valuable players from Polo, including Edwin Lewis, Hilfiger's former CEO who retired in 1994, and at least a dozen other key executives.

At the top of Hilfiger's Polo alums was Silas Chou, the man who was credited with masterminding the Tommy revolution. Born in 1950 in Hong Kong, Chou was also the chairman of Novel Enterprises, a publicly traded apparel manufacturing business founded by his family, which was a key knitwear supplier to companies such as Murjani, Liz Claiborne Inc., Limited Inc., and Polo. Chou had been a partner with Lawrence Stroll in running Polo's Canadian and European licensees in the 1980s.

In 1989, Chou and Stroll stepped in to rescue Hilfiger when he was sinking under the weight of the financially troubled Murjani, which was heading toward collapse. Chou wanted to build his own stable of designer brands for Novel and he believed that Hilfiger could be his first. Having already produced Hilfiger's knitwear for Murjani, Chou always had been impressed with the Hilfiger look. "I saw products I liked," he said. "Tommy's clothes had a personality, a traditional American look but with a modern touch—that 'twist,' as he calls it. I liked the oversized, relaxed fit which was different from Polo shirts, which were tight to the body. Our European customers always thought Polo was too tight."

After Chou negotiated with Murjani to take over Hilfiger, he made it clear that he had big plans. "I told Tommy, 'I don't want to be just a licensee; I want to be with you all the time so we can row in the same direction,' " Chou reminisced. Having incorporated Tommy Hilfiger Corp. in Hong Kong, Chou and Stroll provided the initial financing, and each took a 35 percent stake, while Hilfiger got 22.5 percent, and Horowitz received 7.5 percent. Months later, Chou and Stroll sold their interests in Polo's European and Canadian operations.

As chairman of the venture, Chou remained in Hong Kong, but he knew just where to find the perfect chief executive to work in New York. Chou had his sights set on Edwin Lewis, a fifteen-year veteran of Bidermann Industries, Polo's women's-wear licensee at the time. Prying Lewis away from Polo was a feat, because Lewis was rumored to be the heir apparent to Ralph's business partner, Peter Strom. But Chou won

Lewis over by giving him equity in Hilfiger and free rein to run the show. Tapping into his retail connections, Lewis gave Hilfiger instant credibility with department stores.

Watching from the sidelines over the years, Ralph Lauren resisted the urge to criticize his rival. But privately, his associates said he seethed, dismissing Tommy as a copycat, a Polo markdown, a designer who subsisted only by leaching so many top talents from Polo. Hilfiger "only took off after he hired Ed Lewis," Ralph later reflected privately to a reporter.

While Tommy's role model was Ralph, Chou's corporate model was the venerable Liz Claiborne Inc., one of the most professionally run fashion companies on Seventh Avenue—and a public company since 1981. "From the beginning, Silas set it up with all the proper reporting documents for tracking the business—the types of things that Wall Street would be asking for," said Horowitz. "It made it easy for us when the time came for us to go public."

Tommy Hilfiger Corp. filed for its listing on the New York Stock Exchange in 1992, becoming one of the first fashion houses to jump into the bull run of the 1990s. The company's balance sheet revealed its impressive climb. Between 1990 and 1992, sales had quadrupled to $107 million, with a net income of $9 million. Hilfiger's initial public offering raised $46.9 million, of which $11.3 million was earmarked to develop more than 1,000 in-store shops in department stores. The fashion house would go on to perform splendidly on Wall Street, exceeding analysts' earnings projections every quarter, and impressing institutional investors, who made millions on the stock. Unwittingly, Tommy had repaid his debt to Ralph in the most tangible way. The respect Hilfiger earned on Wall Street made it far safer for Polo to go public on the New York Stock Exchange five years later.

"We are just the luckiest sons of bitches around," Chou reminisced one afternoon at Hilfiger's headquarters in 1997. "We did the right thing in the right place. The right thing was casual wear, the right place was the U.S. in the late eighties and nineties, when America moved into the information age. Ralph was really the pioneer in casual wear, but with our experience, we saw that with Tommy, we could use our expertise to deliver the same product, but at a better price."

The Polo alum with the closest ties to Lauren was Joel Horowitz, who became Hilfiger's CEO after Ed Lewis retired. Joel Horowitz's father, Sidney Horowitz, a close friend of Ricky Lauren's parents, was a veteran apparel production manager who was one of Ralph Lauren's first employees in 1968. After Joel dropped out of Miami (Ohio) University in his sophomore year in 1968, Sidney Horowitz talked his nineteen-year-old son into coming over to Polo, where Joel joined as a production assistant for Polo's new dress-shirt business. Over the years, Horowitz helped manage Polo's first store in Beverly Hills and ran Polo's short-lived jeans division in the 1970s. Horowitz joined Murjani in 1983, where he met Hilfiger.

Horowitz said his experiences during the struggling early years at Polo and later at the freewheeling Murjani taught him that delivering merchandise to stores on time was tantamount to success. "Now I'm not knocking Ralph, because he was successful anyway," Horowitz said. "But the fact is that you have to execute. You have to get all the products into the stores at the same time, which is what we did at Hilfiger. And that's why we were able to skyrocket the way we did."

IN THE LATE 1990s, Hilfiger and Polo were on parallel tracks, having peddled their products across America's malls as well as operating their own boutiques, mainly in Europe and Asia. Both produced merchandise through hundreds of contractors around the world and thus were saddled with the mind-boggling minutiae and logistics of multinational commerce. Thus, they planned out the bulk of their collections about a year before the merchandise reached the stores.

Four times a year, the Hilfiger organization held planning sessions called "adoption meetings," where its designers put the finishing touches on its collections before they went into production. On one hot Friday afternoon in August 1997, Tommy showed up just after lunch to review certain styles that would arrive in stores in the fall of 1998. Tommy was the vision of Pat Boone that day, in a blue seersucker suit, a white pique shirt, and white bucks. Michael Sondag, the company's senior vice president of design, led the way to the meetings.

Two scruffy boys carrying shopping bags got on the same elevator as Hilfiger and Sondag. "Do you want to buy some candy?" they asked in unison. Hilfiger grinned and directed them through glass doors to a receptionist. "Tell them that Tommy sent you." The kids shrugged in disbelief. One of them said, "Awww, you ain't Tommy. Tommy isn't even *here*."

Hilfiger held the elevator door open to watch their reaction as the receptionist pointed, confirming who he was. Incredulous, one kid extended his leg into the air to show off the Hilfiger sneakers he was wearing. Hilfiger cracked up and waved to them as the elevator doors closed.

A crowd of young assistants was sitting on the floor waiting when Sondag and Hilfiger walked into the first of a series of design rooms set up like little vignettes with clothing samples, fabric swatches, and storyboards. There were basketballs, a pair of wooden skis, old ice skates, picture postcards, and ski posters. All in all, a scene very similar to what the people at Polo had described as Ralph's method.

"Okay, here we go again, holiday 1998," said Sondag as everybody settled down. Hilfiger sat on the carpet and rolled up his shirt sleeves, as all eyes were watching him.

Sondag stood next to a display called Athletics and started his spiel: "What we want to do is give everything a real active feel, the basketball shirts, the soccer shirts, and the jerseys. We want to go upscale and go upmarket and come up with more sophisticated athletics. Spectator athletics, that are as good-looking to wear on the streets as they are to work out in." Unfolding a stack of sweaters in gray, black, and white, he said, "Here's that icy look in woven. Tommy, you seemed to have liked this when we were showing it to you last week?"

Hilfiger nodded approvingly, then he piped up to mutter some fashion-speak: "Modern high-tech outerwear fabrics. Texture into the knits . . . That's what we wanna all wear, isn't it? It's much cleaner."

Hilfiger interrupted Sondag to question why there was so much ivory, gray, and black. "If the customer is walking the aisle and sees so much black and gray in one month and comes back another month and sees the same, it may not be different enough. So we need an infusion of color." Sondag agreed, then led everyone to another room.

Standing next to Sondag was Craig Reynolds, senior vice president of merchandising, whom Hilfiger calls his "chief of police." Reynolds's job was "to make sure the licensees don't do anything to conflict. We don't want the same shirts in our jeans line that are in our sportswear line. They all have to be different. But there still has to be a continuity between all categories."

Next were more meetings with licensees: Oxford Industries, for dress shirts, and Hartmarx, for suits and tailored clothing. Hilfiger examined samples for his new dress shirt with a double button under the collar—the extra button allowed a man to wear a tie with a bigger knot. After a model tussled with closing the top button, Hilfiger concluded: "We need to work on the collar."

The next order of business was coming up with a new suit label to distinguish Hilfiger's $750 Italian-made suits from his $395 models. Hilfiger mused: "When the salesmen tell men this is our bridge line, they have to identify it with something else other than just saying it's a better make and better fabric. I think we need to re-color the label, maybe white with navy lettering. Silver? But silver isn't as expensive, it doesn't have the value platinum has . . . call it the platinum collection? Armani has a black and white label but he doesn't advertise it. Ralph does Purple Label. Calvin has white at Saks. Donna does a black and gold label. Can we make up some labels in silver on the midnight background? I want to see what they look like."

It seemed tedious that six people would spend a good half hour dickering over the color of a label that would be hidden inside a suit jacket. But for a fashion image-maker like Hilfiger, the color of the label is a key marketing tool—and just as important as the way the suits looked.

LABELS ON THE inside, logos on the outside. Hilfiger knew the importance of symbols and insignias that would connect with shoppers. Initially, Hilfiger used logos as a merchandising magnet, a clever way to draw attention to his department store displays during his early years when he didn't have in-store shops. There was no way that shoppers could miss the shirts with "Tommy Hilfiger" in letters as big as the E on an eye chart, adorning the mannequins facing the aisles.

But logos would serve another purpose in the 1990s as Hilfiger would update his image into something younger and more textured when he aligned his brand with rap culture, the seminal movement that won over the MTV generation. Hilfiger was one of the first designers to plaster his name on rugby shirts and tops that fit right in with such status logos as Puma, Adidas, and Gucci that rappers loved to wear in music videos.

"We always bought into logos," Russell Simmons, founder of Def Jam records and his own fashion label, Phat Farm, told *Vogue* in 1996. "The reason for it is that it represents all the shit we don't have. We're not ripped-dungarees-rock-n-roll-alternative-culture people. We want to buy into the shit we see on television but we want to put our own twist on it. Part of the fantasy of fashion is about being successful. It's aspirational. I put this on, I'm getting laid. Not because I'm cool and raggedy but because I'm cool and clean. Because I want to buy into this culture."

Hilfiger certainly understood the power of rap culture, a genre to which the forces in the fashion industry couldn't (or wouldn't) relate. The homeboy look had crept onto the runways in the early 1990s when Chanel's Karl Lagerfeld put his runway models in droopy pants and huge CC logos, which made for riveting, drive-by flirtation with street style. But since most fashion houses, including Polo, either feared or didn't know exactly what to make of the hip-hop crowd, they steered clear of any association with the rappers. This was uncharted territory. It was already established that black consumers followed the white mainstream. But fashion wasn't at all prepared for black youths to lead white consumers.

Timberland, the maker of hiking boots and rugged outdoor gear, was caught by surprise when it learned that inner-city kids were buying its $150 hiking boots three and four pairs at a time. When Timberland's sales spiked 46 percent to $295 million in the first nine months of 1993, Jeffrey Swartz, Timberland's executive vice president, gave *The New York Times* a reason: Timberland was just selling more to its core customers, whom he described as "honest working people" who liked Timberland's functional, outdoorsy clothes. Swartz estimated that no more than 5 percent of Timberland's sales came from "urban" shoppers. Of course, Timberland was happy to get the additional business, but Swartz emphasized that Timberland had no intention of courting its swelling number of inner-city fans. "We are not going to build this business on smoke. We are not able to execute trendy," Swartz maintained.

But Tommy Hilfiger saw things differently. Once the rappers started buying his colorful, logo-filled clothes, Tommy saw an opening to broaden his reach to America's youth, black and white, who all liked hip-hop music. It was easy for Hilfiger to get it, because he had always been a pop music buff. As teenagers, Tommy and his younger brother, Andy, played bass guitar in a family rock group called Hippo, which was their father's nickname. In the late 1980s, Hilfiger began wooing the rock world, having provided blazers and polo shirts to British rocker Pete Townshend for a concert tour.

Around the same time, Andy Hilfiger was steeped in the hip-hop world, residing in an apartment in East Harlem and working as a lighting man for rock bands and music videos. Andy always arrived on the set with a bag full of his brother's polo shirts and Tommy Hilfiger logo duffel bags, which he passed out to concert promoters and rap stars who had already seen L.L. Cool J on stage sporting Hilfiger's red, white, and blue jumpsuits, originally designed for the Lotus Formula One auto racing team. Andy knew that dropping a few duds on the right folks could pay off down the road: "I never pushed for them to wear Tommy onstage, but you know, when you give away clothes, somebody's going to wear them *somewhere* where they will be noticed."

Tommy's rap-culture moment finally happened one Saturday evening in 1994 after Andy stopped by the Macklowe Hotel to drop off a few shirts for rapper Snoop Dogg. A smart move. That night, Snoop wore a striped rugby shirt with "Tommy" across the front and "Hilfiger" on the back on *Saturday Night Live*.

The next week, retailers, stylists, and shoppers lit up the phone lines at Hilfiger's showroom, clamoring to get their hands on that rugby shirt. On the cover of his hit CD *Grand Puba 2000*, Grand Puba leaned against his black Lamborghini convertible in a dark-green Tommy jacket over a white Tommy T-shirt. Once Hilfiger became the designer of choice among the rappers and urban youths, the suburban white kids followed, so they could be as "down" as the black kids.

Tommy, who started as a Ralph copycat, was now a fat cat doing his own thing—a hybrid mix of preppy and urban street styles. And Hilfiger was serious about emphasizing multiculturalism. Hilfiger's West Thirty-ninth Street headquarters was unique on Seventh Avenue as its creative ranks swelled with a number of twenty-something African Americans, Latinos, Asians, and foreign expatriates on staff. The company's mission statement sounded as if it came from the United Nations: "By respecting one another, we can reach all cultures and communities."

It remained to be seen whether Hilfiger's reach would someday lift those minorities into the executive suite—which would surely be a first on Seventh Avenue. One of the most promising talents was Lloyd Boston, the company's creative director, an African American who since 1993 had been in charge of designing all of Hilfiger's shopping bags, merchandise hang tags, and other packaging. Hilfiger met Boston in 1990 after a fashion show at Rich's department store in Atlanta, when Boston took him to task. "He didn't use any models of color in his fashion show," Boston recalled. "I told him, 'I love your clothes, but I don't see myself represented.' " Tommy apologized, noting that he always included black models in his shows, but Rich's had chosen the models before he arrived.

Boston, a sophomore art major at Morehouse College, told Hilfiger he wanted to be a graphic designer. Tommy took down his phone number and called him a few days later, offering him a one-year internship in New York. Boston transferred to Rutgers University in New Jersey, where he completed his degree at night school while working for Hilfiger during the day. Hilfiger paid for his final semester at Rutgers and offered him a job after graduation.

Hilfiger's multicultural mosaic was more than just progressive; it was very strategic. After all, Tommy was in his forties, married with four young children and living in Greenwich, Connecticut. He would always need a window into the world's fast-paced pop culture. Kidada Jones—the daughter of *Vibe* founder Quincy Jones—who helped style his fashion ads, kept Hilfiger in check. "Kidada speaks her mind," said Andy Hilfiger. "She will say, 'Tommy, this baby blue isn't happening anymore,' or 'Andy, those pants are *whack*' [out of style].' "

Hip-hop star Coolio once modeled in a Hilfiger fashion show and then joined Tommy onstage for his runway finale. Many fashion editors in the audience shook their heads as the grinning white guy from Elmira became an honorary homeboy.

Rap group Mobb Deep rhymed his praises: "Tommy Hill was my nigga/ and others couldn't figure/How me and Hilfiger used to move through with vigor." Tommy was knocked out. "I thought it was cool—he called me his nigga!" he told *Playboy*.

Unlike the executives at Timberland, the honchos at Tommy Hilfiger Corp. weren't tentative about embracing the rap crowd. "I feel proud that we're able to appeal to such a wide, diverse audience out there," said Horowitz. "That is something I don't think anyone has ever achieved. And I think it is really a tribute to Tommy and how he respects his position and what he's done with it." As for the white people who dissed Hilfiger, claiming that he was nothing more than a "ghetto" brand, Horowitz was unfazed: "You know, I really don't care what *they* think."

Unbeknownst to *them*, Hilfiger had his bases covered—and loaded. White New Yorkers, in particular, couldn't see Hilfiger beyond all those black bike messengers and roughnecks riding the subways who uniformly sported his logo. But Hilfiger was far more than a logo man. In 1997, the number one designer dress shirt in many department stores belonged to Tommy. His $400 business suits were top-sellers at Dillard's, Burdines, Parisian, and Macy's.

"Tommy is a sportswear designer who brought a new life to what was stodgy and expected in tailored clothing," said Ned Allie, an executive at Hartmarx, which made the suits. "Tommy's charcoal gray suit has a beaded stripe that would be bright white or even red. These subtle nuances are what make it so fresh. The market is already flooded with European labels; we don't need another Armani out there. With Tommy, the whole design world in the U.S. started looking at him, and American people are gravitating to him."

And so did establishment types like Britain's Prince Charles, President Bill Clinton, and former U.S. Senator Bill Bradley. Golf sensation David Duval donned Hilfiger's sportswear on the pro tour, and hundreds of middle-aged white men in the suburbs followed.

IN AUGUST 1997 at Macy's in New York, Polo Sport and Tommy Hilfiger were across the aisle from each other on the second floor, bisected by Nautica, another popular menswear brand. These three brands comprised more than 40 percent of all men's sportswear sold in department stores. The Polo Sport outpost resembled a pro shop, with a video wall flashing images of men in flashy Polo Sport togs hang gliding, skiing, and cycling. Across the aisle, Hilfiger's shop was all sunshine and swagger, with a poster featuring three guys strolling on the beach and a corner alcove labeled "Tommy Surf."

The symmetry begged the question: Were they separated at birth? Hardly, declared Lauren. "There are people in this business who are leaders and people who are followers," he expounded in a 1997 interview at his office. "Tommy Hilfiger hasn't anything new to say. His goal was to do Ralph Lauren at a lower price and that's what put Tommy on the map. He's for the younger customer who couldn't afford Polo." Hilfiger's ascent simply meant "There is room in department stores for both McDonald's and Burger King."

Nevertheless, the flame-broiled upstart made him testy. "Tommy gives Ralph the hives," insisted one of Lauren's former publicists. "He is obsessed with all the press Tommy is getting. When *Vanity Fair* published its profile on Tommy in 1996, Ralph was livid. The photos [of Hilfiger's Greenwich, Connecticut, home] included all of Ralph's props, the flags, the boots, the country stuff. Ralph was beside himself."

But Hilfiger, growing more confident and richer by the year—his salary would climb to $13 million in 1996—was now a cult figure in his own right. He relished the horse race. He told *Playboy* in 1997, "Ralph and I are engaged in something like the Pepsi-Coke war, or the BMW-Mercedes war. We're moving fast and forward and we're each conscious of what the other is doing."

Hilfiger was feeling mighty secure in 1996, when he was on the verge of crossing an important threshold—to finally be validated by the fashion establishment. The industry's most prestigious trade group, the Council of Fashion Designers of America, voted Hilfiger the best menswear designer of 1996. As fate would draw him closer to his rival, Tommy picked up his award at the black-tie ceremony at Lincoln Center, sharing the stage with Ralph, who won the CFDA award for women's wear, his third trophy from the CFDA.

FROM 1995 ONWARD, Hilfiger watched with fascination as the tables turned: Lauren, fashion's great interpreter, began to copy his copycat. Polo backed off its elitist stance by introducing new collections for men and women at "accessible" prices. Lauren permanently marked down his core product—polo shirts—from $55 to $49; Hilfiger's sold for $44. Lauren's Polo Sport collection was foundering until 1995, when Lauren showed perfect hip-hop pitch when he signed the exotic African American model Tyson Beckford as his poster boy under an exclusive contract that was reportedly valued at a million dollars a year. As many writers applauded Ralph's move, Tommy shrugged it off, noting that it was he who had put Tyson on the runway, years ahead of Ralph, the man who had initially ignored the hip-hop movement and hardly ever used blacks in his ads. As Tyson's buff, dark-skinned torso jumped from the packages of Polo Sport underwear, the brand's street credibility soared, putting it on par with Tommy.

Lauren explained that his new emphasis on Polo Sport in the late 1990s had nothing to do with Hilfiger or anybody else. "I sensed that people were into health and fitness more than they were into clothes. I am one of them. I've been running and biking for years. Polo Sport is part of that future, for the young and old."

But the ever-image-conscious Lauren wasn't about to bend over too far in the direction of hip. Tempering his mass market push a bit—and trumping Hilfiger's popular suits—Lauren introduced his top-of-the-line Purple Label collection of $1,800 suits in 1995 with a blitz of print ads. "Purple Label just started. It isn't a big business yet," Lauren said two years later. "But what Purple Label is doing is leading a trend. The market is starting to say, 'Wait a minute, even though the masses are wearing jeans on casual Fridays, suits can be sold at high prices.' Purple Label invigorates a company. It shows that you are leading."

Purple Label, Polo Sport, and a mainstream women's collection called Lauren by Lauren all lifted Polo's profile and sales as the fashion house prepared to go public. In 1996, *Fortune* began working on a major profile of Ralph, who invited writer Susan Caminiti to his Colorado ranch where Ricky Lauren and Buffy Birritella were also on hand.

The designer got bossy when *Fortune*'s photographer started taking pictures. "Ralph knows the lighting; he knows his best angle; he knows how a picture should look," she recalled. Lauren loved the shots of him in weathered jeans and a denim shirt, at home on the range—he wanted that image for the cover shot. But the November 11, 1996, cover of *Fortune* featured the distinguished designer as a captain of industry in navy pinstripes, white shirt, and black-and-white-patterned tie, with the caption: "Ralph Lauren: a $5 billion empire built on the fashionably correct."

(Months later, when Caminiti was researching a story on Hilfiger—which was never published—an anxious Tommy Hilfiger kept quizzing her. "Is this going to be on the cover of *Fortune*? Is this going to be like Ralph? His article was six or seven pages. Is it going to be like that?" he kept asking her.)

Tommy seemed obsessed with Ralph who, conversely, seemed obsessed with Tommy. Hilfiger even had the nerve to use Clemente Di Monda, the old-school Italian-born barber who had tended Lauren's hair for years. When Clemente's barbershop lease expired in 1991, Lauren invited him to open a new shop in one of the empty spaces on the eighth floor at Polo's headquarters at 650 Madison Avenue. So, whenever Tommy wanted a haircut, he had to troop over to Ralph's digs.

(And on one such occasion in the spring of 1999, Polo staffers were taken aback when Tommy Hilfiger walked down the hall from the barbershop only to wander inside one of Polo's showroom offices, where sample merchandise was sitting out in full view. He looked around for a moment, but nobody had the nerve to ask him to leave. Hilfiger later explained that he had taken a wrong turn on his way to the men's room.)

RALPH AND TOMMY were running neck and neck in the fall of 1996 when both launched jeans collections. Each designer planned to spend as much as $20 million to advertise his jeans. In coming out with Polo Jeans, Ralph had more on his mind than just outdoing Tommy. He wanted desperately to make a big splash with jeans, a category in which he had failed twice before. It had been downright embarrassing that Lauren had yet to get a handle on jeans—which he practically lived in and which were part of the romantic imagery of his Southwestern and country look over the years. While he kept striking out, Calvin Klein had reigned as the designer-jeans king throughout the 1980s.

Lauren's first jeans licensing venture, Polo Westernwear, was with Gap back in 1978, when Gap's three hundred stores were peddling Levi's and searching for some designer sizzle. Lauren had hoped to stake his claim on the western-wear market, as a designer alternative to jeans such as Wrangler and Lee. But Polo Westernwear didn't lasso enough consumers, primarily due to fit problems. Ralph designed his jeans to be tight, which looked terrific on lithe models, but were too snug for most women and men. "As a matter of fact, even Ralph himself began to wear Levi's," Trachtenberg wrote in his biography of Lauren. Polo Westernwear only sold a paltry $12 million in its first year, riding off into the sunset in a hurry as Gap pulled out of the venture.

It would be nearly ten years before Lauren would dive back into the jeans pool with Double RL jeans, named after his ranch. This time, Lauren's dream client was an upscale bohemian who knocked around in beat-up jeans. The company rolled out Double RL jeans in a store-on-wheels—a $1 million, customized Peterbilt eighteen-wheeler, decorated with a mural of thundering horses. On September 22, 1993, the designer truck pulled onto campuses like New York University and Wesleyan.

The college kids who wandered inside found prices that were insane: $150 for faded flannel shirts and $70 for preweathered jeans—the same kind they could find at vintage clothing shops for a third of that price. After a few months, Double RL stopped trucking.

But Ralph's third attempt, Polo Jeans, was the charm. At $48, the jeans were priced right and they sported Lauren's favorite symbol, the American flag. This time Ralph reclaimed Old Glory with his own personal fillip that Tommy couldn't knock off: Polo Jeans sported a tiny flag insignia, with RL initials in white to replace the stars. In ads, Tyson wore Polo Jeans against a backdrop of a flag with beige and red stripes, reminiscent of Jasper Johns' famous *Flag* painting. A couple of years later, Ralph would sit on top of the flagpole when Polo made its $13 million donation to the Smithsonian.

Polo Jeans sauntered into Macy's in New York in August 1996, unveiled by supermodels Bridget Hall and Tyson Beckford, who, along with fifty Harley-Davidson bikers, came roaring down Broadway into Herald Square in front of Macy's. The models stayed to sign autographs, and the event received a smattering of local press.

Weeks later, Tommy Jeans, which featured a number of baggy styles favored by the hip-hop set, came on board with a familiar stroke of marketing-on-wheels: a Tommy Jeans tour bus. Wrapped in a gigantic Hilfiger ad, the bus cruised its way through twelve more cities for in-store fashion shows and parties, showering fans with freebies like jeans, CDs, and guitars. The bus entourage included Andy Hilfiger and the kids of celebrities: Kidada, Quincy Jones's daughter; Kate Hudson, Goldie Hawn's daughter; and Kentaro Seagal, Steven Seagal's son. "By the time we got to Denver, the crowds were huge," Andy recalled. "People kept telling us that they saw us on CNN when we were in Atlanta and Dallas."

In the battle of the jeans, both designers had impressive first-year sales of more than $100 million. But retailers agreed that Tommy Jeans, by measures of sales and buzz, had outpaced Polo Jeans, winning the first round of the jeans war.

IRONICALLY, WHILE TOMMY AND Ralph had been preoccupied with polishing their images to perfection, they failed to realize that despite all that slick marketing, most young shoppers could hardly tell them apart.

Such were the fashion prerogatives evident on the evening of November 17, 1997, in New York at the Barnes & Noble store in Union Square, where Tommy Hilfiger was appearing in person to sign his new coffee-table book, *American Style*. Barnes & Noble was draped in full Tommy regalia that night, as the soundtrack blared Hilfiger's theme song, "Young Americans" by David Bowie, and while the salesclerks scurried about in Tommy khakis and pinstripe shirts. What was most striking was the way the young people came dressed—in either Tommy or Polo or a bit of both.

Damani Davy and two of his Long Island high school buddies were the first to arrive at Barnes & Noble, displaying their addiction to their main man. Davy, a lanky seventeen-year-old, wore Hilfiger's puffy vest and baggy corduroys sliding down to his hips, revealing "Tommy Hilfiger" on the waistband of his underwear. "Tommy captured street kids 'cause that is mostly who supported him," Davy said. "He gave us what we want to wear, like baggy clothes, lots of color, and reflectors on the back of the jackets." Next to him stood Errol Sanders, in a Polo Sport baseball cap, who chimed in, "Tommy isn't gassed up. He *remembers* who put him there."

Further back in line was Matt Spiro, a thirteen-year-old squirt of a kid with Buster Brown bangs, whose baggy pants, sweater, and jacket all had "Polo Sport" or "Ralph Lauren" logos. Spiro spoke up: "I want to be a designer so I study all the fashion stuff. Ralph Lauren is my favorite. I'm not *really* a big Tommy Hilfiger fan. I have Polo everything—shoes, pants, and underwear"—and one hundred shares of Polo Ralph Lauren Corp. stock. "I bought it the first day it came out at $26," he bragged coolly. "I think it's up around $28 now."

So why had little Mr. Polo bothered to show up for Tommy Night? "I like Tommy, too. He seems more down to earth than Ralph Lauren," Spiro said. "The great thing about Tommy is that he knows what people want."

Behind Spiro stood a handsome guy in a black turtleneck with an RL logo who looked just like Tyson, the Polo Sport model. Tyson's twin, whose name was Edmond, had this to say: "I like Tommy, but I gotta support my boy Tyson, who is the first black person who ever modeled for Ralph Lauren. Tommy uses more black models; I'd rather support him than Ralph. And I do have on Tommy Hilfiger underwear tonight."

So Edmond, like the others, was an equal-opportunity consumer. Nevertheless, he wasn't swallowing all the hype. "The best jeans are still Levi's," he insisted.

IT WAS INEVITABLE that the like-minded designers would finally collide. In the summer of 1997, Hilfiger and Polo ran virtually the same magazine ad with the same model, Letitia, on the beach. In Hilfiger's version, Letitia wore red, white, and blue men's underwear while Polo's ad featured her in a red, white, and blue swimsuit. "I don't know how it happened, but I freaked when I saw it," said Toth, whose agency created Hilfiger's ad. "And I bet that Ralph did, too."

TOMMY HILFIGER WAS in high-fashion heaven in November 1997. He finally had his answer to Ralph's Madison Avenue flagship—his own little White House in Beverly Hills. At the corner of swank Rodeo Drive and Santa Monica Boulevard, Hilfiger built from the ground up a two-story federalist-style fortress with columns and a rotunda dome, in spanking white limestone, at a cost of $20 million. With flags flying on top, it jumped out on the block with Chanel, Giorgio Armani—and Polo, which was located just two doors away.

With its pale pearwood fixtures, enameled "Tommy White" walls, and a grand, winding staircase, the store was an inviting place to shop—and to dine, in the upstairs café run by restaurateur Wolfgang Puck. Hanging on the walls were Andy Warhol originals from Hilfiger's private collection, including a portrait of Mick Jagger, Tommy's neighbor on Mustique island. A glimmering, custom-made Harley-Davidson, parked on the first floor, was for sale for $40,000.

The shop was loaded with apparel for men, women, children, and infants—not to mention Tommy's new, top-drawer $1,200 cashmere sportcoats called Hilfiger, which were made in Italy.

To celebrate his Beverly Hills moment, Hilfiger went for the full-court press. The buzz began on Sunday, November 9, when the *Los Angeles Times Magazine* put Tommy's toothy mug on the cover, with the headline: "Tommy Hilfiger 90210." On Tuesday night, Tommy chatted it up with Sinbad, the host of *Vibe*, the late-night TV talk show. *USA Today*'s cover story on Thursday proclaimed: "It's the Tommy life everyone seems to clamor for now."

Friday night was the curtain-raiser for the Sunday store opening. Hilfiger co-chaired a black-tie benefit and auction at the Century Plaza Hotel, where 1,500 guests, including Dustin Hoffman, Sidney Poitier,

Sean Penn, and Russell Simmons, were entertained by Sheryl Crow and Natalie Cole. Before dinner, there was a fashion show with celebrity models who wore Hilfiger's madras shorts and "huge fit" jeans.

Tommy emceed the show: "Here comes Emily Marcus from *Moesha*! Here's Aleca Donna from *Clueless.* We have Peter Paul, one of my top models in New York, who is an upcoming rap star. Show it to them! Allll-right!" Finally, Hilfiger hit the runway himself, on the arm of supermodel Naomi Campbell. The event was taped and aired later on VH-1, the cable TV music station.

The next morning, Hilfiger, in a crisp navy blazer and chinos, took the press on a tour of his new Beverly Hills digs. Checking out the parked limos and all the hubbub on the corner were the salespeople at Polo, who were naturally quite curious. Ralph had never deigned to put himself and Tommy in the same league, let alone on the same block. But on Rodeo Drive, Tommy was looking good. "People around here were a little worried about Tommy coming here at first," a pretty brunette saleswoman in Polo's shoe department said. "I told the store manager that we need to stock more boots and lug-sole shoes, you know, for all the urban customers who will now be shopping on our block."

After a full week of seducing L.A., Tommy headed back to New York, planning to cram more into his schedule now that he was a client of the William Morris Agency, which was developing movie, music, and publishing projects for him.

The Hilfiger organization was right on track in its growth strategy, which was built around a twenty-five-year plan. Horowitz explained in 1997, "It's a generational thing. It's inevitable. The next generation doesn't want to wear what their parents did and that's how we've planned it. Everybody compares us to Ralph. Well, that's fine because we went into this saying, 'We're the next generation Ralph Lauren, because what better model to follow?'

"We're now about halfway there, so we're starting to see how this all works," Horowitz continued. "Ralph has confronted that. He had to look in the mirror. He did some great things reinventing himself with Polo Sport. Not many people are able to do that. But he built such a solid foundation that even with some jolts along the way, he was able to withstand that and come back strong. We're not in that league yet. But that's where we want to be."

Style marches on, indeed.

AS INGENIOUS MARKETERS backed with solid businesses, Lauren and Hilfiger have designed fashion machines that hum to the pace of modern times. Nevertheless, they will always be challenged to stay on their toes. In 2000 and beyond, Lauren will have to find more ways to captivate Generation X shoppers, while Hilfiger will be pressed to grow along with the young consumers he won over in the 1990s.

Silas Chou is nonetheless convinced that Hilfiger has real staying power. "Maybe we can break this tableau of apparel companies lasting for no more than two generations," he observes. "All the brand names of the past history always stick with a snobbish image. We never built our image on snob appeal and people don't wear Tommy for snobbish reasons. They wear Tommy to have individuality. And luckily, that has coincided with the whole society's transformation."

Truly, society had been transformed, as more people no longer felt compelled to choose between one designer and another. Inevitably, the most formidable competition for Tommy and Ralph was coming from the Gap, and its sister stores Banana Republic and Old Navy, which had brilliantly staked their claim on the American look at lower prices. The Gap divisions had proven that they could have the same clout and cachet with consumers that designer names once had.

What is now critical is the force of personality driving the Tommy and Ralph brands. Can these one-time outsiders continue to cast their spell of insiderness, making the American dream of belonging that much more real and accessible to their followers? If consumers believe in the power of Old Glory, the answer is incredibly clear.

chapter 4

WHAT BECOMES A LEGEND MOST? WHEN GIORGIO ARMANI TAKES HOLLYWOOD

The press gives the readers a distorted image of fashion. They portray it as a world full of mad people who dress imaginary women and men. This is the antithesis of my way of presenting fashion.

GIORGIO ARMANI, July 30, 1998

The Emporio Armani concert on September 12, 1996, was some enchanted evening, even by New York standards. The heat began to rise after 9 P.M., when Lauryn Hill and the Fugees were rocking the stage with their hip-hop version of "Killing Me Softly," the Roberta Flack ballad. The trio was pumping to a groove that sparked a spontaneous eruption in the audience. One by one, spectators sprang to their feet, singing along and bopping in the aisles.

Before leaving the stage, the Fugees gathered at the microphone to give a "shout out" to their fashionable host for the evening: "We just wanna thank Armani for giving a few kids from the ghetto some great suits."

Amid the partying people, about four rows back, stood Giorgio Armani, roaring with glee and blowing kisses toward the stage. The concert was crackling with energy, coming together just the way he had intended. The unscripted plug from the Fugees was sublime, as were the compliments that came later from actress Mira Sorvino. Those kudos telegraphed a powerful message: A lot of very cool people dig Giorgio Armani. And the veteran fashion warrior could look forward to getting even more pop from the event, which would replay to millions on VH-1, the cable network that bought the rights to televise the concert.

The night was another big score for the Milanese maestro of fashion. Armani had come to Manhattan that fall to christen two new flagships on Madison Avenue. The champagne started to flow on September 10, when Armani invited the press for cocktails, and a hundred celebrity friends for supper at his sleek, eponymous boutique at Sixty-fifth Street, where affluent boomers could get their fill of $2,500 "black label" Armani suits.

A couple of days later came the big moment to celebrate the opening of Emporio Armani, at Fifty-eighth and Madison, a sort of "Armani-lite," where thirty-somethings could cop Italian style in an $800 suit. Emporio was Armani's bridge to the future, and he went all out to create a memorable night that would generate lots of buzz.

The Emporio Armani concert was billed as a "high-energy, high-volume celebration of style." Manhattan's legendary florist and party-planner, Robert Isabell, and the Armani people had turned the cavernous, Twenty-sixth Street Armory on Lexington Avenue into a swank cocktail lounge. Cantilevered tiers were carpeted to create a cozy theater where guests sat on thick pillows across from small tables lit with votive candles. A platoon of gorgeous hunks in black T-shirts delivered drinks, and circulated trays of dim sum and skewered chicken.

The sixty-two-year-old Armani, dashing with his deep tan, snowy hair, and true-blue eyes, brimmed with vitality. He showed off his trim, disco body in a snug navy T-shirt and flat-front pants. Starting at 7:30 P.M., the fashion host with the most stood guard at the entrance, where he reached out to shake each and every hand of his thousand invited guests: the downtown club kids, the fashion industry crowd, and enough famous faces to give the paparazzi whiplash, including Arnold Schwarzenegger, Mike Tyson, Robert De Niro, Lauren Bacall, Quincy Jones, Michael Keaton, Spike Lee, Pat Reilly, Winona Ryder, Caroline Kennedy and her brother, John F. Kennedy Jr., and Sarah Ferguson, Duchess of York.

The program served up an eclectic mix from pop music's cutting edge: Hill and the Fugees, Jakob Dylan and the Wallflowers, D'Angelo, Me'Shell Ndegéocello, along with guitarist Eric Clapton, an Armani buddy and walking billboard for the designer. Rounding out the evening was a fashion show, of course, and a wacky video starring Jennifer Tilly as a big-haired mall rat who suddenly turned chic, thanks to the fashion wizardry of "Salvation Armani." After a pasta buffet, everyone moved onto the dance floor, where Armani was still working up a sweat around 2 A.M.

Armani was most definitely in The Zone. He stayed up late to play the evening for all it was worth, an estimated $2 million. A *major* splurge. And a huge shot in the arm at a critical juncture. The triumph proved once more that Giorgio Armani, the man and the brand, was still kicking, amid the onslaught of Gucci, Prada, and Dolce & Gabbana, the latest fashion flavors of the season.

The party was also a testament to Armani's ability to enliven his persona without the direction of Gabriella Forte, the steely executrix who had been the custodian of the Armani image and his conduit to the press for more than fifteen years. In the spring of 1994, Forte had shocked her boss when she bolted for a bigger job: president of Calvin Klein Inc. Armani was livid when he found out she was leaving. "He recruits my people, my collections," Armani snapped to *Women's Wear Daily.* "Next he will be calling me up to head his design studio!"

Forte's sudden resignation stung Armani badly, but a decade before he had recovered from a blow far greater. In 1985, Sergio Galleoti, Armani's dynamic co-founder and intimate friend, died after a long illness. It was Galleoti, a former architectural draftsman, who had encouraged Armani to go out on his own. Together they had pooled a $10,000 investment to open Giorgio Armani SpA, in 1975.

Armani called his relationship with Galleoti one of "great complicity." Each partner resided in his own apartment at the company's Milan headquarters, a magnificent seventeenth-century palazzo on Via Borgunuovo. Pushy and outgoing, Galleoti deftly handled the company's business side, freeing up the serious and reserved Armani to design in his studio.

Galleoti's death was a defining passage in Armani's life. Compelled to tend to the business matters of his burgeoning fashion house from then on, Armani plotted for the long term, positioning the company to be a trademark that didn't depend on the talents of any one individual.

Armani, who would turn sixty-five in 1999, had begun to make the difficult transition of letting go, of delegating more responsibilities to his younger staffers and giving them more credit in public. "For the moment, they still count on me," he said in March 1997. "But I think it is dangerous to depend on the health of one person and that is why I want to depersonalize the house." Armani made such a gesture later that year when, for the first time, he took his runway bow alongside the members of his menswear design team.

And after all those uptight years, Armani was finally ready to loosen up. "I had an image that was too serious—like I was on a pedestal," he reflected in March 1997. "I now feel more at ease, without having a filter, a barrier. I have changed a lot . . . I now take the opportunity to smile."

To be sure, Armani's personal makeover made him more daring. His decision to elevate his profile with the Emporio concert in 1996 was a gamble, especially since the Armani image was about a mature, timeless style. He was way outside of his box in his quest to cultivate a younger, downtown image. But Armani had managed to pull off a glamorous, laid-back event where he came across as effortless and clever—and not as some old fool trying too hard. The party, he revealed months later, "felt very young and it was great fun. There were all the celebrities and it had the *feeling* of Armani. This was one of those influential events that people remember for a long time."

The payoff was both psychic and tangible—the TV coverage, scads of press, and an overflow of goodwill. Clearly, the Italian master who spoke hardly any English was fluent in the language of high-fashion marketing.

Since the early eighties, Giorgio Armani had been one of the world's best-selling designers, a creator who was equal parts steak and sizzle—fashion and marketing. But long before he created a fashion empire and became an icon to the stars, Armani could claim the title of fashion revolutionary. In 1975, he opened his fashion house with a radically chic look: the unconstructed suit, whose slouchy jacket with sloping lapels hung like a sweater. Armani's signature style blurred the distinction between sportswear and business suits by taking linings and shoulder pads out of jackets, the creases out of trousers, and the starch out of shirt collars. His suits came in featherweight wools, cashmeres, and linens, all textured and patterned in shades of taupe and gray. Those supple materials draped and rumpled gracefully, giving men a comfortable, effortless sophistication. And setting himself apart from the rest of high fashion, Armani consistently manufactured high-quality tailored garments on an industrial scale. Nobody did it better, retailers agreed.

Barneys New York was the first American retailer to take a flier on

Armani. In 1976, Barneys' owner, Fred Pressman, ordered a shipment of the rumpled suits, confident that Barneys' progressive clientele would go for Armani, which they did. Barneys' success goaded Saks Fifth Avenue, Bloomingdale's, and swank haberdashers, including Louis of Boston, to do the same. But the most powerful magnet for the designer turned out to be Hollywood. In the 1980 movie *American Gigolo*, actor Richard Gere, playing a swaggering Beverly Hills stud, was a walking Armani fashion show. Best fashion moment: the scene where Gere lovingly tossed a rainbow of folded shirts across a bed. The close-up revealed the Giorgio Armani label inside the neck.

Gigolo put Armani on the public's radar. The next year, Armani's annual sales were an impressive $90 million. From Hollywood to Wall Street to the regular Joe on the street, men of all pinstripes got into the Armani habit. It was amusing to hear men get so worked up over clothes. Mark Girman, an owner of two car washes in Pittsburgh, told *The Wall Street Journal* that Armani had changed his life. After seeing Gere in *Gigolo*, Girman took a new fashion turn. Nine years later, the car-wash connoisseur had collected twenty-five suits, many shirts and ties, an overcoat, and eight pairs of shoes—all by Armani.

Armani had cast the same spell over a new generation of executive women who were unimpressed with the fussy, figure-molding haute couture that was coming out of Paris. Armani's soft, comfortable tailoring went over big in a feminist age; a lady in Armani was sophisticated, and breathing easy—even after a heavy meal. Armani's pantsuits were the pinnacle of power dressing, a conservative yet polished look that CNN anchorwoman Willow Bay liked to wear on camera. "Armani is safe," Bay told *Harper's Bazaar*. Most women appreciated that Armani didn't startle them with unusual new styles every year. "Change has to be subtle," Armani once said. "When a woman alters her look too much from season to season, she becomes a fashion victim."

All you had to say was "Armani"—as generic as Kleenex—and the name instantly conjured the image of modern élan. "Giorgio Armani changed the whole notion of the way the world dresses," said Patrick McCarthy of *Women's Wear Daily.* Italian knitwear designer Rosita Missoni, whose own colorful sweaters were also fashion classics, gushed succinctly: "Armani put women in men's clothes. He is a *genius.*"

ARMANI MAY HAVE invented the unconstructed suit, but he didn't own it for long. In fashion, imitation has always been the fastest path to popularity, and Armani knockoffs popped up faster than dandelions in a backyard. Since the 1980s, scores of Seventh Avenue apparel makers had come out with their versions, which they invariably touted as "*our* Armani jacket." Macy's coattailed the trend with an Italian-style brand whose name rang a bell: "Alfani." And fashionable women on a budget knew where to go shopping: the Calvin Klein department, where high-quality Armani-like suits were priced at least 20 percent lower than the real thing.

Knockoffs would always be a source of validation—and irritation—for Armani. The designer grew more exasperated as others kept taking his ideas to the bank. Armani got so fed up by the fall of 1982 that he abruptly called off his October fashion show. He was incensed because the press refused to play *his* way. In order to get a running start on the knockoffs, Armani tried to convince fashion writers attending his show to hold off writing their reviews until his merchandise had safely arrived at stores months later. No way, the fashion press balked, calling his worries a case of "Armanoia."

But Armani's tantrum was just another melodrama for the gossip columns that soon blew over. The next year he was back to his runway ritual and on July 19, 1983, *The New York Times* reported: "The news was from Europe and most of it had to do with Giorgio Armani, the Italian designer who said he would never stage a fashion show ever again in his life. Well, Mr. Armani did have a fashion show and his collection looks like a winner."

So Armani got real and focused on his designing. A decade later, no longer fretting about knockoffs, he had the gumption to knock himself off. At the suggestion of Colombe Nicholas, who was president of Armani's U.S. division at the time, Armani hired a relatively inexperienced talent, a twenty-three-year-old black American named Patrick Robinson, to design the copies. Nicholas auditioned several job candidates by requisitioning sketches of an imaginary Armani collection. Robinson's sketches were by far the best, in the true spirit of Armani, she said. Gabriella Forte agreed, and told a euphoric Robinson, "I know that Giorgio will just *love* you."

Robinson, a Californian who graduated from Parsons School of Design in New York, moved to Milan in February 1992 to take the $80,000-a-year position as design director for Le Collezioni, Armani's second-tier women's label, priced a notch below his top collection, which everybody in the know referred to simply as "black label," because the label inside was black with white lettering. Armani's black label became the gold standard that none other than Ralph Lauren would imitate when he came out with his "Purple Label" top-drawer suits tailored in England.

"The years I spent at Armani were the best training that a designer could ever have," explained Robinson, who spent his first month in Milan meeting with Armani every day. After that, the boss left him on his own. Yet Armani insisted that Robinson do what Armani himself had done in the 1960s: learn the craft first and the design second. So Robinson commuted regularly to nearby Turin to study how the clothes were made inside the factories owned by Gruppo GFT, the manufacturer licensed to make Le Collezioni.

"Armani taught me that the technical people in the factories aren't always so good at fitting clothes," Robinson reminisced. "Armani knows the way a jacket is supposed to look. He doesn't say, 'It should be twenty-three inches.' He can just look at something on a hanger and tell you that it should fall *this way*."

From the outset, sales of Le Collezioni "went through the roof," Nicholas remembered. Soon, Le Collezioni surpassed black label to become the core of Armani's women's-wear business. "Patrick understood the Armani look completely and they were in perfect synch. But then again, Patrick *did* have a great master to interpret."

Robinson characterized Armani as the consummate perfectionist, who didn't mince words. "We had our yelling fits. Did he *yell*!" he remembered, laughing. "But Armani was pretty cool and pretty amazing. He's running this huge empire all in his head. He knows everything, what every little string is doing. He's in *complete* control." (Robinson resigned from Armani in 1994 to design the Anne Klein collection in New York.)

Successful as Le Collezioni was, Armani would always be wary of his competitors. "I pay attention to what's being copied because I always need to keep a distance," Armani explained.

And to Armani, distance—in terms of design—meant centimeters and not miles. Never one to jump onto the latest runway trends, Armani preferred to stay put, to recycle his core silhouettes, with only a few modifications each season. It didn't hurt, of course, that Armani kept designing plenty of good looks worth repeating.

While Armani's approach seemed pretty logical, this wasn't the usual way high fashion worked. In the 1990s, more designers fell into the habit of shock therapy: runway collections that were provocative, outlandish—and thrilling—to fashion editors who lauded them for moving fashion "forward."

But not Armani. Like Lauren and Hilfiger, Armani knew his customers depended on his surefooted styles, which they continued to buy, knockoffs notwithstanding. His business kept growing steadily, and during most of the 1990s Armani reigned as *the* top-selling designer brand at Saks Fifth Avenue and Neiman Marcus.

As he flaunted fashion's conventions, Armani epitomized the end of fashion. Sophisticated people no longer cared if fashion moved forward or backward; they just wanted fashion to provide them with attractive clothes suited for modern living. Armani's uncontrived, antifashion stance dovetailed with the zeitgeist of casual dressing. People now wore fashion *their* way, like journalist Carl Bernstein, who told *The Wall Street Journal* that he liked to pair his $1,500 Armani jackets with beat-up jeans.

"Fashion is finished, for me the *diktat* is finished," Armani declared to *New York* in September 1997. "That is, 'this is fashion and you must dress this way'—it's finished. Fashion is what a woman makes. She puts on an Armani jacket, a skirt by Gigli. This is fashion."

But the irony of this antifashion philosophy was that it took so long to take hold. While Armani's unconstructed suits were new and original in 1975, variations of his look continued to remain in style for two decades. What's more, he built his billion-dollar empire largely through the sales of expensive clothes—and not perfumes, jeans, and underwear, the way Calvin Klein did.

Firmly established as a high-fashion clothing brand from the start, Armani basked in that heady intangible known as mystique. Among top designers, mystique is usually fast and fleeting. But Armani had a secret weapon: celebrities, who are by far today's most powerful fashion role models to the masses. The whole world associated Armani with the rich and famous. When real estate agents and advertising executives saw how chic and sharp Glenn Close or Lauren Hutton looked in Armani, they went for Armani too.

From *Gigolo* to the Oscars, Armani benefited from a long-standing tradition of dressing the stars, a practice that over the years effectively transformed him and other designers into stars in their own right.

THE SYMBIOTIC RELATIONSHIP between fashion designers and Hollywood dated back to the 1950s, when couturier Hubert de Givenchy began his heady association with Audrey Hepburn, the world's most famous fashion role model of all time. By the late 1990s, many designers could brag that they dressed Sharon Stone, Gwyneth Paltrow, or some other ingenue of the moment. But "gilt by association" was only meaningful when such luminaries delivered the shoppers to the stores. And not many designers, or stars, could make that claim.

Armani could. He was the first designer to milk his celebrity connections by developing a publicity machine to get his clothes on the backs of Hollywood's most influential and most visible A-list of actors, directors, producers, and agents. Such headliners became an integral component of his master marketing plan to keep his trademark in lights.

The centerpiece of Armani's celebrity strategy was the Academy Awards, the biggest photo op of the year. After Armani opened a Beverly Hills boutique in 1988, the designer set out to become *the* designer of choice on Oscar night. By 1991, *WWD* called the Oscars "The Armani Awards," by virtue of the fact that everybody who was anybody was wearing Armani. After his Oscar coup, Armani developed a relationship with dozens of famous people who lived in his clothes and graced the events he hosted. At the October 1990 dinner he gave at New York's Museum of Modern Art to celebrate *Made in Milan,* a documentary on Armani directed by Martin Scorsese, there was a famous face everywhere you turned: Scorsese, Richard Gere, Cindy Crawford, John F. Kennedy Jr., Robert De Niro, and more. Such glitterati assured Armani of getting many mentions in the press and on TV, since his guests were exactly the people the public loved to see.

WHY DOES A celebrity endorsement have so much pull with consumers? "Celebrities work on another level because people think of them as real people more than models," said Martha Nelson, editor of *In Style.* "People have a history with them. With Demi Moore we think, 'I remember when she had that little haircut in *Ghost* and wasn't that amazing she got so buff for *Striptease*?' We feel that we have known her over a long period of time and there is an emotional connection."

In Style, which debuted in September 1994 with Annette Bening—wearing a navy Armani—on the cover, brilliantly tapped into the public's adulation of the style of celebrities. Publisher Time Inc. took a page from its winning formula at *People* and came up with a more fashionable hybrid. *In Style* featured celebrities in full-length shots, out on the town, behind the velvet rope at movie premieres, inside their fabulous homes—and of course, at awards shows like the Oscars. In a record three years, *In Style* had turned a profit, and by the end of 1997, the magazine had a paid circulation of more than 1 million.

As more affluent consumers got hooked on reading *In Style*, more fashion houses flocked to become advertisers in the magazine, led by Gianni Versace, who was one of the first designers to understand its powerful attraction.

"Versace loved the approach of *In Style*," noted Hal Rubenstein, veteran fashion reporter and Versace observer. "Versace thought that people were tired of looking at models. He understood that, oddly enough, movie stars look like real people. Their breasts aren't perfect, their hips are wide, they are more approachable and people relate to them."

Like Armani, Gianni Versace was early to beat a path to celebrities. Versace's association came quite naturally since so many of his signature items, such as shiny print silk shirts for men and skintight gowns for women, were made for the stage. Versace's main man was his close friend, singer Elton John, who sat in the front row of his fashion shows and showed up to knock out a few tunes to launch Versace's boutique on Fifth Avenue in the fall of 1996. Versace also put the stars to work as models for his advertising, including Madonna, the artist formerly known as Prince, and Courtney Love.

In the spirit of Armani, Versace had courted the flashiest of the famous, the likes of Sylvester Stallone, Tina Turner, and actress Elizabeth Hurley. And Versace was just as often linked to the infamous, such as Mike Tyson, who often wore Versace in public. Gianni Versace himself once bragged to a reporter that rapper Tupac Shakur "wore Versace on the day he walked into prison *and* on the day he walked out of prison." Fashion insiders liked to say that a rich man's wife wore Armani, while his mistress favored Versace.

In the aftermath of the murder of Gianni Versace in July 1997, the platinum-haired Donatella Versace, who took over designing for the eponymous house, continued to draw her late brother's celebrity mascots at fashion shows. Turning out for Donatella's first Paris couture show in July 1998 were Sean Puffy Combs, Melanie Griffith, and Jennifer Lopez, all decked out in Versace. Such stardust gilded the Versace trademark, as the fashion house claimed annual sales of more than $500 million in 1997.

So first it was Armani, followed by Versace, who set a new standard by using star power to achieve fashion horsepower, and the rest of the industry followed. The fact that Armani—who never spent much time in America and didn't speak English—managed to captivate all those celebrities, years ahead of such canny marketers as Calvin Klein, was the result not only of keen instincts about modern culture, but also of Italian sensibilities.

"The Italian designers have always been sharp in finding ways to reach the American public," said Sara Forden, a Milan-based reporter for *Women's Wear Daily*. "Italians are grounded in the American mentality and American habits. They are quick to spot what is hot, whether it's a business trend or a lifestyle trend."

Culturally, Italian fashion designers have gravitated toward Hollywood for a long time. Perhaps that is because Italy has always had its own homegrown film industry to promote. The 1950s and 1960s were the golden years of Cinecittà, the famous Rome studio that turned out a slew of international hits like *La Dolce Vita* and *L'Aventura*. Actors Sophia Loren, Gina Lollobrigida, and Marcello Mastroianni became world-class stars. "In Italy, we have no royalty like in France," observed Armando Branchini, a Milanese management consultant. "Movie stars are our royalty."

But inside the haughty Paris couture salons in the 1950s, movie stars weren't shining so brightly. In 1955, Christian Dior refused to provide a wedding gown for a movie starring Brigitte Bardot, who was a fast-rising star at the time. "There was no way Dior would risk incurring the displeasure of some of his most elegant clients by allowing his dresses to be put on vulgar display on the screen," wrote Marie-France Pochna, a Dior biographer. "Dior was a snob. He ranked living, breathing aristocrats far higher aesthetically than their pale imitations on stage and screen."

So while the couturiers staked their claim on European aristocracy and American socialites, the Italians looked up to the stars. When Italian high fashion was centered in Rome in the 1960s, Valentino Garavani, known simply as Valentino, became a favorite of the Hollywood jet set.

Besides being a talented couturier, the darkly handsome and heavy-lidded Valentino prevailed as fashion's most glamorous bon vivant—and the personification of *la dolce vita.* Amid the lush trappings of his yacht and palatial homes, Valentino loved to entertain on a grand scale, surrounded by such Hollywood legends as Elizabeth Taylor and Joan Collins, who were among his favorite clients. Valentino zeroed in on Sharon Stone, Hollywood's fashion plate of the 1990s. Sophia Loren was also among the galaxy of stars Valentino invited to his black-and-white ball to celebrate his thirtieth anniversary in business, where his clients Aretha Franklin and Bette Midler belted out a soulful "Happy Birthday." The 1992 gala was a reprise from a year earlier, when Valentino first celebrated his thirtieth anniversary at his magnificent villa in Rome, with an A-list of stars and European royalty in attendance.

VALENTINO SET A powerful example of Hollywood marketing for Armani, but it was Nino Cerruti, another charismatic Italian designer, who would first expose Armani to the world of movie stars. Armani worked as a design assistant for Cerruti from 1964 to 1970, during the time the house of Cerruti began dressing European actors on the screen.

Nino Cerruti was thirty years old in 1960 when he became the third-generation leader of Cerruti 1881, the Italian textile manufacturer famous for its fine wool fabrics. The young textile heir was all about style. At six two, he was a debonair Cary Grant type whose stunning wife, Chantall, was a former model for Balenciaga. Nino Cerruti relished his role as a menswear designer, in the forefront of the peacock revolution led by Pierre Cardin, whose sculpted suits were the rage of the sixties. Cerruti opened a posh menswear boutique in Paris in the 1960s that became his springboard for penetrating the movie studios in Rome, Paris, and Hollywood.

Cerruti had a penchant for theatrics. In the summer of 1958, he dreamed up a publicity stunt involving Anita Ekberg, the blonde bombshell who was riding high from her role in *La Dolce Vita,* the famous film satire about jet-set decadence starring Marcello Mastroianni. Cerruti hired Ekberg to help him introduce a new color called *battalion,* a greenish or petrol blue, in menswear.

First, Cerruti convinced Italian automaker Lancia to customize forty of its sleek "America" convertibles in the same shade. Cerruti remembered how easy this was: "Lancia charged us absolutely nothing. They did it just for the publicity. Imagine today going to a car manufacturer and telling him, 'Please paint me forty cars!' "

On the day of Cerruti's fashion show, a caravan of Lancias—each with a pretty model in a blue dress—cruised the streets of Rome, then rolled onto the Via Veneto, the famous trolling ground of local playboys and starlets, which had been blocked off to traffic for the occasion.

One Lancia was left on display inside the nearby Excelsior Hotel, where Cerruti 1881 was holding a menswear fashion show. Down the runway came the petrol blue suits, followed by Ekberg in a slinky blue number designed by Cerruti. She broke a bottle of champagne against the hood of the Lancia, as the paparazzi fired away. "That's how we launched the new color. It was very crazy. Very *Dolce Vita,*" Cerruti recalled. And the strategy worked, he maintained, recalling that many of the most fashionable men across Europe turned on to Cerruti blue that year.

Cerruti's Paris boutique, located on the bustling Place de Madelaine in the heart of the Right Bank shopping district, became famous for its exquisite tailoring, and drew actors Terence Stamp, Michael Caine, and Jean-Paul Belmondo, who became regulars. Orson Welles ordered his hats from Cerruti. Before long, Cerruti was dressing his famous clients in front of the camera as well. In 1965, Cerruti outfitted Belmondo and Alain Delon in sharp double-breasted suits for the French production *Borsalino.* Throughout the 1970s, Cerruti's clothes appeared in several French and Italian movies, worn by actors Yves Montand, Catherine Deneuve, and Liv Ullmann.

Giorgio Armani entered the picture in 1964, when Cerruti hired him to design a new menswear line called Hitman. The son of a transport company manager from Piacenza, not far from Milan, Armani arrived at Cerruti 1881 after first dropping out of medical school. He shifted into the world of fashion, spending six years as a window dresser and buyer at the Rinascente department store. Cerruti remembered being impressed by Armani's serious, professional demeanor and his drive to succeed. "What I could spot was that he had all the right sensibilities," Cerruti recalled.

At Cerruti 1881, Armani learned all about fabrics and manufacturing inside the company's factories. Armani said that his six years at Cerruti 1881 were "fruitful years. My experience with the firm's tradition definitely influenced the forging of my own career."

Having exited Cerruti 1881 in 1970 to lay the foundation for opening his own fashion house, Armani wasn't closely involved in Cerruti's movie projects, most of which occurred after he departed. But his seasoning at Cerruti 1881 obviously rubbed off, since Armani moved precipitously to cultivate Hollywood soon after he opened his own house. It came as no surprise to Cerruti to learn that Armani had been in his own business for barely three years when he designed the wardrobe for *American Gigolo.*

Armani flashed back to the time when John Travolta, who was originally cast to play the lead in *Gigolo,* came to Milan to be fitted for his film wardrobe. At the time, Armani didn't realize that Travolta was such a big deal. But one hot July afternoon when the two were kicking back at an outdoor café in the Piazza San Babila, Armani watched the Milanese on the street go crazy for the star of *Saturday Night Fever*. "People were all the way across the street yelling 'Travolta!' " Armani remembered.

Cerruti contended that his former charge was ambitious and a quick study. "Armani had already left when we began doing a lot of movies. But he has a way of knowing and of learning. Armani's approach to movies and his approach to celebrities were exactly the kinds of things we were doing when he was here."

Well, not exactly. From the beginning, Armani made the stars integral to his overall marketing game plan, whereas Cerruti didn't. While Cerruti basked in the reflected glory of the stars he dressed, Cerruti still remained largely anonymous to the American public. Nevertheless, Cerruti 1881 was a solid establishment and had grown into a $350 million-a-year business by the mid-1990s.

After *Gigolo*, Armani enjoyed another windfall of publicity for something he had nothing to do with: rumpled linen jackets with the sleeves pushed up, worn by Don Johnson and Philip-Michael Thomas, who played detectives in the eighties hit TV series *Miami Vice*. The show attracted millions of viewers who tuned in just to check out the clothes. Meanwhile, menswear retailers cashed in on the *Miami Vice* style of unconstructed blazers and pleated pants. The show's costume designers used many sources to outfit the actors. But most people outside the fashion industry weren't aware that it was Nino Cerruti who created *Miami Vice*'s original look. (Cerruti even won a Cutty Sark menswear fashion award for *Miami Vice*.) Most people associated the detective duo's continental élan with Armani, who dined off all the free publicity he was raking in from the series.

Taking a few cues from his famous protégé, Cerruti set out to win over Hollywood starting in 1986, when he hired a full-time publicist in Los Angeles. Cerruti's first movie assignment in America was outfitting

Michael Douglas and Kathleen Turner in *The Jewel of the Nile.* He had designed clothes for Turner in several other films and for her own personal wardrobe. She returned the favor by attending his fashion shows in Paris, becoming his first American muse. "Kathleen was very kind and very helpful to me," he said.

Cerruti thus became one of Hollywood's busiest tailors, commissioned to provide on-screen wardrobes for Jack Nicholson, Jeremy Irons, Clint Eastwood, and Harrison Ford, as well as Richard Gere in *Pretty Woman.* But Cerruti said he was also expected to give, in return for the privilege of dressing Hollywood's leading men. By the early 1990s, there was no shortage of fashion houses willing to bend over backward, ready to pay big bucks to get their styles on the likes of Harrison Ford. Film production companies, taking advantage of an oversupply of designers and an undersupply of big stars, became more demanding. "Hollywood is like a Turkish bazaar where they expect you to give 1,000 percent," Cerruti explained. "The productions used to pay for the clothes we made for the movie, but now we get a credit [at the end of the movie] in exchange for supplying the clothes for free."

But Armani still managed to drive a harder bargain because he had become almost as famous as the actors he outfitted. Armani didn't need to give away his clothes just to see his name roll by in type in the end credits, when moviegoers were filing out of the theater. Still, Armani obliged by giving a discount when his clothes were used in movies, such as *48 Hours* and *The Untouchables*, where his name was prominently featured—in the *opening* credits.

Armani was able to negotiate such visible plugs because by the mid-1980s, he was well on his way to becoming a household name. In addition to his movie projects, Armani had appeared on the cover of *Time* magazine in 1982. His PR people in Milan had already outfitted a number of stars like Glenn Close and Robert De Niro. So the Armani machine was up to speed when the designer opened his first boutique in Beverly Hills on Rodeo Drive in 1988. Armani dispatched Gabriella Forte to America to prepare for his West Coast coming out.

Forte was born in Italy but grew up in New York, where she used to run her own fashion PR firm, which made her the perfect go-between for Armani. She certainly lived up to her surname, which means "hard" or "strong." A dictatorial taskmaster, Forte was known to terrorize employees with her profanity-laced tirades. A petite, broad-faced woman who wore her long black hair in a severe center part, Forte was the *voice* of Armani. She fielded most press calls, furnishing pithy quotes which she attributed to Armani. Steeped in the world of Armani, she wound up marrying Eddie Glantz, a New Yorker who had been a member of Armani's menswear design team in Milan since 1979, the same year Forte joined the company.

Forte was indispensable in bringing Hollywood to Armani. She had become chummy with Jay Cocks, a former film critic who covered Armani for *Time*, who introduced her to many movie people whom she steered into Armani's world. "Gabriella is a true movie buff, and she loved to work with the stars," recalled Pier Filipo Pieri, a publicist who worked for Forte from 1984 to 1989. After Pieri handled the arrangements to send Glenn Close an Armani gown to wear for a big event in Washington, she sent him a huge bowl of red tulips and a gracious note of thanks.

In searching for a West Coast representative, Forte knew Armani was more impressed with pedigree than an impressive résumé. First and foremost, high fashion had always been a business of relationships. The famous houses in Paris and Milan were great believers in hiring fancy foot soldiers to link them to the upper reaches of the upper crust. More often than not, the Europeans recruited countesses or marquesses, or other outgoing ladies who were already entrenched in the international social

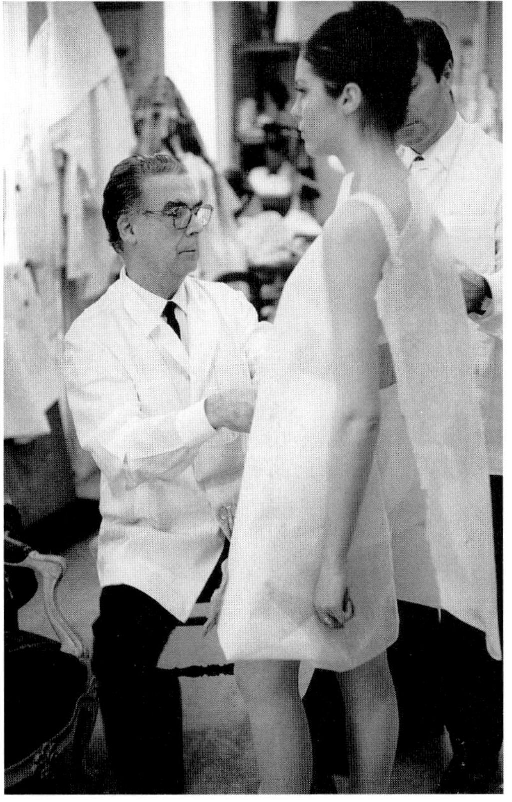

Emanuel Ungaro, with a model in one of his signature couture gowns, in his Paris studio in 1988. PHOTO BY DERRY MOORE

Cristobal Balenciaga, the world's most revered couturier and mentor to Emanuel Ungaro, at his Paris atelier, 1960. "One never knew what one was going to see at a Balenciaga opening. One fainted. It was possible to blow up and die," gushed Diana Vreeland in her 1984 memoir D.V. PHOTO BY HENRI CARTIER-BRESSON, MAGNUM PHOTOS

Now that's Italian! Giorgio Armani with Sophia Loren at the September 12, 1996, concert extravaganza he threw to celebrate the opening of Emporio Armani in New York. The cost of the party: $2 million. PHOTO BY KEVIN MAZUR, COURTESY OF GIORGIO ARMANI

At the 1996 Emporio party, Giorgio Armani and Pat Reilly, the National Basketball Association's most valuable fashion plate who inspired American men to get into the Armani habit. PHOTO BY KEVIN MAZUR, COURTESY OF GIORGIO ARMANI

Giorgio Armani and Glenn Close, one of his earliest celebrity role models on September 12, 1996. Armani's clothes "go with my philosophy of simple, unadorned elegance," Close said. PHOTO BY KEVIN MAZUR, COURTESY OF GIORGIO ARMANI

Nino Cerruti staged a paparazzi moment with La Dolce Vita *star Anita Ekberg, who modeled "battalion" blue at his menswear fashion show in Rome, 1958. Cerruti was one of the first designers to recruit movie stars to promote his name.* COURTESY OF NINO CERRUTI

President Bill Clinton, Ralph Lauren, and Hillary Rodham Clinton in front of the Star-Spangled Banner, at the National Museum of American History in July 1998. Lauren's fashion house donated $13 million to restore the 185-year-old flag.
PHOTO BY JEFF TINSLEY, COURTESY OF THE NATIONAL MUSEUM OF AMERICAN HISTORY, SMITHSONIAN INSTITUTION

Rapper Snoop Dogg with Tommy Hilfiger inside his New York showroom in 1994. Snoop wore a Hilfiger rugby shirt on Saturday Night Live, *which did the trick to inspire youth all across America to go shopping for their own Tommys.*
PHOTO BY MARTHA SWOPE, MARTHA SWOPE ASSOCIATES CAROL ROSEGG, COURTESY OF TOMMY HILFIGER CORP.

Swaddled in silk. Lauren Hutton, Zoran, and Isabella Rossellini, 1992.

PHOTO BY ERIC BOMAN

Saks Fifth Avenue newspaper ad for Zoran, fall 1998.

PHOTO BY SKREBNESKI, COURTESY OF SAKS FIFTH AVENUE

LVMH chairman Bernard Arnault and his wife, Hélène, congratulate Michael Kors backstage after his fashion show for Celine, in Paris on October 17, 1998. With Kors, Arnault finally found a designer who craved commercial success—and not just artistic acclaim. "Fashion is creativity, with the goal of having as many customers as possible," Arnault said. PHOTO BY BERTRAND RINDOFF-PETROFF, COURTESY OF CELINE

In a New York state of mind: Donna Karan and Barbra Streisand, 1993.
PHOTO BY JORN BARRETT, COURTESY OF GLOBE PHOTOS, INC.

After his 1988 debut collection, a star was born. Isaac Mizrahi reclined at the feet of supermodel Dalma, who wears his jumpsuit on the May 2, 1988, cover of W. PHOTO BY GEORGE CHINSEE, *W*/FAIRCHILD PUBLICATIONS

Body double: Ralph Lauren and Tommy Hilfiger party in pinstripes at the Fresh Air Fund benefit on June 9, 1995, in New York. PHOTO BY GEORGE CHINSEE, *WOMEN'S WEAR DAILY*/FAIRCHILD PUBLICATIONS

Fashion with wit and a sense of irony. Advertisements for Target Stores and Marshall Field's in Chicago, which are both owned by Dayton Hudson Corp.

COURTESY OF DAYTON HUDSON CORP.

whirl. At Yves Saint Laurent, for example, the position of *couture directrice* went to Baroness Hélène de Ludinghausen, a descendant of the Russian Stroganoff family, who gave the culinary world its famous beef Stroganoff.

In 1981, Armani enlisted Lee Radziwill, the former princess and sister of Jacqueline Kennedy Onassis, to be his "special events" coordinator on the East Coast, and it would be Radziwill who would suggest a candidate for the Beverly Hills position. Radziwill had mentioned the job to her niece Maria Shriver, who told her close friend, Wanda McDaniel, a former society columnist for the *Los Angeles Herald Examiner* and one of Shriver's bridesmaids when she married Arnold Schwarzenegger.

Blond and fetching, McDaniel, the wife of Al Ruddy, a Hollywood producer whose credits included *The Godfather,* was pretty much the ideal candidate. A graduate of the top-ranked University of Missouri School of Journalism, she had the instincts of a reporter, and she was already hooked into Hollywood. After Forte met with McDaniel, she sent her to Milan to get Armani's final approval. McDaniel then returned to Beverly Hills, where she got down to business.

Forte told her to feel free to pick any title she wanted. But McDaniel preferred not to use a title. She explained to the *Los Angeles Times*, "It'll be a real hands-on job. I'll hostess lunches for the new Armani shop opening on Rodeo, help get Armani clothes in films and generally be a sort of ambassadress."

When Giorgio Armani on Rodeo Drive opened in August 1988, McDaniel got off to a fast start. The first "shopping party" she organized for the boutique was covered by Marylouise Oates, a columnist at the *Los Angeles Times*. One of the first to arrive was producer Dawn Steel, an Armani devotee who just happened to be one of the most powerful women in Hollywood. The day's heavy hitter was Barbara Sinatra, who, Oates reported, "bought up a storm, at least fifteen pieces," while Shriver dropped by with Schwarzenegger and purchased a rose-colored suit.

Given Armani's strength in menswear, McDaniel concentrated on finding a high-profile man to become a billboard for Armani. Choosing the right person wasn't so easy. In 1985, Armani reportedly tried to woo up-and-comer Kevin Costner for one of his advertising campaigns, but Costner turned him down. Actors were accustomed to being hounded by publicists to hawk all kinds of products, and the most serious, intellectual actors weren't interested in being flacks for fashion. Those were the most difficult ones, and they were precisely the types whom Armani wanted to wear his clothes—the actors who seemed to be above it all, yet were still highly visible. As it turned out, the first celebrity Armani would sign up wouldn't even come from Hollywood.

McDaniel set her sights on Pat Reilly, the Los Angeles Lakers basketball coach, who had already been wearing Armani for years. Reilly was a prime catch who had everything going for him. The National Basketball Association was making a resurgence, and the Lakers, led by its famous center, Magic Johnson, were a hot, winning team. Reilly's public profile soared with the Lakers' five NBA championships, and, as luck would have it, Reilly moved on to coach the New York Knicks, another popular team that always made it to the playoffs, and whose hometown just happened to be America's fashion and media capital. (Reilly would remain in the spotlight after he left New York in 1995 to coach the Miami Heat.)

The rugged-handsome Reilly was a fashion role model right out of central casting, a real man's man. Reilly's coat-and-tie years in Catholic schools had left him with perfect carriage and impeccable grooming habits. With his slicked-back hair and manly swagger, Reilly, at six-four, was a sharp dresser with an innate sense of style. "My players always called me *GQ*," he said, laughing, referring to the men's fashion magazine. Reilly was already wearing Armani in the early 1980s when he and his wife were passing through Milan and decided to pay a visit to Armani's showroom. "I always liked his clothes," he said. Reilly didn't get to meet the designer on that trip, but soon he would get to know him quite well.

In January 1990, *GQ* put Reilly in Armani on its cover—which was around the time when McDaniel and Forte first sat down with him and made a proposition: Armani wanted Reilly to be on his team. The relationship started out slowly. Armani initially provided the coach with a couple of customized suits in 56 Long (Italian size), and then everyone waited to see what would happen.

The reaction was swift, as Reilly turned out to be a slam-dunk. The NBA season stretched out over many months and Reilly was constantly on the radar. Whenever the Lakers played, the TV cameras planted at courtside captured Reilly pacing up and down, so spiffy in those suits with the sloping lapels. Sports commentators began to pepper their play-by-play banter with asides about Reilly's wardrobe. Before long, every coach and player in the NBA began to spruce up. They all wanted to be like Reilly, the NBA's most valuable fashion plate. And so did thousands of basketball fans, who started filling their closets with Armani suits.

The natty coach, who described himself as a conservative dresser, preferred Armani's classic one-button navy suits, with Armani's white shirts and subtly patterned ties. Armani's tailors, he said, "made an adjustment in the jacket because I like the button stance right below the buckle."

He emphasized that he wasn't on Armani's payroll, that he was more like an "unofficial spokesman." Each year, both Reilly and his wife, Chris, received a free Armani wardrobe, and the coach gladly obliged to show up for Armani-sponsored charity events and store openings. Armani also flew Reilly to Milan to sit in the front row at his fashion shows. That was hardly a chore; Reilly admitted that he loved to study the clothes Armani sent down the runway.

And indeed, Armani's runway presentations were like no other in fashion. Armani never hired supermodels nor did he use jazzy theatrics, both of which would detract from his low-key designs. Every Armani fashion show, whether in Milan or on the road, required the installation of a special runway—*la pedana*—a long path of frosted tiles that are lit from underneath in order to fully illuminate the textured fabrics, details, and muted shades.

In the 1990s, Armani's fashion presentations became chockablock with the famous—Martin Scorsese, Robert De Niro, Sophia Loren, Isabella Rossellini, and Lauren Hutton—sitting ducks posing to be shot by the paparazzi. Armani flew his VIPs over first class and put them up at one of Milan's top hotels, usually the Principe e Savoia, a few minutes from Armani's headquarters. Then Armani's public relations staffers coddled his special guests, squiring them around Milan to go sightseeing, shopping, and nightclubbing.

Meanwhile, the workaholic designer remained sequestered in his studio, unavailable to meet with his invitees until after his show, when he usually hosted a dinner in his apartment at his headquarters. Armani rarely vacationed with his clients like Versace or Valentino did. Only a few—Michelle Pfeiffer, Eric Clapton, and Lauren Hutton—have visited his beachfront vacation hideaway in Pantelleria, Italy.

It would always be difficult really to get close to Armani if you didn't speak Italian or French, the two languages he spoke fluently. Armani always had an interpreter by his side when he was among Americans, although he appeared to understand more English than he let on. Oddly enough, his ignorance of English worked in his favor, in creating yet another layer of inaccessibility to fuel his already larger-than-life persona.

Over the years, as many designers tried to emulate Armani's stellar front row, they succeeded in recruiting Isabella Rossellini and Tom Cruise, who began as Armani devotees but turned into free agents who flitted from one designer to another. The Armani people usually shrugged off such defections, but not always. Once, a flap ensued over who would dress Anjelica Huston when she picked up her award at the 1992 Council of Fashion Designers of America gala in New York. When the Armani staffers heard that Huston—typically an Armani devotee—would be wearing a white beaded dress by Calvin Klein that night, they didn't like it. Rumors flew that the house of Armani might even cancel its table at the benefit. Lee Radziwill called to pressure the CFDA, as did Forte. After a CFDA official told Forte that the event was "for American designers and American clothes," Forte retorted to *WWD:* "So maybe they shouldn't ask Armani, Chanel and all the rest to buy tables."

But Armani could rest assured that Reilly, who had turned down many offers through the years, wouldn't be tempted to try out another designer. Reilly said: "I'd almost feel like a traitor. Anyway, I'm not interested in endorsements, even if somebody would pay me. I enjoy wearing Armani."

Eric Clapton also relished wearing Armani after he backed off from Versace in 1992. Gianni Versace used Clapton's departure to take a swipe at his Milanese archrival. When Clapton wears Armani, he "looks like an accountant," Gianni Versace cracked to *WWD.* Clapton fired back: "I had a business deal with Versace and now I have a business deal with Armani. The Versace clothes don't cater to me anymore. I appreciate what he does, but I think his clothes are more for the southern Italian male or for Sylvester Stallone types."

GLAMOROUS AS THEY are, fashion shows are fairly low-voltage to the general public, who will probably never see a tape of an Armani runway show to get a glimpse of Pat Reilly or Claudia Cardinale. However, billions of ordinary folks around the world are guaranteed to stargaze for three long hours on Oscar night. As the luminaries paraded into the Dorothy Chandler Pavilion, celebrity interviewer Joan Rivers usually greeted them with the same question, "Who are you wearing?" And more often than not, they responded: "Armani." The designer would forever be remembered as the first designer who swept the Oscars without taking home a single trophy.

The ripple effect of Armani's movieland coup has spread far and wide. After Armani threw down the gauntlet, the Oscars turned into fashion Olympics, as houses from around the world jockeyed for months to get their clothes exposed at the big show. Armani's subdued elegance sent Hollywood fashion victims running for cover, compelling image-conscious actors to find a designer they could call their own, or to hire one of fashion's newest and busiest professionals: freelance stylists.

Long before Armani, the Academy Awards used to be a no-brainer. Back in the years when the Hollywood studios ruled, the contract stars were hemmed into the formulas of musicals, historical spectacles, and plots with happy endings. And when the actors got dressed for the big night, they stayed right on the studio lot, turning themselves over to the professionals, such as costume designers as Jean-Louis at Columbia, Edith Head at Paramount, and Adrian at MGM, the designer who put Joan Crawford in shoulder pads.

"The stars were so used to having stuff made especially for them—the clothes that showed their best features, their best colors, to fit their image on screen," recalled Bob Mackie, a costume designer who formerly worked for Edith Head and Jean-Louis. For the Oscars, "you dressed them as sexpots or grand actresses, or the way the studios wanted them to be perceived by the public."

Back then, all eyes were on the stars, and not the costume designers, who were largely unknown to the public anyway. Mackie was a sketcher for Jean-Louis, who made one of the most memorable gowns of the sixties, the flesh-toned, skintight confection worn by Marilyn Monroe when she sang "Happy Birthday" to President John F. Kennedy at Madison Square Garden in 1962. "That dress was so impressive, but nobody knew who made it," Mackie remembered. "Jean-Louis never got any pop from designing that dress."

But by the 1970s, there was no more studio system to lord over the stars, and the professional costumers began buying more film wardrobes from established fashion houses instead of whipping up original creations. So on Oscar night, Hollywood players were left to their own fashion devices. Staged glamour gave way to individual expression. The men were tucked safely in black tie, while the women, if they were stumped, had a Plan B: Beverly Hills retailer Fred Hayman, who became the Oscars' official fashion coordinator. Hayman served as a clearinghouse, rounding up gowns from a number of designers. And he steered business his way too, for Hayman's Rodeo Drive shop was stocked with fabulous gowns every spring.

Without the old studio standards, the Oscars turned into a showcase of the good, the bad, and the ugly. TV viewers tuned in to scoff at the inevitable Oscar faux pas. In 1990, Demi Moore showed up in sequined biking shorts and Kim Basinger wore a one-sleeved, bouffant Cinderella number. And Cher. Only Cher could get away with wearing feather headdresses and baring her navel in some outrageous getup, compliments of

Bob Mackie. That was the heyday of "Mr. Blackwell," the chief of fashion police, who used to find plenty of Oscar fashion victims for his "worst-dressed list" at the end of the year.

But the Oscars' airbrushed glamour would make a stunning comeback by the mid-1990s. In the age of celebrity worship and TV shows like *Entertainment Tonight,* stars felt as if they were onstage every time they went out in public. As more actors became concerned with their off-screen images, which could enhance—or sabotage—their on-screen careers, they were less willing to experiment with fashion, especially on Oscar night.

"It's not so much about insecurity of the stars but the fact that society is driven so much by clothing, style, taste and beauty," said Wayne Scot Lukas, a freelance stylist who has dressed clients like Janet Jackson, Melanie Griffith, and Tina Turner. "The public nowadays is judging actresses by every facet of their lives. If you smoke, how you sit, who you went out with that night and what you were doing. They have no private lives. We as a public have put them on the pedestal as these fabulous, amazing creatures and now they become the media target. We create these gods and then we make fun of them. We knock them down."

As a few stylists became bosom buddies with the stars, the designers began to court them too. Armani flew Philip Bloch, one of the most influential stylists based in Los Angeles, to Milan to attend one of his fashion shows. For a fee, roughly between $500 to $1,500 a day—or higher—such stylists could be enlisted as fashion fixers. The stylists combed designer showrooms in Los Angeles, New York, Paris, and Milan as well as the racks at Saks Fifth Avenue and Barneys in Beverly Hills, to make their famous clients look at all times, in the words of Lukas, "hip, cool and pulled together."

Lukas contended that he tended to gravitate to the designers who were eager—and equipped—to work with celebrities: "The people at

Armani are selfless. They give you the accessories, the alterations, anything you need. And the same thing goes for Versace."

After his all-stars took over the Oscars in 1990 and 1991, Armani became the fashion standard by which all of Hollywood would be judged. Armani even got listed for a wardrobe credit at the end of the show for dressing Billy Crystal, the 1991 Oscar host. Millions of television viewers got used to hearing Armani's name again and again. When Whoopi Goldberg hosted the ceremony in 1992, she twirled around onstage during her opening monologue to show off her velvet Armani gown. The Armani impact lingered weeks after the fact when *People*, *In Style*, and *W* came out with their Oscar fashion spreads, which were always full of Armani sightings. Invariably, Team Armani—Jodie Foster, Annette Bening, Michelle Pfeiffer, Anjelica Houston, Winona Ryder, Sigourney Weaver, Faye Dunaway, and Salma Hayek—hogged the spotlight in getting the most complimentary mentions in the press.

The celebrities regarded Armani as a sure thing—the safest option on a night when even the most seasoned veterans can suffer a bit of stage fright. "On a night like the Oscars, you're in gobs of makeup, instead of blue jeans, and everybody's looking at you," said Glenn Close. "I lead a very laid-back life: I don't spend a lot of time on myself. Armani makes me feel comfortable. If I'm in a beautiful Armani outfit for a formal occasion, it goes with my philosophy of simple unadorned elegance. I don't need any jewelry."

Armani stitched up a very full, beaded, strapless gown for the very pregnant Glenn Close when she was nominated for best actress for *Fatal Attraction*. Always on Oscar night, Close says she wants to feel as natural as possible—and not look as if she were outfitted for a movie role. "When I'm in Armani I don't feel that I am somebody else. It's important that his clothes make me look better but enhance who I am. The clothes focus on *you*."

Armani got to see all of this for himself when he attended the 1991 ceremonies at which his friend Martin Scorsese was nominated for best director for *Goodfellas*. Amid the movie-star gridlock, Armani still managed to draw a crowd as everyone came over to meet him. He was so overwhelmed by all the attention that he skipped all the after-parties and retreated to the Regent Beverly Wilshire Hotel with his staffers for a quiet dinner.

Even though Armani usually had a long list to dress for the Oscars, the designer managed to take the time to study each individual. He said: "I like to keep a direct rapport with the performers who like what I stand for. In forming my relationship with them I ask them, 'What do you have in mind?' And then, we spend a whole week working on something for them to wear."

As for the men: "My approach to menswear has never been *fashion*. I never put them in things that are too showy. I have to slow them down. When they are handsome or famous, they don't need very much or they look overdone."

While Armani designed in Milan, McDaniel and her Beverly Hills staff of four, along with a few freelancers, toiled all year to make the night come together. Whenever they located new faces to bring into the fold, they knew who to focus on: those young stars who exuded a classic elegance. Armani's understated look meant: You wear the clothes, the clothes don't wear you. So in 1992, when Warren Beatty's *Bugsy* was nominated, his wife, actress Annette Bening, wore a simple black wool crepe gown with cap sleeves and brilliant earrings. The critics in the press agreed; she was a "perfect 10."

The young screenwriting duo Ben Affleck and Matt Damon looked dapper and all grown-up in classic Armani tuxedos when they came to pick up their 1998 award for *Good Will Hunting*. On his way into the ceremony, Damon began the evening with an acceptance speech, telling

Joan Rivers: "We really want to thank Molly over at Armani for giving us these great tuxedos."

According to its official policy, the house of Armani doesn't pay its famous billboards for the night. The nominees and certain regulars, of course, received free gowns and tuxedos, altered to fit them at the Beverly Hills store. Another tier of celebrities was granted a gown or tuxedo on loan. All the trimmings—shoes, handbags, and sunglasses—are part of the package.

Membership in Armani's exclusive club has its privileges. A select list of celebrities are said to receive a year-round discount of as much as 50 percent at his boutiques. And for a few of his favorite clients like Jodie Foster, Armani has furnished wardrobes for movie promotional tours.

In the late 1980s, when dressing the stars was still a novelty, the actors were quite easy to please, bowled over as they were that a famous designer actually wanted to dress *them.* McDaniel explained: "It started out as, 'Oh my god, Armani is going to let me wear something!' It was like a privilege coming into the inner sanctum, it had a mystique."

But by the late 1990s, as more designers relentlessly chased the stars, the tables turned. Designers wooed nominees and presenters with boxes of evening clothes—without any obligation to wear them. In 1997, the record appeared to belong to Lauren Holly, who was married to comedian Jim Carrey at the time, when she received, unsolicited, fifty-six free gowns from thirteen different designers.

The designers' publicists cajoled and begged, and the rumors flew, as the most imperious stars played gimme-gimme, requesting cash payments or free wardrobes in exchange for wearing a designer gown on Oscar night. Joining the scramble were jewelers like Harry Winston, which provided millions of dollars worth of precious gems as loaners for the night.

The Oscar fashion sweepstakes went into full swing on the day the nominees were announced. On Valentine's Day in 1995, Angela Bassett wore a red Escada pantsuit to read the names of the nominees at the official press conference. After the Escada publicists worked the phones, that fashion factoid got at least six media mentions.

Nineteen ninety-five was the year of *Forrest Gump* fashion. The maker of Hush Puppies had crafted a special pair of size 9½D shoes for Tom Hanks (he wore Hush Puppies in the movie) and promised to make a donation to his favorite charity if he wore them on Oscar night. (He didn't. But Hanks did wear the tuxedo Calvin Klein sent over.) *Gump* producer Steve Tisch received a 0.4 carat diamond stick pin, a gift from the International Diamond Council trade group. Donna Karan showered Tisch with two tuxedos and two gowns for his girlfriend for the Golden Globe Awards and the Oscars. "I'm trying to get up the courage to ask Donna for a suit for my niece's bat mitzvah," Tisch joked at the time.

Sharon Stone, the most coveted fashion diva of them all, was "confirmed" to wear a Valentino but pulled a fast one and changed her mind at the last minute. She came out onstage, with co-presenter Quincy Jones, in a $22 Gap turtleneck and a black skirt. Gap sold thousands of what became known in-house as "the Sharon Stone shirt" in the months to follow.

Armani, who had started this horse race, would get his just deserts at the 1995 Oscars, when his tribe included Foster, Pfeiffer, Uma Thurman, and David Letterman, the show's host. But much of the thrill was gone for Armani, who was fed up. *Basta*. An Armani spokesman said in 1995: "Mr. Armani is very much against the idea of buying stars." And in 1997: "We're cutting back. We don't need forty-five names on a press release. Mr. Armani has now made the Oscars a second priority." Freshening his celebrity roster with luminaries outside Hollywood, Armani mined golden names like golfer Tiger Woods, boxer Oscar de la Hoya, and hip-hop diva Lauryn Hill.

Meanwhile, the rest of high fashion pressed on to hustle Hollywood. The house of Christian Dior, aiming to revive interest in its couture collections by John Galliano, went for Nicole Kidman in 1997, who came with her husband, Tom Cruise, in a lime-green embroidered Dior gown. Everyone agreed Kidman looked smashing, but Dior's brief shining moment at the Oscars quickly evaporated, failing to do the trick to induce women to go shopping for Dior suits and gowns—the way Armani had done.

HAVING SCALED BACK his Hollywood pursuits, Armani redirected his energy to his time-tested formula. Consistency, after all, was money in the bank. The Armani mystique had worked its way through the fashion cognoscenti to the celebrities and, finally, to the masses. Giorgio Armani SpA had blanketed the world with 250 boutiques selling everything from $60 A/X jeans to $10,000 beaded gowns. The company's wholesale volume in 1998 reached about $1.2 billion (more than $3 billion at retail), with about a third of sales from the U.S. and Canada.

Even though he stood at fashion's most enviable pole position, Armani still wasn't off the hook. Having established his beachhead long before the rest, he had done the hard part. Now what was left for him to do was to stay focused and continue to make fabulous clothes, while the other designers played catch-up. Still, Armani had to be aware that he was about to hit a generational wall. He had to keep finding ways to keep his trademark young and vital, through advertising, celebrities, and other types of marketing. And as good as he was, even Armani had his limitations. To date, his Armani A/X jeanswear chain—his version of Gap—

has yet to turn on lots of people. Lucky for him that A/X accounts for less than 15 percent of his business.

As for the other designers who played celebrity roulette, they would also need some serendipity: the right stars at the right time—and the hope that their picks would do justice to the clothes. Cutting through the clutter would also be tougher, as there were few opportunities for designers to hog the big screen as Armani had in *Gigolo.* In 1998, several new movies each featured a slew of designer labels, such as Woody Allen's *Celebrity,* starring Leonardo DiCaprio, Gretchen Mol, and Melanie Griffith—who dressed in Karl Lagerfeld, Badgley Mischka, Dolce & Gabbana, and Hervé Leger. And what goes around comes around: Armani and Cerruti would be together again—hanging in wardrobe in *Hurly Burly*, starring Kevin Spacey, Robin Wright Penn, and Sean Penn.

So in the end, what would most fashion designers get from all this exposure? Perhaps not as much as they hoped for. In most cases, designers would find that all that groveling to celebrities turned out to be an expensive distraction keeping them from doing what they needed to do: figuring out what bona fide—paying—customers wanted to wear.

Designers "can overhype the influences of celebrities," observed *In Style*'s editor Martha Nelson. "In the end, it doesn't matter what celebrities wear. People are not willing to be led around by their noses either by some anonymous fashion editor, some designer or even by celebrities, if the clothes don't work for them."

And that summed up Armani's edge: making his designs work for his fans whether they were Broadway ingenues or bank vice presidents in Minneapolis. "Armani is synonymous with fashion at every level," said Sara Forden, the *Women's Wear Daily* reporter based in Milan. "At weddings even in small villages throughout Italy, it's not unusual to find the mother of the bride or members of the wedding party wearing Armani."

Most likely, those wedding guests felt that it was worth splurging for designer finery that was comfortable and flattering, with the added value of feeling like stars when they got dressed. Conversely, Glenn Close favored Armani because she wanted low-key elegance that would let her shine through, as a normal person. Armani had accomplished what seemed impossible. He made ordinary people feel like stars and made stars feel like regular folks. And everybody looked good.

chapter 5

GIVING THE LADY WHAT SHE WANTS: THE NEW MARSHALL FIELD'S

The consumer is king. His preference is law and his whim makes and unmakes merchants, jobbers and manufacturers. Whoever wins his confidence controls the mercantile situation; whoever loses it, is lost.

CHARLES COOLIDGE PARLIN, market researcher

The Windy City skyline, in striking origami relief, adorned the invitation to Chicago's smart set to save the date of September 4, 1988.

On that night, Marshall Field's would kick off the city's fall social season with its most spectacular black-tie benefit in years. The site was the Water Tower Place mall on North Michigan Avenue, along the tony retail stretch known as the "Magnificent Mile," where Field's had just completed a $10 million renovation of its seven-story branch store.

The gala, benefiting Chicago's Lyric Opera, was a bold stroke of bravado for Marshall Field's—a maneuver calculated to underscore position as Chicago's favorite department store now that Bloomingdale's had come to town. The trendy New York emporium had just big-footed into Chicago, landing a bit too close for comfort for Field's, right across the street from Water Tower Place, in a gleaming new six-story building. To commemorate its Chicago debut, Bloomie's had scheduled its own glitzy gala, a September 23rd benefit for the Chicago Symphony.

The festivities took place during the end of that heady era when department stores had plenty to celebrate. Starting in the late 1970s, designer fashions and perfumes were on a roll, accompanying the breakneck expansion of department stores into suburban malls. In 1978, when America was teeming with more than 20,000 shopping malls, Lord & Taylor swept through suburban Detroit, inaugurating three new branches on three successive nights, with glossy benefits at each location. Each black-tie opening featured a designer headliner: Bill Blass, Oscar de la Renta, and Mary McFadden. Such spectacles were integral to Lord & Taylor's marketing strategy to come out swinging, positioning each of its new branches as the "happening" places to shop. And where there was buzz, hordes of shoppers were bound to follow.

Inevitably, the 1988 autumn face-off between Field's and Bloomingdale's played as a swaggering rivalry between Chicago and New York. Bloomingdale's aimed to be the more exclusive—the tickets to its soiree went for $225 apiece, compared to the $175 admission to the throw-down at Field's. Bloomie's also planned to regale Chicago with a French twist: Karl Lagerfeld was jetting in from Paris to show off his latest Chanel couture collection during the gala.

But Field's was astute in throwing the first party of the season, the better to impress Chicago socialites when they would be fresh and expectant, just like back-to-school students. Even though Chicagoans dearly loved *their* Marshall Field's, the home team still needed to score big points. "This was a moment to take a stand, to be the superior store," recalled Michael Francis, who was a Field's marketing executive at the time. "We tried to find out, point by point, what Bloomingdale's was doing and our goal was to do it better. No expense was spared to put on a big show." (Even though local vendors donated thousands of dollars in refreshments and discounted services for both affairs, Bloomingdale's and Field's spent an estimated $250,000 apiece on their fall parties.)

As Chicago suddenly became retail's liveliest battleground, *Vanity Fair* fanned the flames, predicting that "store wars" between Field's and Bloomie's were shaping up to be "the noisiest confrontation in retail history." Philip Miller, Field's dashing fifty-year-old chairman, was ready to rock and roll. "It'll be fun to test our mettle," he said.

The confrontation between the retailers came at a critical juncture in the history of department stores. America's oldest retailing format had been growing stale and unexciting, losing ground to a new generation of discounters, specialty stores, and catalog merchants. By the early 1990s, a number of venerable local chains had either gone out of business or merged with their former rivals. Those who survived the wave of consolidation that started in the mid-1980s were focused on streamlining their operations and filling their floors with more affordable merchandise.

Less than two years after Bloomie's moved to Chicago, Marshall Field's would meet a similar fate. In 1990, Field's was sold to Dayton Hudson Corp., the Minneapolis retail concern best known for its fast-growing Target Stores discount division.

Dayton Hudson proceeded to take Field's down a new path. Under Phil Miller, the high-toned Marshall Field's had shunned the so-called moderate merchandise category. But Dayton Hudson, preoccupied with generating profits, did just the opposite. By adding more moderate goods, Field's could draw many more shoppers, which it sorely needed in the 1990s after so many out-of-town competitors had been closing in. By the early 1990s, Chicagoland was bustling with branches of Bloomingdale's, Nordstrom, Henri Bendel, Lord & Taylor, and an aggressive discounter called Kohl's. Even Carson Pirie Scott, the moderate-priced department store that was Field's State Street neighbor, was showing new signs of life. "Marshall Field's and a little of Carson's used to be the only game in town. But eventually Chicago became a market for everybody," said Gary Witkin, who was Field's chairman from 1990 to 1992.

Under Dayton Hudson's stewardship, Field's shifted more and more of its merchandise from class to mass. The glitzy "store wars" of the eighties were finished. Retailers of every stripe now waged "markdown wars." During its "Field's Days" and "13 Hour" sales, Marshall Field's was filled with such signs as "Look at this bargain."

Gloria Bacon, a Chicago physician and Field's charge-card customer since 1963, didn't like this new agenda. She longed for the return of the Field's of the 1970s, when the ever-obliging sales associates steered her to the unusual and exclusive, like the fabulous Italian wool knitwear that she couldn't find anywhere else in town. Bacon was turned off by the way Field's had practically rolled out the red carpet to welcome the hordes of bargain hunters who pawed through the store's ubiquitous markdown racks. "The ambiance is gone," she lamented in 1997. "Field's isn't special anymore, it's just another generic Midwest department store."

Her sentiments were shared by many Chicago shoppers who, having grown up on the upscale Marshall Field's, had shifted their loyalties to Saks Fifth Avenue and Nordstrom, which felt more like the great Field's they once revered. "Customers [were] telling us we're not what we used to be," Dan Skoda, Field's president, said in July 1997. "We lost the image of what we stood for."

The $64,000 question was: Would Field's ever be able to get it back? It was hard to be optimistic. Field's predicament reflected the decline in department store retailing that coincided with the mass merchandising of fashion that began in the 1990s. In order to survive, department stores were forced to merge with stores they used to compete with, to form national chains, positioning themselves to compete more effectively.

"When you go national, it's an incredible task to tailor your goods by city or market," said Witkin. "This is the reality of running a bigger business." Moreover, he noted, department store buyers were no longer the tastemakers who picked out special merchandise for every branch location. Buyers in the 1990s were loath to experiment like they used to. They couldn't afford to gamble with avante-garde fashions that might catch on with only a handful of the most discriminating shoppers. It was safer to concentrate their business with a few key vendors.

Therein lies the great retail conundrum. Field's had to abandon its white-glove heritage in order to compete in a modern era. But without its distinctive image, Field's was hard-pressed to stand out in a crowd of look-alike department stores.

So just how do department stores create an identity nowadays? It isn't easy. Even the label "department store" is a misnomer, because there are fewer and fewer departments inside them. Most chains have stopped carrying electronics, toys, books, appliances, and furniture. What's left standing are the goods that generate the highest profits—primarily apparel and cosmetics.

"Establishing an identity is much harder today for department stores," observed Arnold Aronson, a New York retail consultant. "The typical customer isn't loyal to any one store; she's looking for the best values on her favorite brands." Furthermore, he added, harried shoppers "have changed their perception of what they value nowadays. They are starved for time; they want a store that's efficient, has decent service, and gets the job done."

Traditionally, department stores have built their reputations by being exciting and glitzy—and now all of that is history. In today's economics, department stores are all about being affordable and predictable—and often dull, which is the safest and surest way to profits.

FOR GENERATIONS, AMERICANS had a love affair with their local department stores. In the mid-nineteenth century, when the first merchant pioneers founded department stores, most towns were just starting to build their central business districts. Retailers, including Marshall Field's, John Wanamaker in Philadelphia, Rich's in Atlanta, and Neiman Marcus in Dallas, exposed their communities to the finest of merchandise. In the process, the locals became sophisticated consumers, as well as members of a big retail family.

At Christmastime, for instance, many families from around the Midwest made a special trip to downtown Chicago to enjoy the storybook window displays at Marshall Field's. They worked their way up to the eighth floor, where Santa was stationed in front of the magnificent seventy-foot Christmas tree in Field's Walnut Room restaurant. For decades, people put their trust in institutions like Field's, whose palatial downtown stores and sleek mall branches were symbols of civic pride, just like the Chicago Cubs and the White Sox. Every town had a JCPenney's and a Sears, which were reliable for kitchen curtains, electric drills, and washing machines. But only department stores delivered style on a grand scale to big cities. Field's took the lead in Chicago as the arbiter of good taste and high quality, and thus became the premier fashion authority of the Midwest.

By the time "designer" became the merchandising hook starting in the late 1970s, Bloomingdale's had become among the most tantalizing of New York retailers, introducing shoppers to Pierre Cardin, Yves Saint Laurent, and a kicky new tie designer named Ralph Lauren. Bloomie's became the quintessential "retailing theater," especially during its famous international promotions, when the entire store brimmed with exotic merchandise from whatever country Bloomie's was promoting that year. In 1978 the theme was "India: The Ultimate Fantasy," while in 1981 it was "China: Heralding the Dawn of a New Era." Shoppers were treated to folk dancers, cooking demonstrations, and commemorative shopping bags. The foreign promotions didn't do much to enhance the bottom line, but they worked wonders to polish Bloomie's mystique. They were the trademark of Marvin Traub, the store's legendary chairman from 1970 to 1991, who transplanted Bloomie's chichi to Washington, D.C., and Boston with stunning success.

In coming to Chicago, Bloomie's took on its stiffest competition outside New York. Marshall Field's was no longer coasting on its fabled carriage-trade laurels. Field's had become flashy and very popular after 1982, when the chain was purchased by BAT Industries PLC, the giant tobacco and retail concern from London. BAT had emerged as a white knight to rescue Field's from the clutches of Wall Street corporate raider Carl Icahn. Flush with cash from its core tobacco business, BAT was determined to fix up Field's, as well as Saks Fifth Avenue, the other stellar-but-dusty department store chain it had purchased a year earlier. Accordingly, BAT spent freely to upgrade Field's—about $70 million in the first two years. "We had an obligation not just to purchase Marshall Field's, but to put our blood and guts and investment into it," said Arnold Aronson, who presided over BAT's retailing division at the time. The British conglomerate even committed itself to a five-year, $110 million renovation of Field's seventy-five-year-old downtown flagship, a questionable indulgence given that State Street was no longer Chicago's shopping mecca. Chicago's business leaders were delighted at the possibilities that a spruced-up Marshall Field's could deliver—the "new" Field's could be just the magnet to pull affluent shoppers back into Chicago's downtown Loop.

In 1983, BAT recruited a seasoned veteran, Phil Miller, the president of Neiman Marcus and a Bloomingdale's alum, to become chairman of Field's. Outgoing and boyishly handsome, the blond, blue-eyed Miller dressed in snappy double-breasted pinstripes and was often referred to as "the Robert Redford of retailing." Miller served on local boards with Chicago's Gold Coast society, and he lured them downtown to posh events in the Walnut Room, such as the 1986 Oakbrook Polo Ball, which Prince Charles attended. Miller also courted the masses, when he invited the stars from the hit TV series *Miami Vice* to make an in-store appearance in 1985. Field's visibility surged, as did Miller's. "People would stop Phil on the street. He was like Mr. Chicago," recalled Phyllis Collins, Field's veteran high-fashion buyer.

Miller's biggest challenge was clarifying Field's merchandise mix. When he arrived, the store was a hodgepodge that ran the gamut from expensive to budget. Miller's ultimate goal: to dominate the Chicago market in what he called the "better-best" category of high-end merchandise—about one-fourth of Field's business—while bolstering the store's core "upper-middle" business. Miller converted Field's bargain basement into "Down Under," a section devoted to Cuisinart food processors, housewares, and electronics that beckoned yuppie homeowners. At the same time, Miller turned Field's into the designer headquarters of the Midwest with brands that included Fendi, Bottega Veneta, Christian Lacroix, Emanuel Ungaro, and Donna Karan. "You can't get some designers' trunk [fashion preview] shows because Marshall Field's has them all sewn up," observed Larry Gore in 1986, as the representative for several Chicago specialty stores. "The designers want Marshall Field's; they want *that* name in Chicago."

Miller's strategy worked wonders. As Field's market share and fortunes climbed, analysts projected that by 1990, Field's annual sales would reach $1 billion—up from $750 million in 1984—with a healthy 10 percent to 12 percent operating profit margin, about double the profit levels at the time of BAT's acquisition.

Moreover, Miller *knew* what it took to wow Chicago. For the Lyric Opera benefit in 1988, all seven floors at Marshall Field's Water Tower Place store were transformed into what the *Chicago Tribune* described as a "Disneyland of party areas." For 1,200 guests, the fantasy began as soon as they walked in and onto a "stage" facing an audience sipping champagne—an effect designed to "make stars out of the guests," a Field's publicist explained.

Chicago had always been Field's kind of town, but on that glorious night, Field's was steeped in "New York, New York." Seventh Avenue's most glamorous designers—Bill Blass, Carolina Herrera, and Carolyne Roehm—were on hand. So was cabaret crooner Bobby Short, who took his act to the seventh floor. There was even a replica of Harlem's famous speakeasy, the Cotton Club. And circulating through the gourmet spread of lobster tails, caviar, and six-foot-tall chocolate bombe cakes (served by waiters on ladders), was Chicago's own talk-show queen Oprah Winfrey, svelte in brocade and black velvet. She told the *Chicago Tribune*, "I'm not eating and I still think this party is great."

Departing guests carried home champagne memories—and little gift bags filled with $165 worth of goodies: a split of Veuve Clicquot champagne, a silk bow tie from Charvet of Paris, Blass and Herrera perfumes, and a box of Field's famous Frango mints. Miller was jubilant: "I hope this will be known as the best party Chicago has seen in a long time. It's to remind Chicago that Marshall Field's and Chicago are synonymous and we can have the most fun together."

Two weeks later, Oprah dolled up again, in 6.5-carat canary yellow diamond earrings, and headed for Bloomingdale's. The requisite red carpet, klieg lights, and blaring trumpets welcomed 3,500 partygoers, including Italian fashion magnates Carla Fendi and Massimo Ferragamo. Ten bands blasted on all six floors, where guests downed flutes of "Bloomie's Blush," a champagne cocktail invented for the occasion. At the end of his Chanel fashion show, Karl Lagerfeld, sporting sunglasses, ponytail, and Japanese fan, sauntered down the runway to take a bow. Amid hundreds of white orchids and roses, Marvin Traub exulted, "This is the most spectacular store we've ever done. Chicago is a marvelous city and we wanted to do it marvelously."

Fred Jackson, publisher of *Town & Country*, was duly impressed. He told the *Chicago Tribune*: "If it's done by Bloomie's, it's on a New York scale. They don't spare a thing."

All in all, an unforgettable evening, made all the more unforgettable by the strange speech made by Robert Campeau, the Canadian real estate developer and owner of Bloomie's through his recent $4 billion purchase of Federated Department Stores. Traub graciously introduced Campeau, who stepped up to the mike and proceeded to ramble on about America's Wild West, the early days of radio, switching back and forth from English to French. Mortified, the guests tittered, and wondered what was going on.

About a year later, they found out. Campeau, the mogul who had piled up mountains of debt to buy Federated, was fast running out of cash. On January 15, 1990, Campeau's retail empire collapsed and filed for Chapter 11 bankruptcy protection. Campeau Corp.'s $7.5 billion filing was the largest retail bankruptcy in U.S. history to date. (Divorced from Campeau, Federated came out of bankruptcy in 1992, when it acquired Macy's and then reorganized to become a healthy, well-run chain of more than 420 stores with annual sales of $15 billion by 1996.)

By the end of 1989, the party was also over for Field's—but not because of Bloomie's. Right before Christmas, BAT had put Field's and

Saks up for sale to thwart a hostile takeover bid from billionaire raider Sir James Goldsmith. Phil Miller countered with his own pitch to rescue his retail empire, by putting together an investor group that made a run on Field's—but with no luck. The winning bid—a stunning $1.4 billion—came instead from Dayton Hudson Corp.

After having failed to acquire Field's a decade earlier, the Minneapolis retailer was thrilled to have at last captured Chicago's crown jewel. Dayton Hudson called the acquisition an "ideal marriage" between like-minded Midwesterners, mainly because its own Dayton's in Minneapolis so closely resembled Field's.

But to Chicagoans, Marshall Field's was far more than a department store. Field's *was* Chicago. Founder Marshall Field and his heirs were among the city's most prominent philanthropists, through their investments in such local landmarks as the Merchandise Mart, the University of Chicago, and the Field Museum of Natural History. Dorothy Fuller, a former Field's fashion director, explained: "Marshall Field's is a Chicago institution and the people of Chicago think it belongs to *them*."

IN THE MIDST of America's industrial revolution, when railroads and factories went up after Reconstruction, Chicago was a bustling, dusty frontier town where the locals hungered for both basic merchandise and pointers on how to live and to dress well. In 1868, a hard-driving wholesale clerk named Marshall Field and his business partner, Levi Z. Leiter, opened their first store, Field and Leiter. In a six-story building on the corner of Washington and State streets, Field and Leiter delighted their community with a dazzling array of the finest goods available. A "marble palace, with enough merchandise to turn almost every female head," reported the *Chicago Tribune*, which marveled at the counters lined with bolts of silk, $1,000 lace tablecloths, horsehair sofas, and

Staffordshire china imported from England. In the first year, the store's sales reached an impressive $8 million, with a $300,000 profit. In 1881, Marshall Field, at age forty-seven, bought out his partner and renamed the store Marshall Field & Co.

A prescient merchant, Field zeroed in on fashion-conscious ladies. Early on, he hired a "style expert" to travel to Europe by sea to bring back "special Parisian frocks" to America's heartland. During the 1880s, when women wore cumbersome hoop skirts, Field & Co. was the first in Chicago to offer the radical "bustle" dress, from the Parisian couture house of Worth. In a move to encourage women to spend the entire day shopping, Field's installed a tea salon and restaurant, which became famous for chicken pot pie and its signature Field's Rose Punch. There was even an "Evening Room" for ladies to see how their gowns looked under artificial light. The wife of U.S. President-elect William McKinley called on Field's to create her inaugural gown. "*Give the lady what she wants*," Marshall Field reportedly declared in a fit, after observing one haughty salesclerk in action. His legendary command became the store's motto, and the gold standard that Field's would maintain for decades to come.

Even though other department stores, such as Carson Pirie Scott, sprang up around Chicago, Marshall Field didn't worry about out-of-town stores invading his turf. According to a Field biographer, Philadelphia merchant John Wanamaker once dropped into the store and told Marshall Field: "I like this city. I think you could use another store here." Field responded coolly: "Probably. But I've been thinking of expanding. You come here and I think we'll open in Philadelphia." Wanamaker reportedly "smiled weakly and shook hands, promptly forgetting about his idea of competing with Field's."

Rebuilt twice after devastating fires, Marshall Field & Co. moved in 1907 into an eleven-story limestone and granite monument—

crowned with a magnificent Tiffany-glass dome—that took up an entire block on State Street. As the dry-goods anchor of Chicago's burgeoning downtown Loop, Field's served every need. Along with a dizzying spread of apparel, furniture, and housewares, the store offered eleven restaurants, workrooms to repair antique furniture and clocks, a dry cleaner, an ice cream kitchen, and more. On Saturdays, parents dropped their children off at Field's for charm school and handicraft classes. Chicago gangster Al Capone bought his $35 silk shirts by the dozen at Field's Men's Store annex, which specialized in shotguns and hunting paraphernalia. Field's reputation for style soared to new heights in 1914, with the publishing of *Fashions of the Hour*, a bimonthly magazine mailed free of charge to Field's customers. It featured photographs of Chicago socialites in the latest fashions and articles on art, travel, and gardening.

In 1941, Marshall Field pulled out all the stops when it designed a special dress salon called "the 28 Shop." During World War II, when the pace-setting Paris fashion houses were shuttered, the 28 Shop filled the void by showcasing America's up-and-coming designers like Adrian, Norman Norrell, and Hattie Carnegie. The marketing of designers by name was a bold new step for Field's, where merchandise had only carried the Marshall Field & Co. store label. Chicago's wealthiest matrons headed to Field's entrance at 28 East Washington Street, where they boarded a private elevator lined with velvet benches. Arriving on the sixth floor into a rotunda foyer, clients were greeted by a butler and a hostess who led them into a lovely pink salon with twenty-eight dressing rooms, designed by Joseph Platt, the former Hollywood set designer for *Gone With the Wind*. Saleswomen whisked gowns out from the stockroom and stood guard to wait on each client. The 28 Shop was an immediate hit and became the fashion headquarters for the most stylish women in the Midwest.

Although the 28 Shop was the place where the elite met at Field's, the salon imparted cachet to everything else in the store. Starting in the 1950s, Kathleen Catlin, Field's legendary fashion director and head buyer for the 28 Shop, prevailed as Field's most influential tastemaker. Catlin dressed the displays for Field's windows, staged fashion shows, and schooled local fashion writers about the latest trends from Paris. Her fame spread far beyond Chicago. "Kathleen was so well-received in Paris because Field's bought more couture than any other retailer back then," recalled Dorothy Fuller, who formerly worked under Catlin.

At the Paris house of Balenciaga in the early 1950s, for instance, Catlin was thoroughly enchanted by the grand couturier's chemise or "sack" dress. She followed her instincts and, unlike the other American buyers, ordered several Balenciagas. Without bust or seam darts, the dresses were so unusual that "we put them on backwards at every fashion show . . . we only discovered that later on," recalled Fuller. Carmel Snow, the editor of *Harper's Bazaar*, wired Catlin to commend her on the Balenciagas: "My dear, how courageous!" And perspicacious. By the late 1950s, every smartly dressed woman in America donned a chemise, and the style lasted throughout the 1960s.

Catlin's sharp instincts made her an invaluable consultant to the leading dress houses on Seventh Avenue. "Kathleen knew that we had to create a desire," Fuller recalled. "The manufacturers flew in from New York, laid the (couture) clothes out on a table, and measured each seam. They went back to New York to copy the dresses and then Field's bought the copies."

In effect, Field's leadership led to the democratization of high fashion. Knockoffs came out of the 28 Shop and trickled all the way down to the budget floor, another Field's invention in 1885. The bargain basement concept was hatched by Harry Selfridge, one of Field's most colorful merchants, "who swept through the store with the dash of a circus promoter and the fervor of a revolutionist [sic]." Selfridge was confident that Field's would attract more working-class clientele by creating a special area for goods that were "trustworthy or less expensive, but reliable." Marshall Field wasn't keen on the idea at first, and he fretted that too many newspaper ads shouting "specially attractive bargains" would tarnish Field's uptown gloss.

But Field's bargain basement worked like magic and became a clever merchandising tactic that other stores across America soon copied. Shoppers who once wistfully window-shopped at Field's reportedly "came by the thousands in the first week to grab the cheaper silks, dress goods, hosiery, handkerchiefs, cloaks, ribbons and shawls." (Selfridge later moved on to London to create his own retail empire, Selfridge's, the first American-style department store in England. He frequently sent his buyers to Chicago to walk the floors at Field's.)

With more than one hundred years of such astute merchants as Catlin and Selfridge, Field's established its authority at opposite ends of the shopping spectrum. The receptionist who bagged a $19.95 budget coat and the Gold Coast socialite who selected a $3,000 original were both loyal clientele, confident that the fashions inside their hunter green Marshall Field's shopping bags represented the best of everything. (Marshall Field & Co. became known as Marshall Field's after 1982.)

IN 1990, FIELD'S was basking in the glow from its years under the charismatic Miller, who moved on after the acquisition by Dayton Hudson to become vice chairman of Saks Fifth Avenue. Having paid dearly for Field's, Dayton Hudson was keen to prune the fat from the store's operations, so the new owner folded Field's right into its existing department store division, in order to reap the advantages of shared expenses and economies of scale. Hundreds of Field's employees were let go. Many Chicagoans feared the worst when they heard that most of Field's buyers would be transferred to Minneapolis headquarters.

Phyllis Collins, the high-fashion buyer whose husband had an established law practice in Chicago, was one of the few Field's merchants allowed to stay. She didn't view the Dayton Hudson people as the enemy. "Never in their minds was this a takeover. They didn't want to fire people; they didn't have a superiority attitude. Everyone was on a first-name basis. They made an effort not to rip us apart."

Nevertheless, Collins believed that Dayton Hudson officials had underestimated what they were taking on. "They thought they were buying another Dayton's—and Dayton's wasn't used to competition in Minneapolis. They thought that with Field's, it was Frango mints and a Christmas tree in the Walnut Room and you've got them [customers]. But this is Chicago, this is a sophisticated city where you've gotta do it better, you've gotta sing and dance."

And just as many locals had feared, Field's began to lose its luster under Dayton Hudson. Gloria Bacon, a Field's aficionado, was appalled when she discovered $19.99 Nine West shoes displayed right next to the $350 Chanels. Field's solicitous saleswomen had disappeared, and almost every month there was a storewide sale.

Furthermore, Field's, the once-proud independent, had been forced into group therapy. Every price tag in Field's read "Dayton's, Hudson's and Marshall Field's." Advertisements for designer fashions in *Vogue* were labeled "Dayton's Oval Room *and* Field's 28 Shop." Even Field's exclusive Frangos were now available at Dayton's, Hudson's—even Target. Finally, when Field's came out with a new, "environmentally friendly" brown shopping bag, shoppers revolted. Field's backed off, and brought back its signature hunter green tote.

In making such moves, management wasn't prepared for such a backlash. "The Chicago customers hated these changes," recalled Gary Witkin, Field's president succeeding Miller. "There was this psychological perception that Field's was no longer Chicago-owned. It created a sensitivity for people to look for differences that they hadn't seen. The customer said, 'You are messing with my Marshall Field's.' "

As more Chicagoans became aware that Field's was being run from Minneapolis, Nordstrom saw an opportunity to win them over. In radio commercials, Nordstrom underscored its unwavering commitment to Chicago with the tagline: "Our buyers are your neighbors."

But whether the buyers were next door or a few hundred miles away in Minneapolis was beside the point. Department store retailing was no longer a buyer's market. Gone was the ritual of the 1970s, when buyers spent half of their time "branching"—that is, visiting store locations to learn the local idiosyncrasies of every community. Retailers believed that America was thoroughly homogenized—that the folks in Chicago loved the same fashions that the people in Detroit did—so it made sense to stock the same merchandise at most every branch store. In any event, the logistics of traveling to all of the sixty-six Marshall Field's, Dayton's, and Hudson's stores scattered throughout the Midwest was impractical. "Our buyers are lucky if they get to each store once a year," explained Dan Skoda, Field's president since 1992.

In short, buyers no longer had the freedom to impose their will (or their taste, for that matter) upon stores that had become fixated on the bottom-line performance above everything else.

This was the assembly-line, bottom-line apparel of the nineties that shoved fashion forever aside. In the 1960s, "before television and communications dictated a lot of the fashion, the department store used to be your first visual contact with fashion," said Allen Questrom, who served as chairman of Federated Department Stores from 1993 to 1998. "You came into the store to see what was available. In those days, the buyers spent a lot of time in the art of fashion; they knew more about fit, construction, and fabric. They could pick things that fit within the context of their store for a certain ilk of customers. They got to know the customers who shopped that store. The downtown store and later the mall had the advertising and special events that made the store *the* authority."

Such retail rituals disappeared by the 1970s, the era of the designer boom and nationally advertised fashion brands. Once designers became household names in apparel, accessories, perfumes, and bedding, their brands "created the ultimate consumer demand which you didn't have twenty years ago," said Philip Miller. "The department store used to be the vehicle that introduced merchandise concepts to the customer, but today, it's the brand. The designer is now communicating directly through national advertising and editorial and through fashion shows. The consumers see it in many instances as fast as we retailers do."

As designer brands moved onto center stage in the 1980s, department stores abandoned their practice of organizing sales floors in categories such as "better dresses" or "women's sportswear." The floors were reconfigured in brand-name boutiques under banners such as Liz Claiborne, Ellen Tracy, or Jones New York, which were among the most popular labels sold in America. As such powerful brands began to dominate department stores, buyers became less inclined to try out new and unfamiliar labels that shoppers would most likely overlook. "Most people don't have a natural sense of fashion and they are insecure," said Questrom. "The person who can afford to stay in the Ritz Carlton Hotel won't go out to experiment and try some exclusive inn they've never heard of. They need an authority, and today the authority is the brand. They have confidence in that label."

DAYTON HUDSON DIDN'T believe in hosting lavish black-tie benefits the way Field's had under Miller. Instead, the corporation quietly donated 5 percent of its annual pretax profits directly to charities—or about a million dollars a week, in the late 1990s. Nevertheless, Dayton Hudson knew the significance of maintaining ties to Chicago society. So Field's continued its longtime tradition of hosting a major fashion show benefit every fall. Traditionally Field's fashion shows were posh and elegant, where couture originals were shown on Chicago's top models—the teenage Cindy Crawford had once been a runway favorite. But Dayton Hudson decided that Field's shows needed to be more populist, to reach the broad audience that management now wanted to attract.

In August 1991, Field's added a new fashion show to its calendar, "Cause for Applause," which was billed as "a show of entertainment and fashion trends, rather than designer fashions presented on a runway." The program was modeled after Dayton's annual "Fash Bash" musical revue which had been a big hit with Minneapolis audiences for years.

"Cause for Applause," held at the Chicago Theater near Field's on State Street, indeed turned out to be a fashion show that made the headlines, but not the ones Dayton Hudson was expecting. Actor Mandy Patinkin, a Chicago native, was a jovial host. He got a few laughs when he passed out boxes of Frangos to the people in the front rows. But the evening droned on for nearly two hours, during which sixty models and dancers paraded the new fall styles, consisting of career clothes from Nippon, J.H. Collectibles, and Adrienne Vittadini—and hardly an evening gown in sight. Clearly, there wasn't much cause for applause from the Gold Coast crowd.

Genevieve Buck, the *Tribune*'s fashion editor, was sarcastic in her review: " 'Cause for Applause' was obviously ushering in a new fashion era at Field's," she wrote. "Gone were the upscale Calvin Kleins, Oscar de la Rentas, the Giorgio Armanis and Yves Saint Laurents of past shows that opened the fall season after Labor Day."

"Cause for Applause" encored in 1992, when carnival jugglers shared the stage with models, only to get another thumbs-down from Buck and her Gold Coast readers. Dayton Hudson gave up after that, and Field's returned to its high-toned fashion-show benefits for the fall season.

But that didn't mean a return to Field's upscale agenda of the eighties. "The way we do it today is different," explained Gerald Storch, Dayton Hudson's executive vice president of store planning, in 1997. "Our ultimate goal is to have the merchandise that most [shoppers] want, the national brands like DKNY, Dana Buchman, Perry Ellis, and Tommy Hilfiger."

BUT WHAT DID America's shoppers really want? Since the 1980s, designer brands had a spotty track record as they grappled with focusing on what to produce while department stores weren't sure of what to mark down and what to sell at full price.

Still, the chains kept multiplying. By the early 1990s, retail space across the nation had mushroomed at an astonishing pace. America overflowed with thousands of shopping centers—but fewer customers. There were more than 35,000 malls in operation by 1992, an estimated 18 square feet of retail space for every man, woman, and child in America, or nearly triple the number that existed in 1972. As America's suburban migration slowed in the late 1980s, the population of young women trawling the malls began shrinking as well. More and more, supply was exceeding demand, but unfettered, retailers continued to open more branch locations.

"The way retailers made money in the past was to open new stores every season," said Carl Steidtmann, an economist at Management Horizons, a retail consulting firm. "They are so wedded to this experience that it is difficult for them to change."

Beginning in the 1970s, retailers had a reason to expand so rapidly: a new generation of baby-boomer career women who were filling their closets with clothes to wear to work. Thus began the explosion of women's brands like Liz Claiborne, Jones New York, Chaus, and J.H. Collectibles, which dominated the women's floors in department stores. Those mighty labels were joined by dozens of specialty chains like The Limited, its sister, Express, and Casual Corner and Ann Taylor, all with their own private-label fashion lines. Discounted women's fashions were plentiful at Marshall's, Loehmann's, T.J. Maxx, and the factory outlet malls, while Sears and Penney's beefed up their fashion selections. Even Wal-Mart couldn't resist. By 1992, the Bentonville, Arkansas–based powerhouse had $82 billion in annual sales—with nearly $30 billion coming from apparel and sheets and towels.

Ironically, it would also be fashion that eventually put retailing on the skids. The buoyant women's apparel industry hit a pothole in the fall of 1987 when designers made a concerted push to bring back short skirts—at a time when women had spent the past few years building wardrobes of calf-length hemlines. The miniskirt revival that began in spring 1987 was universally endorsed on the high-fashion runways and tested on such popular prime time TV series as *Dynasty*, where actress Joan Collins could be seen plotting her schemes in sexy short dresses. One Bloomingdale's newspaper ad blared "SHORT" in three-inch type: "Never ones to flash a leg in vain, we applaud the outright appeal of a hemline above the knee." Chasing the wave, Liz Claiborne spent hundreds of thousands of dollars to shorten skirts already in production for its fall deliveries.

But the minis suffered a maxi-crash that year because millions of women just said no. National Public Radio's Nina Totenberg, for one, was outraged, and on the air, she urged women not to buy into the hype. Sisterhood was indeed powerful. For the first time in a decade, there was a drop in the sales of women's apparel. The backlash took the industry by surprise, and fashion writer Irene Daria concluded, "the female American population seemed to mature overnight."

Apparel marketers were stumped—and panic-stricken. Racks and racks of short skirts languished unsold, alongside blazers, blouses, and sweaters, as more women boycotted fashion in general. Claiborne, Limited, and U.S. Shoe, the holding company of Casual Corner, pointed to fashion as the reason their profits fell in 1987. A few years later, shorter skirts finally did catch on with most women, but apparel marketers were starting to learn a hard lesson: They couldn't dictate fashion as they used to.

Maybe if they just tried harder, or made fashions cheaper, lightning might strike again. But alas, Seventh Avenue continued to suffer with a string of designer flops in the 1990s—like the "waif" look of frilly velvet and droopy ruffled blouses, the unkempt "grunge" look, and the "fishtail" dress with its asymmetrical hemline.

The apparel industry had laid the groundwork for this rebellion by disrupting its own fashion cycles, which had always induced women to update their wardrobes. By espousing the notion of "individual style" and "investment dressing," designers had unwittingly persuaded women to stop buying so many clothes.

By 1994, the apparel industry had entered a third straight year of slumping sales, and retailers and designers alike were baffled. In 1993, women's apparel prices fell 4.4 percent from the previous year, the sharpest price decline since 1952. During the 1994 Christmas season, Liz

Claiborne revealed just how bad things had gotten: Only about 20 percent of Claiborne's fashions had moved at full price in department stores.

As for those enthusiasts who kept shopping, many women were buying far fewer clothes and paying less for them. The average retail price of a dress fell in 1994 to $35.78 from $39.30 in 1991; blazers dropped to $37 from $41.

The fallout of women's apparel had more to do with working women than fashion. As everybody shifted into wearing casual clothes most of the time, it was easy for women to become blasé about fashion. Indeed, American women were focusing more on their careers instead of their clothes. In the early 1980s, the New York advertising agency Wells, Rich and Green had surveyed hundreds of women about their fashion habits, concluding that "the more confident and independent women became, the less they liked to shop; and the more they enjoyed their work, the less they cared about clothes." Demographics were another vital component. As America's population skewed older, many women already had closets bulging with clothes they could still wear. They were also saddled with mortgages and bills for their children's education. So keeping up with the latest fashions was simply no longer a priority.

Such signals were immensely distressing to apparel marketers, who realized women's cooling attitudes toward fashion were likely to be permanent. "In women's apparel, what you're seeing in many ways is the end of an era," Carl Steidtmann, the economist, told *The Wall Street Journal* in 1994. "Businesses which grew up in the past fifteen years when the industry was growing dramatically and everything seemed to work are now in an era of no growth when nothing they are doing seems to work."

Across America, there were just too many retailers selling too many clothes at a time when many women were winnowing their wardrobes. Starting in the early 1990s, a retail shakeout began, when The Limited

Inc., which had 3,300 stores in 1990, began shuttering hundreds of its Limited, Express, and Lerner's stores. Some of the most popular apparel marketers like Merry-Go-Round, Gillian Group, and J.H. Collectibles went out of business altogether. Even the mighty Liz Claiborne was forced to shutter its seventy-five-store First Issue chain.

NOT EVERY RETAILER was confounded by fashion, however. As more women shopped for clothes that were affordable, comfortable, and casual, the retailer they now turned to was the Gap. With its combination of well-made classic clothes, the right price, and a hip, modern image, Gap had became the new fashion destination for millions of women and men. The Gap, along with its sister divisions Banana Republic and Old Navy, gained an incredible market share in the 1990s and became the world's second largest apparel brand, behind Levi's. In 1998—the year in which it opened a new store every day—Gap generated $8.3 billion in sales in its 2,237 stores, which included 953 Gap Stores, 637 Gap Kids stores, 258 Banana Republic stores, and 282 Old Navy stores in the U.S., with the remaining Gap stores in Japan, the UK, Canada, France, and Germany.

"For years, we and so many others defined fashion as 'designers,' but fashion is no longer that," said Patrick McCarthy, editor of *Women's Wear Daily,* in December 1997. "The big shift started about 18 years ago, but didn't reach fruition until the last 5 to 7 years . . . [when fashion] went from designer to moderate and everything in between. People are now defining Gap and Banana Republic as fashion, even though those stores are charging $30 for a dress."

Gap was founded in 1969 by Donald Fisher, a California real estate developer, who opened his first Gap (as in generation gap) boutique in San Francisco selling Levi's jeans and discounted records and tapes. As

Gap caught on and expanded into hundreds of stores over the next decade, Fisher bought Banana Republic in 1983, the year he made the best decision in his professional career, hiring Mickey Drexler, the former president of Ann Taylor. An MBA with the instincts of a designer and extraordinary vision, Drexler hired designers to create Gap's own extensive collections of jeans, T-shirts, and sweaters in a broad range of sizes and colors. And thus began Gap's antifashion explosion.

Gap's unpretentious, "real clothes" stance reflected the changing consumer attitudes across America starting in the late 1980s. "Fashion had ground to a halt in the 1990s, and Gap was right there to initiate the casual, dress-down trend in a big way," said David Wolfe of Doneger Group retail consultants in New York. "Gap slowed down the evolution of fashion. Every six weeks, Gap has a totally fresh assortment—not necessarily based on new designs, but on new colors. You walk into a Gap store and the consumer gets the message right away."

But just as important as Gap's easy-to-read clothes was its image. Gap began with its "Individuals of Style" campaign of black-and-white ads, putting Kim Basinger in an oversize white Gap men's shirt and pearls and Dizzy Gillespie in a Gap mock turtleneck. With its ubiquitous, seductive advertising, Gap created its own fashion moment in 1984 with a $12.50 pocket T-shirt that continues to be a wardrobe staple for millions of Americans. Next came Gap's vintage photographs of celebrities with the tagline "Humphrey Bogart wore khakis," and "Gordon Parks wore khakis." In the world according to Gap, fashion was beyond the clothes, and all about the individual who wore them.

As Gap's credibility climbed, the chain became retail's most formidable fashion authority, usurping the role department stores had owned for years. Gap didn't need designer pedigree, it didn't need snob appeal, it didn't need high prices. And, ignoring fashion's revolving door, Gap still managed to make money, even though its clothes didn't go out of style each year. Shoppers kept coming back for more Gap basics, attracted by the new colors and other flourishes Gap created to keep its styles fresh—underscored with Gap's marketing magic.

Like Marshall Field's in its heyday, Gap played big to both ends of the spectrum. Whether they were affluent or working class, folks were proud to admit that their clothes came from Gap. They were members of a modern elite: individuals secure in their own style and beyond designer hype. "That is the big shift in fashion. People now consider moderate, inexpensive clothes as chic," McCarthy said.

Department stores could only look at Gap—and take notes.

THE WOMEN'S APPAREL debacle of the early 1990s, and the triumph of Gap and its many imitators, hastened the already declining fortunes of department stores. Much more business had shifted to the discounters, who became the powerhouses of retailing. By 1996, discounters accounted for about 41 percent of general retail sales (up from 27 percent in 1987). Wal-Mart now sold more apparel than all department stores combined. And department stores' overall market share had slipped to 14 percent, down from 20 percent in 1987.

It was against this backdrop that so many entrenched local department stores were either driven out of business or compelled to merge with their one-time competitors. By 1997, more than half of all department store sales came from four conglomerates: Federated Department Stores (the owner of Bloomingdale's, Macy's, Burdines), May Department Stores, Dillard's, and Nordstrom.

Taking advantage of size, these conglomerates learned how to make more money by operating more efficiently. They centralized their buying operations—as much as 85 percent of the merchandise sold in any one location could be sold in virtually any other store in the chain.

Returning to the origins of America's first department stores in the nineteenth century—and copying the success of Gap—the amalgamated chains further democratized fashion. Federated dropped high-end merchandise from almost all its stores. "Outside of Bloomingdale's, we have an eyedropper of designer merchandise," said Terry Lundgren, vice chairman of Federated. In 1997, only 45 of Federated's 420 stores carried bridge brands—such as Ellen Tracy, Emanuel, Anne Klein, and DKNY—priced a notch below top designer labels. Across the rest of Federated, the likes of Liz Claiborne were the top of the line.

Department store retailing had become increasingly about minimizing fashion risks. But even though department stores had revamped their strategies, they would never reign supreme again. In 1997, economists at Management Horizons predicted that the department store industry "is not growing and probably won't for the foreseeable future." Management Horizons projected that sales at department stores from 1996 to 2001 would rise annually at a meager 0.5 percent, compared to growth of 2.2 percent between 1991 and 1996.

Department stores now depended on getting their fashion authority from their key suppliers, known as "matrix" brands. In menswear, for example, the big three were Polo Ralph Lauren, Tommy Hilfiger, and Nautica, which accounted for 40 percent of the men's sportswear sold in department stores in 1997. "There are maybe eight key women's apparel brands and three or four men's brands who have their systems hooked into the computers at the stores," explained Robert Buchanan, a former Wall Street retail analyst. "The matrix puts stores on automatic pilot, and relieves the buyers from having to go to so many meetings. It's just easier and more efficient for stores to operate that way."

Stores also depended on matrix brands to take on many of their former responsibilities. A typical example was Eileen Fisher, a New York designer of loose-fitting women's casual apparel priced from $40 to $250. Fisher, who founded her company in 1984, was one of the lucky ones. She felt fortunate to be on the matrix at Field's, where her collection was carried at all of its fourteen stores. She depended on getting big orders from department stores after the independent shops she used to sell to in the 1980s went out of business in the 1990s.

Fisher personified the modern fashion house of the 1990s. She designed her business to be as straightforward and conservative as her styles. Fisher didn't get distracted by throwing expensive fashion shows and hobnobbing with the press. She knew that in order to be popular with women, she first had to be an important player inside department stores.

So Fisher took care of business: designing, manufacturing, and shipping merchandise to stores. She shared the cost of building in-store shops—at a cost of several thousand dollars each—in department stores. She also forked over thousands to subsidize newspaper ads and store catalogs where her merchandise appeared.

Fisher dispatched her own team of retail coordinators to pay visits to every store branch—just like buyers did in the old days—to set up in-store displays in department stores and orient the salespeople. The designer also did her part to make certain that Eileen Fisher fashions sold before markdowns. Whenever full-price sales fell below a certain level, Fisher had to pay a rebate—in the form of a discount on future orders—to department stores. "Retailers are very serious about making their profit margins," she said.

And that's why Fisher went the extra mile to ascertain what the computer printouts couldn't tell her. What styles were missing from her collections? Did women prefer silk to rayon? Fisher fine-tuned her collections from consumer feedback she gleaned from her own chain of a dozen Eileen Fisher boutiques—and not from Field's. "At the department stores, their buyer isn't on the floor; she doesn't know," Fisher said.

As department stores directed more and more of their business to powerful matrix brands such as Eileen Fisher, they began to look alike. "The worst thing that happened to fashion in department stores was when they got carved up into all of those in-store boutiques. That's what turned stores boring," said Ellin Saltzman, a former fashion director of Saks Fifth Avenue and Macy's.

Nevertheless, boring spelled success for May Department Stores, the 240-store chain that had the best annual growth rate among department stores in the 1990s. Industry experts dubbed May's aggressive use of matrix brands the "May-onnaising" of department stores.

May's divisions included Lord & Taylor in New York, Foley's in Houston, Hecht's in Washington, D.C., and May/Robinson in Los Angeles. May's stores were clean, brightly lit, and neat, and well-stocked with the most popular mainstream brands—merchandise that was conservative, affordable, and satisfactory to May's clientele. "May has never had any pretenses," explained Aronson, the retail consultant. "It's a middle-class Sears dictated out of St. Louis."

May even managed to give the discounters a real run. Lord & Taylor, for example, frequently tempted shoppers with 20 percent off coupons on any single item already on the markdown racks. During such promotions, a dress originally priced $180 could go for as little as $54, or 70 percent off the original price.

But if Lord & Taylor could afford to give away a dress at such a steep discount, was the dress overpriced at $180 to begin with? Such steep sales made more people more skeptical. The original prices on clothes had come to resemble the "list" prices on items like stereos, prices that were steeply marked up so that they could be marked down.

As more shoppers became trained to hold out for the best deals, markdowns had indeed become a way of life. In a 1996 consumer survey of 6,300 households, 80 percent said they were motivated to buy clothes because they were advertised bargains, up from 71.7 percent in 1992. "Shoppers say, 'I can wait until the next sale or go to factory outlet malls and get it today,' " said Field's Skoda.

With so many retailers overflowing with fashion merchandise, markdowns were indeed the only way to keep the goods flowing through stores. Department store powerhouse Liz Claiborne sent fresh merchandise to stores every four to six weeks. Most department stores started marking down those goods nine weeks after the clothes hit the sales floor—if not sooner. The rationale behind this practice was that the longer merchandise was hanging on the racks, the harder it was to sell. So retailers wasted no time moving out their mistakes and moving in fresh fashions at full price.

But this revolving door also worked against fashion. When a new trend didn't sell promptly, the style disappeared before shoppers ever had a chance to catch up. A 1995 study by the retail consulting firm Management Horizons observed that the markdown syndrome had effectively blocked fashion novelties from ever reaching department stores, in an era when the chains "desperately need to be more unique." Retailers "focus on keeping the goods moving rather than experimenting with new merchandise that might differentiate them with their competitors. The unhappy result is that many department stores look shockingly similar and risk losing market share to smaller innovative specialty stores," Management Horizons concluded.

So if conventional department stores had turned into cookie-cutter operations with the same brands, what happened to the best designer fashions, the crème de la crème? Where are the 28 Shops of today? Field's continued with its 28 Shop at only two locations: State Street and Water Tower Place. But the 28 Shop of the 1990s bore little resemblance to its glorious past incarnation. At State Street, the special elevator and rotunda foyer were gone. The 28 Shop was simply another department on the eighth floor, with designer dresses from Yves Saint Laurent, Christian Lacroix, and Bill Blass grouped together on metal T-stands.

Stepping up to claim the best designer business in the late 1990s were the few high-end specialty department store chains, namely Saks Fifth Avenue, Neiman Marcus, and Barneys New York—as well as the designers themselves, such as Gucci, Escada, Jil Sander, and Giorgio Armani, who opened their own stores in cities like New York, Chicago, Houston, Los Angeles, and San Francisco.

Meanwhile, the young designers like Isaac Mizrahi, who emerged in the early 1990s, had fewer retailers left to support them. Bloomingdale's, for one, used to nurture new designers by carrying their money-losing collections for a few years until they caught on. "If we really believed in a designer, we would continue to buy them for several seasons, even if the line didn't sell well," said Kal Ruttenstein, fashion director at Bloomingdale's. He recalled that back in 1989 Bloomie's even bought a big ad in *The New York Times* to help expose Mizrahi to the public. "But today, we wouldn't do that anymore," Ruttenstein lamented. And now everybody knows that even Bloomie's sponsorship failed to save Mizrahi a decade later.

With fashion's new condensed time frame, new designer brands came and went—in a hurry. There was no point in standing behind a slow-selling newcomer when there were plenty of other new designers that stood, perhaps, a better chance at selling. "We give them about a year and if they don't make our projections, we tend to drop them," said Joan Kaner, fashion director at Neiman Marcus.

Meanwhile, the fashion authority poised to lead in the next millennium is Gap, the juggernaut which, through its various divisions, serves shoppers' needs for apparel, shoes, cosmetics, fragrances, and underwear at every price range. And at the top of its pyramid, Gap's $1 billion-a-year Banana Republic chain distinguished itself in the late 1990s as formidable competition to tonier designer brands. Its 280 shops generated retail sales of about $636 a square foot, or more than twice as much as similar mall chains.

In the fall of 1998, when Banana Republic draped itself in suede jackets, shirts, pants, and vests, the retailer pulled off an unprecedented fashion coup. Ignoring cues from Paris, Milan, or Seventh Avenue, Banana Republic decided to push suede—a material that nobody was using of late—into a major fashion statement. "We felt the opportunity in the marketplace that we could go aggressively after suede," said Gap's CEO Drexler. "Suede was a luxurious fabric and it speaks to the consumer about high quality."

And once again, the Gap organization designed the way it knew best, putting its familiar casual silhouettes, shirts, jackets, vests, and pants into buttery suede fabric imported from Italy and priced reasonably at $100 to $400. Then Banana Republic blitzed magazines and the TV airwaves with ads with stark images of the lush sportswear above the caption: "Banana Republic. Suede." The store provided free alterations on suede, which helped move almost all of the merchandise before markdowns. After Banana Republic's suede crusade, a number of the sharp-eyed merchants on Seventh Avenue began whispering the unthinkable; they were ready to copy Banana Republic, to come out with their own suede fashions for fall 1999. Banana Republic had effectively turned suede into what's known in retailing parlance as a "category killer," by creating such a demand that suede merchandise alone drew thousands of shoppers into the store.

The end of fashion has led straight to Gap, which has mastered a modern way of marketing clothes that is working according to the principle that Marshall Field's had drummed into his people long ago: "give the lady what she wants." To borrow a 1998 cover line from *Fortune* magazine: "Gap Gets It." Which means the shoppers get it, too.

IN 1995, MARSHALL Field's marked its fifth year under Dayton Hudson—but there was little to celebrate. Field's had become more populist with its "13-Hour" sales, but the novelty of a more affordable Field's wore off because every other store in Chicago was promoting lower prices as aggressively as Field's was. "We were promotionally driven into the mid-1990s but it didn't feel good and we didn't do it as well as our competition," admitted Field's Skoda. "We kept hearing from our guests [what Field's always called their customers] that this isn't what they want. This isn't why they shop here. 'I want better merchandise, great service and exciting new things. I want to be proud to have it in a Marshall Field's box.' "

Finally, management stepped back in search of a new solution that would revive its upscale image—at the expense of turning off all those bargain hunters. Phase two began when Field's gutted many of its storewide promotions—causing sales to plummet; Dayton Hudson reported that operating profit at all of its department stores plunged 41 percent in 1995 from 1994.

As Dayton Hudson management finally saw the wisdom of catering more to Field's sophisticated, hometown market, it transferred twenty-five buyers back to Chicago. "Chicago is the fashion capital of the Midwest and having more buyers here allows us to sense the pulse of a fashion city and Michigan Avenue," said Skoda.

Field's had a lot of making up to do on the fashion and image front. Field's used to rank along with Nordstrom and Crate and Barrel as a top-quality place to shop, according to Series Industry Research Systems, a market research firm that based its findings on telephone interviews with consumers. But in the 1990s, consumers had given Field's lower marks. "We're not looking at Kmart, but they have certainly dropped from the elite," Chris Ohlinger of Series Industry told the *Chicago Tribune* in September 1997. Even so, shoppers ranked Field's ahead of Bloomingdale's in terms of quality and service.

Dayton Hudson could afford to be patient while it revamped Field's, Dayton's, and Hudson's, because its core business, Target Stores, was growing faster than ever and shoring up the corporation's balance sheet. By 1997, Target's 736 locations accounted for $17 billion, or 70 percent, of Dayton Hudson's revenue and 80 percent of its operating profits, while the department stores registered 12 percent of revenue and 8 percent of profits.

Target had carved out a niche as an upscale discounter by offering apparel and household merchandise—and it became one of the most sophisticated and efficient retail operators in America. Target used the same tactics as supermarkets: It knew exactly how much space on each shelf went to a particular brand of deodorant.

Just like Gap's Old Navy, Target had given $10 knit shirts and $19.99 jeans a fashion image. Target's apparel and housewares were a notch above budget, but its merchandise didn't look cheesy. It became fashionable for well-to-do shoppers to visit the store they nicknamed "Tarjay," with a French pronunciation.

In 1997, Target rolled out an arch, high-fashion ad campaign, "Fashion and Housewares," that wooed shoppers with humor. One of the first ads shows a bald man in a $7.99 knit shirt with an $18.99 desk fan slung across his back. Target became the first discounter that successfully positioned itself as hip.

Field's, Dayton's, and Hudson's benefited by being a part of Target's family, not only because of its profits, but also its model efficiency. Accordingly, the department store division trimmed its expenses by $50 million in 1997, sharpened its list of vendors, and hired more salespeople. Moreover, the division maximized its productivity. "In the old days it would take us maybe three or four days to unload a fifty-three-foot trailer that was full of merchandise," said Hank Lorant, Field's regional director of stores, in 1998. "Now we can get all that merchandise unloaded and onto the sales floor in three or four hours."

Field's was also busy designing a new image for itself, as a department store that offered value and customer service, tarted up with a dash of glamour. The cheeky advertising strategy that worked wonders on Target did the same for Field's. In 1997, Field's came out with a new advertising tagline: "Where else? Marshall Field's." The ads were shot throughout the expansive, historic State Street store in order to underscore the breadth of merchandise that shoppers could find only at Field's. In one of the TV commercials in the Walnut Room restaurant, three modern Holly Golightlys—in black sheath dresses and big black hats—were seated at a table. The announcer recited breathlessly, "Yves Saint Laurent, Ungaro, Escada, Missoni—and *Vivienne*," referring to the smiling waitress who suddenly appeared to serve them.

The message from this commercial—that Field's employees aimed to serve its shoppers—reflected the store's new emphasis on training its sales associates to perform specific duties. Some staffers were assigned to "push teams," whose jobs were to rearrange merchandise on markdown displays, while others concentrated on selling to customers full time. Field's also motivated salespeople by paying commissions for the first time, to individuals in such key areas as fashion apparel and shoes, which attracted a better caliber of salespeople.

While Field's was still wedded to its matrix list of national brands, the store was also beginning to benefit from having more of its buyers in Chicago. "They are now on hand to attend the local social events, to see where the trends are, and they convey this to our partners in Minneapolis," Skoda said.

While such tinkering began to take effect, Field's still had a long way to go. In 1997, Donna Karan agreed to be the featured designer at Field's annual fall fashion benefit. But after executives from Donna Karan International made a visit to Field's, the designer changed her mind and pulled out of the event. Karan begged off, citing conflicts in her hectic schedule, but that wasn't the real reason why she wasn't coming to Chicago.

"We couldn't believe how Field's had gone down," said one Donna Karan official who recalled his walk through Field's. "I mean, they put *one* Saint Laurent dress on a hanger and call that their designer department. There are practically no designer goods at the store. It would have been bad for our image for Donna to do that event."

But if the Donna Karan people had returned to Chicago a year later, they might have felt better about Field's, where improvements were starting to kick in. One Field's shopper, Kathy Robinson, told the *Chicago Tribune* in July 1998 that she had recently bought furniture, shoes, and clothes at Field's on State Street. "They're slowly but surely roping me in. If I'm going to a department store, it's Field's," Robinson said.

Field's new polish penetrated more than just the surface. Dayton Hudson reported that its department store division had risen impressively all through 1997, when pretax profit grew 59 percent to $240 million from the year before. And Field's was on track in 1998 to post another stellar year. In August 1998, an executive at Field's hometown rival,

Carson Pirie Scott, paid a rare compliment to Field's in the *Chicago Tribune.* "They recognized they weren't going in the direction they should have been. They did something about it and it seems to be paying off," said Ed Carroll, Carson's executive vice president of marketing.

Basking in its recent good fortune, Field's threw its September 11, 1998, fashion benefit with a newfound confidence. It was a night of déjà vu as designer Carolina Herrera was the featured designer at the black-tie benefit at the Museum of Contemporary Art, which was only a few blocks away from Water Tower Place, where Herrera had attended Field's most memorable bash a decade ago.

"An Evening of Fashion and Art" was the theme of the party, which began with cocktails under a tent behind the museum. After a fashion show featuring Herrera, Sonia Rykiel, Ungaro, and Calvin Klein designs, the Venezuelan-born Herrera, regal in her white satin shirt and a full gray taffeta skirt, took her runway bow, caressing a bouquet of white calla lilies.

An Andy Warhol portrait of Herrera hung on the wall in the corridor at the museum where a gourmet dinner of lamb chops and grilled shrimp salad was served. The evening was elegant and low-key, with guests going home around 11 P.M. carrying gift bags with two miniature Herrera perfume samples.

While some Chicagoans still believed that Field's fared better without Dayton Hudson, the truth was that Field's would have never would have survived on its own. Under the stewardship of Dayton Hudson, Field's initially stumbled badly, but also remade itself for the future by adopting many of Target's best practices.

Working the room at the party was the blond and bubbly Sugar Rautbord, a fixture on Chicago's Gold Coast scene for more than twenty years, who was dressed in a steel-gray Herrera gown from Field's. She was having a swell time, smiling and posing for photographers. She didn't seem to mind at all that the party wasn't so lavish.

"Thank God, the eighties are over!" she declared. "Everything is now pared down; people don't want to be overdone nowadays. This is the smart way to do philanthropy in the nineties." Then Rautbord let it be known that she loved to shop at Field's again: "Field's is on its way back. The store is making a renaissance."

chapter 6

GORED IN A BULL MARKET: WHEN DONNA KARAN WENT TO WALL STREET

No, I'm not your typical CEO—far from it. But to take a company from zero to $700 million says something about how we operate. Do we do it by the straight and narrow? Of course not. We cut on the bias. I'm a creative thinker with a vision.

—DONNA KARAN, May 1997

I don't watch the stock price. The stock price is like hemlines. It goes up and it goes down.

—DONNA KARAN, October 1996

For Donna Karan, the last week of October 1996 was about as harried as it gets. The first lady of American fashion was once again caught up in the frenzy of producing two major fashion shows—and more. She opened the week with the introduction of D, an experimental collection of avant-garde sportswear, and closed it with a fashion show of her Donna Karan New York couture collection. In between the traffic on the runways, Karan had to be *on*, especially on

Wednesday evening when she met with a group of Wall Street money managers—a group that was decidedly not in her fashion tribe.

The Week That Was began on Sunday, October 27, under the fashion-show tents set up in Bryant Park behind the New York Public Library, the venue where Bill Blass, Todd Oldham, and Nicole Miller and forty other designers were unveiling their spring 1997 women's collections. That afternoon, D debuted under a special tent designed to meet Karan's exacting specifications.

The big tent was now a study in beige, its ceiling and walls draped with hundreds of yards of filmy gauze fabric. The rows of folding chairs were gone, replaced with long benches with individual seat cushions covered in creamy muslin. The atmosphere was intimate and ethereal, a setting in keeping with Donna Karan's recent embrace of spiritualism and New Age philosophy. Behind the gauzy layers were models, hairdressers, makeup artists, and technicians whose efforts would culminate in a twenty-minute presentation that would cost nearly half a million dollars.

Seated under the beige top were about 650 fashion editors, photographers, and retailers. In the front row—and oblivious to flashing cameras pointed at her—was actress Demi Moore, still sporting her *GI Jane* buzz cut. (Earlier that year, she and her husband, Bruce Willis, had modeled in Karan's print ads.) The press release placed in each seat described D in a flurry of alliteration: "directional, definitive, distinctive, downtown and daring." Models paraded down the runway in see-through asymmetrical tops worn in layers with tight tube skirts.

D was also derivative, in the minds of a number of fashion sharpshooters in the audience, who whispered to each other as they spotted the references to minimalist German designers Helmut Lang and Jil Sander. Retail buyers, who had had their fill of such looks during the Paris and Milan shows just weeks earlier, were perplexed, figuring that

D, which was pricier than Karan's sporty DKNY line, would be difficult to sell to women. In any event, the press reviews of the show were generally upbeat, if guarded. "Women will decide whether they enjoy playing with Karan's lean, body-clinging pieces to create an effortless effect," opined Mimi Avins in the *Los Angeles Times.*

Meanwhile, back in the heart of New York's garment district at 550 Seventh Avenue, Donna Karan's corporate headquarters, staffers scrambled to prepare her showroom for the rest of the week. The long, black-walled space on the fourteenth floor would be doing double duty, as the venue for Friday's fashion show as well as the Wednesday night dinner Karan was hosting for fifty Wall Street institutional investors.

Of all the hectic weeks for Donna Karan to play hostess! It wasn't her idea. But then, there was no way she could turn down Morgan Stanley, the investment bank that had led her namesake fashion house to Wall Street in a $258 million initial public offering four months earlier. Josie Esquivel, Morgan Stanley's apparel industry analyst, talked her into it, insisting that it would be a good idea for Karan, the chairman and CEO, to get acquainted with some of the key people who would hold considerable sway over her stock.

On Wednesday evening, Karan came dressed in all-black, as usual, her hair in a floppy cheerleader ponytail with long bangs. She was with Stephen Ruzow, her trusted chief operating officer. They led the group on a tour throughout the building and through more offices around the corner at 240 East Thirty-ninth Street, to give them a feel for what was behind the $510-million-a-year Donna Karan franchise: women's and men's apparel, sunglasses, handbags, athletic shoes, backpacks, perfumes, and cosmetics. Afterward, everybody sat down at tables on the showroom runway, which was now dim and cozy, with dozens of flickering scented candles from the Donna Karan Home Collection. While they dined on chicken and salad, two models strolled around in the styles from the spring couture line that would be shown on Friday.

What grade did the Wall Street suits give Karan for the evening? Somewhere between Satisfactory and Incomplete.

"It was all very opulent, very impressive," recalled one portfolio manager who was there. "But I can tell you that I didn't leave there feeling any more optimistic about the outlook for the stock."

He and the other money managers had reason to be skeptical about Donna Karan International. Back in June, when the company made its bow on the New York Stock Exchange, investors were psyched, lining up for the 10.8 million shares, representing 50 percent of the company, that were for sale in the initial public offering, or IPO. As investors deemed Donna Karan the most fashionable deal of the season, the stock commanded a respectable opening price of $24 a share.

But the excitement surrounding Donna Karan, listed under the symbol DK, didn't last long. On June 28, the first day of trading, DK bounced up to $30, then settled to close at a respectable $28, as many investors flipped their holdings, collected their one-day profits, and bailed out. Just thirty days later, DK slumped below its offering price to $21—and then the race to the bottom began, as the shares skidded like a run in a pair of sheer DKNY pantyhose.

By October, DK had tumbled to $15.50, in response to the company's lower-than-expected third-quarter earnings. A few months later, more bad news surfaced: a $1.7 million net loss in the fourth quarter. The company red-flagged some troubling signs: Its businesses were "too broadly focused" and internal expenses had ballooned way over budget. CEO Karan vowed to slash costs, and she ordered "management to take measures to insure that this trend doesn't continue." By the end of 1996, barely six months after the opening day, DK shares had tanked to the $9 range.

As speculation swirled that DK was headed for a meltdown, stockbrokers started wisecracking about the glossy fashion issue that was now as deceptive as a well-placed shoulder pad. Among traders, DK just happened to have another meaning, as in "don't know." A stock is "DK'd" when a broker can't complete a trade because he doesn't recognize the transaction, arguing that he didn't make it and doesn't know who did. And DK shares were certainly an enigma.

The House of Karan was now in the thick of it, taking a hazing on Wall Street. There was no escaping the reality that it was no longer business as usual. The very fact that Karan had been forced to entertain those Wall Streeters right in the middle of the hectic fashion-show week was a wake-up call if ever there was one.

Many people acquainted with Karan weren't at all surprised, suspecting that the pressures of being a chief executive with real fiscal responsibilities hadn't sunk in yet for the forty-seven-year-old designer. And they were right. Karan was clueless about the rules of Wall Street. Public companies are under pressure to keep everything up: revenue, earnings, and the stock price. There's nowhere to hide, because securities regulations require public companies to issue quarterly income statements as well as to disclose promptly any material developments that could affect future earnings, such as the sales of assets, lawsuits, and executive changes. And whenever bad news comes out, the reaction is swift: The stock price takes a tumble, followed by a flurry of negative news articles.

Accustomed to setting her own agenda and projecting upbeat, larger-than-life images of herself and her fashion house, Karan wasn't ready for prime time on Wall Street, which was like living in a fishbowl. She wasn't used to people questioning her abilities. Every so often, fashion editors would nix her runway collections, but they never grilled her about business matters.

So why did Karan go to the trouble to take her fashion house public and put herself under such a hammer? She was up against a wall. Takihyo Inc., the financial backer who had launched her company in 1985 and owned 50 percent of it, was ready to cash out. Takihyo partners Tomio Taki and Frank Mori had become embittered with Karan, after having locked horns with her on the company's business strategies during the 1990s.

When a divorce between the parties became imminent, going public was the obvious option. "Unfortunately, we never really discussed the concept of why we were going public and what that meant. It was not just getting the money," Taki recalled. "Now, we had different objectives than she did. . . . The investment banker explained everything to her in advance. But I just don't think it registered in her mind."

After the offering, Mori and Taki took their share of the proceeds—$58 million in cash and about 25 percent of the outstanding shares in the public company—and bowed out, leaving Karan to fend for herself for the first time in the company's eleven-year history.

Karan had always held the title of chief executive officer, but hers was largely a ceremonial role without real fiduciary responsibilities. Back in 1993, when Karan first floated the idea of going public, Wall Street analysts immediately raised concerns about her ability to run the company without Taki and Mori. But she didn't heed that warning. Karan refused to give up her CEO title then and she refused again in 1996. She loved the title and she felt confident that Ruzow would continue to do the heavy lifting on financial matters, as he had done in the past.

For years, Karan relished her role as the company's creative visionary, an artsy image that had played well for her, and she fully expected her expanded role with the big boys on Wall Street would play even better. Anna Wintour, editor of *Vogue*, thought her readers might like to see Karan up close and personal, as a CEO on the verge of taking her company public. Karan had kept a diary during the sixty road-show presentations she and Ruzow made before institutional investors in America and Europe, in the effort to drum up interest in DK shares. "Going Public," by Donna Karan, ran in the September 1996 issue of *Vogue*.

Poking fun at herself as a fashion creature trapped inside a world full of suits, Karan recounted how, on the long plane rides between stops, she got up to speed, memorizing accounting lingo like "EBIT" (earnings before income and taxes). She was incredulous at how nosy those professional money managers could be: "What going public really means is that everybody gets into your business quite literally."

Her entry for Day Six in Portland, Oregon: "These guys are really most interested in margins—what makes money? Growth and how to support it. It's not about luxury and cashmere and fabric and color. It's the bottom line."

While the designer CEO came across as amusing, if a bit flaky, in *Vogue*, the shareholders who read the article weren't laughing, because their DK holdings were tanking. Taki was among the exasperated. "She made it sound like a game," he said of the article. "Everybody already thinks that she doesn't know anything about [being a CEO]. The investors are thinking, 'She is the CEO and I am depending on *her* to manage the company with my money?' It is ridiculous!" Taki and Mori, as selling shareholders in the original offering, were obliged to hold on to that big block of shares they owned for at least a year before they could start cashing in. Their wait would be painful. By mid-September, their DK holdings had lost more than $40 million in value since the June offering.

In July 1997, after a full year of hard knocks in the stock market, Karan aired her frustrations in a speech before an audience of fashion industry executives: "I have been a CEO for ten years, yet nothing in my experience prepared me for the challenge of going public. Like having a baby, it doesn't matter how much advice you get, how much reading you do—until you go through it yourself, you have no idea what's coming."

By then, it had become clear that Karan's days as chief executive officer were numbered. But the jury was still out on how long the celebrated fashion house would stay in style on Wall Street.

DURING THE 1990S, the "monastic" look, "grunge," and fishtail hemlines were among the fleeting runway fads that barely lasted a season before they disappeared into fashion oblivion. But what did catch on, the trend that every fashion house wanted to knock off, was going public. The climate was perfect for new stock issues, with interest rates low and a roaring, unstoppable bull market. A record number of retail and fashion issues went public starting in 1992, with forty such companies coming to market between October 1995 and November 1997.

Besides Donna Karan, the newcomers to the New York Stock Exchange and the Nasdaq over-the-counter market included Gucci, Tommy Hilfiger, St. John Knits, Jones Apparel Group, Kenneth Cole Productions, Polo Ralph Lauren, Mossimo, Marisa Christina, Starter, He-Ro Group, North Face, Nautica, and Guess.

A number of these new issues seemed highly unlikely to produce the long-term growth and profits that public companies were supposed to sustain. For one, there was Mossimo, a West Coast maker of casual menswear best known for its $28 volleyball shorts with a funny script logo. Another questionable contender was He-Ro Group, which specialized in cocktail dresses marketed under the designer label Oleg Cassini—not a familiar name to most women. Cassini's big moment occurred more than thirty years before when he dressed First Lady Jacqueline Kennedy. Compared to those companies, Donna Karan International looked downright solid. Nevertheless, Donna Karan was vulnerable to instability given that 70 percent of its business came from expensive and trendy clothes for women and men.

Traditionally, the companies behind some of the top-performing apparel stocks projected an aura of invincibility. For example, VF Corp. (1998 sales of $5.5 billion) marketed commodity staples—Lee and Wrangler jeans and Vanity Fair bras—items that millions of people would always need to replace, regardless of what was in style. Likewise, Warnaco Group Inc. (1998 sales of $2 billion) contained a good balance of sturdy fashion licensed brands: Victoria's Secret lingerie, Chaps by Ralph Lauren, and Calvin Klein underwear. And the longtime stronghold in department stores Liz Claiborne Inc. (1998 sales of $2.5 billion) had been the apparel maker favored by legions of career women since the early 1980s. Such consistently solid performers made a lot of sense as public companies.

Nevertheless, Wall Street rolled out the welcome mat to a number of iconoclastic businesses during the go-go stock market of the 1990s. "The market has broadened," observed Linda Killian of Renaissance Capital Corp., a firm that specializes in evaluating new stock issues. "When you look back in the sixties, seventies and eighties, the typical IPOs were bio-tech and high-tech companies. But companies that were never viewed as being suitable for the public market were suddenly attractive in the 1990s. The list includes pet supermarkets, Internet stocks, gaming, and fashion—they all are the new industries in the IPO market."

Despite the ephemeral and unpredictable nature of fashion, more apparel companies were viewed as attractive investments in the nineties because designer names and fashion brands had become powerful hooks in the marketplace. "Part of the valuation that goes into a company is brand equity," Killian explained. "The fashion companies now have the ability to license across a number of products not only at the high end but at the lower price points."

Never before had apparel companies had such reach. For example, Guess Inc. (founded in 1981) was one of the hundreds of apparel makers that cashed in on the designer jeans boom. Guess marketed the sexy "three-zip Marilyn jean," which it advertised on the fetching German model Claudia Schiffer. As demand for designer jeans ebbed and flowed over the years, Guess could have easily slipped off the fashion radar. But instead, Guess spent millions on advertising to position itself as a power brand and a full-fledged fashion house, which attracted many licensees. In 1995, the year before it went public, Guess had sales of $440 million, $48 million of which came from royalties it collected from twenty-six licensees that made Guess infants' and children's wear, eyewear, footwear, active sportswear, and sheets and towels.

As fashion moved into the forefront of pop culture, Wall Street became seduced by the celebrity of designers. Donna Karan's best design effort ever may have been her road shows for investors. Her campaign began with a stock prospectus sporting an unusual black cover that resembled her fashion-show invitations. Investors who attended the presentations took home a DKNY baseball cap, sunglasses, a T-shirt, and cosmetics.

Karan played to standing-room crowds on most stops on the circuit. Instead of lecturing her audiences, she dazzled them with a touch of glamour: a little fashion show. Apologizing for not looking like a supermodel, Karan made quick changes behind a folding screen near the podium. She switched jackets—from black to white to lime green—to demonstrate the versatility of her signature "seven easy pieces" formula, suitable for day-to-night, office-to-black-tie dressing. A video montage followed, featuring Karan alongside her pal Barbra Streisand. There was

President Bill Clinton in one of Karan's draped wool crepe suits and First Lady Hillary Rodham Clinton hosting her first White House state dinner in 1992 in Karan's famous "cold shoulder" gown in black.

"Investors were starstruck to watch her up there," recalled Esquivel of Morgan Stanley. "It was the whole celebrity aspect of her. Everybody felt this was a deal they *had* to be in."

The glamour factor "certainly helps sell the stock initially," said Killian. "But ultimately, a fashion stock reverts to form over time." In other words, "what investors are looking for are not accolades for their fashions or from their peer group, but more consistent growth—sound financial growth and management."

As always in the erratic world of fashion, past performance was never any guarantee of future results, which was why fashion issues would always be high-risk investments.

"Fashion companies can be good, family-owned businesses, but most of them aren't cut out to be public companies," asserted Arnold Cohen, the principal of Mahoney Cohen, a leading accounting firm on Seventh Avenue. Cohen knew this first-hand from his years as chief financial officer of Puritan Fashions, a popular New York dress manufacturer in the sixties and seventies. When Puritan began trading on the New York Stock Exchange in 1965, its annual sales exceeded $100 million and its top-selling dress label was Forever Young by Gloria Swanson, a licensed brand named for the ageless star of *Sunset Boulevard*. But in the late sixties, when the fashion winds blew in the opposite direction—pantsuits—Puritan was caught flat-footed, and it scrambled to shift into slacks. Cohen remembered: "Puritan couldn't survive in this environment."

Thanks to the tenacity of Carl Rosen, Puritan's visionary chairman, the dressmaker managed to hang on and even enjoyed a renaissance in the late 1970s, when Rosen took the leap to become the jeans licensee for Calvin Klein. But like so many apparel companies, Puritan had no executive management to speak of. So when Rosen died in 1983, Calvin Klein Inc. rushed to acquire Puritan in order to protect what had been Klein's core designer jeans business.

Cohen related a story about one of his clients, a privately owned maker of women's coats, that illustrated a recurring theme in the rag trade. This coatmaker had enjoyed healthy sales gains for years until two consecutive warm winters hammered sales, leaving the maker stuck with too much unsold inventory. So the owner elected to cut back sharply on the number of coats he produced in 1997, a decision that caused his annual sales to plummet to $74 million from $100 million. The owner had no one to answer to but himself. It would be *his* call when—if ever—to pump up the volume again. "Now that doesn't smack of a public company, does it?" Cohen asked. "Once you are public, no way can you go backwards, even if the bottom line is better at $74 million than it was at $100 million. There is always that pressure for public companies to grow."

Still, going public offered many advantages to owners, such as when aging founders were ready to cash out of their businesses. And when more fashion houses were looking for growth outside the U.S., which was another trend in the 1990s, being a public company, with an enhanced ability to raise capital, made it far easier to expand internationally.

In the early 1990s, a handful of showcase fashion IPOs started the stampede to Wall Street. All of Seventh Avenue looked on with envy and awe as Jones Apparel Group, maker of Jones New York women's apparel, went public in 1991 at $14 a share. Jones's fortunes rose with its stock price—and its founder, Sidney Kimmel, became much richer. By selling blocks of shares he owned at the right time, Kimmel personally pocketed more than $300 million between 1991 and 1997. And shareholders made out quite handsomely, too. A $1,000 investment in Jones at the May 1991 offering was valued at $5,607 by March 1997.

Then along came Tommy in 1992. Menswear maker Tommy Hilfiger Corp. issued a $15-a-share IPO on the New York Stock Exchange. Hilfiger's fashions at retail became hotter than a pistol in the ensuing years, as the popular brand gained market share to become one of the top three menswear brands in department stores, along with Polo Ralph Lauren and Nautica. An initial $1,000 investment from the Hilfiger offering at $7.50 a share (adjusted for a stock split) was worth $6,866 by March 1997.

Those fashion issues were among the few best-case scenarios—and the examples everybody on Seventh Avenue repeated as the justification to go public. But some of the most touted fashion issues also turned out to be dogs, whose stocks collapsed within a year of their coming to the market. A $1,000 investment in Guess Inc. at the time of its August 1996 IPO had shrunk in value to $611 by March 1997. Likewise, $1,000 spent on Mossimo's shares in February 1996 were worth $548 twelve months later. And only nine months after Donna Karan's June 1996 IPO, a $1,000 investment in DK had a value of $458.

Donna Karan's sorry performance broke the spell and cast a dark shadow around the entire sector. "The Donna Karan IPO did a lot to hurt the perception of the apparel business among today's investors," Margaret Mager, apparel analyst at Goldman Sachs, told *WWD* in 1998. Subsequently, there were far fewer new issues after Donna Karan, as Wall Street began losing its taste for fashion.

Clearly, Donna Karan's travails were unique to its operations, but Wall Street wasn't necessarily buying that argument. To quell the skeptics, at least one apparel maker adopted a new spin for its IPO. When Columbia Sportswear, a Portland, Oregon, maker of parkas and jackets geared to snowboarding, skiing, and fishing (1997 sales of $350 million), went to the market in early 1998, it took pains to distance itself from the likes of Donna Karan and Mossimo. In road-show presentations to institutional investors, Columbia skirted the F-word, preferring to describe clothes as "outdoor" apparel instead of fashion.

"High fashion and Wall Street are like oil and vinegar. They don't mix," declared Alan Millstein, a New York fashion industry consultant. "The best public companies out there, like Liz Claiborne, Jones Apparel, and St. John Knits, are safer than the others because they don't depend on selling runway clothes." But for Donna Karan, the runway was the center of her fashion universe, where the yellow-brick road to going public all began.

IN 1985, KARAN opened the doors of her fashion house to such fanfare that in record time, she shot to the top as America's best-known designer, beloved by executive women. And she became the last women's designer to cross the threshold into the major leagues. There have been no shortage of promising, media-savvy talents coming on the scene since then—such as Isaac Mizrahi, Marc Jacobs, Michael Kors, Todd Oldham, and Cynthia Rowley—but none of them flew very high, nowhere near the $100-million-a-year mark in sales. And many crashed, notably the celebrated Mizrahi, who shuttered his business in 1998 after ten unprofitable years. "Donna is an innovator; the only world-class designer to ever come out of Seventh Avenue since Anne Klein," said Millstein.

After Karan, it was as if some invisible hand had pulled up the drawbridge. The fact that Karan had managed to break through the ranks when so many others couldn't owed a great deal to her extraordinary talents as a designer and marketer. But Karan also lucked out, with a number of pluses that greatly facilitated her ascent.

Timing, for one. Karan got in on the ground floor during the designer wave of the 1980s, when she was able to fill a need for a new generation of affluent women, many of whom were advertising executives and investment bankers over thirty. These women could afford to wear the luxurious designer creations by Bill Blass or Oscar de la Renta, who were the favorites of Nancy Reagan and the ladies-who-lunch set. But high-powered baby boomers wanted a designer of their own generation and there weren't many to choose from—Giorgio Armani had barely begun his push into women's wear. So women gravitated to Karan, who gave them clothes that were glamorous, sophisticated, and very modern. What's more, Karan's target customers could easily identify with a designer who was an ambitious career woman, married with a daughter.

Furthermore, Karan had been blessed by having secured what young designers didn't get anymore: deep-pocketed private investors who were also experienced managers in apparel manufacturing. When Ralph Lauren and Calvin Klein went into business in the late 1960s, they didn't need a wealthy benefactor—each was able to scrape together the $10,000 or so that it took to open a fashion company. But that was long before the marketplace became inundated with fashion designers and the price of entry rose dramatically. Launching a prestigous designer business in New York in the 1990s required real capital, at least a million dollars. And because establishing a new fashion house took years, and success was such a crapshoot, few independent investors were willing to take a flier on an untested designer who was more likely to fail than to succeed.

Financiers such as Taki and Mori were rare and the last of their kind. They poured more than $10 million of capital into Donna Karan for more than a decade, and their business acumen was critical in turning Karan's dream into a thriving enterprise.

It has often been said that fashion designers are born, not made. And true to legend, Donna Ivy Faske had fashion in her bloodline. She grew up in the sixties in suburban Woodmere, Long Island, where her mother,

Helen Richie Faske, known as "Queenie," was a showroom model and sales representative for manufacturers in New York's garment district. Her father, who died when she was three, was a tailor, while her stepfather, Harold Flaxman, toiled in the rough and tumble of the rag trade's dress business.

Young Donna, by her own admission, was a terrible student, one who cut classes and lied about her age to land her first job, selling clothes at a neighborhood boutique at age fourteen. "I was always a working person," she once recalled. "I knew fashion was a part of me whether I'd be a retailer or an illustrator or what. I knew I was artistic. Whether I was artistic enough was a real question in my mind."

With her shaky high school record, Donna had to use her mother's connections with Seventh Avenue designer Chester Weinberg in order to get admitted into New York's Parsons School of Design, one of the top fashion schools. Finally in her element, Donna flourished at Parsons alongside classmates Louis Dell'Olio, Bill Robinson, and Willi Smith, who would go on to become famous designers. Donna stood out by winning student awards for her designs, and she caught the eye of designer Anne Klein, the doyenne of American sportswear at the time. Klein took a shine to the spirited young talent, who dropped out of Parsons to become one of her assistants.

But Donna was unfocused on the job and proved to be a handful for the demanding Klein, who fired her after a few months. Over the next eighteen months, Donna finally got herself together, as she moved on to another sportswear house, then settled down and got married to Mark Karan, a Long Island boutique owner. In 1974, she went back to Anne Klein, who gave her a second chance.

Knocking on Anne Klein's door the year before was Tomio Taki, a wealthy Tokyo businessman who had come to Manhattan to buy a fashion company. Taki had no experience on Seventh Avenue, but he was deeply rooted in apparel making, having spent his early career in his family's business, Takihyo Group, a two-hundred-year-old apparel, textile, and consumer products company based in Nagoya, Japan.

In 1960, Taki's father put him through a test. Young Taki had to develop an apparel factory in Okinawa, an island where labor costs were high. Taki first had to determine which garments the Okinawan workers could make efficiently and would also generate healthy profit margins. He settled on producing cotton raincoats, which the factory eventually exported to the U.S. by the thousands.

Landing in New York, Taki once again had to figure things out. He went about doing some practical market research. With the help of several business contacts, he sent dozens of ordinary women on a shopping mission: to secretly cut out the hang tags from clothes by their favorite upscale designers. From the thickest stacks of tags—Bill Blass, Halston, and Anne Klein—Taki began making overtures. He ultimately bought a 50 percent stake in Anne Klein & Co. from investors Gunther Oppenheim and Sandy Smith, leaving designer Anne Klein and her husband, Chip, who ran her sales showroom, owning the other half of the business.

Gunther Oppenheim was a legendary garment district impresario, who liked to make his money fast, without a lot of hassles, to "get the order, make it, ship it," remembered Dexter Levy, an accountant who worked at Anne Klein back then. As America's most acclaimed designer sportswear brand, Anne Klein was a perennial top seller at department stores—so Oppenheim had no complaints about sales.

But what made him furious were the spiraling expenses Klein incurred in the design studio, where she spent lavishly on fabrics and samples to create her famous collections. Levy remembered: "Anne was legendary for flying all over the world, looking for the best fabrics, at any and all costs." He estimated that she spent as much as $1 million a year just in sample fabrics, at a time when the company's sales were about

$10 million. As the studio's bills swelled with her creative whims, Oppenheim flew off the handle. "Gunther was always battling with Anne, telling her 'You've gotta sell this! I ain't Chase Manhattan Bank!' " Levy recalled, adding that Oppenheim was obsessed about costs because "half of the money in the company was his, and he was tightfisted."

When Taki showed up, Oppenheim was in his seventies, had recently remarried, and was good and ready to cash out of Anne Klein. Levy said: "Gunther wasn't interested in fighting the fights with Anne and Chip anymore. Tom [Taki] made them [Oppenheim and Smith] a fair offer and they left the business."

Less than a year after Taki entered the picture, in October 1974, Klein suddenly died of cancer. Taki promptly promoted her top assistant, Donna Karan, who was twenty-six and about to give birth to her first child at the time, and he hired her Parson's buddy Louis Dell'Olio to help her. (Taki eventually acquired the rest of Anne Klein from widower Chip Klein.)

In the beginning, according to Levy, Taki was more of a passive investor in Anne Klein, spending most of his time in Tokyo in his family's business. But in 1975, he hired Frank Mori, a seasoned garment industry veteran and Harvard MBA, to run Anne Klein. The fashion house continued to thrive under Karan and Dell'Olio, and Karan quickly gained confidence, Levy noted. "Donna grew in the job. When the Saks buyers came in, she sold the line herself in the showroom. She began to think she was Anne Klein reincarnate, that *she* represented the organization."

And Karan, just like her late mentor, was a big spender. "She had picked up all of Anne's bad habits," said Levy, who remembered one time in the mid-1970s: "I went to what I thought was a dry run for the fashion show and I came back the next day and Donna had worked all night, completely changing the second half of the show." Karan and Mori often argued bitterly about her penchant to waste money. "They had some life and death struggles, but generally she would cave in to Frank," Levy said.

Taki and Mori, partners in Takihyo USA, however, got along quite well in business. "There are no power plays here," Mori once said about their relationship. Taki's low-key cerebral style was a sharp contrast to Seventh Avenue's tightly controlled family businesses. When managers visited Taki's office in New York, they had little reason to be intimidated. Instead of a traditional desk in his office, there was a round mahogany table with four armchairs. Taki invited visitors to "sit wherever you want."

Over the next decade, Karan and Dell'Olio proved that the Anne Klein trademark could have a long afterlife. The formidable design duo won three Coty Awards, fashion's equivalent to the Oscars at the time. They also designed Anne Klein II, which was one of the first bridge collections, priced a notch below designer brands and sold in department stores. Anne Klein had more than twenty licensees for jewelry, scarves, belts, and such, and its annual sales grew to more than $400 million at its peak in the late 1980s.

By 1983, Karan felt she had outgrown Anne Klein. She wanted to stretch, to express herself with her own high-fashion collection. As she became harder to manage, Mori made it easy for her to leave: He fired her. Karan had an employment contract with an annual salary of $1 million, which meant that Mori and Taki were obliged to pay her for the remaining years of the contract.

"Donna pushed this thing to the brink—and they realized the liability," said Levy. "So they made an arrangement with her to use her severance pay to back her in business. They felt that they could cap their liability and control how much they would have to put in the business. They didn't worry because Donna was a great designer, a proven commodity."

In 1985, Taki and Mori spun off Karan into her own house, leaving Dell'Olio to continue at Anne Klein. Karan now had everything going for her. She had divorced Mark Karan and married an old flame, Stephan Weiss, a sculptor and a divorcee with two children. And she had her very own fashion house where she wasn't simply an employee, but an equal partner.

The fact that Karan always owned 50 percent of her company seemed highly unusual because moneymen typically weren't so generous. Financial backers always retained the majority stake so that they could retain the power to control. But when Karan negotiated with Taki and Mori, she insisted on owning half of her namesake company. Taki, who was known to be generous in his business dealings, came around to agree that she needed a substantial stake in the venture. Taki recalled: "I wanted her to be confident and by owning half of the company she would have that confidence. I gave it to her to encourage her to build her own equity base." But down the road, he would regret his largess.

Karan also got something else that Taki agreed was important for the company's image: the title of chief executive officer. Although they never put it in writing, Taki claimed, "it was always understood that she made the marketing and fashion decisions, and we made the financial decisions. This is the way it was supposed to be. And it wasn't a problem at the beginning. At the start, it was the three of us. Usually if we said no to anything, she wouldn't say anything more."

But this harmony would change after Karan's husband, Weiss, became more involved with the company. During the first few seasons, when the fashion house was mired in production and delivery problems, Weiss stepped in to help. "I needed a fire helmet because I was putting out fires all day," he told *Working Woman* in 1993. Weiss also admitted that he wasn't comfortable during the times his position put him in an "adversarial role with Donna, which I didn't like." Eventually, Weiss bowed out of the day-to-day management and shifted his energies to directing the company's new ventures and licensing.

Taki characterized Weiss as a diligent, hard worker, one who was learning on the job about the fashion business. Weiss once approached Taki to seek his own stake for himself in Donna Karan. Taki responded to him: "Go talk to Donna," who eventually split her 50 percent interest in her house with him. Soon, Weiss was attending the partners' quarterly planning meetings, where all the company's key decisions were made.

With Weiss joining in the mix, the meetings became more confrontational, since Karan now had an ally. Taki remembered, "Unfortunately, the combination of Donna and Steve became too much of a problem. Sometimes, it was Donna and Steve against me and Frank, or Steve and Frank against Donna. I had to calm them down."

The high-strung Karan was famous for throwing fits when she couldn't get her way with Taki and Mori. According to Taki: "She would sit down on the couch, scream, yell, and cry to influence us. She'd walk out of the meeting. So what were we going to do? I might have to say, 'Okay, Donna.' " In other words, "Donna always gets what she wants."

And to some observers, Karan had been getting what she wanted for a very long time. When Karan finally arrived on Seventh Avenue, all the fashion editors and top retail executives, like Dawn Mello, president of Bergdorf Goodman, were rooting for her. Her fashions hit the ground selling—first at wholesale, then in stores. The fact that Takihyo owned Anne Klein provided real leverage with department store buyers; every major retailer who carried Anne Klein was inclined to give Karan's fashions good play on the sales floor.

It wasn't as if retailers needed much convincing, because Karan designed clothes that were special and very salable. Her fashion concept was built around the idea of a man's wardrobe—interchangeable tops and bottoms, rather than outfits. Women loved Karan's staples: a body suit—a fitted blouse that snapped in the crotch so that it never came untucked—a slim dress, a wrap skirt, pants, and a jacket. Everything came in sophisticated solids like navy, black, burgundy, or cream in luxurious silk, cashmere, and fine wool. The collection, priced from $150 for a bodysuit to $2,000 for a skirt and jacket, had an urban edge with a touch of sexiness. In addition, Karan got plenty of mileage from her earliest celebrity customers such as Candice Bergen, Diane Sawyer, and Barbara Walters, who were fashion role models to millions of women.

But the best role model for Donna Karan New York was Karan herself. She had the ultimate credibility because she looked like her customers: big-boned and hippy, a healthy size 12. Her designs were slimming and flattering: Her gathered wrap skirts hid tummies while her wedge-shaped dress made women look taller. And women swore by Donna Karan's opaque pantyhose, made by Hanes. The designer stockings were a breakthrough, fortified with Lycra, which made women's legs look firmer and longer—and every hosiery maker rushed to copy them.

Indeed, she had the golden touch. Never bothering to do any market research, Karan confessed, "I design from my guts. Before every season, I open up my closet and see what's missing. Then I design what I want to wear." From her guts came another winner—the casual, urbane DKNY sportswear collection that became a $100 million business in its first year, 1989, and ultimately the backbone of her company. Karan herself dreamed up the catchy name; she said that DKNY had a nice ring to it, like NYPD.

But coupled with Karan's canny fashion sense were her quirky work habits, which threw a wrench into the system. Donna Karan's signature collection always came in late, arriving weeks after other designer collections were already on the sales floor. Late deliveries were a chronic problem that plagued the company from the start and continued to wreak havoc a decade later. It seemed illogical that Karan couldn't meet a deadline.

"In my opinion, Donna is the most brilliant designer in the market," said Stephen Ruzow, "but the collection is her personal signature and it changes as Donna changes." While other designers prepared their spring collections in time for buyers to order in February for June delivery, Karan's collection was never ready until after her April fashion show, which made it impossible to turn orders around quickly. "Retailers complain about this consistently, but Donna is on her own time frame," Ruzow explained. To work around her habits, the company created another label called Donna Karan Signature, designed by a team of her closest assistants, which arrived at the stores ahead of her top collection, to ensure that the store shelves weren't empty. Fortunately, her bread-and-butter DKNY collections, which was designed by a separate staff, made it to the stores on time.

Late deliveries were more than a mere inconvenience to stores. In the 1990s, designers stepped up their pace in delivering fresh merchandise to stores every few weeks. Stores marked down slow sellers to make room for the next round of deliveries. So Karan, running on her own clock, was ruining the flow of merchandise—and causing her company to miss out on sales. Timing played a big role in how Escada, a German fashion house, built a mighty $700-million-a-year business in the 1980s. Escada didn't do fashion shows and instead designed its production timetable so that Escada fashions always beat other designer brands to the sales floor.

Nevertheless, retailers put up with Karan's late deliveries for years because during most seasons, her clothes managed to sell briskly whenever they arrived, which was a testament to her tremendous pull with women. Karan built a cult following of well-to-do women who dressed head-to-toe in whatever Karan served up each season. Karan herself was the consummate saleswoman when she made in-store appearances like the one she did one February morning in 1993 at Bergdorf's. Karan was a whirling dervish, darting from one dressing room to another, telling perfect strangers exactly what to try on and what to buy—just like girlfriends do when they shop at the mall. Bergdorf's clients were wide-eyed, hanging on her every word, and many left with shopping bags full of Donna Karans. During those heady years when Karan played personal shopper, Bergdorf's could sell as much as $800,000 worth of merchandise over the span of a few days.

Karan achieved this loyalty by designing her fashion image to be as important as her clothes. Image marketing was the mark of fashion houses in the 1990s, and Karan, along with Calvin Klein and Ralph Lauren, was among the best. Karan was already thinking about fashioning her image back in 1984, before her house even opened, when she hired advertising whiz Peter Arnell. He helped her create a persona that permeated everything, starting with her sleek Donna Karan New York black and gold logo. Karan's advertising was evocative without having to show clothes—such as a black-and-white shot of the Brooklyn Bridge on a foggy day. In the early years, Karan always took her runway bow to the recording of her chosen anthem, "A New York State of Mind," belted out by her buddy Barbra Streisand.

Karan's ads also featured an idealized image of herself: brunette model Rosemary McGrotha, who once was shown in a speeding limousine, balancing a Filofax and a baby. Another memorable ad, "In woman we trust," featured McGrotha being sworn in as president, with a lacy black bustier peeking out from the top of her blouse. Karan fortified her feminist, go-getter message through a dialogue with her fans in her *Woman to Woman* newsletter. A typical excerpt:

"To me, the future is all about personal style, not designer dictates. My role is to offer women the freedom and tools to pull it together in a completely modern, sexy way—with simplified pieces that are timeless, luxurious, and flexible enough to go day into evening. This is not about a season; it's about everything I stand for. . . . That's why I think of these clothes as a celebration of personal style. From one woman to another."

With her squinty smile, a sweater tied around her waist, snuggling next to her handsome hunk of an artist husband, Karan seemed to be having it all. She came across as one smart cookie with a head for numbers. In a September 1989 cover story for *Manhattan Inc.*, writer Jennet Conant noted that Karan was "intimately acquainted with the bottom line."

But four years later, during another interview, she revealed more honestly to *Working Woman*, "What's business to me isn't about facts and figures but the image of the company that all begins with product. When I see a balance sheet the small print drives me crazy. For me, it all has to be visual."

So while Karan wrapped herself around the "product," Mori and Taki and Ruzow and others took care of the nitty-gritty fine print. As Ron Frasch, a former Neiman Marcus executive, explained to *Working Woman:* Ruzow "insures that a company with a creative head and diverse divisions is pulled together—and that Donna gets the credit."

Once a week, Karan broke away from her creative agenda when she and Ruzow got into the habit of meeting in her Manhattan apartment to review business matters from a long to-do list that tumbled out of her overstuffed leather tote. Often, Ruzow had to rein her in to keep her from taking on too many new projects. "She would do everything tomorrow because she is so prolific. My job is to keep the business in focus," Ruzow said.

As a private company, the fashion house was cleverly designed just like a Donna Karan pantsuit: to capitalize on Karan's strengths and compensate for her flaws. But harking back to the years of Anne Klein, Taki and Mori would always object to the outrageous expenses coming from the design studio, which was the deep, black hole at every fashion house.

In the trial-and-error process of creating high-fashion collections, designers spent hundreds of thousands of dollars to make sample garments for every collection. Karan's studio was her baby—her special sanctuary where she created her runway collections, where her ego and her artistic reputation were on the line. Accordingly, Karan pulled out the stops, just like her mentor Anne Klein had done. "We creative types like to spend," an unflinching Karan said in October 1996.

Every year, Karan and her design team traveled to Paris to *Premier Vision*, the leading fabric trade show, which drew the top producers from around the world. Such business trips, and side trips to London and Milan, yielded a bounty: scores of seven-meter fabric samples and lots of research material, clothes bought from auctions and flea markets and from the trendiest independent boutiques, like Egg, Karan's favorite haunt in London.

Returning to her New York studio, alongside pattern makers, sewers, fitting models, and other design assistants, Karan got down to the nuts and bolts of designing a collection. Some designers such as Dell'Olio worked from their own sketches, from which they envisioned an entire collection. This was the efficient way to design, minimizing the number of sample garments that needed to be made.

But Karan, who didn't sketch well, tinkered painstakingly with sample garments that were made many times over. And because Karan manufactured her samples in Italy as well as New York, and made many, many changes along the way, costs mounted quickly.

"Donna is the most brilliant artist, but she has a hard time deciding," said one of her former studio assistants. "Right up until the day before the show, she is still making changes on the collection." (According to this assistant, Karan would be so taxed during this process that she began taking vitamin B_{12} injections to fortify her for the countdown crunch right before her fashion shows, and she encouraged her assistants to do the same.) The design team got used to the company's bean counters, who carped about the problem of "oversampling" and the need to cut back. "But nothing ever happened, because nobody ever says no to Donna," this former staffer said. "She'll have a hundred fabrics pinned up against the wall and she wants to see how all of them look made up."

So why didn't anyone stop her before she killed the budget again and again? Taki and Mori swallowed hard when Karan overspent, but they stopped short of turning off the spigot. "In creating financial success, you have to support creative people and what they want to do. That is an obligation," Taki said.

So then it was left to Ruzow to juggle, to work around Karan's unorthodox ways. "Whenever the costs got over budget, we shipped more goods to stores to help fix the bottom line," said Ruzow.

But Karan's overspending and constant bickering wore down Taki and Mori. The drama finally came to a head in 1992, when Karan was ready to introduce her first perfume.

Since the 1980s, designer perfumes had become like a license to print money. A popular designer perfume could generate fat profits year after year—and the beauty of it all was that it had to be designed only once. Given the mystique surrounding Donna Karan, her first fragrance was certain to be a sure thing. But in order to take off, the perfume needed a high-octane launch: tens of millions of dollars in advertising and marketing. That's how Calvin Klein created his succession of blockbuster fragrances like Obsession, Eternity, and CK One. He left the marketing to the experts, which in his case happened to be his fragrance licensee, Unilever, which, as is typical in licensing deals, was responsible for all development costs and advertising. Calvin Klein rolled up his sleeves during the development phase, but after that he could sit back and collect a big royalty check every year, amounting to millions of dollars that were virtually free and clear of expenses.

But not Donna. After she made the rounds to experts Estée Lauder, Revlon, and Cosmair, she wasn't satisfied. She wanted a higher-than-usual royalty fee and, not surprisingly, total control. She and Weiss talked it over and agreed that they could do it better themselves, so the perfume should be done in-house.

That's when Taki and Mori hit the roof. They were apparel makers who knew their limitations—even if Karan didn't. "We had so many people who wanted to give us money to do her fragrance. We didn't need to do it ourselves," Taki said.

But again, Donna had it *her* way. Weiss, the sculptor, designed the black and gold bottle for the Donna Karan New York fragrance, which was meant to resemble the torso of a female nude seen from the back. The high-concept scent was a blend of cashmere, suede, Casablanca lilies, "and the back of my husband's neck," in Karan's words. The smell was faint, perhaps too subtle. "The scent was meant for me and my husband and not for someone across the room or the next woman in the elevator," Karan told *Vogue*.

"I know this is not the way fragrances get developed. But we wanted to make something so special and precious, it needed plenty of tender loving care. We have started something from nothing and if I'm going to make a mistake, it had better be a small one! Because it could damage the heartbeat of our huge apparel company."

Those were famous last words. The Donna Karan New York fragrance became a cautionary tale on how *not* to do it. In the first six months, the perfume registered losses of $5.9 million, on sales of $4.1 million. That seemed implausible. No designer as high-profile as Karan had ever *lost* money on a perfume!

But this was amateur hour—a case study of a fragrance launched on the cheap. There was no advertising blitz—not even scent strips inserted into magazines. Furthermore, Donna Karan fans were forced to hunt for the perfume, which was initially available only at Bloomingdale's or through a toll-free mail-order line. The telemarketers taking the orders couldn't even pronounce the designer's name correctly, greeting callers with a chipper "Hello, Donna KO-ran." And Weiss's sculpture-of-a-spray-bottle was prone to leakage, leaving a trail of unsatisfied customers.

The fragrance debacle was a watershed, the coup de grâce for Taki and Mori, who were tired of tussling with Karan. The backers got ready to back out.

SO IT WAS time to head to Wall Street. With the help of investment bankers at Bear Stearns, the company began to make the necessary preparations for an initial public offering. The preliminary prospectus, filed in August 1993, revealed that Taki and Mori would be exiting the company, leaving Karan and Weiss to become the company's co-chief executive officers. The company's annual sales at the time were $258.5 million, with a net income of $29 million—and 90 percent of the sales came from DKNY and other women's wear. All of the newer divisions—children's wear, menswear, and fragrance—were unprofitable to date.

Understandably, the institutional investors who read that first outline were reluctant to jump on board. Despite its popularity, the House of Karan had a long road ahead to prove that it could succeed moving other merchandise besides women's clothes. And leading the charge in the future would be two creative, nonbusiness people, Karan and Weiss.

Just as Wall Streeters began to take a closer look, to search for the substance behind the Donna Karan style, many would-be investors got cold feet. Some unsettling news had hit the fan involving Leslie Fay Companies.

In 1993, the venerable Seventh Avenue dressmaker was embroiled in a messy accounting scandal. During a year-end audit that January, Leslie Fay's corporate controller admitted that he and others in the back offices had been overstating the company's sales and income by making false entries into the company's books. When Leslie Fay dropped this bombshell in February, its shares took a nosedive on the New York Stock Exchange. By April, the beleaguered company was forced to reorganize under Chapter 11 bankruptcy.

During an internal investigation of Leslie Fay in the following months, so much bad news trickled out that the company's reputation was forever ruined. As it turned out, the books had been cooked at Leslie Fay for years. Leslie Fay wound up having to restate its earnings for the past three years, effectively wiping out $81 million of previously reported net income that never existed. The price of Leslie Fay shares fell to under a dollar a share, which forced the company off the New York Stock Exchange. The controller who blew the whistle and the company's chief financial officer were eventually indicted by a federal grand jury, while John Pomerantz, Leslie Fay's CEO, who claimed absolutely no knowledge of the scheme, managed to escape charges—but not embarrassment—and was eventually cleared of any wrongdoing after the investigation. The mystery of Leslie Fay continues as the two indictments have yet to result in any punitive damages or jail terms, seven years after the fact.

As the Leslie Fay soap opera played out during 1993, all of Seventh Avenue was aghast and sullied by association. Leslie Fay personified the ugly stereotype of the old-time garmento who played it fast and loose—a depiction that legitimate apparel makers had been trying to shake for years. With the overhang of the Leslie Fay scandal, 1993 was hardly the climate for Donna Karan to go public.

What's more, Donna Karan had its own problems to contend with, since the sales of its women's collections began to slump that year. There was no way the fashion house would meet its internal earnings projections. Any stock offering embarked upon against that backdrop—if indeed it managed to squeak through—would depress the overall value of the company. So Karan, Weiss, and Mori held a press conference in New York to call the whole thing off, for the time being.

After that very public false start, the Donna Karan organization retreated back to business, somewhat as usual. Weiss was now in the executive suite, with Karan as the company's co-chief executive. As Weiss went about issuing orders around the office, he crossed many people at the company, especially Frank Mori. Most people in the industry thought that Weiss, the artist-turned-CEO, was in way over his head.

"He wasn't credible," said Millstein, the consultant. "He was inexperienced. . . . He had the job because his wife wanted him to come to work every day in a suit and tie, not in [an artist's] smock."

Karan told *New York* in May 1996 that the relentless bashing of Weiss "burns my butt. I cannot believe after all these years we are still discussing that about my husband who has done an extraordinary job. . . . If anybody thinks I did it [alone], we did it."

SOMEWHERE ALONG THE way, Karan got religion. During the early 1990s, she had embarked on a new personal journey of self-introspection and she began to explore her spirituality through Eastern philosophy and the teachings of New Age guru Deepak Chopra. Eventually, Karan's newfound beliefs found their way into her business. Her fashion-show music also became more ethereal, like the time the models walked down the catwalk to a recording of Chopra reading his poetry. And the clothes looked otherworldly, too. Karan had all but abandoned her signature sexy sleek and began experimenting with dowdy-looking long skirts and baggy tops. A lot of retailers and customers missed the sexy Donna look, but Karan didn't seem to care. She had to keep evolving.

Given her rocky relations with Mori and Taki, Karan had to hold her company together in order to make another pass at Wall Street. She must have been heartened after watching Gucci make a splash with its IPO in 1995. The Italian fashion house had been riding high with Tom Ford, the hottest designer of the moment, and a red-hot stock. Investcorp, the Bahrain-based investment bank that bought Gucci in 1987 for $245 million, made $1.6 billion on selling Gucci shares, in two deals: an October 1995 IPO and a secondary offering five months later.

By the spring of 1996, the house of Karan was all dressed up and ready to go to the stock market again. The company's balance sheet was now cleaned up, and the fashion house looked a lot more promising: annual sales were $510 million, or about double the 1993 sales. There were no more losses in menswear—the men's division was actually profitable and growing—and children's wear had been discontinued. Only the beauty business—the fragrance, lotions, and skin-care line—still wasn't making money.

In the 1996 offering, Karan was now listed as the chairman and the sole CEO of the company, while Weiss held the title of vice chairman, continuing to oversee the company's beauty business and legal and licensing departments. The prospectus gave a cryptic definition of his new role: "While Mr. Weiss's office will not necessarily be a full-time position, he will spend substantial amounts of time as vice chairman." No one understood what that meant.

Surprisingly, one aspect of the offering, a royalty payment to Karan and Weiss, managed to pass muster with prospective investors. The royalty payment was in connection with the company's most valuable asset, its trademarks, which after the offer would belong to Karan and Weiss through Gabrielle Studio, a company named after Karan's daughter. For the use of the "Donna Karan," "DKNY," and "DK" trademarks, the public company agreed to pay an annual royalty, based on a percentage of sales, starting at 1.75 percent for the first $250 million plus 2.5 percent of the next $500 million in sales, and so forth. It seemed unusual—and downright greedy—that Karan and Weiss would take ownership of the trademarks, which were the most valuable asset the company had other than Karan herself. At other publicly owned designer companies such as Tommy Hilfiger, Liz Claiborne, and Polo Ralph Lauren, the trademarks belonged to the company, not the designers.

Here's how it worked. In the offering, Karan and Weiss collected the same as Taki and Mori—$58 million, and about a 25 percent stake in the public company. In addition, the creative couple was entitled to a $5 million royalty from Gabrielle Studio. After the IPO, the company would continue to pay millions in royalties to Gabrielle Studio every year.

Morgan Stanley, the lead underwriter in the deal, advised against this arrangement, as did Taki and Mori. But Karan and Weiss flatly refused to relinquish the royalty stream, claiming that it was Karan, after all, who was the company's visionary and who deserved to own the trademarks that she alone had made valuable. Taki was pissed. He countered that if anybody deserved to share in the ownership of the trademarks, it should have been him and Mori, who put the fashion house in business and had put up with Donna all those years.

But the royalty payment didn't seem to faze all those wide-eyed investors, who couldn't wait to get their hands on DK shares. Later, when the company's fortunes began to evaporate, most institutional shareholders felt as if they had been duped.

One bright spot that DK shareholders had been looking forward to was the company's plan to grow through lucrative licensing deals. Everything was right on track in early 1996, after Donna Karan had signed an agreement with jeans maker Designer Holdings Inc. to make DKNY jeans. Designer Holdings made an initial $6 million payment to the public company, and agreed to pay $54 million more over the next four years, plus 7 percent royalties on sales every year.

Designer Holdings, itself a recent new listing on the New York Stock Exchange, had done a fine job with Calvin Klein's jeanswear. In just two years Designer Holdings had more than tripled sales of Calvin Klein jeans to more than $400 million in 1996. Arnold Simon, Designer Holdings' chairman, vowed to do the same for DKNY jeans, whose sales were about $50 million in 1995. Simon had visions of a $300 million DKNY jeans business after only about three years.

But the DKNY jeans deal came unzipped only months after it was signed. In March 1997, Donna Karan and Designer Holdings agreed to dissolve the partnership, citing "unexpected difficulties." The day the news broke, DK shares dropped again to $11.25—or less than half the offering price.

After the fact, Simon spilled the back story: the frustrating back-and-forth exchanges he endured in dealing with Karan and a number of the company's executives, all of whom, it seemed, wanted to put their two cents in about the terms of his contract. The sticking point was fundamental: Karan wanted to limit Designer Holdings to making denim jeans and nothing else; Simon insisted on making a jeanswear collection, as he had for Calvin Klein.

"The contract stated I will have a jeanswear license comparable to other jeanswear licensees in the industry," asserted Simon. "Of course I know what that means. I can't just make five-pocket jeans, but a whole collection of tops and bottoms. But they were only going to let me do jeans and two T-shirts. I mean, how do you go into this business with *two T-shirts*?"

But Ruzow sustained that the deal with Designer Holdings was "very explicit" because Donna Karan had never intended for its licensee to produce a jeanswear collection that could cannibalize its own DKNY sportswear collections made in-house. "Arnie signed the license knowing that. He just went ahead, knowing that he would eventually get what he wanted," Ruzow said.

In canceling the contract, Donna Karan agreed to give back the $6 million payment to Designer Holdings and $4 million more in development costs. But having already counted on the $6 million windfall, Donna Karan had already splurged on a new advertising campaign starring Demi Moore and Bruce Willis. The stars were paid in clothes, and $2.3 million went to buy ad space, mainly in Europe, where the company was getting ready to open boutiques in Stockholm, Moscow, Amsterdam, Berlin, and Barcelona. Management figured it could afford to spend more on advertising because, according to Ruzow, "We were on track to make our ad budget for the year and the pictures were fabulous. It was a once-in-a-lifetime shot, we felt that it was a good time to increase our exposure."

But at year-end, those ad expenses stood out like a sore thumb on the company's income statement in a year that Donna Karan didn't meet its earnings targets. DK shareholders reacted bitterly to the broken deal with Designer Holdings. They promptly filed a class-action lawsuit against the company in federal court, charging Karan and her top officers with mismanagement. (The suit was dismissed in 1998.)

Because Takihyo still owned Anne Klein, a competitor with Donna

Karan, Mori and Taki were legally barred from being involved with internal Donna Karan matters. But Mori was too frustrated to stand by and watch Takihyo's stake of 5.4 million DK shares slip any further in value. Mori appealed to the board of directors to waive the restriction and let him back in so that he could restructure the company he had built. But the Donna Karan board members said no. Still, the directors were motivated to act, and thus began a search for a new CEO to replace Karan.

Karan got a phone call from an eager thirty-nine-year-old candidate, John Idol, who was president of Polo Ralph Lauren's licensing divisions. The polished executive, who resembled a young Harrison Ford, was determined to win Karan and the board over, which he did. When the company announced his appointment as CEO in May 1997, Karan told reporters how impressed she was with him, remarking that he was also "cute." Karan held on to her titles as chairman and chief designer.

To be sure, Idol's arrival didn't sit well with Ruzow, who for so many years had been the de facto CEO without having the title or real authority over Karan. In the public offering, Ruzow had received a $5 million onetime payment for his efforts over the years. But there was no way that Ruzow was going to report to Idol, so he resigned from the company. He became CEO of Kate Spade, a designer handbag company, then left there after three months and became president of Calvin Klein underwear at Warnaco Group Inc., Klein's licensee.

Idol quickly began polishing the company for Wall Street, signing up Liz Claiborne to make DKNY jeans and Estée Lauder to take over the troubled beauty division in 1997. The beauty division had chalked up an estimated $100 million in losses since 1992, with its lineup of skin treatment products and fragrances named Chaos, Water Mist, Ice, Sunlight, and Rain.

Idol went about cost cutting, slashing some $40 million in annual expenses, which included layoffs of 285 employees, about 15 percent of the total workforce. Employees saw many of their perks, like clothing allowances and cellular phones, disappear. There would be no more free clothes given away to movie stars, including Barbra Streisand. And Idol was determined to come up with a new system to get the collection delivered to the stores earlier. The aggressive restructuring write-offs took the company deep into red ink in 1997—a net loss of $81.4 million on sales of $639 million. Nevertheless, Karan and Weiss enjoyed a splendid payday, collecting $17.6 million in Gabrielle Studio royalties in addition to their combined salaries of $3 million.

Having cleaned house, Idol promised good times and profits in 1998, but excessive spending wasn't the only problem at the House of Karan. Fashion was, too. Donna Karan's $37-million-a-year menswear division was doing just fine until 1997, the year Donna suddenly had a thing for men in tight suits.

Karan was playing with fire when she decided to change her menswear silhouettes. Her men's suits were expensive—$800 and up—and a big part of their appeal had always been the loose, draped silhouette that flattered men over forty, her target market. But Karan had gotten carried away with the trends coming out of Milan from Prada and Gucci, where the jackets were tight, with high armholes, worn with skinny pants. And so tight became the order of the season—on virtually all of Donna Karan's menswear.

The results were disastrous at stores like Barneys New York and Saks Fifth Avenue. It was said that some retailers didn't even bother with markdowns, they just sent the collection back to Donna Karan. During the closeouts, delighted Donna Karan fans had a field day finding bargains at Men's Wearhouse—that is, the ones who could fit into tight suits.

The fallout was even more stunning as the brand lost credibility with men who moved on to other brands like Zegna and Armani. "Consistency in menswear is critical," said Ruzow. "It's hard to win the customer back once you've disappointed them."

The tight suits didn't appear on John Idol's watch, so he had no qualms about criticizing them as a "one-time fashion moment" that would never happen again. "We will continue to break new ground in fashion, but in the future we will try to evolve and not radically move completely off into something new."

The rain poured on the women's collections as well. Idol pulled the plug on the experimental D line that had never caught on. In the past, the company had goosed up sales by shipping DKNY sportswear indiscriminately to many accounts, disregarding the fact that $400 blazers would never move in certain store locations. Idol finally cut off one hundred store locations and slashed prices of DKNY by about a third, noting that it was "ridiculous that DKNY's khaki pants were $130 when Banana Republic was selling them at $68." What's more, Donna Karan's fifty-odd outlet stores were so poorly merchandised that they weren't making money. There would be no more of that. "This is The New Donna Karan," Idol promised to investors at the Goldman Sachs Global Retailing Conference in September 1998.

Idol had much to prove—and an incentive to prevail. His $898,000 annual salary guaranteed him lucrative stock options based on the company's future stock price. "I think this will be one of the great turnaround stories on Wall Street," he promised. But with the stock trading in the $5 to $7 range at the end of 1998, he still had a lot of turning around to do.

In the meantime there was no way that Karan would be denied. She dug into her own pocket to make up for the shortfall in her design studio budget. In 1998, Karan was said to be still spending heavily, continuing to buy as much expensive fabric as she wanted. "I'll pay for it myself," she was said to have told one of her assistants. Later, in corporate filings, the company disclosed that at the end of 1997, Karan made a personal loan to the company of $7 million. The loan was characterized as a "cash cushion" for the company. "We may have to borrow from her again. We don't intend to, but we could," Joseph Parsons, the chief financial officer, explained in a statement.

But the next time Karan pulled out her checkbook, she weighed in with a gift instead of a loaner. She had found a great location on the corner of Sixtieth Street and Madison Avenue across from Calvin Klein, where she set out to build her first flagship store, to open in 1999. Her magnanimous commitment, to spend "many millions" of her own money to fund the store, played like another DK joke around Wall Street.

Meanwhile, Idol continued to sweat to make his earnings targets. In 1998, the company eked out a profit of $128,000, or one cent a share. Spinning out this thread of good news, an assured Idol pronounced, "We've turned the corner," on March 24, 1999, the day of the 1998 earnings release.

Still Wall Street wasn't impressed; the stock remained stuck in the mud at $7.25.

The year 1998 was supposed to be pivotal for Donna Karan, whose underwriter, Morgan Stanley (which became Morgan Stanley Dean Witter in 1997), had visions of DK shares bubbling up in the mid-thirties range in 1998. One of the investment bankers involved in the deal remarked in hindsight in May 1998: "Had I known then what I knew later, I would have never recommended that we do the stock offering."

WHILE DONNA KARAN'S travails stayed in the headlines, other fashion stocks were also having trouble staying afloat, including Guess, Marisa Christina, and Mossimo. "The post IPO of certain companies has been sloppy," said Elizabeth Evillard, managing director of PaineWebber specializing in fashion stocks. "For the first one, two, or three quarters, if the company does not make the estimates that were projected by the analysts, the market is unforgiving."

While Donna Karan International performed its comedy of errors, fashion's theater of the absurd starred Mossimo Inc., the maker of volleyball shorts, in Irvine, California. Mossimo, which took Wall Street on a wild ride, was the parable of the overhyped designer who landed into an overheated stock market.

The stock charted like a parabola. In February 1996 Mossimo went public at $18 a share, and soared steadily within months to a remarkable $51 a share, buoyed by Mossimo's grand plans to expand. But as Mossimo failed to deliver and started to screw up, the stock crashed to under $10 a year later. By October 1998, Mossimo's share price had plummeted to $2.50.

The tale of Mossimo had a storybook beginning, fueled by extraordinary luck. In 1987, Mossimo Gianulli dropped out of the University of Southern California to begin a modest apparel business in a garage with a $100,000 loan from his father, a landscape architect. Always more of a salesman than a designer, Gianulli hit the jackpot on a fluke. He put his name, "Mossimo"—scribbled in a bold, black flourish—on the T-shirts and shorts he produced. It didn't take long for the Mossimo signature to become the coolest of logos at surf shops along the West Coast. Gianulli began to think big. He hired designers to help him expand into woven shirts and casual sportswear.

It wasn't fashion innovation that caused Mossimo to pull in $44 million in sales by 1994. It was Gianulli's ability to market himself as a latter-day version of rat-packer Dean Martin, who was his idol. With his swarthy good looks, pompadour hairstyle, and sideburns, Gianulli was hired in 1994 to play a hunk in Janet Jackson's "You Want This?" music video. Moss, as his buddies called him, was a smooth, martini-drinking swinger on Hollywood's celebrity circuit, who became a cult figure among Generation X-ers on the West Coast. Starstruck young women and beach boys lined up to meet him whenever he appeared in stores.

When Mossimo went public, Gianulli entered the record books. At thirty-two, he became the youngest CEO of a New York Stock Exchange company; all of his senior executives were in their early thirties and none had ever run a public company. Mossimo's shares doubled to $37 after just three months on the stock market, giving the plucky Gianulli, who owned 70 percent of the shares, a net worth of more than $500 million, which got him listed in *Forbes* as one of the 400 richest people in America in 1996.

The cocky young fashion mogul set his sights on becoming the next Calvin Klein. Mossimo pulled out of Pacific Sunwear shops and *Surfer* magazine, and sallied into the world of Bloomingdale's, *GQ*, and *Vogue*. His luck was holding out through 1996, when Mossimo's sales climbed 30 percent to $108 million, with $10.7 million in net income, reflecting Mossimo's push into casual men's sportswear and a new women's line.

But overexpansion and inexperience did Mossimo in. By early 1997, the company was sinking under the weight of design problems, cost overruns, late deliveries, and slumping retail sales. The Mossimo logo now seemed like a short beer in a very tall glass. By fall, shareholders headed into court to sue Mossimo, alleging that the company's officers made false and misleading statements about Mossimo's financial condition. The class-action suit charged that as Mossimo expanded, it had lost control of its operations and finances. Mossimo denied the allegations and vowed to fight the charges in court.

In March 1998, Gianulli relinquished his CEO title to become the company's "visionary." Replacing him as CEO and president was John Brinko, fifty-five, a turnaround specialist whose last rescue effort was at the troubled Barneys New York chain after it fell into Chapter 11 bankruptcy in 1996.

But Mossimo's stock only started to show signs of new life in January 1999 after the company hired a new CEO, Edwin Lewis, the former Tommy Hilfiger Corp. chief executive who retired in 1994. Ready for a new challenge, Lewis, who was fifty-four, poached a few of his trusted Hilfiger executives to help him build Mossimo into the next Hilfiger. The news of Lewis's arrival lifted Mossimo's shares to the $7 to $9 range in early 1999.

IRVINE ALSO HAPPENED to be the home of one of the strongest fashion companies on the New York Stock Exchange, St. John Knits. With 1996 sales of $200 million, St. John Knits was unique—a maker of $1,200 women's knit suits that was grounded in conservative practices for more than thirty years.

For starters, St. John had amassed a loyal following of executive businesswomen who loved its Chanel-inspired suits, which had become fashion classics. At Saks Fifth Avenue, St. John's sales rose to $75 million to become Saks' most profitable vendor.

Founded in 1962 by the husband and wife team of Robert and Marie Gray, St. John invented a silk and rayon knit yarn called Santana, which it patented. Santana gave St. John's garments an edge; the clothes retained their shape and remained wrinkle-free—appealing properties that made St. John a favorite of traveling executives. St. John had few quality problems it couldn't control; the company spun and dyed Santana yarn, and produced all of its garments, buttons, and jewelry inside a sprawling industrial park in Irvine.

St. John advertised in *Vogue, Harper's Bazaar*, and the rest, but stayed clear of the hype on Seventh Avenue. "I never believed in fashion shows," said Robert Gray, St. John's CEO, in November 1997. "Whenever you get good press from those shows it always comes from some outrageous fashions—and we don't make outrageous fashions. We aren't part of that scene. If you try to create 'fashion,' that's a pretty tough job to make something different that is still wearable. We make something that is stable, with three different skirt lengths, that looks good on women. We try to satisfy the biggest customer base we can."

For a long time, the Grays, who were joined in business by their designer daughter, Kelly, didn't consider their company as a candidate for Wall Street. "It was never in my plans to go public," Gray said. "All of our growth came internally. We kept putting money back in our own company. It felt good to be running my own ship."

In 1989, the Grays sold 80 percent of their interest in St. John to Escada, the German fashion house, for about $56 million. The Grays continued running St. John, using the funds to open seventeen boutiques in Europe and Asia. But when Escada ran into its own financial troubles, it spun off St. John onto the New York Stock Exchange for $117 million in March 1993, which landed the Grays on Wall Street.

During St. John's pre-IPO road shows, Gray didn't try to fascinate potential investors with the glamour of the fashion business the way Donna had. Gray said he played it straight when he told them: "I'm a product man. What I try to do is sell product. We have had the same team for thirty-five years. We know what we are doing. We aren't trying to sell fashion or reinvent the wheel. We are trying to invest in clothes that women enjoy wearing."

St. John's impressive five-year earnings growth rates—averaging 31 percent a year on sales gains of 24 percent—made institutional investors salivate for higher and higher earnings. Gray knew he could push more merchandise out the door, but he was thinking long term. He had watched too many luxury brands lose their cachet because their merchandise was sold in too many stores. "We're not going to flood the market with goods," he said.

But even the rock-solid St. John demonstrated that old Seventh Avenue adage: You're only as good as your last season in stores.The knitwear maker got snagged in the spring of 1998 when it came out with more complicated, trendier designs. It was a wise fashion move to draw younger women into St. John's fold, but too many of the new styles had too-short skirts, which its traditional customers didn't like. And disappointing its fans even more, St. John's spring line suffered from uneven quality: dyes that didn't match, crooked pockets, and loose buttons. Red-faced, the company recalled the irregular goods from irate retailers. As expected, Wall Street was unforgiving. When St. John disclosed that for the first time in five years it wouldn't meet its earnings targets, the stock tumbled 11.5 percent to $39 on the very same day.

The market turmoil in the fall of 1998, and other internal problems at St. John's struggling Amen Wardy home furnishings division, depressed its earnings for the rest of the year. There was also an embarrassing class-action suit from shareholders, charging that management had misled investors. St. John vigorously denied the charges alleged in the lawsuit. When Gray came to New York to speak to Wall Street money managers in October 1998, he was visibly grumpy. "You know we have been getting a lot of bad press lately."

As St. John struggled to unravel its recent mistakes, there was reason to be optimistic about its future. After its long, stellar run, St. John had hit an iceberg when it got sidetracked by fashion and production problems. But the company was still profitable and imminently fixable. Women who loved the brand would be patient, at least for a while, because St. John offered a look that was unique in fashion. Nevertheless, Wall Street would make St. John pay for its errors, and the stock wouldn't recover until the company proved itself again.

But Gray didn't wait for St. John's stock to rebound. In December 1998, Gray and his family launched a $500 million buyout offer for all the outstanding St. John shares they didn't already own, in a move to become a private business again—distancing itself far from the prying eyes of Wall Street.

CLEARLY, WALL STREET is a level playing field that throws all types of companies onto the same track and expects them all to perform up to par every quarter. In the mid-1990s, Wall Street had been drawn to fashion issues, like moths to a flame, but such stocks were an enigma—glamorous, yet highly volatile—as well as investments where they could get burned. Conversely, fashion companies such as Donna Karan viewed Wall Street as a cash machine, without taking into account that institutional investors were essentially gamblers who didn't understand fashion cycles and who shot from the hip. Whenever weaker apparel stocks underperformed, everybody paid, and fashion stocks across the board took a hit.

But that's the way the Street plays fashion—tough and quick. The fashion businesses that made the leap to Wall Street had raised the bar for themselves, putting their brands under financial pressure beyond the day-to-day challenge they already had in designing and second-guessing consumer tastes. Publicly traded fashion companies had to meet a financial standard, which by definition is at odds with what is traditionally defined as fashion: that is, a trendy and unpredictable product. When a company goes public, it's the end of fashion. It means the end of too-tight pants and fashion for fashion's sake. It means commodity merchandise—polo shirts, jeans, sweaters, and blazers—that sell year in and year out. Such consistency kept the earnings up and the stock price rising at Liz Claiborne, Warnaco, VF Corp., and others.

In the mid-1990s, when Liz Claiborne's sales peaked at $2.2 billion, and its stock floundered at less than $30 a share, the apparel maker didn't find an answer from fashion. Instead Claiborne took its case directly to the people. Claiborne spent $1 million to conduct an exhaustive market research study of more than six hundred consumers, mostly in focus groups. The study, conducted in 1995 and 1996 by Arc Research in New York, employed psychologists who visited women at home, looked into their closets, and spent the day shopping with them. The intelligence Claiborne gleaned about women's preferences in fabrics, styles, fit, accessories, and colors were used by Claiborne's design teams. The strategy worked, as Claiborne's sales and profits started rising again in 1996.

But Donna Karan couldn't let go of fashion. The predicament at Donna Karan was deep-seated. John Idol's grand restructuring eliminated most of the waste, but his plans were merely scaffolding. He couldn't fix the core problem, which was Donna Karan herself. She was through and through a victim of the old school of fashion, and her spoiled habits had been tolerated, even nurtured, by Takihyo for years.

As Donna went about her personal fashion discovery, she had broken her promise: "from one woman to another." Where were the magnificent seven—the easy-to-wear wardrobe pieces that her fans depended on? They got drowned out, replaced by "twisted parachute" skirts, padded dresses, and D tube tops. Idol vowed that "The New Donna Karan" would give women what they wanted. But just as Dayton Hudson learned when it tried to make over Marshall Field's, the consumer will let you know when you get it right. The House of Karan had miles to go—at least a couple of years—before it could turn itself around, while New Age Donna had yet to find herself in the religion of Wall Street.

chapter 7

OUTSIDE OF THE BOX: ZORAN

You don't have to be scientist to do fashion.

You have to **sell,** *and that's that.*

ZORAN, February 1998

The two hundred fashion enthusiasts who showed up for the noon session of a fashion symposium at New York University on November 6, 1998, were primed to meet Oscar de la Renta, the dashing, Dominican-born couture designer who caters to American socialites and First Lady Hillary Rodham Clinton. But de la Renta—jockeying between couture assignments for Balmain in Paris and for his own Seventh Avenue house—was forced to cancel at the last minute. Instead, the audience would get a heady dose of high-fashion stimulation from Zoran Ladicorbic, a New York designer who they probably didn't know sold clothes that were more expensive than de la Renta's. In the world of fashion, he was known simply as Zoran. The Z in his logotype was a bold slash, the mark of a swashbuckler. And if ever there was a designer who had cut through the established order, it was Zoran.

Zoran was the vision of a modern Einstein that day, with his bushy gray hair and thick beard, in a baggy black pullover and loose black pants. Instead of making a speech, Zoran answered questions, expounding on his minimalist take on fashion, which had served him splendidly for more than twenty years. As he held forth in his scratchy Slavic accent, dropping his articles and prepositions, a blond model canvassed the room dressed in several combinations of his luxurious styles: a sarong skirt, a quilted jacket, pants, and a floor-length shift gown, all in cashmere, silk lamé, taffeta, or wool. About thirty minutes later, Zoran turned to the left of the stage and asked the model, "Are you ready?" She walked toward him, toting a Zero Halliburton stainless steel briefcase, the same type that hip L.A. lawyers carry.

The Halliburton contained every garment she had just modeled, all neatly folded inside. A collective gasp swept the room, as many women in the audience stood up to get a closer look. Zoran had cooked up this little gimmick to illustrate what he called "jet-pack fashion." A Zoran wardrobe—from day to evening wear—was not only chic, but portable enough to fit into a small bag, ready to be tossed in the overhead compartment on a plane.

No fuss. But surely some muss, ventured one woman in the audience. Stuffed into that tiny case "the clothes will get wrinkled," she contested. Zoran countered that his fine fabrics weren't prone to wrinkles, and besides, "Woman arrives in hotel, hangs clothes in shower, and wrinkles fall out." His presentation finished, Zoran snapped the briefcase shut and walked off, toting his compact collection like the top secret that it was.

Zoran was an enigma, a fashion creature stranger than fiction. Colorful, difficult, and often outrageous, Zoran was a Yugoslavian immigrant in New York, a hairy bohemian whom some nicknamed Rasputin, after the mystical, nineteenth-century Russian spiritual adviser. Zoran was indeed otherwordly, among the breed of eccentric designers, those who made fashion the edgy and exciting industry it had become. Fashion had always been a sanctuary for strange birds like Zoran, but all too many of these exotics were destined for extinction. All show and little substance, they usually burst on the scene for a moment of glory, only to burn out, making room for the next wave of young talents.

Not so with Zoran. He was weird, yet purposeful. His unconventional ways hadn't prevented him from building one of the most successful high-fashion businesses in America. Since 1976, when Zoran launched his first collection, he had managed to grow his business steadily in what was indisputably the most difficult sector to turn a dollar: expensive women's clothes. Zoran had succeeded on his own terms—not Seventh Avenue's. And his unique success sprang from two sources: an intimate understanding of his customer and a business approach that worked perfectly for a company his size.

IN CONTRAST TO Emanuel Ungaro's ornate couture frocks, festooned with bells and whistles that screamed "expensive," Zoran's fashions were spartan, lacking what was known as "hanger appeal." Without sharp tailoring, shoulder pads, or linings, the clothes looked downright humble as they drooped and slouched on hangers. It wasn't obvious, for example, that Zoran's pull-on pants with an elastic waistband were made from the finest $60-a-yard Tasmanian wool and retailed for ten times that amount. Or that a long folded square was really a lush $1,000 silk sarong, the bottom half of an elegant black-tie ensemble. But it just so happened that Zoran's untailored look was right on target, hitting the spot where a growing number of well-to-do women had landed in recent years.

What's more, Zoran's economic accomplishments were as unexpected as his designs. Right from the start, Zoran's clothes stood out because they always *sold.* By the late 1990s, when Zoran's contemporaries such as Calvin Klein were pushing millions of jeans and underwear—and hardly any high fashion—Zoran was still focusing on a single collection, whose pared-down simplicity was in the height of fashion in the 1990s. Saks Fifth Avenue became Zoran's best wholesale account; his collection was sold at twenty of Saks' fifty-five branch stores by 1998. At Saks alone, Zoran's business amounted to an estimated $30 million, at retail—which meant Zoran outsold the couture collections of every other high-end designer. More startling were the profit margins that Zoran pulled in; his fashions always retailed at full price—and never went on sale. Ever. Zoran's solid success without markdowns was an anomaly in fashion. (At Saks Fifth Avenue, no more than 50 percent of designer merchandise sold regularly sold at full price.)

Zoran ran an exemplary fashion house that offered a successful business model for designers large and small. He proved that a niche player could survive in a cutthroat marketplace, where affluent women were buying fewer designer clothes and were more likely to trade down than up when they did. Zoran's little business was an exquisite combination of all the designer businesses profiled in this book, one that incorporated many of their strengths and avoided most of their mistakes and pitfalls.

Granted, Zoran had neither the fame nor the fortune of de la Renta, Blass, or Ralph Lauren. Nonetheless, Zoran was very much a multimillionaire, having succeeded at playing the same game as the top industry players. In the spirit of Armani, Zoran offered simple styles that delivered the tangibles and the intangibles: high quality, as well as the cachet that his well-to-do clients expected. Zoran kept repeating the same styles, making him an extreme version of fashion's great recyclers like Armani and Gap. Like Karan in her early years, Zoran devised a formula that revolved around the functionality of a few good staples that were the basis for a wardrobe. The venerable St. John Knits didn't court the fashion press or hold fashion shows—and neither did Zoran. It took Zoran all of nineteen years to run his first paid advertising in magazines, and even then, he advertised in the most economical, low-key way possible, by sharing a space with Saks Fifth Avenue.

Unlike his peers, Zoran was adamant about keeping his business small, distributing his merchandise to a select group of the best retailers. Zoran knew his own limitations—and the limitations of luxury goods, which derived much of their allure from being scarce, forcing people to search for them. This strategy was a mind game grounded in reality. There would always be a finite market for expensive clothes.

Zoran's narrow focus allowed him to operate at maximum efficiency with minimal hassle. If he ever had any inclination to "think pink" or to fiddle with his signature style, he had thus far resisted, saving his company millions in research and design expenses, and sparing himself the nerve-racking creative stress that hounded designers like Donna Karan.

What goes around in fashion had come around to Zoran, whose business was reminiscent of couture's legendary renegade, Cristobal Balenciaga. Fashion editors had often used the expression "the ease of Balenciaga" to convey the wearability and comfort of his styles. And the same could be said of Zoran.

BORN IN 1947, Zoran grew up in a well-to-do family in Kikinda, near Belgrade, where his father was a landowner and a banker. He studied architecture at the University of Belgrade before leaving Yugoslavia in 1971 after his sister, who had earlier emigrated to Long Island, sent him a plane ticket to America.

In New York, Zoran shifted into fashion's fast lane. He checked coats at the Candy Store disco; he sold clothes at designer Pierre Balmain's Madison Avenue boutique, and worked as a collaborator with designer Scott Barrie. In those days, Zoran was a dandy who loved to wear expensive suits and rakish fedoras—a happy-go-lucky party boy who hung out until he figured out his next move.

Halston's sleek simplicity was all the rage in 1976 when Zoran dreamed up his own formula of basic pieces, which he first turned out in $8-a-yard silk crepe de chine. Zoran recalled spending $100 to buy the fabric and then hiring a Manhattan handkerchief maker to sew the garments for $3 apiece. He was lucky to land his first retail order with Marion Greenberg, an enthusiastic buyer at Henri Bendel, who bought his first run of about forty garments. Bendel's sold them quickly and immediately ordered more. Zoran claimed he sold about $40,000 at wholesale in his first year.

While Greenberg proved to be an invaluable sponsor to Zoran in his early years, the two later parted bitterly in 1983 after Greenberg sued Zoran, charging that she was an equal partner in his business by oral agreement, and that Zoran couldn't have made it without her input and professional connections. A New York state court judge eventually dismissed the suit in 1995.

While the extent of Greenberg's contribution was debatable, there was no denying that Zoran benefited from his early round of fawning coverage by the fashion press. For a few years, Zoran was even a favorite of *WWD*'s editor, John Fairchild, "who was initially quite impressed by him," recalled Ben Brantley, who was *WWD*'s fashion editor at the time. "Zoran's clothes were so damn photogenic. He was always very canny about hiring models who would make the clothes look good—like Esme and Josie Borain. Zoran got a lot of page-one pictures. And so many women in the office really got into wearing Zoran."

But *WWD*'s reporters were always searching for novelty in fashion, and Zoran wasn't delivering, which meant that he was no longer newsworthy. Fairchild cooled on Zoran and began deriding Zoran's plain clothes as "furniture covers," Brantley remembered. Fairchild, who loved

Paris couture, didn't consider Zoran a true craftsman. "It bored him ultimately," said Brantley, who recalled a *WWD* photo layout of a model dressed as a nun next to Zoran with the headline "Chairman of the Bored." Eventually Zoran disappeared from the pages of *WWD*. Without a PR machine of his own, Zoran stopped getting covered in the press.

But Zoran didn't lose much sleep. By that time, he was off and running with a thriving little business, so he hardly fretted that *Vogue* and *Harper's Bazaar* didn't come calling. He *had* the customers. And how those clients came into the Zoran fold is a story unto itself.

Zoran always chose to fly below the fashion radar. Ever the contrarian, Zoran refused to join the Council of Fashion Designers of America, the prestigious New York fashion industry trade group, which had repeatedly invited him to join. Zoran hated the fawning ways of the fashion establishment, the big parties, the hype, and the "hullabaloo," as he called it. Like Garbo, he wanted to be left alone. This pretense worked splendidly to his advantage. Keeping a distance from Seventh Avenue fueled the mystique he had cultivated as New York's most difficult fashion artiste. Most people were self-conscious around him, having heard all the tales about his quirky temperament—they didn't want to risk being insulted, or worse, rejected. Whenever his name came up, many fashion insiders dismissed him as a drunk and a crazy man.

"Zoran is a man of great mood swings," said Brantley. "I have seen him be very kind and generous to people, and I've seen him be very cruel. He doesn't mean to be cruel, but to be outrageous, he must be confrontational."

ZORAN WAS A night owl who cut up after hours when springloaded with his beloved Stolichnaya vodka. Late one night in November 1994, in his lower Manhattan loft showroom, Zoran was holding his usual salon around a large table with about a dozen friends and clients, most of whom happened to be in his clothes that night. The talk turned to hair. Suzanne Orenstein, a Minneapolis buyer, casually asked Zoran whether she should continue to let her shoulder-grazing locks grow. Zoran hated long hair on women, so she knew what he was about to say.

"NO!" Zoran boomed. "You need to cut it—now." He sprang from his chair, leaving a trail of Marlboro smoke, and disappeared behind a long white wall. Zoran came back with two huge pairs of fabric scissors. He grabbed the tablecloth from a nearby table and draped it around Orenstein. Working by candlelight, Zoran started whacking away. He wasn't *that* drunk; he slowed down when he got to the nape of her neck. "Zoran is always cutting somebody's hair. He did mine once," one woman said.

A fast ten minutes later, he was done. Orenstein grabbed a hand mirror to inspect her ear-length bob. A little lopsided, but her hair looked better. She laughed and gave Zoran a big hug as everyone clapped. Why did she let him do it? Orenstein insisted that it never crossed her mind to question Zoran. "He wanted to do it," she said. "I know he is strong-willed and I have confidence in him."

On another evening, Zoran was primed for a little mischief, hours after having a steak dinner at Peter Luger's in Brooklyn. He was celebrating the birthday of one of his few buddies in the press, Cathy Horyn, a fashion writer for *Vanity Fair*. Their last stop, around 2 A.M., was at a bar in lower Manhattan. Although Horyn said she was ready to call it a night, Zoran wasn't. Just one more round of Stolis for the road, he insisted as he lit up another Marlboro.

The bar's jaded regulars weren't sure what to make of Zoran. Who was this homeless-looking fellow? Why couldn't he sit still? Why wouldn't he shut up? Zoran zeroed in on two city sanitation workers who were now seated at the bar after having parked their garbage truck outside.

"I want you to take her to hotel in garbage truck," he demanded in his raspy, thick accent.

The garbage guys barely looked up. Zoran persisted. "I want Cathy to ride in garbage truck." He dug into his pocket and pulled out a crisp $100 bill. "For birthday."

Moments later, Horyn was perched high above the street, waving good night to Zoran while seated next to a driver whom she remembered "was quite cute, a really good-looking man." As the white truck rolled through the silent streets toward the Wyndham Hotel, Horyn was tickled but wistful. "I just wish somebody had seen me *get out of that truck*."

Passion and humor certainly summed up Zoran when he was at play, when he could sometimes be quite calculating. Actress Lauren Hutton recalled the evening she was at his studio in the early 1980s, not long before she was due to appear on stage as a presenter at the Academy Awards. "I told him I was planning to wear this puffy red Halston dress," Hutton said. Zoran walked over to a long rack of clothes and pulled out something of his. "Take a look at this," he demanded.

"It was a pair of long boxer shorts in this incredible gold material and a sweatshirt top that matched. He said, 'I think this looks better,' " she remembered. "And I wore it."

Amid a sea of big hair and ballgowns, Hutton was starkly simple—and smashing on stage. Photos of her Oscar fashion coup cropped up in a number of publications. "When I got home, people kept calling me up; I kept getting all these messages about my outfit," she remembered. Zoran got a number of calls, too, from friends who spotted his clothes on TV. Long before Armani had conquered the Oscars, Zoran was feeling quite smug.

Yet for all his bluster and his aloof facade, Zoran kept abreast of all the to-ings and fro-ings inside the fashion loop. He burned the phone lines daily, gossiping with his circle of well-connected clients, buyers, and a few fashion editors. Zoran's friends were often surprised at how plugged in he was. Often, it was Zoran who told them first about the drop in the price of Donna Karan's stock or who showed up out at Armani's latest store opening.

Zoran was crazy—like a fox—when it came to running his business. In the world of expensive clothes, Zoran had mastered the art of marketing luxury fashion, the art of getting the most bang for the buck. He accomplished this without any offshoots from his one and only collection. There were no Zoran perfumes, jeans, or handbags, none of the sundry extras that designers like Blass relied on to compensate for the money they didn't make from their top-drawer couture designs.

Zoran's success exemplified the end of fashion. He proved that high fashion lived on, but under a new definition that was actually quite old-fashioned—a throwback to the era of Balenciaga, when couture houses were small and exquisite. By staying focused on his own special niche—and by not being too greedy—Zoran made sure that his company grew steadily and profitably for more than a decade. Then came the 1990s, the best of times for Zoran, when his business exploded. Suddenly, more and more affluent women had a yen for Zoran's low-voltage, casual style.

Zoran got rich on the most primary of concepts. His fashion formula was essentially a top-of-the-line Gap: T-shirts, tops, tunics, pants and skirts, boxy shifts, and loose jackets. These were clothes that you just threw on, without any embellishments or fastenings. No zippers. No buttons. Everything came in only one size, and always in the best fabrics. The woman who loved the look of a $50 slouchy cotton sweater from Gap could finally get perhaps the best version of that classic from Zoran, in the richest cotton for about $600, or in four-ply cashmere for $1,200.

This was a luxury that was anonymous, a tad frumpy and appealing to Wasp sensibilities—and checkbooks, as it was quite common for women to spend $30,000 or so a year on a Zoran wardrobe. "With their implicit disdain for frippery they are also, perhaps, the ultimate snob clothes," wrote Ben Brantley in a 1992 profile of Zoran in *Vanity Fair*.

And among the sexiest too. Curiously, Zoran's loose, covered-up styles were a turn-on to some men. Brantley, for one, was amazed when he once observed how a group of men reacted to one woman in Zoran. "There was this sexual charge that came out of her; men were just falling over her. I think that part of the appeal is that these are clothes that you can slide out of very quickly."

ZORAN WOULD LIKE everyone to believe that he had his successful strategy all figured out from the start. But he wasn't *that* savvy. He was just stubborn. He loved simple, plain clothes and saw no reason to change them every season. This turned out to be a brilliant business tactic. Zoran's classics built a steady consumer following, effectively turning his label into a potent trademark.

Fashion's Rasputin was also a guru who instilled fear, respect, and unwavering loyalty in his most faithful private clients, about a hundred women known as the Zoranians. They were his truest believers, the ones who trooped downtown to visit him at his white-walled loft showroom—first on Sullivan Street and then on Chambers Street—where Zoran made them over. It was there that he told them what they *needed* to wear—his clothes, of course—which they tried on right in front of him, *before* he permitted them to look in the mirror. "I am your two eyes and *I* tell you what looks good," he said.

Zoran was brutally frank in his assessments of women. He never failed to point out when someone was too fat or when clothes were too tight: "You like to look like slut," Zoran barked to one journalist in noting her penchant for short, fitted dresses. Short, carefree hairstyles completed the Zoran look, which was why he was so scissor-happy to create a nifty bob. He told the Zoranians to ditch their fussy trimmings, their scarves, their belts, to "give jewelry and diamonds to housekeeper."

Zoran's "don'ts" went right down to the feet, where stiletto heels and slingbacks were verboten. "Woman should be like man," he said. Of course he suggested the only footwear that complemented his look: his own high-tongued $400 suede loafer. There was nothing more chic than a woman who didn't have to think about what she was going to wear, he said. "I don't talk them into dressing simple and plain. You either get it or you don't, and if you don't, I don't sell to you."

It sounds like a cult, doesn't it? But Zoranians said their gruff leader hadn't washed their brains; he simply cleaned up their fashion sensibilities and shored up their own sense of personal style. "Zoran has an incredible eye, this great sense of proportion; he can look right at a person and tell you what is right for you," said Ann Free, a former Washington lobbyist who bought her first Zorans in 1985. "These are fabulous, understated clothes. Once you open your eyes and get acquainted with his approach, you get the feel of being simple and unadorned and that gives you a real confidence. As women get older, they get a lot smarter. You find a style that works for you. And once you get there, it's effortless."

Like Balenciaga, Zoran figured out long ago who the true customers of expensive clothes were: wealthy women over thirty-five, those who led active professional and social lives and who weren't fashion victims. Accordingly, Zoran's styles flattered mature women: Nothing was tight or clingy. His skirts and pants had elastic waists and his dresses, jackets, and loose coats draped gracefully when a woman walked.

Like Armani, Zoran had his share of famous clients, such as Gloria Vanderbilt, Candice Bergen, Diane von Furstenberg, Lauren Bacall,

Isabella Rossellini, Queen Noor, Elizabeth Taylor, and the late Jacqueline Onassis, who bought her Zorans at Henri Bendel but never met the man.

But celebrities weren't Zoran's favorite customers. The stars required high maintenance—too much trouble for him to be bothered with. Zoran liked to sit on his throne waiting for women seek him out, instead of chasing them. He wouldn't suck up, and with few exceptions, he wasn't giving away clothes, which the stars expected. "If they want to wear my clothes," he snapped, "let them go to Saks, like Elizabeth Taylor does."

Zoran was much more impressed with the self-made millionairesses next door, the executive women who were elegant, understated dressers such as Roberta Arena, a former executive vice president of Citicorp. A fervent Zoranian since the mid-1980s, Arena looked the part with her short brunette bob and slender figure. Arena owned hundreds of pieces of his clothes, with her favorite styles in every fabric he'd ever offered—alongside a few sweaters from Gap. A jet-pack Zoranian, Arena logged in hundreds of thousands of miles of business travel; she regularly boarded the Concorde clutching a small carry-on bag packed with enough Zorans to take her through two weeks' worth of board meetings, dinners, and cocktails. Naturally, she and Zoran got chummy along the way, hanging out together in Naples, Florida, where they both had vacation homes.

Another longtime enthusiast was Nancy Friday, the best-selling author, who fondly referred to her favorite Zoran outfits in her books. On the back of the dust jacket of her 1996 book, *The Power of Beauty*, Friday was pictured in a black boatneck sweater and pull-on pants, both by Zoran. "I feel that I look as good as I can in Zoran," Friday said. At five ten and a half with cropped blond hair, Friday said she wore Zoran not to blend in but to stand out. "Zoran's clothes are plain in the same way that a Picasso line drawing is plain, absolutely elegant and perfect. I have Zorans that are twenty years old and I can wear them and wear them."

Friday and her husband, Norman Pearlstine, Time Inc.'s managing editor, passed many a cocktail hour at Zoran's downtown studio, where Friday took her time scouring Zoran's wall-length rack of clothes.

Of course, Zoran's kooky persona added some juice to his curious mystique. Zoran had treated many women to one of his spontaneous shearings. But the vast majority of Zoran's clients would never get a haircut or share a Stoli with him. One Bendel's client had been spending between $30,000 to $40,000 a year on her Zorans for a decade before she finally got around to meeting the designer in 1996.

Fashion trends have always been a sign of the times. And Zoran's surging popularity in the late 1990s came as more wealthy women had put aside the eighties frou-frou to recast themselves as serious people. "They are separating what they consume from who they are. These women don't need to be reaffirmed with expensive jewelry," said Steve Barnett, a New York management consultant whose clients include international marketers of luxury goods.

Thus, Zoran's highly nuanced "dog-whistle fashion" summoned that woman who could discriminate from afar that his $2,200 six-ply cashmere cardigan was as precious as any fur. "The smaller the group that recognizes it, the more luxurious it is," said Barnett.

Zoran's snob appeal and cachet endured because he saw the virtues of staying small for the long haul. He never forgot what happened to Halston when the celebrated minimalist got greedy in the 1970s and rolled out a cheap Halston III collection for JCPenney. The tony Bergdorf Goodman promptly dumped Halston's couture line—and suddenly the golden Halston trademark had turned to rust. That message wasn't lost on Zoran, who was keenly aware of the limitations of his simple formula—try to stretch it too far and disaster would follow.

Indeed, Zoran had already watched such a collapse. In 1987, an ambitious young Dallas designer, Sandra Garratt, introduced Multiples, a collection of cheap polyester-cotton knit sportswear that was the hottest label during the eighties trend known as "modular" dressing.

Multiples' connect-the-dots concept was easy and affordable: For $200 a woman could buy several of its twenty-four components, including pants, shirts, skirts, jumpsuits—and put together a stylish, versatile wardrobe. Each piece came in only one size, packed in a plastic bag with a how-to chart that tempted women to experiment mixing and matching the pieces, which was easy enough to do.

Multiples, as it turned out, was also a Zoran rip-off, or so he claimed. Zoran believed that Garratt was no creative genius, just a former employee of his who quit working for him after only a few months. Garratt maintained all along that she had already dreamed up modular clothes a couple of years before Zoran went into business. Back in 1974, Garratt won a student award as the "most promising star" at the Los Angeles Fashion Institute of Design and Merchandising, for her senior project: a collection of one-size knit sportswear pieces made to be worn in layers. Garratt said that Zoran had hired her based on her work for her student portfolio.

During the late 1980s, Zoran watched on the sidelines as Garratt basked in the spotlight. Garratt's first year with Multiples yielded her a fat $2 million royalty check on sales that hit $100 million at retail. But Zoran guessed—and probably hoped—that Multiples would be a flash in the pan that would stumble on its own success. It was a reasonable bet. Fashion gimmicks tend to have a short shelf life, and Multiples was no exception. Indeed, Multiples' flimsy knits hardly had much life left in them after several machine washings—a problem that caused many early enthusiasts not to buy more.

Furthermore, the idea was so simple to execute that in no time there were multiples of Multiples—such knockoffs as Elements, Switches, and Linkup. Ironically, Multiples' biggest rival was Units, a brand that Garratt herself created. Garratt had launched Units in 1986 with the help of venture capital partners. But after a few months, Garratt fell out and split with her financiers, who retained the rights to Units. The financiers sold the trademark to JCPenney, which pressed on with a chain of two hundred Units boutiques.

Months later, Jerrell Inc., a Dallas apparel maker, offered Garratt a licensing deal to come up with another version of Units. And thus Multiples was born. But after one terrific year of sales, Garratt sued Jerrell, claiming that Jerell's own line of knockoffs was cannibalizing her Multiples business. A court settlement left the beleaguered Garratt with $130,000, and by October 1989 she was out of business. (Units lasted until 1994 before folding.)

Zoran delighted in recounting the rise and fall of Multiples, if only to underscore that *he* knew the marketplace. More to the point, he was still around to get the last laugh. "I knew I could make big money if I did cheap clothes, but I wanted this to last long time," he explained. And the sure way to command couture prices year after year was to do what Zoran did: remain exclusive, maintain the highest quality, and—fundamentally—design the styles that women want.

Quality was easier to maintain when a fashion house was like Zoran's and filling orders by the dozens and not the thousands of dozens. Zoran's seamstresses cut each garment individually, finishing the edges by machine with perfectly straight topstitching. His signature label was then barely tacked on, making it easy to remove, if it didn't fall off on its own. This was done on purpose because, as Zoran liked to say: "Labels scratch." His aversion to labels later became a sore spot when the Federal Trade Commission took issue that missing from Zoran's clothes were fabric-care labels that are required by law. Without admitting or denying guilt, Zoran paid $14,000 in 1998 to settle with the FTC. He then began attaching a "dry clean only" label to his garments.

Ever the purist when it came to natural materials, Zoran refused to use the new high-tech synthetic blends that designers like Armani now favored. "My clients expect the best fabrics. Only 100 percent," he said.

As Zoranians paid dearly for his heavy "double georgette" silks, they expected not to see themselves coming and going. Wisely, he had the good sense not to produce too much. Women couldn't just breeze into the mall to Nordstrom or Lord & Taylor, for example, and pick up a few Zorans. The only chain that stocked Zoran in America was Saks. (He finally added Neiman Marcus in the fall of 1999.)

Worldwide, Zoran did business with only about sixty retail locations, usually no more than one specialty store in each city. For the entire state of New York, Zoran sold only in Manhattan, and only at two locations: Saks Fifth Avenue and, more recently, Bergdorf Goodman, which he added to replace Henri Bendel in 1998. Both Saks and Bergdorf's bustled with business; it was more typical than unusual for either store to move $40,000 worth of Zorans in a single day.

This kind of clout gave Zoran the upper hand over his retail clients. He shipped merchandise to stores not necessarily when they requisitioned an order, but when *he* thought it would sell. All too often, retailers required designers to ship seasonal fashions too early—spring fashions in December, for example, when shoppers were still buying winter clothes. Zoran knew this was ridiculous—and he refused to go along. He continued to ship linen clothes to stores in the middle of July, when the summer goods in the rest of the store were marked down to 50 percent off. And since his retailers weren't going to mark down the linens at the end of the season, it didn't matter when they sold—which was usually sooner rather than later.

AS FAR BACK as 1983, when Zoran thrived on small orders from more retailers, he flew into a rage, abruptly canceling accounts that he accused of selling knockoffs of his designs, stores such as Bergdorf's and Saks Fifth Avenue, and I. Magnin in San Francisco.

Linda Dresner, who operates boutiques on Park Avenue and in Birmingham, Michigan, said she cut off Zoran by her own design in the early 1990s. After having "great success with Zoran for about eight years," Dresner decided to drop the line—ironically, for the same reason some women swear by Zoran. "Our sales slacked off with him because he stuck with too much of the same things and our customers needed more change. It was just too repetitious." She also bridled at Zoran's rude treatment of women. "He could be insulting to people. He would tell them to lose weight. I guess some people like to be insulted, but I found it was too much."

Imperious as Zoran was, he continued to satisfy Chicago's Ultimo, whose twenty-year-relationship with Zoran grew into a $2 million annual business in the late 1990s. Since Zoran personally followed the sales of all his retail accounts—the stores faxed him reports daily—he could fill Ultimo's needs as ably as Joan Weinstein, Ultimo's owner. Zoran "understands his product better than anybody," Weinstein said.

Over the years, Weinstein evolved into a Zoranian herself, as she wore Zoran "95 percent of the time." The blond Weinstein, who resembled actress Jeanne Moreau, usually dressed in all-black or charcoal Zorans that she wore *her* way, layering a silk top asymmetrically across her shoulder, tied at the waist. She also piled on stacks of cinnabar bangles at each wrist—a flourish Zoran chose to ignore. "Zoran covers all the bases," said Weinstein. "You can wear it sexy, you can make it look young. It looks different on everybody."

For a long time, Zoran also protected Ultimo's local monopoly; Zoran wouldn't sell to any other store in Chicago. Zoran finally relented in 1998, adding Saks in Chicago. Weinstein wasn't happy about that—but she couldn't complain because her Zoran business still remained steady.

ZORAN'S ONE-SIZE concept wasn't as simplistic as an extra-large T-shirt that fit everybody. Only Zoran's sarongs fit all; the other styles flattered different body types: the "skinny pant" fit sizes 4 through 6; the "regular pant" fit up to a size 10, and the "pajama pant" fit sizes 10 up to 14. The same went for his "square top," which came in four or five different silhouettes.

Eliminating sizes was just one way Zoran made business simple and kept costs down. Most fashion houses spent millions to create samples to prepare every collection; Zoran spent zero. His seamstresses kept using those same patterns—some so old they were held together with yellowing tape. Whenever he was in a creative mood, he thought about new shapes and fabrics, nervously twisting his beard. Once he decided to shorten a sleeve by a few inches. He walked over and told the seamstresses to make the change.

Zoran held up a 1976 version of his tunic top next to the 1995 model. The difference? "I close up side slits." After years of opening and closing slits and shifting around fabrics, Zoran said his collections provided infinite variety—more than 25,000 combinations—enough to keep his fans intrigued and collecting the latest variations on his theme.

But designing still had its challenges and frustrations, namely scouting out mills that could deliver the precious fabrics that Zoran required to make his simple shapes pop. Nowadays, it was harder to locate the $100-a-yard fabrics he favored in the past—not even the top Paris couturiers ordered such materials in quantity anymore. Thus, many of the best mills in Italy and Switzerland that Zoran relied on for years had closed down—or stopped making the materials he needed.

Instead of pure fashion, Zoran was selling fabulous fabrics. And his clients knew it. Some of his fans admitted that they tried to cut corners by taking their old Zorans to their local dressmakers to copy. "But they don't come out the same because you can't get those fabrics," said Ann Free.

AFTER A TWELVE-YEAR absence, Zoran agreed to return to Saks Fifth Avenue in 1993, and Saks soon became his biggest account. Saks chairman, Philip Miller, assigned June Horne, a senior buyer, to work with Zoran. Miller made it clear that he expected Horne to bond with the difficult designer because Saks had big plans for him. Horne recalled that she was anxious: "I had heard all the stories about him."

In 1995, Horne made her first visit to Zoran's Chambers Street headquarters, inside a huge twelfth-floor loft that functioned as design studio and factory. A long white wall bisected the room. The factory side was crammed with bolts of fabric, a long plywood cutting table, and rows of sewing machines for ten seamstresses. On the other side was a vast open space, virtually empty except for an endless rack of finished garments arranged by color, mostly black.

Horne arrived at sunset, when Zoran "was sitting with his back to the wall, so there was this silhouette of him and his beard. I thought, oh my, he is sitting there like God. He reminded me of Jerry Garcia," she remembered.

She came equipped with a Polaroid camera and an order pad, ready to get down to business. But at five o'clock, Zoran was just sitting down to a late lunch of salmon and pasta, sent over by Balducci's. Out came the Stoli and champagne. Horne hung around for three hours during which they discussed everything except his clothes, though they were "over on that wall staring me in the face the whole time." Their repartee was lively. "I remember we got into a slightly heated argument about politics."

Weeks later, after three or four of these get-togethers, Horne finally got around to writing Saks's order. She fully expected to do the paperwork with assistants, but it was Zoran who sat down beside her and told her what to buy. "I've never met any designer who is so involved with the line on a day-to-day basis. He stays on top of every detail," she marveled.

Zoran was adamant and pushy, of course. He insisted on sending alpaca to Saks through April, even though Horne told him not to. The twenty $2,000 alpaca jackets he sent to the store "all sold immediately," she confirmed. Zoran agreed, just for the hell of it, to meet Saks shoppers in Palm Beach in December 1997 where he parceled out bits of fashion advice to shoppers, something he generally avoided. "The most time you have with customer is five minutes, and there is nothing I can do for you," he said.

Zoran refused to disclose profits, but given his low overhead and frugal habits, he was clearly cleaning up. His operations were as stripped down as his fashions. All garments were made in-house, by thirty or so employees in New York and Milan, except for sweaters, which were knitted by outside contractors near Milan. The employees who didn't sew performed many odd jobs. Jude Goldin, a former waiter at Mr. Chow's, managed Zoran's New York office, answered the phone, did paperwork, packed boxes of clothes, and styled store windows at Saks and Bergdorf's. Still playing the waiter, Goldin also served Stoli and champagne whenever the Zoranians dropped by.

Zoran found many ways to save money. In 1997, he left his Chambers Street loft and moved his factory into the garage of his nearby townhouse residence. So, while seamstresses toiled in the ground-floor garage at his townhouse, Zoran turned the second floor into his showroom and hangout for the Zoranians, leaving the third level for his private living quarters. The seamstresses liked their new garage factory, which was air-conditioned, while the Chambers Street studio wasn't. ("I'm European," he said about his indifference to air-conditioning.)

Frugality, indeed, was the byword at the house of Zoran, where there were few indulgences. The fashion master cut his own hair and wore the same outfit every day—a white T-shirt (bought at Wal-Mart), black or khaki pants (made in his studio), and Cole-Haan black moccasins without socks. He spotted a nifty $19 black nylon windbreaker at Old Navy and bought a dozen for himself. Zoran either walked or cabbed around Manhattan, and when he traveled to Milan or Florida, he always flew coach.

In keeping with his love of architecture, Zoran had bought and sold several homes over the years. Besides his TriBeCa townhouse, he owned an 1831 plantation home in Charleston, South Carolina, and a beachfront spread in Naples, Florida.

While Zoran managed just fine without secretaries and design assistants, he couldn't mind his business without an excellent chief executive. In another sign of his head for business, Zoran didn't find his CEO on Seventh Avenue, but on Wall Street: Gary Galleberg, a lawyer and former mergers and acquisitions associate at the prestigious Wall Street law firm Cravath, Swaine & Moore. Handsome, urbane, and terse, Galleberg, who was born in 1957, was the kind of guy who would be successful at running any type of business. He was also modest, discreet, and a calculated risk taker—a casual fellow who came to work in a polo shirt and Zoran chinos, accompanied by his dog, a Rhodesian Ridge-back named Red.

Galleberg and Zoran met by chance, when they struck up a conversation over drinks at a downtown bar in 1985. After they became friends, Zoran asked Galleberg in 1988 to work for him. "I was intrigued by the challenge of running a small business," recalled Galleberg. "I didn't know anything about fashion, but that didn't matter to me. The company was already in good shape when I came. It was a solid company with a good brand and I thought it would be fun to be involved in that."

So Galleberg became Zoran's first official CEO. He computerized the company's books and became an active investor in the stock market, for himself and for Zoran's own portfolio. By the late 1990s, Galleberg was pulling down the equivalent of a senior law partner's salary, without the killer hours and the stuffy protocol.

Zoran provided the creative brains and Galleberg the business brawn. Galleberg came along at the perfect time, just as sales spiked in the late 1980s and paperwork began to take up too much of Zoran's time. Galleberg liked that the business was no-nonsense and hummed with profits. "The hardest part about the business is controlling growth," Galleberg said. Zoran's business with Saks alone more than doubled between 1995 and 1997. "We are doing a lot more work with virtually the same number of people," Galleberg said. "Except for the seamstresses, we haven't added any more senior assistants, so we're trying to operate more efficiently. And that takes a great deal more coordination."

Galleberg was relieved that he didn't have to bother with coordinating fashion shows, which Zoran hated. "I always thought fashion shows were a waste of time, because buyers write orders in showroom, not runway," Zoran observed.

About once or twice a year, Zoran got the urge to host a modest fashion soiree, a dinner party for about one hundred guests in his showroom, where he presented a few outfits on a couple of models. In March 1995, Zoran staged such a dinner in Milan at the start of Milan's fashion week, when designers like Giorgio Armani and Gianni Versace were doing their big runway shows. Zoran's dinner for 150 at Biffi Scala was a prized invitation to a select group of wealthy Italian clients—an A-list of what he called "the contessas and marquessas"—and a few members of the fashion press and European boutique owners, including Milan's Marisa and Pupi Solari, among his biggest accounts.

Zoran hardly needed to enlist the three models he hired for the night. His guests were a walking Zoran fashion show. The Italian women, regal in carriage, faithfully turned out in their Zorans, demonstrating the endless ways his designs could be worn—spare, the way he loved them, or gussied up with antique earrings and pearl necklaces, the way most Italians preferred.

Helping Zoran host the dinner was Mirella Pettini Haggiag, herself a striking Italian socialite who wore her Zorans with panache. Haggiag was another one of Zoran's lucky finds. A former model who worked for Valentino, Haggiag was a fixture on the Italian social whirl. With her movie producer husband, Roberto Haggiag, she owns homes in Rome, Milan, Venice, and New York.

Before dinner, Zoran rolled in a long rack of clothes and set up a makeshift changing room for the models: a folding screen in front of the restaurant's bar. While guests were finishing their tiramisù and espresso, Zoran pulled a few items from the rack, handing them to his assistant, who dressed the models. Zoran, in a baggy black sweater, escorted each model through the dining room. "The cut is marvelous," purred Gae Aulenti, the noted Italian architect, when a model twirled by her in a stiff white silk gazar shift. At the end of dinner, the guests headed over to the clothes rack and began sifting through the clothes. Zoran shooed them away, inviting them to come over to his Milan showroom, which many did for the next few weeks.

The tab for Zoran's veal and risotto dinner party came to about $10,000—far less than the $500,000 designers usually spend on a runway show. Later that week, Armani and his licensees spent nearly $1 million on a black-tie fashion-show dinner party and disco.

When Zoran traveled to Milan in the springtime, he usually stayed over for his birthday, March 7, when he liked to do a little celebrating. After his triumphant dinner party, Zoran decided to return to Biffi Scala with a party of six for his birthday. But instead of reserving a cozy banquette in the corner, where he most likely would be recognized, he called with a special request. "Is kitchen available?" he asked the maître d'. "Kitchen is chic-est place in restaurant," he explained.

Kitchen dining became popular in Italy during the late 1970s, when acts of terrorism attributed to the Red Brigade were prevalent. Back then, many rich people and politicians didn't like to dine in restaurants, fearing they'd be gunned down, *Godfather*-style, over a plate of pasta. So several fine Italian eateries allowed their most special clients to dine incognito in the kitchen. Restaurant kitchens thus became the height of inverse chic in Italy, where danger could be not only exclusive but glamorous.

Zoran loved this sort of thing. Biffi Scala's kitchen was in the basement, a cozy place where the scurrying chefs were in full view. A waiter prepared a table with small stools for Zoran. After that fancy party earlier in the week, Zoran sipped his Stoli, relieved not to have to play the gracious host.

But not quite. Halfway through the pasta course, a video crew from a local TV station and a Milanese socialite bolted down the steps in search of Zoran. He came in on cue, complimenting the woman who was dressed in navy taffeta and velvet Zoran. "You look great," he said.

Suddenly, blinding strobe lights came on, as the camera rolled. "Here we are downstairs in the kitchen of Biffi Scala with the famous Zoran," the reporter began, in heavily accented English, shoving a microphone in Zoran's face. "Tell us about what you do," he asked. Zoran, who was smoking, didn't flinch: "I do fashion." Then the reporter posed the same question to Galleberg. "I work for him," he deadpanned.

IN THE SUMMER of 1997, Zoran was feeling a bit restless—but serious, for a change. He was getting ready to reintroduce his signature suede loafers, which he had stopped making a few years ago. And he thought about creating his first handbag.

But what Zoran was really thinking about was expanding—perhaps even buying an existing fashion house. And he couldn't think of any finer name than one of America's premier couture houses, Bill Blass.

At seventy-five, the debonair Blass was Seventh Avenue's most prominent designer-statesman, a philanthropist who once bestowed a $10 million gift on the New York Public Library. Blass's couture collections sold mostly in trunk shows—and hadn't been profitable in years. But Blass had a cash cow: a valuable network of forty licensees that made his sheets, perfumes, jeans, and menswear. Zoran said that Galleberg could further exploit those licensees while he would update Blass's couture line. "Bill and I have same customer," Zoran said, referring to some of his socialite clients.

Zoran had bumped into Blass in 1996 on a freezing night after a CFDA fashion awards ceremony at Lincoln Center. Zoran was shivering in a nylon windbreaker, standing outside beside Ron Gallela—Jacqueline Onassis's famous stalker—and other paparazzi, who were waiting for Mick Jagger and other celebrities to leave the party. Zoran almost got hauled off by the police because he had attracted a group of homeless people who watched him give out twenty-dollar bills to other street people. One police officer tried to stop Zoran and they got into an argument.

Blass suddenly emerged, carrying the silver CFDA trophy he had received for his lifetime achievement in fashion. Zoran walked over to say hello. Stunned, Blass muttered something and scurried off to his limousine. Lauren Hutton, also leaving the event, recognized Zoran and wondered what he was doing outside when all the fashion people were inside. Zoran never attended such affairs, but that evening he just happened to be in the neighborhood and decided to wander over to Lincoln Center for the hell of it. Zoran cracked up as he remembered the look on people's faces who recognized him: "They all thought I was drunk!"

A few months later, Zoran called Blass and invited him for lunch at Da Silvano, an Italian restaurant popular with the fashion crowd, in the West Village. Both Blass and Zoran liked to smoke and drink, and they were having a fine time when Zoran finally leaned in and told Blass that he wanted to buy his fashion house. Incredulous, Blass thought Zoran was only kidding—and besides, where would Zoran get the millions to buy his business? Zoran insisted that he could afford to buy Blass out, but only at the right price. He wanted Blass—cheap. Zoran told Blass that he would send Galleberg to go over the numbers and perhaps they could strike a deal whenever Blass was ready to sell.

Blass's reaction to Zoran's proposition was more intrigue than real interest. Blass was hardly ready to retire, having enjoyed excellent sales from his 1997 spring couture line. So nothing came of Zoran's initial pursuit. Undeterred, he vowed to pursue Blass again, confiding to his buddies that eventually "Bill will sell to me."

It seemed incredible that Zoran, the stellar model for the future of fashion, and not its past, would be genuinely interested in Blass and his old-school way of business. How serious was Zoran about Blass? Clearly, he seemed to relish the impossibility of it all—that David *could* actually buy Goliath. Zoran would have gotten a kick out of flipping the finger at all those fashionistas. He could just hear the gasps reverberate across Seventh Avenue.

But after Zoran's initial overture to Blass in 1997, and Galleberg's subsequent meeting with Blass in 1998, no business combination resulted from the talks. So Zoran settled back down to concentrate on his own company, which continued to advance quite smartly. In the fall of 1999, Zoran added a major new client, Neiman Marcus, which he said placed an initial wholesale order for about $8 million for the first year. Neiman's would keep Zoran occupied and stimulated for a while. But fashion's Rasputin, who liked to brag that he hadn't designed anything new in fifteen years, was still searching for something more to do.

epilogue

ON MARCH 29, 1999, the longest-running bull market on record crossed a monumental threshold when the Dow Jones Industrial average broke the 10,000 barrier, encapsulating America's stunning economic rebirth, energized by the boom in information technology that now compelled every sector in business to learn to operate faster, cheaper, and more efficiently. "Companies that stumble in the computer room are all too likely to be devastated in the marketplace," opined *The Wall Street Journal.*

Devastation engulfed Levi Strauss & Co., the world's largest clothing maker, which announced in early 1999 that its annual sales had plunged 13 percent to $6 billion. It seemed unfathomable that Levi's, the inventor of jeans, American fashion's calling card for nearly 150 years, had lost its groove with young people who once swore by Levi's as the coolest jeans on the planet. But that was before brands like Gap, Polo Jeans, Tommy Hilfiger, Sears' Canyon River Blues, and Penney's Arizona Jean Co. began chipping away at Levi's market share. Moreover, Levi's classic, tight-fitting denim was no longer the height of cool, after the baggy, oversized hip-hop look had become the rage among young jeans wearers during the late 1990s.

Just as the French couture houses fell out of touch, Levi's had become too inbred, too complacent, and too slow to react to changing fashion trends and encroaching competition. Embarking on the biggest worldwide restructuring in its history, Levi's said it would close half of its U.S. factories, lay off thousands of workers, and search for new leadership from outside its ranks.

Peter Jacobi, Levi's president and chief operating officer, who announced his resignation in 1999, admitted to a group of textile industry executives: "The alarms were going off, but frankly, we hit the snooze button a few too many times. We were left behind, stuck in a rut of internal focus, the same old business model and the same old products. . . . In the last several years, we the manufacturers and marketers have seen our authority falter. Our consumers know what they want, and whether or not we want to believe it or not, we no longer have much choice in the matter. . . . unfortunately what's the most common among [consumers] is their lack of commonality."

At the end of fashion, even a brand as pervasive and dependable as Levi's could no longer take its dominance for granted. Consumers had become far too sophisticated to stick by the same old Levi's when there were a dizzying array of jeans brands and styles being waved in front of them at every turn.

And given the cyclical nature of fahion, retailers couldn't afford to stake their future on jeans and khakis just because everybody was dressing casually. It was inevitable that fashion's revolving door would eventually spin again, and promote a new way of dressing up that would inspire millions of people to change their wardrobes once more. But whether fashion promoted jeans or strapless gowns, the rewards would always go to the companies that expertly marketed their way into the collective consciousness of a critical mass of consumers.

IN 1999, THE war to capture Gucci waged on bitterly. By early March, Bernard Arnault's LVMH had amassed a 34 percent stake in Gucci and appeared to be closing in for the kill.

But weeks later, Gucci launched a stunning poison-pill counterattack that pitted LVMH against Gucci via a formidable ally: François Pinault, the French billionaire who controlled Pinault-Printemps-Redoute, the biggest nonfood retail group in Europe. In its role as Gucci's white knight, Pinault snapped up a 40 percent stake in newly issued Gucci shares for $3 billion after just having shelled out another $1 billion to buy Sanofi's beauty products division, including the House of Saint Laurent. Pinault planned to resell the Sanofi unit to Gucci, in a play to create a multibrand luxury group, run by Gucci's CEO Domenico De Sole and designer Tom Ford. This time, Arnault, the champion of corporate takeovers for more than a decade, had been brilliantly outmanuevered.

Amid a flurry of litigation, bidding wars, and harsh words between the parties, the slugfest between the French tycoons came to a head on May 27, 1999, when a commercial court in Amsterdam upheld Pinault's alliance with Gucci, finally putting the brakes on LVMH's five-month battle to win control of Gucci. But the losing side in the "war of the handbags" refused to retreat. LVMH was still Gucci's second largest shareholder—and a raging bull—that charged right back to court with another round of lawsuits, desperately seeking to overturn the outcome.

Ironically, the end of fashion had circled back to Paris, where the walls that had been hastily erected at the start of the decade to protect French designers from the encroaching Italians and Americans had fallen down. Only five years ago, Saint Laurent had shamed Ralph Lauren for knocking off his couture gowns. Now the House of Saint Laurent was on the brink of becoming the ward of two Americans—De Sole and Ford—at the helm of a new Italian fashion group.

On March 22, 1999, *The Wall Street Journal*'s Thomas Kamm reported from Paris: "The brewing battle for Gucci is emblematic of the New Europe that is taking shape with the launch of the common currency and the globalization of industry: two Frenchmen squaring off for control of a Dutch-based Italian company, run by a U.S.-educated lawyer and an American designer advised by London-based American investment bankers."

Meanwhile, Pierre Cardin, having flourished splendidly on his own for more than forty years, revealed that he was just about ready to leave the helm of his fashion house. Cardin insisted that he had no plans for entertaining offers from bankers or financiers, including LVMH. He said: "My brand must go to an important company, all the better if it's Italian, because Italy is truly number one in this field."

RALPH LAUREN AND Tommy Hilfiger continued their rivalry to dominate the all-American look, and each veered off into new directions in 1999. In February, Polo Ralph Lauren Corp. surprised the industry with its first acquisition: Club Monaco, a Toronto-based fashion retailer known for its affordable knockoffs of fashions by designers like Marc Jacobs and Prada. In buying Club Monaco for $56 million, Lauren was facing the hard truth: the limitations of his maturing brand, which he had already exploited to the hilt under all his Polo and Lauren labels.

Yet Lauren maintained that after he took Polo public in 1997, he had always intended to stretch beyond his franchise. "This company has the talent to do many things," he told *The Wall Street Journal*. "It could be a hotel, a restaurant or Club Monaco."

In 1999, Tommy Hilfiger would make his move into the upper reaches of New York's glitterati. The Hilfiger Corporation stepped up to underwrite the annual December gala benefiting the Metropolitan Museum of Art's Costume Institute, the heady event that had become known as "the party of the year." Hilfiger would co-chair the party alongside *Vogue*'s Anna Wintour and Aerin Lauder, the fetching young heiress of the Estée Lauder cosmetics empire.

In contrast to the past, when the Met gala centered around the exquisite couture exhibits of legends such as Balenciaga and Christian Dior, the party theme for 1999 was decidedly haute-hip: "Icons of Rock

Style," in keeping with fashion's current penchant for celebrities and pop culture. The Hilfiger organization vowed that the bash would be an unforgettable throw down, the likes of which New York had never seen.

In 1999, Marshall Field's kept up its campaign to be the hometown favorite again—but not without sticking another thorn in Chicago's side. In March, Chicagoans were outraged when they learned that Field's famous Frango chocolate mints, produced at its State Street store for more than seventy years, were leaving town. Dayton Hudson announced it would close Field's candy kitchens, in favor of making Frangos in Pittsburgh, where a local candy maker would be better able to fill the burgeoning demand for Frangos, which generated $17 million in yearly sales at its Marshall Field's, Dayton's, Hudson's, and Target Stores.

Harking back to the years when Dayton Hudson first took over Field's—and caused a ruckus when it tried to banish Field's signature green shopping bag—the flight of the Frangos played as a snub to civic pride. The Frango fracas dominated front-page headlines in the *Chicago Tribune,* as Chicago Mayor Richard M. Daley held a press conference where he blasted Dayton Hudson's sudden decision to upend a Chicago institution. "This is the candy capital of the United States," he declared. "You cannot find a candy company here to make Frango mints? Why do you have to go someplace else?"

Mayor Daley met with the store's executives but failed to change their minds. City officials would get even, however, by delaying a zoning request by Target to expand one of its stores on Chicago's North Side.

DESIGNER GRIDLOCK AT the Oscars continued in 1999, with the likes of Ralph Lauren, Valentino, Gucci, Prada, and Chanel among those grabbing a piece of the fashion action. But Giorgio Armani still managed to pull off a major upset: The ever-glorious Sophia Loren upstaged all starlets when she came out on stage in Armani's fitted black gown with a wisp of chiffon caressing her cleavage.

As for Donna Karan International, 1999 would be a year in which the restructured fashion house would try to make its earnings' targets and boost its stock price that was stalled at around $9 a share in June. Whatever buzz was left in the DKNY trademark would be put to a test in the fall of 1999, when Estée Lauder would launch the first DKNY fragrance and DKNY would inaugurate its first American flagship on Madison Avenue at Sixty-first Street, across from Calvin Klein and Barneys New York.

At the dawn of a new millinneum, fashion's top players are now undergoing corporate makeovers to position themselves for the future. Those who are most committed to staying in style have their work cut out for them because the old rules no longer apply.

At the end of fashion, rich people don't care to wear their affluence on their sleeves; women aren't fixated with chasing the trends; intrinsic value often trumps designer logos; nobody's dressing up and everybody loves a bargain. Especially socialite Blaine Trump, who was the fashion plate at Christian Lacroix's New York gala in 1987. In an article headlined "Cheapskate Chic," Trump boasted to *The Wall Street Journal* in June 1999 that she buys her denim shorts for "something ridiculous like $9.99 at Kmart."

At the end of fashion, it takes a whole lot of clever marketing to weave ordinary clothes into silken dreams.

a note on research

The End of Fashion is based on 140 interviews, which I conducted between July 1996 and April 1999 in New York, Chicago, Los Angeles, Paris, and Milan, with all of the principal subjects of each chapter and people close to them. I attended all of the parties, fashion shows, and other events that took place during this period that I describe in detail. I have also used considerable secondary material from books, newspapers, magazines, and financial documents issued by publicly traded companies, in addition to my own articles from the ten years I have served as the fashion writer for *The Wall Street Journal*. In the few instances where I have used anonymous quotes in the text, I attempted to verify the account by checking with at least one other source.

A.I.=author's interview

notes

INTRODUCTION

3 "We sold Isaac . . .": Kal Ruttenstein, A.I., 11/26/97.

4 "It looks *divine* . . .": Isaac Mizrahi, A.I., 7/2/97.

4 "All my life . . .": Michael Gross, "Slave of Fashion," *New York*, 10/1/1990.

5 "I just got . . .": Isaac Mizrahi, A.I.

6 "Look, it is all . . .": Ibid.

6 "I will always have . . .": "Isaac Mizrahi Shutting Down," *WWD*, 10/2/98.

9 "Today my style . . .": Teri Agins, "Way of All Flash: The Decline of Couture Is Seen in the Closing of a New York Salon," *The Wall Street Journal*, 4/28/92.

10 "There used to be . . .": Teri Agins, "Breaking Out of the Gray Flannel Suit," *The Wall Street Journal*, 3/23/92.

11 "Have We Become . . .": Jerry Adler, "Have We Become a Nation of Slobs?" *Newsweek*, 2/20/95.

12 "I got more . . .": Teri Agins, "Out of Fashion: Many Women Lose Interest in Clothes to Retailers' Dismay," *The Wall Street Journal*, 2/28/95.

12 "was only a bit . . .": "How to Buy a Sweater," *Consumer Reports*, December 1994.

12 "In another trial . . .": "Wash and Worry," *Consumer Reports*, May 1997.

14 "The fact is . . .": Martha Nelson, A.I., 8/4/97.

CHAPTER 1

17 "We will know . . .": Karl Lagerfeld, A.I., 4/24/98.

18 "The fact is . . .": Holly Brubach, "In Fashion: The Rites of Spring," *The New Yorker*, 6/6/88.

19 "You know, you . . .": "Lacroix Takes New York," *WWD*, 10/30/87.

19 "she felt forced, . . .": Dennis Thim, "The New Lacroix," *WWD*, 7/19/91.

20 "I believe I have . . .": Lacroix fashion show program, July 1997.

20 "When I wrote . . .": Bernadine Morris, A.I., 6/26/97.

21 "It's the same . . .": Teri Agins, "Not So Haute: French Fashion Loses Its Primacy as Women Leave Couture Behind," *The Wall Street Journal*, 8/29/95.

22 "Nowhere else in . . .": Marilyn Bender, *The Beautiful People*, New York: Coward McCann, 1966, p. 205.

22 "Worth, who invented . . .": Caroline Rennolds Milbank, *Couture*, New York: Stewart, Tabori & Chang, 1985, p. 26.

22 "The fashion system . . .": Pascal Morand, A.I., 7/9/97.

23 "They were all snobs . . .": Gerry Dryansky, A.I., 1/23/97.

24 "Christian Dior darted . . .": Bettina Ballard, *In My Fashion*, New York: David McKay, 1960, p. 60.

24 "Right after the shows . . .": Agins, "Not So Haute."

24 "better to wait . . .": Ballard, *In My Fashion*, op. cit.

25 "Most every French home . . .": Veronique Vienne, *French Style*, Columbus, Ohio: Express, 1993, p. 81.

26 "The women who . . .": James Brady, A.I., 1/9/97.

27 "The real issue . . .": John Fairchild, *Chic Savages*, New York: Pocket Books, 1989.

27 "What was amusing . . .": Karl Lagerfeld, A.I.

28 "From then on . . .": Bender, *Beautiful People*, p. 228.

28 "Dior rejected an initial offer . . .": Alice Rawsthorn, *Yves Saint Laurent*, New York: Nan A. Talese, 1996, p. 20.

29 "From 1983 to 1989 . . .": Marie Fournier, A.I., 4/23/98.

29 "all that horrible . . .": Marc Bohan, A.I., 1/24/97.

29 "suffered from 'inconsistency' . . ." and following: Colombe Nicholas, A.I., 5/2/97.

31 "My name is more . . .": Richard Morais, *Pierre Cardin*, London: Bantam, 1991, p. 150.

31 "Cardin is a very . . .": Henri Berghauer, A.I., 7/28/97.

31 "when he was forced . . .": Morais, op. cit., p. 164.

32 "His fortune was . . .": Ibid., p. 234.

32 "I don't understand . . .": Pierre Cardin, A.I., 1/22/97.

32 "Pierre was considered . . .": Henri Berghauer, A.I.

33 "A name is like . . .": Joan Kron, "Fashion Empire: Haute Couture Means High Finance at the House of Yves Saint Laurent," *The Wall Street Journal*, 9/10/84.

34 "The perfume business . . .": Patrick McCarthy, A.I., 12/10/97.

34 "was valued at . . .": Bryan Burrough, "The Selling of Saint Laurent," *Vanity Fair*, 4/93.

34 "In the next . . .": Philip Revzin and Teri Agins, "All About Yves: Saint Laurent Remains Idol of French Fashion but He Isn't Immortal," *The Wall Street Journal*, 4/6/89.

35 "If he dies . . .": Burrough, "Selling of Saint Laurent."

35 "developed a marketing . . .": Armando Branchini, A.I., 3/8/97.

35 "In one sense . . .": Fairchild, op. cit., p. 29.

36 "In 1984, Arab . . .": Kron, "Fashion Empire."

36 "It was Pierre . . .": Morais, op. cit., p. 119.

38 "In 1996, bridge . . .": Katherine Weisman, "Secondary Collections Can't Seem to Make a French Connection," *WWD*, 10/15/97.

38 "French designer brands . . .": Ibid.

38 "Mugler and Montana . . ." and following: Armand Hadida, A.I., 1/21/97.

39 "I just couldn't . . .": Elizabeth Snead, A.I., 4/99.

39 "We're really not . . ." and following: Joan Kaner, A.I., 5/23/97.

40 "When you look . . .": Agins, "Not So Haute."

41 "It is better . . .": Didier Grumbach, A.I., 7/4/97.

41 "Fashion in France . . .": Pascal Morand, A.I.

43 "Mouclier claimed that . . ." and following: Jacques Mouclier, A.I., 7/11/97.

43 "I know something . . .": Godfrey Deeney, "Ralph Cries Foul in Yves Saint Laurent Copycat Suit," *WWD*, 4/28/94.

44 "line for line . . ." and following: Godfrey Deeney, "Lauren Fined by Paris Court and So Is Bergé," *WWD*, 5/19/94.

44 "The French respondents . . .": Susan Rice, A.I., 7/95.

46 "Karl is a . . .": Bernadine Morris, A.I.

46 "All this media . . .": Karl Lagerfeld, A.I.

46 "no longer impressed . . .": Agins, "Not So Haute."

47 "Behind his angelic . . .": Nadege Forestier and Nazanine Ravai, *The Taste of Luxury*, London: Bloomsbury Publishing, 1992, p. 41.

47 "There was always . . .": Colombe Nicholas, A.I.

47 "My relationship to . . .": Forestier and Ravai, *Taste of Luxury*, p. 106.

48 "It is a massive . . .": Patrick McCarthy, A.I.

49 "looks 'like vomit' . . .": Laurence Benaim, "La Revolution de Soie," *Paris Match*, 1/19/97.

49 "People aren't going to . . .": James Fallon, "Alexander de Paris," *W*.

49 "crude and vulgar . . .": Karl Lagerfeld, A.I.

49 "For Bernard Arnault . . .": David Wolfe, A.I., 4/16/97.

50 "What is the press . . .": Colombe Nicholas, A.I.

50 "guaranteed to pill . . ." and following: Zoe Heller, "Jacob's Ladder," *The New Yorker*, 9/22/97.

51 "It isn't a question . . ." and following: Bernard Arnault, A.I., 3/19/99.

CHAPTER 2

54 "My colleagues always . . .": Charlotte Aillaud, "Emanuel Ungaro," *Architectural Digest*, 9/88,

55 "Ferragamo was prepared . . .": Ferrucio Ferragamo, A.I., 8/96.

55 "I want this . . .": Emanuel Ungaro, A.I., 7/96.

56 "Emanuel had such . . .": Grace Mirabella, A.I., 4/5/97.

56 "Nearly all of . . .": Carlo Valerio, A.I., 1/21/97.

57 "These are huge . . .": Katherine Weisman, "Ungaro's New Marriage," *WWD*, 7/8/96.

58 "had stashed them . . .": Pier Filipo Pieri, A.I., 1/21/97.

59 "During that time . . .": Ferrucio Ferragamo, A.I., 8/96.

59 "It was easy . . .": Ibid.

60 "had a perfect . . .": Aillaud, op. cit.

61 "What I can . . .": Gruppo GFT, *Emanuel Ungaro,* Milan: Electa, Milan Elemond Editori Associati, 1992, p. 38.

61 "When Balenciaga changed . . .": Beverly Rice, A.I., 6/11/97.

62 "Knapp hocked her . . .": Emanuel Ungaro, A.I., 1/29/97.

62 "One name on . . .": *WWD*, 7/65.

63 "GFT said . . .": Emanuel Ungaro, A.I., 7/12/97.

63 "But the couturier . . .": René Ungaro, A.I., 4/24/98.

63 "He makes what . . .": Catherine de Limur, from an unpublished 1984 interview with Joan Kron.

63 "Research just shows . . .": Emanuel Ungaro, A.I., 4/24/98.

64 "I sew the sleeves . . .": Emanuel Ungaro, A.I., 1/29/97.

64 "Everything evolves from . . .": Pamela Golbin, A.I., 1/29/97.

64 "full of suffering . . .": Emanuel Ungaro, A.I., 1/21/97.

65 "I try to teach . . .": Emanuel Ungaro, A.I., 1/21/97.

66 "After twenty-three years . . .": Jennet Conant, "The Heat Is On," *Newsweek,* 4/4/88.

66 "Emanuel puts a woman . . .": Lynn Wyatt, 4/17/97.

66 "turning off lights . . .": "Rich, Rich, Rich," *WWD,* 1/1/86.

67 "never spent more . . .": Carlo Valerio, A.I., 1/21/97.

67 "We have a . . .": Maura De Visscher, A.I., 6/97.

67 "I knew the . . .": Kyra Sedgwick, A.I., 7/97.

68 "hearts were shattered . . .": Ben Brantley, "Ungaro Undone," *Vanity Fair,* 3/90.

68 "I like to play . . .": Laura Ungaro, A.I., 7/11/97.

69 "heavy, clumsy and brutal . . .": Salvatore Ferragamo, *Salvatore Ferragamo, Shoemaker of Dreams,* Florence: Centro di Della Edifimi srl, 1985 (originally published in 1957), p. 42.

69 "Salvatore became famous . . ." and following history: Stefania Ricci, *Salvatore Ferragamo, The Art of the Shoe,* New York: Rizzoli International Publications, 1992, pp. 60–86.

71 "For *them,* it was . . ." and following: Steven Slowick, A.I., 7/9/97.

72 "The Bain review . . .": Carlo Valerio, A.I., 9/97.

72 "We know he gets . . .": Ferrucio Ferragamo, A.I.

73 "thought it might . . ." and following: Peter Arnell, A.I., 6/2/97.

73 "Valerio worried that . . .": Carlo Valerio, 1/8/98.

73 "zero for the . . .": Ferragamo, A.I. With regard to Ferragamo's aversion to licensing, see Harvard Business School case study N 9-391-159 on Salvatore Ferragamo SpA, in which Fulvia Ferragamo is quoted: "If the label says Ferragamo, then there is a Ferragamo behind it from design to sale."

74 "There was little . . ." and following: Carlo Valerio, A.I.

74 "The division had . . .": Carlo Valerio, A.I., and confidential source.

75 "difficult opportunity . . .": Thierry Andretta, A.I., 4/23/98.

75 "I like the history . . .": Ibid.

76 "Laura Ungaro hit the . . .": Thierry Andretta, A.I., 9/10/98.

76 "Ferrucio is more . . ." and following: Laura Ungaro, A.I., 4/24/98.

77 "The Ferragamos are . . ." and following: Emanuel Ungaro, A.I., 4/24/98.

78 "We can't force . . ." and following: Ferrucio Ferragamo, A.I., 4/11/99.

CHAPTER 3

80 "I don't respect . . .": Ralph Lauren, A.I., 4/9/97.

81 "Lauren couldn't get . . .": Confidential sources.

81 "You know, most . . .": Frank Rich, "Stars and Stripes for Polo," *The New York Times,* 7/18/98.

81 "We've been assured . . .": Patricia Leigh Brown, "Hillary Clinton Inaugurates Presentation Campaign," *The New York Times,* 7/14/98.

81 *The Washington Times* cartoon ran on 7/19/98.

81 "A shopper at . . .": Rich, "Stars and Stripes."

82 "Congress was considering, . . ."and following quote from Rich: Ibid.

84 "It's not the jeans . . .": Terry Lundgren, A.I., 12/23/97.

85 "Ralph Lauren, who . . .": Ralph Lauren, A.I., 4/9/97.

86 "Young Ralph set . . .": Jeffrey A. Trachtenberg, *Ralph Lauren: The Man Behind the Mystique,* Boston: Little, Brown, 1998, p. 26.

86 "as Brooksy as . . .": Cathy Horyn, "Ralph Lauren, Suiting Himself; Sometimes, Criticism Can Wear a Little Thin," *The Washington Post,* 5/24/92.

86 "Frank Lifshitz was . . .": Jeffrey A. Trachtenberg, p. 20.

86 "millionaire . . .": Ibid., p. 26.

87 "Nobody was interested . . ." and following: Ibid., p. 29.

87 "The age of elegance . . .": Ibid., p. 60.

87 "buoyed by a . . .": Ibid.

88 "I elevated the . . .": Ralph Lauren, A.I.

88 "I would be . . .": Lang Philips, "Confessions of a Young Wasp," *New York,* 9/2/91.

88 "The only difference . . .": Jonathan Yardley, "King Lauren Conferring Nobility," *The Washington Post,* 12/15/86.

89 "I don't put . . .": Ralph Lauren, A.I.

89 "LVMH's Bernard Arnault . . .": Bernard Arnault, A.I., 3/19/99.

89 "Polo's licensees generated . . ." (for fiscal year ending 3/31/86): Trachtenberg, p. 263.

90 "In 1894, the . . .": Trachtenberg, p. 9. Author's note: "The Madison Avenue store generated sales of $33.8 million in fiscal 1993. Given the significant original investment in construction, as well as the ongoing expenses associated with maintaining it as a perfect prototype for Polo's customers and licensees, management expects that the store's expenses will continue to exceed its revenues." From a confidential financial document on Polo Ralph Lauren Corp. prepared by the company.

91 "Everyone loves M&M's . . .": Ralph Lauren, A.I.

91 "Ralph is demanding . . .": Confidential source.

91 "Ralph was always . . .": Confidential source.

91 "The salespeople were . . .": Confidential source.

92 "Think of this . . .": Confidential source.

92 "I always see . . .": Mimi Avins, "The Good Life for 30 Years. Ralph Lauren Has Set the Standard for American Style," *Los Angeles Times*, 9/12/96.

92 "Now I think . . .": Ibid.

93 "stuff inside there . . .": "Ralph's Teepee," *W*, 12/1/95.

94 "Ralph is busy . . .": Confidential source.

94 "We work with . . .": Ralph Lauren, A.I.

94 "Every year the . . .": Confidential source.

95 "Ralph is the . . ." and following: Confidential source.

96 "Do I need . . .": Ralph Lauren, A.I.

97 "Ralph wanted the . . .": Teri Agins, "Gang of Five," *Avenue*, 9/89.

97 "When you see him . . .": Confidential source.

97 "There probably isn't . . .": Horyn, "Suiting Himself."

98 "gobbled up and . . .": Michael Gross, "Ralph's World," *New York*, 9/20/93.

98 "In 1990, Calvin . . ." and following: Teri Agins and Jeffrey A. Trachtenberg, "Designer Troubles: Calvin Klein Is Facing a Bind as Magic Touch Appears to Be Slipping," *The Wall Street Journal*, 11/22/91.

99 "Klein's reversal of . . .": Teri Agins, "Shaken by a Series of Business Setbacks, Calvin Klein Inc. Is Redesigning Itself," *The Wall Street Journal*, 3/21/94.

101 "preppy classics with . . .": Hilfiger Corp. press releases.

101 "Murjani's Polo-lite . . ." and following: Teri Agins, *The Wall Street Journal*.

101 "Every decade someone . . .": Trachtenberg, p. 220.

101 "He may have . . .": Agins, "Tommy Hilfiger," op. cit.

101 "To the consumer . . .": Vicki Vasilopoulous, "U.S. Designers Set Out to Redefine Themselves," *DNR*, 12/24/90.

102 "By setting his . . .": Amy M. Spindler, "Hilfiger's New Blueprint," *The New York Times*, 6/11/96.

102 "Tommy came down . . .": Michael Toth, A.I., 6/19/97.

103 "I haven't done . . .": Ralph Lauren, A.I.

103 “He chatted up . . .”: Tommy Hilfiger, A.I., 8/5/97.

104 “They couldn’t believe . . .”: Jim Moore, A.I., 4/97.

105 “I saw products . . .” and following: Silas Chou, A.I., 8/5/98.

106 “Tapping into his . . .”: Joel Horowitz, A.I., 8/18/97.

106 “From the beginning . . .”: Ibid.

106 “Hilfiger’s initial public . . .”: Hilfiger Corp. stock prospectus, 6/12/92.

106 “We are just . . .”: Silas Chou, A.I.

107 “Now I’m not . . .”: Joel Horowitz, A.I.

108 “Four times a year . . .”: The author attended Hilfiger’s adoption meeting.

111 “We always bought . . .”: Jonathan Van Meter, “Hip Hop Hilfiger,” *Vogue*, 11/96.

111 “honest working people . . .” and following: Michel Marriott, “Inner-City Outer Gear, Urban Youth Take to Clothing of the Outdoors,” *The New York Times*, 2/17/94.

112 “Andy knew that . . .” and following quote: Andy Hilfiger, A.I.

113 “The next week . . .”: Ibid.

113 “He didn’t use . . .” and following: Lloyd Boston, A.I., 8/5/97.

114 “Kidada speaks her . . .”: Andy Hilfiger, A.I.

114 “Tommy Hill was my . . .” and following quote: Alex Foege, “Playboy Interview: Tommy Hilfiger,” *Playboy*, 10/97.

114 “I feel proud . . .”: Joel Horowitz, A.I.

115 “the number one . . .”: According to spokesman from Oxford Industries, Hilfiger’s shirt licensee, 8/97.

115 “Tommy is a . . .” and following quote: Ned Allie, A.I., 8/5/97.

116 “There are people . . .”: Ralph Lauren, A.I.

116 “Tommy gives Ralph . . .”: Confidential source.

116 “his salary would climb . . .”: Hilfiger Corp. 1996 proxy statement.

116 “Ralph and I . . .”: Alex Foege, op. cit.

117 “Tommy shrugged it . . .” Tommy Hilfiger, A.I.

117 “I sensed that . . .” and following quote: Ralph Lauren, A.I.

118 "Ralph knows the . . .": Susan Caminiti, A.I., 98.

118 "Is this going to be on the cover . . .": Ibid.

118 "And on one . . .": Spokespersons for Lauren and Hilfiger, A.I., 5/99.

119 "Lauren's first jeans . . .": Trachtenberg, pp. 200–201.

119 "As a matter . . ." Ibid. p. 202.

119 "The company rolled out . . .": Mary Ellen Gordon, "Double RL Hits Some Bumps Along the Way," *WWD*, 9/93.

120 "By the time . . .": Andy Hilfiger, A.I.

121 "Such were the . . .": The author attended Hilfiger's book signing in New York.

122 "I don't know . . .": Michael Toth, A.I.

123 "Friday night was . . .": The author attended the Hilfiger party.

124 "People around here . . .": Confidential source.

124 "It's a generational . . ." and following quote: Joel Horowitz, A.I.

125 "Maybe we can . . .": Silas Chou, A.I.

CHAPTER 4

127 "The press gives . . .": Giorgio Armani, A.I., 7/30/98.

128 "high-energy . . .": Armani press release, 9/19/96.

129 "an estimated $2 million . . .": Estimate provided by Armani officials. The Emporio Armani concert was largely underwritten by its licensees.

129 "He recruits my . . .": Sara Gay Forden, "Armani Ballistic as Forte Leaves Him for Calvin," *WWD*, 5/24/94.

130 "great complicity . . .": Giorgio Armani, A.I., 3/14/97.

130 "For the moment . . ." and following quote: Ibid.

131 "felt very young . . .": Ibid.

132 "an impressive $90 million . . .": Jay Cocks, "Suiting Up for Easy Street; Giorgio Armani Defines the New Shape of Style," *Time*, 4/5/82.

132 "changed his life . . .": Teri Agins, "Who Loves Armani? Actors, Car Washers, and Senior V.P.'s," *The Wall Street Journal*, 10/31/90.

132 "Armani is safe . . .": James Servin, "Look Who's Watching," *Harper's Bazaar*, 9/98.

132 "Change has to . . .": Suzanne Somers, *Italian Chic*, New York: Villard Books, 1992, p. 19.

133 "Armani changed the . . .": Patrick McCarthy, A.I.

133 "Armani put women . . .": Rosita Missoni, A.I., 3/6/97.

133 "The news from . . .": "Notes on Fashion," *The New York Times*, 7/18/83.

134 "Nicholas auditioned several . . ." and following: Colombe Nicholas, A.I.

134 "I know that . . ." and following: Patrick Robinson, A.I., 4/5/97.

135 "went through the . . .": Colombe Nicholas, A.I.

135 "We had our . . .": Patrick Robinson, A.I.

135 "I pay attention, . . ." Giorgio Armani, A.I.

136 "journalist Carl Bernstein . . .": Agins, "Who Loves Armani?" op. cit.

136 "Fashion is finished . . .": Rebecca Mead, "Giorgio Armani Designer," *New York*, 9/16/96.

138 "Celebrities work on . . .": Martha Nelson, A.I., 8/4/97.

138 "Versace loved the . . .": Hal Rubenstein, A.I., 8/97.

139 "wore Versace on . . .": Cathy Horyn, A.I.

140 "The Italian designers have . . .": Sara Gay Forden, A.I., 7/98.

140 "In Italy, we . . .": Armando Branchini, A.I., 3/9/97.

140 "There was no way . . .": Marie-France Pochna, *Christian Dior*, New York: Arcade Publishing, 1996, p. 161.

142 "Lancia charged us . . .": Nino Cerruti, A.I., 7/8/97.

142 "Cerruti's Paris boutique . . .": Ibid.

143 "What I could spot . . .": Ibid.

143 "fruitful years . . .": Cocks, "Suiting Up," op. cit.

144 "People were all . . .": Giorgio Armani, A.I.

144 "Armani had already . . .": Nino Cerruti, A.I.

145 “Kathleen was very . . .”: Nino Cerruti, A.I.

145 “Hollywood is like . . .”: Ibid.

146 “Gabriella is a true . . .”: Pier Filipo Pieri, A.I., 1/21/97.

147 “Radziwill had mentioned . . .”: Karen Stabiner, “Dressing Well Is the Best Revenge, or How a Former Reporter Went from Missouri to Milan—and a Job That Pays Her to Wear $2,000 Designer Suits,” *Los Angeles Times*, 12/11/88.

147 “It’ll be a . . .”: *Los Angeles Times*, “Listen,” 6/10/88.

148 “bought up a storm . . .”: Marylouise Oates, “Marylouise Oates: Broadway at the Bowl: Bet on a Sequel,” *Los Angeles Times*, 8/31/88.

148 “Costner turned . . .”: Wanda McDaniel, A.I., 11/15/97.

148 “Catholic schools had . . .”: Pat Reilly, A.I., 11/24/97.

148 “My players always . . .” and following: Ibid.

149 “Armani initially provided . . .”: Ibid.

149 “made an adjustment . . .” and following: Ibid.

150 “also flew Reilly . . .”: Confidential source.

151 “Lee Radziwill called to . . .”: Bridget Foley, “CFDA: A Bumpy Trip to Its Lincoln Center Bash,” *WWD*, 2/3/92.

151 “So maybe they . . .”: Ibid.

151 “I’d almost feel . . .”: Pat Reilly, A.I.

151 “looks like an . . .”: Kevin Doyle, “Armani’s True Confessions: The Magician of the Jacket, Giorgio Armani Is a Secret Dreamer Who’s Putting His Fantasy on Display in His First Major Retrospective,” *WWD*, 6/25/92.

151 “I had a business . . .”: Ibid.

152 “The stars were . . .”: Bob Mackie, A.I., 1/6/98.

153 “That dress was so . . .”: Ibid.

154 “It’s not so . . .”: Wayne Scot Lukas, A.I., 10/97.

154 “hip, cool and . . .” and following: Ibid.

155 “On a night . . .”: Glenn Close, A.I., 9/20/98.

155 “When I’m in . . .”: Ibid.

156 "He was so . . .": Armani spokeswoman, A.I., 11/15/97.

156 "I like to keep . . ." and following quote: Giorgio Armani, A.I.

157 "According to its . . .": Armani spokeswoman, A.I.

157 "It started out . . .": Wanda McDaniel, A.I.

157 "she received, unsolicited . . .": Lisa Bannon, "And the Winner Is: Anybody Who Has an Oscar-Night Gig," *The Wall Street Journal*, 3/21/97.

158 "After the Escada . . .": Teri Agins, "Will Tom Hanks Wear Hush Puppies on Oscar Night?" *The Wall Street Journal*, 3/24/95.

158 "The maker of . . .": Ibid.

158 "I'm trying to . . .": Ibid.

158 "Gap sold thousands . . .": Gap spokeswoman, A.I., 1998.

158 "Mr. Armani is . . .": Agins, "Will Tom Hanks."

158 "We're cutting back . . .": Armani spokeswoman.

159 "The company's wholesale . . .": Armani spokeswoman.

160 "In 1998, several . . .": Heidi Parker, "Film Fashion Frenzy," *Movieline*, 9/98.

160 "can overhype . . .": Martha Nelson, A.I.

160 "Armani is synonymous . . .": Sara Gay Forden, A.I.

CHAPTER 5

162 "The consumer is . . .": Daniel J. Boorstin, *The Americans: The Democratic Experience*, New York: Random House, 1973.

163 "This was a moment . . .": Michael Francis, A.I., 1/97.

164 "the noisiest confrontation . . .": Peter Wilkinson, "Store Wars: Marshall Field's and the Bloomingdale's Invasion," *Vanity Fair*, 10/88.

164 "It'll be fun . . .": Ibid.

165 "Marshall Field's and a little . . .": Gary Witkin, A.I., 6/30/97.

165 "The ambiance is . . .": Gloria Bacon, A.I., 6/10/97.

165 "Customers [were] telling . . .": Dan Skoda, A.I., 7/22/97.

166 "When you go . . .": Gary Witkin, A.I.

166 "Establishing an identity . . .": Arnold Aronson, A.I., 8/12/97.

168 "about $70 million . . .": Janet Key, "Field's Keeps Legend Alive, Still Chicago's Number One," 9/9/85, *Chicago Tribune.*

168 "We had an . . .": Arnold Aronson, A.I.

169 "People would stop . . .": Phyllis Collins, A.I., 8/23/97.

169 "Miller's biggest challenge . . ." and following description: Key, *Chicago Tribune,* op. cit.

169 "You can't get . . .": Ibid.

170 "Disneyland of party . . ." and following: Jon Anderson, Barbara Mahany, Ron Grossman, "Social Studies: Chicago Pops the Cork on a Magnum Party Season," *Chicago Tribune,* 9/11/88.

170 "I'm not eating . . .": Ibid.

170 "I hope this . . .": Jon Anderson, Barbara Mahany, Genevieve Buck, John Teets, "Party Wars: 3,400 Cheer on the Blast on Boul Mich," *Chicago Tribune,* 2/25/88.

171 "This is the . . .": Ibid.

171 "If it's done . . .": Ibid.

171 Description of Robert Campeau's speech: Dorothy Fuller, A.I., 8/24/97.

171 "$7.5 billion . . .": Jeffrey A. Trachtenberg, "Campeau's Federated and Allied Stores Take Step Toward Leaving Chapter 11," *The Wall Street Journal,* 10/29/91.

172 "an 'ideal marriage' . . .": Genevieve Buck, "Can Crown Jewel Be Restored? Dayton Hudson Will Need Magic Wand to Revive Field's Mystique," *Chicago Tribune,* 12/25/95.

172 "Marshall Field's is . . .": Dorothy Fuller, A.I.

172 Descriptions of Field and Leiter and Marshall Field & Co.: Lloyd Wendt and Herman Kogan, *Give the Lady What She Wants: The Story of Marshall Field & Co.* New York: Rand McNally, 1950.

172 "marble palace . . .": Charles Collins, *Chicago Tribune,* 2/10/52.

173 "style expert . . ." and bustle dress: Homer Sharp, A.I., 2/23/97.

173 "I like this . . .": Wendt and Kogan, *Give the Lady What She Wants,* p. 237.

174 "Chicago gangster Al Capone . . .": Ibid., p. 355

175 "Kathleen was so . . .": Dorothy Fuller, A.I.

175 "we put them . . ." and following Carmel Snow quote: Ibid.

175 "Kathleen knew that . . .": Ibid.

176 "who swept through . . ." and following: Wendt and Kogan, *Give the Lady What She Wants*, pp. 204–207.

176 "came by the . . .": Ibid.

176 "Dayton Hudson was keen . . .": Gary Witkin, A.I.

177 "Never in their minds . . ." and following: Phyllis Collins, A.I.

177 "Gloria Bacon, a Field's . . .": Gloria Bacon, A.I.

178 "The Chicago customers . . .": Gary Witkin, A.I.

178 "Our buyers are your . . .": Homer Sharp, A.I., 8/23/97.

178 "Our buyers are lucky . . .": Dan Skoda, A.I.

178 "before television and . . .": Allen Questrom, A.I., 4/16/97.

179 "created the ultimate . . .": Philip Miller, A.I., 4/30/97.

179 "Most people don't . . .": Allen Questrom, A.I.

180 "or about a million . . ." Dayton Hudson Corp. 1997, 1998 annual reports.

180 "a show of . . .": Genevieve Buck, "Marshall Field's for Fall: Fashion and Theatre Share the Same Stage," *Chicago Tribune*, 5/8/91.

180 " 'Cause for Applause' was . . .": Genevieve Buck, "Fashion Show a Festive Affair with Patinkin," *Chicago Tribune*, 8/11/91.

181 "The way we . . .": Gerald Storch, A.I., 7/97.

181 "There were more . . .": Teri Agins, "Out of Fashion, Many Women Lose Interest in Clothes to Retailers' Dismay," *The Wall Street Journal*, 2/28/95.

181 "The way retailers . . .": Carl Steidtmann, A.I., 6/23/97.

182 "Never ones to . . .": Ann Hagedorn, "Will Many Go Mini? The Fashion World Awaits the Answer," *The Wall Street Journal*, 6/22/87.

182 "Claiborne spent hundreds of . . .": Irene Daria, *The Fashion Cycle*, New York, Simon & Schuster, 1990, p. 14.

183 "Nina Totenberg . . .": Ibid., p. 7.

183 "apparel prices fell . . .": Agins, "Out of Fashion," op. cit.

184 "Only about 20 percent . . .": Teri Agins, "Liz Claiborne to Close Stores but Problems Remain," *The Wall Street Journal,* 12/29/94.

184 "The average retail . . .": Agins, "Out of Fashion," op. cit.

184 "the more confident . . .": Susan Faludi, *Backlash,* p. 174.

184 "In women's apparel . . .": Agins, "Out of Fashion," op. cit.

185 Gap brand has been the second most popular brand after Levi's since 1991: Russell Mitchell, "The Gap," *Business Week,* 3/9/92.

185 Gap 1998 results from company reports.

185 "For years, we . . .": Patrick McCarthy, A.I.

186 "Fashion had ground . . .": David Wolfe, A.I.

187 "That is the big . . .": Patrick McCarthy, A.I.

187 "By 1996, discounters . . ." and following on Wal-Mart and department stores' market share: Ira P. Schneiderman, "Discounters Snag More Apparel Shoppers," *WWD,* 6/11/97.

188 "Outside of Bloomingdale's . . .": Terry Lundgren, A.I., 12/23/97

188 "is not growing . . .": Management Horizons report "North American Retail Outlook to 2001," 5/97.

188 "There are maybe . . .": Robert Buchanan, A.I., 3/97.

189 Description of Eileen Fisher's relationship with department stores: Eileen Fisher, A.I., 9/97.

190 "The worst thing . . .": Ellin Saltzman, A.I., 2/25/97.

190 "May has never . . .": Arnold Aronson, A.I.

191 "I can wait . . .": Dan Skoda, A.I.

191 "desperately need to . . .": Management Horizons.

192 "If we really . . .": Kal Ruttenstein, A.I.

192 "We give them . . .": Joan Kaner, A.I.

193 Banana Republic estimates are for 1998 from Richard Baum, Goldman, Sachs & Co., A.I., 3/99.

193 "We felt the . . .": Mickey Drexler speech at Goldman, Sachs & Co. Retailing Conference in New York, 9/11/98.

194 "Gap Gets It . . .": Nina Munk, *Fortune,* 8/3/98.

194 "We were promotionally . . ." and following quote: Dan Skoda, A.I., 8/22/97.

196 "In the old . . .": Hank Lorant, A.I., 9/11/98.

197 "They are now . . .": Dan Skoda, A.I., 9/11/98.

197 "We couldn't believe . . .": Confidential source.

197 "They're slowly . . .": Susan Chandler, "Field's Re-Wooing of Upscale Shoppers May Be Winning Strategy: Parent Has Seen Payoff in the Last Four Months," *Chicago Tribune,* 7/26/98.

198 "They recognized . . .": Ibid.

198 The author attended Field's 9/11/98 party in Chicago.

199 "Thank God, the . . .": Sugar Rautbord, A.I., 9/11/98.

CHAPTER 6

200 "No, I'm not . . .": *WWD,* 5/97.

200 "I don't watch . . .": Teri Agins and Wendy Bounds, "Donna Karan CEO Is Sobered by Wall Street Fling," *The Wall Street Journal,* 11/13/96.

202 "Women will decide . . .": Mimi Avins, "Karan Layers It on with Her New Line," *Los Angeles Times,* 10/30/96.

202 "talked her into . . .": Josie Esquivel, A.I., 97.

203 "It was all . . .": Confidential source.

205 "Unfortunately, we never . . .": Tomio Taki, A.I., 2/5/97.

206 The description of the road show and quotes from Karan are all from "Going Public," Donna Karan, *Vogue,* 9/96.

206 "She made it . . .": Tomio Taki, A.I.

206 At the $24-a-share June 1996 offering, Takihyo's 24.7 percent stake in Donna Karan was valued at about $127.5 million. By October, DK traded at around $15.50, making Takihyo's stake worth about $82 million.

206 "I have been a . . .": "Donna Karan's Agenda: Find a Co-chief Executive, Firm Up Licensing Deals," *WWD*, 6/6/97.

208 "The market has . . ." and following quote: Linda Killian, A.I., 4/14/97.

209 "Donna Karan's best . . .": Linda Sandler and Teri Agins, "Donna Karan IPO Got a Warm Reception but Designer's Earnings Outlook Is Uncertain," *The Wall Street Journal*, 7/1/96.

210 "Investors were starstruck . . .": Josie Esquivel, A.I. 5/97.

210 "Fashion companies can . . .": Arnold Cohen, A.I., 7/97.

210 "Puritan couldn't survive . . ." and following quote: Ibid.

211 "Kimmel personally pocketed . . ." and following: Thomas J. Ryan and Lisa Lockwood, "The Age of the IPO: Fashion Execs Wear Crowns of Royalty," *WWD*, 4/17/97.

213 "Columbia skirted the . . .": Thomas J. Ryan, "Columbia's IPO Wows Wall Street," *WWD*, 3/30/98.

213 "High fashion and . . .": Alan Millstein, A.I., 2/97.

213 "Donna is an . . .": Ibid.

214 "poured more than $10 million . . .": Tomio Taki, A.I.

215 "a terrible student . . .": Jennet Conant, "The New Queen of New York," *Manhattan Inc.*, 10/89.

215 "I was always a . . .": Ibid.

215 "But Donna was unfocused . . .": Ibid.

216 "Young Taki had . . .": Teri Agins, "Tomio Taki Is Hoping to Stay in Fashion," *The Wall Street Journal*, 8/30/88.

216 "he sent dozens . . ." Ibid.

216 "get the order . . .": Dexter Levy, A.I., 7/27/98.

216 "Oppenheim had no . . .": Ibid.

216 "Anne was legendary . . ." and following: Ibid.

218 "There are no . . .": Agins, "Tomio Taki Is Hoping," op. cit.

218 "sit wherever you . . .": Ibid.

219 "I wanted her . . .": Tomio Taki, A.I.

219 "it was always . . .": Ibid.

219 "I needed a . . ." and following quote: Teri Agins, "Woman on the Verge," *Working Woman*, 5/93.

220 "Go talk to . . .": Tomio Taki, Ibid.

220 "Unfortunately, the combination . . ." and following quote: Ibid.

221 "I design from . . .": Agins, "Woman on the Verge."

222 "In my opinion . . .": Stephen Ruzow, A.I., 2/98.

222 "Fortunately, her bread-and-butter . . .": Ibid.

223 "Karan was a . . .": Agins, "Woman on the Verge."

224 "intimately acquainted . . .": Conant, "The New Queen."

224 "What's business to . . .": Agins, "Woman on the Verge."

224 "insures that a . . .": Ibid.

224 "She would do . . .": Ibid.

225 "We creative types . . .": Agins and Bounds, "Donna Karan CEO."

225 "Donna is the . . .": Confidential source.

226 "In creating financial . . .": Tomio Taki, A.I.

226 "Whenever the costs . . .": Stephen Ruzow, A.I.

227 "She and Weiss . . .": Agins, "Woman on the Verge."

227 "We had so . . .": Tomio Taki, A.I.

227 "The scent was . . ." and following quote: Georgina Howell, "Donna's Prime Time," *Vogue*, 8/92.

227 "losses of $5.9 million . . .": Teri Agins, "With IPO in the Wing Is Donna Karan in Fashion?" *The Wall Street Journal*, 8/16/93.

228 "The fragrance debacle . . .": Tomio Taki, A.I.

229 Details of Leslie Fay accounting scandal: Teri Agins, "Loose Threads: Dress Maker

Leslie Fay Is an Old Style Firm That's in a Modern Fix," *The Wall Street Journal*, 2/23/93.

230 "So Karan, Weiss, and . . .": Teri Agins and Sara Calian, "Donna Karan Suspends Plan for Public Offer," *The Wall Street Journal*, 11/18/93.

230 "He wasn't credible . . .": Rebecca Mead, "Donna Sells Her Soul," *New York*, 5/6/96.

230 "burns my butt . . .": Ibid.

231 Gucci results from 1995 and 1996 offerings from Gucci Group press releases.

231 "The company's balance . . .": Donna Karan International stock prospectus, 6/10/96.

232 "For the use . . .": Ibid.

232 "advised against . . .": Josie Esquivel, A.I., and Tomio Taki, A.I.

232 "claiming that it . . .": Tomio Taki, A.I.

232 "if anybody deserved . . .": Ibid.

233 "Designer Holdings made . . .": Wendy Bounds, "Donna Karan Shares Sink After Pact with Designer Holdings Is Terminated," *The Wall Street Journal*, 3/6/97.

233 "The contract stated . . .": Arnold Simon, A.I., 6/11/97.

234 "We were on track . . .": Stephen Ruzow, A.I.

235 "Mori appealed to . . .": Jennifer Steinhauer, "Donna Karan in the Cutting Room," *The New York Times*, 6/28/97.

235 "didn't sit well . . .": "Karan Reflects on Her Week's Development," *WWD*, 8/4/97.

235 "But there was . . .": Stephen Ruzow, A.I.

235 "estimated $100 million . . .": Ibid.

236 "Employees saw many . . ." and following: John Idol, A.I., 3/10/99.

236 "But Karan had gotten . . .": Ibid.

237 "Consistency in menswear . . .": Stephen Ruzow, A.I.

237 "one-time fashion . . .": John Idol, A.I.

237 "ridiculous that DKNY's . . .": John Idol speech at Goldman Sachs & Co. Retailing Conference, 9/9/98.

237 "This is The . . .": Ibid.

238 "I'll pay for . . .": Confidential source.

238 "We may have . . .": Wendy Bounds, Donna Karan interview on Dow Jones News Service, 4/27/97.

238 "We've turned the . . .": Teri Agins, "Donna Karan Reports Much Narrowed Loss and Cost Cutting," *The Wall Street Journal,* 3/25/99.

239 "The post IPO . . .": Valerie Seckler, "Wall Street Runway, Why Some Stocks Fly and Others Don't," *WWD,* 5/11/98.

239 "to pull in $44 million . . .": Russ Stanton, "The Rise and Fall of Mossimo Giannulli," *Los Angeles Times,* 3/8/98.

240 "latter-day version of rat-packer . . .": Frederick Rose and Teri Agins, "Fashion Designer Becomes Fashion Victim on Wall Street," *The Wall Street Journal,* 10/23/96.

240 "shareholders headed into . . .": Frederick Rose, "Designer Mossimo to Wear New Title of Firm's 'Visionary,' " *The Wall Street Journal,* 3/6/98.

242 "I never believed . . ." and following: Robert Gray, A.I., 11/10/97.

242 "the Grays sold . . ." and following: Ibid.

243 "We're not going . . .": Ibid.

243 "You know we . . .": Gray speech to analysts at Robertson Stephens Retailing Conference in New York on 10/11/98.

245 Claiborne study: Al Shapiro, A.I., 1/98.

CHAPTER 7

247 "You don't have to . . .": Zoran, A.I., 2/98.

250 "amounted to an estimated . . .": Estimates from retail executives.

252 "Zoran recalled spending . . .": Teri Agins, "Uniquely Chic: If Zoran Doesn't Ring a Bell That's Fine with Quirky Designer," *The Wall Street Journal*, 5/8/95.

252 "was an equal . . .": *Marion Greenberg v. Zoran Ladicorbic,* State Supreme Court of New York, 7/1/83.

252 "who was initially . . ." and following: Ben Brantley, A.I., 97.

253 "didn't consider Zoran . . .": Ibid.

253 "Zoran is a man . . .": Ibid.

254 "You need to . . .": Agins, "Uniquely Chic."

254 "He wanted to . . .": Ibid.

255 "I want you . . ." and following: Cathy Horyn, A.I., and Zoran, A.I.

255 "I told him . . ." and following: Lauren Hutton, A.I., 11/12/97.

257 "With their implicit . . .": Ben Brantley, "Zoran Zeitgeist," *Vanity Fair*, 3/92.

257 "There was this . . .": Ben Brantley, A.I.

257 "I am your . . .": Agins, "Uniquely Chic."

258 "You like to look . . .": Zoran, A.I., 3/95.

258 "give jewelry . . .": Agins, "Uniquely Chic."

258 "Woman should be . . ." and following: Zoran, A.I.

258 "Zoran has an incredible . . .": Ann Free, A.I., 95 and 5/97.

259 "If they want . . .": Zoran, A.I.

259 "Arena logged . . .": Roberta Arena, A.I., 95.

259 "I feel that . . ." and following: Nancy Friday, A.I., 97.

260 "One Bendel's client . . .": Ted Marlow, A.I., 4/29/97.

260 "They are separating, . . ." and following: Agins, "Uniquely Chic."

261 "Zoran believed that . . .": Zoran, A.I.

261 "Garratt maintained all . . .": Sandra Garratt, A.I., 3/98.

261 "Garratt's first year . . ." and following: Diane Reischel, "Units Creator Wrapped up in Legal Woes," *Los Angeles Times*, 5/4/90.

262 "I knew I could . . .": Zoran, A.I., 3/97.

262 "Labels scratch . . .": Agins, "Uniquely Chic."

262 "$14,000 in 1998 . . .": "Designer Agrees to Label Fine," *WWD*, 7/28/98.

263 "it was more typical . . .": June Horne, A.I., 3/97, and Gary Galleberg, A.I., 3/97.

264 "great success with . . ." and following: Agins, "Uniquely Chic."

264 "Zoran grew into a . . .": Joan Weinstein, A.I., 7/97.

264 "understands his . . ." and following: Ibid.

265 "His seamstresses kept . . .": Agins, "Uniquely Chic."

265 "I close up . . .": Ibid.

265 "More than 25,000 combinations . . .": Zoran, A.I., 2/98.

265 “the best mills . . .”: Gary Galleberg, A.I.

266 “But they don’t . . .”: Ann Free, A.I., 4/95.

266 “I had heard . . .” and following quotes: June Horne, A.I.

267 “The most time . . .”: Zoran, A.I.

268 “I was intrigued . . .” and following: Gary Galleberg, A.I., 6/17/97.

270 “The tab for . . .” and following: Agins, “Uniquely Chic.”

271 “Is kitchen available?” and following: Author attended the 3/7/95 dinner in Milan.

272 “hadn’t been profitable . . .”: Bill Blass, A.I., 7/1/97.

EPILOGUE

275 “Companies that stumble . . .”: George Anders and Scott Thurm, “The Innovators—The Rocket Under the Tech Boom: Heavy Spending by Basic Industries,” *The Wall Street Journal,* 3/30/99.

276 “The alarms were . . .”: From Peter Jacobi speech to the American Textile Manufacturers Institute, 3/13/99.

277 “ ‘war of the handbags’ . . .”: Thomas Kamm, “War of the Handbags Escalates as LVMH Revives Gucci Quest,” *The Wall Street Journal*, Dow Jones News Service, 6/10/99.

277 “The brewing battle . . .”: Thomas Kamm, “Gucci Watch: Behind the Competition for Luxury-Goods Firm Is a New European Ethic,” *The Wall Street Journal,* 3/22/99.

278 “Cardin insisted that . . .”: “Pierre Cardin Says Prefers to Sell to Italian Group,” Dow Jones News Service, 3/15/99.

278 “This company has . . .”: Teri Agins, “Polo Ralph Lauren Agrees to Acquire Canadian Chain,” *The Wall Street Journal,* 3/2/99.

279 “The Hilfiger organization . . .”: Hilfiger spokeswoman, A.I., 5/99.

279 “which generated $17 million . . .”: Susan Chandler, “Outsourcing Risks, Rewards: The Decision to Farm Out Production of Frango Mints Has Left a Not-So-Sweet Aftertaste in Chicago, but Field’s Is Hardly Alone in Retailing or Other Sectors in Taking That Route,” *Chicago Tribune,* 3/14/99.

279 “This is the candy capital . . .” and following on zoning proposal: Gary Washburn and Susan Chandler, “A Taste of Politics of Field’s Daley Message Hits Target on Frango Jobs,” *Chicago Tribune,* 3/12/99.

selected bibliography

Ballard, Bettina. *In My Fashion*. New York: David McKay, 1960.

Bender, Marilyn. *The Beautiful People*. New York: Coward McCann, 1966.

Birmingham, Nan Tillson. *Store*. New York: J. P. Putnam Sons, 1978.

Brady, James. *Superchic*. Boston: Little, Brown, 1974.

Coleridge, Nicholas. *The Fashion Conspiracy*. London: William Heinemann, 1988.

Daria, Irene. *The Fashion Cycle*. New York: Simon & Schuster, 1990.

Fairchild, John. *Chic Savages*. New York: Pocket Books, 1989.

Ferragamo, Salvatore *Salvatore Ferragamo, Shoemaker of Dreams*. Florence: Centro di Della Edifini srl, 1985 (originally published 1957).

Forestier, Nadege, and Ravai Nazanine. *The Taste of Luxury*. London: Bloomsbury Publishing, 1992.

Grumbach, Didier. *Histories de la mode*. Paris: Éditions du Seuil, 1993.

Gruppo GFT. *Emanuel Ungaro*. Milan: Electa, Milan Elemond Editori Associati, 1992.

Jarnow, Jeannette A., Miriam Guerriero, and Beatrice Judelle. *Inside the Fashion Business*. 4th ed. New York: Macmillan, 1987.

Milbank, Caroline Rennolds. *Couture: The Great Designers*. New York: Stewart, Tabori & Chang, 1985.

Mirabella, Grace. *In and Out of Vogue*. New York: Doubleday, 1994.

Morais, Richard. *Pierre Cardin*. London: Bantam Press, 1991.

Pochna, Marie-France. *Christian Dior*. New York: Arcade Publishing, 1996.

Rawsthorn, Alice. *Yves Saint Laurent*. New York: Doubleday, Nan A. Talese, 1996.

Ricci, Stefania. *Salavatore Ferragamo: The Art of the Shoe*. New York: Rizzoli International Publications, 1992.

Roscho, Bernard. *The Rag Race: How New York and Paris Run the Breakneck Business of Dressing American Women*. New York: Funk and Wagnalls Co., 1963.

Rubinstein, Ruth P. *Dress Codes: Meanings and Messages in American Culture*. Boulder, Col.: Westview Press, 1995.

Sices, Murray. *Seventh Avenue*. New York: Fairchild Publications, 1953.

Somers, Suzanne. *Italian Chic*. New York: Villard Books, 1992.

Trachtenberg, Jeffrey A. *Ralph Lauren: The Man Behind the Mystique*. Boston: Little, Brown, 1988.

———. *The Rain on Macy's Parade*. New York: Times Business, 1996.

Traub, Marvin, and Tom Teicholz. *Like No Other Store . . . the Bloomingdale's Legend and the Revolution in American Marketing*. New York: Times Books, 1993.

Vienne, Veronique. *French Style*. Columbus, Oh.: Express, 1993.

Vreeland, Diana. *D.V.* New York: Alfred A. Knopf, 1984.

Wendt, Lloyd, and Herman Kogan. *Give the Lady What She Wants: The Story of Marshall Field & Co.* New York: Rand McNally, 1950.

index